THE COLLAPSE OF THE MYCENAEAN ECONOMY

In this book, Sarah C. Murray provides a comprehensive treatment of textual and archaeological evidence for the long-distance trade economy of Greece across 600 years, during the transition from the Late Bronze to the Early Iron Age. In analyzing the finished objects that sustained this kind of trade, she also situates its artifacts within the broader context of the ancient Mediterranean economy, which includes evidence for the import and export of commodities as well as demographic change. Murray argues that our current model of exchange during the Late Bronze Age is in need of a thoroughgoing reformulation. She demonstrates that the association of imported objects with elite self-fashioning is not clearly supported by the evidence from early Greek history. Moreover, the notional "decline" in trade during Greece's purported Dark Age appears to be the result of severe economic contraction, rather than a severance of access to trade routes.

Sarah C. Murray is an Assistant Professor of Classics and Religious Studies and a Faculty Fellow of the Center for Digital Research in the Humanities at the University of Nebraska–Lincoln. She has also taught at the University of Notre Dame, where she was a Visiting Assistant Professor. She has over ten years of field experience as an archaeologist in Greece, most recently as photogrammetry specialist at the Mazi Archaeological Project in West Attica. Murray has written articles on digital field methods, historiography, and early Greece for the *Journal of Field Archaeology*, *Hesperia*, and the *Archaeological Journal of America*.

THE COLLAPSE OF THE MYCENAEAN ECONOMY

IMPORTS, TRADE, AND
INSTITUTIONS 1300–700 BCE

SARAH C. MURRAY

University of Nebraska–Lincoln

CAMBRIDGE
UNIVERSITY PRESS

One Liberty Plaza, 20th Floor, New York, NY 10006, USA

Cambridge University Press is part of the University of Cambridge.

It furthers the University's mission by disseminating knowledge in the pursuit of
education, learning, and research at the highest international levels of excellence.

www.cambridge.org
Information on this title: www.cambridge.org/9781107186378
DOI: 10.1017/9781316890424

© Sarah C. Murray 2017

This publication is in copyright. Subject to statutory exception
and to the provisions of relevant collective licensing agreements,
no reproduction of any part may take place without the written
permission of Cambridge University Press.

First published 2017

Printed in Great Britain by Clays Ltd, St Ives plc

A catalogue record for this publication is available from the British Library.

Library of Congress Cataloging-in-Publication Data
Murray, Sarah (Sarah C.), author.
The collapse of the Mycenaean economy : imports, trade, and institutions, 1300-700 BCE / Sarah
Murray (University of Nebraska, Lincoln).
New York, NY : Cambridge University Press, 2017. | Includes bibliographical references and index.
LCCN 2017009645 | ISBN 9781107186378 (hardback : alkaline paper)
LCSH: Mycenae (Extinct city) – Commerce – Mediterranean Region. | Mediterranean Region –
Commerce – Greece – Mycenae (Extinct city) | Imports – Greece – Mycenae (Extinct city) |
Imports – Mediterranean Region – History – To 1500. | Social change – Greece – Mycenae
(Extinct city) | Bronze age – Mediterranean Region. | Iron age–Mediterranean Region. | Mycenae
(Extinct city) – Economic conditions. | Mediterranean Region – Economic conditions. |
Mediterranean Region –Antiquities. | BISAC: SOCIAL SCIENCE / Archaeology.
LCC HF376.M9 M87 2017 | DDC 382.0939/18–dc23
LC record available at https://lccn.loc.gov/2017009645

ISBN 978-1-107-18637-8 Hardback

Cambridge University Press has no responsibility for the persistence or accuracy of
URLs for external or third-party Internet Web sites referred to in this publication
and does not guarantee that any content on such Web sites is, or will remain,
accurate or appropriate.

"Time counts and keeps countin', and we know now finding the trick of what's been and lost ain't no easy ride."

Mad Max: Beyond Thunderdome

To everyone who has helped

CONTENTS

List of Figures, Maps, and Tables	page viii
Preface	xi
Acknowledgments	xiii
INTRODUCTION	1
1 THE DARK LIGHT OF EARLY GREEK TEXTS ON TRADE	31
2 DIRECT EVIDENCE FOR LONG-DISTANCE TRADE IN EARLY GREECE	73
3 ASSESSING QUANTITATIVE CHANGE IN THE ARCHAEOLOGICAL RECORD	130
4 BRONZE DEPOSITION (AND CIRCULATION?), TRADE IN COMMODITIES, AND EVIDENCE FROM AROUND THE MEDITERRANEAN	160
5 DEMOGRAPHIC AND DOMESTIC ECONOMIC CHANGE IN EARLY GREECE: FACTORS OF SUPPLY AND DEMAND	210
6 SNAPSHOTS OF A TRADE SYSTEM IN FLUX	247
CONCLUSIONS: IMPORTS AND ECONOMY, CRISIS AND RESILIENCE, BRONZE AGE AND IRON AGE	275
Works Cited	283
Index	345

FIGURES, MAPS, AND TABLES

Figures

2.1	Import findspots at LH IIIB Mycenae	page 78
2.2	Import findspots at LH IIIB Tiryns	80
2.3	Import findspots at LH IIIC Perati	87
2.4	An inscribed amulet made out of a Hittite *bulla* from tomb 24 at Perati (simplified drawing of bulla from Tomb 24)	89
2.5	Distribution of finds and imports in [undisturbed] chamber tombs at Perati	90
2.6	Distribution of finds and imports in PG burials at Lefkandi Toumba	97
2.7	Distribution of finds and imports in SPG (G) burials at Lefkandi Toumba	97
2.8	Location and distribution of imports in PG Lefkandi Toumba burials	98
2.9	Change in qualitative characteristics of imports, IIIB-G	99
3.1	Accumulation of archaeological sites for the LB IIIB, LB IIIC, PG, and G periods, 1900–2015	138
3.2	Comparison of survey site incidence	139
3.3	Surface finds in select regions	140
3.4	Sites per 10 km in some individual surveys	140
3.5	Agency of archaeological discovery, IIIB-G	142
3.6	Visualization of "indirect observables"	152
5.1	LBA and EIA sites from surveys in Greece	217

Maps

1.1	Sites mentioned in the Introduction, Greece and Crete	2
2.1	Distribution of imports at sites on the mainland, LH IIIB – Geometric	118
2.2	Distribution of imports at sites on Crete, LM IIIB – Geometric	120
4.1	Greek ceramic exports around the Mediterranean, thirteenth to eighth centuries	194
5.1	Distribution of Protogeometric sites in central Crete	218
5.2	Distribution of Protogeometric sites in Thessaly	220
5.3	Distribution of Protogeometric sites in central Greece	222
5.4	Distribution of Protogeometric sites in the southern Peloponnese	224
5.5	Distribution of Protogeometric sites in the northern Argolid	226
5.6	Distribution of Protogeometric sites in Attica	228

Tables

1.1	Comparison of some aspects of trade in the texts	66
1.2	[Minimalist] comparison of some aspects of trade in the texts	71
2.1	Imported objects in Greece from the IIIB period	83
2.2	Summary of imported objects in tombs in the Perati Necropolis containing one import	88
2.3	Imported objects in Greece from the IIIC period	92
2.4	Summary of imported objects in tombs at Lefkandi containing only one import each	96
2.5	Imported objects in Greece from the PG period	102
2.6	Imported objects in Greece from the G period	108
2.7	Minimum, maximum, and weighted middle import counts	113
2.8	Chronological schemes and durations for the end of the Aegean Late Bronze Age	114
2.9	Approximate imports per annum according to the traditional chronology	116
2.10	Approximate imports per annum according to a modified "low" chronology	117
2.11	Function of imports (some categories omitted)	126
2.12	Material of imports (some categories omitted)	126
2.13	Putative origin of imported objects (some categories omitted)	127
2.14	Regional trade: Origin of imports in West Greece, East Greece, and Crete	127
3.1	Data used for chi-squared test of statistical significance.	133
3.2	95 percent confidence intervals for IIIB import counts: Cumulative, mainland, and Crete	134
3.3	Example of extrapolation from actual data into approximate 200 year totals for each period, assuming a hypothetical accumulation of imports at observed p/a rates for each period	134
3.4	95 percent confidence intervals for IIIB import counts: Mainland	135
3.5	95 percent confidence intervals for IIIC import counts: Mainland	135
3.6	95 percent confidence intervals for PG import counts: Mainland	135
3.7	95 percent confidence intervals for G import counts: Mainland	135
3.8	95 percent confidence intervals for IIIB import counts: Crete	135
3.9	95 percent confidence intervals for IIIC import counts: Crete	135
3.10	95 percent confidence intervals for PG import counts: Crete	136
3.11	95 percent confidence intervals for G import counts: Crete	136
3.12	Breakdown of sites by type, IIIB–G	141
3.13	Impact on import quantities if beads are excluded from the counts	150
3.14	Tribute brought to Egypt by Aegeans in the Tomb of Rekhmire, Thebes	154
3.15	Exchanges in the *Iliad* and the *Odyssey*	155
3.16	Exchanged goods in the Homeric poems	157
4.1	Number of bronzes on the Greek mainland, bronzes present at a sample of IIIB–G sites, import counts, and period durations	168

4.2	Ratio of mortuary to nonmortuary sites in the sample of excavated sites from which bronze data was collected and distribution of bronzes in mortuary and nonmortuary sites from the IIIB, IIIC, PG, and G periods	171
4.3	Bronze and other metal objects in PG cemeteries	176
4.4	Summary of exported Greek pottery in the Mediterranean from IIIB–G	191
4.5	Summary of evidence from exports, IIIB-G periods	206
5.1	Proposed population growth and growth rates in the EIA	234
5.2	Range of "Urban/Polity" population in Bronze Age centers	236
5.3	Change in population vs. change in various categories of material evidence	239
6.1	Metal use in a sample of regional groupings of EPG-LPG tombs	262
7.1	Summary of evidence for trade in the Aegean	278

PREFACE

Cataloging "imported" and "exported" objects and discussing their meaning has long constituted something of a subfield within Greek archaeology. This has been a productive avenue of scholarship. The academic desire to understand movements and exchanges of goods and peoples around the Mediterranean has produced reams of thorough, interpretatively subtle, methodologically nuanced and productive analysis, driving important advances in the application of materials science within Aegean archaeology and beyond. Yet, in some ways, imported and exported objects have received an amount of analytical attention that outweighs their relatively puny presence in the archaeological record. Perhaps as a result, one can sense a palpable fatigue with studies of long-distance exchange in some quarters within Aegean and Iron Age archaeology. In the years that I have spent putting together this book, I have encountered variations on this sentiment in print, during job interviews, in casual discussions with colleagues over coffee, while troweling away sediments in archaeological trenches, and elsewhere. Similarly, the transition from the Late Bronze Age (LBA) to the Early Iron Age, (EIA) though neglected as an area of study during the earlier parts of the twentieth century, has formed the backbone of so many dissertations in the last twenty years that the mention of such a topic usually engenders a sigh from senior scholars tired of hearing about institutional change and continuity across this horizon.

So, what do I think I am doing in this book? Why should we keep flogging the same dead horses again and again? I hope to provide something of an answer to these questions in what follows. In short, I intend the book to be as much about the process of interpreting difficult assemblages in the archaeological record as it is about imports and exports themselves or about the LBA–EIA transition. While many have promoted or disparaged the value of imported and exported objects for telling us something about ancient economic or personal networks, an extended inquiry into whether or not such assemblages are reliable as indicators of exchange systems over a relatively long time span, with a notional cultural break complicating things has never been effected. If there is one thing I would like archaeologists to take away from the work here, it is that import and export assemblages, like all human-generated collections of artifacts, are too contingent on a frighteningly random gauntlet of factors – including but not limited to formation processes, the whims of archaeologists, a lack of standardized recording and categorization systems across subdisciplinary boundaries, and (as always) the ubiquitous and ever-oppressive unevenness of the archaeological record – to be interpreted meaningfully on their own. However, I also show that if we immerse contingent datasets within the greater pool of the archaeological record, we can often distinguish random or spurious changes in such assemblages from real variation in the past and tell the history of prehistory from a surer footing. This is no crystal ball, but I think it is the best we've got.

ACKNOWLEDGMENTS

It has been over a decade since I set foot on my first archaeological project in Greece. The year was 2005. I had two seasons of toils – on a massive field school in the nostril-singeing garbage incinerator of modern Pompeii, where we lived in a tourist tent campground that doubled as the local stray dog latrine – under my belt. The contrast with rural Greece was sharp, and I was immediately enchanted by the dazzling world of bright sun, sparkling seas, clear air, and jagged topography. For me, it was a beginning and an end: the end of a period of relatively angst-ridden, alienated adolescence and the beginning of a *joie*-filled life of traveling, reading, learning, thinking, and writing through the puzzles of the past. The reassuring rhythm of the year, with its hibernatory winters spent counting down to the next flight to Athens, and the punctuation mark of the first glimpse of the familiar contours of Attic topography from the plane every summer marks the time, but it's still hard to imagine that ten years have gone by. Mostly because of random, blind luck and the generosity of others, I have been able to continue pursuing this most glorious life, through jobs on archaeological digs and surveys as well as in labs and research consortia, a funded Ph.D. at Stanford, generous travel and research allowances, and even a good professional position. I have a hard time believing how it all came up aces, despite my questionable decision-making skills and shortcomings. To paraphrase Jacques Cousteau, anybody who has an opportunity to lead an extraordinary life has no right to keep it to themselves. The people that make up the Greek archaeological community make this the best profession in the world, and I dedicate this book to them, and especially to everyone who has helped make my career in archaeology possible.

The research here grows out of my doctoral dissertation, defended at Stanford University in 2013 and advised by Ian Morris, Jerry Rutter, Eric Cline, Josh Ober, and Richard Martin. Many thanks are due to Ian, whose work inspired my interest in the topic of Early Iron Age Greece and who provided incisive and galvanizing feedback on the early, anemic drafts of my dissertation chapters. Jerry generously applied his unmatched expertise on Late Bronze Age material culture and read the whole thing (!) with a characteristically keen eye. I am fortunate to have had the opportunity to work closely with both Ian and Jerry during my graduate career, and I never could have even dreamed of imagining trying to attempt a book on this sprawling subject without their guidance. This project would not have been possible without Eric Cline's work, and I am grateful to him for his many contributions to the field of Late Bronze Age trade, for taking the time to be an outside reader for my dissertation and for introducing me to the editors at Cambridge University Press. Along the way, the support and fellowship of my Stanford colleagues, especially John Sutherland and Robert Stephan, was instrumental in all senses. Many colleagues – notably Phil Sapirstein, Alex Knodell, Dimitri Nakassis, Miriam Clinton, Catherine Pratt, Tom Strasser, Tom Tartaron, Bartek Lis, and Stepan Rückl – have helped me to advance my work on this topic through stimulating discussions and general encouragement. I am grateful to Dimitri Nakassis, Stepan Rückl, and Alex Knodell for sharing unpublished copies of their work on the early Greek economy, along with many productive conversations.

Generous funding for the dissertation research was provided by the Stanford Classics Department, the Stanford University G.R.O. Fund, the Stanford Humanities Center, and the Mellon Foundation. Since 2013, I have continued to work on improving and expanding the study. The Classics Department at the University of Notre Dame gave me a job fresh out of graduate school, allowing me to continue actively researching the early Greek economy. At the University of Nebraska-Lincoln, the Department of Classics and Religious Studies and the Center for Digital Research in the Humanities have both given generous financial support for the final stages of the research, along with something even more valuable – a congenial professional environment. The American School of Classical Studies at Athens' Blegen Library has been my "Battle Stations" from the beginning. I wrote most of the book there, and couldn't have done it anywhere else.

The editorial team at Cambridge University Press guided me through the publishing process with great patience and professionalism, and I am thankful to Anastasia Graf, Beatrice Rehl, Edgar Mendez, and Joshua Penney, as well as to three anonymous readers whose excellent critiques are largely responsible for the final shape of the book and for the existence of what turned out to be its best parts. Remaining errors and oversights are my own responsibility.

Finally, I want to thank all of my amazing friends, who make everything both worthwhile and possible.

INTRODUCTION

During the last several decades, the extent and variety of movements and relationships between peoples of the Mediterranean during the Late Bronze Age and Early Iron Age have been the subject of much debate.[1] Likewise, the intertwined nexus of problems concerning the nature and cadence of the notional "collapse" of the Mycenaean world at the end of

---

[1] No longer can it be said, as Renfrew did in 1969, that "trade is one of the activities of prehistoric man that has received much less attention than it deserves" (Renfrew 1969, 151). A list of published work on the topic since 1990 (in chronological order) includes, but is not limited to Knapp 1990, Lambrou-Phillipson 1990; Liverani 1990; Gale 1991; Peltenburg 1991; Sherratt and Sherratt 1991; Crielaard 1992; Haldane 1993; Knapp 1993; Cline 1994; Popham 1994; Waldbaum 1994; Budd et al. 1995; Day and Haskell 1995; Gale and Stos-Gale 1995; Palaima 1995; Popham 1995; Cline 1996; Hirschfeld 1996; Lebessi 1996; Artzy 1997; Bass 1997a; Bass 1997b; Hoffman 1997; Artzy 1998; Cline and Harris-Cline 1998; Crielaard 1998; Foxhall 1998; Gale 1998; Knapp 1998; Mountjoy 1998; Muhly 1998; Sherratt 1998; Crielaard 1999; Haskell 1999; Hirschfeld 1999; Karageorghis 1999; Parker 1999; Sherratt 1999; Hirschfeld 2000; Jones 2000; Liverani 2001; Matthäus 2001; Sherratt 2001; van Wijngaarden 2002; Bryce 2003; Liverani 2003; Luke 2003; Sherratt 2003; Hirschfeld 2004; Maran 2004; Braun-Holzinger and Rehm 2005; Eder and Jung 2005; Jones et al. 2005; Laffineur & Greco 2005; Manning and Hulin 2005; Vianello 2005; Bell 2006; Fletcher 2007; Kristiansen and Larsson 2007; Maggidis 2007; Gillis and Clayton 2008; Kopanias 2008; Pulak 2008; Jung 2009; Kelder 2009; Lolos 2009a; Maier et al. 2009; Monroe 2009; Muhly 2009; Routledge and McGeough 2009; Vagnetti et al. 2009; Burns 2010b; Cline 2010; Kardulias 2010; Schon 2010; Sherratt 2010; Cohen, Maran, and Vetters 2010; Tomlinson et al. 2010; Yasur-Landau 2010; Betelli 2011; Gates 2011; Haskell 2011; Hughes-Brock 2011; Vetters 2011; Vianello 2011; Bell 2012; Gale and Stos-Gale 2012; van Wijngaarden 2012; Brysbaert and Vetters 2013; Tartaron 2013; Rutter 2014; Vacek 2014; Crielaard 2015.

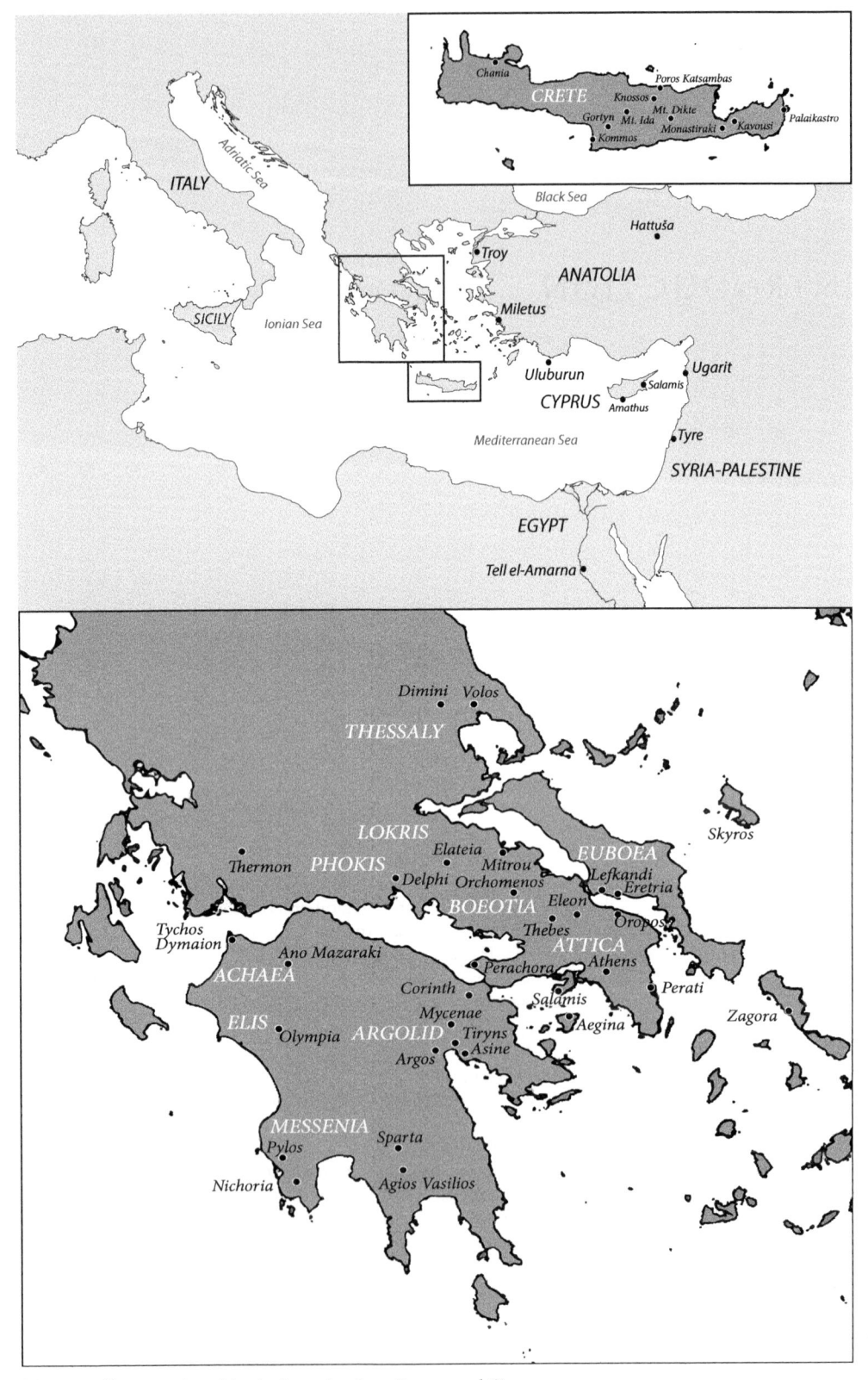

Map 1.1. Sites mentioned in the Introduction, Greece and Crete

the Late Bronze Age (LBA), its relationship with the following Early Iron Age (EIA), and the articulation of both periods with Archaic and Classical history comprise a similarly popular area of research.[2] This book is an historical study, based on textual and archaeological evidence, that lies at the intersection of these topics. Geographically the focus is Greece, both the mainland and Crete, but given that this is a study of long-distance trade, a broadening of spatial scope to the wider Mediterranean will occasionally be appropriate.

In general, the goal is to answer a simple question with no simple solution: how and why did the exchange economy (and the economy overall) of the Greek world change in scale and structure between the thirteenth and the eighth century? Specifically, the book has three aims: (1) to present a synthesis of the existing evidence for long-distance trade through the transition from Greek prehistory to history, (2) to investigate whether the archaeological evidence can be relied upon to provide a sense of the cadence of economic change that has some fidelity to past patterns, and (3) to show that there were major, far-reaching adjustments to both the scale and the structure of the Greek trade economy (and the economy overall) after the LB IIIB period. This process of adjustment was complex and can only be properly understood with the aid of methodological advances in the way that we study the total archive of the archaeological record and research that elides traditional disciplinary boundaries separating the Bronze from the Iron Age.

1. AN ABBREVIATED ECONOMIC AND POLITICAL BACKGROUND TO THE LATE BRONZE AGE AND EARLY IRON AGE IN GREECE

To begin, I provide a brief introduction to the period and the issues at stake for the reader who is not already familiar with the general characteristics of the LBA–EIA transition in Greece, specifically its economic aspect and the history of long-distance exchange. The purpose of this introduction is to provide some orientation and background for readers not versed in the details of the early Greek world who may be interested in the general methodological and

---

[2] Works on social, political, architectural, and economic aspects of Greece during the transition between the LBA and EIA to appear since 1990 (in chronological order) include Carlier 1991; Negbi 1991; Powell 1991; Whitley 1991a; Whitley 1991b; S. Morris 1992; Rutter 1992; Deger-Jalkotzy 1994; Papadopoulos 1994; Foxhall 1995; de Polignac 1995; Morgan 1996; Osborne 1996a; Osborne 1996b; Langdon 1997; Mazarakis-Ainian 1997; Tandy 1997; Deger-Jalkotzy 1998a; Deger-Jalkotzy 1998b; Lemos 1998b; I. Morris 1999; Georganas 2000; Morris 2000; Wallace 2000; Eder 2001b; Mazarakis-Ainian 2001; Weiler 2001; Georganas 2002; Kyrieleis 2002; Wallace 2003; Eder 2004; Hatzaki 2004; Wallace 2005; Crielaard 2006; Deger-Jalkotzy and Lemos 2006; Dickinson 2006; Rystedt 2006; Snodgrass 2006; Wallace 2006; Wedde 2006; Lemos 2007c; Georganas 2008; Giannopoulos 2008; Deger-Jalkotzy & Bächle 2009; Dickinson 2009; Heymans and van Wijngaarden 2009; Jung 2009; Wallace 2010; Crielaard 2011; Mazarakis-Ainian 2011 (2 vols.); Lantzas 2012; Knodell 2013; Feldman 2014; Rizza 2014; Kotsonas 2016.

interpretive aspects of the book, rather than the specific regional historical implications and contexts. Those already fluent in the basic details of the period and the history of interpretations of the LBA–EIA transition will be best served by skipping ahead to Section 2. Many of the general issues surrounding the period, its chronology, and related economic, social, and political developments remain controversial, so it is fair to hedge by stating that what follows necessarily smooths over many complex points in an attempt at concision and clarity.

In its relative chronological terminology, the field of Aegean prehistory divides the Bronze Age (roughly 3000–1100 BCE) into a sequence of Beginning, Middle, and Late. Traditional nomenclature also internally divides the study of the Bronze Age by region, with specific designations and ceramic sequences for the Greek mainland (Early, Middle, and Late Helladic, as well as the transitional Submycenaean), Crete (Early, Middle, Late, and Sub-Minoan), and the Cycladic islands (Early, Middle, and Late Cycladic). On Crete, a separate phasing system has been developed to describe architectural and political developments (protopalatial, neopalatial, final palatial, and postpalatial).

For the EIA (c. 1100–700 BCE), subphases are usually referred to by designations from the extensively documented ceramic sequence. Like LBA sequences, these vary in some significant ways by region in ways that are too complex to cover in the current context, but in general follow the usual tripartite development from Early, Middle, and Late Protogeometric (c. 1100/1050–900 BCE) to Early, Middle, and Late Geometric (c. 900–700 BCE).[3]

The Middle and Late Bronze Ages in mainland Greece and Crete witnessed what has been traditionally interpreted as a classic rise and fall of complex societies. Beginning on Crete in the Middle Bronze Age (c. 2000–1600 BCE), the appearance large court-centered architectural complexes, communal sanctuaries, and other signs of increasing social complexity, economic development, and political hierarchy signal the beginning of what is known as "palatial" Minoan society.[4] Though it was once assumed that authorities at Knossos, home to the earliest excavated and most widely known of Crete's palaces, ruled over the entire island, work throughout the twentieth and twenty-first centuries has uncovered so many additional buildings with characteristics usually associated with palatial architecture that archaeologists now puzzle over the exact nature of Minoan authority and political structure.[5] Some

---

[3] The absolute chronology of Greek prehistory is hotly debated. The numbers I provide here are meant only to orient an unfamiliar reader to the general timeframe involved, and are inexact. For LBA chronology see discussion in Knapp and Manning 2016; table at Manning 2010, 23. For the EIA, Dickinson 2006, 23; Coldstream [1977] 2003, 435. Papadopoulos 2003, 146 suggested extending the G period down into the seventh century.

[4] Cherry 1986; Warren 1987; Branigan 1988; Catapoti 2005.

[5] Godart, Kanta, and Tzigounaki 1996; Knappett 1999; Schoep 2006.

clues might be contained in the written records kept by Cretan scribes during this period, but the script in which those records are written, Linear A, remains undeciphered. However power was organized, evidence from both Minoan Crete and the greater Mediterranean shows convincingly that an important characteristic of protopalatial and neopalatial Minoan society was integration into wider Mediterranean maritime networks (with a cultural correlate often termed a *koinê*).[6] The discovery of many imported exotica in palatial deposits on Crete suggests that there were strong ties binding Crete to the wider world and that palatial Minoan society was generally cosmopolitan in nature.

On the mainland, signs of political and economic complexity are largely absent from the Middle Bronze Age, but intensify during the Late Helladic (c. 1600–1100 BCE), roughly contemporary with the neopalatial period on Crete. At the beginning of this period, something like a Mycenaean state system seems to have solidified economic and political capital in the hands of groups occupying building complexes that – as on Crete – are known as palatial centers.[7] As on Crete, there are so many of these complexes (at Mycenae, Tiryns, Argos, Pylos, Thebes, Orchomenos, Agios Vasilios) that control from a single center has often been considered improbable. Some Mycenaean documentary evidence (unlike Linear A, the mainland script called Linear B has been deciphered)[8] suggests that political power rested in regional authorities, but in least one region (the Argolid) so many "palaces" are clustered together in a small space that archaeologists remain at a loss to explain the relationships between them.[9] The architecture of the mainland palatial centers, and the tastes and social organization of Mycenaean elites in general, were probably largely influenced by Minoan exemplars, although they differed in a number of important ways.[10]

Compared to Crete, the mainland appears to have had fewer ties to the wider Mediterranean during the earlier Mycenaean period, but this changed by the fourteenth century, when many scholars agree that Mycenaeans either conquered or became politically and culturally dominant over Crete.[11] At its pinnacle in the LBA (especially the fourteenth and thirteenth

---

[6] Cline 1994; Watrous 1998; Knappett, Evans, and Rivers 2008.

[7] On Mycenaean state formation, see Dickinson 1977; Voutsaki 2001; 2010; Parkinson and Galaty 2007; Wright 2008.

[8] See Chapter 1.

[9] Kilian 1988; Bennet 2007, 186–187. For evidence of regional organization in the form of variation in material culture, see Mountjoy 1999; Mommsen et al. 2002; Darcque 2005.

[10] For example, conspicuous and formidable fortification walls are characteristic of Mycenaean palaces but not Cretan ones (though see Alusik 2007 for a corrective to the view that Minoans were uninterested in defensive architecture), and the iconographic repertoire of Mycenaean art tends to feature more martial themes than that of the Minoans (catalog of depictions of warfare and combat in Vonhoff 2008).

[11] For some discussion of Crete and Mycenaean relations during the LBA, see Popham 1976; Bouzek 1996; Cline 1997; Haskell 1997.

centuries BCE), the mainland Mycenaean culture was clearly involved in affairs – political, military, and economic – around the Mediterranean, as we know from Near Eastern correspondence (see Chapter 1), the widespread distribution of Mycenaean or Mycenaeanizing pottery in Egypt, Cyprus, Anatolia, Syria-Palestine, and Italy (see Chapter 4), and the increasing (though still relatively modest) appearance of imported exotica at sites in mainland Greece.[12]

Beginning in the late thirteenth and coming to a head in the twelfth century (late Helladic/Minoan IIIC) a series of complex crises, which continue to challenge scholars' explanatory models, beset the world-system of the LBA Mediterranean.[13] Many of the characteristics that had defined the LBA world, such as the palatial complexes, the economic organizations and structures documented in the Linear B texts, and relative system-wide uniformity of ceramic shapes and decorative styles disappeared over the course of the late thirteenth and twelfth centuries. On the mainland, palaces at Pylos and Mycenae smoldered, while other centers like Tiryns suffered destructions, but limped on. Strong traditions in large-scale wall-painting, ivory- and gold-working, and glyptic seem to have been abandoned altogether as political and economic leadership devolved to a local level. The major engineering and infrastructural projects of the Mycenaeans probably began to fall into disrepair, making travel and communication more difficult. The appearance of a new class of "warrior burials," and the prominence of figural scenes depicting what appear to be sea raids or battles on contemporary pottery suggest the emergence of just the kind of might-makes-right Hobbesian struggle for survival that is commonly depicted in postapocalyptic literature. At least on the mainland, the population appears to have decreased drastically, if settlement numbers can be taken as any guide to this.[14] On Crete and in the islands, evidence for a dramatic decrease in population is not as convincing. However, most settlements from the IIIC period are located in highly defensible positions (the most extreme example being the cliffside settlement at Monastiraki Katalimata) suggesting that inhabitants who remained on the island harbored real fears about security and stability, either due to the threat of invaders from the sea or attacks from their neighbors.[15] It is no surprise, then, that most scholars have envisioned a collapse not only of palatial society but also of the dense network of long-distance interactions that characterized the LBA *koiné*, and a gradual cessation of cross-Mediterranean exchange.[16]

---

[12] Data for the entire BA collected in Cline 1994.
[13] For a general treatment of the LBA collapse, Cline 2014; see also Knapp and Manning 2016 for a denser but selective review of related evidence.
[14] See demographic evidence in Chapter 5.
[15] Nowicki 2000; 2008; Wallace 2000; 2006; 2010; on the islands, Deger-Jalkotzy 1998b.
[16] Deger-Jalkotzy 1991; Bell 2009; Routledge and McGeough 2009.

Overall, the IIIC period in Greece appears to have been one characterized by a lack of clearly defined or standardized authorities or institutions, either political or economic, and we can be relatively confident that this was a time of general disarray, uncertainty, and flux. This flux clearly created chaos, but also opened chasms of opportunity in the sociopolitical and economic hierarchy. Regions outside of the former palatial centers seem to have benefited from the demise of the erstwhile economic prominence of places like Mycenae, Thebes, and Pylos. Former peripheral settlements, like Mitrou, Elateia, and Eleon in central Greece (perhaps the regions of Phokis and Lokris in general) and Tychos Dymaion in Achaea flourished.[17] At Perati in east Attica, tombs were furnished with exotic objects suggesting that some kind of long-distance trade may have carried on through the collapse of the palatial institutions.[18] On Crete, there are signs of continuing prosperity at a few coastal sites like Chania, despite the general move up to refuge settlements, and contacts with Italy and western Greece remained intact.[19]

By the eleventh and tenth centuries (Protogeometric Period/Early Iron Age), however, most of these postpalatial points of light on the mainland had been extinguished, and the archaeological record becomes rather sparse indeed.[20] All indications are that the population must have remained low throughout this period, unless the material record is seriously misleading. Excavated settlements, like Nichoria in Messenia, Asine in the Argolid, and Mitrou in Lokris are characterized by simple architecture, mostly mud-brick on a stone socle or base, and lacking much decorative elaboration.[21] On Crete many refuge sites were abandoned for more convenient locations, but the persistence of settlements throughout the island to hew to defensible locations (the Gortyn acropolis and the settlement at Kavousi Vronda) may point to a continuing period of troubled intra- or interisland instability.[22] Craft traditions seem limited to small-scale metalworking (simple pins and fibulae), textile

---

[17] On Central Greece, see Deger-Jalkotzy 1983; Kramer-Hajos 2008; Knodell 2013; for Achaea, Giannopoulos 2008 is a good recent review of the evidence. Latacz 2004 on the primacy of Thebes in Mycenaean times is relevant.

[18] Iakovidis 1980, 111; Desborough 1964, 69–70; Dickinson 2006, 185; Muhly 2003, 26; Thomatos 2006, 178; Lewartowksi 1989, 75; Dickinson 2006, 58; 2010. Short considerations at Dickinson 2006, 179–180; Thomatos 2006, 157–158; on "warrior graves," Deger-Jalkotzy 2006, 155–157.

[19] Hallager and Hallager 2000.

[20] The number of sites from Greece dating to the EPG period is sufficiently small to have prompted scholars to seek out explanations for its paucity other than actual paucity of remains in antiquity. See Dietz 1982, 102; Rutter 1983; Snodgrass 1993, 30; Foxhall 1995; Papadopoulos 1996, 254; Mazarakis Ainian 1997, 100; Morgan 2006, 237, n. 25; Morris 2007, 213.

[21] Nichoria in Messenia (MacDonald et al. 1983); Asine (Wells 1983a); Mitrou (Rückl 2008).

[22] For general discussion of the transition from IIIC–PG on Crete, Ksipharas 2004, 324–328; cf. Nowicki 2000; 2002; Wallace 2006; 2010.

manufacture, and the ceramic production of figurines and finewares, some of high quality. Signs of interaction with the wider world are rare and styles developed separately in different regions.[23] Protogeometric Greece is usually considered to have been mostly inward-looking and isolated.

Nonetheless – as did the twelfth century – the eleventh and tenth centuries in Greece saw their fair share of exceptions and innovations. On Crete we may reconstruct a certain standard of continuous stability and connectedness through the collapse and the local Protogeometric, as attested by the impressive wealth and exotica in early tombs at Knossos (though our resolution on the data is problematic) and the troves of imported and local luxury goods deposited in cave sanctuaries on Mts. Ida and Dikte.[24] Rich burials at Lefkandi in Euboea, on the island of Skyros, and at Athens show that the story of the Greek mainland during this period is likewise more complicated than a simple model of decline would suggest, and a few exported objects in Cyprus and the Syro-Palestinian littoral point to some modest sustained contacts (see Chapters 2 and 4). A new feature of the material culture is the replacement of bronze with iron as the primary metal used for making weapons. Debate about the nature and causes of the introduction of iron to Greece during the EIA has not produced a completely convincing model to explain this transition, but Cyprus was almost certainly involved.[25]

From the Geometric period, and especially in the eighth century, the archaeological evidence is more plentiful.[26] The number of settlements appears to increase, while the urban fabric at sites like Oropos[27] and Zagora[28] becomes more complex. Large "monumental" sacred buildings at some sites (e.g. Eretria[29] and Ano Mazaraki)[30] attest to the increasing investment of communities in cult sites, as do the valuable offerings (including imported materials and artifacts) deposited in major local and regional sanctuaries.[31] After many centuries during which writing was apparently not a feature of the cultural landscape, Greeks adapted the Phoenician alphabet and began to produce written texts, including Homer's *Iliad* and *Odyssey* and Hesiod's

---

[23] Snodgrass 1971; Coldstream 1983; Desborough 1952; Morgan 1990; 2003.
[24] Rutkowski and Nowicki 1996; Coldstream 2006; Sakellarakis 2013.
[25] Waldbaum 1978; 1982; Snodgrass 1989; Sherratt 1994; Kayafa 2000. Given the apparent emigration of some Greeks to Cyprus during the twelfth century, technological communication between these two regions would likely not have presented insuperable obstacles. I intend to return to this topic in future work.
[26] Antonaccio 1995, 3.
[27] Mazarakis Ainian 2002a; 2002b; essays in Mazarakis Ainian 2007.
[28] Most recently Gounaris 2015.
[29] Auberson and Schefold 1972; Bérard 1982; Verdan 2012; 2015. Verdan suggests that the *Daphnephoreion* might have been intended as a banquet hall instead of a temple.
[30] Petropoulos 2002, cf. Kolia 2011 for a smaller temple near Ano Mazaraki.
[31] Sourvinou-Inwood 1993; Morgan 1997; 2003; Kilian-Dirlmeier 1985; Muscarella 1992; Crielaard 2015.

Theogony and *Works and Days*. The population probably grew considerably, perhaps creating new tensions in economic class relationships based on changing proportions of available labor and land,[32] and possibly feeding a rash of land hunger that pushed Greeks to send colonizing parties from cities like Eretria and Corinth to Italy and to the North and East.[33] The eighth century has long been termed a "renaissance" because it appears to have been a period of increasing complexity, wealth, and interconnectedness between Greece and the wider Mediterranean.

2. THE ESTABLISHED NARRATIVE OF TRADE WITHIN EARLY GREEK HISTORY

The previous section represents an attempt to briefly sketch the currently accepted model of the rise, fall, and regeneration of complex societies over roughly a thousand years of early Greek history. Although it has not been uncontroversial, as we shall see, a key component of this narrative centers on the perceived cadence of long-distance exchange and contacts. The world of the Greek LBA was characterized by considerable commercial and political relations with social groups and institutions throughout the eastern and western Mediterranean, which (many argue) helped elites create social difference and solidify political capital. These relationships were jolted and largely severed at some point in the late thirteenth or twelfth century, as chaos gripped the complex societies of Syria-Palestine, Egypt, Anatolia, and Greece collectively. During the ensuing EIA, Greece was largely isolated and limped along through what has long been known as a Dark Age, although a few communities retained contacts with the East and maintained relative prosperity. Eventually, in the late tenth or ninth century, the Mediterranean networks that had once linked the Mycenaeans to the Near East began to hum once more and by the eighth century Greeks were crossing the seas for profit and to find new homes in great numbers again.

In what follows I want to examine the evidence for this story as far as identifiable commercial or reciprocal trade is concerned,[34] and test its major plot points against a vigorous analysis of the relevant material remains and textual records pertaining to long-distance trade over the transition from the

---

[32] Most have interpreted this as a clash between elites and commoners (e.g. St. de Croix 1981; Morris 1987; Donlan 1997). For a recent interpretation of the evolution of communities that proposes a more fluid process see Duplouy 2006 (reviewed in Power 2006).

[33] Though the desire for more land probably played a role, the colonizing movement itself is a topic that is far too complex, multicausal and multifaceted to treat properly here (see Crielaard 1992, 239–242; recent summary in Papadopoulos 2014, 187–188).

[34] Throughout the work I use the terms "trade" and "exchange" as synonyms, mostly for stylistic variation, with specific terms such as gift exchange, commercial exchange, tramping, and so forth used to specify particular sorts of relationships where appropriate.

Late Bronze to Early Iron Age. For, despite the frequency with which international trade is discussed in literature on the LBA, and the increasing number of works appearing on the transitional periods between the LBA and the "rise of the polis" in the eighth century, no synthetic work on this topic exists. Given the centrality of the study of LBA/EIA trade and interaction to much fresh research, it thus seems both timely and prudent to collect the relevant evidence in one place, and to assess how far it is possible to stretch this evidence to reconstruct a well-grounded and logically consistent history of the Greek trade economy between 1300 and 700 BCE.[35]

I do my best here to review the basis on which arguments about change in the Greek trade economy have been made, to summarize both the direct and the corroborating evidence, and to contextualize this evidence in a broader picture of the economy. The book confirms a few long-held notions of early Mediterranean trade, confounds a few others, and, most importantly, gives other scholars a useful summary and background against which to confirm or confound the conclusions I am able to reach in my own modest way.

The evidence is at times difficult to work with (a classic situation of "indirect traces in bad samples"),[36] and pushes against aggregation, meaningful comparison, and simple results. Despite these difficulties, it is clear that there is one major takeaway from a quantitatively-geared approach to the material cultural evidence for the economic transition under study. There appears to have been a major and far-reaching economic decline after the end of the thirteenth century. This decline in the scale and complexity of the economy was probably associated with some relatively major population movements, and probably took effect in full force by 1100 BCE. Though the recent trend has been to reconceptualize this period in a more positive light, the economic data, as far as

---

[35] Long-distance trade has been a major focus of debate in LBA studies. The recent bibliography listed previously (n. 1) is hefty. But the EIA has rarely been integrated into the story. The focus on LBA exchange is, no doubt, more than a product of disciplinary circumstance: there is far more evidence to examine for this period, including shipwrecks, related texts from both Greece and the Near East, and ample Mycenaean pottery in foreign contexts. Early EIA trade and commerce have been subjected to less scrutiny (though Geometric colonization has flourished as a disciplinary focus). We have made gains in assembling the relevant data in this area in recent years (see Tandy 1997; Foxhall 1998; Crielaard 1999; Jones 2000; Fletcher 2007; Maier et al. 2009; Knodell 2013; Nakassis forthcoming). Nonetheless, Sherratt and Sherratt's observation from 1993 (p. 361), that "[o]ne of the most crucial but poorly understood phases in the development of the Mediterranean economy is the transition from the Bronze Age to the Iron Age" continues to ring true. In large part this is because the EIA evidence, in terms of Greek products found abroad, shipwrecks, written testimony, and imported objects within Greece, is not as plentiful. However, as Papadopoulos has repeatedly emphasized (i.e. Papadopoulos 1993; 1996; 2001; 2014, 181–184) the biggest obstacle may be the "iron curtain" that has long stood between LBA and EIA studies. This curtain has begun to come down among younger scholars (see recent history of the discipline in Kotsonas 2016).

[36] Clarke 1973, 16. See comments at Muhly 1973, 167: "The study of trade in the Bronze Age is a difficult and often unrewarding endeavor."

we can gather them, support a gloomier view, at least on a macroscopic scale. Recovery was slow, but by the eighth century BCE there are signs that the Greek economy had outstripped its LBA predecessor, and that Greeks were interacting with the wider Mediterranean in thoroughgoing ways once again. Though we may only be able to measure the intervening economic decline with the rough toolkit of archaeology, its scope and scale are, in broad brushstrokes, so clearly manifest in the material culture that we do a great disservice to the evidence to dismiss it as unimportant or insignificant. Economic decline is not an abstract concept; the evidence shows that the LBA–EIA transition almost certainly must have been a traumatic period for people living in Greece, full of difficulty, uncertainty, and insecurity (if also opportunity). There is clear evidence that institutions for trade and exchange had to be rebuilt entirely from scratch during the Geometric period, when recovery finally began. However difficult the hard times of the eleventh and tenth centuries were, it is equally clear that the Greeks who stayed in Greece through the contraction survived, adapted, and eventually built something new in apparently challenging circumstances.

That, in sum, is the argument I undertake to lay out in what follows. But why is it a mission worthy of dispatch? Ultimately, what is at stake in a book interrogating the early history of the Greek trade economy? Why will story of the transition between Greek history and prehistory be broadly and usefully enlightened by the study of long-distance commercial and political relationships? The reason is that trade has always been central to the narrative of social and economic development concerning the transformation of LBA society to the EIA. Why should this have been so? A variety of notions hang in the balance.

3. PREHISTORIC ECONOMIES, LONG-DISTANCE CONTACTS AND POLITICAL STRUCTURE

In addressing this topic, I come face to face with an old anthropological and archaeological debate about the fundamental relationship between trade, commerce, and rulership, and – ultimately – with questions about why people engage in long-distance trade at all. We can think of some obvious reasons that trade at a certain geographic resolution might exist independently of the ambitions and assertions of social leaders, especially in cases that revolve around the acquisition of goods needed for survival in the absence of local resources. However, the acquisition of goods that are "unnecessary" and/or perceived as irrelevant from a survivalist point of view, is usually considered as part of a social, political, or economic strategy.

In the relevant archaeological literature, it is generally assumed that the acquisition of locally unavailable, not-strictly-necessary goods from afar indicates the desire of some local population to collectively better its economic situation, through diversification of resources, or of individuals to elevate themselves above the group by possession of exotic materials or finished products.[37] It has even been argued that the acquisition and management of goods unavailable locally might be a prime mover toward social differentiation and the development of complex states in the first place, and that loss of trade routes may often lead to collapse.[38] If these premises are true, we would imagine that a history of Greek trade would bear usefully on our knowledge of how the LBA–EIA transition progressed from a politico-economic point of view – changes in the scale and nature of trade might be instrumental in reconstructing political and economic history of early Greece. But before proceeding it is a good idea to set out with some diligence the scholarly background on relationships between trade and economy, trade and politics.

This discussion began among anthropologists, dating back to Malinowski's *Argonauts of the Western Pacific* in 1922 and Mauss's related work on exchange and authority in early societies.[39] According to Mauss and Malinowski, island chieftains gained prestige and power by virtue of their access to special objects acquired from distant lands. However, these exchanges were not economic in nature; the gains accrued from exchange were socially embedded and symbolic. This socially embedded view of trade (known as substantivism or primitivism)[40] is traditionally opposed to formalist models, which presume that industrial and preindustrial humans operate and have always operated based upon identical models of rational economic maximization.[41] The primitivist/substantivist versus formalist debate has grown stale, and recent work in the field of economics has shown emphatically that almost all economies share aspects of both models: people act in their own self-interest, but always in ways that are uniquely mediated by institutional and cultural frameworks.[42] Evidence from the LBA Mediterranean economy bears out notions of this "new institutional" approach with great clarity. While heads of state certainly

---

[37] Cf. Polanyi 1966; Schortman and Urban 1987; Tainter 1988, 23–24; Sherratt and Sherratt 1991; Sherratt 1999; Helms 1979; 1988; 1993. For the impact of imported goods on local hierarchies and politics for the Aegean in particular, see examples at Renfrew 1975; Voutsaki 1995; 1998; 1999; 2001; Kilian 1988b; I. Morris 1999. Summary of relevant evidence and literature at Manning and Hulin 2005, 273–274. See also review of literature on trade, power, and elites in Oka and Kusimba 2008, 352–357.

[38] For the role of exotic commodity acquisition in building states, see Rathje 1971. For its role in their demise, Eckholm 1980; Hodges and Whitehouse 1983; Cipolla 1970.

[39] Malinowski 1922; Mauss 1923.

[40] Important studies include Hasebroek 1928; Dalton 1975; Polanyi 1963; Bohannon and Dalton 1962; Brunton 1971; Rotstein 1972. On the ancient world: Finley 1970; Renfrew 1975; 1977; Snodgrass 1991.

[41] See, for example, Earle 1982; Monroe 2000, 6; Earle 2002.

[42] North 1990; 1991; 1996; for examples of use in historical study see Kowaleski 1995; Williamson 1985; 1996. In the Mycenaean economy, Parkinson, Nakassis, and Galaty 2013, 415.

exchanged goods via relationships that were essentially and overtly political, these exchanges also had economic underpinnings, and other exchanges outside of the political "symbolic" realm existed alongside of those relationships in ways that look quite modern.[43]

In what follows, I presume that we cannot necessarily rebuild entire economic systems or the motivations that drove individuals within them from the meager evidence left behind in the archaeological record. The bottom line is that long-distance interaction was complex, as are all aspects of the ancient economy; the artifacts we find will never tell the whole story that lurks in the shadows behind them.[44] In general, however, I think that our best chance at getting a decent idea of the relationship between surviving artifacts and overall economic systems lies in (1) beginning with a thorough and systematic assemblage of all of the relevant evidence that could be brought to bear on the discussion and (2) assessing patterns of evidence over time, rather than staring fixedly at individual periods.

The first point is self-evident, and needs little justification. The only plausible reason *not* to begin analysis with a comprehensive grasp of relevant evidence is that assembling evidence is often logistically difficult and time consuming. But this is more of an excuse than a logical stepping-stone. The second point adheres to the overall principles of a diachronic and comparative approach to history.[45] That is to say, the central objective of comparative history should be to discover which variables precipitated different outcomes in varying historical circumstances by "identifying critical differences between similar situations" and to trace processes in order to validate conclusions. Along with Goldstone, I consider the success or failure of a historical project by judging whether it "identifies relationships heretofore unrecognized or misunderstood in particular sequences of historical events that have occurred." It is often not possible to achieve total explanatory success that covers all historical details: "Elucidation of a process that connects many details

---

[43] For the diverse and multilayered nature of LBA trade systems, Monroe 2009; Bell 2012; 2006; Whitelaw 2001b; Sherratt and Sherratt 1993; Nakassis forthcoming. For debates touching on these subjects in the wider archaeological literature, see, recently, McKllop 2005; Bellina 2003.

[44] Cf. comments at Fletcher 2007, 32. On the shadows, Sherratt 2011. One is reminded of Herodotus's story of the jars in Egypt (Hdt. 3.6): "Every year Egypt imports from all over Greece, and from Phoenicia as well, clay jars full of wine, and yet it is hardly an exaggeration to say that there is not a single empty wine-jar to be seen there. One might well ask: where do they all disappear to? This is yet another issue I can clarify. Every headman has to collect all the jars from his community and take them to Memphis, and then the people of Memphis fill them with water and take them out into the waterless regions of Syria we have been talking about. That is how every jar that is imported into Egypt is taken, once empty, into Syria to join all the earlier jars" (trans. A. Purvis).

[45] Goldstone 1991, 52.

of what happened is sufficient to produce a work of great value."[46] Analysis here has attempted to satisfy all of Goldstone's conditions in a way that at least "connects many details of what happened" by comparing the evidence for trade systems across a scholarly divide that has resisted porosity. In other words, when we look at the overall economic scene of trade in a geographically and physically static area across different periods that present different political, social, economic, and military realities, the crucial factors shaping and shaped by the realities of trade are revealed in a clearer light.

So much for my general approach to the movement of objects in the archaeological record, and the way that the study of these objects can be assessed in relation to society more broadly. In the particular context of the early Aegean, trade has been central to discussions of elite self-fashioning and even the construction and cementation of social and political difference. Within the LBA world, scholars have often seen access to trade networks, and the luxury goods and commodities that moved through them, as a key underpinning factor in the ability of Bronze Age elites to both acquire and maintain control over subordinate groups. These elites used imports to create and reify their identities as privileged and special by way of conspicuous consumption. In addition, the redistribution of exotica helped consolidate power and garner loyalty amongst vassals.[47] According to this view, trade in the LBA was not only an economic institution, but also a tool used to consolidate power, maintain long-distance contacts and relationships, and entrench social differences within Greek society.[48]

If the acquisition of exotic goods from afar was controlled by the Mycenaean palace states during the LBA, and if palatial elites leveraged special relationships with kings in the Near East in order to both establish and legitimate political power as well as to enrich themselves economically, the corollary is that any disruption of trade would likewise have brought about political disaster.[49] If authority is based upon preferential access to goods from abroad, and that access disappears, authority will soon go with it. Alternatively, we might assume that, if the primary reason that the Mycenaeans cultivated long-distance trade relationships was for the preservation of political power, and that the political system within which this mechanism operated no longer

---

[46] Goldstone 1991, 60–61.
[47] Knapp 1990; 1998; Sherratt 2001; Burns 2010a; 2010b; Bennet 2008; Voutsaki 1997; 2001; 2010; Schon 2010; Monroe 2011.
[48] Similar formulations have been made about the relationship between imports and elites in the EIA: Tandy 1997, 113–127; I. Morris 2000, 195–257; Lemos 2002 (Appendix 2: "At the same time it is possible that members of the Euboean *koiné* could have reached the eastern Mediterranean by the second half of the tenth century as their elite groups were eager to acquire imported goods to reinforce their status."); Wallace 2010, 195–200.
[49] Bell 2012, 180; Singer 1999, 733; Singer 2000; Monroe 2009, 361–363; Bell 2006, 1; Cline 2014, 148–153.

existed, trade would disappear, having lost its raison-d'être.[50] In either case, exchange has a central role within current understandings of LBA political economy, both as a prosperous system and a failed one.

If we accept, whatever the precise relationship between political collapse and long-distance trade relations, that trade was meaningful socially, politically, and economically during the LBA, and that trade systems in the LBA were closely connected to entities which held political and social power, then we might expect the material residues of trade in the archaeological record to accompany meaningful changes in political and economic reality. So, dramatic changes in the material remains of trade after the end of the Mycenaean period should be strong indicators for change in trade systems, but also for change in the political organization of society. On the other hand, if the evidence for long-distance trade does not change much through time, it might suggest that the social and political relationships and structures that obtained in the LBA remained largely intact right on through the traumatic events at the end of the Mycenaean period.

So, given our understanding of how long-distance trade and political structure articulated in the LBA, we can reasonably expect that evidence for the evolution of trade should have meaningful things to say about political realities as well as economic ones. In addition, looking at the nature and extent of long-distance trade over the centuries is likely to provide clues relevant to reconstructing ancient economies and societies, and the way they grew and changed over time. The scale of long-distance trade economies does not only tell us about the economy, but also about culture. Flux in trade volumes over time will vary according to the willingness or reticence with which groups pursue relationships with people they see as different. It can show evidence of people's facility with culturally embedded ideals such as trust, cooperation, and honesty, and the degree to which they extend these ideals outward to unknown parties. Trade can also play into the development of new technologies, of the amount of resistance to our acceptance of tradition or innovation, and the relationship of people to their past and to their future. We should not underestimate the centrality of long-distance relationships, commercial or otherwise, in shaping a diverse menu of social conditions.

Thus, while Tartaron (2013, 10–11) has recently advocated "a reorientation of our intellectual energies away from international-scale maritime relations" it remains true, I think, that we still have much to learn on this front, and should not leave its study aside just yet. For all of the reasons given previously, clarity in regard to the systems underlying this kind of exchange are uniquely appropriate

---

[50] For the role of long-distance exchange in the growth and beginnings of legitimation in the palatial mainland see Cavanagh and Mee 1998, 41–60; Dickinson 1977; Voutsaki 1997; 2001; 2010; Bennet 2007, 186; Nakassis 2007, 133; Wright 2008.

to certain lines of inquiry about the important economic transition that the Greek world experienced in the late second and early first millennium.

4. DISCONTINUITY OR CONTINUITY? THE LBA TO EIA TRANSITION

The second area in which a study of trade in early Greek history is likely to make an impact is in the debate over whether we should see the Greek LBA to EIA transition as a story of disruption, stagnation, and reinvention, or as a continuous and unified spectrum of development. The only way to resolve this debate is to put the study of the LBA and EIA in the same scholarly arena, an arena that had not attracted a great deal of attention until the past few decades.[51]

As the period has gained traction in scholarship more recently, the most prominent debate concerning the LBA–EIA transition has concerned whether it should be seen as a period of institutional, economic, and political rupture from the Bronze Age or a time of gradual development during which many characteristics of Mycenaean/Minoan culture were retained.[52] The terms of this discussion were more or less set by Desborough, Coldstream, and Snodgrass in the 1970s, when the study of the era between the collapse of the Bronze Age palaces and the Archaic/Classical Greek city-states first underwent intensive study.[53] The synthetic works of all three scholars have been highly influential, but Snodgrass's study has had the most lasting effect on the shape of current discourse about the nature of the EIA. Snodgrass argued that the Aegean region disengaged from the rest of the Mediterranean world after the end of the postpalatial period in the eleventh century, and that this period of disengagement only ended with the so-called renaissance of the eighth century. Basing his narrative on the archaeological evidence available at the time, he envisioned the EIA as a time of depopulated egalitarian communities. This, he reasoned, represents a big change from the complex, highly stratified, urbanized society of the LBA.

Since Snodgrass's work in the 1970s, scholars have taken a variety of approaches to the EIA. Initially, most archaeologists and historians agreed with Snodgrass, maintaining an emphasis on sharp discontinuities marking out the EIA from what came before and after. I. Morris has since shown that

---

[51] Papadopoulos 2001, 444; history of scholarship in I. Morris 2000, 77–106 and more recently Kotsonas 2016; also relevant is Whitley 1991a, 5–8.
[52] Snodgrass 1971; I. Morris 1993; 2007; Papadopoulos 1993; 1994; 1996; Morgan 1993; Mazarakis-Ainian 1997; Marakas 2010; van Effenterre 1985. Lemos 2002 gives a comprehensive bibliography, though it is now a bit out of date.
[53] Coldstream [1977] 2003; Desborough 1952; 1972; Snodgrass 1971. Other important early work was done by Schachermeyr (1979; 1980; 1984) though this has been less influential.

quality of life in the EIA was in fact considerably worse than life in the periods that preceded and followed it, supporting the notion that the Snodgrass model was more or less correct.[54] Others, however, have focused more on continuity and sought to overturn the view that major ruptures followed the end of the Bronze Age. Philologists have seen similarities between the uses and word forms of Linear B and Greek,[55] and have read into this a link between eighth century authors and their Mycenaean predecessors. Religion has also been widely cited as an area of particular continuity between Bronze and Iron ages.[56]

In the context of the continuity/discontinuity debate, the relationship between Greece and the East has been a particularly rich area of study. The notion that there was little trade in the Protogeometric period – that Greece was isolated from the wider world, and especially from the Near East – at the transition to Greek history has formed an important part of the traditional narrative of the formation of Western Society. In an older model of Classical scholarship, part of the appeal of the existing narrative of trade (with isolation in the Dark Age) is that it conveniently wipes clean the slate from a period in which Greek and Near Eastern cultures were tightly intermingled.[57] This severing of historic from Mycenaean age Greece has allowed a description of western heritage in which things like democracy, western art, and philosophy arose in an unsullied EIA crucible free from eastern influence.[58] The demolition of this reductionist and no-longer sustainable rhetorical isolation of early Greece from the Orient has been salutary. However, debate continues over whether and to what degree ties (elite or otherwise) lapsed or were largely retained in the EIA. The recent trend has shifted from emphasizing a rupture to showing the breadth and depth of the connections that Greece retained through the EIA, as part of the wider school of thought arguing that there was not much that fundamentally distinguished the EIA Greek from the LBA Mycenaean world.[59]

If accepted, this position is quite important, because it implies the need for a major overhaul of the way scholars reconstruct early Greece. Rather than an instance of the collapse and regeneration of complex society, this period would rather represent a beat in an altogether different rhythm of social development,

---

[54] Tandy 1997; Dickinson 2006, 88–103; I. Morris 2007; Papadopoulos 1993; Foxhall 1995; Papadopoulos 1996 for contrary arguments.
[55] Carlier 1984, 68; van Effenterre 1985, 155.
[56] Marakas 2010; de Polignac 1995; Morgan 1996.
[57] G. Murray 1907, 50; Botsford 1922, 31; Botsford 1922, 52–55; Burn 1936, 1; Beazley and Robertson 1926, 580; Nilsson 1933, 246; Starr 1961, 59.
[58] Political aspects of narratives about the transition: Kotsonas 2016.
[59] See Themelis 1976, 37; Luce 1975, 12; Wells 1983a, 17; Calligas 1987, 17; Calligas 1988, 229; S. Morris 1989, 48; Whitley 1991a, 5; Papadopoulos 1993, 195; Papadopoulos 1996, 255; Papadopoulos 1997, 192; Lemos 1998; Papadopoulos 2001; Nakassis 2013; Papadopoulos 2014, 181; Nakassis forthcoming.

demanding a revision of our most basic narrative of early Greek history. Unfortunately, despite many years of debate, scholars remain at a stalemate about the underlying basis upon which the ancient Greeks developed a complex and exceptional social and economic system after a period of remarkable stagnation – whether it was due mostly to the preservation of a fundamentally Mycenaean ideology, to influence from the east, to entirely independent developments, or some combination of the above.[60] The study undertaken here, a careful examination of the relevant evidence that might weigh on our ultimate judgment in this context, aims to answer this question with greater precision than existing qualitative studies have managed to do.

5. THE QUANTITATIVE ARCHAEOLOGICAL RECORD

The final contribution that I want to make in this book is to vigorously investigate how much quantitative analysis can tell us about prehistory, in a straightforward and transparent way that takes seriously two key notions that might at first seem at odds with one another, but which I see as ultimately complementary. First, I contend that the recent tack away from quantitative analysis in archaeology[61] is a major problem, because when we dismiss quantitative change in the archaeological record we simultaneously discard our only chance of obtaining a clear picture of flux in ancient economies. Second, despite its potential to clarify big patterns in past economies, we must proceed with quantitative analysis as extreme skeptics, and prove beyond possible doubt that the patterns we see in the evidence are likely to reflect meaningful ancient realities.

Of course, the quantitative analysis of evidence for prehistoric trade, and of archaeological material in general, is fraught with difficulties.[62] Since the

[60] While many authors have sided with the gradualist view of the EIA representing a time of smooth development from the LBA, many continue to call the period a Dark Age and to retain the older notion that there was a major episode of collapse and regeneration. See I. Morris 2007; Tandy 1997; Bouzek 1997, 24; Coldstream 1998, 1. Most general works and textbooks on Greek history maintain this view (see S. Murray forthcoming b).

[61] Formally quantitative approaches gained traction in archaeology relatively recently in the history of the discipline (Spaulding 1953, 93; Ammerman 1992, 233). Spaulding's innovation was an early example of the application of quantitative methods to archaeological material. He argued that existing statistical methods could make patterns in the archaeological record clear in ways that traditional humanistic analysis could not. During the 1960s and 1970s archaeologists became more interested in quantitative analysis (Heizer and Cook 1960; Binford and Binford 1966; Clarke 1968; Papers in Hodson, Kendall, and Tauta 1971). Though great enthusiasm has often surrounded the adoption of scientific methods in archaeology, most agree that quantification has not lived up to the expectations that archaeologists of the 1970s and 1980s had for it. Postprocessual archaeologists have criticized the semiscientific methods of quantitative archaeology for masking subjective interpretations with numbers and charts and for losing sight of historical context and of the individual (Hodder 1985).

[62] Manning and Hulin 2005, 283; Dickinson 2006, 201; Cherry 2010, 111–112; cf. Cline 2010, 164–165; Tartaron 2013, 34.

postprocessual turn of archaeology in the 1980s, quantitative analysis has frequently come under fire for presenting an artificially scientific and beguilingly systematic view of an ancient world that was as complex and full of changing meanings as our own.[63] In addition, archaeologists have become increasingly aware that the patterns apparent in the archaeological record often reflect the activities, research priorities, and methodological proclivities of archaeologists more than ancient realities.[64]

Regarding ancient patterns in Mediterranean trade the influence of quantitative archaeology has not been pervasive[65] and scholars remain divided about how much counting up imported goods from sites can tell us about the nature of Aegean trade. Cline's oeuvre still represents the most thorough attempt to quantify the evidence for long-distance trade in the LBA Aegean.[66] Parkinson (2010) and Schon (2010) have made use of Cline's catalogs of Bronze Age imports to draw some tentative conclusions about the scale and characteristics of early Greek trade. On a less "global" scale, others have made significant strides in the quantitative study of single artifact types[67] or of imports found in individual excavations or regions.[68]

Many scholars are not convinced of the utility of such efforts. Discussing EIA trade, Dickinson states that "basing any detailed conclusions on the quantities actually found involves highly questionable assumptions."[69] According to Dickinson, exotica show only that a site was connected in some way with "the outside world." No further conclusions can be drawn from imported artifacts, since these items could indicate a variety of things including but not in any way limited to trade and foreign exchange.[70] Likewise, Manning and Hulin have criticized Cline's data as an "inadequate, if not misleading, basis on which to analyze trade," and Cherry asserts that the fact that "most scholars imagine a vigorous trade in a wide variety of materials taking place throughout the entire Eastern Mediterranean" should take precedence over the quantitative evidence, i.e. the surprisingly small number of artifacts (1,118 items, working out to about 0.5/year over the entire LBA) tallied up by Cline.[71]

---

[63] See Hodder 1982; 1984; 1985; Miller and Tilley 1984; Spriggs 1984.
[64] Helpful recent discussion in Lucas 2013; see also Collins 1975.
[65] Although world-systems theory (usually categorized as a tenet of processual archaeology) has played a significant role in framing the debate. There are useful reviews in Kardulias 2010; Sherratt 2010.
[66] Cline 1994; Cline and Yasur-Landau 2007; Cline 2010.
[67] Haskell 2011; also worth noting are Gale and Stos-Gale 1986 (ingots); Mangou and Ioannou 2000 (ingots); Kayafa 2000 (metals); Ingram 2005 (beads); Rutter 2014 (Canaanite Jars).
[68] Hoffman 1997 (Crete); Bikai 2000 (Kommos); Lemos 2003 (Lefkandi); Rutter 2006 (Kommos); Rahmstorf 2008 (Tiryns); Tomlinson et al. 2010 (Kommos).
[69] Dickinson 2006, 201; cf. Tartaron 2013, 34.
[70] Dickinson 2006, 201.
[71] Cherry 2010, 112.

According to this critique, the scholarly consensus – formed out of general impressions gleaned from anecdotal evidence, literary sources, and educated hypotheses – is preferable to the archaeological data as a basis for drawing conclusions. Such a standpoint on the evidence calls into question the entire project of archaeology – how are reconstructions of the past made by individual scholars to be evaluated if not in reference to the evidence? Cline has rightly made the counterargument that the evidence exists, and to dismiss its value out of hand without giving careful critical thought to the reasons behind disparities between scholarly opinion and archaeological data is unhelpful.[72]

Few would argue that import counts tell the whole story, but as Cline points out, "[i]t does no good to disparage the only material evidence we currently possess." Cline argues that this evidence must be taken into account in any discussion involving possible trade and contact between the Aegean, Egypt, and the Near East.[73] Fantalkin summarizes the middle-of-the-road view that "[t]he accumulation of data, an essential beginning, should lead to contextualization involving the understanding that different chronological settings may represent different geopolitical dynamics."[74] While gathering the evidence is key, putting this information into a historical/chronological context is a necessary follow-up. According to this view, the best way forward is to neither disparage nor dismiss the material remains of trade but to get the evidence together and then have a contextually informed discussion about what it might mean.[75]

Regarding the economic transition between the LBA and the EIA, neither of these goals have been accomplished yet. Here, I aim to tackle them, but not only in the sense that I have gathered the evidence. Despite the broadly stated, almost superstitious skepticism about numbers that has been expressed in existing scholarship on Mediterranean trade, few have articulated with much clarity how we might distinguish meaningful quantitative change from change that can be discounted as a product of postdepositional factors, or as so insignificant that it can reasonably be dismissed. In regard to LBA and EIA trade, we have long been vaguely aware that we know of "fewer" imported and exported objects from EIA, but little effort has been made to distinguish levels of magnitude and/or statistical significance of these trends, let alone how they compare to other quantitative economic measures such as demography, or how they reflect archaeological research priorities rather than change in the ancient past.

---

[72] Cline 2010, 165.
[73] Cline 2010, 165.
[74] Fantalkin 2006, 199.
[75] Ammerman 1992, 239: "This is essentially a problem of formalism; most practicing archaeologists who have spent years assembling a data set are likely to have a dense network of ideas, albeit imperfect and incomplete, about their data."

In order to get a sense of all these factors, and in order for analysis to be meaningful, the evidence for trade needs necessarily to be contextualized within the overall human-generated dataset of archaeological knowledge for the relevant periods. Prehistoric archaeologists reconstruct the past by weaving together narratives that unify scattered pieces of information into a coherent whole. Since only a small, often randomly preserved, fraction of written sources and material evidence from the prehistoric world survives and is thus already partial and contingent, it is of the utmost importance that this material be considered within a matrix of all the information that we have managed to assemble into the archaeological record. Here, I attempt to project the evidence for trade against a systematically constructed background of the archaeological record as we have it, so that it is possible to put it in perspective. The hope is that this will put us in a much better position to distinguish random patterns from meaningful change.

6. APPROACHES TO ANCIENT TRADE FROM THE MATERIAL EVIDENCE

I hope that it will not be controversial to assert without too much further pleading that sorting out all of these topics is crucial to our ability to clearly tell the story of Greece's historical economic development. In addition, I hope that it will become clear throughout the progress of the argument that evidence for trade can be a fruitful source of answers to bigger questions about the realities of social and political developments over time.

A bit of further articulation is appropriate in regard to the intellectual orientation of much of what follows. For the prehistoric period, the only evidence we have to rely upon when examining the external connections of any group are archaeological artifacts. As we have already seen, these objects are unlikely to have a straightforward relationship with ancient trade or the ancient economy.[76] As Bennet states, "[t]he core problem with understanding past exchange patterns is that objects tend not to be recovered archaeologically in contexts where they were consumed, not in the process of distribution, or even at their point of arrival."[77] There are many difficulties that go along with trying to read the nature of "trade" into the number and type of surviving objects found lying around archaeological sites. Traded goods may not be well represented by the finished, recognizably imported objects that end up getting deposited and excavated in archaeological sites. While the presence of nonlocal pottery and other foreign goods tends to indicate some kind of cultural contact, it does not necessarily indicate direct participation in trade by the community

---

[76] Jones 2000, 50; Cherry 2010, 111–112; Parkinson and Galaty 2010, 16–25; Tartaron 2013, 34.
[77] Bennet 2007, 201.

or individuals that possessed them. Likewise, the absence of imported goods at a site does not necessarily indicate the total disengagement of that site from exchange networks, but could be indicative of anything from taphonomic/postdepositional processes to the archaeological invisibility of traded goods, to cultural choices about what to do with imports.

Despite the oft-stated maxim that it is impossible to excavate trade networks, many scholars have attempted to create economic models based on the archaeological evidence of traded goods. A variety of theoretical approaches have been used in the study of ancient trade, and some have contributed to our understanding of exchange networks and mechanisms in the prehistoric past.[78] It will be useful to define the framework which underlies this book, especially in relation to these theoretical approaches.

Existing analyses of trade in the archaeological record have most often taken a model-based approach. While some of these models of trade networks have analytical value, archaeological models of artifact distributions have been extensively criticized and problematized and should therefore be approached with caution. In what follows, I review the way in which archaeologists have interpreted the meaning of import and export distributions, and assess their value for the current study. I then articulate my own approach to the evidence, which largely eschews existing theoretical models in order to create space for a more rigorous interrogation of the basic facts underlying our ideas about ancient trade.

Historians and archaeologists have identified numerous categories of trade systems, which some believe can be traced in the distribution of material in the archaeological record. Polanyi isolated three main modes of exchange: reciprocity, redistribution, and market exchange.[79] Inherent to these models is the presumption that geographical patterns in the evidence would be shaped by and therefore reflect the nature of the trade system.[80] Renfrew later elaborated on these three basic types, diagramming ten models of trade: direct access, home-base reciprocity, boundary reciprocity, down-the-line, central-place redistribution, central-place market exchange, freelance (middleman) trading, emissary trading, colonial enclaves, and port-of-trade. Renfrew explicitly linked these different systems to different spatial patterns in artifact distribution that could be recognized archaeologically.[81] He theorized that we could distinguish different kinds of trade by looking at the distribution of traded goods.[82] Gift exchange between elites, for example, would result in a different

---

[78] For example, discussion of the evidence of imports from Al Mina (and to a lesser extent Pithekussai) in Luke 2003.
[79] Polanyi 1957.
[80] Polanyi in Dalton 1968, 163.
[81] Renfrew 1975.
[82] Renfrew 1975, 46.

pattern of import deposition than independent, freelance market trade.[83] Renfrew applied this framework to obsidian in the Near East. He argued that this material was traded in a "down-the-line" fashion, apparent from the changing density of finds relative to distance from their source.[84] In turn, associating different trade systems with specific social and cultural relationships allowed Renfrew to link the spatial pattern of traded objects to social and political structures.

Others have proposed alternative interpretative frameworks for the spatial distribution patterns of commodities and artifacts. In the World Systems model, first developed by Wallerstein for the early modern world, but modified by archaeologists to suit the conditions of archaic states,[85] finished products from well-developed "core" states are exchanged for necessary bulk commodities from outlying, less-developed "peripheries."[86] Because of the diverse interests of the parties in a World System, and the model's assumptions regarding asymmetric exchange relationships, it is expected that certain patterns in the deposition of artifacts should be evident in the spatial data. In a Core/Periphery World System, we would expect finished value-added imported products to accumulate in areas with strong control over commodities that would have been of interest to their trading partners.[87] For example, if timber were of interest to a core state, we would expect imports from that core state to accumulate in areas with good access to timber resources, and so on. Most Aegeanists using a World Systems perspective see Greece as a peripheral state, subsidiary (though not subordinate) to powerful, more mature Near Eastern states, although the explicit tenets of the world systems model do not seem to have won over many adherents in this context.[88] Other scholars have attempted to make sense of trade systems using different spatial models, often at least loosely related to the ideas of Renfrew and Polanyi.[89] For example, Hirth, working on ancient Mesoamerica, developed the notion of "gateway communities."[90] The gateway community model is a variation of a port of trade model that predicts a dendritic distribution of goods throughout a site hierarchy rather than a distribution in which goods are accumulated in areas that are a short distance from a "central place."[91]

---

[83] Renfrew 1975, 48–50.
[84] Renfrew, Dixon, and Cann 1968.
[85] Wallerstein 1974; Hopkins and Wallerstein 1982; Chase-Dunn and Hall 1991.
[86] Stein 2002, 904.
[87] Kristiansen 1998.
[88] Sherratt and Sherratt 1991; Kardulias 2010; Burns 2011.
[89] Smith 2004, 84–85.
[90] Hirth 1978.
[91] Hirth 1978, 38. In this model, one powerful community monopolizes most of a region's market activity, while a "gateway community" is located at a regional boundary and operates as a commercial middleman. Imports and economic activity are funneled through

The idea that patterns in the distribution of imports might be a good indicator of the mechanisms of trade, or the organizational structures through which goods moved around, is therefore well-established in the archaeological literature.[92] According to this approach, change in distributions of imported objects over time, fed through the lens of a model such as World Systems Theory or gateway communities, should indicate of adjustments in prevailing trade systems and, by extension, political and social institutions. On the other hand, the notion that archaeologically evident patterns of artifact consumption, production, or circulation – even when considered synthetically – have anything to tell us about exchange systems has been criticized in recent years. Critics have argued that modifications archaeologists apply to Wallerstein's World Systems model rob this heuristic tool of any explanatory value, effectively rendering it so broad and amorphous that it is unsuitable for distinguishing between differently functioning systems.[93] Perhaps more importantly, even the components of the World Systems model that archaeological applications preserve rest on the assumption that external forces and dynamics are the primary drivers of trade and exchange.[94] Recent studies of trade argue instead that individuals within systems, rather than imposed economic forces, determine the material characteristics of societies. Thus, studies of trade and exchange now tend to focus more on the social aspects of intercultural interactions rather than economic or structural ones.[95]

According to these studies, approaching trade from the point of view of the internal dynamics of consumption not only explains social development better, but also treats the archaeological evidence in a manner that is more appropriate to its limitations.[96] Spatial studies of artifact distributions depend on a number of problematic assumptions: for instance, that the archaeological evidence for trade accurately represents the original circulation of goods, that different types of circulation will result in archaeologically distinguishable patterns of deposition,[97] and that the normal coexistence of multiple types and levels of

---

the gateway community because it is an important point of cultural mediation, not because it is a center of power.

[92] Galaty et al. 2010, 48.

[93] For example Stein's critiques (Stein 1999a; 1999b; 2002) as well as more general debates about the value of broad and generalizing approaches at Kohl 2008; Hegmon 2003; 2005; Watkins 2003. For recent defenses of the model even in its most general form, recently Galaty 2011; Hall, Kardulias, and Chase-Dunn 2011.

[94] Forces such as geographic realities or determinants, Knapp and Cherry 1994, 141 ("Bronze Age maritime centers in the eastern Mediterranean likely owed their commercial and social success to their location along the most commonly used sea-lanes.")

[95] Stein 2002, 904–905.

[96] Hodder and Orton 1976; Manning and Hulin 2005, 270–271; Cherry 2010, 111–112; Sherratt 2011.

[97] Hodder and Orton 1976.

exchange will not muddle up the archaeological footprint.[98] For example, if archaeologists focus on excavating large, important sites, it is likely that they will have more evidence for trade at these sites, and will argue accordingly.[99] If there was trade in organic products, this will be less apparent in the archaeological record than trade in durable goods. If people took imported goods with them when they abandoned one site, and left them behind at another, this will likewise affect the spatial distribution of evidence for trade in ways that do not reflect the dynamics of the circulation of goods with fidelity.

By focusing on the evidence of exchange in its depositional context, archaeologists hope to sidestep these problems while still saying something useful about the way in which cultures interacted. Something about the nature of demand can be inferred from the way that imported products functioned in society.[100] People are likely to consume objects in ways that are meaningful to them, in places that the objects are considered appropriate, useful, or desirable. But even if we focus on import consumption in studying trade dynamics, we still do so under the assumption that the archaeological record is not hopelessly distorted, and that we can draw meaningful conclusions from it.

In sum, although I do not in any way think that theoretical and model-based approaches to the trade economy of the early Aegean are valueless, it seems to me that we are currently not in a position to use them to their fullest potential, because we do not yet understand the evidence: is the material residua of long-distance trade hopelessly distorted? Are the differences we see in the geographical distributions and quantities of imports over time significant, or random? Are they related to the overall distribution of sites and apparent demographic fluctuations? Or do certain areas in certain periods truly see more apparent trade on a per capita as well as aggregate level? We do not yet have any decent answers to these questions. How, if we do not understand basic aspects of the evidence, can we hope to usefully apply generalizing models to it? Along these lines, one purpose of this book is to provide scholars some traction on these issues, as a precursor to opening the doors for more useful theoretical modeling of ancient trade.

In light of this goal, the primary tenets underlying this work surround the notion of formation processes: how did the patterns we see in the archaeological record get there, and how can we interpret them meaningfully while retaining a strong grasp of the relevant taphonomic complications involved? I hold the position that more elaborate theoretical approaches and models are best applied to data at a later stage of analysis, once the basic

---

[98] Vianello 2011, 411; cf. Lamberg-Karlovsky 1975, 348.
[99] Manning and Hulin 2005, 287.
[100] For the Mycenaean world, most clearly formulated in Burns 2010b; Brysbaert and Vetters 2013; cf. Kayafa 2008; Hoffman 1997 for early Crete; I. Morris 2000, 195–256; Crielaard 1999; Sherratt 1999 for early Greece.

mathematical patterns of quantities and distributions have been established. The archaeological record is highly contingent, incomplete, and taphonomically random[101] and applying synthetic models to data that has not yet been fully synthesized simply exacerbates, instead of helping to solve, the intractable interpretive problems at stake, and frequently obscures more than it enlightens. Therefore, in what follows I largely eschew the most popular models and approaches to ancient trade, including network theory and world systems theory, in favor of a relatively naïve and hardheaded attempt to sort out what the data really can do in helping us to reconstruct past "systems." Instead of applying models to evidence, I prioritize discussion of the basic interpretive problems we must face when coming to terms with both the scale and distribution of evidence for trade and the pesky problem of how much faith to put into that data. The purpose of this approach is to ensure that future scholars who wish to show that models can be helpful in evaluating ancient commercial and political relationships at a distance can easily keep their applied theory embedded in the data.

7. DEFINITION OF TERMS AND GEOGRAPHICAL SCOPE OF THE WORK

A few final preliminary remarks on definitions and the geographical scope of the work are necessary before proceeding with the argument. When I speak about trade, I use this term in a basic sense, to be taken as effectively synonymous with exchange, as any kind of movement of materials or objects from their place of origin or manufacture to another place where they cannot have originated or where the local material culture can be clearly distinguished from them. Long-distance exchange is a bit trickier to define, since the term *long* carries no precision. In this work, I take long-distance exchange to mean primarily maritime exchange that would have necessitated significant voyaging to and from regions with social, cultural, political, and/or economic systems that were clearly distinct from one another. Thus, this book covers exchange at a distance both geographically and socially, rather than small-scale exchanges that took place amongst neighbors operating within a similar cultural framework.[102]

As for defining imports themselves, this is another problem that looms large over the study, and the issue of how representative the surviving archaeological materials that we recognize as imports are of an original body of circulating

---

[101] Earle 1982, 7; cf. Renfrew 1972, 441.
[102] Not because I think the latter kind of exchange is less important; but this is a topic complex and rich enough to demand its own book-length treatments and cannot be covered in the current context. For small-scale networks see Knappett 2011; Tartaron 2013; Knodell 2013; Kramer-Hajos 2016.

imports is at the center of much of the discussion that follows. In general terms, I use a working definition of a finished import as a manmade object that is recovered in a context that is outside its "cultural unit" of manufacture. In Greece cultural boundaries have always been fluid,[103] and for the period under study they often seem arbitrary, so choosing whether to call something an import or not under the working definition I have given is not beyond criticism. However, for analytical purposes, it seems both practical and necessary to define a coarsely uniform area of cultural practice, while accepting that its boundaries are not fixed lines in the sand. In addition to problems of defining cultural boundaries, in the absence of scientific analysis of thin sections or clay content, separating imports from locally made imitations can be complex.[104] Largely, we are at the mercy of individual field project members and their bespoke definitions about or ability to recognize these objects, a problem that I return to occasionally in what follows. Commodities are subject to some of the same issues of recovery and fuzzy boundaries, but the working definition of an imported commodity I use here, which is any object found in a region that is made from a material that does not naturally occur in that region, should be less controversial.

Geographically, I limit my analysis to the part of Greece that is generally understood to have been culturally Mycenaean during the Bronze Age,[105] since my analytical goals have to do with figuring out how much the Greek economy changed after the Mycenaean collapse. Within the Greek world, I do not include Macedonia, Thrace, or the Cycladic and East Greek islands in my analyses. This decision is likely to frustrate some, especially those archaeologists working to bring to light the many, fascinating, and important new sites from the LBA and EIA in northern Greece and eastern Greece. Aside from the already cited reasoning (that northern Greece was not clearly part of the same Bronze Age cultural trajectory that seems to be evident in the southern Greek mainland) this limitation is also driven by sheer logistics. The long timespan covered and the data-intensive approach I take here make the work difficult to scale geographically. Gathering and sorting out over a hundred years' worth of evidence for imports, exports, systems of production, and comprehensive excavation and survey data at a certain resolution presents serious obstacles to the researcher in Greek archaeology, especially since many smaller excavation reports are scattered throughout a variety of perfunctory polyglot publications which are not available in most libraries. Anyone who has hefted the annual *ArchDelt* volumes on Macedonia and Thrace, and

---

[103] A theme that runs throughout the influential works of Horden and Purcell 2000 and Broodbank 2013.
[104] See, for instance, the collected essays in Kerschner and Lemos 2014.
[105] Again, not an entirely unproblematic notion: see Feuer 1983; Parkinson and Galaty 2007, 8–9; Tartaron 2004, 165–167.

seen their bulging spines on the bookshelf, will perhaps sympathize with my decision to draw a line of data collection at the Thessalian border. For similar reasons, I also largely set aside the evidence from the Cyclades and East Greece, though parts of the coastal regions of these areas probably had greater-or-lesser cultural affiliations with the mainland in the LBA.[106] I recognize this as a shortcoming of the present work, and expect that future endeavors, either my own or other scholars', will move in the direction of full geographic coverage. I do include Crete in the discussion, though this presents certain difficulties. At many points I will treat Crete largely as a separate entity from the Greek mainland, since its economic history and ceramic chronology diverge in important ways throughout the period under study, and I will often have occasion to comment on the ways I deal with these divergences.

Finally, a term that appears in both the title of the book and throughout the discussion that follows is "institutions," which I believe to provide a convenient structuring frame for diachronic comparative analysis. I understand institutions to be constituted by the social, political, and logistical scaffoldings within which exchanges and transactions took place, and which in turn shaped the nature and possibilities of those exchanges and transactions (in essence, the performance of exchange economies).[107] While "formal" institutions in the shape of hierarchically, coercively mandated rules and regulations are occasionally apparent in the evidence from early Greece,[108] I am more interested in what we can discover about the history of "informal" institutions, that is, habitual and customary behaviors that are the product of countless individual decisions that are structured by and structure the way that people behave.[109]

8. OUTLINE OF THE BOOK

The book falls into six chapters, along with this introduction and a brief concluding section. The structure of the argument is both progressive and cumulative, with the overall aim to work systematically through all available

---

[106] The "true" limits of a Mycenaean world are difficult to establish, and the issue has wrought much discussion, dating back at least to Feuer 1983. According to Snodgrass (2000, xxvi) the limits should be drawn south of Thessaly, as Mycenaean culture becomes diluted and "fleeting" in Phokis, Lokris, and Aetolia (see also Wardle and Wardle 2003; Kramer-Hajos 2008). However, due to the presence of many chamber tombs with finds in the Mycenaean style in Lokris, Phokis, and southern Aetolia, as well as the Mycenaean palace at Dimini, it seems unwise to exclude these regions from a loosely defined "Mycenaean world." See also comments at Dickinson 2006, 24–25.

[107] On the role of institutions in shaping economic practice and performance from a comparativist perspective, see Harriss, Hunter, and Lewis 1995.

[108] For example, the systems of taxation and allotment (*ta-ra-si-ja*) in the Linear B texts.

[109] Drawing generally from the framework laid out in Giddens 1984, but also the tenets of New Institutional Economics (see n. 42 above).

categories of evidence, from textual evidence to ancient demography, for change in exchange systems, showing gradually that the case to be made for a dynamic economic history from the LBA to the EIA is a strong one. In Chapter 1, I review the textual materials that might bear on our reconstruction of early Greek trade, and explain why they are so problematic in their likely relationship to each other and past trade systems as to be largely useless in a rigorous attempt to write history. Having dismissed the textual evidence as deeply unhelpful for my project here, I move on to the next obvious place to look for a history of economic interactions in Chapter 2. This chapter examines the most direct evidence for early Greek long-distance exchange, imported objects discovered in Greece, from a quantitative and qualitative point of view. An attempt is made to clarify the major patterns in the evidence (an overall decline in imports between 1200 and 800 BCE, and significant changes in the type and depositional context of these imports), before challenging the robustness of these patterns in Chapter 3. I conclude that the evidence is probably distorted in a variety of ways, and that we must seek additional lines of logic in order to be sure that the rough trends apparent in the import evidence are reliable.

This proposition is taken up in Chapters 4 and 5. First, in Chapter 4 I test the notion that the long-distance commodities trade suffered an even greater decline after the Mycenaean collapse than did trade in small personal objects and "trinkets" by considering the evidence for trade in raw metals (especially copper and tin) and other commodities from the LBA and EIA. In addition, I summarize the evidence of Greek exports around the Mediterranean. Finally, in Chapter 5, I evaluate likely fluctuations in demography, another factor that should be taken into account when assessing growth and decline in economic systems. This is a key moment in the argument, because demographic analysis allows us to evaluate the relative importance of supply and demand as drivers of economic change. The gist of these first five chapters is to show with unprecedented empirical thoroughness that a decline in aggregate trade volume commensurate with a major period of depopulation is highly likely after the early twelfth century BCE, but that per capita change is not as dramatic. With all of the evidence arrayed, I take a look back in Chapter 6 and attempt to provide a narrative history of long-distance exchange, and its social and political parameters, using the bigger trends apparent in the evidence as jumping-off points for a (necessarily broad-brushed) explanation of the transformations visible in the archaeological record.

The new conclusions reached in the book ought to have an impact on the way in which we view long-distance exchange across the LBA–EIA transition. First, the entrenched notion that Mycenaean elites used imported exotica to create and express social difference, or that they controlled or depended on long-distance exchange, does not appear to be borne out by the distribution and context of the import evidence, at least during the thirteenth and twelfth centuries, and should be reevaluated. Second, Greece does not appear to have been particularly "isolated" during the EIA, though there is evidence that a severe economic depression was indeed a characteristic of the later twelfth and eleventh centuries. Third, the institutions through which long-distance interaction operated when this economic crisis lifted in the Geometric period appear to have been meaningfully different from those present during the thirteenth century, though there are some fascinating strains of continuity. Thus, from the standpoint of the long-distance exchange economy, we should conceptualize the LBA–EIA transition as a period of significant transformation, a crucible in which a new template of exchange and Mediterranean interaction was forged.

ONE

THE DARK LIGHT OF EARLY GREEK TEXTS ON TRADE

ONE OF THE GOALS OF THIS BOOK IS TO SHOW THE MERITS OF AN evidence-forward approach to the economic history of the LBA to EIA transition. Thus, in the majority of the book I will focus on the story told by archaeology alone. To begin, however, I wish to show in detail how and why the textual evidence traditionally called into service in comparing the LBA and EIA trade economies is deeply problematic and can tell us remarkably little about diachronic change. The comparison of documentary evidence from the LBA with literary evidence from the eighth century is a methodological nightmare that produces only tentative and schematic conclusions. The implication is clear: if we are to understand the Greek EIA on its own terms, we must come to terms with this reality and become more aggressive in squeezing patterns and meaning out of the archaeological record, independent of the texts, rather than constantly appealing to Linear B or Homer to come to our aid when the evidence is difficult to deal with.

In this chapter, I compare the systems of exchange and economy that are evident in LBA and EIA texts to one another, in order to show how little this comparison can really tell us about Early Greek economic collapse. I argue that although comparison of the texts in question can demonstrate a few obtuse realities about the nature of the Greek economy before and after the Mycenaean collapse, a variety of complex factors obviate any likely relation of these texts to (1) each other and (2) the realities of LBA and EIA Greece.

1.1. TRADE FROM THE TEXTS: THE LATE BRONZE AGE

If we want to reconstruct the "history" of LBA trade, we can try to work with a number of different resources (letters, archival documents, accounting registers, legal treatises) from a variety of sources (mainland Greece, Hattuša, Amarna, Ugarit), but for various reasons their use as historical sources is not straightforward. In what follows, I summarize the textual evidence for trade in the palatial period of the Mediterranean LBA and then examine the impression we get from these texts about how that institution functioned.

Mycenaean Greece

Bronze Age Greeks were not highly literate by modern standards, but they did leave behind some texts. For direct written evidence of Mycenaean Greece, we are reliant on the corpus of Linear B texts. Most of these date to the thirteenth century BCE.[1] Most are in the form of inscribed clay tablets, but some Linear B texts have also been discovered in other formats, such as *dipinti* on transport vessels. These texts have come to light in quantity at only a few sites (Pylos, Thebes, Mycenae, Tiryns, Agios Vasilios, and Midea on the mainland, Knossos and Chania on Crete), all of which have been characterized as administrative centers.[2] The existing Linear B tablets were not preserved because they were particularly important, but because they happened to be baked in accidental or destructive fires. These texts thus constitute a skewed sample with an unknowable relationship to the original textual corpus.[3] As a result of all these factors, it is reasonable to conclude that the Linear B texts tell us only about a portion of the Mycenaean economy that may or may not be representative of the entire system.[4]

Among the many idiosyncrasies of the Mycenaean Linear B tablets is their silence on the topic of long-distance trade and/or commerce.[5] No word for

---

[1] Although two groups of tablets from the palace at Knossos date to the fifteenth and fourteenth centuries (Chadwick et al. 1987–1998; Driessen 1990; Driessen 2000), the majority of the existing texts date to the thirteenth century.

[2] Because of the limited distribution of Linear B texts, scholars have concluded that this script existed to fill a particular set of needs for a small subsection of society associated with palatial administration and thus reflects only the economic and administrative interests of the state (Finley 1957, 129; Shelmerdine 2008, 115; although nb that the discovery of Linear B tablets is usually cause enough to label a site as palatial).

[3] Although Bennet (2001, 30) has suggested a way to reconstruct the administrative cycle through which tablets were written, stored, and disposed of.

[4] Nakassis 2013, 2–3, 16.

[5] Palaima 1991, 276. Attempts to reconstruct long-distance trade mechanisms on the basis of the surviving Linear B evidence: Killen 1985; Palaima and Wright 1985; Olivier 1990; Palaima 1990; Palaima 1991, 276; Halstead 1992; Dickinson 1994, 73–86. See also Tartaron 2013, 24, for a brief but incisive discussion of the relevant problems with and limitations of these data.

trader, merchant, or entrepreneur has yet been identified in Linear B.[6] Although some texts mention exotic goods that must have been obtained outside of Greece,[7] there are only two tablets in which the movement of a commodity across territorial boundaries is explicitly mentioned, and these both record shipments from one location in Greece to another (cloth transferred from Mycenae to Thebes in one instance and the movement of goods from Thebes to Euboea in the other) rather than a shipment further abroad.[8] The near-absence of trade in the Linear B texts is made conspicuous by the economic and transactional content of most of the tablets and the existence of archaeological evidence suggesting that long-distance trade did play a role in the palatial economies of the LBA.

Scholars have repeatedly sought to explain this dissonance, but no consensus exists about why the Linear B texts should be silent on the subject of long-distance or extra-Mycenaean trade.[9] One possibility is that the absence of trade in the documentary evidence is due to random chance. This possibility is not an attractive one, given that over 5,000 documents from a number of different sites throughout the geographical scope of the Greek world are preserved.[10] It is more probable that long-distance trade was simply not within the purview of

---

[6] Palaima 1991. However, many names in Linear B indicate familiarity with maritime transport. These terms, as catalogued by Palaima (1991, 284) occur in texts from both Pylos and Knossos and include *na-u-si-ke-re[-we]* (ship-famous), *e-u-na-wo* (good-ship), *o-ku-na-wo* (fast-ship), *o-ti-na-wo* (ship-starter), *na-wi-ro* (ship-man), *e-u-o-mo* (fine-harborer), *e-u-po-ro-wo* (fine-sailing).

[7] These goods include both raw materials not available in Greece – such as ivory, exotic foodstuffs and spices– and captive women taken during presumed fracases in the Eastern Aegean. See Palaima 1991, 289–295 for a summary of the relevant texts.

[8] From Mycenae, tablet MY X 508: cloth destined for Thebes. It is interesting to note (along with Killen 1985, 268) that this tablet, our only preserved Linear B tablet recording the export of manufactured goods, was found in the West Houses at Mycenae. This complex may have been a clearinghouse for manufactured goods (Tournavitou 1995). Four documents from Knossos (Ld (1) series) record the earmarking of cloth destined for *xenwia*. In addition, a set of inscribed sealings from Thebes indicate the transport of some commodities, including wool and/or livestock, to toponyms on Euboea, which may have been outside of the Theban territory (Aravantinos 1991; Melena and Olivier 1991, 116–133; Palaima 1991, 277–278). For the movement of goods from Thebes to Euboea, see Aravantinos et al. 2001.

[9] Killen 1985, 265–270; Bennet 2007, 202. Killen provides the most exhaustive and thoughtful treatment of the possible explanations for the absence of trade from the Linear B record. His suggestions include the following: (1) "Trade was essentially an occasional and marginal activity for the palaces, and the records of a single year . . . would not therefore be expected to contain many references to it."; (2) "We do have more records of trading activity in the archives, but these are not recognizable as such."; (3) "There were originally more records in the archives dealing with external trade, but these, by chance, have not survived."

[10] We do not have a large number of Linear B texts from Mycenae or from the Argolid (fewer than a hundred), where imports from the IIIB period are most frequently encountered in the archaeological record. It is possible that the Pylos texts, which dominate our record for the thirteenth century, are particularly short on evidence of long-distance trade because Pylos was not involved in this sector of the economy. However, the nature of the archaeological evidence at Pylos – where most objects of value appear to have been packed up and removed from the palace before its destruction – makes this hypothesis less appealing.

an administrative system that was designed to regulate "normal," predictable inputs and outputs of taxation and tribute. If long-distance trade "events" either happened so infrequently as to obviate the need for detailed accounting or took place at such a high level that the record keeping associated with them was beyond the purview of humble scribes, it might not have made much logical sense to keep extensive records on these events.[11]

Whatever the reason, the fact remains that the Linear B texts we possess do not provide us with a direct view of Mycenaean trade. On the other hand, the tablets do give us some oblique glances at the integration of the Mycenaean palaces with the peoples of the wider Mediterranean. Tablets and sealings contain occasional references to locations within or people/things from/relating to Egypt and the Near East.[12] In several tablets, the modifier *ku-pi-ri-jo* is used to describe individuals and commodities in texts from Pylos.[13] This is only one example of an indication that many of the dependent workers of the Pylian state came from abroad. Overall, the evidence suggests that many of the dependent workers at Pylos were nonnative women.[14]

Taken together, this evidence does not constitute a robust body of information from which to reconstruct Mycenaean trade systems.[15] In order to get a more detailed sense of how trade may have worked during the LBA, we must attempt to draw on analogies to ancient Near Eastern trade, since there is more surviving documentary evidence from that side of the Mediterranean.[16] The commercial activities of the major LBA empires – the Hittites, Egyptians, Babylonians, and Assyrians – are recorded in a variety of media that survive in quantity and dwarf the corpus of Mycenaean texts in both scale and scope. Among the many archives surviving from these empires, the most important sources for reconstructing Bronze Age Mediterranean trade are records from Hattuša, Amarna, and Ugarit that describe gift exchange and commercial transactions.

---

[11] This scenario aligns with a "minimalist" interpretation of Mycenaean trade. A related issue is the identification of the "agency" behind long-distance exchange events. As Crielaard (2000, 55) suggests, "one explanation is that private entrepreneurs independent of the palace conducted overseas trade."

[12] Cline 1994, 128–131.

[13] Palaima 1991, 279–280; Himmelhoch 1990-1991. Tablets about Cypriots are as follows: PY Cn 131 (one of 25 shepherds at *pi-*82*, *ku-pi-ri-jo* is in charge of 50 sheep); also a *ku-pi-ri-jo* shepherd in PY Cn 719; PY Jn 320 (*ku-pi-ri-jo* holds a quantity of bronze); PY Un 443 + 998 (*ku-pi-ri-jo* in charge of quantities of alum, wool, and cloth). Also see Cline 1994, 130, with list of tablets and bibliography. For more work on smiths at Pylos, see Gillis 1997; Nakassis 2013, 73–116.

[14] Chadwick 1988, 83, 91–93; Hiller 1988; Palaima 1991, 279–80; Bennet 1997, 519; Bryce 1998, 321–324; Bryce 2002, 259–260; Magiddis 2007, 81–82; Olsen 2014.

[15] Killen 1985, 262–270. These texts are problematic for other reasons. They represent a random sample and give us insight into the functioning of only a small cross-section of society.

[16] A fact already appreciated in Ventris and Chadwick 1956, 106.

Hittite Sources

Hittite written documents survive in abundance and contain compelling evidence that the Mycenaeans and Hittites had significant relations throughout the Late Mycenaean period.[17] However, the cuneiform documents from Hattuša and a few other sites scattered around Anatolia are relatively quiet in regard to trade.[18] Moreover, objects from distant lands are even sparser in the Hittite heartland than they are in Greece.[19] That said, there is some indication in the cuneiform sources that have been excavated in central Anatolia of the way in which Hittite kings interacted economically with the outside world. Inventory records and tax registers from Hattuša reveal the intakes and outputs of the state, and also shed light on the kinds of materials that the Hittite state was interested in acquiring during the late thirteenth century.[20]

Amarna Letters

The so-called Amarna letters (here abbreviated EA), a group of nearly four hundred clay tablets found at el-'Amarna, the capital of Egypt during the reign of the Pharaoh Akhenaten in the fourteenth century, are also useful for reconstructing trade in the LBA Mediterranean. Most of the corpus of Amarna letters comprises letters or inventories attached to letters.[21] The tablets on which the letters were inscribed come from one context, a cache identified by inscriptions as "the Place of the Letters of the Pharaoh." These depositional circumstances suggest that the Amarna letters were purposely maintained in an archive and therefore may have been considered particularly important by the Pharaoh.[22] Some of the letters were written to the Pharaoh from kings of other states that engaged with Egypt on a more-or-less equal footing, while others relay communication between the Pharaoh and subordinate vassals. Many of the letters between the Pharaoh and other kings record the exchange of gifts, thus providing

---

[17] van den Hout 2011, 47, 56. Documentary texts from the Hittite kingdom span the period from ca. 1650 BCE to ca. 1180 BCE. About 30,000 cuneiform texts have been studied so far, in Hittite and Luwian scripts, on clay tablets, one bronze tablet, stone surfaces, and seals and seal impressions. Sites that have produced substantial numbers of clay tablets include Hattuša, Maşat Höyük-Tapikka, Ortaköy-Šapinuwa, and Kuşaklı-Sarissa. A few stray finds come from Alaca Höyük, İnandık, Kayalıpınar, Tarsus, Ugarit, Emar, and Alalakh.

[18] Genz 2011, 301.

[19] Bryce (2003, 60–61) gives thoughtful consideration to the surprising lack of Aegean imports (limited to a few ceramics and some weapons of possible Aegean derivation; see Taracha 2003) in the Hittite heartland. For further discussion of imports in the Hittite heartland and references, see this book's conclusions.

[20] The best collection of Hittite documents available in English remains Beckman 1995. There is also a recent summary in van den Hout 2011.

[21] Thirty-two of the tablets, on the other hand, represent a miscellaneous collection of myths, epics, syllabaries, lexical texts, a list of gods, and so forth (Moran 1992, xvi). All translations of the Amarna Letters in the following come from Moran 1992.

[22] Kühne 1973, 70, n. 345.

insight into a system of long-distance exchange that was in operation during the LBA.

Ugarit

Finally, texts from the port town of Ugarit provide a nonpalatial perspective on trade. Ugarit was probably the most important port in the LBA Mediterranean.[23] Excavations at the site (modern-day Ras-Shamra on the Syrian coast) have turned up many inscriptions in the Akkadian, Cypro-Minoan, and Ugaritic languages since the 1950s. These record the nature of trade within and among a variety of states and individuals.[24] The evidence from these texts suggests that Ugarit was a major nexus of trade through which goods and commodities from inland and coastal regions traveled during the thirteenth century.[25]

Relevance of Near Eastern Texts to Mycenaean Trade

Despite the fact that the Mycenaean Linear B texts are not really helpful for reconstructing an exchange economy, then, documentary evidence from which to build an impression of the manner in which LBA trade in the Mediterranean worked does exist. Before proceeding, however, the inclusion of Near Eastern texts in an analysis of Aegean trade demands justification. A lateral move is required in order to successfully wed this textual evidence to a discussion of the early Greek economy, since it is roughly contemporary with the world of the Linear B texts but not explicitly related to the world of Mycenaean Greece. Any inference made about Mycenaean Greece based on these texts necessarily presupposes the existence of institutional parallels between Hittite, Egyptian, and Mycenaean trade mechanisms. Demonstrating that such parallels probably existed presents real, but not insuperable, obstacles to analysis. Regardless of these obstacles, the Near Eastern material is so potentially valuable that it is worth harnessing despite the potential flaws of cross-Mediterranean analogy, especially since the Linear B texts provide only thin gruel for a reconstruction of trade.

Why is it justifiable to think that Near Eastern texts give us any insight whatsoever into Mycenaean trade? The main reason is that we have compelling evidence that the Mycenaeans participated in the kinds of long-distance transactions that are documented in these texts. Hittite documents naming the king of "Ahhiyawa" as a diplomatic peer allow us to tentatively reconstruct an active Ahhiyawan presence on the west coast of Anatolia and probably in Ugarit in

---

[23] Heltzer 1978; Brody 1998, 46; Bell 2012, 181.
[24] Nougayrol 1955; Nougayrol 1956; Virolleaud 1957; Virolleaud 1965; Nougayrol 1970; Bordreuil and Pardee 1989.
[25] van Soldt 1995; Akkermans and Schwartz 2003, 335; van de Mieroop 2007; Monroe 2009, 31.

the fifteenth through thirteenth centuries.[26] And many scholars believe that Ahhiyawa is the Hittite name for a or the centralized Mycenaean state located in mainland Greece or a larger entity constituted by the united Mycenaean world (including but not limited to parts of the Anatolian coast).[27]

If Ahhiyawa is both Mycenaean and located on the Greek mainland, then we can conclude that mainland Greek entities (either individuals or institutions) were active participants in the kinds of diplomatic and economic interaction that we read about in Hittite and Egyptian texts. Some evidence for this is provided by the explicit mention of gift exchange between Hittites and Ahhiyawans in at least a few Hittite documents.[28] In addition, a pair of letters sent from Hattuša to the Ugaritic king Ammurapi shows that Mycenae was involved not only in the exchange of gifts with the great kings, but may also have participated in commodities markets. In AhT 27A (§7), the author of the letter (most likely the Hittite king Šuppiluliuma II) states, "[n]ow I have been told that the (Ah)hiyawan is tarrying in [the land] of Lukka, but that there are no (copper) ingots for him … give ships to Šatalli, so that he may take the ingots to the (Ah)hiyawans." In addition, in AhT 27B (§6), the king again instructs his Babylonian correspondent to allow the same Šatalli to "take (copper) ingots to the (Ah)hiyawan," who is apparently waiting in the land of Lukka.

Taken together, this evidence, along with the abundant archaeological indications of a contemporary Mycenaean presence in the Eastern Mediterranean,[29] makes it appear likely that the Mycenaeans were at least occasionally players in the same kinds of exchange that were evidently conducted on a regular basis among the better-documented Eastern Mediterranean states of the LBA. Thus, the Near Eastern archival material is of plausible relevance to a reconstruction of

---

[26] Texts now collected in Beckman, Bryce, and Cline 2011. For further discussion of these texts, see Güterbock 1983, 136; Lackenbacher and Malbran-Labat 2005, 237–238; Cline 2010, 178; Singer 2006, 250–252; Singer 2011; Lackenbacher and Malbran-Labat 2016. All translations and citations of the Ahhiyawa Texts (AhT) are from Beckman, Bryce, and Cline.

[27] This conclusion is based largely on a series of documents dating to the thirteenth century BCE that seem to firmly establish that Ahhiyawa had come to be known as a kingdom on mainland Greece rather than a segment of Mycenaean civilization limited to western Anatolia by the LH IIIB period. Mee 1998, 143; Kelder 2010, 93–99; Beckman, Bryce, and Cline 2011, 4–6; Bryce 2011, 10. Cf. Latacz 2004 for an argument that Ahhiyawa should be associated with Thebes/Boeotia.

[28] Gift exchange detailed in AhT 8. In AhT 19 (= CTH 243.6), a copper vessel of Ahhiyawan manufacture is listed as part of the Hittite king's inventory. It is not implausible that this vessel may have been a gift from the Ahhiyawan king in the past. However, as Beckman, Bryce, and Cline (2011, 182) note, "[w]e have no idea how the item was acquired – whether through trade, as a gift perhaps presented to the palace by a traveler returning from the west, or by other means."

[29] Cadogan 1973; Mee 1978; Bouzek 1985; Åström 1996; Mee 1998; Mountjoy 1998; Hirschfeld 2004; Artzy 2005; Laffineur and Greco 2005.

trade institutions in LBA Greece, although its relationship with the reality of the Greek economy overall is likely to be less than straightforward.[30]

Elite Gift Exchange as an Economic Institution

Royal correspondence from the Near East contains rich information about kingly gift exchanges. Gift exchange was an important institutional mechanism in the LBA Mediterranean world. The kings of Egypt, Assyria, Babylon, Hatti, Alašiya, Ahhiyawa, and Mitanni were tied together in a fraternal brotherhood, according to which the kings assumed mutual obligations and responsibilities to one another and agreed to deal with each other as equals.[31] These brotherhoods were made manifest by way of frequent correspondence,[32] which allowed the kings to constantly monitor the health of their relationships and to cash in on or fulfill the obligations assumed under its terms. In the kingly correspondence, letters invariably begin with a formulaic greeting assuring the recipient that the sender is doing well and that both parties wish one another equally well. In general, the tone of the texts is collegial: the great kings commonly acclaim mutual respect, piety, and admiration for one another in the letters.[33] Beyond the office of king, the rest of the royal family (queens or brothers, for instance) also participated in the exchange of letters.[34]

Despite strongly professed concern for each other's mutual well-being and the apparent brotherly bond between kingly peers, it is apparent that the great kings are not likely to have ever met one another in person. For example, in letter EA 7, Burnaburiash, the king of Babylon, expresses dismay because the king of Egypt has not sent him a note of sympathy about the sickness he has been experiencing recently. The king of Egypt sends his messenger with a reply explaining that Egypt is far away and that it would be difficult indeed for him to obtain updated information about his brother's illness. When this letter arrives,

---

[30] There is, in addition, convincing evidence that at least some Mycenaean institutions were modeled on or closely resembled Near Eastern ones. See, for example, Killen's (1983) incisive comparison of the system of mobilization and recruitment of rowers at Ugarit and Pylos.

[31] Beckman 1995, 4: "In contrast to vassal treaties, where the overlord imposes certain provisions on the vassal and obliges him to swear to observe them, in these parity treaties neither party imposes anything on the other. Rather, each monarch in turn voluntarily assumes certain obligations. Then the other party takes on identical – or better, symmetrical – responsibilities. In particular, the Hattusili-Ramses agreement calls for the reaffirmation of former treaties, the mutual renunciation of aggression, a mutual defense pact, the guarantee of succession to the throne for the designated heir of the Hittite ruler, and the extradition of fugitives." Although not many of these kinds of treaties survive, two well-known examples are a treaty between an unknown Hittite king and Padatissu of Kizzuwatna and another between Hattusili III of Hatti and Ramesses II of Egypt.

[32] Bryce 2003, 48; Beckman 1995, 5. For example, Hattusili III to Kadashman-Enlil II: "Only if kings are hostile do their messengers not travel continuously between them" (EA 7: 8–32).

[33] Moran 1992, xxiii.

[34] Bryce 2003, 52.

the king of Babylon has to ask one of his advisors to make sure that Egypt is, in fact, far away. The Babylonian king's ignorance of Near Eastern geography makes it apparent that the great kings of the LBA did not travel much outside of their own seats of power and may never have met face to face,[35] despite their claims of abiding mutual brotherly love.[36]

From the large proportion of the letters that pertain to gift exchange we may deduce that one important aspect of the relationships maintained among the great kings was a mutually beneficial reciprocity through which goods and commodities circulated.[37] Gifts served as important material correlates of the political relationships that they cemented.[38] Among the gifts attested in the correspondence, gold features prominently, in the form of gold figurines, oil containers, cosmetic flasks, razors, ladles, goblets, necklaces, bracelets, rings, plated chariots, gold-plated ships, beds, chairs, and thrones. In addition, large shipments of pure ingot gold circulated.[39] Although gold is the material most frequently discussed in the existing records, this may be a product of the fact that correspondence with Egypt is overrepresented in the corpus of letters, and, as is frequently remarked in the Amarna correspondence, gold was approximately more plentiful than dust in Egypt. Each kingdom possessed particular commodities in relative abundance – lapis lazuli was frequently sent from the Mitanni and Babylonian kings to Egypt, Alašiya/Cyprus was well supplied with copper and timber, and the Hittites may have specialized in trading horses and iron. Talented individuals were also exchanged.[40] From slaves and horses, to elaborate and valuable linens and handicrafts, to unworked

---

[35] Indeed, as far as we know, none of the royal brothers ever actually met, despite their frequent communication (Bryce 2003, 48). On the other hand, the noninvitation in EA 3 ("When you celebrated a great festival, you did not send your messenger to me, saying 'come to eat and drink'") may suggest that royal travel was not completely out of the question.

[36] Tushratta of Mitanni to Egypt's Queen Tiye: "I will never forget my love for your husband, and as for Naphurreya your son, my love for him will be ten times greater!" (EA 26: 25–29); Tushratta to the Pharaoh: "Since my brother is desirous of my love, shall I not be desirous of my brother's love? At this moment I show you ten times more love than I did to your father!" See also EA 27: 9–12; EA 29: 55–59.

[37] Moran 1992, xxiv–xxv; Zaccagnini 2000, 144–145; Bryce 2003, 89.

[38] Zaccagnini 1973; Liverani 1972, 297; Expressions of this notion in the letters: "From the time my ancestors and your ancestors declared a mutual friendship, they sent beautiful gifts to one another and did not refuse each other any request for beautiful things . . . " (EA 9:7–10 [Letter of Burnaburiash]); "Mane, my brother's messenger, [came and] I heard the greeting and I rejoiced greatly. I saw the goods that my brother sent and I rejoiced greatly." (EA 27: 7–8).

[39] Many letters specifically state a demand for bulk gold rather than fine finished goods; for example, Tushratta, king of Mitanni: "May my brother send me much gold that has not been worked" (EA 20: 71–74).

[40] Beckman 1995, Letter 23 (Hattusili III of Hatti to Kadashman-Enlil II of Babylon): "Furthermore, my brother: My brother, [send me] a sculptor. [When the sculptor] finishes the images, I will send him off, and he will go home . . . [and] send me one of the experts in vulture augury."; cf. Zaccagnini 2000, 146 for the trade in medical and magical personnel; on movement and exchange of expert personnel generally in the Hittite empire, Bachvarova 2009, 30.

or worked metal and stone, the goods that the royals shipped to their peers covered seemingly every category of ancient material culture. Conspicuous in absence is the exchange of agricultural produce and livestock (although the Hittites did sometimes send cattle to Egypt).[41]

The grandiosity of gifts recorded as having moved across political boundaries in the Near East varies widely, but sometimes was spectacular. In a single shipment from Akhenaten to Burnaburiash, approximately 600 kilograms of gold were accompanied by other lavish gifts that are impressive for both their quantity and variety.[42] The context of the gift is not entirely clear. Presumably the scale of this shipment, documented in over 1,000 itemized entries, must have been exceptional. Other single shipments of this size are usually wedding gifts, such as the ones presented to the Mitannian princess Taduhepa when she was married off to Egypt, or shipments for other special occasions, such as the accession of a new king.[43]

A standard greeting gift must have been more modest. An envoy carrying a letter of minor diplomatic importance from Prince Sutahapshap of Egypt to Hattusili III of Hatti carried a gift of "[one] drinking cup of good gold, inlaid, with the face of an ox whose horns are of white stone, [and whose] eyes are of black stone. [Its weight] is 93 shekels of good gold … [One] new [linen garment] of good fine thread … [One] new two-sided [linen bed] spread of good fine thread."[44] Similarly, a message from Burnaburiash to Egypt carries with it only a bulk amount of lapis lazuli: "As a greeting-gift I send you 1 mina of lapis lazuli. Send off my messenger immediately so I may know my brother's decision. Do not detain my messenger."[45]

---

[41] Also, Letter 22E (Beckman 1995, 131–133) from Queen Puduhepa of Hatti to Ramesses II of Egypt appears to imply that civilian captives, cattle, and sheep might be an appropriate dowry for a queen's daughter. The situation is quite different in regard to the gifts/tributes sent from vassals/inferiors to the kings (EA 161, 54–56). There is one instance of an attempt to transmit freshly killed game birds over long distances. This ended badly (Liverani 2001, 63: "One wonders at the stupidity of the official who sent freshly killed birds, undoubtedly without preserving ice, on a 160 km trip from Alalakh to Carchemish [text 125] and thought the king of Carchemish would find them tasty!")

[42] EA 14; see also EA 12 for a similarly lavish gift inventory written in Babylonia.

[43] EA 22 (gifts for the Pharaoh/father of the bride) and EA 25 (a dowry for the princess) according to Kitchen's (1998, 258) reading.

[44] Beckman 1995, Letter 22A. Similar in scope are letter 22B from Queen Naptera of Egypt to Puduhepa of Hatti ("[O]ne colorful necklace of good gold, made up of twelve strands. Its weight is 88 shekels. One dyed cloak of byssus. One dyed tunic of byssus. Five dyed linen garments of good fine thread. Five dyed linen tunics of good fine thread. A grand total of 12 linen garments.") and letter 22C from Ramesses II to Prince Tashmi-Sharrumma of Hatti ("One cup of good gold. Its weight is 49 shekels. Two dyed cloaks of byssus; two dyed tunics of byssus.").

[45] EA 8. The gift here might have been restrained, given that the letter referred to the murder of Burnaburiash's merchants in Egyptian territory. Gifts of a similar quantity appear frequently in the Amarna correspondence (EA 10, §43–49; EA 7; EA 5).

Given the apparent existence of such a wide scalar range of magnanimity within the structure of royal gift exchanges, conflicts among the kings regarding the appropriate generosity or meanness of individual gifts were perhaps inevitable. Royals were sensitive to perceived slights, which could include the lack of proper attention to the size and quality of gifts sent to their ally. Hence Hattusili III is palpably annoyed when he chides the Babylonian king Kadashman-Enlil for sending him lapis lazuli that is not up to par ("Why did you send me lapis lazuli of poor quality? The lapis lazuli which you sent me . . . . Now send me the silver which I need for my work . . . anything else my brother needs let him write to me . . . what will I not send my brother that is in my household?").[46] Likewise, Burnaburiash complains to Akhenaten that he has slackened off in his generosity since the good old days, through teeth that we might well reconstruct as having been clenched: "From the time my ancestors and your ancestors made a mutual declaration of friendship, they sent beautiful greeting gifts to each other and refused no request for anything beautiful. My brother has now sent me two minas of gold as my greeting gift . . . [W]hy have you sent me only 2 minas of gold?"[47] Kadašman-Enlil also takes the Egyptian king to task for his laxity in gold distribution in EA 3.[48] In another letter, Hattusili III tries to head off similar peevishness on the part of the Assyrian king Adad-nirari I by providing a full explanation of why an expected gift of iron blades is delayed.[49] The pervasive anxiety suggests that there was indeed a "vital connection between good diplomatic *entente* and the dispatch of luxury goods" among the kings.[50]

It remains unclear, however, whether these exchanges represented pure diplomatic bombast or encompassed, at least in part, commercial and/or utilitarian exchange that was masquerading under the guise of gift exchange. According to the rhetoric of the great kings, each was self-sufficient and had no pure economic need for inputs from brother kings, thus eliminating any trade motivated by demand rather than kingly reciprocity.[51] This is, I submit, likely to be egotistical posturing. Most of the evidence points to a system in which

---

[46] Beckman 1995, 143, from EA 23.
[47] EA 9 §6–16.
[48] EA 3 §13–22: "It was just 30 minas of gold that you sent me. My gift does not amount to what I have given you every year."
[49] Beckman 1995, Letter 24B: ". . . they have not yet finished making the iron. When they finish, I will send them to you."
[50] Zaccagnini 2000, 145; EA 11.
[51] EA 7, Burnaburiash to Akhenaten: "I am told that in my brother's country everything is available and my brother needs absolutely nothing. So too in my own country everything is available and I too need absolutely nothing. But since we have inherited warm relations from our predecessors, let us send greeting gifts to each other"; Liverani 2001, 155.

purely symbolic gifts and the exchange of goods that were in demand coexisted within the mechanism of kingly diplomacy.[52]

The existence of raw commodities such as unworked gold and copper[53] and functional goods like swords and armor in documented gifts[54] – along with specific mentions of direct payment for goods in silver[55] and references to duty-free passage for merchants, ships, and cargoes[56] – makes this undercurrent of economic exchange particularly apparent. In addition, it is clear in many cases that frank demands for "gifts" from allied kings are motivated by specific economic needs. Thus, in EA 9, Burnaburiash asks the Egyptian king for gold *because* he is working on a temple, and thus has a greater need for gold than usual.[57] Similar project-fueled requests for gold were made by Tushratta of Mitanni when he was building a tomb and by a Babylonian king for work on an undeclared building project.[58] Thus, the "gifts" are requested in accord with demand, and rather than being hoarded in the treasury of the king, they are pumped into the domestic economy by way of building projects. Further evidence that the influx of gold provided by Egyptian largesse was intended for use in the domestic economy comes from Babylonia, where the intensive relationship with Egypt cultivated under Burnaburiash II caused gold to replace silver as the normal standard of equivalence.[59] Thus, it does not seem implausible to characterize the gift-exchange relationships among the great kings as hybrid politico-economic partnerships, whereby abundant goods from each region were spread around, to the mutual benefit and enrichment (though not always full satisfaction) of all parties.[60]

Those who stood to benefit from healthy exchange relationships were not limited to the royal families. Incoming wealth stood to filter from the royal coffers outward at least into the immediate neighborhood of the palace. The exchanges between kings were an abundantly public matter, and rich gifts from a brother king were not only distributed economically throughout the realm, but also generated a sense of the prosperity of the kingdom and the esteem it held among peer groups. A glorious gift brought a king respect

---

[52] Avruch 2000, 155: "In the [l]etters ... trade is conflated with more archaic-looking gift exchange, so that commerce appears in the guise of reciprocity"; Bryce 2003, 94; Druckman and Güner 2000, 175.

[53] EA 20, cf. note 69; EA 35, from Alašiya to Egypt; also from Assyria (Ebeling 1927, No. 249 = Ass. 14410, stating that 1 mina of tin was acquired from an official merchant of Hatti and 25 mina of copper from an official *tamkaru* (agent) from Ninevah).

[54] Beckman 1995, letter 24B, cf. note 79.

[55] EA 35; EA 37, according to Avruch 2000, 155.

[56] EA 8; complaint that merchants have been murdered and demands for compensation; EA 39, EA 40: request for duty-free passage.

[57] EA 9 §17–18.

[58] EA 19 § 43–48; EA 4: "And as to the gold I wrote you about, send me ... as much as possible ... right now in all haste, this summer, so I can finish the work I am engaged on."

[59] Sommerfeld 1995, 920.

[60] Kohl 1987, 15.

"before his country and foreign guests"[61] and spread national pride and prestige to the entire empire, whereas gifts that slighted or disappointed could be a source of great distress and shame for the state, especially if witnessed by foreign dignitaries in addition to a king's own court.[62]

It may have often been the case that gifts arrived looking tarnished or meager not because a king decided to disrespect his royal trading partner, but because of the mechanisms by which kingly gift exchange took place in the LBA world. Kings did not take their gifts directly to one another. Rather, royal envoys were put in charge of moving goods across the vast distances between seats of power, across territories that were often thick with raiders and pillagers.[63] Elaborate means were therefore taken to ensure that nothing in the inventory of gifts was lost in between origin and destination.[64] These means included the extensive use of royal seals and guards for shipping containers.[65] That the precautionary measures were not always effective is made clear by one set of letters describing an incident in which a shipment of gold from Egypt to the Mitannian king Tushratta arrived looking dull and gray, having been debased by dishonest merchants en route.[66]

According to the Near Eastern texts, then, long-distance trade between royal powers was directional, from one palace to another, but intermediaries (not the king-traders themselves) did the work on the ground. The kings themselves did not meet one another, despite proclamations about their deep personal ties. Trade goods ran the gamut, from finished luxury goods and raw materials to craftspeople and slaves.[67] Although Ahhiyawa is not well represented in the textual evidence, circumstances suggest that the Mycenaean state probably engaged with the Near East on terms dictated by the system of kingly gift exchange outlined here.

Other Kinds of Long-Distance Exchange in LBA Texts

Kingly exchange operated within social, economic, and diplomatic systems that defined the way in which goods moved to and from states. Commercial exchange also played a part in the circulation of both materials and finished

---

[61] Tushratta of Mitanni, EA 20 §71–74.
[62] Zaccagnini 2000, 152.
[63] EA 7 §73–82; EA 161 §41–46.
[64] Bryce 2002, 88, 102; Zaccagnini 2000, 151; EA 39 (The ruler of Alašiya asks the Pharaoh to allow his messengers to leave Egypt without delay for those men also serve as merchants): "My brother, let my messengers go promptly and safely so that I may hear my brother's greetings. These men are my merchants. My brother let them go safely and promptly."; EA 255 §12–25: "Let the king, my lord, send a caravan even to Karaduniyas. I will personally conduct it under heavy guard."
[65] For sealing practices in NE trade, see Monroe 2009, 56–65.
[66] EA 20 §46–56.
[67] Liverani 1987, 67.

goods among institutions and individuals. It is sometimes difficult to distinguish whether nonpalatial market/commercial exchange occurred across or only within borders, but on balance it looks likely that long-distance commerce occurred in contexts other than royal gift exchange, at least in some cases, and that even kings occasionally participated openly in these commercial transactions. In other words, although exchange in royal correspondence is mostly concerned with a neatly contained, formalized system of gift exchange, the bigger picture is much more complicated.

Exchange outside of the purview of gift exchange appears occasionally in the Amarna letters, as in EA 369, when the Egyptian Pharaoh requests forty female slaves in exchange for a payment of "silver, gold, and linen garments: *ma-al-ba-si*, carnelian, all sorts of precious stones, an ebony chair; all alike, fine things. Total (value): 160 *diban*."[68] An Assyrian text from the archive of Babu-aha-iddina provides another example of royal commerce, when one of Shalmaneser I's chancellors explains that his trip to a vassal town was made in order to make payments to the local builders there who were working on a canal.[69]

Near Eastern merchants trading across recognized territorial borders were not always palatial attachés carrying goods from one court to another.[70] They must have had busy ledger books of their own. Documentary evidence from the ancient Near East, in particular from the port of Ugarit, sheds some light on the complex, far-reaching business practices conducted by merchants and traders outside of the palatial diplomatic sphere discussed earlier.[71] It is quite obvious from these texts that merchants at Ugarit sought individual gain and conducted transactions on the basis of rules that were distinct from those apparent in kingly gift exchange. One letter received by the entrepreneur Rapanu from a man named Enbiyanu reads, "How have I cast the copper? It is concerning the donkey(s) (of) the son of Agalibi for which I have cast it. Now that I have cast the copper, you first release the donkeys, and I will then release the copper. May Ba'al-alu come, and may he enter into an oath on account of the silver (price) of the donkeys and may he take it."[72] Other texts from Rapanu's house included royal correspondence with the kings of Hatti, Alašiya, and Egypt, and he was probably an advisor to the king who took care of many royal transactions, including sending a shipment of oil to King Niqmadu III of Alašiya (RS 20.168).[73] Thus, merchants like Rapanu worked for the

---

[68] §9–14: 40 shekels "of silver is the price of a female cupbearer."
[69] Ebeling 1927, No. 178 (=Ass. 14445d).
[70] Though many of the best-documented traders at Ugarit had close ties to and obtained considerable capital from the palace (Monroe 2009, 107).
[71] Over 550 weights have been found at the port to date, demonstrating the transactional density of activity here (Courtois 1990, 119).
[72] Excavation No. RS 20.015 (= Ug. 5 N 53), trans. Monroe (2009, 72).
[73] Bordreuil and Pardee 1989, 228–274; Nougayrol et al. 1968, 42; Ferrara 2012, 139–40.

palace, were in charge of long-distance shipments, *and* conducted business in their own interests.

Likewise, Urtenu, another Ugaritic merchant, was frequently in touch with the kings of Alašiya (he received a shipment of ingots from the palace at the end of the thirteenth century) and with an Ugaritian scribe who lived in Cyprus, who requested a shipment of furniture.[74] One Assyrian text, meanwhile, recounts the receipt of a loan of silver intended to fund an independent caravan trip by a Sutean (non-Assyrian)[75] merchant from two Assyrians.[76] Another transaction that cannot be tied to a royal archive records that a *tamkaru* brought tin and bronze for the making of fifty axes from Nineveh to Assur.[77] Most of these transactions could best be described as long distance, commercial, and nonpalatial.

The notion that individual merchants were engaged in trade operations that were not directly related to the palatial sector is corroborated by the New Kingdom Egyptian text known as the "Satire on the Trades," in which "merchants fare upstream and downstream as they do business with copper, carrying goods <from> one town to another and supplying him that has not, although the taxmen carry gold, the most precious of all the minerals."[78] The distinction between the merchants cargo of copper and the palatial cargoes of gold may indicate that there were multiple, hierarchically organized, palatial and independent tiers of exchange in Egypt, though other Egyptian evidence calls this into question. An inscription at Abydos from the reign of Ramesses II states that "I gave thee a ship laden with cargo upon the sea, and great [marvels] of God's Land are brought in to thee; and the merchants ply their trade under orders, their labor being gold, silver, and copper."[79] Does this mean that all merchants plying the sea with metals were under orders? Given the rhetoric inherent in a dedicatory inscription, it does not rule out independent trade.[80]

Overall, the impressive variety of scripts, weight standards, and transactions documented at Ugarit make it clear that intercultural, long-distance exchanges among nonroyal parties took place at the port.[81] It is unclear whether activity at the site is meaningfully relevant to the activities of the Mycenaean state.[82] The major issue with all of the evidence regarding independent, commercial

---

[74] RS 94.275.
[75] Monroe 2009, 119.
[76] Ebeling 1927, No. 39 = Ass. 14446ab: "3 and 2/3 minas silver ... was received for the caravan of the Sutean's firm. Upon return of their caravan they will pay the principal silver."
[77] Ebeling 1927, No. 249; Freydank 1979.
[78] Papyrus Lansing 4,8–5,2; Caminos 1954; trans. in Monroe 2009, 73–74.
[79] Redford 1992, 227.
[80] Monroe 2009, 192 (partly quoting Menu and Gasse 2001, 249).
[81] Or alongside palatial ventures, as in RS 19.050.
[82] Monroe 2009, 217–218, Table 6.2 (list of textual references to the presence of foreign merchants at international ports).

trade is that, although we have compelling reason to believe that Ahhiyawa as a state was involved in the *kinds* of royal gift exchange diplomacy that we know about from the Amarna letters and similar texts, there is no concrete reason to believe that Mycenaean long-distance, commercial, nonpalatial trade necessarily followed the model that existed in places like Ugarit. While it is likely that nonpalatial long-distance commerce took place in the Eastern Mediterranean during the Bronze Age, we cannot say definitively whether the Mycenaeans participated in this kind of trade or were the destination of nonroyal shipments.[83]

Postpalatial Interlude

In the early twelfth century BCE, Ugarit was destroyed and abandoned, the Mycenaean palatial state system crumbled, and Egypt lost control of large swathes of its empire. The impression that we have of the twelfth century is that it was a time of widespread chaos, the movement of populations, and the dynamic transformation of political, social, and economic institutions, although will probably never know exactly what happened. There are some indications in LBA texts from the end of the thirteenth and beginning of the twelfth centuries that the disruptions which rocked Greece and the Near East at this time may have had a deleterious effect on long-distance trade.[84] But contemporary texts relevant to the Greek economy from the period between the collapse of the Mycenaean palace states and the eighth century BCE are wanting. The system of Linear B documentation fell out of use with the end of the palatial states, and as far as we are able to tell written communication was not a feature of life in the Aegean during the postpalatial period or during the centuries that followed.[85]

There is, nonetheless, some oblique textual evidence from Greece that sea-going travel may have become more dangerous at the end of the Mycenaean period, a situation which could plausibly have carried through into the twelfth century. A few texts from Pylos describing the organization of a large contingent of coastal guards could testify to a situation of deteriorating

---

[83] Ahhiyawa is mentioned only once in commercial texts from Ugarit, in correspondence between the king of Ugarit (Ammurapi) and the king of Hatti (Šuppiluliuma II), RS 94.2530. Lukka is probably to be equated with Lycia, in southwestern Anatolia but the association is not considered to be fully philologically proven (Otten 1993).

[84] Cline 1994, 10–11, 16–23; 32; Yasur-Landau 2010, 102.

[85] In Cyprus the Cypro-Minoan script probably continued in use during the IIIC and PG periods in a modified form known as Cypro-Greek; if Greeks traveled to and from Cyprus during the period, it is possible that some of them continued to communicate using Cypro-Greek script, but we lack any direct evidence for this. See Egetmeyer 2013 for a brief review.

maritime stability.[86] At the same time, tablet PY Jn 829 records the collection of bronze from the gods "for javelins and spears," possibly in order to arm the Pylians against an undefined threat. Another tablet (PY Tn 316) *might* suggest that humans were sacrificed to the gods at the last minute in order to stave off impending doom.[87]

From the Near East, we have more concrete evidence of trouble. The inscription of year eight from Medinet Habu in Egypt gives a contemporary account of the "invasion" of the Sea Peoples, but the superficial reading is problematic.[88] At Ugarit the evidence demonstrates real chaos in the early twelfth century BCE, with destruction coming from the sea.[89] Awful famines struck even the formerly prosperous royal trader Urtenu (RS 34.152, 9–14) in whose house was discovered a letter naming the enemy: "the Šikila people who live on boats."[90] Finally, there are explicit reports that enemy ships had landed and were setting fire to towns in Ugarit's territory.[91]

In the Hittite empire instability is also evident. From the reign of Šuppiluliuma II comes a report on a battle against both Alašhiya and the "enemy of Alašhiya."[92] We hear of combined efforts by the Hittites and by Ugarit to suppress a maritime enemy in the land of Lukka (RS 20.238). Although this evidence does not necessarily tell us much about the Aegean, except insofar as the world must have lost a major commercial hub in Ugarit, we can probably feel confident that there were seagoing groups who created logistical problems for established powers at this time. This may or may not have had deleterious effects on maritime travel during the succeeding LB IIIC period, but there is no definitive evidence in the texts about whether it did or did not precipitate "the ruin for the time being of ... trade routes."[93]

1.2. TEXTUAL EVIDENCE FOR TRADE IN EARLY IRON AGE GREECE

In order to rationalize the application of evidence from Near Eastern texts to Bronze Age Greece, it is necessary to move laterally in space – to show

---

[86] PY An 657. The force would have amounted to about 800 men for about 100 miles of coastline. Due to sampling problems we cannot be sure whether or not this was normal practice. For discussion of the watchers and the meaning of these texts see Hooker 1982; Baumbach 1983; Palaima 1995; Deger-Jalkotzy 2008.
[87] Chadwick 1987, 41–43; Smith 1992–93; for opposition to the argument see Muhly 1992.
[88] Redford 2000, 7–18; O'Connor 2000, 94–100.
[89] Yon 1992a; Yon 1992b.
[90] RS 34.129.
[91] RS 20.238.
[92] "I mobilized, and I Šuppiluliuma, the Great King, [sailed out(?)] at once to the sea. The ships of Alašhiya met me in battle at sea three times, but I smote them ... " (= KBo 12, 38, as translated in Beckman 1996, 33).
[93] Lorimer 1950, 65.

that texts from contemporary but distant cultures could be applicable to the Mycenaean economy. For the Homeric evidence, it is a move backward in time rather than outward in space that is required. Becuase written records largely disappear after the disturbances that rocked the Mediterranean during the early twelfth century, scholars are uncontroversially "in the dark" about the Greek economy from a textual standpoint until late in the Geometric period, when written records in the Greek alphabet began to appear. The only written evidence that might possibly pertain to this period of early Greek history between the twelfth and eighth centuries is the tradition of bardic poetry best represented in the works of Homer (the *Iliad* and *Odyssey*) and Hesiod (*Theogony* and *Works & Days*). The versions of these poems that we possess are probably rooted in traditional oral compositions passed down from one generation to the next (possibly since the sixteenth century BCE).[94]

Homer's epics describe fictional events set near the end of and closely following upon the legendary Trojan War, while Hesiod's poems describe the origins of the Greek pantheon of gods and the plight of a peasant farmer in central Greece, respectively. Their content may reflect some material realities or social conventions that pertain to the LBA and/or EIA, but this is highly controversial. In particular, it is clear that the poems are problematic as evidence for prehistoric periods because it is generally agreed that they were not written down until eighth century BCE or significantly later.[95] They are likely to give us some indication of economic life in the eighth century, but even for this contemporary period we must keep in mind the interpretive complications involved.[96] What is the point of attempting to make eighth century (or later) written material relevant to the preceding several centuries of society and economy?

---

[94] Bennet 1997, 527; Bachvarova 2016. For a possible shared Luwian/Mycenaean tradition see Hawkins 2010, 218; for a possible Minoan tradition, S. Morris (1989) and Hiller (1990) have argued that the frescoes in the West House at Akrotiri support the notion that hexameter poetry originated or existed in the LBA. There are many visual similes and instances of human/nature opposition in LBA art which is similar in spirit to much in the Homeric repertoire. Finally, the depiction of a lyre player in a fresco from the megaron at the Palace of Nestor may suggest that bards like those in the Homeric poems sang at the feasts of Mycenaean kings (Immerwahr 1990, pl. XVIII; cf. Younger 1998).

[95] Most believe that the period of Homeric and Hesiodic transmission should be placed between 750 and 650 BCE, with a general consensus that Homer's work was composed earlier. But this does not necessarily stand on firm evidence, and some have even claimed priority for Hesiod. For a review, see Rosen 1997.

[96] Some argument could be made for the inclusion of Biblical texts, which provide evidence for exchange institutions dating to the eleventh and tenth centuries (for instance, 2 Kings, 12–13), but since we have little reason to believe that eleventh century Israel and eleventh century Greece were characterized by similar socio-economic conditions or institutions, this evidence is of limited use for reconstructing the EIA Greek economy. For gift exchange and trade in the Book of Kings, see Nam 2012.

The debate over the historicity, and applicability to historical study, of early Greek poetry is far too complex to cover in detail in the current context, but a brief summary is appropriate in order to bring into focus the difficulties involved.[97] In the early days, the world portrayed in the Homeric poems was considered to be totally imaginary, a mytho-historical fantasy that could not be related in any way to history.[98] Greek history began with Herodotus and Thucydides, and everything before that was beyond the reach of human knowledge. However, Heinrich Schliemann's excavations at Troy and Mycenae turned up material culture that looked Homeric, and his work convinced many scholars that Homer described a real, Bronze Age, world.[99] But when Linear B was deciphered it became clear that Mycenaean social structure did not look much like what Homer describes.[100] Furthermore, work by Lord and Parry showed that the poems were composed orally, making it difficult for many to believe that the details in them could have been preserved faithfully over the 500 years between the collapse of the Mycenaean palaces and the invention of the Greek alphabet in the mid-eighth century BCE, which allowed them to be permanently brought into captivity.[101] Even if the Homeric world was not the Mycenaean world, some historians were still convinced it must line up with a real phase in Greek history – it was just a matter of finding the one that provided the best fit. Finley argued emphatically that Homer was a reliable guide only to social and economic standards between the twelfth and ninth centuries, rather than to the Mycenaean period.[102] Lorimer and Snodgrass, however, did not agree that Homer's world was real; both argued instead that the poems present a jumble of information that cannot be taken to represent any single period.[103] Along the

---

[97] For a relatively recent review, see Latacz 2004.
[98] Grote 1846–1856 I, 321.
[99] Schliemann 1880, 336–345; Followed by Allen 1921; Nilsson 1933; Page 1959; most pieces in Wace and Stubbings 1962; Blegen 1962; Mylonas 1966; Luce 1975.
[100] Though some (e.g. Bennet 1997; Monroe 2009, 227–230) believe that there may still be good reasons to link up some aspects of Homer to the world of the Mycenaean palaces, e.g. the attestation of Homeric names of places (including Troy) and people (including Atreus) in Hittite texts, archaeological evidence demonstrating that Mycenaeans were active on the Anatolian coast in the LBA (Mee 1978; van Wijngaarden 2002), evidence in the Linear B tablets that Mycenaeans took women from the Eastern Mediterranean home to work as palatial dependents (Olsen 2014, 95–100, 111–113), and the fact that Troy was in fact a large and important settlement during the LBA and that Mycenaean pottery is present there (Korfmann 1995; Mee 1984). In addition, there is linguistic evidence that some aspects of Homeric language originate in a version of Greek that is older than that used in the Linear B texts – specifically tmesis and -oιo stems in the genitive (Horrocks 1980, 9; Janko 1982, 50–54; West 1988, 158–159).
[101] Bennet 1997, 513.
[102] Finley 1957; 1981, 199–212, 232. The position is similar to that followed by Andrewes (1961) and Dickinson (1986) (though Andrewes places Homeric society slightly earlier, in the twelfth/eleventh centuries).
[103] Lorimer, 1950, 452; Snodgrass 1971, 389; 1974; cf. Nilsson 1933, 212.

same lines I. Morris, Kurtz and Boardman, and van Wees argue, albeit on different grounds, that the Homeric poems are most relevant to the time in which they were crystallized – in the Late Geometric or Archaic periods, but that they do not present faithful representations of any single historical milieu.[104]

Most scholars now accept the limitations of these poems for telling us something about life during the LBA and earlier EIA. The role and function of material culture within the *Iliad* and *Odyssey* is far too complex, nuanced, and purposefully deployed to be distilled down into a reflection of an existing archaeological or chronological correlate. However, there remain strains of thinking that read the poems as a garbled memory of these earlier periods, and the Homeric readings of culture, politics, and economy remain an entrenched feature in studies of early Greek archaeology.[105] Indeed, the notion that certain aspects of EIA life, including the economy, may be enlightened by the social and economic systems that are apparent in the world portrayed by Homer's *Iliad* and *Odyssey* and Hesiod's *Theogony* and *Works and Days* remains relatively widely accepted,[106] despite the methodological concerns expressed by some.[107] The integration of Homeric evidence into interpretations of EIA material culture has long been a major current of most work on the period overall. In general, however, I maintain that it is best to adopt a minimalistic interpretation of the *Iliad* and the *Odyssey* according to which the material and cultural attributes of the world portrayed in the poems represent eighth century (or later) ideals and agendas and/or an unsalvageable potpourri of elements from various periods that are largely not relatable to earlier Greek history or archaeology in any coherent way.

The evidence from Hesiod is easier to accept as straightforward information about economic realities, because that is what it is supposed to be (see *WD* 10: "ἐγὼ δε κε Πέρση ἐτήτυμα μυθησαίμην." "I will declare to Perses things as they are."). Hesiod's *Works and Days* purports to provide a sort of self-help manual for early Greek peasants, providing instructions such as when to plant, which direction in which to urinate, and how to ward off baneful ruin in the harsh environment of his home region of Boeotia. Given its late date, applying it to eleventh, tenth, and ninth century economies is probably not

---

[104] I. Morris (1986) argues for an eighth century context. Kurtz and Boardman (1971) argue that burial rites in the poems only make sense for the eighth century or later. van Wees (1999) places the poems later, to the seventh or early sixth centuries. Crielaard (1995) thinks that the eighth and the seventh centuries are equally plausible settings. Persistent efforts to determine the relationship between Homeric and archaeological worlds are represented in the *Archaeologia Homerica* series.
[105] In the words of Antonaccio 1995, 4: "Homer cannot be ignored."
[106] Some examples can be found in Crielaard 2006; Crielaard 1995; Papadopoulos 1994; Lemos 2007b; Mazarakis-Ainian 2006.
[107] I. Morris 1986; I. Morris 1997b; Tandy 1997, 8–14.

methodologically sound. On the other hand, it is possible that the Greek agricultural economy did not change dramatically for the average peasant farmer during this time, in which case we might be able to acquire some valuable information about the EIA economy in general from Hesiod. But even if we accept the idea that Hesiod's poems have a strong relationship with the earlier EIA, we still must keep in mind that, like the Homeric poems, the *Theogony* and *Works and Days* were part of a bardic song culture, likely aimed at aristocrats, the context of which we struggle to fully understand.[108] So, like the Homeric poems, this text likely represents something that is not entirely divorced from, but has a complicated relationship with, reality.

To sum up, although they are probably not a reflection of any single material reality, early Greek hexameter poetry may provide us instead with an idealized image of the way some eighth century Greeks thought trade and the economy ought to have worked in a world like theirs.[109] For the purpose of understanding economic transitions, then, we should tread carefully. Essentially, the textual evidence lets us watch a speeding train of elite views on exchange enter a long tunnel, and then emerge again out of the other side centuries later. If we are happy to read this evidence in a straightforward way, it could be of use. If the material residua of trade that appears in the archaeological record from the EIA fits well with an eighth century impression of trade/exchange taken from the texts, and if both the eighth century ideal of trade/exchange *and* the EIA evidence fit poorly with the LBA evidence, then that could convincingly demonstrate a crucial point: economic institutions must have changed substantially, and not simply contracted, after the Mycenaean collapse. Otherwise, these institutions would have come out in the eighth century looking similar to the way they looked in the thirteenth. The implication would presumably be that meaningful institutional change must have occurred at some time during the period between 1200 and 800 BCE. But if we are not so sanguine about the reliability of our view on trade from the texts, and its relationship to reality in either period, then pinpointing any kind of change or continuity will require attention to the archaeology alone.

Trade in the Iliad *and the* Odyssey

As previous scholars have noted, there is little direct engagement with the theme of commercial economy in the *Iliad* and the *Odyssey* and it is thus difficult to discern a clearly articulated sense of systematic exchange institutions in the poems.[110] That said, there is plenty of material exchange to go along with the trading of winged words within early Greek poetry. On the basis of this

[108] Rosen 1990; Martin 1992; Tandy and Neale 1996.
[109] I. Morris 1997b, 558.
[110] Wace and Stubbings 1962, 531.

evidence, most commentators have discerned two separate registers of trade in the Homeric world.[111] Most prominent is the exchange of goods among the *basileis* (usually translated as chiefs or chieftains), either in the context of *xenia* (loosely, hospitality) relationships or as prizes, wedding gifts, ransom, and the like, while an undercurrent of commercial exchange runs steadily in the background of the action.

I take the more evasive of these subjects first. The world of commercial exchange is not a central concern of the Homeric poems. This is not surprising, given that poetic works on the subject of long-distance trade are scarce throughout ancient history. Nonetheless, the world of profit-motivated maritime exchange can be glimpsed obliquely at several points in both the *Iliad* and the *Odyssey*.

There is plenty of reason to believe that both wealth-seeking and commerce had a place in the World of Odysseus. In book one of the *Odyssey*, we hear that Mentes, the king of the Taphians, once traveled to Temese, where the men are "of strange speech" in order to exchange iron for copper.[112] Odysseus travels frequently to conduct his business: abroad to Ephyre in order to acquire a desired pharmaceutical,[113] but also locally to look into collecting on a debt in Messenia.[114] In the context of the Trojan War, the Lemnians cross over to the Greek camp in order to sell their wine to the Achaeans for bronze, iron, hides, cattle, and slaves.[115] Achilles sells war captives to the islanders along the Anatolian coast in exchange for a variety of goods.[116] Some other Greeks end up traveling abroad for gain (for example, Menelaos gathers much gold when swept off to Egypt after the war).[117] However, given the length of the poems, these instances of explicit commercial action do not amount to much.

It seems to be true that most of these are isolated instances, and do not necessarily constitute commerce by traditional definitions. In general, most of the examples in which Greeks act with a profit motive look like they took place under exceptional circumstances (no doubt the war camp provided a different cultural and social context, with its own set of rules for kingly behavior, than did normal village life). Outside of these exceptional circumstances, the Greeks themselves (and Homeric *basileis* in particular) are rarely the ones who initiate or conduct exchange that is profit or need-driven.

---

[111] There is a vast bibliography on the topic of the role of commerce within the Homeric economy. Some pertinent discussions can be found in Finley 1954; Van Wees 1992, 47–48, 228–34; Raaflaub 1997, 636–38; von Reden 1995, 58; Crielaard 2000.
[112] *Od.* 1.179–184.
[113] *Od.* 1.253–262.
[114] *Od.* 2.328–330; *Od* 21.20–22.
[115] *Il.* 7.467–75.
[116] *Il.* 21.40–41; *Il.* 23.740–47; 24.751–753.
[117] *Od.* 3.299–302.

Homeric heroes gain wealth by might or guile or diplomacy, but not by commercial exchange.

Instead, most of the commerce in the poetic world is the concern of foreign merchants, a shady and suspicious lot by all accounts.[118] Mentes, agent of the bulk metal exchange in *Odyssey* book 1, is the leader of a group of *lēistēres* (pirates) and a trader, and thus an outsider to the social world of the *basileis*. Otherwise, most impersonal Homeric long-distance exchange is conducted by the Phoenicians, and they are not portrayed in a flattering light. Rather, these traders are wily, "greedy knaves" who peddle trinkets, are guilty of most dastardly child-snatchings,[119] and are not to be trusted.[120] It is no wonder that Odysseus is offended when his hosts mistake him for a trader in book 8,[121] and that strangers are generally treated in a circumspect manner in the epics.[122] When we find Greeks frothing about profit at home, it is not usually part of a positive character portrait, as in the case of Melanthius, Odysseus's goatherd, who threatens Eumaeus: "Him I will someday take on a black benched ship far from Ithaca, that he may bring me in much wealth."[123]

Although Homeric trade was largely in the hands of foreigners and other rogues, there is a remarkable sense of pan-Mediterranean awareness among the characters in the poem, suggesting that their lack of apparent participation in distant markets is not indicative of an overall provincialism.[124] Cyprus is visited at least seven times by Homeric heroes, who also make stops in Phoenicia, Africa, Egypt, and Arabia.[125] A remarkably detailed description of Egypt by Achilles (*Il.* 9.381–384) is further proof of the cosmopolitan

---

[118] *Od* 9.125–130; cf. Hesiod *Op*. 352–353. The consensus is that the conception of foreigners, and especially Phoenicians, as masters of maritime commerce hews closely to the reality of eighth century Greece. However, some scholars, in particular Bass (1997b, 84–93), have argued that the Phoenician/Canaanite domination of overseas transport and commerce, and especially directional commerce to the Aegean, is just as compatible with a Bronze Age world. For a sophisticated discussion of the Phoenicians in Homer see Winter 1995.

[119] *Od*. 15.445–473; Winter 1995, 249: "These traits go beyond mere description to serve a moralizing subtext, the underlying message of which is that hunger for commercial profit leads to the breaking of higher laws of social honor, punishable by divine retribution."

[120] *Od*. 15.415–429.

[121] *Od* 8.159–164. For attitudes toward *basileis* who trade, see Andrewes 1967, 46–47; Finley 1954, 66–71; Coldstream 1982; Reed 1984; Kopcke 1990; von Reden 1995, 58–76.

[122] The attitude of the Cyclops in *Od*. 9 is one example, as are the suspicions of the Phaiakians of book 7 (*Od*. 7.32–33).

[123] *Od*. 17.248–250.

[124] It is no surprise that the Homeric *basileis* were well traveled, since ships were apparently widely available in the Homeric world. Although Telemachus has to recruit a ship and a team of volunteer sailors from his townsman in order to pursue news of his father across the sea, he has little trouble doing so, and there are other hints at the ease and commonness of oversea travel woven into the *Odyssey* (*Od*. 2.288–293; *Od*. 3.69–74; *Od*. 4.634–6370. On the commonness of travel and travelers: *Od*. 17.419–444; *Od*. 17. 485–487; *Od*. 19.75–79).

[125] S. Morris 1997, 610–611.

knowledge possessed by heroes, regardless of their distaste for commercial expeditions.[126]

But why did *basileis* travel, if not in order to pursue profitable exchange? Clearly there were many reasons that Homeric heroes moved around, including warfare, accident, exile, and so forth. Among these motivations, one of the apparent perks of Homeric mobility was the opportunity it created to generate intra-*basileis* relationships of kingly *xenia* through gift exchange. This kind of exchange is the most visible form of trade in the epics.

Gift giving in Homer fulfills a wide variety of sub-categorical needs – gifts are used to pay ransom, to assuage the pain of battered pride, to reward military service, to facilitate long-term *xenia* friendships, in compensation for past acts or perceived debts, or in anticipation of future good will.[127] Most of the gift exchanges that transpire among the characters in Homer are not strictly relevant to a discussion of long-distance maritime exchange. By and large, the transactions that we hear about are intra-Greek exchanges, and so it is problematic to extrapolate anything about trade at a distance directly from them. However, in some cases, goods are passed between Greek *basileis* and non-Greek political leaders. These exchanges are similar enough to "domestic" (intra-Greek) gift-giving in both form and function that we may hypothesize that the system governing the apparatus of Greek *basileus*-to-*basileus* exchange was analogous to the one that pertained to relationships abroad.

Instances of truly cross-cultural gift exchange are rare, but they do exist. One example is Agamemnon's receipt of a *xenia* gift from Kinyras, a Cypriot king. The gift is a multimedia cuirass crafted of the finest metals and inlaid with gold, tin, and glass.[128] Another relevant *xenia* relationship comes to light in Telemachus' visit to Sparta. Phylo brings out a silver basket "which

---

[126] Although part of the awareness of the wider world apparent among *basileis* in the poems may not be due to the fact that *basileis* traveled frequently, but because the bards who sang the tales had covered a lot of ground. The poems attest to the fact that professional craftsmen and experts, such as builders, artists, and bards, traveled as needed among communities (*Od.* 17.382–386; *Od.*19.135; Raaflaub 1997, 636; Donlan 1997, 650–651). While most craftwork in the poems appears to be generated within the realm of the *oikos* and its surrounding community, there are explicit instances in which outsiders arrive in a community in order to perform special services, one of the most important of which was the singing of tales (Eckstein 1974, part 1; Rössler 1981; Schneider 1991; S. Morris 1992, ch. 1; Donlan 1997). For local markets (essentially village-scale production), see *Il.* 7.467; *Il.* 9.71–72 (wine) and 23.834–835 (a possible local metallurgy market). The craftsmen most commonly encountered in the poems are the *kerameus*, *chalkeus*, and *tektôn*, but we have little sense of whether these were full- or part-time occupations or whether the individuals involved stuck to one village or were itinerant (*Od.* 18.328 may suggest a village smithy; cf. Donlan 1997, 653). There is also an intriguing instance of short-distance travel to collect an owed debt in *Od.* book 3, which may hint at more complex regional economic systems (3.365–368; cf. *Od.* 21.5–41) descendant from the old Mycenaean economy of "collectors."

[127] Donlan 1989a, 1–3; Raaflaub 1997, 637; Qviller 1981, 124–127.

[128] *Il* 11.19–28.

Alcandre ... who dwelt in Thebes of Egypt, where greatest store of wealth is lied up in men's houses" had given to Helen, along with a gold distaff and a basket with wheels underneath, a basket of silver with gold-rimmed wheels, and similar gifts. Menelaos received two silver baths, two tripods, and ten talents of gold from the Egyptian as well.[129] At the end of his visit, Helen gives Telemachus a silver mixing bowl that Menelaus received from the Sidonians,[130] probably as a gift (and recalling the silver bowl which Achilles gives out in Patroklos' funeral games, which likewise originated in Sidon).[131] The exchange of bronze and gold armor between Glaukos and Diomedes on the battlefield in the *Iliad* and their ancestral ties of *xenia* also should number amongst long-distance/cross-cultural exchanges, since we can regard the Lycians and Argives as representatives of different cultures.[132]

The gifts exchanged between Greeks and their Sidonian or Phoenician guest friends look quite similar to the ones that pass between the Homeric heroes of Pylos, Sparta, Ithaca, and other cities. The exchanged goods, as listed in the preceding paragraph, included a majority of fine finished objects – armor, metal vessels, a belt – but also unworked talents of gold. This mixture of finished goods and raw metal is echoed quite closely in intra-*basileis* exchange. We are taught by the poet that the paradigmatic beggar comes to the door looking for scraps, in opposition to a normal visitor, who would be expecting "swords and cauldrons" for his troubles.[133] Odysseus gets a whole shipload of tunics, gold talents, and tripod cauldrons when he leaves Phaiakian shores,[134] and also carries home a fancy sword that Euryalus gave him to make up for rude remarks.[135] Fake Odysseus claims to have given himself "a sword of bronze and a cloak of double fold, as well as a fringed tunic" on his fictional stopover in

---

[129] *Od.* 4.123–132.
[130] *Od.* 4.615–619; *Od.* 15.99–129; after Telemachus turns down an offer of gold cups and a chariot, *Od.* 4.587–592: "... I will send you forth with honor and give you splendid gifts, three horses and a well-polished chariot; and besides I will give you a beautiful cup, that you may pour libations to the immortal gods and remember me all your days." Here we see the Sidonians/Phoenicians in a totally different light than they portrayed in during the course of their normal trading activities abroad.
[131] *Il.* 23.741–747 (although this bowl came into Achilles' hands via Patroklos, Euneus, Thoas, and the Phoenicians rather than by way of a direct relationship).
[132] *Il.* 6.215–236. While exchange occurs among the Greek heroes of the poem, kingly exchange across cultural boundaries outside of military contexts (e.g. looting, ransom, or the taking of booty) appears to have occurred mainly in the context of guest-friendship relationships – weddings of Greeks to non-Greeks are not common (with the exception of Bellerophon who married a Lycian), and we do not hear of prizes or awards given to non-Greeks. For a full analysis of the Glaucus/Diomedes exchange, see Donlan 1989a. Donlan argues (14–15) that the exchange is indistinguishable from intra-Greek gift-giving and is governed by the same rules that underpin all *xenia* relationships. Other discussions of the exchange can be found in Maftei 1976; Calder 1984.
[133] *Od.* 17.221–222.
[134] *Od.* 8.390–397; 13.4–22; 13.217–219.
[135] *Od.* 8.403–405.

Crete.[136] During his adventures with Iphitus in Messene Odysseus received a fine bow.[137] Later, he picked up some sought-after wine, several talents of gold, and a silver bowl from Maro.[138]

Overall, then, from a Homeric perspective, we could reconstruct the ideal form of trade as gift exchange between perceived equals, with trade goods consisting "mainly of artifacts of metal or cloth and unworked metal (chiefly gold and iron)."[139] The terminology used for these objects is usually *keimêlia*, "things stored up," which points toward some of their most important features – they are not generally used for anything, but remain in storerooms until a king decides to pass them on to another friend down the line. Gifts are of special manufacture, not everyday objects. They are sought after because they are scarce and beautiful, not because they are useful. Usually the gifts traded are generous, but not lavish, encompassing from one to three items on average.[140] Kings themselves traveled to see one another, rather than sending emissaries around to pass off gifts to known trading partners. As a result, relationships among kings were durable but flexible, as new and old friendships and networks of obligation were constantly evolving. Kings felt strong personal ties to one another. Trade for profit also existed in the Homeric world, but it was not considered appropriate for kings to participate in commercial enterprise, with some wartime exceptions.

Trade in Hesiod's Works and Days

Hesiod's poetry presents a view of exchange from another perspective. Homer's travelers were self-consciously aware that their class should distance itself from the appearance of actively seeking profit. Hesiod, on the other hand, proscribes to his audience exactly how best to do so in a variety of situations likely to confront a peasant farmer. In particular, he explains to a common man exactly which parts of the year are best for taking up maritime expeditions and how best to decide what proportion of his own produce to pack on a sailing ship to sell abroad.[141] Hesiod does not express any disdain for profit-seeking expeditions, and his matter-of-fact, technical discussion of the realities involved with travel and commerce suggests that sailing and trading to augment a basic subsistence income were a regular part of his affairs. Hesiod's farmer may have been trying to become rich, to gain *kerdos* (profit), but it is difficult to parse exactly where his mercantile efforts fell on a scale of social mobility. He may not have been discussing profit-seeking behavior, but simply advocating

---

[136] *Od.* 19.241–243.
[137] *Od.* 21.5–41.
[138] *Od.* 9.196–198.
[139] Donlan 1997, 663.
[140] Donlan 1981, 102–103: "... high numerical and value ratios between animals and *keimêlia* are observed in the few instances where actual equivalencies are given."
[141] *Op.* 619–694. See also Osborne 1996b.

a strategy for mitigating the risk of having a single, agricultural source of income in a world of great uncertainty.

So there is, on the one hand, an impression that the common farmer in EIA Greece might have engaged in trade at some distance from his home (sometimes involving seafaring) from time to time. However, Hesiod's admission that he "has never yet sailed the broad sea"[142] outside of one trip to Euboea (only a few hundred feet away from the Boeotian coast) adds confusion to the matter, although some scholars have proposed deleting this problematic statement.[143] Even if someone like Hesiod really did sail frequently for trade, we do not have clarity on exactly how Hesiod would have effected his sea journeys, and by extension how his trade activities were financed. According to a direct interpretation of the poetry (*Op.* 622–632; 684–688) we should imagine that Hesiod not only had relatively detailed knowledge of seafaring, markets, and the appropriate quantities one should expect to exchange on his trips, but even had adequate resources to maintain his own boat (in landlocked Ascra nonetheless!). On the other hand, the passage at *Op.* 643, in which Hesiod describes how to choose a small or large boat, may suggest that the boats were owned in common and kept at a harbor, then rented out by people like Hesiod on an *ad hoc* basis,[144] or even that what Hesiod describes is taking a common passage on a larger merchantmen with other farmers-*cum*-traders.[145]

Whatever the exact details of his activities, Hesiod's narrative provides convincing corroboration to the Homeric glimpses into an active profit-motivated trade economy in the EIA, whether or not he ever participated in something like "long-distance" trade. As in the LBA texts that juxtapose elite gift exchange with the basic transactional activities of Ugaritian merchants, textual evidence for trade in the EIA suggests that exchanges operated on a variety of levels and involved actors that pursued their interests in a variety of ways. On the one hand, elites exchanged luxury goods with one another as a part of embedded political economies, while more practical trade by those seeking to improve their lot by way of active profit-seeking transactions took place at a different register of society.

1.3. COMPARISON OF LATE BRONZE AGE AND EARLY IRON AGE TRADE

In a more specific sense, how does trade in the LBA texts compare to trade in early Greek texts? There are many intriguing similarities and differences.

---

[142] *Op.* 650: οὐ γάρ πώ ποτε νηί γ'ἐπέπλων εὐρέα πόντον (for I never have set sail in a ship on the wide sea).
[143] West 1978, 55–56; Lamberton 1988, 131.
[144] Edwards 2004, 60.
[145] Bravo 1977, 8–9, 25–42. Mele 1979 (40–46) agrees with this point of view, but see Snodgrass 1983 for a criticism.

In what follows I compare five aspects of trade as it is portrayed in the LBA texts and in Homer and Hesiod.

1.3.1. Agency

One of the primary points of similarity between the texts is that the most visible agents of long-distance trade are political leaders. If the Near Eastern evidence is any guide to LBA trade, we should conclude that the Mycenaean king(s) would have had exclusive access to gift-exchange transactions with rulers of other Mediterranean states. There is evidence that royal gift exchange occurred among powerful kings, that the Mycenaeans were on equal footing with these kings for part of the Late Mycenaean period, and that traffic in exotic luxury gifts and dear commodities made up an important sector of the trade economy in the LBA Mediterranean. We could thus likely conclude that royals and their families were the principal agents driving trade during the Bronze Age. Likewise, Homeric kings exchange gifts with one another and with foreign kings, and their transactions comprise a majority of the long-distance trade economy that is visible in early Greek poetry.[146]

It is impossible to imagine that source bias has not skewed our sense of the most important players in the game. Most surviving written sources from the LBA come from palatial contexts or deal with royal business, and the Homeric poems no doubt privilege exchange between heroes because those are the main subjects of the stories that they tell. However, in both sets of material, and in Hesiod's poetry, there is a visible current of long-distance trade that is separate from kingly exchange. Merchants worked for the palaces in order to facilitate the movement of royal shipments, both within and beyond the state, but also acted independently in order to maximize their own investments. They clearly engaged in trade on their own terms, although that trade was still governed by the laws and standards agreed on by the king's law. Foreign traders, such as the Suteans, had a place in this economy as well. In Homer, Phoenician merchants and roguish pirates notoriously roamed the seas plying their wares for gain, operating totally outside of and beyond the authority of the *basileis*. And in Hesiod, we hear of a lowly peasant farmer who can participate in maritime exchange, although whether or not he ever reached distant (instead of local) shores is not

---

[146] Those ranking below kings in Homeric society are not supposed to participate in gift exchanges (*Il.* 24.428–439: Priam offers Hermes, in the guise of Achilles' clansman a drinking cup, and Hermes responds, "you try me out, old man, for I am young, but you will not persuade me, telling me to accept your gifts when Achilles does not know. I fear him at heart and have too much reverence to rob him.")

clear.[147] Thus, multiple levels of agency are apparent in both sources, but kingly gift exchange is best documented.

1.3.2. Mechanisms

The contrast in trade mechanisms at both levels of exchange between the LBA and EIA evidence is sharp. In the royal exchanges of the LBA, kings were the agents both sending and receiving goods, but they did not carry out any of the actual logistical steps of the exchange. Once the size and content of the gift was determined, it was up to the royal scribe to write down the letter that would accompany the gift, the storeroom keepers to gather the inventory, and merchants of some sort (either royal attachés or foreign contractors) to make the actual trip to deliver the gift. Seals and guards were sent to ensure that enclosures arrived intact, and the written communication did the job of making sure important messages that went along with the gifts were accurately conveyed. The kings exchanging gifts did not meet face to face, and hardly had to lift a finger in order to carry out the large transactions recorded in the texts.

In the Near East, elaborate and sophisticated infrastructure ensured a fair shakeout if things went badly on the road or at sea,[148] as entire classes of officials took charge of various aspects of the vigorous trade economy. Even at a nonkingly level, juridical texts and merchants' records attest to a highly organized and managed business environment for all kinds of transactions. Ports appear to have been well organized, administered by officials of a whole spectrum of types, ethnicities and levels of authority ensuring that arrivals and departures were orderly and lawful. Whether or not the same conditions applied within Greece cannot be determined with much certainty. The evidence from the Linear B tablets suggests that the main ports of the Mycenaean world *might* have been managed in similarly complex ways,[149] though it seems unlikely that Tiryns could have ever approached Ugarit as a "Bronze Age Venice" of sorts.[150] The archaeological evidence, meanwhile, remains murky. Although we eagerly await the full publication of pioneering studies of Mycenaean harbors like the one at Korfos-Kalamianos on the mainland and the Cretan site of Poros-Katsambas, detailed material evidence

---

[147] See Edwards 2004 for a discussion of the Ascran economy and its reach; we do know that Hesiod could enjoy delights from afar, such as Byblian wine (*Op.* 589) but this does not mean that he procured it himself.

[148] RS 18.031.

[149] Palaima 1991, 296–301. The Linear B evidence, especially Tablet PY Vn 46, supports the idea that Mycenaean Knossos and Pylos had organized systems for building, maintaining and manning sizeable fleets, although these may have been for military rather than commercial purposes.

[150] As argued by Astour 1972, 26.

for the organization of power and access at LBA harbors in Greece does not yet exist.[151]

Unlike LBA kings, Homeric heroes did not dispense gifts by proxy at a distance. Gifts in Homer were exchanged under the same general rhetorical headings (let us cement the bond between our houses), but under vastly different circumstances. Gifts among Homeric heroes were exchanged only when they encountered one another face-to-face, and after at least one party had undergone a long and hazardous journey. The artifices that had allowed diplomacy to function at a distance in the LBA no longer existed in the Homeric poems. Not only did Telemachus not have a scribe to take down a letter asking Nestor about his father and make a list of gifts he planned to send to Pylos along with his message, he did not even live in a society that utilized the technology of writing.[152] Instead of dispatching his (nonexistent) diplomatic agents to gather the inventory, finding the appropriate intermediaries who could be trusted to take the cargo to its destination, and waiting about for word of Odysseus's adventures, he asks someone to loan him a ship, gets a few rations together, and sets out on the dangerous and unpatrolled seas on his own. Once he arrives at his destination, he has to convince his hosts that he is not a pirate,[153] something an elaborate royal envoy from Egypt to Hattuša probably never had to worry about.

In general, everything about trade in the EIA texts looks informal and individual-driven rather than formalized and state-driven. Foreign merchants in the LBA were integrated into the larger mechanisms that had been developed to govern trade, while the Phoenicians that brought trinkets to the shores of Greece in Homer, the Lemnians ferrying wine over to the Greek army, and Achilles selling his captives along the Anatolian coast all look like total free agents. In an ungoverned world of long-distance maritime trade, informal commercial exchange took place *ad hoc*, with no universal standards or codes of behavior guaranteeing transactions.

1.3.3. Materials and Magnitude

Just as the technological and logistical apparatus around trade is far less developed in Homer than it appears to be in LBA texts, the volume and variety of goods exchanged in texts are distinct in the two sets of evidence. Kingly gift

---

[151] For the finds from Kalamianos-Korfos, see Tartaron et al. 2011; Tartaron 2013, 243–265 (see also pp. 286–288 for insightful summary of the problems facing the study of harbors and their ancient dynamics). Poros-Katsambas preliminary reports can be found in Dimopoulou 1997; Dimopoulou-Rethemiotaki 2004; Dimopoulou 2012.

[152] With the exception of the Bellerophon episode (*Il.* 6.119–236), which may be a garbled interpolation of a Near Eastern mythical motif, there is no evidence or mention of literacy in the Homeric poems. (S. Morris 1997, 619; Bryce 2002, 56).

[153] von Reden 1995, 65.

exchanges are on a legendary scale, with gifts of 1,000 or more items changing hands on special occasions. Gifts in these texts represent a huge range of objects. A partial list of gifts in a single instance of exchange between Burnaburiash and Akhenaten includes: gold necklaces, golden oil containers, gold pins, silver goblets, gold figurines, silver figurines, gold goblets, gold pails, gold rings, golden sandals, ivory bracelets, bronze razors, gold bowls, gold necklace plaques, tubes of eye paint, gold knives, gold ladles, a statue of the king and his family, chariots overlaid with gold, seven ships overlaid with gold, gold-embellished furniture, silver braziers, monkey figurines, abundant sweet oil, silver ladles, silver sandals, silver mirrors, hundreds of bronze mirrors, bronze tripods and braziers, horse tack, bronze razors, bronze ladles "for the barber," hundreds of fine linen garments and bed furnishings, hundreds of jars of perfumed oils, stone vessels and figurines, stone headrests, whetstones, ebony and ivory boxes, and over four hundred ivory containers of various types.[154]

The variety and richness of the goods sent from one king to the other in the LBA are consistently lavish, though rarely are they on the scale of Burnaburiash's gift. The most common gifts in the Amarna letters are gold (unworked or finished items), lapis lazuli (either individual seals or bulk quantities), linens in a variety of forms, silver vessels, stone vessels, copper or tin in ingot form, horses and slaves, and fine handiwork of ivory or precious stone. Nonroyal commercial exchanges, on the other hand, usually involve commodities, primarily metals, cloth, livestock, wine, salt, and so forth, with only the exceptional occasion of exchange in finished luxury goods. Thus, in the LBA, it was perfectly appropriate for kings to send to one another any combination of menu items from the entire range of imaginable shippable goods, both commodities and finished objects, depending on the needs of the recipient, the resources of the sender, and the context of the interaction. On the other hand, merchants seeking to maximize profit and perhaps lacking the means to come by hundreds of gold ladles, focused on raw materials, simple handicrafts, and agricultural goods.

In Homer, we see a scaled-down version of trade,[155] and less distinction between the two levels of intra-*basileis* exchange and other type of exchange. The most commonly traded objects among *basileis* in Homer are fancy metal vessels (mostly for drinking or mixing wine),[156] gold ingots,[157] jewelry,[158]

---

[154] EA 14. Evidence from the Uluburun shipwreck confirms this picture, and provides an unusually revealing window into the kinds of exchange described in the texts.
[155] Crielaard 2000, 56.
[156] *Il.* 6.212–236; *Il.* 9.121–161; *Il.* 23.259–271; *Il.* 23.651–653; *Od.* 4.125; *Od.* 4.127–130; *Od.* 4.589–592; *Od.* 4.611–619; *Od.* 8.430–432; *Od.* 9.201–205; *Od.* 13.13–15; *Od.* 15.102–108; *Od.* 16.13.
[157] *Il.* 9.121–161; *Od.* 4.127–130; *Od.* 8.386–397; *Od.* 9.201–205.
[158] *Od.* 15.459–463; *Od.* 18.290–300.

fancy belts,[159] wine,[160] clothing,[161] horses,[162] women,[163] and arms.[164] Gone in large part are many of the materials and artifact types attested in documents about Bronze Age trade: lapis lazuli, ebony and ivory, and precious stones among materials; seals, statues, figurines, mirrors, footwear, ships, and furniture among classes of artifact. The largest single gift within the poems, the one offered by Agamemnon to Achilles, consists of seven tripods, ten talents of gold, twenty cauldrons, twelve horses, and seven Lesbian women.[165] It is telling that this is the case regardless of the fact that this gift is meant to be so vastly overwhelming in its generosity that the audience is supposed to be shocked at Achilles' refusal to accept it. We can imagine that a gift on the scale of a major Bronze Age royal dispensation would have been beyond the wildest dreams of Homer and his audience.[166]

The merchants in Homer deal in similar goods as the kings do. Bulk metals like iron and bronze as well as fine jewelry, wine, slaves, gold goblets, and other merchandise are omnivorously acquired by the Phoenicians and other merchant traders that make brief appearances in the *Iliad* and *Odyssey*. In large part, then, while Homeric heroes trade in a different context and with different aims than merchants in the epics, the kinds of materials that circulate in the trade networks of these two distinct groups are difficult to distinguish from one another.[167]

1.3.4. Purpose

What was the point of exchange? This is a complex question in any circumstance, and we can hardly hope to really answer it for a period of such sketchy and biased evidence. However, from the point of view of the texts, it appears that the motivations of the LBA monarchs were more varied than the motivations of the Homeric heroes. In the LBA world, the exchanges that took place in the context of royal gift exchange were explicitly not purely symbolic, while Homeric exchange appears closer to anthropological models of gift exchange.[168]

---

[159] *Il.* 6.212–236; *Il.* 7.299–302.
[160] *Il.* 7.464–482; *Od.* 9.164–166; *Od.* 9.201–205.
[161] *Il.* 23.560–563; *Od.* 8.386–397; *Od.* 19.241–243.
[162] *Od.* 4.589–592.
[163] *Il.* 6.212–236; *Il.* 7.299–302; *Od.* 7.7–10.
[164] *Il.* 23.560–563; *Od.* 19.241–243; *Il.* 23.798–800.
[165] *Il.* 9.120–135.
[166] For similar disparity between the maximum scale of the imagination in Homer and documented reality in Mycenaean times when it comes to the size of herds and the pastoral economy, see van Wees 1999, 20 with bibliography at note 61.
[167] Although unworked gold talents are not traded outside of the *basileis*-level elites in the Homeric texts. This may indicate that there was at least some notion of varying classes or categories of exchange good.
[168] Finley (1970, 120) was among the first to recognize that Homeric "gift-giving was part of the network of competitive, honorific activity." He drew on Polanyi's (1957) integration of

Gift exchange in the LBA is symbolically important. Individual kings express their dismay about perceived dishonors in the form of gifts that are of less value than expected, and maintain a constant inflow and outflow of diplomacy and the attendant riches. But the point of the gifts obtained from brother kings is also pragmatic. While golden sandals and gold-plated ships may not be practical gifts, there is clear evidence that some gifts, though couched in the rhetoric of greeting-gifts, were eventually circulated into the local economy rather than treasured as precious heirlooms to be piled in a storeroom or kept as mementos of special friendship. Gifts of gold and lumber were converted into wealth that fueled particular building projects and helped the individual empires to prosper. Kingly gift exchange in the LBA texts is a hybrid – gifts for royalty to treasure[169] and lavish upon their family members circulated together in the same system as unadulterated raw materials meant to finance the state's activities. Commodities look like the more important partner in this binary, if the constant appeals for gold in the Amarna letters are any indication. Thus, the evidence suggests that there was a combined purpose behind LBA royal gift exchange. Besides binding kingdoms together in virtuous cycles of reciprocity, this trade was also about the long-term economic and diplomatic well-being of the state.

In Homer, gift exchange looks more like purely symbolic gift exchange.[170] Gifts are given in anticipation not of a future compensatory gift per se, but in order to cement a long-term relationship that binds the two parties together.[171] The recipient of a guest-gift assumes the responsibility of honoring the relationship that the gift generates whenever the appropriate circumstances for reciprocation should arise. The recipient does not usually demand the gift, nor does he make stipulations about what the gift should be, or explain what he intends to do with it. The gift itself is usually something beautiful, and can sometimes be useful. However, the point of the gift is not to proffer things for a utilitarian purpose, but to cement a close relationship, which might come in handy in a variety of scenarios in a Homeric world in which movement, travel, and military action appear to have been quite common (a place of refuge in case of exile, alliances in a distant war, sources of valuable information in uncertain times, and so forth).[172]

Because Homeric objects thus constituted the material embodiment of powerful and useful personal ties,[173] they could take on great social value

---

Mauss (1923) and Malinowski's (1922) anthropological work into the study of early economies. A more recent work on the topic is von Reden 1995.

[169] EA 21, 33–41.
[170] Herman 1987; Donlan 1989b, 6–10; Donlan 1997, 663.
[171] Donlan 1997, 663: "Gift-giving among the Homeric elite, by contrast, has maximum social and political purpose, but little economic purpose."
[172] However, see Qviller 1981 for a convincing explication of the more pugilistic aspects of gift exchange in Homer.
[173] Finley 1954, 100.

beyond a fair market price, precluding their circulation in commercial exchange.[174] Nobody in Homer, for instance, melts down his silver gift in order to put a new addition onto his swineherd's hut. Rather, the treasures are locked in the treasure room, worn for strutting around on the battlefield, or regifted to cement other important relationships. Homeric gifts thus represent true relationships that are meaningful to both givers and recipients.[175] The wider community does not stand to benefit in straightforward ways from Homeric gift-exchange transactions and may have had to bear the burden of the costs of such gift exchanges, at least in part.[176] The Homeric hero builds up wealth and reputation for his own *oikos*, not to provide funding for state or community projects.[177]

1.3.5. Values and Ideology

Both LBA kings and Homeric kings display a reluctance to admit that there is any economic motivation for their exchange activities.[178] Neither Near Eastern kings nor Homeric heroes are happy to express the need for things, and they do not want to appear to be greedy or to desire a profit. In the Homeric poems, *basileis* like Odysseus consider themselves to be distinct from those who "wander at random over the sea" causing trouble and peddling goods. The Phoenicians presented in Homer are not tightly integrated into the world of the Greeks or their economy.[179] Rather, they exist on the margins,

---

[174] A good example is the scepter of Agamemnon, described at *Il.* 2.101–108, which was passed from Zeus to Hermes to Pelops to Atreus to Thyestes to Agamemnon and which granted widely-recognized authority to its owner.

[175] von Reden 1995, 69: "[In Homer] gifts had histories and created obligations, thus being somewhat closer to persons than objects of sale."

[176] In *Od.* 13.13–15, Alcinous suggests that each man present at the departure of Odysseus should give him a tripod and a cauldron, and that "we will recoup the cost having gathered it from the people." This statement provides an interesting window into what may have been a system of informal, *ad hoc* taxation.

[177] *Od.* 1.392–393; *Od.* 14.323–326. Once again, Hesoid's *Works and Days* provides us with a different perspective, although one that is not at odds with the idea of trade as a purely individual or *oikos*-centered pursuit. Hesiod is clearly *not* interested in using trade as a means of developing personal ties or with increasing his own status through trade, but instead seeks explicitly to increase the economic prosperity of his *oikos*. His purpose in taking to the seas is to sell his surplus agricultural products for profit. Hesiod's attitude expresses ambivalence about taking to the seas even under these circumstances, and we should imagine that whenever possible he forewent sailing trips, because they were risky. Once again, however, the issue with the evidence from Hesiod is that it does not seem to be relevant to long-distance exchange, and so it is largely not relevant to the discussion here (see comments in Tartaron 2013, 198, 294, n. 6).

[178] Monroe 2009, 204; Finley 1954, 73.

[179] Although the guest-friend relationships between Greeks and Sidonians cited previously muddle the picture somewhat. It is possible that only certain groups of Phoenicians we seen as antagonistic to Greeks in certain circumstances.

intermittently showing their faces on the Homeric stage to serve as profit-seeking foils to the honorable Homeric heroes, more often at odds with proper social functioning than harmonizing with it.

On the other hand, merchants and traders of the LBA world were integrated tightly into exchange at all levels, including royal exchange, and stigmatization of trade for profit as unacceptable or undesirable does not appear to have been widespread. On the contrary, merchants at Ugarit were among the most highly regarded members of the community,[180] and even foreign traders are subsumed comfortably within the state.[181]

How much does this tell us about the role of merchants or traders in mainland Greece? Not necessarily much. The lack of vocabulary words in Linear B for merchant or trader or entrepreneur may be totally misleading, since it is only negative evidence from a random sample of texts. Alternatively, it may indicate that trading functionaries and foreign merchants were not a part of the Mycenaean palatial society, but operated on their own, outside of the sector of palatial control. The evidence is inconclusive – it is possible to guess that Mycenaean economies worked like those in parts of the Near East or to argue the lack of evidence for trade in Linear B proves that the Mycenaeans shared the Homeric distaste for merchants and traders.[182]

1.4. RELEVANCE OF TEXTS TO ONE ANOTHER

There are, then, both differences and similarities between trade and exchange in the LBA and the EIA texts. I have already addressed the issue of whether and how these texts are relevant to archaeological material. However, before I consider the way in which this evidence may weigh on my interpretation of the archaeology, it is necessary to consider how comparable the texts are to one another. To what extent can the differences in the role and function of trade between the LBA and Homeric material be attributed to the different biases inherent in the genres and priorities of the texts themselves? In general, while the comparability of the evidence is dubious at best, there are some salvageable conclusions.

---

[180] Monroe 2009, 203.
[181] One Syrian text (KTU 4.102) records the existence of a "Cyprus-town" near Ugarit. For evidence of a community of Canaanite seafarers at Ugarit with their own temple on the city's acropolis see Brody 1998, 46–49; for the integration of royal and merchant business, Monroe 2009, 20; Bell 2012, 185.
[182] There is some limited evidence for foreign merchants' and traders' interaction with the palaces in the Mycenaean period. It is possible but not certain that an Egyptian became a Cretan shepherd (KN Db 1105 + 1446: a3-ku-pi-ti-jo (Αἰγύπτιος) from the Cretan site of su-ri-mo in charge of 80 sheep). At Pylos, individuals named "Cypriot" associated with sheep, bronzeworking, and various commodities are attested. See Himmelhoch 1990–1991 for discussion of these texts, and n. 13, above.

TABLE 1.1. *Comparison of some aspects of trade in the texts*

	LBA Texts	Homeric Poems/Hesiod
Agency	both great kings and merchants/traders	both "kings" and merchants/traders
Mechanisms	proxies and contractors	do-it-yourself
Materials	(a) commodities and value-added goods (great kings): gold and lapis lazuli prominent, but also all kinds of finished goods (b) mostly commodities (merchants): copper and tin prominent	commodities and value-added goods (both kings and merchants): gold and metal vessels prominent
Magnitude	large	small
Function of Gift Exchange	commercial and symbolic	symbolic
Ideology	kings express self-sufficiency, but merchants respected	commercial exchange broadly frowned upon

In order to compare the two sets of texts to one another, we must confront the fact that textual evidence suffers from many of the same shortcomings as archaeological evidence. Just as there is no point in comparing archaeological material from one period to the evidence from another period if there seem to be major differences in the history of exploration or preservation of the sites we have documented from each one, it is impossible to fruitfully compare bodies of textual evidence if we predict that they (a) both represent totally different perspectives, with unknowable biases skewing the evidence in directions that are hard to guess at and thus impossible to correct for and (b) each stand as an imperfect sample of an original corpus of textual material and may or may not be representative of the overall quality and characteristics of contemporary written documents.

Consider, for instance, the LBA royal correspondence. When we attempt to bring evidence like the Amarna letters into a discussion on ancient society or political economy, what we are aiming for is essentially a form of content analysis, for which the evidence is inherently inappropriate. Content analysis should be "limited to negotiations in which complete transcripts are available or the material consists of a sample taken from a known population of negotiating interactions."[183] None of these conditions apply to the Near Eastern correspondence. We do not know, and have no way of knowing, the original population of letters that were sent among kings in the Ancient Near East, so we have sampling problems. The letters that we have left might give us

---

[183] Druckman and Güner 2000, 175.

a representative impression of the correspondence between Akhenaten and his brother kings. But if the unknown quantity of unknown, "uncoded" data differed qualitatively from the known data, entire parts of the correspondence system would remain hidden from view.

Second, we can safely guess that these letters give us a single, formalized perspective on the way that kingly gift exchange worked, but we can only speculate about the underlying particularities of the system that generated the letters.[184] And even if we had all of the written data from the original body of evidence, and an understanding of the biases inherent in the correspondence system, any data about the way in which the great kings interacted that materialized in nontextual ways would remain hidden from view. Thus, we can neither easily evaluate the social meaning of the material that we do have, nor assess how well this material informs us about normal practice.

These complications apply in amplified form to any attempt at a content analysis of the Homeric poems. The way in which characters in the *Iliad* and the *Odyssey* conduct trade and exchange, and their attitudes about these pursuits, might or might not have been normal within the original corpus of eighth century Greek epic poetry, and might or might not have any relationship with a real world that once existed in the eighth century or before. While we have some firm ground for texts like the Amarna letters – we know the audience and the author, and can get a firm grasp of the contexts in which the letters were composed and read – almost every platform from which one tries to approach the Homeric poems turns out to be slippery. We might imagine, for instance, that the main characters in the poems correspond to real chieftains in early Greece who listened to traveling bards like the one we think composed the *Iliad* and the *Odyssey* singing similar epic tales in their own halls. If we accepted this, we would reconstruct lives and attitudes of these *basileis* that were something like the ones depicted in the poems, with the exception of a few touches of Las Vegas sparkle.[185] If this were the case, we might have some basis from which to at least begin to extract the characteristics of life among the highest echelons of eighth century society,[186] and we might be able to compare these details to the ones about life among Bronze Age kings in the Amarna letters.

---

[184] See Nakassis (2013, 19) on similar problems that obtain in the attempt to discern the relationship between the Linear B texts and society: "...because the Linear B tablets are laconic administrative documents, they provide only the information that was directly relevant to the scribes." In the case of the letters, these are diplomatic exchanges and present only the information that kings wished to express to their addressees, a category of evidence that does not necessarily line up directly with their true ideas or sentiments.

[185] Dalby 1995, 271.

[186] Raaflaub 1997, 633.

But what if wandering bards kept away from the richest households, and tried to pitch their songs to a more humble class of patrons, as Dalby has argued?[187] If this were the case, the simple "do-it-yourself" lifestyles of the *basileis* and the small-scale gift exchanges that took place between Greeks and foreigners would take on a different meaning, something to which even a humble farmer like Hesiod could have aspired. The "scaling down" of bureaucracy and exchange might then have been part of the poet's effort to make the story and heroes relatable to the audience. Most Homeric scholars would prefer the former view, that the material in the epics represents a *basileus*-eye view on eighth century culture. But given the nature of the evidence we will simply never be able to know for certain who the poems were supposed to be for and about, whether they represent any real group's life, whether they are pure amalgamation and fantasy, whether they represent a coherent ideal from a material-cultural level, or any number of other permutations on these themes.

Thus, it is clear that some of the "aspects of trade" set out in Table 1.1 cannot usefully be compared across the texts. Because we have no idea how representative the individual instances of trade that we know about are, we cannot rely on existing descriptions of the types of artifacts exchanged as a point of systematic comparison. For instance, because we have so many letters from Egypt, gold is well represented in LBA correspondence as an exchange item, while Aegean or Alašhiyan commodities like olive oil and copper may be underrepresented. It is, then, unwise to draw conclusions about the materials that dominated trade in either period based on comparing the texts.

In addition, because we do not know the nature of the audience or the motivations of the author of the Homeric or Hesiodic poems, we cannot tell whether scorn and distrust for foreign merchants like the Phoenicians was widespread or limited to particular segments of society. Hesiod's work suggests that profit seeking and risk mitigation were a part of life for many Greeks, but attitudes toward merchants who were not also or mainly farmers might have been different. Similarly, attitudes toward merchants based on texts found in the kinds of royal and industrial contexts from which the LBA texts originate should likewise not be taken to represent the views of everyone else. Not surprisingly then, the available literary evidence is not helpful for sorting out diachronic change in pervasive social attitudes toward commerce and marginal ethnic groups.

Likewise, the motivations behind trade are difficult to compare across the texts. Near Eastern kings report that they are not demanding commodity wealth just to hoard it up in their storerooms, but that they need it to build

---

[187] Dalby 1995, 279.

something. In Homer, the emphasis is on hoarding up treasure and cherishing gifts as dear reminders of good times around the bonfire with friends. Neither stated function should be taken at face value. A letter to the king of Egypt requesting gold for greed's sake, rather than because it was needed to complete a specific project, was probably not likely to get a positive response, and so the emphasis on utility gold in the Amarna letters could be misleading. Likewise, it is difficult to imagine that the gold talents passed from one Homeric hero to another were kept in the storerooms forever. If the texts are any indication, *some* greeting gifts *may* have been imbued with more social and sentimental meaning in Homer's world than they were among Bronze Age kings, but this remains mostly speculative.

In sum, it is difficult to get the LBA and Homeric texts to articulate with one another in productive ways. The most reliably comparable "aspects of trade" are those dealing with mechanisms and magnitudes. There is no reason to doubt the veracity of the highly complex, multilayered, vertically hierarchical organization of trade described in the LBA texts. Even if the texts we have are not representative of the whole, the logistical infrastructure of trade that they describe must have existed. That is to say, the material practices of trade described in the texts (sealing, generating inventories of shipments, demonstrating and proving ownership and authority over commodities and other resources, securing reliable intermediaries, and providing for safety and security of investments and associates) are clearly documented in both kingly and extrapalatial contexts, and seem to constitute real, consistent features of trade infrastructures in the Near East. Linear B texts attest a similar bureaucratic complexity in contemporary Greece.[188]

The scale of gifts or other trade shipments that we read about in LBA texts is probably reliable too. Shipment inventories like the ones in the Amarna letters are as close as we will ever get to hard evidence that gifts of a certain size really once existed, and even if the gifts in the surviving texts are not necessarily representative or normal, they do give us some outer limits – we know that a gift of over 1,000 items was not totally out of the question within the context of royal gift exchange in the thirteenth century BCE. There is no reason to suspect that these inventories are forged or trumped up. Indeed, they were in part intended to provide an official receipt that could be checked against the batch at arrival.

Both the scale and mechanisms of Homeric trade look much smaller and simpler, and I believe that this is likely to be faithful to actual conditions in the EIA. Whether or not the Homeric poems represent an eighth century reality[189] or a fantasy of "exaggerated wealth"[190] it is hard to avoid the conclusion that

[188] Finley 1957; Killen 1985, 241.
[189] Redfield 1975, 75.
[190] I. Morris 1986, 89.

the kind of gift sent from Burnaburiash to Akhenaten was beyond the wildest dreams of the eighth century bards and audiences, and that the technologies used to send this kind of gift simply did not exist in the EIA. Materially speaking, everything about the way trade worked in the LBA looks completely impossible in a world that was anything like what Homer describes. Perhaps most importantly, writing and sealing are not features of this world, but these technologies form the spine of the functional apparatus of LBA trade. Without the insurance of legitimacy and authority that written documents and seals provide,[191] any attempt to dispatch trusted representatives with valuable goods or messages was bound to get messy. Even if he found a good system of delegation, a *basileus* had a limited staff, mostly agricultural retainers with limited skills,[192] to dispatch for errands.[193] His resources were tiny compared with those at the disposal of the king of Pylos, who commanded the ear of a veritable army of specialized attachés, so it is no surprise that he made his own journeys to acquire information and conduct diplomacy. The Homeric hero went abroad with the hopes of "bringing many treasures home"[194] with which to add glory to his *oikos*.[195] In general, we might conclude that trade in the Homeric world, especially trade across cultural boundaries, must have become an occupation of individuals acting on their own initiative, with their own resources, and at their own risk.

On the other hand, it is possible that the absence of trade by intermediaries acting for a "state" or hired hands working for a *basileus* in the Homeric poems is the result of the narrative function of the poems, to entertain. After all, a story in which each king strikes out on his own to acquire glory and treasure is far more exciting than a poem about kings sitting on their thrones and complaining about how much gold they never get from Egypt. But the scale of trade reinforces the notion that the grandiosity, and perhaps also the ceremonial pomp, of kingly exchange faded out after the LBA. Let us say that the Homeric poems are a total fantasy – we would imagine, then, that the glorious prizes given out among traders would have been scaled up, if anything. But gifts in Homer are tiny compared to LBA exchange

---

[191] Liverani 2001, 73.

[192] Dalby 1995, 275.

[193] In the area of trade: *Od.* 2.337–355; for Homeric heroes doing their own work in general: *Od. Il.* 5.313 (Anchises called ox-herd); *Od.* 18.366–375 (Odysseus challenges Eurymachus to a reaping or ploughing contest); *Od.* 24.205–212 (Laertes working hard at his farm).

[194] *Od.* 17.527.

[195] The self-sufficiency of the Homeric king in the area of establishing long-distance trade ties probably echoes the weakness of Homeric leadership overall. While the great kings of the LBA held the authority to trust their orders would be carried out by intermediaries, the Homeric king continually had to prove the authority that was vested in him by his own demonstration of kingliness (Qviller 1981).

TABLE 1.2. *[Minimalist] Comparison of some aspects of trade in the texts*

	LBA Texts	Homeric Poems
Agency	both great kings and merchants/traders	both "kings" and merchants/traders
Mechanisms	proxies and contractors	do-it-yourself
~~Materials~~	~~(a) commodities and value-added goods (Great Kings): gold and lapis lazuli prominent, but also all kinds of finished goods (b) mostly commodities (merchants): copper and tin prominent~~	~~commodities and value-added goods (both kings and merchants): gold and metal vessels prominent~~
Magnitude	large	small
~~Function of Gift Exchange~~	~~commercial and symbolic~~	~~symbolic~~
~~Ideology~~	~~kings express self-sufficiency, but merchants respected~~	~~commercial exchange broadly frowned upon~~

items — a few necklaces or goblets, or some tripods and horses.[196] If this is the biggest exaggeration that Homer can muster, it must have been that Homeric life was simpler yet, with only the highest strata of society managing to acquire even small tokens of relationships abroad.

If we are realistic about our evidence the comparison of trade in the texts can realistically tell us only that trade changed in mechanism and magnitude between the thirteenth and eighth centuries — about the rest, we cannot be sure.

1.5. CONCLUSIONS

Taking the documentary evidence at face value, we see a scenario in which trade in the LBA was conducted on two tiers. First, spectacular royal gift exchanges between great kings were sent directionally between centers of power and comprised both finished goods and commodities. Second, merchants who worked for their own personal gain conducted a bustling trade in commodities (but not gold) that was unrelated to kingly gift exchange, but which still operated within the legal and infrastructural apparatus of states. A variety of indicators suggest that this system broke down around 1200 BCE as a result of maritime disturbances that tore apart

---

[196] The size of gifts may have been limited to the amount that would be expected to fit in the small storage spaces of the Homeric house (Dalby 1995, 273), read by Dalby as the kind of structure known from the Geometric period in Greece.

the political and commercial status quo of the LBA Mediterranean. Unfortunately, texts do not shed much light on the conditions of the twelfth century, but if we take the Homeric texts at face value, the new system eventually reconstituted as something that looks quite different than the LBA status quo. However, the Homeric evidence does not do much to elucidate the precise nature of the new trade economy of the eighth century, except that it was smaller in scale and probably entailed an embedded "do it yourself" element. Even the largest gifts in EIA texts are small by Bronze Age standards, and the technological mechanisms needed to support the kind of elaborate exchange infrastructures that we read about from the Mycenaean period simply no longer existed in the world of the *Iliad* and *Odyssey*.

Ultimately, these texts are fraught with difficulties and provide us little in the way of a basis for reconstructing a complex economic process of transformation which precipitated the chiefly exchanges in Homer from a highly developed world of busy ports and elaborate laws. They paint a tantalizing picture of a complete reconfiguration of economic systems over a period of several hundred years, with some threads that run right through the tale and others that are clearly torn clean out and rewoven in new and unexpected ways. However, the texts can only take us so far, and obviously have serious shortcomings as a matrix through which to reconstruct several hundred years of complex social, political, and economic developments. The only way that we can reconstruct the details of what happened inside the textual tunnel of the post-Mycenaean world is to turn to the material evidence that enlightens early Greek history and try to make sense of the gap as best we can. That is the project I will undertake in the next five chapters.

TWO

DIRECT EVIDENCE FOR LONG-DISTANCE TRADE IN EARLY GREECE

IF THERE IS ONE CONCLUSION WE CAN DRAW WITH CONFIDENCE FROM the textual evidence, it is that the scale of trade must have declined at some point during the period that intervened between the collapse of the Mycenaean palaces and the reemergence of writing in Greece in the eighth century. But that conclusion is hardly satisfying. The devil, as usual, is in the details. What exactly is meant by decline? How much trade was there in the Bronze Age? In the EIA? Can we quantify the difference? Describe it with clarity? Or even explain it?

Since the texts are unreliable when it comes to the details of change in trade systems, we begin a history of early Greek trade from a position of empirical weakness and uncertainty. To limit our conclusions to what the texts show clearly is schematic to the point of banality. The major challenge that lies ahead entails clawing out some precise sense of change in a trade economy from the material evidence that is left for us to analyze, despite the inherent problems that this material presents. The following chapters represent an attempt to tackle this challenge head on. It may appear at times that this study is overly focused on quantities and arithmetic; that is intentional. When dealing with a prehistoric period from which little reliable documentary evidence survives, it is crucial to hew closely to the evidence when coming to conclusions.[1] Concomitant to an effort to build prehistoric narratives

---

[1] For a different view, Sherratt 2011, 3–4.

based on what the archaeological record preserves is a level-headed assessment of that record. In my view, solid footing for that kind of assessment requires quantification.

There is a vast body of theoretical and empirical research that considers strategies and approaches for understanding trade in the ancient world, and much of this work is subtle and enlightening. However, in this book, as stated in the introduction, I am interested in a synthetic accounting of the evidence that we have for trade, and an intensely critical assessment of how traditional metrics for the scale and nature of a trade economy fail to properly ground themselves in a realistic view of that evidence. Therefore, I will for the most part steer clear of theoretical models for reconstructing trade systems, and leave that bold venture for future scholars.

2.1. DIRECT EVIDENCE FOR LONG-DISTANCE TRADE FROM EARLY GREECE

However sophisticated the approach to trade, the starting point of most discussions of intercultural contact (in the absence of useful textual evidence) are the objects or materials found within a region that must have originated on distant shores.[2] While archaeologists have counted and cataloged these objects with care, determining what they actually mean has proven to be a problem. As with the textual evidence, there are gaps and biases that must be considered before we accept the message that these objects convey at face value, and scholars have often crossed swords over the many ways in which the evidence of imports and exports (or lack thereof) might be interpreted.[3]

An obvious place to start an assessment of our story of early Greek trade then, is with a careful accounting of these categories of evidence. Since both imports and exports represent internally complex bodies of evidence and require careful handling based on the potpourri of interpretative problems that come with materials deposited, excavated, and studied in a wide variety of regional contexts, by archaeological practitioners from diverse disciplinary traditions possessing a range of levels of expertise concerning such material, I treat them separately in this book. In this chapter and the next, I compile and discuss the evidence of imported objects; in Chapter 4, I turn to commodities and raw materials and the known corpus of Greek exports.

---

[2] Some examples are: Cline 1994; Lambrou-Phillipson 1990; Skon-Jedele 1994; Leonard 1994; van Wijngaarten 2002; Stampolidis and Kotsonas 2006; Phillips 2008; Parkinson 2010. For other studies operating under similar premises, see Crielaard 1998; Hodos 2006; Fletcher 2007.

[3] Snodgrass 1991, 18; Manning and Hulin 2005; Cherry 2010, 111–112; Cline 2010, 167–168; Parkinson 2010; Parkinson and Galaty 2010 16–25; Tartaron 2013, 23–26.

Background to the Evidence

Interest in and cataloguing of exotic objects found within Aegean contexts both have a long history in Greek archaeology going back to its very earliest days.[4] The import record is the result of a steady accumulation of evidence over some 200 years of research.[5] Until the 1990s however, little of this evidence had been investigated in a systematic way. As Cline has pointed out, earlier debates were about whether there was trade between Greece and other early Mediterranean states, rather than about what the corpus of known imports could tell archaeologists about trade.[6] Except for Pendlebury's *Aegyptica* (1930), most work on early trade in the Aegean Bronze Age did not take much of the archaeological data into account, focusing instead on things like Egyptian wall paintings and Near Eastern texts. In 1990 and 1994, respectively, Lambrou-Phillipson and Cline published catalogues of foreign objects found in Bronze Age Greece.[7] These catalogues were a major step forward in the study of interstate relations in early Greece, since they gave scholars rapid, convenient access to a complete body of archaeological evidence.

Meanwhile, the subject of long-distance trade in EIA Greece did not warrant much detailed work until the discoveries at Lefkandi prompted scholars to take a fresh look at the hypothesis that Greece was mired in an isolated Dark Age during the period between the eleventh and ninth centuries.[8] Both Hoffman (1997) and Jones (2000) have collected the data for EIA Crete,[9] while Skon-Jedele covers

---

[4] Early catalog of imports in Pendlebury 1930; early finds at Knossos, Evans 1925; at Mycenae, Wace 1979; Taylour 1981; imports at Tiryns in Kilian 1988a; Rahmstorf 2003; at Thebes, Porada 1981; Kopanias 2009; at Kommos, Watrous 1985; at Perati Iakovidis 1969; Iakovidis 1970; cf. Iakovidis 1980; in the IIIC period Maran 2006; Halbherr and Orsi 1888; Hogarth 1900; Watrous 1996; at early Greek sanctuaries, Dawkins 1906–07; Dawkins 1929; Payne 1940.

[5] Far more effort has gone into researching imports from the LBA than the EIA. For the former, Cline's oeuvre represents the most thorough investigation of the evidence for long-distance trade (see especially Cline 1994; Cline and Yasur-Landau 2007; Cline 2010). Parkinson (2010) and Schon (2010) have made use of Cline's catalogs of LBA imports to draw some tentative conclusions about the scale and characteristics of early Greek trade. On a less "global" scale, others have made significant strides in the quantitative study of artifact types or imports found in individual excavations or regions. For artifact types: Haskell 2011a and 2011b (coarse-ware transport amphorae); Gale and Stos-Gale 1986 (ingots); Mangou and Ioannou 2000 (ingots); Kayafa 2000 (metals); Ingram 2005 (beads); Rutter 2014 (Canaanite Jars). For sites or regions: Hoffman 1997 (Crete); Bikai 2000 (Kommos); Lemos 2003 (Lefkandi); Rutter 2006 (Kommos); Rahmstorf 2008 (Tiryns); Tomlinson et al. 2010 (Kommos). For the EIA, some catalogs have recently appeared (Markoe 1985; Skon-Jedele 1994; Jones 2000; Lemos 2002, Appendix B; Braun-Holzinger and Rehm 2015) alongside catalogs in individual site publications.

[6] Cline 2010, 163.

[7] These two catalogs are not identical. Cline rejects many imports that Lambrou-Philipson accepts. For Cline's criticism of Lambrou-Phillipson see Cline 2010, 162. For a review of the differences between the two catalogs see Burns 2010b, 36–37. For a more recent catalog of Egyptian imports in particular see Phillips 2008.

[8] Lack of systematic work: Knodell 2013, 62.

[9] Updated in Stampolidis and Kotsonas 2006.

Egyptian imports specifically and Lemos (2002) produced a catalog of PG imports in the eastern (Aegean) part of the Greek mainland. The Geometric material has been well-documented for Crete.[10] Less work has been directed at assembling a record of exotica from the Geometric period on the mainland,[11] but some catalogs of particular or limited classes of artifacts exist.[12]

The tables and quantities I present in this chapter are cumulative of the efforts of all of these scholars, with many modifications and additions: revisions of data where objects have been shown to be either of domestic manufacture or redated, additions of objects that had not been identified as imports at the time of the publication of the preexisting catalogues,[13] and additions of new objects discovered in recent excavations.[14] It should be stated from the outset that the deceptively precise-looking (relative and absolute) quantities presented are far from "facts," as will be discussed in many specific cases, and in Chapter 3. They represent, at best, an honest effort to assemble and sort a deeply problematic dataset.

Imports in Greece in the Late Mycenaean Period

The distribution of LH IIIB imports is spatially characterized by concentrations where we would expect them to be: at major palatial sites, specifically Mycenae, Tiryns, and Thebes.[15] A majority of securely dated IIIB imports were found in or close to the Argolid, at Mycenae and Tiryns especially, but

---

[10] Boardman 1970; Hoffman 1997; Jones 2000; Kourou 2000; Stampolidis and Kotsonas 2006.
[11] Strøm 1992; Muscarella 1992; Gunter 2009; recent review in Kourou 2015.
[12] Markoe 1985; Skon-Jedele 1994.
[13] In the first category of updates, the primary changes have to do with ceramic imports at Kommos and wall brackets from Tiryns. According to Rutter, some imported ceramics at Kommos had previously been misidentified as to their origin (Rutter 2006, 649–653), or unrecognized as imports entirely (Rutter 2006, 658). In addition, some of the objects originally dated too ambiguously to be included in my "firmly dated" import catalog have been subjected to further study and assigned to a specific period. Further complications are presented by the PG import data from the Temple A/B deposits at Kommos. See n. 75 in this chapter for the system I settled on for quantifying imported sherds from Kommos Temple A/B. Recent discoveries have impacted counts for the wall brackets found in LH IIIB and LH IIIC deposits at Tiryns (see n. 26 in this chapter) and Jones's counts for EIA Crete (see Stampolidis and Kotsonas 2006). For a thorough object-by-object accounting of these imports from the IIIB–PG periods and a detailed catalog, see S. Murray 2013 (all imported artifacts are examined in their contexts at 378–464); since imported *exotica* from the Geometric period were not included in that study, I provide notes and bibliography for these Table 2.6.
[14] For detailed summary of the newly discovered imports from LB IIIB–PG, see S. Murray 2013, Appendix B.
[15] Hofstra 2000; Ventris and Chadwick 1973, 341–346 (texts no. 240–246 = PY Ta 713, PY Ta 715, PY Ta 707, PY Ta 708, PY Ta 714, PY Ta 721, PY Ta 722: lists of furnishings provided with gold, ivory, and glass inlays). The example of Pylos is important to keep in mind when we approach the evidence for imports from the IIIB period, since most sites almost certainly would have undergone transformational processes both during and after the destructions attested at the end of the period. These processes probably impacted the distribution of imported objects.

also at Dendra, Tsoungiza, Midea, and Prosymna. There are also imports at Thebes and at the Boeotian coastal site of Pharos/Dexameni. A couple of imports are known from Attica, and a few have been identified in the western Peloponnese, at Monodendri, Spiliareika Lousikon, and Pylos.

The paucity of imports from Pylos is conspicuous. However, there are mitigating factors to keep in mind when considering this information. The palace appears to have been cleared of most precious artifacts before its destruction, unlike Mycenae and Tiryns, and (as Hofstra's dissertation (2000) and the Pylos Linear B tablets document) there is compelling evidence that the site did have access to exotic materials such as gold and ivory during the IIIB period.[16]

At Mycenae, imports have been recovered from a number of areas both within and outside of the citadel proper: from the "Citadel House" area at the south of the Citadel,[17] from the area NE of the Lion Gate,[18] from the West/Ivory houses,[19] and from Petsas House in the lower town.[20] While the complex

[16] This fact is likewise confirmed by the recovery of imports from IIIA contexts at Pylos (Hofstra 2000; Murphy 2014) and by the presence at the site of glass beads made of Egyptian and Mesopotamian materials (Polikreti et al. 2011).

[17] The structures of the Citadel House area include a series of storage facilities as well as a number of spaces that have been interpreted as cult locations. Imports from this area include two fragments from a faience plaque inscribed with the name of Amenhotep III, "the good god Neb Ma'at Re, son of Re." Such plaques were used in Egypt to consecrate foundation deposits (Cline 1990, 206). The plaque was found inside the mouth of a lead vessel that was part of the floor deposit in room 31, the Room with the Fresco (French 1981 45; Taylour 1981, 9, 10, 17). In the Room with the Idols was a vessel containing objects of glass, stone, ivory, and faience, including a faience scarab. Taylour suggested that these were originally strung together with the scarab to create a necklace (Taylour 1970, 277). Imports were found in the nearby areas of Tsountas' house and the South House as well. Three imports, all Near Eastern faience objects (one statuette, one pendant, and one plaque) were found in the Tsountas' House Shrine area (Iakovidis 1983; for its identification as a shrine, French 1981, 45). Burns has suggested that these imports were part of a stored cache of religious votives, since two of the three seem to be heirlooms (Burns 2011, 150). Near the South House and dating to the IIIB period were found two fragments of Canaanite jars. One came from Room 1 of the South House annex, a storage context containing other large jars and a group of Linear B tablets (MY Oi 701–708). The other was found in an area of debris (fallen from above) on the ramp to the north of the South House, together with an imported Syro-Palestinian hematite weight (Wardle 1973, 303–304).

[18] Four (or more) imports were found in the buildings excavated to the NE of the Lion Gate. A fragmentary faience dish and seven fragments of a faience plaque bearing the same inscription as the faience plaque found in the Citadel House ("the good god Neb Ma'at Re, son of Re"; for the possibility that the fragments may belong to more than one plaque, see Cline 1990, 202–205) were found in early excavations in this area (Tsountas 1891, 18–24). Two more fragments from a single plaque were later found in the same area (building M) (Iakovidis 1983, 54).

[19] Tournavitou 1995. All of the imports from the House of the Shields consist of faience or alabaster vessels discovered in the West room and the West half of the North room (Tournavitou 1995, 695–712). The vessels consist of shapes that would not be out of place in ritual contexts, including rhyta, alabastra, kylikes and one bowl, in addition to vessel fragments that are too small to be attributable to a particular shape (Wace 1956, 111–112; Foster 1979, 127; Peltenburg 1991, 164; Cline 1994 nos: 652–661; Tournavitou 1995, 695–712).

[20] Two imports have been found in recent excavations at Mycenae outside of the citadel. One is a faience cartouche from a large dump of LH IIIB2 pottery (Whitley et al. 2005–2006, 33). In

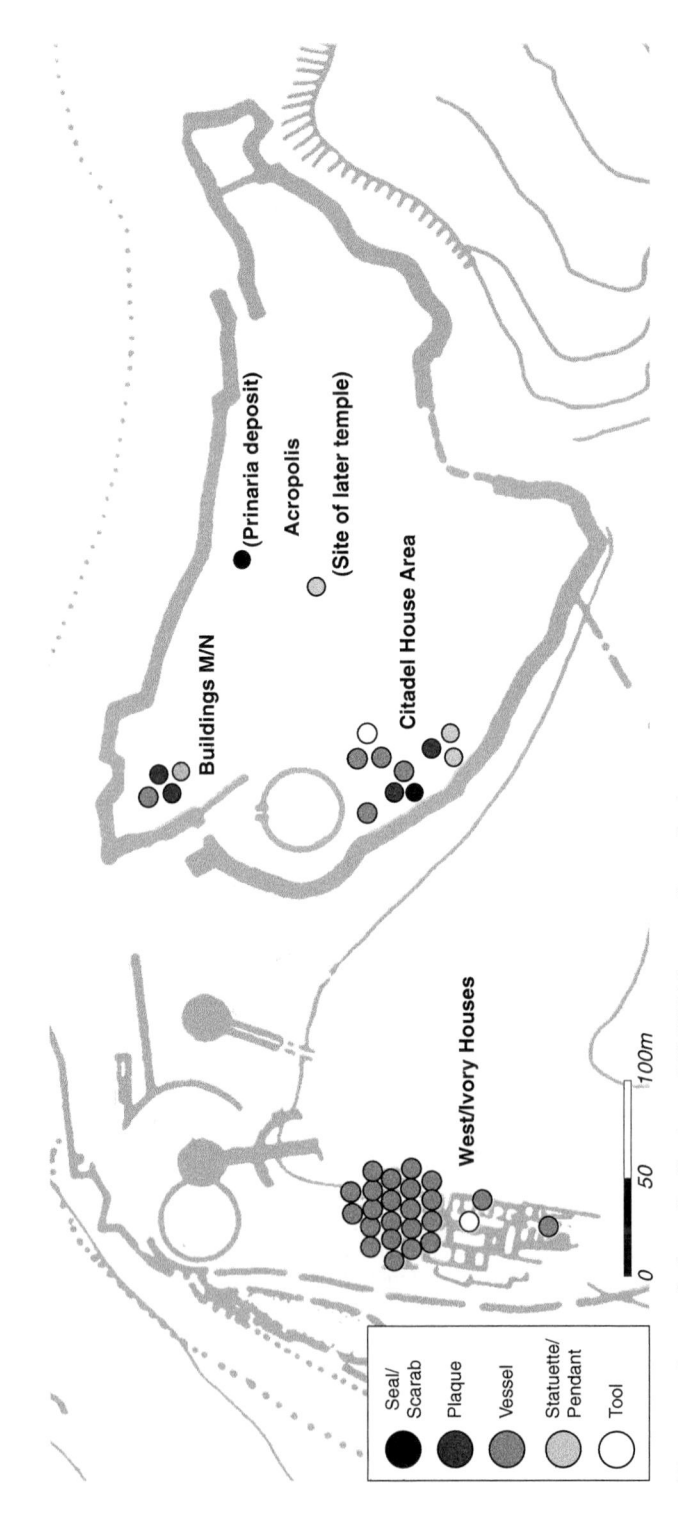

Figure 2.1. Import findspot distribution at LH IIIB Mycenae (by author)

stratigraphy and history of excavation at the site makes many of these imports difficult to interpret with certainty,[21] a number of patterns are apparent in the nature and intrasite distribution of the imports. First, the majority of identified imports from the site come from contexts associated with religious/cultic activities or with the manufacture of crafts, the intended use of which may have been in ritual/cult activities.[22] This may or may not be a function of the state of preservation of the site, since deposits from the upper citadel did not survive antiquity in good stead. Second, the imported objects from Mycenae can be divided into two clear types – faience objects and Canaanite jars.

At Tiryns, the characteristics of known exotica are quite different. Though results of excavation in the lower town and lower citadel await full publication, at least twenty-one imports from Tiryns can be dated to the IIIB period. The largest concentration of IIIB imports is in the area around Building VI in the lower citadel, which contained cult materials and Linear B tablets.[23] Another import-rich deposit was excavated just inside the North gate of the lower citadel.[24] Tirynthian imports are similar in kind and context to the Mycenaean imports – Canaanite jars and faience objects are present, and imports are located preferentially in workshops or areas with evidence of ritual activity. However, the Tirynthian import assemblage is notable for the additional presence of several Cypriot open and closed ceramic vessels, as well as a few highly unusual imports, such as the inscribed ivory rod (Vetters interprets this as a tally stick) and wall brackets (one imported, along with local imitations) which were probably intended to hold torches.[25]

---

addition to this cartouche, the Petsas house excavations have yielded one fragment of a Canaanite jar from a late IIIA or early IIIB context and a number of other Canaanite jar fragments dating to late IIIA (Shelton 2010, 197). The discovery of an elephant's tooth also indicates that this area was a place where nonlocal goods circulated.

[21] The cemeteries at Mycenae have produced a significant number of LH III imports, but the nature of the data does not allow most of these to be firmly dated to one subperiod or another. Eleven of the imports from Mycenae's cemeteries date either generally to the LH III period. Three of these objects are Canaanite jars; Xenaki-Sakellariou 1985.

[22] Tournavitou 1995, 244. Shelmerdine also concluded that the buildings were repositories for special goods that would later be distributed elsewhere, though not necessarily for cult purposes (Shelmerdine 1997, 394).

[23] Kilian 1981 58; Kilian 1982, 401–403; Kilian 1983a, 304. According to preliminary reports, the floor to which the Cypriot juglet belonged may have been part of a workshop. This conclusion is based on the presence of a central hearth within the room and the discovery of an associated pit filled with stone tools and metal scraps. A milk bowl was also found in this area (Cline 1994, 180), as was the Canaanite jar. Fragments of this were found in an ashy deposit showing traces of metalworking (Kilian 1988a, 121). The other Cypriot sherd identified at Tiryns was likewise found in a workshop deposit, also in building VI. To the NW of building VI another Canaanite jar fragment was found together with a locally manufactured wall bracket. For recent analysis of these deposits see Brysbaert and Vetters 2013).

[24] Maran 2004, 13; Brysbaert and Vetters 2013, 195–199.

[25] Rahmstorf 2008. Rahmstorf's work has had a major impact on our understanding of the wall brackets found in LH IIIB and LH IIIC deposits at Tiryns. Cline (1994) counted all wall

80   COLLAPSE OF THE MYCENAEAN ECONOMY

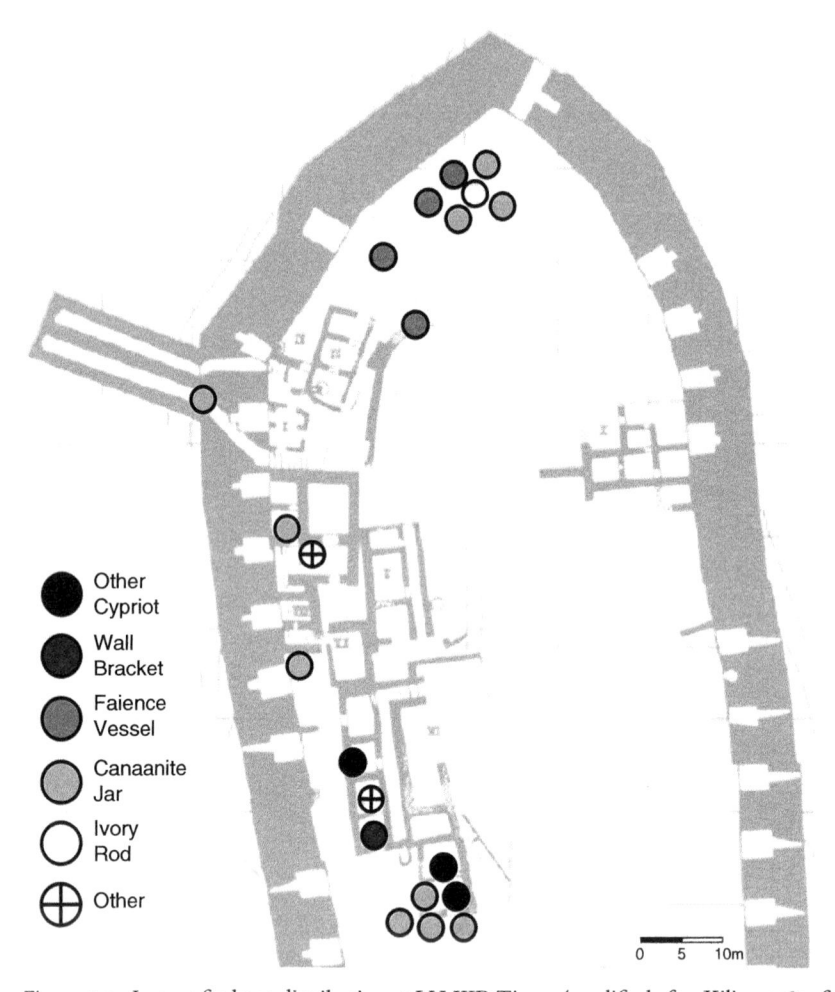

Figure 2.2. Import findspot distribution at LH IIIB Tiryns (modified after Kilian 1982, fig. 23)

Overall, Tirynthian imports are characterized by (1) exclusive presence in the lower citadel and lower town, (2) an unusual number of widely distributed Canaanite jar fragments[26] and (3) the association of imported objects with workshop areas, and with metalworking areas in particular. Maran has pointed out that metalworking at Tiryns is often associated with ritual or

brackets as imports, because the artifact type originated in the Eastern Mediterranean (Cyprus and the Levant). However, Rahmstorf convincingly demonstrated that the Tirynthian wall brackets are a distinct local type (Rahmstorf 2008, 135–136; Rahmstorf 2003, 65; Maran 2004, 12–13). He argues that all but one of the Tirynthian brackets are of local manufacture (Rahmstorf 2008, 108). For the inscribed ivory rod, its context and meaning, see Cohen et al. 2010.

[26] Rutter (2014) argues that the known number of Canaanite jars from Tiryns is likely to increase in the coming years, because many Canaanite Jar body sherds have been observed in the Tiryns storerooms but not yet officially registered or published as imports. This may also apply to other sites.

cult,[27] and Vetters has fleshed out this observation to suggest that Tiryns is likely to have been home to resident Cypriot craftsmen whose presence ought to account for the significant number of imports excavated in the lower citadel.[28]

Finally, at Thebes, the disposition of known imports is quite different again. In contrast to the situations at Mycenae and Tiryns, a small fraction of the Mycenaean complex at Thebes has been excavated.[29] Perhaps as a result, the import corpus at Thebes is both more spatially concentrated and more internally homogenous than those from Mycenae and Tiryns. All but one of the IIIB Theban imports were found in a single cache in a late IIIB deposit in the New Kadmeion.[30] This is the largest single deposit of imported objects from the IIIB period on the Aegean mainland.[31] The seals are mostly made of lapis lazuli, but a few are of other materials, such as faience and jasper. The subject matter depicted on the seals is varied, and includes animal-headed demons, deities, Hittite inscriptions, Cypro-Minoan human-headed bulls, bull-headed men, lions, chariots, archers, and a variety of other motifs. Also found in the Kadmeion was the only other IIIB import from Thebes, a Syro-Palestinian ivory scepter head.[32]

The final owners of these seals probably did not have much interest in the scenes depicted on them, or their original function as seals, undercutting the idea that they would have been shown off by palatial officials as talismans of elite cosmopolitanism. Most of the seals show evidence of having been recut, recarved, or significantly abraded before their final deposition.[33] In addition, the seals were found along with an assemblage of other semiprecious stone objects, both finished and raw, including a set of cylinder seal shaped stones that had not been cut at all. Burns suggests this is because the cylinder seals at

---

[27] Maran 2004, 25.
[28] Cohen, Maran, and Vetters 2010; Vetters 2011. The authors suggest that the function of the craftsmen was to make fine faience vessels and other finished goods for the palatial authorities. See also Brysbaert and Vetters 2013 with a detailed consideration of the specific contexts and assemblages of late palatial exotica.
[29] The excavations that have taken place have revealed two phases of Mycenaean remains, labeled as the Old and New Kadmeia. The site was abandoned after a destruction horizon at the end of LH IIIB1. Over 300 Linear B tablets have been found at Thebes, demonstrating convincingly that some kind of complex administration took place here in the Mycenaean period (Symeonoglou 1985, 40–50).
[30] Porada 1981 is the original publication of the cylinder seals. For the context see Falkenstein 1964; Platon & Touloupa 1964; Touloupa 1964a; 1964b; 1965; 1966. Porada has shown that the seals may have passed through a variety of hands before their deposition in Thebes. The carved designs on the seals are executed in a range of styles including Cypriot, Mesopotamian, and Syro-Palestinian and their production dates vary widely, between the middle of the third millennium and the middle of the second millennium.
[31] Cline 1994, 25.
[32] Thebes Museum no. 13275 (Cline 1994, no. 19).
[33] Aruz 1997, 277–278.

Thebes had been subsumed into a stone-cutting industry for their value as raw materials, rather than because of their value as imported objects.[34] Indeed, as emphasized by Kopanias in his recent reevaluation of the seals, this deposit of lapis lazuli, one of the rarest and most elusive stones in the prehistoric world, is extraordinarily large and must have been worth a great deal as a commodity.[35]

Elsewhere on the mainland, imports are not found in large concentrations during the IIIB period. In general, the finds discovered outside of the major palatial centers come from a combination of mortuary and settlement contexts. Typologically they are not dissimilar from imports discovered in and around the palaces: Canaanite jars, Egyptian vessels, seals, and amulets, and Mitannian cylinder seals comprise the majority of the corpus. In addition, a few sherds of Italian ceramic vessels and daggers or knives are known from LH IIIB sites.

On Crete, imported objects dated to LM IIIB have been identified at Kommos. Careful treatment of the ceramic and architectural phasing at the site has contributed a great deal to our understanding of trade and cultural interaction during the LBA. As Rutter notes, "Kommos has been recognized for over a decade as the single most important settlement not only on Crete but throughout the Aegean for ceramics imported from outside the [Greek] cultural sphere."[36] The imported ceramics at Kommos have been treated thoroughly by Rutter,[37] and so only a brief summary is necessary here. Imports from Anatolia,[38] Cyprus, and Egypt are concentrated in the Southern area and the Hilltop settlement in particular while Syro-Palestinian imports are entirely limited to the Southern area.[39] As opposed to imports from Egypt, Syria-Palestine, Cyprus, and West Anatolia, which seem to become less common in the final phase of occupation, Italian pottery from the site comes particularly from LM IIIB contexts.[40]

---

[34] Burns 2010b, 155. Porada likewise pointed out (1981, 68) that the overall weight of the seals is about one mina and that this suggests the entire set of objects actually came into the Theban palace as part of one gift to the wanax.

[35] Kopanias 2008, 55–56. Kopanias follows Burns in suggesting that the seals were likely intended to be recarved as jewels in the associated workshop in the Kadmeion.

[36] Rutter 2006, 646. Cf. Watrous 1985; 1989; 1992, 149–183; Watrous, Day, and Jones 1998; Shaw 1998; Rutter 2004.

[37] Rutter 2006.

[38] Rutter 2006, 659. Eight sherds of Western Anatolian manufacture have been recognized from LM IIIA2–LM IIIB contexts, though Rutter has postulated that we are probably missing a fair amount of this material, because "lack of published indigenous pottery assemblages of LBA from coastal W. Anatolia" makes it difficult to make identifications. Rutter also suggests that they may be kick ups from earlier levels (Rutter 2006, 653).

[39] Rutter 2006, 653.

[40] Rutter 2006, 675–676; mostly around building N and in the levels washed out to the south of Court 6, but also in the residential areas of the site.

TABLE 2.1. *IIIB imports*

Site	Imports	Possible Imports[41]	Description of Imports
Mainland			
Mycenae	43	16	A variety of imports, including Egyptian faience objects, Canaanite jars, an Egyptian alabastron, a Syro-Palestinian smiting god statuette in bronze, a stone axe, and a diorite bowl, mainly from the acropolis and the West/Ivory houses (Some imports from the tombs, including Canaanite jars, might date to the IIIB period.)
Thebes	40	2	Cache of Mitannian cylinder seals and an ivory scepter head from Syria-Palestine (Possibly IIIB: Canaanite jar and glass Egyptian vase (LH III))
Tiryns	21	3	Canaanite jars, faience vessels, and some unusual Cypriot objects with seeming cult or commercial associations, concentrated in the lower citadel (Possibly IIIB: Cypriot bronze tripod, gold earring; hematite seal (LH III))
Menidi	4	–	Canaanite jars from the tholos tomb
Dendra	3	–	Egyptian alabastra and a set of beads from a garment in chamber tombs 2 and 6
Tsoungiza	3	–	Italian Pertosa dagger, shoulder of a Canaanite jar, and sherd from an Italian impasto vessel from the settlement
Pylos	2	–	Canaanite jar from tholos tomb 2; Porphyrite Egyptian bowl from the settlement
Monodendri	2	1	2 Mitannian faience seals (Italian ring (LH IIIA-C)) in a tomb
Spiliareika Lousikon	1	–	Syro-Palestinian unguent vase from a chamber tomb
Prosymna	1	2	Mitannian faience seal from tomb 38; Carnelian amulet and faience scarab from Egypt (LH III)
Pharos/Dexameni	1	–	Mitannian faience seal from tomb 5
Athens	1	–	Italian impasto jar from a well
Midea	1	–	A Syro-Palestinian leather-working knife
Dimini	–	2	Canaanite jars (LH IIIB-C)
Agios Ilias	–	1	Faience amulet from a tholos tomb (L
Asine	–	1	Egyptian stone amulet (LH II-III)
Chalkis	–	1	Egyptian alabaster alabastron (LH III)
Dendra	–	1	Egyptian/Cypriot silver spoon (LH IIIA or B)
Iyrisa	–	1	Faience Mitannian cylinder seal (LH IIIA-B)
Larisa (Argos)	–	1	Hematite seal (Syrian?) (LH III?)
	–	1	Canaanite jar (LH II-IIIB)

(continued)

[41] The number of imports dated to a range (i.e. LH III?, LH IIIA–B, etc.) that *might* include IIIB.

TABLE 2.1. *(continued)*

Site	Imports	Possible Imports	Description of Imports
Megali Magoula Velanidi			
Mega Monastiri	-	1	Faience S-P seal (LH IIIA1-B1)
Nafplio	-	1	Egyptian alabastron (LH III)
Nemea	-	1	Italian bronze dagger (LH III?)
Tanagra	-	2	Faience seal and bronze bowl (LH III)
Voudeni	-	1	Egyptian stone seal (LH IIIA-C)
Vrysarion	-	1	Faience seal (Egypt/Cyprus) (LH IIIA-B)
Stavros	-	1	Faience Mitannian seal (LH IIIA-B)
	(123)	(41)	
Crete			
Kommos	78	17	Ceramic imports (see extended description to follow)
Chania	5	2	Fragments of Cypriot open vessels (Faience scarab from Egypt (LM IIIA-B) and Italian bowl (LM IIIB-C))
Knossos	1	6	A series of imported objects (Cypriot and Egyptian vessels) from poorly dated settlement contexts that could be IIIB; Italian bronze dagger from tomb 6 at Zapher Papoura
Mochlos	1	-	Canaanite jar from the settlement
Armenoi	1	-	Faience Mitannian seal from grave 108.
Agia Pelagia	1	-	Fragment of an Italian vessel (unknown context)
Agia Triada	-	1	Bronze Syrian figurine (from Cyprus?) (LM IIIA-B)
Amnisos	-	1	Egyptian glass flask (LM III)
Kalyvia	-	2	Glass flask and krateriskos from Egypt (LM III)
Katsamba	-	1	Cypriot bowl (LM III)
Pseira	-	2	Canaanite jars (LM IIIA-B)
	(87)	(32)	
Total	210	73	

Elsewhere on Crete, a few imports have been identified from secure IIIB contexts and include, at Chania, a faience scarab in addition to the more unusual Cypriot and Italian open vessels, an Italian dagger at Knossos, a Canaanite jar sherd at Mochlos, and a Mitannian seal from Armenoi.[42]

The primary characteristics of imports from the IIIB period can be summarized as follows:

(1) Imports are spatially concentrated near palatial settlement sites on the mainland, are rare except at Kommos on Crete, and are sparsely distributed

[42] Descriptions of imports, their find contexts, and associated bibliography can be found in S. Murray 2013, 378–464.

elsewhere. While imports from cemetery contexts are not particularly common from the IIIB period, this may be an accident of preservation, since the precise dating of many artifacts from elaborate tombs at sites like Mycenae is not possible.[43]

(2) Imports originate from a relatively diverse set of locations overall (including, Cyprus, Italy, and Syria-Palestine), but from relatively homogenous origins within individual assemblages (that is, Egyptian finds at Mycenae, Cypriot finds at Tiryns, Syro-Palestinian finds at Thebes, Italian finds at Kommos).

(3) The assemblage is dominated by a small repertoire of import categories – above all Canaanite jars, but also Egyptian scarabs, plaques or amulets, Mitannian cylinder seals of faience, lapis lazuli, or another semiprecious stone, and Italian ceramic vessels – though a potpourri of additional object categories, including Italian blades and Syrian statuettes, fills out the corpus.

(4) Imported objects on the mainland, although located preferentially in palatial centers, do not come from contexts that suggest imported exotica were especially prized by palatial officials as "status symbols." Most are found in the context of workshops or areas that suggest ritual use.

Imports in Greece in the Final Mycenaean "Twilight" (LH/LM IIIC)[44]

According to our traditional narrative of historical economy, it would be reasonable to expect a significant decrease in the quantity of imported objects in Greece in the twelfth century, concomitant with the dissolution of the major political powers of the LBA and their inability to maintain long-distance trade links in a maritime world of deteriorating stability and security. While it is true that there are fewer total imported objects from the IIIC period, it is not immediately clear how their distribution or quantity relates directly to historical events, a point I will return to in greater detail in Chapter 6 of this book.

The majority of documented imported exotica dating to the LH IIIC period were excavated at the cemetery of Perati in east Attica. Imports are known from fourteen other LH IIIC sites scattered throughout the Peloponnese and Central Greece. These include Mycenae and Tiryns in the Argolid, Anthedon, Elateia, and Lefkandi in central Greece, Teichos Dymaion, Achaea Klauss, Aigio, Agia Varvara, and Portes in Achaea, Kanakia in the Saronic Gulf, Pisaskion near Pylos in Messenia, and Kouvaras Fyteion in Aetolo-Akarnania. On Crete, imports are concentrated at two sites (the cemeteries at Knossos and the Diktaean Cave

---

[43] Xenaki–Sakellariou 1985 on Tsountas's nineteenth century exacavations.
[44] I fold Submycenaean and Subminoan into the "postpalatial" phase. While there are a variety of compelling arguments for distinctness of Submycenaean and Subminoan from LH/LM IIIC (see Papadopoulos et al. 2011 for recent summary), I group them together with IIIC here because I am interested in assessing trade intensity during the time between the palatial collapse and the beginning of the Protogeometric period.

sanctuary) during LM IIIC, but imports have also been recorded at ten other LM IIIC sites spread evenly between central Crete (Knossos, Tylissos, the Idaean Cave, Patso Cave, and Phaistos) and eastern Crete (Dikte, Karfi, Vrokastro, Krya Siteias, and Kato Syme).[45] An interesting feature of this distribution is the fact that imports have been discovered at a far greater percentage of excavated sites from the LH IIIC period (around 18 percent) than of sites from the LH IIIB period (around 5 percent).[46]

On the mainland, the most striking characteristic of the import record for the LH IIIC period is the overwhelming concentration of imports at the cemetery of Perati in east Attica. The prehistoric cemetery of Perati is located at the foot of this hill, on the west bank of a dry gully.[47] Of the excavated tombs, 192 were chamber tombs, and the others were pit graves. Most tombs contained multiple burials (150) while others (sixty-one) were occupied by only a single skeleton. Eight of the tombs were found empty.[48] Eighteen cremations were present among a mortuary population that had primarily been inhumed.[49] The cemetery was in use throughout the LH IIIC period.[50] Imported objects were found in nineteen different tombs (8 percent of the nonlooted tombs). The tombs from which imports are documented are found only in the western portion of the cemetery (see Figure 2.3). While a few tombs (30, 13, 147)[51] contained several imported objects, in most cases exotica were found in ones and twos, in a couple of identifiable spatial clusters in the cemetery (see Table 2.2). The imported objects comprise an unusual, motley collection of objects that are not similar to the kinds of imports common in the IIIB period, including a number of Egyptian faience figurines of Bes and crocodiles, hematite weights, single Cypriot earrings, and one amulet inscribed in Luwian

---

[45] The concentration of IIIC imports in central and eastern Crete might be a product of the fact that we have few excavated sites from western Crete that date to this period. For example, only nine IIIC sites are known in the Chania region, compared to forty-eight in the IIIB period. On the other hand, the number of sites in the Rethymno region stays stable, from thirty-four IIIB sites to thirty-two in IIIC.

[46] These figures are calculated based on the site catalog I generated as part of this project, explained in Chapter 3, in S. Murray 2013, S. Murray 2015, and in S. Murray forthcoming b.

[47] Iakovidis 1980, 1. These tombs are numbered sX in the excavation reports. An import remained in one of the looted tombs, s19.

[48] Iakovidis 1980, 10.

[49] Iakovidis 1980, 10–11.

[50] Iakovidis 1980, 109–110.

[51] Tomb 30 was the most import-rich in the cemetery, containing twelve individual imported objects (Iakovidis 1969, 301–304). The imports are almost all small Egyptian faience figurines – three crocodile amulets, seven figurines of Bes, and a figurine of the goddess Toeris. The other import in the tomb was a small Syro-Palestinian domed hematite weight. Tombs 13 (Iakovidis 1969, 285–289) and 147 (Iakovidis 1969, 117–122) were the only other two tombs with more than a couple of imports. In tomb 13 five Egyptian scarabs were mixed among the rich finds. Tomb 147 contained an impressive array of gold and silver jewelry (rings, gold sheet and wire), hundreds of faience and glass beads, along with Syro-Palestinian amulets and an Egyptian scarab.

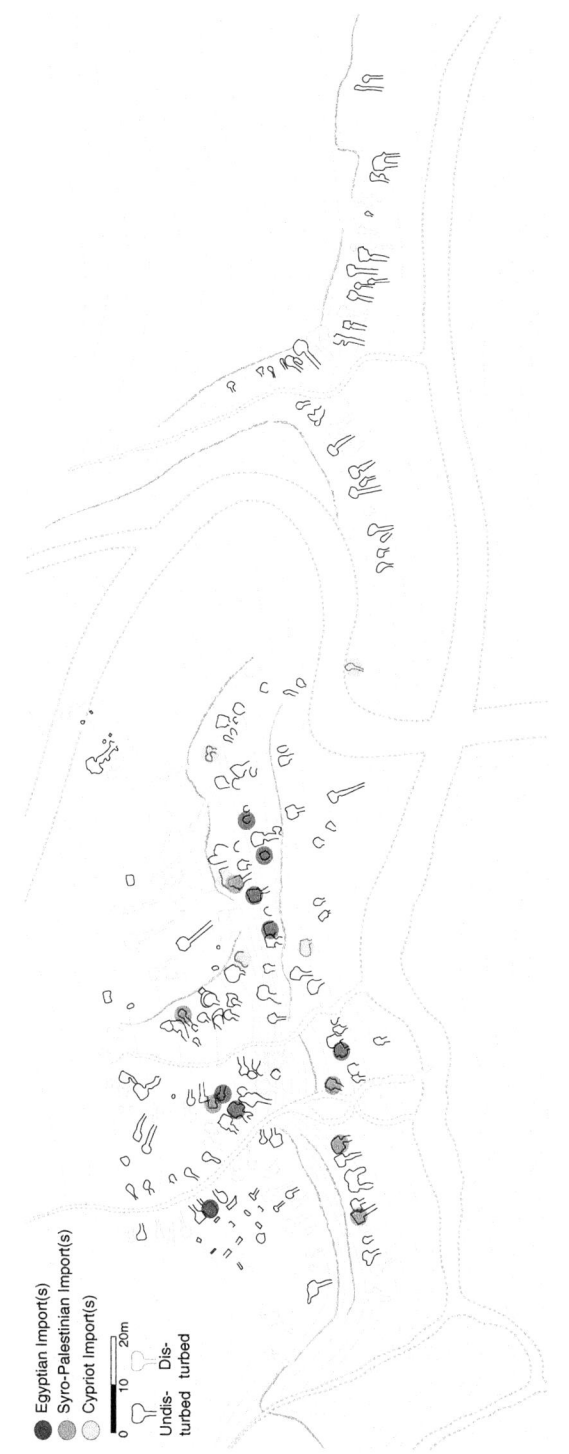

Figure 2.3. Import findspot distribution at LH IIIC Perati (modified after Iakovidis 1969, 12 σχεδ.1)

TABLE 2.2. *Single-import tombs from Perati*

Tomb #	Import	Other Finds	Phase	Burials	Objects/ Burial
1	Egyptian cartouche of Ramses II, pierced	23 vessels, steatite beads and buttons, gold and jewelry	I-II	8	7.4
9	Cypriot gold earring	10 vessels, 1 glass bead	I-II	3	4.7
11	Cypriot gold earring	7 vessels, some miniature, a gold ring, gold wire, bit of ivory, five gold beads	I-II	2	6.5
12	Syro-Palestinian bronze knife	41 vessels, 14 semi-precious stone beads or buttons, a bronze sword, glass beads, gold beads and wire, silver rings, lead wire	I-III	disturbed	unk
S19	Cypriot gold earring, stylized bull's head	Psi figurine, two steatite beads, faience beads	robbed	robbed	unk
34	fragment of an Egyptian faience vessel	13 vessels, steatite buttons	II	1	3.5
49	Syro-Palestinian gold amulet	stone bead	?	1	2
90	Scarab inscribed "Ptah lord of Truth"	8 vessels, bone needles, bronze needle, steatite buttons	I	2	4
100	Syro-Palestinian hematite weight	three vessels, rock crystal beads, seashells	I	3	2
142	Cypriot hematite seal	10 vessels, agate seal, steatite buttons, faience beads, ivory fragments, silver ring, strange clay beads	II	5	7.8

script (see Figure 2.4). Although some of the tombs containing imports contain many finds overall, there is no clear correlation between the sheer number of objects in a tomb and import presence, at least by the very rough sense of this provided by such a blunt metric (see Figure 2.5).[52]

[52] In the current context it is not possible to expand an analysis of wealth and exotica in the complex burial assemblages at Perati, where chamber tombs were reused so often that it is difficult to associate individual finds with excavated skeletons. I use instead a very obtuse measure of wealth, in the hope that this provides some general sense of whether tombs with

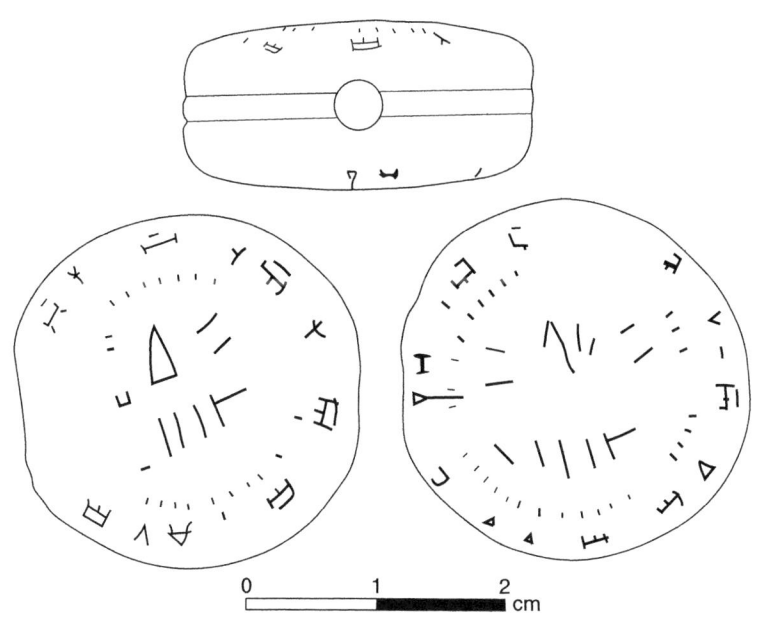

Figure 2.4. An inscribed amulet in the shape of a Hittite *bulla* from tomb 24 at Perati (simplified drawing of bulla from Tomb 24 (after Iakovidis 1970a, 317 εικ. 134))

The only other mainland site with a significant concentration of imported finds from the IIIC period is Tiryns.[53] Of special interest among these is a Syro-Palestinian armor scale that was deposited underneath a hearth in the courtyard of a building in the northeastern section of the lower town.[54] The hearth consisted of a smooth clay surface, below which a pavement made of sherds

---

more objects also are more likely to contain imports (for more sophisticated approaches to the assessment of wealth in burials, see, for example Voutsaki 1995; 1998; 2001). For a fuller analysis of the Perati tombs and their exotica, with bibliography and history of scholarship, see Murray forthcoming a. Further discussion of Perati can also be found in Chapter 6 of the current book. The secondary bibliography is not extensive. Self-standing secondary studies is essentially as follows: Iakovidis 1954, 1966, 1967, 1987 (a summary of Iakovidis 1980 in German rather than an independent analysis), 2003; Paidoussis and Sbarounis 1975; Tomlinson 1995; Cavanagh and Mee 2009; and shorter considerations within Thomatos 2006, Cavanagh and Mee 1998, and Hölbl 1987.

[53] Four fragments of Canaanite jars are included in the import count for IIIC Tiryns. Two of these fragments were found in building IX in the lower town, and the other two near buildings III and VI in the lower citadel. Another IIIC sherd from an unidentified Syro-Palestinian vessel comes from one of the western casemates. Given the position of the Canaanite Jar fragments in relation to similar artifacts from the LH IIIB period, it is possible that at least one of these fragments may be an earlier kick up. However, the two sherds from the lower town probably come from the IIIC period. Maran notes elsewhere (2005, 420) that "[i]n contrast to the Lower Citadel, the LH IIIB and IIIC levels in this area do not immediately follow on top of each other, but are separated by thick stream deposits" (see also Stockhammer 2008, 157; Stockhammer 2012).

[54] Maran 2004, 18.

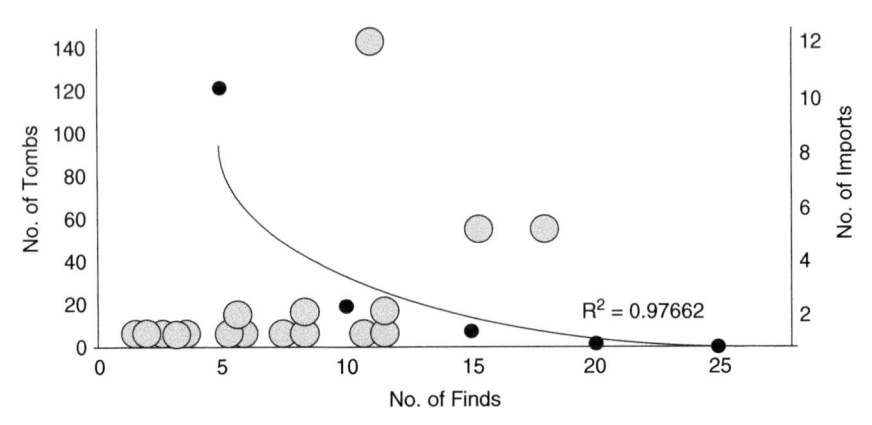

Figure 2.5. Distribution of finds and imports in [undisturbed] chamber tombs at Perati (by author).

covered the carefully placed bronze armor scale. The armor scale, and its deposition in a clearly ritual context that has its closest parallels among Cypriot metalworkers at Hala Sultan Tekke, has suggested to many that Cypriot merchants were still resident within the lower citadel at Tiryns in the LH IIIC period.[55] This conclusion is further reinforced by Stockhammer's reevaluation of the ceramic evidence from the lower citadel. He has identified a number of Cypriot simple style stirrup jars and further fragments of imported wares in the immediate vicinity, as well as an assemblage of pottery that ought to be associated with opium-smoking rituals typical of Cypriot practice.[56] Moreover, in the same phase from Tiryns was discovered a small clay ball inscribed with Cypro-Minoan markings, another object that finds its closest parallels in contexts associated with merchants and trade in Cyprus.[57] Finally, Maran argues that the so-called Tiryns treasure, a hoard of metal goods that has generally been interpreted as belonging to palatial times and which contains a number of Cypriot (tripod stand, iron knife) and Cretan (rings), belongs to the LH IIIC period, and that we should reconstruct robust links between Tiryns, Crete, and Cyprus during post-palatial times.[58]

---

[55] Bibliography cited in Vetters 2011, 13, n.115–117; 30.

[56] Stockhammer 2008, 156, cat. 1182 (Cypriot or Near Eastern lamp); Stockhammer 2008, 90–91 for simple style Cypriot imports. For a combination of a small cylinder of clay and an amphoriskos as an assemblage for opium smoking in Cyprus and Ugarit, see Stockhammer 2008, 172–173.

[57] Full publication and analysis in Vetters 2011. This is the only site on the mainland where significant numbers of Cretan coarseware transport vessels continue to be found during the IIIC period (Maran 2005).

[58] Maran 2005, 426–427; Maran 2006.

On Crete, most LH IIIC imports come either from Knossos or from the Diktaean Cave (Italian daggers and knives) in the Lasithi plain, though assigning dates for the material from the latter deposits is difficult.[59] At Knossos, fourteen imported items are known from LM IIIC deposits.[60] One imported Italian knife was found in excavations west of the stratigraphic museum in a layer associated with an apsidal building.[61] Two items, a necklace of faience beads and an ivory pin, were discovered in Tomb V in the Agios Ioannis cemetery.[62] The other eleven imported objects were all in the complex containing Tombs 200–202 in the North Cemetery, dated to the end of LM IIIC/SM.[63] It should be kept in mind that counts of imported objects from tombs in Crete throughout the IIIC–Geometric period are difficult to assess on a diachronic basis, because of mortuary practices characterized by burial in collective tombs that remained in use over long periods of time.[64]

To summarize, there are fewer imports known from the IIIC period than from the preceding IIIB period. The character of the imports changes both spatially and in apparent use and meaning. At Tiryns, the inhabitants of the lower citadel appear to have maintained some long-distance contacts, or else kept company with individuals from beyond the Mycenaean cultural sphere. An apparently new and well-connected community at Porto Rafti in Attica buried their dead in tombs at Perati with offerings from Cyprus, Egypt, and Syria-Palestine. Finally, a significant number of warrior burials in Achaea contain imported weapons from Italy and Cypriot artifacts. On Crete, later IIIC burials from Knossos contained Italian and Cypriot imports.[65]

The primary characteristics of IIIC imports can be summarized as follows:

(1) The distribution of imports on the mainland is dispersed to an unusually large number of sites overall, compared with the IIIB, PG, and Geometric periods. On Crete, most imports come from central inland or eastern sites.

---

[59] Dating for objects from the cave is almost exclusively by style or typology.
[60] Hallager 1985, 303.
[61] Hallager 1985, 295; Cline 1994, no. 839.
[62] Jones 2000, cat. no. 1.4.17.
[63] Tombs 200 and 201 contained many offerings, including "an SM decorated stirrup jar, a bronze pin head of Italian type, an ivory comb, beads of glass, frit, and faience, a necklace of eighty spherical beads of solid gold and two rosettes of gold leaf" (Catling 1979, 46). The imports in tomb 200 included the pin head (Italy), the ivory comb (North Syria), the necklace of glass, frit, and faience (Egypt), the gold beads (Cyprus), the gold rosettes (Cyprus), and a set of imported gold finger rings (Cyprus). Tomb 201 was a warrior grave, containing a bronze spearhead, five large bronze arrowheads, a type II sword, an openwork tripod of Cypriot manufacture, a group of four other imports comprising two elaborate ivory sword hilts (Levant?), an ivory poppy head pin (North Syria), and a necklace of faience beads (Egypt). (Coldstream and Catling 1996, 194–195).
[64] Whitley 1986, 275–276; comments in Kotsonas 2006, 150, n. 3.
[65] See also Cultraro 2005, for indications that IIIC imports from Italy might also exist in the assemblages at Palaikastro, Tegea, and Gourtsouli in Arcadia.

TABLE 2.3. *IIIC imports*[66]

Site	Imports	Possible Imports[67]	Description of Imports
Mainland			
Perati	45	–	Near Eastern imports consisting largely of amulets and scarabs, as well as some hematite weights and jewelry, from Egypt, Cyprus, and Syria-Palestine.
Tiryns	10	4	Canaanite jars, Cypriot pottery, bronze scale (haematite weight, gold earring and bronze tripod from Cyprus (LH IIIA-C); Syrian bronze statuette (LH IIIC?))
Teichos Dymaion	5	–	Two Cypriot iron knives, an Italian bronze fibula, a Pescheira dagger, and an Italian bronze openwork wheel
Mycenae	4	9	A haematite sphendenoid weight, a Syro-Palestinian armor scale, fragments of a Canaanite jar and an Egyptian alabastron (also various imported objects with no good context, dated somewhere in LH III, but these may likely belong earlier rather than later)
Lefkandi	3	–	A bronze Italian knife and two fragments of Italian vessels
Kanakia	3	–	Two Cypriot spindle whorls and a Syro-Palestinian armor scale
Aigio	3	–	Three bronze spearheads of a type not known in the Aegean – Cypriot or Italian?[68]
Portes	2	–	Two sherds from different Cypriot vessels
Elateia	1	–	Italian pin and sword from a cemetery
Anthedon	1	–	Cypriot tripod stands from the hoard
Achaia Klauss	1	–	Italian bronze knives
Agia Varvara	1	–	Mitannian cylinder seal of faience in a chamber tomb
Pylos	1	–	Cypriot bowl from tomb near former palace
Kouvaras Fyteion	1	–	Naue II sword from Italy in a IIIC tomb
Salamis	1	–	Faience bead from cist grave (Desborough 1971, 67)
Voudeni	–	1	Egyptian seal (LH IIIA-C)
Thebes	–	1	Canaanite jar and Egyptian glass vase (LH III)
Tanagra	–	1	Bronze bowl (LH III)
Prosymna	–	2	Carnelian amulet and faience scarab from Egypt (LH III?)
Dimini	–	2	Canaanite jars (LH IIIB-C)
Nemea	–	1	Italian bronze dagger (LH III)
Nafplio	–	1	Egyptian alabaster alabastron (LH III)
Monodendri	–	1	Italian bronze ring (LH IIIA-C)
Larisa (Argos)	–	1	Haematite seal from Syria-Palestine (LH III?)

(continued)

---

[66] See also Cultraro 2005, for some indication that IIIC imports from Italy might also exist from Palaikastro, Tegea, and Gourtsouli in Arcadia.

[67] Indicates number of imports dated to a range that might include IIIC.

[68] See discussion in Lambrou-Philipson 1990, 326; Cline 1994, 251.

TABLE 2.3. *(continued)*

Site	Imports	Possible Imports	Description of Imports
Agios Ilias	–	1	Faience Egyptian amulet (LH II-IIIC)
Asine	–	1	Egyptian stone amulet (LH III?)
Chalkis	–	1	Egyptian alabaster bowl (LH III)
	(82)	(27)	
Crete			
Knossos	15	5	Near Eastern finds from Egypt, Cyprus, and Syria-Palestine from the cemeteries, including jewelry and weapons (also a series of imported objects (Cypriot and Egyptian vessels) from uncertainly dated settlement contexts that could be IIIC).
Dikte	9	3	Italian daggers and knives (two Egyptian bronze statues, one Carnelian bead (LM IIIC-G))
Karfi	3	1	Near Eastern faience beads and an Italian fibula (a pendant from Cyprus (LM IIIC-PG))
Vrokastro	1	16	Cypriot iron knife from chamber tomb 5
Tylissos	1	–	Italian razor (context unknown)
Phaistos	1	–	Cypriot fibula from a burial at the foot of the hill
Patso Cave	1	–	Syro-Palestinian reshef figurine
Krya Siteias	1	–	Gold Cypriot earring from the cemetery[69]
Kato Syme Viannou	1	–	A Cypriot bronze tripod in the burnt layer above the IIIB sanctuary
Idaean Cave	1	1	Inlaid ivory box (Cypriot bronze bowl (LM IIIC-G))
Amnisos	–	1	Egyptian glass flask (LM III)
Katsamba	–	1	Cypriot bowl (LM III)
Kalyvia	–	1	Egyptian glass vessels (LM III)
	(34)	(29)	
Total	116	56	

(2) Imports come from both settlements and cemeteries. As in the IIIB period, the contexts are ambiguous in their attestation of a tight link between elites and imported exotica.

(3) With the exception of finds from Perati, Cypriot and Italian imports dominate the record for the IIIC period, both on Crete and on the mainland. Due to the variety of imports found from the IIIC period, it is difficult to

[69] Kanta 2005, 701–706.

generalize about their characteristics. An increase in the variety of import categories contrasts with relative homogeneity in both the preceding IIIB and following PG import records.

Imports in Greece in the Protogeometric Period

The existing literature on trade in the Iron Age repeatedly asserts that there was probably more imported material in Greece before the end of the palatial period than there was in the postpalatial or Protogeometric periods.[70] But until now this decrease has neither been proven empirically nor explored in much detail.[71] What evidence do we have to prove that there was a decrease in long-distance maritime connectedness in Greece during the PG period? The first, and most obvious piece of evidence is that there are fewer known imports dating to this period. During the Protogeometric period, documented imports are fewer in number than they were during the palatial Mycenaean period. The number is comparable to the number known from the IIIC period.

As was the case in the IIIC period on the mainland, most imports in Greece dating to the Protogeometric period come from a single cemetery site in central Greece, in this case Lefkandi on Euboea. On Crete, most imports come from Knossos and Kommos.[72] The context of the imports at all of these sites, with

---

[70] For example Coldstream 2003a, 342; Desborough 1972, 80–81; Dickinson 2006, 206–7; Lemos 2002, 216; I. Morris 2000, 216–217; Snodgrass 1971, 296–297; Crielaard 1998, 187; Wallace 2010, 171–172.

[71] For example Dickinson 2006, 205; Crielaard 1998; The best effort is Parkinson 2010, but this is mostly geared toward the LBA.

[72] Calculating a number to attach to the imported ceramics deposited in the PG period at Kommos presents problems of quantification. In his catalog of imports to Crete, Jones counted the 366 Phoenician sherds from Temple A/B as one "bucket" rather than attempting to determine how many individual pieces of pottery these artifacts may have originally represented (Jones 2000, 245 (C.1.5.1): all tenth/ninth century amphora fragments from Kommos counted as a single catalog entry). Jones also dated this material broadly (Jones 2000, 245 (C.1.5.1): Phoenician sherds dated to tenth/ninth or late ninth/eighth century) in a way that would make it necessary for me to place all of these imports into my ambiguously dated category rather than into the PG category. While many of the sherds come from dumps or floors that could date to the later, post-PG phases of the temple, some should be dated to the Cretan LPG. I counted all the deposits from the Temple A floors and half of the deposits from the Temple B floors as PG imports, since Temple A is dated firmly to the Cretan PG and Temple B straddles the end of the Cretan PG and the beginning of the Cretan G periods (Bikai 2000, 302–312) Instead of counting each sherd as an individual import (Bikai (2000, 302) thinks that the sherds did not belong to a large number of vessels), I counted one import for each fabric group and each type of vessel in each distinct deposit. For example, Temple A deposit 34A2/45 contained three storage jar sherds, all from the same fabric group, and so this deposit received one entry. However, deposit 47A/39 in Temple A contained twenty-five sherds. Nineteen of these were storage jar sherds of fabric group A, while the other two were both of the same non-A fabric group. The deposit also included four nonstorage jar sherds of a single fabric. For this deposit I made three entries, one for the fabric group A sherds, one for the two other SJ sherds, and one for the nonstorage jar sherds. While this

the exceptions of a couple of finds at Knossos and the finds at Kommos and Tylissos, is mortuary. On Crete, imports in the PG are mostly limited to central Crete, as they were in the LM IIIC period, but the distribution is more concentrated at Knossos and Kommos, rather than spreading out to a combination of sites and sanctuaries.

With the exception of four artifacts from the Palia Perivolia cemetery and one from the Skoubris cemetery, PG imports from Lefkandi come from Toumba, the wealthiest overall cemetery at the site.[73] Three imports come from the burials within the floor of the Toumba building. A total of fourteen of the forty-one MPG/LPG and LPG/SPG burials (33 percent) in the Toumba cemetery also contain imports, primarily dating to the LPG (the total excludes SPG imports, since these are equivalent to EG imports in the rest of mainland Greece). The monumental MPG building (*heroon*) at Toumba was probably built as part of an elaborate funeral rite for an important individual from the community.[74] Underneath the floor of the building were two shaft burials containing the remains of a man (cremated), a woman (inhumed), and, in the second shaft, four horses. The man's ashes were contained in a Cypriot bronze amphora manufactured at least one hundred years before the burial occurred. The amphora was sealed with a bronze bowl, and an iron sword, sharpening stone, spearhead, and razor were found with the burial. In the same shaft were the woman's bones, accompanied by wealthy jewelry including an electrum ring, bronze pins, iron pins, and gold pectoral and chest plates, including an elaborately granulated gold pendant that is likely to have been imported. Around the woman's neck was a gold pendant from the Old Babylonian period, dated to about 1700 BCE.[75]

In the Toumba cemetery that came into use following the burial and destruction of the *heroon*, imports were discovered in several graves. Tombs with multiple imports include T.39[76] (LPG), T.70[77] (LPG), T.59[78]

---

is not a perfect system, my hope is that it is a serviceable compromise between including all 300+ sherds as individual entries and ignoring them all, either of which approach would clearly distort the evidence in significant ways. I took a similar approach to calculating an approximate number of G imports to Kommos (Table 2.6).

[73] Lemos 2002, 165.
[74] I. Morris 2000, 195–256.
[75] Popham et al. 1982a, 172; Lemos 2002, 165.
[76] Among the ceramic finds in the tomb were a terracotta wheeled cart and a few miniature vessels. Metal finds included gold (diadem, attachments from a garment, a gold band, and gold cylindrical beads), iron (trunnion axe, spear butt, dagger, arched fibula), and bronze (fibula, set of bronze wheels, imported bronze jug). Faience and glass objects included a ram-headed figurine attached to a ring, a necklace, and an imported glass seal.
[77] A single woman's burial (Popham 1995, 103) containing nine gold rings, six fibulae, two iron pins with rock crystal globes, an amphora, a PSC skyphos, and a pyxis, bronze containers, including two bowls, a situla, and a squat lotus-handled jug, faience beads of two types, and fragments of one faience ring.
[78] Popham et al. 1989, 119. T.59 contained a pomegranate vase and a faience bowl as well as two faience bead necklaces, a faience scarab detached from its bezel, and a faience ring similar to the one in T.39.

TABLE 2.4. *Imports in PG tombs at Lefkandi (tombs with only one import)*

Tomb #	Imports	Other Finds	Phase	Total Objects	Adult/Child?
T.12a[79]	Faience disk beads	Two soft-fired jugs, a bronze fibula	LPG	4	Adult
T.44[80]	Faience beads	Seven miniature vessels, two bronze fibulae, one bronze bracelet	LPG	11	Child
T.62a[81]	Elongated pendant	Jug, high-footed skyphos, kalathos, bronze fibula	LPG	5	Adult
T.63[82]	Faience necklace	Sixteen vessels (kalathoi, jugs, etc.) gold rings, necklace and attachments, steatite beads, bronze fibulae	LPG	30	Adult
T.15[83]	Faience bead	Eight vessels, four gold rings, bronze pin, three iron pins	LPG/SPG	17	Adult
T.41[84]	Faience beads	Twelve vessels, including miniatures, gold attachments, iron knife	LPG/SPG	15	Adult
T.55[85]	Bronze bowl	Fifteen cups, four fibulae, gold sheet with oriental design, seven gold rings, gold pin with rock crystal bead	LPG/SPG	29	Adult

(LPG/SPG), T.42[86] (LPG), T.46[87] (LPG), T.1[88] (LPG), and T.40 (LPG).[89] A number of other tombs contained only one import each, as outlined in Table 2.4.

Most of the imports at Lefkandi come from LPG or LPG/SPG contexts instead of EPG or MPG contexts. This is not entirely surprising, considering that the majority of PG tombs excavated at the site date to the LPG or LPG/

---

[79] Popham, Sackett, and Themelis 1980, 173–174.
[80] Popham, Touloupa, and Sackett 1982b, 226.
[81] Popham and Lemos 1996, pl. 67.
[82] Popham and Lemos 1996, pl. 68–69.
[83] Popham, Sackett, and Themelis 1980, 176–177.
[84] Popham, Touloupa, and Sackett 1982b, 223–224.
[85] Popham and Lemos 1996, pl. 62–63.
[86] Popham, Touloupa, and Sackett 1982b, 223–224. Tomb 42, just to the north of T.39, contained 4 imports and "a rich and varied group" of other finds.
[87] A single inhumation. Grave goods included two gold earrings, a bronze fibula and bracelet, an iron pin, two faience necklaces and a faience head seal, depicting a male figure wearing a conical helmet.
[88] A necklace of faience beads and two glass beads, along with a centaur head, a trefoil oinochoe, a bowl, a dipper, a lekythos, two gold earrings, two bronze bracelets, and two bronze fibulae.
[89] Popham, Touloupa and Sackett 1982b, 221–222.

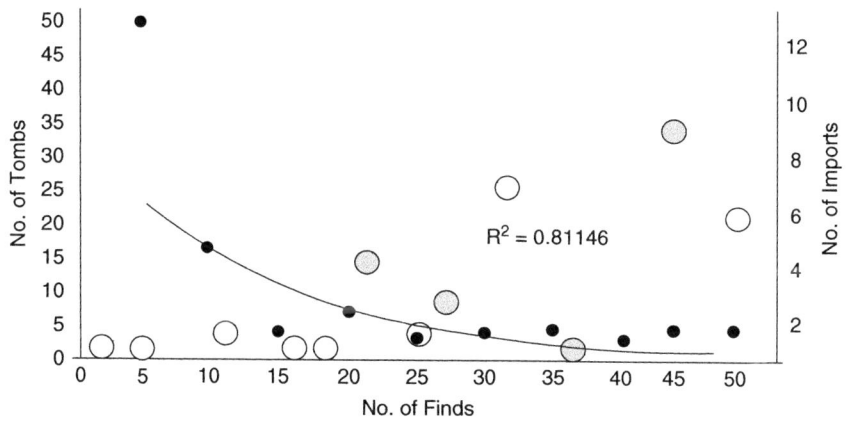

DIRECT EVIDENCE FOR LONG-DISTANCE EXCHANGE   97

Figure 2.6. Distribution of wealth in PG burials at Lefkandi Toumba (by author)

- ● = # of tombs with x finds per burial
- ○ = tomb with imported beads located along X axis according to total finds/burial, and along Y axis according to # imports
- ◉ = tomb with non-bead imports located along X axis according to total finds/burial, and along Y axis according to # imports

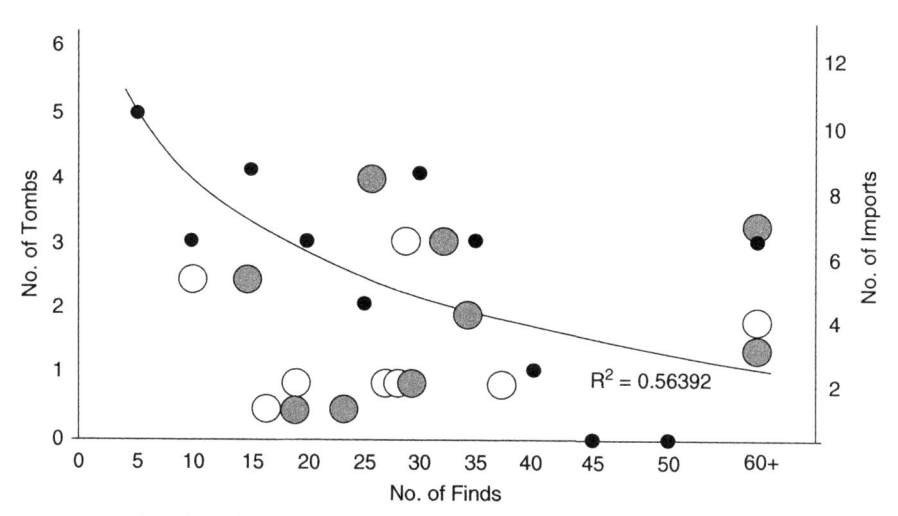

Figure 2.7. Distribution of wealth in SPG (G) burials at Lefkandi Toumba (by author)

- ● = # of tombs with x finds per burial
- ○ = tomb with imported beads located along X axis according to total finds and along Y axis accorging to # imports
- ◉ = tomb with non-bead imports located along X axis according to total find and along Y axis accorging to # imports

SPG period (47/72; 65 percent). But the percentage of imports dated to the LPG/SPG should probably not simply be taken as a reflection of the overall chronological distribution of the tombs, since only seven total imports (15 percent of the total) come from the EPG/MPG period. Aside from one

98 COLLAPSE OF THE MYCENAEAN ECONOMY

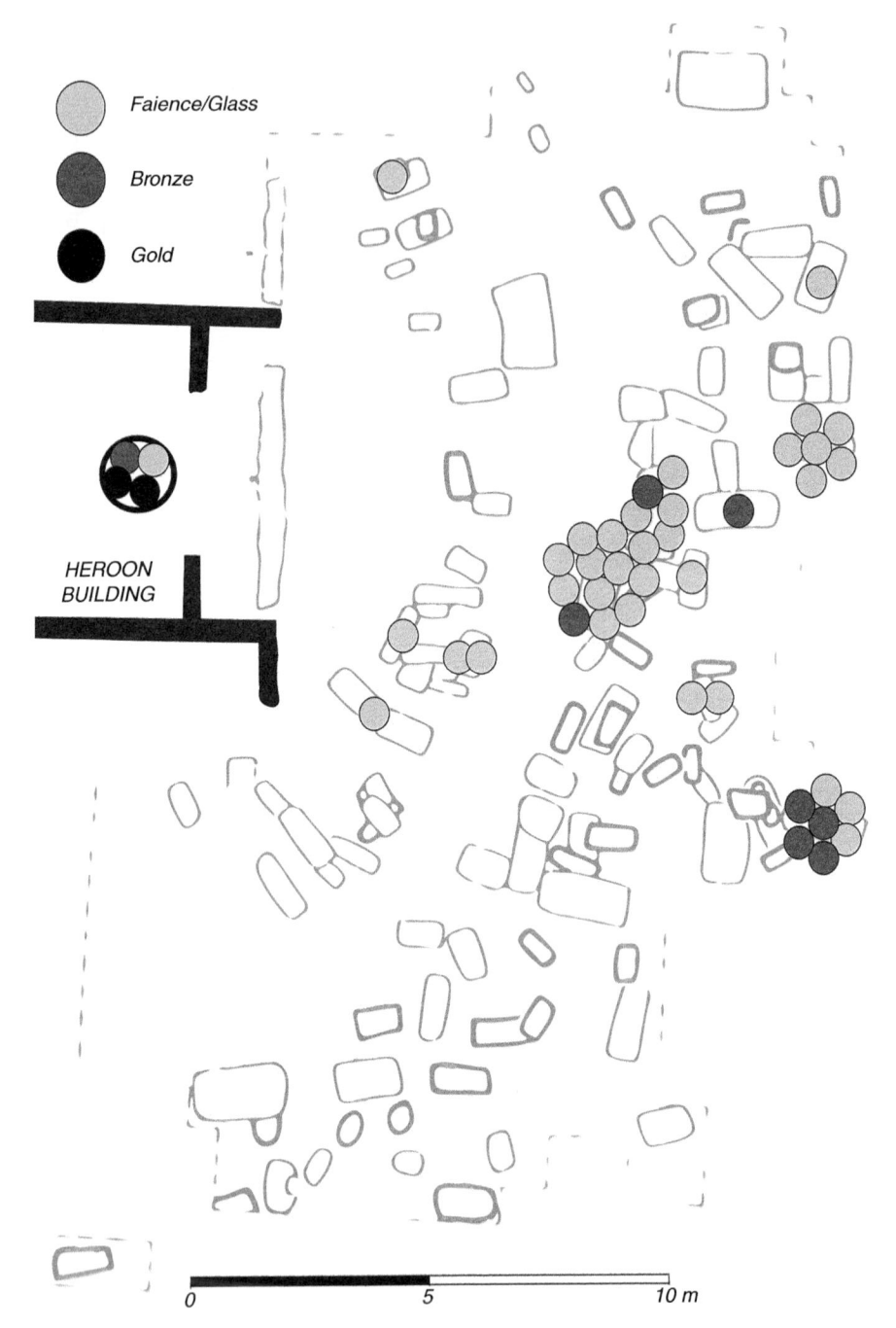

Figure 2.8. Location and distribution of imports in PG Lefkandi Toumba burials (modified by author, after Popham and Lemos 1996, plate 3)

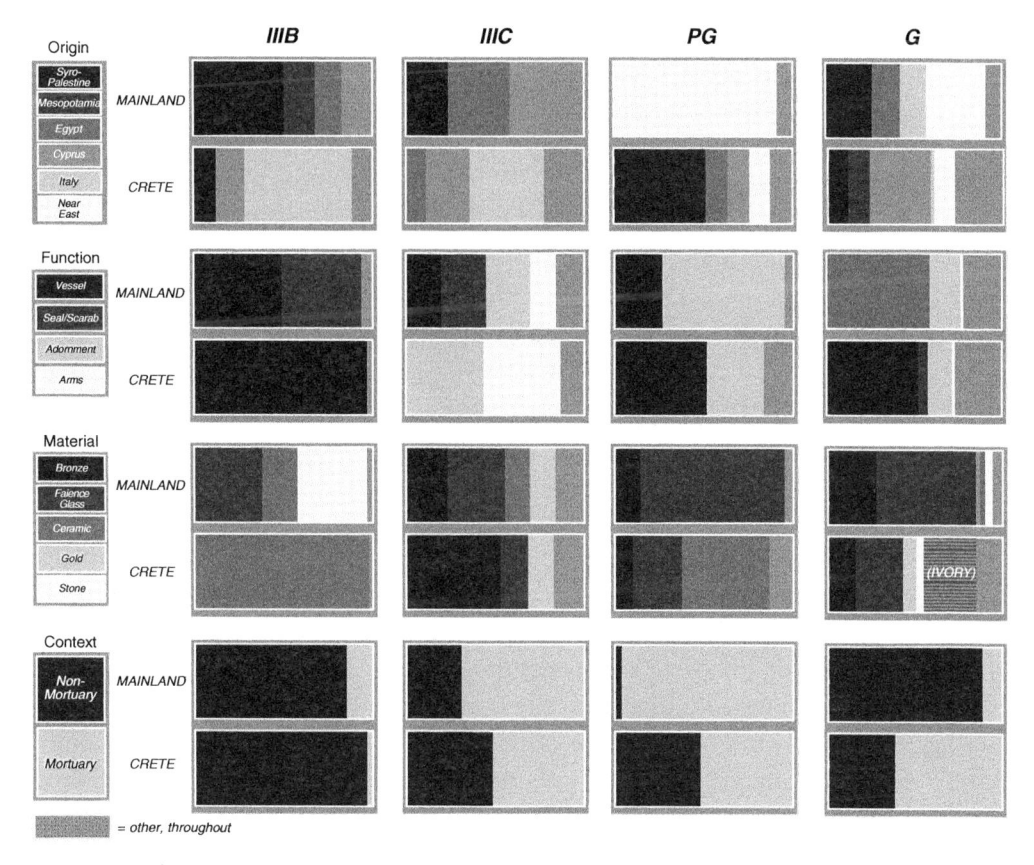

Figure 2.9. Change in qualitative characteristics of imports, IIIB-G (by author)

EPG juglet, the only materials represented are metal (mostly bronze) and faience/glass. Many imports are associated with grave goods that otherwise suggest the burial of women or children.[90]

The correlation of import access to overall quantity of goods contained within each burial at PG Lefkandi Toumba is greater than it was at Perati (see Figures 2.5 and 2.6; counted, again, in the very rough terms of number of objects per individual). This is especially true for imported objects other than faience beads. There are other reasons to believe that exotica and status were correlated at Lefkandi. Besides the obvious connection between exotic goods and high status that is evident in the Toumba Heroon of the MPG, the four wealthiest tombs in the Toumba cemetery in terms of overall finds also have

---

[90] See Arrington 2016 for an argument that Lefkandi's exotica can primarily be explained as talismanic trinkets deposited in accordance with a general system of mortuary ritual, rather than special objects accessible only to a small fraction of society; for talismanic practice on PG and Geometric Crete, M. Shaw 2000, 168–170. For association of wealth with Lefkandi imports, Crielaard 2006, 286–289.

high import counts (T.39, 55, 63, and 59).[91] In addition, the imported objects from the PG phase in the cemetery are noticeably clustered in burials that are directly in front of the door of the heroon, perhaps suggesting a close affiliation with the important figure buried within (Figure 2.7).[92]

Outside of Lefkandi's cemeteries, the distribution of imports on the mainland in the PG period includes more sites in the north and east than was true in the preceding periods. A few imports are known from the Argolid – four from Argos, three from Tiryns, and one from Asine – but the rest come from Central Greece and Thessaly. Roughly half of the imported objects from PG contexts on the mainland consist of beads made of faience,[93] but Phoenician and Cypriot bronze vessels are also represented.

On Crete, the collection of PG imports is more diverse. Faience beads and bronze vessels appear, but so do Phoenician jars, iron spits from Cyprus, and Egyptian seals and scarabs. This evidence is difficult to handle with precision because much debate remains about whether many orientalizing metal artifacts are the product of local workshops or truly imports.[94] Geographically, finds are concentrated at Knossos and Kommos. At Knossos imports are known from a number of tombs, primarily in the Fortetsa and North Cemeteries. The Fortetsa tombs are located to the northwest of the Palace of Minos.[95] They are of a normal Minoan type, with a rock-cut chamber entered via a dromos. Pithoi normally contained the cremated remains of the dead, which were surrounded by grave goods, often placed on a small built stone platform.[96] The tombs contained multiple burials, and were in use from the PG to the Orientalizing period,[97] but those reentering the chamber usually respected earlier burials. At Fortetsa, fifteen imports were found in five different tombs.[98]

---

[91] Imports were recovered from 33 percent of PG Toumba tombs, but only 8 percent of unlooted tombs at Perati contained imports.

[92] In general it seems likely that the population buried at Toumba (as opposed to Skoubris and Palia Perivolia) always represented a limited segment of the community (Crielaard 2006, 289).

[93] See Chapter 3, for discussion of beads as imports.

[94] Hoffman 1997; Stampolidis 1998; Matthäus 1998, 129; Kotsonas 2006; Kopanias 2009.

[95] Brock 1957, xi.

[96] Brock 1957, 2.

[97] Though new tomb construction stopped after the end of PG (Brock 1957, 4).

[98] Brock 1957, 18. Tomb XI was early (EPG) and contained the largest collection of imports (seven) of any tomb from the cemetery. In the tomb were four burial vessels and forty-one other vases. These included a Cypriot tripod stand, Cypriot iron spits, an imported ivory pin, a faience necklace, a lead Hittite lion, five spherical imported carnelian beads, and an ivory pendant in the shape of a bull's head (Jones 2000, 86). Tomb VI contained three imports, a faience ring, two faience necklaces, and some gold jewelry (Brock 1957, 11). Tomb II is one of the richest; associated with one of the LPG burials (pithos x) was a faience necklace and a glass bead (Brock 1957, 97, 208, no. 1113; Skon-Jedele 1994, 1827, 1870, no. 2928). In Tomb IX was a fragment of a faience figurine (Brock 1957, 30). Tomb P, dated mostly to the LG and Early Orientalizing periods, contained only one PG import – a bronze pendant from Luristan found with an LPG krater (Brock 1957, 30; Hoffman 1997, 29). Finally, one import comes from Tomb L (Louka's Tomb), where excavators uncovered a burial from the LPG period

In the Knossos North Cemetery about three hundred tombs were found, demonstrating continuous use from SM to Early Christian times.[99] Five tombs contained a total of ten imports that could be dated to the end of the Cretan PG period.[100] There are six other PG imports from Knossos, all from burial groups scattered around the area.[101] Of these a Cypriot bowl inscribed with a Phoenician indication of ownership, perhaps from late in the tenth century, is particularly eloquent in attesting to the existence of close relationships between Cypriots, Phoenicians, and Cretans by the end of this period.[102] Imported objects were probably being deposited in sacred caves on Mts. Dikte and Ida in the PG[103] and at the harbor of Kommos imported ceramic jars begin to appear again after an apparent hiatus in the IIIC period.[104]

Overall, we can observe the following characteristics of imports known from Greece dating to the PG period:

1. Contexts are geographically concentrated along the Euboean gulf and in Thessaly, or in the Argolid on the mainland. On Crete, most imports come from Knossos or Kommos. Most imports are presumed to be Phoenician products, although in many cases we cannot say more than that they come from the "Near East"; imports from the west are not well-represented.

---

that had been furnished with a Cypriot style gold diadem as well as a couple of Cypriot-influenced pots (a flask and a duck askos).

[99] Coldstream and Catling 1996, 55. It was apparent to the excavators that much of the PG cemetery had been destroyed by later burials, but many important PG remains came to light notwithstanding this later disturbance. At the same time, many imports from these tombs were not included in my catalog, because the great level of disturbance usually made it nearly impossible to date an imported object to a particular period with precision.

[100] Knossos North Cemetery/Medical Facility (KNC/MF) 285 (four different sets of faience beads contained in four different vases (Coldstream and Catling 1996, 239–243, vases 89 (an LPG East Greek krater), 136 (a duck askos), 61 (a coarse-necked burial pithos), 121 (Attic kantharos)); one was a burial urn (61) also containing mature bones, bronze pins, and gold leaf attachments and covered over with a bronze cauldron and several pieces of iron spits and firedogs (Coldstream and Catling 1996, 241)); KNC/MF 100 (three more sets of faience beads; Coldstream and Catling 1996, 132–138); KNC/MF 219 (a faience bead which had been tucked inside an EPG skyphos (Coldstream and Catling 1996, 214, no. 21); KNC/MF 107 and 292 (Phoenician jugs).

[101] Teke tomb 2, ivory handle, probably Phoenician (Boardman 1967, 63–64); Hogarth's Tomb 6, a lapis lazuli bead and a faience bead (Coldstream 2002, 212–215); Hogarth's Tomb 3, imported Cypriot tripod stand (Coldstream 2002, 206–209); tomb on the Kephala ridge, Egyptian scarab (Coldstream 1963, 43). A final two PG Knossian imports are a Cypriot jug (Coldstream, Callaghan, and Musgrave 1981, 153–154) and an eastern Mediterranean iron knife dating to the tenth century, from a tomb on lower Gypsadhes hill (Hood, Huxley, and Sandars 1958–1959, 225).

[102] Hoffman 1997, 12–13, 120–123; Catling 1996, 563–564; Stampolidis and Kotsonas 2006, 347, fig. 17.4 for an illustration.

[103] For Ida, Sakellarakis 2013. On Dikte, Rutkowski and Nowicki 1996; Ksifaras 2004 (206–208) summarizes the evidence. On a variety of sites including these caves, Matthäus 1998.

[104] Bikai 2000, 303. For hiatus in the IIIC period, see Shaw 1998, 17–18.

TABLE 2.5. *Imported objects in Greece from the PG period*

Site	Imports	Possible Imports[105]	Description of Imports
Mainland			
Lefkandi	42	7	A variety of Cypriot and Near Eastern finds in wealthy tombs (also perhaps PG an imported ceramic plate (PG-G) from the settlement)
Atalanti	5	–	Two bronze bowls and faience beads from burials in the town
Argos	4	–	Faience beads and a faience bracelet from burials
Nea Ionia	3	–	Faience beads from burials
Marmariani	3	–	Faience beads from burials
Tiryns	2	–	Faience beads from burials
Athens	2	1	Faience necklace and a bronze bowl both Near Eastern (Cypriot/North Syrian bronze bowl (PG-G))
Neo Monastiri	1	–	Faience beads from a tholos tomb
Mitrou	1	–	Necklace made of pierced shells and green faience beads
Asine	1	–	Faience beads from a tomb
Delphi	–	1	Cypriot/North Syrian bronze bowl (PG-G)
Sparta	–	1	Near Eastern bronze bowl (PG-G)
	(64)	(10)	
Crete			
Knossos	32	2	A variety of exotica from the tombs date to the EIA (also: Phoenician jar and Near Eastern iron knife (PG-G))
Kommos	30	–	Phoenician vessels from the port
Eleutherna	2	3	Cypriot Lekane, Egyptian situla; bronze bowl (PGB–EG); Faience Egyptian seal (SM-LG); faience beads on floor of tombs A1K1 (PG-G)
Prinias Patela	1	–	Faience necklace from a burial
Gortyn	1	–	Cypriot iron spits from a tomb
Tylissos	1	–	Syrian bronze statuette of a man and a bull
Amari	1	–	Cypriot amphoroid krater[106]
Vrokastro	–	16	Egyptian faience seals and a bronze tripod from Cyprus (SM-EG)
Dikte	–	3	Two Egyptian bronze statues, one Carnelian bead (LM IIIC-G)
Idaean cave	–	1	Cypriot bronzebowl (LM IIIC-G)
Karphi	–	2	Cypriot bronze pendant (LM IIIC-PG) and Anatolian bronze arrowhead (SM-PG)
Kavousi	–	2	Egyptian faience object and bronze Italian fibula (SM-G)
Priansos	–	1	Wall bracket (PG-O)

(continued)

[105] Number of imprecisely dated imports from a chronological range that might include PG.
[106] Kourou 2012, 33–50.

TABLE 2.5. *(continued)*

Site	Imports	Possible Imports	Description of Imports
Phaistos	–	2	Egyptian scarabs dated to the thirteenth to eleventh centuries (IIIB-PG)
Arkades	–	1	Egyptian scarab from a tomb (PG-G)
Palaikastro	–	1	Scarab dated to the tenth/ninth centuries[107]
	(68)	(34)	
Total	132	44	

2. Imports from the PG period come almost exclusively from mortuary contexts, with the exception of Phoenician transport jars from Kommos. There are probably more imported exotica being deposited in sacred caves on Crete from this period than the number suggests, but these are hard to date.
3. Import finds from the PG period consist (again with the exception of jars from Kommos) of small "personal" objects like scarabs or faience necklaces, along with bronze vessels.
4. The use-value of the objects is not clear; some may be amulets with a function association with supernatural belief. Nonfaience finds are especially associated with other signs of elite status in mortuary assemblages.

Geometric Imports

During the Geometric period, the number of imports known from Greece increases, exceeding the number known from the final Mycenaean period. While imports come from a few tombs in Attica (Athens, Eleusis, Anavyssos), on Crete, and at Lefkandi (from the Euboean SPG, equivalent to the ninth century), major changes in import distribution occur in Greece in the Geometric period. By far the most important of these is that the densest collections of imports appear in sanctuaries, especially sanctuaries of the Peloponnese, where exotica are not known in quantity from the Protogeometric period.[108] The imports deposited in Geometric sanctuaries, including at Eretria, Perachora, Olympia, and Artemis Orthia, are impressively numerous, especially when compared to the small overall number of all known

---

[107] Karetsou, Andreadaki-Vlazaki, and Papadaki 2000, 332, no. 353.
[108] I could find no evidence of Geometric imports from sites in Thessaly. At the same time, deposits in Thessalian sites continue include significant quantities of metals, such as gold and bronze. See Georganas (2000, 2002) as well as the publications for the sanctuaries of Philia and Velestino (Theocharis 1963; Kilian 1983b; Béquignon 1937, 57–74). As always, it is important to think carefully about whether these contextual and geographic shifts represent change in ancient behaviors, or whether it is likely to be a product of the vagaries of the archaeological record. I will return to this topic later.

imports from the PG mainland. The objects themselves are similar in type to PG imports – bronze vessels are prominent, as are faience objects – but the classes of objects within these categories becomes more diverse. Beads make up only a small portion of the assemblage, while small statuettes, figurines, and (predominantly) scarabs appear as a new feature of Greek exotica. Among bronzes, shallow bowls, Egyptian lotus handled jugs, and large bronze cauldrons with siren and bull-head attachments are all well represented.[109]

At some sanctuaries (Olympia, Perachora, Argive Heraion) the presence of imported objects in the Geometric period represents the beginning of a steady ramping up of the deposition of large amounts of wealth, and of imported or stylistically orientalizing objects, that would continue in the ensuing Archaic period. At others (Eretria, Sparta), the Geometric period was apparently a peak of depositional activity that would tail off during the seventh century. At Perachora, the staggering quantity of nearly a thousand so-called "Egyptian-type" objects were catalogued I the excavations from the early twentieth century.[110] The majority, 750, were scarabs, mostly of faience but a few of steatite, leading analysts to suppose that the majority were Egyptianizing imitations made by Greeks at Naukratis, or by Phoenicians elsewhere on the Syro-Palestinian littoral.[111] A few figurines (of Amun-Re and Bes), beads, and rosettes,[112] were recovered from the Geometric "Egyptian pit." The pit, dating to the late eighth century and early seventh century, was located to the east of the temple.[113] The possibility remains that these objects were made in Greece (perhaps in Rhodes), and brought to Perachora by Greeks returning from the east or by Phoenicians visiting the sanctuary,[114] but close study by Skon-Jedele suggests most of the early examples are probably from Egypt.[115]

Likewise, the dedication of exotica appears to have been a characteristic of ritual activity in other important Peloponnesian communities, specifically at Olympia and at the sanctuary of Artemis Orthia in Lakonia. At Olympia, imported bronzes from the east (Phoenician bowls and North Syrian and

---

[109] Boardman 1964, 63–71; Markoe 1985; Braun-Holzinger and Rehm 2005; Muscarella 1992 (reviewing the vast literature on cataloguing and taxonomizing cauldron attachments, and updating the study in Herrmann 1966a, at 17–18).

[110] James 1962, 461.

[111] James 1962 (461) points out that a similar assemblage in Egypt would contain a far higher proportion of stone to glass paste scarabs, suggesting that most of the finds at Perachora come from a Phoenician, or perhaps Rhodian workshop.

[112] It is interesting to note a surprisingly harmonious correlation with the themes of the exotica from Perati (where figurines of Bes, a scarab inscribed Amun-Re, and rosettes were present) and from Lefkandi (Bes figurine in T.46) from the preceding IIIC and PG periods.

[113] James 1962, 464.

[114] An idea that originated with Dunbabin (1957), according to whom these objects were "personal effects which may have been brought to Greece by Phoenician visitors [or] picked up in Syria or Phoenicia by Greek sailors."

[115] Skon-Jedele 1994.

Urartian cauldron attachments (presumably with cauldrons)[116] and west (fibulae from Italy) were among early votive deposits.[117] At the sanctuary of Artemis Orthia in Lakonia, finds from the end of the Geometric period (from 740 BCE onward) yielded numerous oriental or orientalizing finds, especially carved ivory objects and some scarabs.[118] Finally, Late Geometric and early Archaic deposits of scarabs, beads, and a variety of other kinds of *orientalia* have been published from the open air sanctuary northeast of the temple of Apollo Daphnephoros at Eretria.[119] A few Geometric scarabs and bronzes also come from the sanctuaries of Aphrodite on Aegina[120] and Apollo at Delphi,[121] suggesting that the trend toward the deposition of exotica in sanctuaries that is apparent at Sparta, Olympia, and the Corinthia was not isolated to Peloponnesian communities.

At both Sparta and Eretria imported objects appear not only in sanctuaries but at least sporadically in tombs, as they do in Athens and elsewhere.[122] At Eretria, especially impressive is the burial of a presumable warrior, whose remains were wrapped in a cloth before being buried along with a gold/serpentine scarab, an Italian bronze spearhead, and other swords and spearheads in a great bronze cauldron.[123] Remains found in the pyre suggest that a horse was sacrificed at the burial, a scene reminiscent of the burial within the Lefkandi *heroon* from the MPG. At Lefkandi, imported objects appear in tombs dated to the local SPG period,[124] equivalent to the EG–MG period on the mainland

---

[116] For detailed analysis of the bowls, see Markoe 1985 (Olympia bowls at G1–11). For the cauldron attachments, Kilian-Dirlmeier 1985 and Muscarella 1992 review the evidence. There remains uncertainty (Muscarella 1992, 33; Kyrieleis 1977, 80) about the exact division between imported cauldron attachments (sirens and winged bowls) that were imported, and those that were imitated locally, so the numbers presented here should (as with many classes of imported objects) be considered with some caution.

[117] Philipp 1981 on bronzework from Olympia (entries 1031–1068); cf. Kilian-Dirlmeier 1985; Muscarella 1992; Strøm 1992.

[118] Dawkins 1929, 203.

[119] Huber 2003, 69–108; 169–174. Identifying the origin of many of the objects (Rhodes? Egypt? Phoenicia?) is something of a guessing game. There is an interesting contrast between the corpus of scarabs from Eretria and the ones from Perachora: the latter are almost entirely faience examples, while the former are at least half stone, which is more consistent with an Egyptian manufacture.

[120] At the sanctuary of Aphrodite, several faience scarabs, an Egyptianizing figurine (the type is not described), and pieces of faience Egyptian vessels were discovered in a foundation deposit beneath the temenos along with late eighth century pottery (Staï 1895 241, 261–264).

[121] Rolley 1977; further discussion and bibliography in Muscarella 1992.

[122] Spartan tomb containing an imported bronze bowl, Dussaud 1940 92–95, fig. 1); at Anavyssos, the scarab was found in the most well-furnished grave in the cemetery (Skon-Jedele 1994, 74).

[123] For Eretria, Bérard 1970; Bérard 1982; for Athens, Smithson 1968; Skon-Jedele 1994, 12–29.

[124] In tombs T.22 (7; faience necklaces and amulets); T.51 (1; faience); T.45 (1; faience beads); T.79A (10; a Phoenician bichrome, Cypriot white painted, and Cypriot BoR vase, a cylinder seal, stone weights, and bronzes); T.47 (1; a bronze bucket); and T.78 (1; a bronze vase); T.36 (3; scarab in gold fitting with hieroglyphs in three registers, beads also ivory flakes); T.33

(Figure 2.7). Faience and glass necklaces (including one spectacular example made entirely of Egyptianizing figurines)[125] continued to appear in tombs at Toumba throughout the ninth century, along with bronze bowls and other vessels from the Near East, imported gold earrings, a seal, and a scarab. The appearance, in tomb 59, of a scale plate of the exact same variety as ones deposited apparently as part of (foundation?) rituals at Tiryns, Mycenae, and Kanakia in the final phases of the LBA raises interesting questions.[126]

In general, the burials become richer and imports more diverse in quality and size during the SPG period. The lack of a clear devolution of offering abundance in the cemetery, a different pattern from the one apparent in the PG burials, suggests either that hierarchies within the burial population at Toumba may have begun to erode (Figure 2.6). It seems likely that individuals that were eligible to be buried in front of the heroon monument belonged to a special subset of society to begin with. Thus, divisions of wealth within the burials might be less meaningful than divisions in a burial population with more internal diversity, as at Perati.[127] By 825, the cemetery had fallen out of use; a few glass beads and other likely imports have been discovered from the Geometric layers of the settlement, and we may expect more to appear going forward.[128]

During the Geometric period Crete was receptive to influences from the East, a receptiveness that is expressed in a variety of media.[129] Perhaps not surprisingly given the thoroughgoing nature of this influence, there is plenty of evidence for a deep and broad distribution of imported objects as well as stylistic affinities with the east in the archaeological record of Geometric Crete. The distribution of small objects of generically "Near Eastern" type is wide, ranging all over the island.[130]

The cave sanctuaries at Mt. Dikte and Mt. Ida continued to accumulate imported metal goods in the Geometric period, though in general import deposition is more dispersed in Crete than it is on the mainland. It should be kept in mind that only a small fraction of exotic objects and materials deposited in sacred Cretan caves can be properly assessed from a historical standpoint, since the mixed nature of the deposits (and early date of some excavations)

(2; lotus-bud handled Egyptian jug and bronze bowl); T.74 (1; bronze bowl); T.31 (2; faience figurine with bronze bowl); T.32 (1; Ptah amulet); T.33 (5; lotus oinochoe, glass beads).

[125] Popham et al. 1980, 179–180, no. 28.
[126] Discussion at Popham et al. 1980, 251; Karageorghis and Masson 1975, 209–222; Matthäus and Schumacher-Matthäus 1986, 166; Maran 2004, 21–24.
[127] Popham et al. 1980, 362.
[128] Popham et al. 1980, 84–88.
[129] For summaries of oriental themes in Cretan art of the PG and Geometric periods: Hoffman 1997; Markoe 1996; S. Morris 1997; among others.
[130] General studies of imports in early Crete include Hoffman 1997 and Jones 2000. See recent and upated discussion in Stampolidis and Kotsonas 2006. For the Idaean cave, Halberr 1888; Carter 1998; Sakellarakis 2013.

create serious problems for diachronic sorting. Nonetheless, there are indications that the cave sanctuaries saw increased quantities of wealth being dedicated beginning in the eighth century. Carved ivories from the cave seem to belong to this period based on stylistic analysis, and many have been attributed to Phoenician or otherwise Syro-Palestinian hands. There is also evidence that some of these objects were made locally, or date to the seventh or sixth centuries instead.[131] Quantities of bronze objects, many either certainly manufactured in the east or clearly manufactured in Crete with an eye to eastern styles, add to the impression that the Idaean cave was an exceptional place both in regard to the amount of resources Cretans dedicated to adorning the sanctuary with riches and the strong connection of its patrons and craftsmen to the wider world.[132] The close relationship between the cave and the nearby site of Eleutherna has recently been emphasized by Stampolidis and Kotsonas, and is supported by the fact that the cemetery at that site is also rich in imports and external influences during the Geometric and Archaic periods.[133]

As on the mainland, imports also turn up relatively widely scattered in burials throughout the island, including in the west, but Knossos overwhelmingly dominates the record, in part because excavated tombs from the site are numerous, and in part because a large number of these have been published. Cypriot and Phoenician vessels, as well as orientalizing and oriental gold jewelry are prominent in the body of imports recovered.[134]

As if the wealthy finds from cave sanctuaries and from burials did not underline it enough, evidence from the harbor at Kommos reiterates the fact that special connections with both Cyprus and Phoenicia were operational on Crete during the Geometric period.[135] At Kommos, where imported objects were already unusually common in the PG period, Phoenician and Cypriot vessels appear in significant numbers again in the Geometric period. The appearance of a Phoenician-style shrine at the site around the same time provides a stunning glimpse into the cosmopolitan nature of life at this important port in early Greece.[136]

---

[131] Hoffman 1997, 53–65; Sakellarakis 1992, 92. Imported ivories from the Idaean cave from the North Syrian and Phoenician area may date to the eighth century, but could also be later. See also Jones 2000, 109–114. The number of ivories may overstate the quantity of objects in question, since many were probably inlays or attachments to composite pieces like furniture. For further summary and discussion of the Idaean cave, see Hoffman 1997, 146–147, 156–160; Pappalardo 2004.

[132] See impressive finds now published with images and descriptions in Sakellarakis 2013.

[133] Stampolidis and Kotsonas 2006, 349. See also Themelis 2000, 31 for the discovery of bronze molds from the site dated to the seventh century.

[134] Coldstream and Catling 1996; Boardman 2005; Kotsonas 2006.

[135] Three hundred imported ceramic sherds in addition to faience figurines are known from the Geometric Greek temple (M. Shaw 2000; Bikai 2000).

[136] For ceramics, see Bikai 2000; Bikai 2000, 302–8; Johnston 2000, 197; Johnston 2005. For the Phoenician shrine in Temple B, see Shaw 1989; Shaw 1998, 18–21; J. Shaw 2000, 711–713. Pappalardo 2002 presents the idea that the Kommos shrine represents a common Near Eastern type rather than a special link with Phoenicia.

TABLE 2.6. *Imported objects in Greece from the G period*

Site	Imports	Possible Imports[137]	Description of Imports
Mainland			
Eretria	97	19	Italian spearhead from Italy in "prince's tomb;"[138] a perfume flask from Cyprus and Syrian scarab seal from the Geometric pyre;[139] Cypriot and Phoenician ceramics,[140] as well as other Near Eastern imports of bronze (eastern and Italian including horse blinkers[141]) & faience from various areas in the sanctuary of Apollo Daphnephoros;[142] scarabs & Egyptian figurines.[143] Some likely to be seventh century/archaic. Phoenician beads and scarabs in burials near the *heroon*[144]
Olympia	59	5	Group of Phoenician bronze bowls; numerous Italian fibulae; siren and bull-head cauldron attachments (some perhaps seventh century and some perhaps locally made)[145]
Perachora	36	38	Phoenician frit scarabs and figurines from the sanctuary (James 1962; Skon-Jedele 1994, 253–673);[146] Egyptian mirror dated by style to 750–650; a bronze bowl dates to the eighth/seventh centuries (Markoe 1985, G11)
Lefkandi	35	7	Imported ceramic plate (LPG/SPG) from burial; imported iron knife and pin/nail from Xeropolis; numerous imported rock-crystal beads and glass/faience beads, including compound beads and two pendants of faience in the form of Egyptian gods (Ptah/Seker/Osiris) and Isis; three imported seals from Phoenicia; scale of armor in bronze; mace head[147]
Artemis Orthia	20	14	Variety of Phoenician/Egyptian scarabs, Phoenician ivory needles & a griffin head, a Hittite ivory seal & a glass Syrian seal (Dawkins 1929; Kopanias 2009; Skon-Jedele 1994, 809–831

(continued)

[137] The import data from the Geometric period is quite difficult to pin down precisely. Much of it comes from mixed sanctuary deposits so dating is based on stylistic analysis. Many imports probably date to the last half or quarter of the eighth century, but in many cases could have been deposited in Greece in the early seventh.
[138] Bettelli 2000; Blandin 2007, 115–117.
[139] Martin Pruvot 2010, no. 264 & 272.
[140] Verdan 2013, 95–97, 98–99.
[141] Charbonnet 1986, 117–156; Verdan 2013.
[142] Huber 2003; Verdan 2013.
[143] Huber 2003, discussion of various kinds of imports at vol. 1 69–108; 169–174.
[144] Blandin 2007, 107–108.
[145] Markoe 1985, G3, G5–7; Furtwängler 1890, 141, 142, 884, and pl. 52
[146] The Egyptianizing imports come from the "Egyptian pit" dated to 735–670 BCE and some may be Rhodian products; I assume that half are late eighth century, while half might be.
[147] See publications at Popham et al. 1980; Popham et al. 1989; Popham and Lemos 1996.

TABLE 2.6. *(continued)*

Site	Imports	Possible Imports	Description of Imports
Eleusis	20	–	Cache of twenty Egyptian or Phoenician faience scarabs from the "Isis Grave," probably early eighth century;[148] other scarabs come from the Telesterion but cannot be dated
Athens	15	5	Egyptian faience figurine from LG burial in Odos Kavalotti; electrum figurine, bronze bowl from the Kerameikos;[149] Egyptian necklaces and Cypriot rings from EG graves; Phoenician bronze bowl from the Acropolis; glass seal from Odos Piraeus, glass pendant and two faience scarabs in the Agora, three faience lions in grave (possible: Cypriot/North Syrian bronze bowls (PG-G and G/A)); MG tomb of the Rich Lady w/ Sidonian necklace[150]
Aegina	12	–	Egyptian or Phoenician faience scarabs, a figurine, and two vessels (*ArchEph* 1895 241, 261–4, pin.12)
Delphi	11	5	A Phoenician jar, Cypriot piece of revetment, and an Egyptian or Phoenician scarab; Cypriot/North Syrian bronze bowl (PG-G); some cauldron attachments that may be eighth/seventh century and may be local imitations; openwork bronze stands from eighth/seventh century, probably Cypriot (or Cretan?)[151]
Argos	7	2	Six plain Cypriot bronze bowls and a clay chariot figurine group;[152] beads from a MG tomb (Courbin 1974, 36–37); votive deposits from the Larisa (Bes figurines and scarab), MG-G (Beaufils 2000, 418)
Argive Heraion	3	7	Imported siren attachments for cauldrons;[153] Ivory Egyptian figurine; Bes? Also noted are a piece of an ostrich egg and Phoenician glass bottles; two bronze bowls are dated to the eighth/seventh centuries along with Phrygian fibulae and bowls.
Sparta	1	1	bronze bowl (PG-G) (Markoe 1985, G8)
Paralimni Kamilovrisi	1	?	At least one scarab (*ArchDelt* 1966 Chr 198–201; *ArchDelt* 1971 Chr 216–217)
Marmariani	1	?	Min. one bead, parallels from Syria and Italy (Heurtley and Skeat 1930-31, 39, fig. 16, no. 32)

(continued)

[148] Philios 1889, 171–187; Skias 1898, 84–114.
[149] Coldstream 2003a, 59–60; Kübler 1954, fig 5, plate 162; Herrmann 1966b, 131–133.
[150] For recent discussion of these finds with good references, see Kourou 2015; for full catalog of Egyptian finds, see Skon-Jedele 1994, 12–29.
[151] Rolley 1977, 23, pl. 18–20; Muscarella 1992.
[152] Courbin 1974, 129–130; Strøm 1992, 59.
[153] Waldstein 1902, 191–339; Blegen 1937a, 19–111; Blegen 1937b, 378–383; Muscarella 1992; Strøm 1992 for discussion of cauldrons and other imports.

TABLE 2.6. *(continued)*

Site	Imports	Possible Imports	Description of Imports
Thermon	1	–	Bronze Syrian statuette from the sanctuary[154]
Anavyssos	1	–	Egyptian scarab from a burial[155]
Tragana	1	–	Anatolian bronze phiale (*ArchDelt* 1981 Mel 21–22)
Aigio Plastiras	1		One Egyptian scarab in a pithos burial (*ArchDelt* 45 1990 Chr 137)
Orchomenos	1	–	Beads from burials (Bulle 1907, pl. 30)
Ptoion	1	–	siren cauldron attachments from the same cauldron (Herrmann 1966a, 58, nos. 52–53)
Amyclae	1	–	Bull-attachment from cauldron (Muscarella 1968)
Sounion	1	–	Phoenician bronze statuette (Athens NM 14.926)
Corinth	1	–	Scarab from eighth century grave below Roman agora (*Corinth xii*, 223–224)
Pherai	–	1	A bronze situla that fits well with G imports, but seems to date to the seventh c. (Pendlebury 1930, 92) like most other imports from the site
Thebes	–	1	Scarab of G or A date (Pendlebury 1930, 88)
Brauron	?	?	Excavation report mentions scarabs but number not known; the deposit dates eighth to fifth centuries[156]
	(327)	(105)	
Crete[157]			
Knossos	79	2	Wide variety of NE finds in cemeteries of Knossos (Coldstream and Catling 1996)
Idaean cave	25	1	Various imported bronzes, faience objects, and ivories; Cypriot bronze bowl (LM IIIC-G)
Kommos	13	3	Phoenician and Cypriot vessels from the sanctuary;[158] a possibly Cypriot horse and chariot group;[159] faience figurines dated to the eighth/seventh century
Eleutherna	11	8	Phrygian oinochoe, three Cypriot vessels, bronze bowl; two bronze carinated cauldrons; faience vessels; two gold decorations from the east?; faience Egyptian seal (SM-LG); possibly a Phoenician juglet & scarabs from the late eighth or seventh century; glass bowls and beads[160]
Dikte	9	3	Two Egyptian bronze statues, one Carnelian bead (LM IIIC-G)

(continued)

---

[154] Sotiriadis 1900, 179–181; Romaiou 1916, 227–8; 249–50.
[155] Lazaridis 1968, 97–98; Themelis 1979, 108–110.
[156] Papadimitriou 1963, 113.
[157] Cretan imports assembled from data in Jones (2000), Hoffman (1997), and Stampolidis and Kotsonas (2006) unless otherwise noted.
[158] Bikai 2000, 302–308; Shaw 1998, 19–21; Johnston 2000, 197; Johnston 2005.
[159] Shaw 2000, 142.
[160] Stampolidis 1998; Stampolidis 2004, 255; Stampolidis 2011, 760–762; Karetsou, Anreadaki-Vlazaki and Papadaki 2000, 332, n. 352.

TABLE 2.6. *(continued)*

Site	Imports	Possible Imports	Description of Imports
Amnisos	6	–	Cypriot and Egyptian imported objects, including a bronze figurine, a limestone statue head, bronze tripod fragment from sanctuary of Zeus Thanatos
Kavousi	5	2	Egyptian faience object and bronzeItalian fibula (SM-G); possible Cypriot vessel
Praisos	3	–	Faience scarab and beads
Kissamos	2	–	Cypriot bronze pomegranate pendant from a burial; Egyptian biconical bead
Arkades	2	1	Phrygian iron fibula from an unknown context; Scarab maybe dating to the eleventh-eighth centuries (PG-G)
Zakros	1	–	Egyptian faience beads from the settlement at Hellenika
Inatos	1	–	Ivory/bone goddess figurine from the Eileithyia cave sanctuary
Agia Triada	1	–	Syrian cauldron attachment
Kourtes	1	–	Syrian vessel
Prinias	1	–	Egyptian scarab
Dreros	1	–	Faience beads from tomb 10
Kounavoi	1	–	Phoenician jug/juglet[161]
Phaistos	1	1	Phoenician jug/juglet;[162] possible G scarab[163]
Vrokastro	–	16	Egyptian faience seals and a bronze tripod from Cyprus (SM-EG)
Priansos		1	Wall bracket (PG-O)
Kato Syme	–	1	Scarab dating to G-A (750–600)[164]
	(163)	(39)	
Total	490	144	

The corpus of Geometric imports therefore has clear similarities with the body of known PG imports, although there are new developments, like the appearance of specialized bronze products, major increases in the quantity of imported stone and faience scarabs, a much wider geographical distribution of imports, and the concentration of exotica in sanctuary deposits, especially in the later eighth century.

The most important characteristics of the Geometric data are as follows:

1. While some imports continue to be deposited in graves in Attica, Central Greece, and Euboea, sanctuaries become the most common context from

---

[161] Stampolidis and Karetsou 1998, 124, 181, no, 184.
[162] Stampolidis and Karetsou 1998, 124, 181–182, nos. 185–186.
[163] Karetsou, Andreadaki-Vlazaki, and Papadaki 2000, 330, no. 348.
[164] Karetsou, Andreadaki-Vlazaki, and Papadaki 2000, 331, no. 351.

which exotic materials are recovered in the eighth century. The variety of origin points is impressive, including Italy, Egypt, Syria-Palestine, and Cyprus.

2. Imports appear widely in most regions, with no obvious concentration regionally, though the Peloponnese has a larger share of imports than had been the case in the preceding IIIC and PG periods.

3. As in preceding periods, the function of imported objects is not completely clear, but with the exception of Phoenician bronze bowls that may have been used for pouring libations, most imported objects do not have an obvious use-value. Most interpret the jewelry from tombs as evidence of elite self-aggrandizement, but we should consider some kind of ritual or supernatural function as well.

4. The influx of identifiable imported objects is accompanied by the apparently local production of objects that adopt many of their characteristics of style and technique (in a wide variety of media including bronze, gold, and ceramic (especially in Crete)) in ways that were not apparent in earlier periods. Many have suggested, then, that the deposition of imports had to do with the movement of people, especially craftsmen, instead of with trade.

2.2. OVERALL QUANTITATIVE AND QUALITATIVE PATTERNS IN THE IMPORT DATA

That, in brief, is the basic distribution and character of imports from the LB IIIB, LB IIIC, PG, and G periods in Greece.[165] In what follows, I lay out the general patterns in the data on five separate axes – overall abundance, archaeological context, (presumable) object function, object material, and (presumable) object origin, in order to see what impression the most direct category of evidence for early Greek long-distance interaction, the import data, leaves regarding changes in the structure, scale and organization of trade. In the next chapter, I will subject these patterns to further scrutiny.

2.2.1. Number of Imports

While we have long been generally aware that we know of fewer imports from the periods immediately following the Mycenaean collapse than we do from the periods preceding and following it, the scale of these magnitudes has never been clear. In this section, I attempt to provide a bit more solid traction on the numbers involved, though these should continue to be considered as

---

[165] A much more detailed exegesis on the objects from the IIIB–PG periods, their precise quantification, and lengthy considerations of the archaeological contexts and circumstances, can be found in S. Murray 2013, chapter 6.

TABLE 2.7. *Minimum, maximum, and weighted middle import counts*

	Min[166]	*Max*[167]	*Weighted Middle*[168]
IIIB			**228**
LHIIIB	123	164	132
LMIIIB	87	119	96
IIIC			**136**
LHIIIC	82	109	89
LMIIIC	34	63	47
PG			**152**
Mainland PG	64	74	69
Cretan PG	68	102	83
G			**543**
Mainland G	327	432	364
Cretan G	163	202	179

approximations, given the complexity of counting objects in the archaeological record.[169]

These absolute numbers mean little, because each period is of a different duration. Breaking them down into per annum statistics allows us to compare them directly, but is less straightforward than it ideally would be, because Aegean Bronze Age chronology is controversial. There are two major systems of chronology that have gained wide acceptance, the traditional chronology, based largely on synchronisms with the Near East, and a modified "low"

[166] The fewest possible imports we might have from the period. This indicates the number of imports that are securely dated by archaeologists to the period in question.

[167] The maximum possible imports that could date to this period. This quantity presumes that all ambiguously dated imports that could date to the period do in fact belong within it.

[168] Many of the ambiguously dated objects identified as imports in the import record are dated coarsely (e.g., anywhere within LB III or somewhere between LH I/II and III), while some are dated relatively tightly (i.e. LPG or EG) so there is not an equal probability that each ambiguously dated import is or is not datable within any specific period. Adjusting the figures for each broad category of ambiguously dated objects (LM I-LM III, LM III?, etc.) according to the probability that the total number of objects within that category dates to LB IIIB, LB IIIC, PG or G specifically I have generated "weighted middle" number of imports for each period. This effectively represents a compromise figure between the minimum and maximum possible imports that date to that period, according to the resolution of dating for ambiguously dated imports.

[169] Parkinson (2010) attempts to model the quantity of imported objects by number of "contacts," on the assumption that we can identify tranches of trade goods that arrived in the Aegean in batches. While this approach is innovative and might elide certain inconsistencies in the data due to extraordinary finds like the Theban cylinder seals, I am not comfortable adopting it here, because it requires us to assume things about how prehistoric trade functioned that we simply cannot know, assumptions that would be nearly impossible to apply systematically and evenly across the dataset. However, it is interesting to note that if we eliminated the Theban cylinder seals from the LBA import corpus or reduced them to a single entry, this would effectively negate the difference between IIIB, IIIC, and PG imports).

TABLE 2.8. *Chronology*[170]

Chronological Schemes for the end of the Aegean Late Bronze Age, Mainland		
Period	Traditional	Modified Low
LH IIIB	1300–1175	1300–1190
LH IIIC/SM	1175–1050	1190–1015
PG	1050–900	1015–900
G	900–700	900–700
Duration of Chronological Phases, Mainland		
Period	Traditional	Modified Low
LH IIIB	125 yrs.	110 yrs.
LH IIIC/SM	125 yrs.	175 yrs.
PG	150 yrs.	115 yrs.
G	200 yrs.	200 yrs.
Chronological Schemes for the end of the Aegean Late Bronze Age, Crete		
Period	Traditional	Modified Low
LM IIIB	1300–1190	1300–1190
LM IIIC/SM	1190–970	1190–945
Cretan PG	970–810	945–810
Cretan G	810–700	810–700
Duration of Chronological Phases, Crete		
Period	Traditional	Modified Low
LM IIIB	110 yrs.	110 yrs.
LM IIIC/SM	230 yrs.	245 yrs.
Cretan PG	160 yrs.	135 yrs.
Cretan G	110 yrs.	110 yrs.

chronology.[171] The possible chronologies are summarized in Table 2.8. The differences between the duration of periods according to each chronological scheme are dramatic. In Crete, the absolute chronology of cultural phases presents different problems. Generally speaking, Cretan LM IIIB is thought to follow the dates of LH IIIB, since culturally Crete was "Mycenaean" during this period.[172] However, the Cretan IIIC/SM phase lasts longer than the

---

[170] The date for the Uluburun shipwreck at the beginning of IIIB stands on relatively firm ground (Manning et al. 2009), but beyond that little within any of these chronologies seems fixed. The modified low chronology has the merits of integrating a variety of scientific and traditional chronological results to produce a timeline that attempts to account for all of the evidence. However, radical revisions have been proposed to both the traditional and low chronologies. See review in Knapp and Manning 2016, 116–118.

[171] Tartaron 2008, 84, table 1; cf. Popham 1970, 81–84; Kanta 1980, 298–301; B. Hallager 1988; B. Hallager 1993; Dickinson 2006, 23, fig. 1.1. Recent work suggests that this synchronism is not as straightforward as usually thought. B. Hallager (2007, 196–197) reports that LM IIIB2 shapes appear on the mainland in LH IIIC Early rather than in LH IIIB, indicating "possible dislocations between the LM/LH IIIB2 and C periods." However, the end of LH/LM IIIA should not be affected by these, and the evidence for the absolute date of either region's IIIB/IIIC transition is so opaque that the still uncertain proposal by Hallager (2007, 196) that "LH IIIC Early may have started before the end of LM IIIB2" is difficult to integrate into the analysis here, though in theory it would be possible to generate another chronology in which LM IIIB extends further into the twelfth century.

[172] Snodgrass 1971, 138–139.

equivalent mainland phases, extending down to 970 on the traditional chronology, and PG ceramics persist to 810.[173]

Due to limitations of space, it is impossible to properly treat the complex issue of absolute chronology here.[174] Ceramic chronology, dendrochronology, and radiocarbon dating each proceed according to different professional dictums and standards, and sorting out their intersections and contradictions is a fraught process not likely to be resolved in the near future.[175] This creates serious problems for our attempt to precisely define quantitative metrics of past economic performance, since such metrics must necessarily scale according to the length of chronological periods for internal consistency. For instance, if the absolute chronology revisions suggested by Wardle[176] for the end of the LBA are accepted, the placement and duration of all subphases of the LBA–EIA transition would change, and major upheavals would be appropriate in all treatments of this period. As frightening it is to contemplate the void of this pea soup environment, the existential dread that comes with realizing that we may or may not be largely mistaken about the periodization of prehistory must not stop us from attempting to come to terms with the archaeological record.

A particular issue for the analysis here is the disagreement of the absolute chronologies for the mainland and the Cretan PG. Here we confront one of the generally awkward scenarios generated by the tendency in Greek prehistory to define cultural periods by ceramic typologies. While mainland PG ends around 900 BCE, Cretan PG and PGB extend well into the ninth century. The implication is that many of the PG sites and imports that I have cataloged probably date later than the mainland ones, and that the Cretan PG data reflects partly a ninth century instead of an eleventh and tenth century reality. For example, in the Cretan PG import corpus, a number date to the local LPG, well after the beginning of the ninth century. While it would be ideal to sort all of the data so that its divisions reflected absolute chronological realities, it is impossible to do this evenly across the dataset, because many brief site reports (which I used to populate the import catalog and an overall site dataset within which to contextualize the import data) refer to finds only according to rough ceramic chronology. Since the Cretan PG chronologically straddles the

---

[173] Evidence from excavations at Assiros in northern Greece has prompted the suggestion of another chronology, impacting especially the dates of the end of the IIIC period and the beginning and duration of PG. This evidence remains the subject of debate. Since it is not accepted by the majority of scholars currently (and could easily be reconciled with the traditional chronologies if an unsubstantiated belief that pottery styles must have all originated in Athens is released) I do not take this new chronological scheme into account in my calculations here. For the most recent summary of the debates on the Assiros chronology and related vitriol, see Toffolo et al. 2013; Weninger and Jung 2009.
[174] See fuller treatment in S. Murray 2013, 32–39.
[175] Manning 2014; see also Toffolo et al. 2013 and Fantalkin et al. 2015 for recent data on the EIA; James et al. 1991, refuted by Manning and Weninger 1992, and supported by Weninger and Jung 2009 and Papadopoulos 2011; for revisions of ceramic typology, French and Stockhammer 2009.
[176] Wardle et al. 2014.

lower end of mainland PG, in most cases, without specific EPG, MPG, or LPG designations, hardly any of this data would be possible to place in one category (1050–900 or 900–700 BCE) with certainty. In order to avoid having to toss such a large percentage of the total dataset, I have chosen to categorize the Cretan and Mainland PG data according to their own local chronologies, rather than trying to split them into absolute chronological units (which we are not sure about anyway), and provide separate figures for each region. The overall result of this is probably to slightly exaggerate the figures for the Cretan and overall PG periods and underestimate the ones for the Geometric – since a number of "PG" imports on Crete probably date to 900–700 BCE instead.[177]

In what follows, while keeping in mind interpretational difficulties and various obvious problems with prehistoric absolute chronology that are not within the scope of this work, I do my best present per annum import rates as they would work out based on each of the two separate chronologies.[178] While these figures (like the raw import quantities) look precise, it should be kept in mind that they are best considered as rough, ballpark figures that give us a sense of "orders of magnitude."

TABLE 2.9. *Imports per annum (min/max/weighted) according to the traditional chronology*

		Imports	Weighted Average Per Year[179]
Cumulative	LB IIIB	228	~2.0
	LB IIIC/SM	136	~.9
	PG	152	~.9
	G	543	~3.4
Mainland	LH IIIB	132	1.1
	LH IIIC/SM	89	.7
	PG	69	.45
	G	364	1.8
Crete	LM IIIB	96	.9
	LM IIIC/SM	47	.2
	PG	83	.5
	G	179	1.6

[177] For an argument that the mainland Geometric sequence should be extended into the seventh century, see Papadopoulos 2003, 146.

[178] In order to determine a cumulative rate of imports in each period (IIIB, IIIC, PG) despite the fact that the chronologies for the mainland and Crete vary significantly, I calculate the Cretan and mainland rates separately to reflect the nonequivalent chronologies, and then add those rates together to arrive at the cumulative rates per year.

[179] The per annum rates are calculated as a total of the rates on Crete and the mainland, since the chronologies are different.

TABLE 2.10. *Imports per annum (min/max/weighted) according to a modified "low" chronology*

		Weighted Average Imports	Per Year
Cumulative	LB IIIB	228	~2.1
	LB IIIC/SM	136	~.7
	PG	152	~1.2
	G	543	~3.4
Mainland	LH IIIB	132	1.2
	LH IIIC/SM	89	.5
	PG	69	.6
	G	364	1.8
Crete	LM IIIB	96	.9
	LM IIIC/SM	47	.2
	PG	83	.6
	G	179	1.6

A consistent pattern emerges: import numbers drop off after the end of IIIB, and stay low throughout the periods of the postpalatial Bronze Age and the beginning of the EIA, with recovery in the Geometric period. This generalization applies across the board, on Crete and on the mainland, regardless of the chronology preferred. Other subtleties of the trends apparent in the data depend on the chronological scheme utilized or the regional context. On Crete, those that adhere to a "low" chronology will see a dramatically steep drop off in import totals after the IIIB period on Crete to almost nothing compared with the situation on the mainland, and then a modest recovery in the PG period. According to a traditional chronology, the lull in import totals looks more consistent after 1200 or so. Regardless of some play in the data depending on how long we think these periods might have lasted, the general trend consistently shows an overall decrease in import totals by about half on a per annum basis after the end of the thirteenth century, with recovery in the ninth and eighth centuries.

This is an important point to establish. I will return to the significance of the figures, and their implications for our understanding of ancient economies, in Chapter 3. For now, I continue to explore the raw trends in the data. In addition to being fewer in number, are Dark Age imports different in kind from imports dated to the IIIB or the Geometric period? In what follows I provide a brief survey of diachronic changes in the import data. A more synthetic and interpretatively bold reading of these simple patterns follows in Chapter 6, once the context and background of the bare facts has been filled out, to allow for that kind of reading to hold its footing.

Map 2.1. Distribution of imports at sites on the mainland, LH IIIB – Geometric (by author)

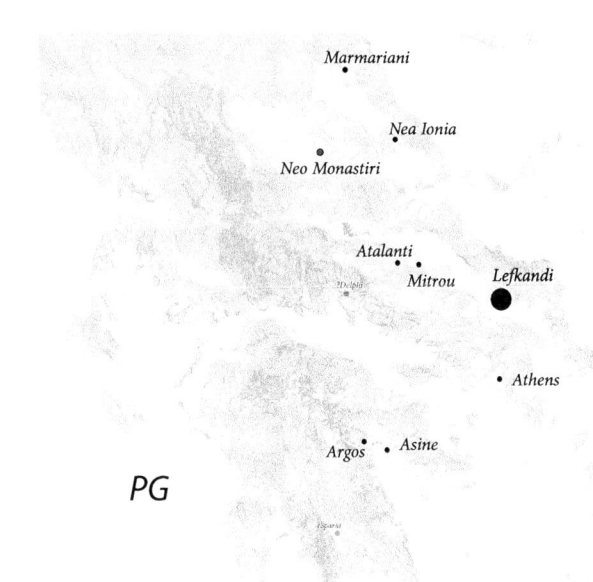

DIRECT EVIDENCE FOR LONG-DISTANCE EXCHANGE 119

Marmariani

Nea Ionia

Neo Monastiri

Atalanti
Mitrou *Lefkandi*

Athens

Argos *Asine*

PG

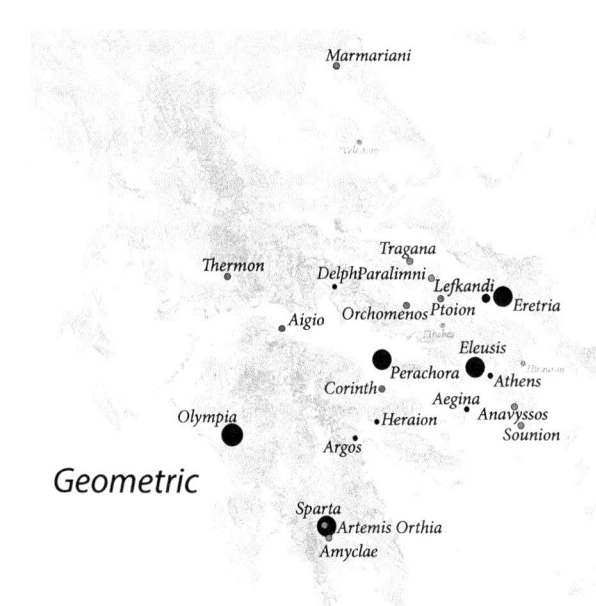

Marmariani

Tragana
Thermon *Delph* *Paralimni* *Lefkandi* *Eretria*
Aigio *Orchomenos* *Ptoion*
Eleusis
Perachora *Athens*
Corinth *Aegina*
Heraion *Anavyssos*
Olympia *Sounion*
Argos

Geometric

Sparta
Artemis Orthia
Amyclae

Map 2.1. (cont.)

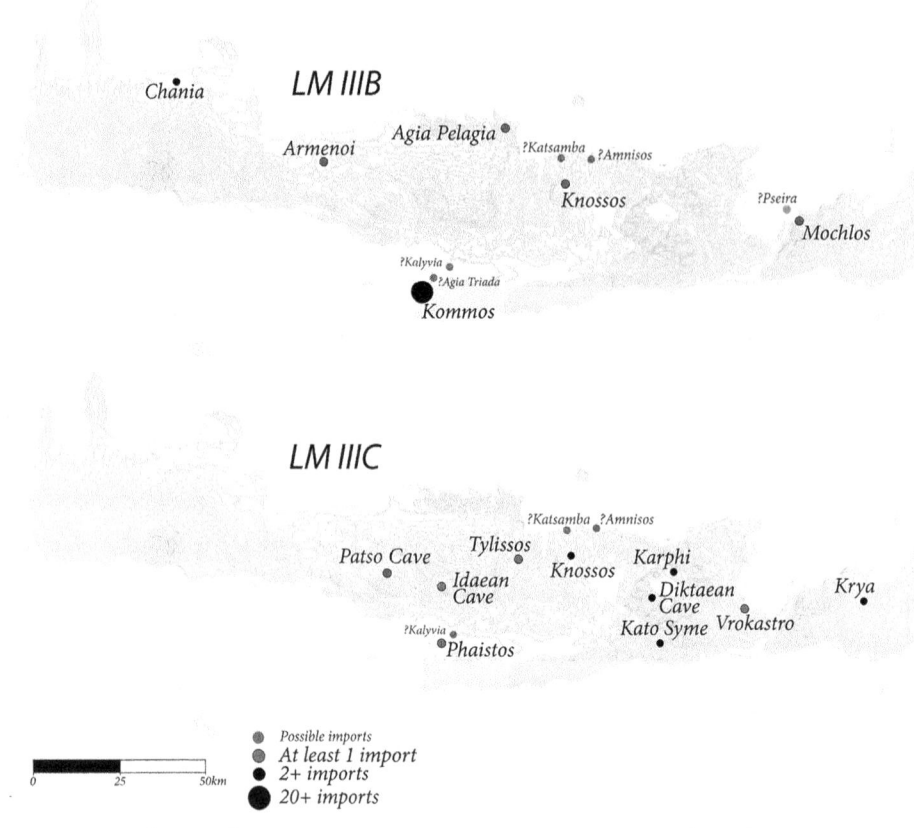

Map 2.2. Distribution of imports at sites on Crete, LM IIIB – Geometric (by author)

2.2.2. Change in Import Deposition Contexts: Context of Consumption and Geographical Patterns

While most securely-dated imports from the IIIB period were found in nonmortuary contexts,[180] and the same is true of Geometric imports,[181] most imports from the IIIC and PG periods come from mortuary contexts. Is this a significant pattern? On the mainland, the general distribution of site types in the total archaeological dataset[182] is comparable for the LH IIIB and LH IIIC periods (settlements comprise 22 and 20 percent of the dataset, respectively), so the trend toward mortuary deposition may be significant over the switch from

---

[180] In the discussion I use "nonmortuary" as a generic catchall term to refer to nonburial contexts. This avoids the necessity to draw hard lines between "cult spaces" and "domestic spaces," a division that is often ambiguous. I consider possible cult contexts for imports on a case-by-case basis, while using the general charts for archaeological context to simply distinguish between mortuary and nonmortuary deposition.

[181] For the Geometric period, the trends diverge between Crete and the mainland. On the mainland, 88 percent of G imports are found in sanctuaries, while Cretan imports are more evenly distributed, between mortuary (60 percent) and nonmortuary (40 percent) contexts.

[182] For full discussion of this dataset, see S. Murray 2013, 47–54; Chapter 3.

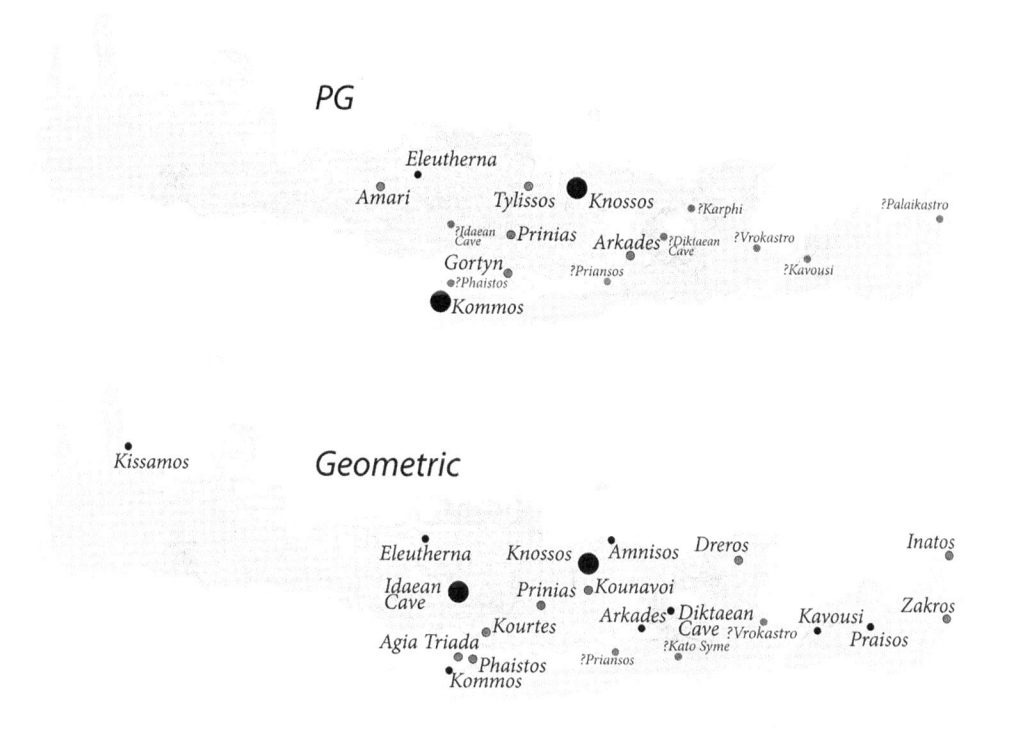

DIRECT EVIDENCE FOR LONG-DISTANCE EXCHANGE 121

PG

Eleutherna
Amari *Tylissos* *Knossos* *?Karphi* *?Palaikastro*
?Idaean Cave *Prinias* *Arkades* *?Diktaean Cave* *?Vrokastro*
Gortyn *?Priansos* *?Kavousi*
?Phaistos
Kommos

Kissamos *Geometric*

Eleutherna *Knossos* *Amnisos* *Dreros* *Inatos*
Idaean Cave *Prinias* *Kounavoi*
Kourtes *Arkades* *Diktaean Cave* *?Vrokastro* *Kavousi* *Zakros*
Agia Triada *?Kato Syme* *Praisos*
Phaistos *?Priansos*
Kommos

Map 2.2. (cont.)

LH IIIB to LH IIIC. In other words, there are enough known tombs from the IIIB period and enough known settlement contexts from the IIIC period to allow us to reasonably expect that if imports were commonly deposited in these contexts, we would have found more of them. One the other hand, we want to continue to keep in mind the fact that our chronological precision for dating finds from many tombs in the IIIB period is poor, especially for important sites like Mycenae, where many tombs were also looted before archaeologists could investigate them.

In the PG period on the mainland, imports are known almost exclusively from mortuary contexts. This might be the product of the archaeological record (the proportion of nonmortuary to mortuary deposits known from the PG mainland is relatively low, at 17 percent overall, an approximately 20 percent decrease from the IIIB and IIIC periods).[183] Most PG imports were found at sites in central Greece, and here (as opposed to the "global" dataset) only 14 percent (c. 17/119) of known PG sites are settlement deposits. This is certainly a low proportion

[183] See S. Murray 2015, 67, fig. 2.

suggesting that we do indeed lack a robust archaeological record for settlements in central Greece, but it does represent some evidence. We might expect that if imports existed in quantity in PG mainland settlement deposits, we might have found them somewhere. In addition, the representation of nonmortuary sites amongst Geometric sites and PG sites is identical at 17 percent, but deposition of imports in the Geometric period is documented from nonmortuary deposits. Overall, putting the contextual changes in import deposition within a larger dataset of the archaeological record suggests that there may have been real change from nonmortuary to mortuary contexts (and back) in import deposition over the transition from the Bronze to the Iron Age.

Of the LH IIIB imports found in settlement contexts, the majority were found in special circumstances of some sort or another, either in areas particularly set aside for the production of special equipment or valuable goods (Thebes "treasure room," the House of the Shields at Mycenae), in areas that are thought to be associated with cult or ritual activity (The Citadel House area, Mycenae acropolis), or in areas with intimations of both (Tiryns: metalworking/cult areas). Exceptions to this rule are the Canaanite jars in the lower citadel of Tiryns, but dating and interpreting these precisely is challenging.

The context of imports from the LH IIIC period is different. Imports continue to be found both in nonmortuary and mortuary contexts, though the distribution begins to tilt toward mortuary deposition. In settlements, the association between imported objects and workshop or cult spaces is not as pronounced as it had been in the IIIB period. At Mycenae, imports continue to cluster directly around the Citadel House area,. The carefully deposited Syrian armor scale underneath a hearth at Tiryns suggests that exotica retained ritual or cultic significance within Greece after the palatial collapse.[184] Many of the mortuary contexts from which imports have been recovered are located in western Greece, where imports are not plentiful from the IIIB period. The tombs containing imports do not particularly stand out, though the ones in Achaea fit in with the class of "warrior burials" which seem to indicate the rise of a new elite in the postpalatial period.[185] At Perati, the amuletic nature of many finds suggests some supernatural function of imports.

By the PG period, imports have disappeared almost entirely from nonmortuary contexts on the mainland. Most imports come from tombs; most of these tombs are located in the east and north of Greece rather than the west and south. West of the Isthmus, only Asine and Argos have yielded any PG imports at all, while on the eastern seaboard of Central Greece there are imports in Velestino, Neo Monastiri, Marmariani, and Nea Ionia in Thessaly, Atalanti and

---

[184] Maran 2004.
[185] Papazoglou-Manioudaki 1994; Kanta 2003; Deger-Jalkotzy 2006; Giannopoulos 2008. Tombs in IIIC were generally modest, according to Cavanagh and Mee 1998, 89–97.

Mitrou in East Lokris, and Lefkandi in Euboea. Most imports are found in tombs that are well furnished relative to the tombs in the cemeteries where they are located. At Lefkandi import access seems to correlate well with overall abundance of goods in tombs (see Figures 2.5–2.6), and at sites like Atalanti, the excavators noted particularly that the tombs containing imports were among the wealthiest in their respective cemeteries.[186]

Beginning in the ninth century, and rapidly becoming common in the eighth century, the practice of depositing imported objects in sanctuaries on the Greek mainland transforms the dataset dramatically. Most Geometric imports come from deposits in sanctuaries.[187] Compared to the limited geographical spread of imports in the PG period, the deposition of these objects is not concentrated in a particular region (that is, the Euboean gulf or the Argolid). The transfer of import deposition patterns from tombs or settlements to collective sanctuaries is clearly important, and confirms many previously stated notions about the ideological and political restructuring that were concomitant with broader developments in eighth century Greece.[188]

The distribution of imports on Crete is superficially comparable to that on the mainland, though there are important differences. Imports in the LM IIIB period are found primarily in nonmortuary contexts, while mortuary deposition attains parity in the LM IIIC (53 percent) and PG (52 percent) periods. In the Geometric period, imports on Crete are found in wealthy tombs like the ones at Knossos or Eleutherna and from nonmortuary sites like the port at Kommos, as well as at sanctuaries across the island. On Crete the ratio of mortuary and nonmortuary sites known from subphases throughout the Bronze-Iron Age transition is highly consistent (nonmortuary sites in the IIIB, IIIC, PG, and Geometric periods represent 22 percent, 19 percent, 19 percent, and 20 percent, respectively, of the overall number of known sites), so we can be relatively confident in the meaningful rather than random nature of these distributions. The great variety of depositional contexts, both geographically and typologically, of Cretan Geometric imports probably indicates that these objects were circulating relatively widely in eighth century Crete.[189]

---

[186] Dakoronia 2006.
[187] See Salmon 1984, 146 and Skon-Jedele 1994, 285–286 for a minimalist interpretation, that these objects arrived on only one or two shiploads.
[188] Research on the rise of sanctuaries in the eighth century is abundant. Some of the most relevant publications include Morgan 1996; Morgan 1997; Morgan 2003; Marakas 2010; Mazarakis Ainian 2001; de Polignac 1995; Sourvinou-Inwood 1993.
[189] In the Geometric period imports are found in eastern (at Zakros, Praisos, Kavousi, and Inatos) and western (Kissamos) Crete, whereas they had been concentrated in central Crete during the IIIB, IIIC, and PG periods. This pattern probably cannot be aligned to an increase in population in the west and east. The number of overall sites known from all regions of Crete is remarkably stable over the transition from the PG period to the G period. The site breakdown by region is as follows: Iraklio, ninty-seven in PG, ninty-eight in G; Lasithi

During LM IIIB, most imports on Crete consist of imported ceramics found at the harbor site of Kommos. Only a couple of other imported objects from Crete can be dated with confidence: five sherds from Chania (Italian and Cypriot), one seal from Armenoi, one Italian sherd from Agia Pelagia, and an Italian dagger from Knossos (Zafer Papoura). Suffice it to say that the archaeological record suggests that imports were not circulating widely in Crete during this period, even though Kommos must have constituted a participatory node in a pan-Mediterranean trade network with partners in Egypt, Anatolia, Cyprus, Syria-Palestine (maybe), and Italy. The picture changes in the LM IIIC period, when datable imports are smaller in number, plausibly due to the demise of a carry trade through Kommos, concomitant with the seeming abandonment of the site,[190] but more evenly distributed throughout the island's sites and cemeteries. Overall, in LM IIIC Crete, imports are found in sanctuaries, presumably as dedications to gods and in (generally) wealthy tombs. In later PG and Geometric Crete, imports return to Kommos, appear in increasing numbers in votive deposits at sacred caves, and continue to be deposited in wealthy tombs at Knossos. Due to the nature of the Knossos chamber tombs, which pile burials of many periods into individual chambers and have been much disturbed by looting and reuse, it is nearly impossible to make much sense of the distribution of the imports in the tombs. There are few differences between the patterns of contextual deposition in Geometric Cretan as opposed to PG patterns, except that imports become more widespread and greater in number

2.2.3. Function and Material of Imported Objects

On both Crete and on the mainland, vessels or containers (especially faience vessels and Canaanite jars) are the most common type of imports documented from the LB IIIB Period. The function of these objects in their original social context is likely to have been complicated – Canaanite jars evidently carried bulk agricultural produce of some kind to Greece, but may also have had carried symbolic capital: their distribution is limited and they are occasionally found in mortuary contexts.[191] The faience vessels at Mycenae and Tiryns come from contexts that suggest they were used in ritual or industrial practice.[192] Cretan imports during this period are almost entirely limited to the (mostly

---

seventy-six in PG, eighty-six in G; Rethymno twenty-three in PG, eighteen in G; Chania twelve in PG, twelve in G.

[190] J. Shaw 1998, 21.
[191] Canaanite jars, with bibliography, in Rutter 2014.
[192] See discussion of Tirynthian imports at Cohen, Maran and Vetters 2010; Vetters 2011; Brysbaert and Vetters 2010; Brysbaert and Vetters 2013. For a thorough description of the context of the imported finds at Mycenae, with bibliography, see Burns 2010b, 139–156. For the idea that these objects represent instead totems of elite interaction, van Wijngaarden 2011.

Italian) ceramics from Kommos, which have been conceptualized as the limited remaining evidence of a carry trade in agricultural commodities.[193] The function/use-value of the cache of seals from Thebes is unclear. Mitannian seals also appear in some chamber tombs.

In the LH IIIC period, Italian weapons and Cypriot and Near Eastern jewelry are the most commonly documented categories of exotica. The existence of ritual practice or individuals of nonlocal origin on the postpalatial Greek mainland is also suggested by the appearance of Syro-Palestinian armor scales deposited in special contexts at Tiryns and Kanakia, and amulets in the burials at Perati. Cypriot metalworkers may have been present at Tiryns in LH IIIC.[194] Offensive weapons from Italy discovered in western Greek contexts from the LH IIIC periods represent a new development in the import record in the twelfth century, and may attest to the rise of a new warrior elite or tightening social and political bonds with the west.

Faience jewelry (mostly beads) and bronze vessels are the only well-represented categories of import known from Protogeometric Greece, with the exception of the Phoenician jars at Kommos, which probably date to the end of the tenth century, if not later. The imported jewelry documented from PG Greece is almost entirely made up of faience or glass beads, with a few exceptions like the striking accoutrements of the woman buried with the *heroon* warrior at Lefkandi. On Crete, the LM IIIC and PG periods are a bit hard to parse from the point of view of import function, since many of the contexts are jumbled, but here too Italian and Cypriot imports, including weapons, and jewelry or bronze vessels are prominent in the records for the IIIC and PG periods.

In the Geometric period, further shifts in the nature of imported objects are apparent, and we see something of a composite corpus, representing aspects of the salient features of all other preceding periods, though often with important wrinkles. Containers (bronze vessels; Cypriot, Egyptian, and Phoenician pottery) form a sizable proportion of identified Geometric imports, but comprise a wide array of shapes, including amphorae and amphoriskoi, aryballoi, bowls, tripod cauldrons, flasks, jugs, lekythoi and pithoi, than imported vessels from previous periods. Likewise, just as seals formed a sizable fraction of recognized imports in both the IIIB and IIIC periods, scarabs and seals are the single most common category of imported object known from the Geometric period. Most of these seals and scarabs come from sanctuaries, and so discerning their functional use-value is not a straightforward process. Imported jewelry, including faience beads, ivory pins, and bronze fibulae are known from mortuary contexts dating to the the ninth and eighth centuries. An additional feature of

---

[193] Rutter 2006.
[194] Vetters 2011.

TABLE 2.11. *Function of imports (overall; some categories omitted)*

	IIIB	IIIC	PG	G
Vessel	145	19	56	147
Seals/Scarabs	54	17	4	166
Adornment	3	33	67	82
Figural Art	2	9	3	34
Arms	2	26	1	3

TABLE 2.12. *Material of imports (overall; some categories omitted)*

	IIIB	IIIC	PG	G
ceramic	112	12	35	80
stone	46	10	2	21
glass/faience	45	29	73	201
bronze	3	35	18	120
ivory	2	5	2	41
gold	–	14	2	5
iron	–	3	3	3

the Geometric import record is the appearance within it of small statues and figurines of foreign gods or goddesses.[195]

Diachronic changes in apparent import function are reemphasized by changes in the material of imports over time. Stone seals, Canaanite/Italian jars, and faience vessels in LB IIIB give way to Italian and Cypriot bronzes, Cypriot gold, glass/faience amulets, and stone weights in IIIC, then to glass/faience beads, Phoenician jars, and bronze bowls/vessels in PG, then a similar material distribution, with the addition of ivory objects of adornment and decoration in the Geometric period.

[195] Similar objects appear in LH IIIC graves at Perati, but otherwise these are largely unknown from the rest of the early Greek import corpus. For the novelty of Egyptianizing figures and figurines from the LH IIIC period, which may be related to their history of production in Egypt, see Hölbl 1987. Few such amulets occur on Cyprus (a couple of amulets from Late Cypriot IIIA:1 Enkomi (Jacobsson 1994, 55 nos. 300–301 and 91–94, cf. Peltenburg 1986)). They appear in the fourteenth through twelfth centuries at Megiddo, which suggested to Hölbl that they may have reached Greece in the hands of Syro-Palestinian traders rather than Egyptian ones. If true, this would obviate the claim of Deger-Jalkotzy (2002, 68) that the objects show direct contact between Egypt and Greece. For regular use of amulets in Egypt, see Sternberg 2004, 454. The only other (roughly) similar figurines from all of the LBA in the Aegean are a monkey figurine of Egyptian blue found on the Mycenae acropolis (LH IIIB2) (Cline 1994, 132, no. 5) and a similar monkey figurine from the citadel at Tiryns (LH IIIA) (Cline 1994, 132, no. 6). Possibly in the same category could belong a Serpentine figurine of a sphinx from MM III/LM I Ayia Triada (Cline 1994, 133, no. 10).

TABLE 2.13. *Origin of imported objects IIIB-G (some categories omitted)*

	IIIB	IIIC	PG	G
Syria-Palestine/Phoenicia	68	20	35	175
Italy	54	25	0	51
Cyprus	23	25	10	64
North Syria/Mesopotamia	23	2	1	46
Egypt	22	30	14	80
Anatolia	8	0	0	3
"Near East"	1	4	72	27

TABLE 2.14. *Origin of imports in West Greece, East Greece, and Crete*

Origin	IIIB	IIIC	PG	G
East Greece	3	13	1	7
West Greece	0	5	0	0
Crete	13	8	16	59
NE General				
East Greece	67	21	65	123
West Greece	1	0	0	63
Crete	18	4	47	70
Egypt				
East Greece	37	24	2	66
West Greece	3	0	0	6
Crete	4	3	5	27
Italy				
East Greece	2	3	0	7
West Greece	0	8	0	38
Crete	51	14	0	6

2.2.4. *Origin of Imported Objects*

It is not always possible to assign an area of origin for imported exotica.[196] Published data for the specific origin of imported objects categorizes most of these as Syro-Palestinian, Egyptian, Italian, and Cypriot throughout the

---

[196] This is especially an issue for imported faience objects dated to the PG and G periods, which are mostly assigned to the Near East generally, and for imported scarabs from the G period, which are most likely Phoenician-made, but could in some cases be Egyptian. Bibliography on the scarabs and other faience and glass objects from early Crete includes Stampolidis 1998 (distribution and agents for movement in EIA Crete); Webb in Coldstream and Catling 1996, 609–610 (Fortetsa and Crete); Banou 2002, 313; Hoffman 1997, 135–137; Stampolidis 2003, 70–75. There has been less intensive study of these items on the mainland, although see the review in Gorton 1996.

Bronze-Iron Age transition. Pottery from Anatolia is known only from Kommos during the LM IIIB period, and Mesopotamian seals come particularly from Thebes in the LH IIIB period and from Crete in the Geometric period. It appears that interaction with Italy was most intense in West Greece and Crete. The apparent cessation of trade with Italy during the PG period (or the lack of imported objects discovered) might be related to the fact that West Greece in particular appears to have been more significantly affected by depopulation after the end of the LBA.[197] Trade with Italy may have depended on participation from Greeks in Achaea[198] and Messenia, and thus was not sustainable when these areas were depopulated. On the other hand, we may simply lack evidence for trade between Italy and western Greece from this period because we have not done a good job of finding Peloponnesian Protogeometric sites.

Interactions between Greece and Egypt appear to have been locally particularized in the East part of the mainland and in Crete throughout the periods under study. Cypriots look like they had stronger ties with Cretans than with mainlanders, with the exception of the community of Lefkandi. In the Geometric period deposition of Near Eastern imports in the western portions of the mainland is a new pattern not evident in the archaeological record from the preceding several centuries.

2.3. CONCLUSIONS

One of the goals of this book is to establish that there was significant change in the Greek trade economy across the LBA–EIA transition, both quantitatively and in terms of the structures, institutions, and individuals driving long-distance trade relations. The first place to start in establishing this position is to square it with the most obvious and direct category of evidence that we have for the Greek trade economy during this period: identified imported objects. This evidence is problematic, but because it is the most direct indicator of long-distance exchange that we have in the archaeological record, it must be taken into account.

---

[197] The dramatic decrease in the number of documented sites in the western Peloponnese is striking after the IIIC period. Region by region, the breakdown is as follows: Achaea, fifty-one IIIC sites, fourteen PG sites, forty G sites; Arkadia, seven IIIC sites, six PG sites, twenty G sites; Elis, twenty-six IIIC sites, twelve PG sites; seventeen G sites; Messenia, twenty-three IIIC sites, twenty-five PG sites; nineteen G sites. This distribution of sites may be a product of any number of factors, including the difficulty with which local pottery styles in the PG in these regions are defined, and so the conclusion that a severance of some kind in West Greek/Italian exchanges could have been based on depopulation must remain tentative for now. See Tanasi 2010a for possible continuing connections between Crete and Malta in the EIA.

[198] Eder 2006, 557.

Even reading this evidence with a skeptical eye, we can see some indications that there was meaningful change along a number of different quantitative and qualitative axes between 1300 and 700 BCE. Archaeologists have identified about half as many imports from contexts dating to the IIIC and PG periods as they have from contexts dating to the LB IIIB period. The number of imported objects identified from Geometric contexts is larger than any other period under study here. While it might be possible to maintain that a decrease in the known number of a category of evidence from the archaeological record by half does not represent significant, meaningful change in an assemblage, this would require special pleading. Likewise, the degree of diachronic variation in the qualitative attributes of identified imported objects constitutes compelling evidence to suggest that some aspects of exchange networks changed significantly during the period under study here. In each period I have singled out for study here, import deposition patterns are distinct. In the LBA there is a concentration in and around palaces. In the IIIC and PG period east Greek cemeteries have produced the most exotica. In the Geometric period, sanctuary deposits are rich in imports. Within these broad patterns, there exists a diverse array of subtrends and locally specific variations (summarized in Figure 2.6). It is not obvious to me how these patterns could have come about if the trade system were characterized by stability in structure, purpose, and extent between 1300 and 700 BCE.

In sum, a straightforward reading of the most *direct* category of evidence for change in the Greek long-distance exchange economy after the end of the LBA would lead us to rapidly conclude there is both quantitative and qualitative systemic change on a variety of axes. However, given the fact that we are dealing with a highly contingent assemblage of evidence documented over many generations by archaeological practitioners within different subfields of archaeology, working in a variety of practical and historical contexts, reading the evidence in a straightforward way would be inappropriate. In Chapters 3, 4, and 5, I seek to interrogate the basic reliability of the patterns evident in the import data, and to contextualize that data against a thick carpet of corroborating material, so that we may reconstruct the economic context of the LBA–EIA transition with more confidence than a simple assessment of imported objects allows.

THREE

ASSESSING QUANTITATIVE CHANGE IN THE ARCHAEOLOGICAL RECORD

How much can we really say about quantitative change in an archaeological record that is deeply contingent and reliant upon the whims of archaeologists for its existence?[1] While it is clear from the evidence laid out in the preceding chapter that archaeologists have documented fewer imports from the PG and IIIC periods than they have from the G and IIIB periods, we have a long way to go before we can agree that these numerical changes reflect changes in ancient realities with any fidelity. In this chapter, I consider the possibility that the import record is seriously distorted by factors of archaeological practice and taphonomy, before testing the distortions I detect against other evidence that might confirm or deny their existence in Chapters 4 and 5.

Do larger or smaller quantities of known imports really indicate scalar change in trade in the past? To the extent that exchanged objects represent the clearest surviving and identifiable archaeological correlate of long-distance exchange, it is important to consider why they appear, when, where, and in the quantities that they do.[2] The quantitative trends might indicate that trade decreased in scale and intensity after the Mycenaean collapse, with recovery again in the Geometric period. But we need to think very carefully about the evidence before drawing this conclusion. In this chapter, I interrogate a number of

---

[1] See, recently, Lucas 2013, a book that has had a profound impact on my own reading of the "archive" that the archaeological record represents.
[2] Blench 1982; Bloch and Parry 1989; Oka and Kusimba 2008, 340.

factors other than change in the scale of trade networks that could account for the trends in quantitative evidence laid out in Chapter 2. First, I test whether the fluctuation in import counts from one period to the next is likely to be random. Second, I investigate whether it is likely that an historical bias against the investigation of post-Mycenaean sites might have resulted in lower cumulative import totals from IIIC and PG sites. Third, I determine whether different practices in counting imports among LBA and EIA archaeologists respectively might be affecting the import counts. Finally, I consider whether the change in the nature of trade goods between the LBA and EIA might be impacting the impression made by the import counts. In the end, I conclude that the evidence is so problematic and prone to distortions of all kinds that inferences about scalar change in trade systems cannot be made based on import quantities alone. While imported objects can tell us some things about how trade systems worked, we must look beyond imports to tell a convincing story of the Greek trade economy after the Mycenaean collapse.

3.1. ARE THE DIFFERENCES IN IMPORT COUNTS FROM PERIOD TO PERIOD STATISTICALLY SIGNIFICANT?

One characteristic of the evidence of Greek imports from all periods is consistent rarity. Among scholars of exchange in the ancient Aegean, this rarity has caused significant head scratching and wrought a debate between minimalists – who believe that Greeks were never deeply involved in intense, regular trade relationships with the wider Mediterranean – and maximalists, who believe that the imports we have represent a tiny fragment of the original quantity of traded goods, which would have been substantial.[3] This debate is thought-provoking. It calls attention to the many difficulties confronting us when we try to find meaning in quantities from the archaeological record. But even before moving onto this intellectual conundrum, it is important to consider some basic circumstances surrounding the number of imports we have counted. First, when approaching imported objects as an indicator of change through time, we must confront the distribution of the evidence. Because the absolute numeric differences between known imports from each period are small, and because exceptional sites often account for a large percentage of imported objects, we can easily imagine that the discovery of one new site with an exceptional number of imported objects would change the patterns laid out in Chapter 2 significantly. Archaeologists cannot give up on identifying patterns simply because they might be altered by any new discovery. However, when dealing with numbers as small as those we have in the import corpus, this is a serious concern.

---

[3] Snodgrass 1991; Cline 2010; Manning and Hulin 2005; Summary in Tartaron 2013, 23–27.

Even more elementary, however, is a basic question of whether the differences in the numbers as they exist now is likely to be random or meaningful. In other words, are the numbers that we see in Table 2.7 likely to vary due to random chance, or are they potentially the result of real variation within a reasonable range of error from a mean quantity of imports per year? This question is worth asking because the numbers involved are so small. If the change in import quantities over time is not statistically significant, then we effectively have no reason, at least based on recognized imports, to hypothesize a decline in trade after the IIIB period.

While not common in archaeological publications, tests of statistical significance are a standard tool used to determine whether differences noted in observed data are likely to have occurred randomly if the source "populations" represented by those observations were in fact equal. In the case of imports, it is practical to use the notion of confidence levels or intervals to make some basic inquiries into the observed differences between import quantities in the IIIB–G periods. The confidence interval for an observed quantity expresses the range of numbers within which differences would not be considered meaningful. In other words, within a small corpus of data like known imports from Greece, minor differences in observed numbers from period to period could be totally random, rather than meaningful, and the 95 percent confidence interval gives us a range of numbers outside of which change is not likely to be random. In essence, the test is designed to determine whether or not observed quantitative changes in imports signify anything. Using statistics, we can also calculate a probability value (p value) for the "null hypothesis" that the distribution of imports among different periods underlies a truly random distribution among periods without real meaning. Conventionally, a probability test is thought to disprove the null hypothesis when the p value is below 0.05.

I have used a chi-squared test of statistical significance in order to calculate a p value for the import quantities laid out in Chapter 2. In conducting a chi-squared test, both observed and expected frequencies are required inputs. Since my null hypothesis assumes that the known imports from 1300–700 BCE in Greece were distributed randomly through time, and that the counts given in Chapter 2 are meaningless, I input the expected frequency as the number of imports we would have expected to find in a given period if these were distributed evenly through time. That is to say, I set up the test to answer the question: if the number of imported objects from these four periods were in fact equal, what is the probability that we would observe the distribution laid out in Chapter 2?

According to the outcomes of the chi-squared test, the overall distribution of imports among the IIIB, IIIC, PG, and G periods is unlikely to be random. The chance that the null hypothesis is correct, given the actual distribution of the data, is close to zero, making the distribution of imports overall extremely

TABLE 3.1. *Data used for chi-squared test of statistical significance*

Mainland

Total Imports (assuming my "weighted average" quantities): 654

Traditional Chronology distribution of years/period: IIIB: 125yrs/21%; IIIC: 125yrs/21%; PG: 150yrs/25%; G: 200yrs/33%

Expected distribution of imports: IIIB: 137; IIIC: 137; PG: 164; G: 216

Chi squared equals 255.761 with 3 degrees of freedom

Low Chronology distribution of years/period: IIIB: 110yrs/18%; IIIC: 175yrs/29%; PG 115yrs/19%; G: 200yrs/33%

Expected distribution of imports: IIIB: 117; IIIC: 190; PG: 124; G: 215

Chi squared equals 256.539 with 3 degrees of freedom.

The two-tailed *p* value is less than 0.0001

Crete

Total Imports (assuming my "weighted average" quantities): 405

Traditional Chronology distribution of years/period: IIIB: 110yrs/18%; IIIC: 230yrs/38%; PG: 160yrs/26%; G: 110yrs/18%

Expected distribution of imports: IIIB: 73; IIIC: 154; PG; 105; G: 73

Chi squared equals 240.118 with 3 degrees of freedom

The two-tailed *p* value is less than 0.0001

Low Chronology distribution of years/period: IIIB: 110yrs/18%; IIIC: 245yrs/41%; PG 135yrs/22%; G: 110yrs/18%

Expected distribution of imports: IIIB: 73; IIIC: 166; PG: 89; G: 73

Chi squared equals 242.299 with 3 degrees of freedom.

The two-tailed *p* value is less than 0.0001

significant in statistical terms. However, this does not necessarily tell us that the variation in known import quantities from period to period over each individual transition is necessarily significant. For this assessment we may turn to confidence intervals, which allow us to calculate, within a given population, an interval wherein variation is likely to be random.

For example, the 95 percent confidence interval for a total of 132 imports (the "weighted middle" for all LH IIIB imports) in our corpus of 654 mainland imports is between 113 and 154, meaning that any number within these brackets might be likely to represent an equivalent original "population" of imports, at least 95 percent of the time. So if we knew of 115 imports from the IIIC period and 132 from the IIIB period, we ought to assume that this small difference is due to random variation rather than indicative of a small decrease in imports. In the import dataset, the cumulative weighted totals for the IIIC, PG, and G periods, at 89, 69, and 364, respectively, fall outside of this range, suggesting that the difference between import totals from the IIIB and later periods is significant.[4] Given this result, we could accept the notion that these

---

[4] All confidence intervals were calculated according to the modified Wald method recommended in Agresti and Coull 1998, 119–126.

TABLE 3.2. *95 percent confidence intervals for IIIB raw import counts: Cumulative, mainland, and Crete*

	IIIB 95% CI	IIIC Imports	PG Imports	G Imports
Overall	202–256	136	152	543
Mainland	113–154	89	69	364
Crete	80–114	47	83	179

TABLE 3.3. *Example of extrapolation from actual data into approximate 200-year totals for each period, assuming a hypothetical accumulation of imports at observed p/a rates for each period*

Traditional chronology (mainland)				
	Imports	Years	p/a rate	200 Year Approx.
IIIB	132	125	1.1	220
IIIC	89	125	.7	140
PG	69	150	.45	90
G	364	200	1.8	360
Low chronology (mainland)				
	Imports	Years	p/a rate	200 year approx.
IIIB	132	110	1.2	240
IIIC	89	175	.5	100
PG	67	115	.6	120
G	364	200	1.8	360

counts do represent some real change in the quantity of imports over time, rather than random variation.

However, once again, we need to modify these results, keeping in mind that some periods were longer than others according to our (admittedly vague) understanding of the relevant absolute chronology. Since the Geometric period, for instance, was probably significantly longer than the IIIB period, it is problematic to compare import quantities for these periods directly. In the calculations that follow, I correct for this using simple arithmetic to come up with hypothetical but probably realistic equivalencies for import totals. Going back to the basic quantitative data, I use the per annum "rates" of import deposition as a hypothetical metric for calculating equivalent import totals under the assumption that each period could be stretched out to equal 200 years (examples in Table 3.3). So, we can imagine that if 2.0 imports per year were deposited in IIIB contexts, after 200 years we would have 400 imports from this period, a number that could then be compared fairly with the totals from the approximately 200-year-long Geometric period. Comparing these

TABLE 3.4. *95 percent confidence intervals for IIIB import counts: Mainland*

	IIIB 95% CI	IIIC Imports	PG Imports	G Imports
Traditional Chronology	196–246	140	90	360
Low Chronology	215–266	100	120	360

TABLE 3.5. *95 percent confidence intervals for IIIC import counts: Mainland*

	IIIC 95% CI	IIIB Imports	PG Imports	G Imports
Traditional Chronology	120–162	220	90	360
Low Chronology	83–120	240	120	360

TABLE 3.6. *95 percent confidence intervals for PG import counts: Mainland*

	PG 95% CI	IIIB Imports	IIIC Imports	G Imports
Traditional Chronology	74–109	220	140	360
Low Chronology	100–140	240	100	360

TABLE 3.7. *95 percent confidence intervals for G import counts: Mainland*

	G 95% CI	IIIB Imports	IIIC Imports	PG Imports
Traditional Chronology	333–388	220	140	80
Low Chronology	332–388	240	100	140

TABLE 3.8. *95 percent confidence intervals for IIIB import counts: Crete*

	IIIB 95% CI	IIIC Imports	PG Imports	G Imports
Traditional Chronology	159–203	40	100	320
Low Chronology	159–203	40	120	320

TABLE 3.9. *95 percent confidence intervals for IIIC import counts: Crete*

	IIIC 95% CI	IIIB Imports	PG Imports	G Imports
Traditional Chronology	30–54	180	100	320
Low Chronology	30–54	180	120	320

TABLE 3.10. *95 percent confidence intervals for PG import counts: Crete*

	PG 95% CI	IIIB Imports	IIIC Imports	G Imports
Traditional Chronology	83–119	180	40	320
Low Chronology	102–140	180	40	320

TABLE 3.11. *95 percent confidence intervals for G import counts: Crete*

	G 95% CI	IIIB Imports	IIIC Imports	PG Imports
Traditional Chronology	295–345	180	40	100
Low Chronology	286–334	180	40	120

approximate hypothetical import totals along this line of reasoning allows us to get a sense of statistical significance using confidence intervals.

In Tables 3.4–3.11, I repeat this exercise for the two macroregions into which I have sorted the import data (the mainland and Crete), using each period as the benchmark in turn to see how import totals do or do not vary meaningfully across the other three periods. A shaded entry indicates that this count is *not* statistically significant compared to the benchmark. When we divide up the data into its constituent regions, and modify the raw import figures to make comparison among time periods of differing length possible, we see that for the most part a null hypothesis positing complete insignificance of the trends apparent in the import data cannot be sustained. Despite the small corpus of imports known from early Greece, their distribution through time does not appear to be random, although meaningful variation on the mainland from IIIC to PG is questionable. We can, then, move forward with our analysis confident that the fluctuations we see in the imports as they have been catalogued and dated by other archaeologists and by myself in Chapter 2 are, at a basic level, statistically significant.

3.2. IS IT LIKELY THAT THE HISTORY OF ARCHAEOLOGICAL EXCAVATION AND/OR THE DIFFERENT NATURE OF LBA AND EIA REMAINS, RATHER THAN REAL TRENDS, ACCOUNT FOR THE PATTERNS IN THE DATA?

With these tests completed, it is possible to move on to more complex interrogations of the quantitative evidence. Even if the differences in total estimated import counts from period to period are statistically significant, this does not necessarily mean that they accurately resemble past trends.

Discovery of Sites in the Twentieth Century

One important possible source of distortion in the data could be a historical bias in the investment of archaeological resources. That is to say, we could know of fewer imports from IIIC and PG sites because we have spent less time and effort investigating sites from those periods, not because fewer of them existed in Greece between 1200 and 900 BCE.[5] Given the history of archaeological practice in prehistoric Greece, this seems like an entirely plausible scenario, and must be seriously investigated before the import counts from Chapter 2 can be accepted as meaningful.

The late stages of the Greek Bronze Age were the focus of the earliest excavations in Greece and continue to be the subject of much scholarly attention, while periods following the collapse of the LBA palatial culture were not intensively studied until the 1970s and 1980s.[6] Could this disciplinary history account for the fact that we know of fewer imports from the EIA than from the LBA? In order to answer this question, it is useful to have a sense of the rate of discovery of palatial, postpalatial, Protogeometric, and Geometric sites over the course of the twentieth century.[7] If the rate of discovery of EIA sites changed significantly in the last few decades of the twentieth century, this might be an indication that archaeologists ignored EIA material before that, and that EIA material is therefore underrepresented in the archaeological record.

However, as I have shown elsewhere[8] plotting the discovery of sites that archaeologists have discovered since the beginning of the twentieth century shows good correlation for the curves of sites from all phases across the LBA to EIA transition.[9] This suggests that the rate of discovery of EIA sites is not increasing at a pace that is significantly greater than the rate of discovery of IIIB sites, that archaeologists have done their job and recorded EIA sites with fidelity throughout the twentieth century, and that the ratio of IIIB/G and IIIC/PG sites will not change significantly in the near future.

LBA versus EIA Sites

So the history of archaeological excavation suggests that the difference between the amount of known material culture from each phase is not the result of biases in archaeological practices during the twentieth century. Still, there could be

---

[5] Morgan 2006, 237, n. 25.
[6] Early major syntheses include Snodgrass 1971; Desborough 1972; Coldstream 2003a.
[7] Table 8.1 in I. Morris 2007, 213 (based on Snodgrass 1993, 30) suggests that the rate of discovery of EIA sites has picked up since 1970. This data does not alone indicate that archaeologists are prioritizing EIA sites, because discovery of all sites (i.e. the rate of archaeological fieldwork) has increased in the aggregate in the same period.
[8] See S. Murray 2013, 54–57; 2015; forthcoming b.
[9] See curve of discovery and analysis in Murray 2015, 56–57, fig. 1.3–1.4; see also discussion of data in Murray forthcoming b.

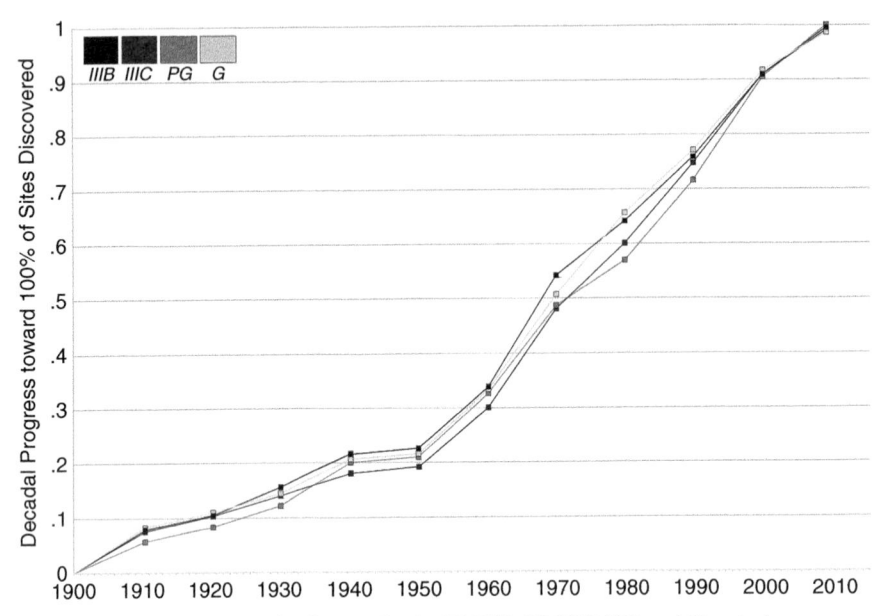

Figure 3.1. Accumulation of arch. sites for the LB IIIB, LB IIIC, PG, and G periods, 1900–2015 (by author)

some other reason that we do not find existing PG material even though we are looking for it. Some scholars argue that the small number of known sites dating to the EIA is a result of the way that archaeologists go about their work, focusing on concentrated settlements rather than small-scale dwellings scattered throughout an agricultural landscape. If the latter settlement pattern were more representative of the PG, then we might be missing large numbers of the earlier EIA population.[10] If this were true, and if we were missing material because it is not concentrated in settlements, we might expect PG sites to score well in archaeological surveys, where archaeologists look for cultural material that is spread around in the landscape. This does not appear to be the case. Though I have not included the data for all archaeological surveys in my site database, the ratio of IIIB/PG sites found by surveys that I have sampled is more than 3:1, higher than the overall ratio of IIIB/PG sites of something in the range of 3:2. In addition, the percentage of all known PG sites known from surface finds in the countryside is not inordinately high.

In general, areas that have been more intensively surveyed (Central Greece, the Peloponnese) have even higher ratios of LBA to PG sites than areas with less intensive survey history (Thessaly, West Greece), so I hypothesize that the

[10] Papadopoulos (1996, 254) argues that many EIA sites remain undocumented because most eleventh century inhabitants moved out of concentrated settlements and into the countryside. Dietz (1982, 102) likewise believes that much of the EIA population is archaeologically invisible because individuals lived near their agricultural plots rather than grouping together in communities during this period.

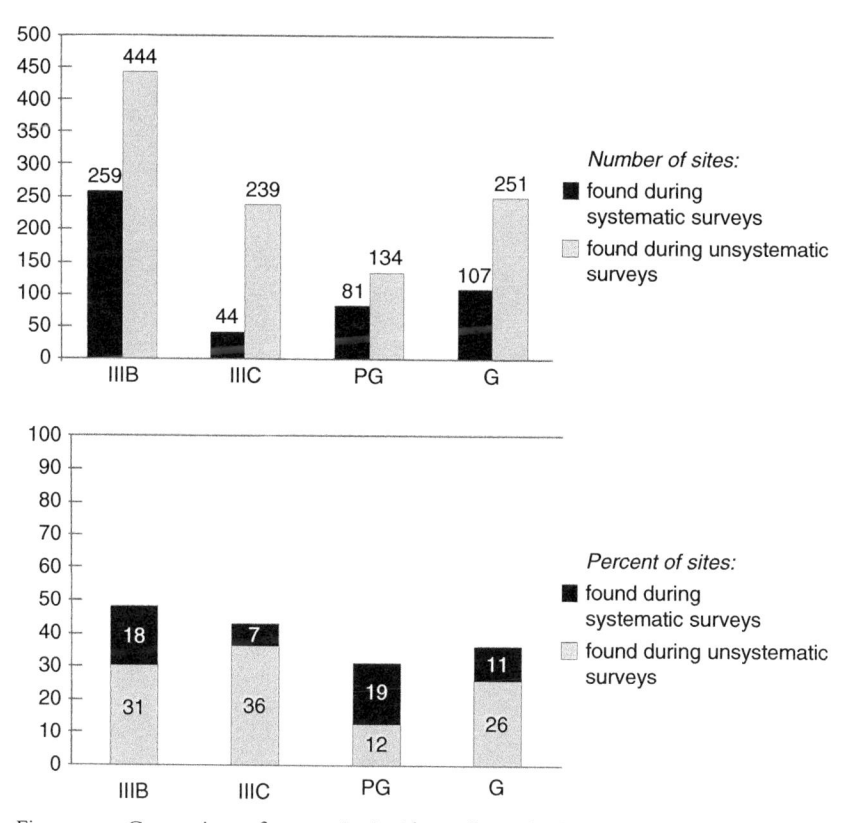

Figure 3.2. Comparison of survey site incidence (by author)

inclusion of more survey data would push the ratio of IIIB/G to IIIC/PG sites higher rather than the other way around.

At first glance, then, it does not appear that we are missing a great deal of EIA material that is spread around in the countryside. Are there other reasons that we could be misreading the survey evidence? We know that pottery from different periods survives through time at different rates.[11] If IIIC and PG ceramics were hard to detect or easily destroyed in the plough soil, we would expect to see little of this material in any survey results. However, we do find this material from some surveys. Overall, 31 percent of all known PG sites come from the identification of artifacts in either intensive or extensive surveys.

---

[11] Rutter 1983. See comments also in Foxhall 1995 on the possibility of confusing PG pottery with later black glaze ware. This seems unlikely, since black glaze is far shinier than PG material, and is painted both inside and outside. Another possibility is distortion based on the famous "wet biscuit" phenomenon (Bintliff, Howard, and Snodgrass 1999, 164), but PG fineware sherds are not likely to crumble in surveyors' hands. This problem is far more likely to impact counts for prehistoric periods, especially the EH and MH. Most compelling is the idea that PG Greeks may have been too poor to acquire much pottery, and the lack of PG material in survey reflects a time of decreased consumption of pottery rather than depopulation.

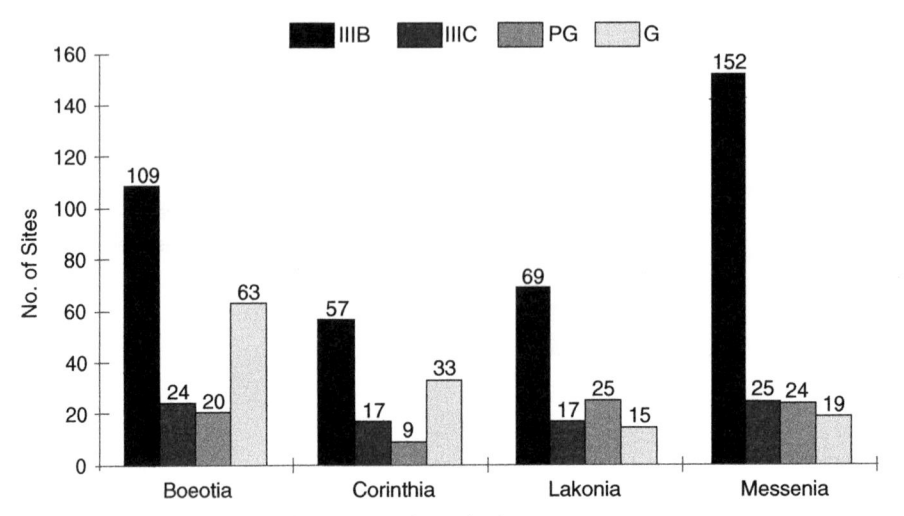

Figure 3.3. Surface finds in select regions (by author)

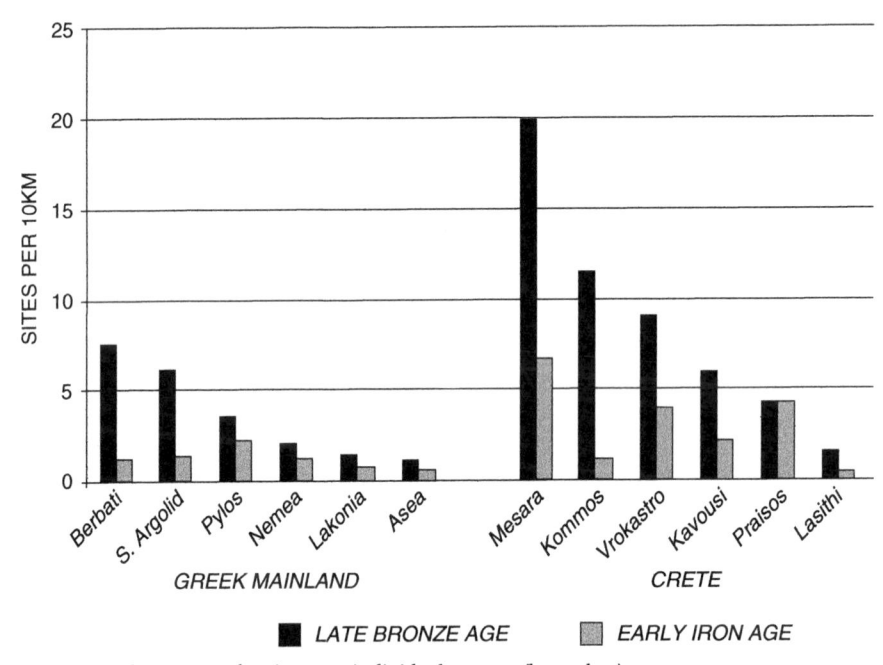

Figure 3.4. Sites per 10 km in some individual surveys (by author)

In some areas, like the Skourta plain survey, PG material was found, but Geometric finds were almost nonexistent.[12] We should deduce, based on the clear regional variation in survey data, that our methods are doing a decent job of picking this up when it exists.

---

[12] Munn and Munn 1989.

TABLE 3.12. *Distribution of IIIB–G sites by type, absolute numbers and percentages*

		IIIB	IIIC	PG	G
Settlements	#	306	132	95	166
	%	22	20	17	17
Cemeteries	#	450	205	245	332
	%	33	31	40	35
Artifacts	#	610	318	260	450
	%	45	49	43	48

Another possibility is that we do not have many EIA sites because the remains of PG settlements are flimsy and do not tend to survive to be discovered.[13] If this were the case, we would expect tombs to dominate the archaeological record for EIA Greece. That is to say, if settlements from the EIA do not survive well, or if most EIA people were transhumant pastoralists who left little in the way of settlement remains behind, we would end up knowing most about the EIA from cemeteries, suggesting that we are missing EIA settlement material. In order to get a better sense of whether or not this is true, I have broken down known sites according to Type (Settlement, Settlement/Cemetery, Isolated Tomb, or Artifacts) (Table 3.12). According to this distribution, approximately the same proportion of IIIB, PG, and G sites consist of artifacts only.[14] These are sites known from survey, or sites where only sherds or some other datable artifacts have been found, in the absence of architectural remains or burials. The proportion of sites where archaeologists have found stratified architectural remains is slightly higher for IIIB and IIIC sites than it is for EIA sites. Likewise, the percentage of cemeteries known from the PG period is, as a total percentage of the data, high relative to the percentages from the IIIB, IIIC, and G periods. These differences confirm the notion, long-recognized, that archaeologists find more PG cemeteries than they do PG settlements. The difference between the percentage of IIIB Settlements (21 percent) and PG Settlements (17 percent) is significant, suggesting that we may in fact be missing some of the settlement evidence for the EIA due to taphonomic factors or issues of archaeological priorities that continue to this day, despite the recent surge in popularity of the EIA as an area of study.

---

[13] Mazarakis Ainian 1997, 100.
[14] Though note that there are many subtleties of the data masked in this apparent uniformity. For instance, in IIIB, most of these artifact-only sites (87 percent) are surface scatters, while PG ones are a mix between excavated deposits (40 percent) and surface scatters (60 percent). There is regional variation here as well, though unfortunately it is not possible to delve into the nuanced characteristics of the data in the current context. See expanded discussion in S. Murray forthcoming b.

142 COLLAPSE OF THE MYCENAEAN ECONOMY

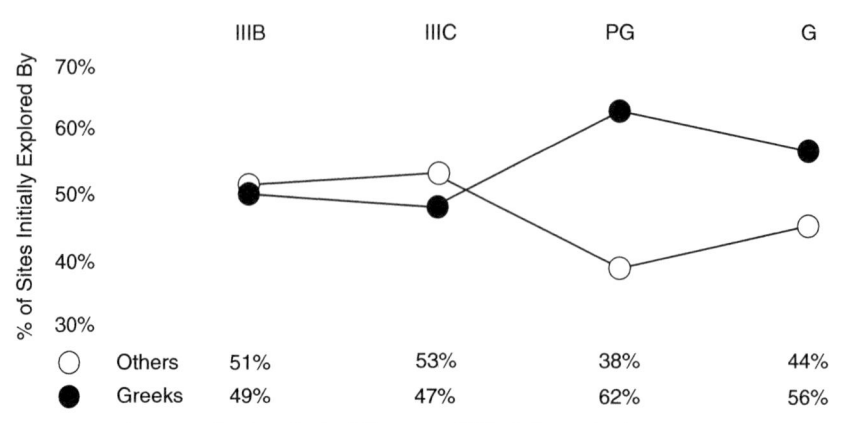

	IIIB	IIIC	PG	G
Others	51%	53%	38%	44%
Greeks	49%	47%	62%	56%

Figure 3.5. Agency of archaeological discovery, IIIB-G (by author)

However, the differences in the "data demographies" between IIIB and PG/G are not as huge as one might expect, based on the general impressions stated in current scholarship. Based on the data, I do not consider it likely that the differences are large enough to account for the overall 2:1 ratio of Mycenaean settlement sites to PG settlement sites observed in the total dataset. In general, the remarkable similarity of site-type distribution between all four of these periods strongly suggests that we have a comparable, if not totally equivalent, knowledge base for each.

If so many PG settlement deposits exist, why do we still have the pervasive sense that the EIA record is so impoverished in settlement evidence? One possible explanation for the dissonance is suggested in the data – an unusually high number of PG settlement deposits consist of modest structures, found in rescue excavations and published primarily in Greek. We may not be aware of their existence because these publications are often not available in marginal library collections.

Summary

Based on various lines of inquiry, we can conclude with some confidence that the limited number of imports known from post-Mycenaean, pre-Geometric sites is not the result of the longer and more intensive history of archaeological exploration for the earlier and later periods, or of a systematic bias by archaeologists who ignore EIA material in favor of more glamorous periods.[15] Neither does it look like the nature of EIA sites is distorting the data in ways that would prevent us from reading the import record in a (relatively) straightforward way.

---

[15] The conclusion is based on a simple, overall evaluation of an incomplete database. There are interesting microtrends in this dataset, which shows variation between regions, and the dataset could usefully be expanded to include more chronological periods (especially IIIA), but for the purposes of answering the question under consideration here, the overall trend apparent in thousands of identified site components should be sufficient.

3.3. IS IT LIKELY THAT DIFFERENT WAYS OF COUNTING IMPORTS IN DIFFERENT PERIODS ACCOUNT FOR THE PATTERNS IN THE DATA?

Even if we do have a reasonably even and fair record of LBA and EIA sites and material, there are other factors of disciplinary practice that could be affecting the counts of imports from various periods. This is especially true because comparing IIIB/IIIC and PG/G material involves comparing archaeological evidence from sites on both sides of a Bronze Age/Iron Age subdisciplinary divide.[16] Most Aegean Bronze Age archaeologists do not work on periods following the decline of the Mycenaean palaces and the final disappearance of Minoan and Mycenaean cultural indicators (around 1100 BCE). Likewise, archaeologists who work on the EIA have historically tended to approach the period from the viewpoint of the later Archaic and Classical periods rather than from the preceding Bronze Age cultures, which they see as culturally disconnected from their subject. It is possible, therefore, that discrepancies in the way that researchers define and count imports across these subdisciplinary boundaries might affect the number of imports that have been catalogued and identified.

Import Catalogs

Much of the import data presented here has been compiled from previous studies, each representing the work of a different scholar with different expertises and intentions. It is therefore worth considering whether disciplinary backgrounds or varying agendas might have led scholars to compile import catalogues according to different standards or different definitions of what ought to be included and excluded. If we discover that this were the case, it would cast serious doubts on the reliability of any quantitative data resulting from a synthetic comparison.

Cline gives his definition of imports as "objects of foreign origin that have been found in the ... Aegean area."[17] Neither Jones nor Lemos give explicit definitions for imports.[18] However, it is apparent that all three count as imports only objects that were made into finished objects abroad and then transported into Greece, and do not cover all objects made of or including foreign material resources.[19] In making my additions to the catalog, I adopted the same approach, and counted only objects that were manufactured as finished goods outside of Greece. There is, therefore, no insuperable obstacle to comparing

---

[16] Snodgrass 1987; Coulsen 1990; S. Morris 1995; I. Morris 1997a; 2000; Dialismas 2004; Knodell 2013; Kotsonas 2016.
[17] Cline 1994, xvi.
[18] Jones lists his interest as simply "apparently exotic artifacts in datable contexts" (Jones 2000, 1). Lemos (2002, 226–227) provides an appendix of "Near Eastern Imports".
[19] Cline also lists foreign commodities found on the Uluburun ship, such as tusks and ingots, but keeps them separate from the finished objects.

LBA and EIA imports due to differences in the fundamental definition of "import" across the relevant object catalogs.

As discussed previously (n. 312), Rutter's latest work revised the list of imports from Kommos in Cline's catalog and Rahmstorf has shown that the wall brackets from Tiryns, originally thought to be imports, were actually produced locally. These revisions demonstrate the general contingency of raw counts of imports. Just as new excavations can add new imports to the archaeological record, research on old material can produce new knowledge and change our understanding of artifacts. In the case of imports, new interpretations of evidence like ceramics from Kommos and Tirynthian wall brackets changed the approximate counts for IIIB and IIIC in significant ways. When the number of imports is as low as it is for prehistoric Greece, these kinds of adjustments have the potential to change the picture of diachronic trends dramatically. That emphasizes the degree to which anyone studying imports on a scale larger than one or a few sites depends on even and accurate reporting of finds in archaeological publications. Though Lemos, Cline, and Jones have certainly each taken all possible care to count imports in a thorough and careful way, Aegean-wide import syntheses can usually only include objects that are tagged as imports in reports published by excavators.

Excavation Reports

Since the information in import catalogs mostly originates in excavation reports, it is important to confront the possibility that excavators working on different periods tend to count or identify imports in nonequivalent ways. Hypothetically, we could imagine that less notice might be taken of small or unimpressive imports from Bronze Age and Geometric sites since they tend to be much more artifact-dense than IIIC and PG ones. On the other hand, since we have comparatively few IIIC and PG sites and since these sites do not tend to be artifact-dense, all objects found at these sites might be given more relative prominence in reporting. Indeed, Coldstream comments that the imports from Lefkandi are little more than trinkets, suggesting that EIA excavators have trumped up their import finds simply because of their rarity within the PG/EG.[20]

Tables 2.11 and 2.12 show how identified imports break down into typological categories. IIIB imports are mostly ceramics and seals, IIIC and G imports represent a wide range of items bridging ceramics, weapons, talismans, and objects of adornment, and PG imports consist mostly of jewelry, faience objects and bronze vessels, or ceramics. The period with the lowest rate of imports (IIIC) has considerable diversity of import types, while imports from both IIIB

---

[20] Coldstream 2003a, 29; cf. more recently Skon-Jedele 1994, 2–3; Tartaron 2013, 22–23; Arrington 2016.

and PG tend to fall into one of two categories. Imports from the G period are the most numerous, and also show a relatively even spread of import types across the board.

The evaluation of Coldstream's "trinket theory" largely depends on the interpretation of the importance of seals vs. faience beads, an issue of value judgment upon which I will refrain from speculating. Regardless of one's valuation of imports, the quantitative comparison of imports could be affected if Coldstream is correct in general terms and small bits of imported jewelry, for instance, are being undercounted at rich LBA sites and overcounted at PG sites, where they are more likely to stand out prominently against the sparse background of PG material culture.. If this were the case, we would have an artificially high ratio of PG imports to IIIB and Geometric ones.

How likely is it that archaeologists have not been assiduous in counting LBA and Geometric imports? Due to the special interest that has always been paid to the notion of external contacts since the early days of Aegean archaeology, I consider it to be unlikely that a large number of imports from LBA or Geometric sites have been willfully ignored by archaeologists, or even lost in the "noise" of artifact-rich sites.

But even if archaeologists have been doing their best to identify all imported objects that emerge from the ground, it remains possible that we are missing a big part of the picture and that methodological variance across the LBA/EIA divide is distorting the data for import volume over early Greek history. This becomes immediately obvious when we consider how scholars excavate and analyze two important categories of artifacts: imported ceramics and imported beads.

Ceramics

Ceramic imports are difficult to identify. In order to make an accurate identification of a sherd as nonlocal, a ceramicist must be thoroughly familiar with all local fabrics and shapes. Then, in order to label that nonlocal fabric or shape as an import from somewhere else, the ceramicist must be familiar with the source fabric, the origin of the shape, or at least have the available resources or knowledge networks to pin one of these down to another point of origin. Ceramicists working in Greece might be familiar enough with Cypriot or Italian wares to identify them within an assemblage. However, if a ceramicist is confronted with an unfamiliar imported sherd and cannot identify that sherd in any meaningful way, the artifact in question might simply be ignored or categorized and published in a way that would preclude its inclusion in synthetic studies of imported material.[21] If we imagine a period during which

---

[21] For instance, consider the following passage from the recent publication of the Mycenaean settlement at Mochlos: "[T]he Gray Ware carinated cup (IIB.149; P 1673) might have had its origins farther afield in Italy. It is also likely that Syro-Palestinian transport amphorae

ceramics constituted a high portion of traded goods, and predict that a significant number of imported sherds from that period are going unidentified by archeologists, then we would conclude that a troublingly large percentage of imports from that period might be missing from the import data. Thus, we might suppose that we are likely to have artificially low counts of imports for periods during which ceramics were commonly imported.

In the Early Greek data, this problem might be affecting the ratio of known imports between IIIB, IIIC, PG, and G. Ceramics are more prevalent in the IIIB data than in the import data from later periods. Accordingly, we might conclude that since more ceramics appear to have been imported to the Aegean in the IIIB period, more IIIB ceramic imports may have gone unnoticed, making our rough count of imports from the IIIB period artificially small.[22] Put another way, we might conclude that because a lot of trade in the IIIB period involved ceramic vessels, and imported ceramic vessels are notoriously difficult to identify, we are almost certainly missing an unreconstructible number of imports from the IIIB period. Since ceramic imports seem not to have constituted a major component of IIIC, PG, or Geometric import assemblages, then we might be missing a smaller percentage of IIIC/PG/G imports.

On the other hand, we could interpret the lower ratio of ceramics within the corpus of IIIC, PG, and Geometric imports to mean that ceramic imports in these periods are being more severely undercounted than IIIB ceramic imports. This argument would presume that the underrepresentation of ceramics in IIIC, PG, and Geometric assemblages can be attributed to the fact that EIA imported ceramics are less recognizable than IIIB ones and are therefore being missed by archaeologists more frequently. If this were the case, the import totals for the EIA would be artificially deflated by the failure of ceramicists to identify imported sherds. If we accept either scenario, we should conclude that different depths of knowledge regarding Mediterranean ceramic types among LBA and EIA ceramicists are impacting the comparability of import counts between the two phases.

Faience and Glass

The second group of imports that is likely to be distorting the counts for LBA and EIA Greece is the corpus of faience of glass beads.[23] While faience and

---

continued to be imported in this phase" (Smith 2010, 136). Long-distance contacts are opaquely evident in the characteristics of the site's ceramics. However, imported objects are not identified in a committed way. A similar phenomenon is evident at EIA sites, such as Lefkandi, where one vessel is identified as nonlocal, with no further specification (Popham et al. 1980, 353, pl. 181).

[22] This seems especially likely in the case of LBA pottery from Anatolia and Canaanite Jars, according to Rutter (Rutter 2006, 653; 2014).

[23] In theory, there could be a problem with the way in which the number of faience/glass objects are tallied (not with how they are identified). A necklace of glass beads could be

glass beads are found regularly and in quantity in a variety of LBA and Geometric contexts, these objects are quite rare in PG Greece.[24] For example, chamber tomb 2 at Dendra alone contained over 40,000 beads,[25] while I estimate the total number of faience beads from PG Greece to be around 30,000.[26]

Perhaps because of their ubiquity during the period (but not because of compelling or abundant evidence for local manufacture) faience and glass beads and vases are not usually counted as finished imported artifacts in the LBA.[27] Sometimes an object of faience or glass is counted as an import if it can be identified as such typologically or stylistically. This is sometimes the case for scarabs, seals, and some vessels whose type of material or method of production is a hallmark of a particular extra-Aegean center.[28] However, in general most Mycenaean glass is considered to be the product of local industry. This notion of domestic production is largely based on "the abundance, diversity, and standardization of Mycenaean glass jewelry, and its wide distribution all over the Mycenaean world."[29] It has long been clear that there must have been some amount of secondary production of glass artifacts by the Mycenaeans, which is to say that glass and faience were imported in ingot form and then melted and recast upon arrival in Greece.[30] This notion is supported by the discovery of glass ingots from

---

counted in different ways. I could count a necklace of 200 red, blue, and white beads as (a) 200 individual beads, (b) three groups of different colored beads, or (c) as one conceptual original object (e.g. one necklace). Fortunately, existing catalogs of imports do treat these objects in roughly equivalent ways. Usually, a group of beads that is found together as a single artifact is treated as one imported object. That is to say, 200 blue faience beads from one tomb count as one necklace rather than as 200 individual imports. However, a single exceptional bead or pendant that is part of a large item such as a necklace or bracelet is usually counted separately. Overall, it appears that the method of counting of beaded jewelry is probably comparable from period to period (based on my assessments of various import catalogs and site reports, though there are exceptions, e.g. Huber 2003 on Eretria).

[24] Nightingale 2008, 88–89; Nikita et al. 2009, 43: "The breakdown of the political and economic system of the Mycenaean palaces apparently ended the production of Mycenaean glass and faience beads."

[25] Persson 1931, 106, no. 51 (Catalog no. 27).

[26] The total number of faience beads counted up in site reports is 13,731. Some excavation reports do not specify the number associated with a find of beads. For these entries I assume n = 300, because the average number of beads in entries with a count is 312. Assuming that an average of 300 individual beads compose all entries with no specific bead count yields a total number of PG beads of 19,431. Considering that there are likely to be other unreported faience beads, or beads that were too small to be recovered in dry sieving processes, I multiply this figure by about 1.5 to get a figure of around 30,000 beads.

[27] Hughes-Brock 2011, 98: "Glass became so thoroughly naturalized in the Aegean that one barely thinks of it as exotic."

[28] For evidence of a glass industry at Mycenae, see Burns 1999; Bennet 2008.

[29] Nightingale 2000; Nightingale 2002; Nightingale 2008; Nikita et al. 2009, 39.

[30] Tite et al. 2008, 115. See Jackson and Nicholson 2010 for evidence that the ingots from the Uluburun ship are from Egypt.

the Uluburun ship, by the lack of industrial installations from LBA Greece for producing raw glass,[31] by the discovery of molds for jewelry manufacture found at Knossos and Mycenae, and by some chemical analyses of Mycenaean glass that show close correlations in chemical makeup between Mycenaean and Egyptian or Mesopotamian material.[32]

Other work complicates this picture. There is evidence for both the import of finished beads that are indistinguishable from locally made beads and for the local (Greek) production of the raw material of glass. The Uluburun ship carried several jars full of faience beads (c. 75,000 individual beads), and glass beads (c. 9,500 individual beads) of a type often observed at sites throughout Greece[33] suggesting that finished beads as well as glass ingots circulated in LBA trade networks.[34] Furthermore, isotopic analysis of Mycenaean glass and faience from Elateia-Alonaki suggests that some raw glass was being produced locally (particularly at Thebes).[35] In most cases (that is, for the vast majority of the hundreds of thousands of beads known from the IIIB period) we are currently unable to distinguish between beads made locally from imported materials, beads made abroad and imported, and locally made beads that are indistinguishable from imported beads to the naked eye. Considering the sheer volume of beads from Mycenaean contexts, the number of Mycenaean beads almost certainly lost in spoil heaps before sieving was a common archaeological practice, and the impracticability of detailed study of any representative sample of this vast body of evidence, this is a problem that is unlikely to be resolved in the near future.

---

[31] There is some archaeological evidence that glass manufacturing took place in Bronze Age centers such as Mycenae (West Houses, see Tournavitou 1995, 456), Tiryns (Panagiotaki et al. 2005, 15), and Kommos (Dabney 1996, 264), but the evidence is not conclusive.

[32] Henderson, Evans, and Nikita 2010, 16: "On present isotopic evidence we can state that in the LBA glass was imported from both Egypt and Mesopotamia to Greece." A thirteenth century cobalt plaque found at Thebes plotted well within the normal Mesopotamian field (Henderson et al. 2010, 9–12), while most of the glass items sampled from Mycenae match Egyptian samples (Tite et al. 2008, 113). XRF analysis of beads from Pylos (Polikreti et al. 2011) show that these were mostly made of Egyptian and Mesopotamian material, though the authors assume that the beads were manufactured within Greece and reached Pylos through internal exchange.

[33] Ingram 2005, 23–27, 122. Tiny beads identical to those found in the concreted masses in the cargo of the ship have been found at Dendra, Mycenae, Menidi, Prosymna, Argos, Tiryns, Aidonia, and Pylos.

[34] Tite et al. 2008, 114: A blue bead from Isopata in Crete has been positively identified as an import from Egypt. Most glass and faience objects subjected to chemical analysis have shown connections with Egypt rather than Mesopotamia.

[35] Nikita 2009, 43: "[There] is the possibility that raw glass was not only imported but actually produced in Mycenaean Greece." Nikita argues that Thebes was a major glass producing center, refuting earlier notions that Mycenaean Greece was entirely reliant on imported raw glass resources.

The same problem applies to the Geometric evidence. While faience and glass beads are sufficiently rare to be noted specially and catalogued as imports when they appear in PG deposits, the increasing number of such artifacts once again in Geometric deposits does not necessarily receive the same treatment.[36] Given the ambiguity of this evidence, it is clear that there are likely to be serious problems involved in comparing the number of IIIB, IIIC, and G imports with PG imports because of differences in the way that faience and glass objects are treated. On the one hand, it is likely that all of the faience and glass objects counted as imports for the PG period are, in fact, imports.[37] There is thus far no evidence for even secondary manufacture of glass objects in Greece during this period, and because the artifacts match up typologically with contemporary Near Eastern beads.[38] It is, moreover, likely that these objects have been counted with relative thoroughness, owing to the rarity with which they are found at PG sites. On the other hand, glass and faience objects are rarely either precisely counted or included within the corpus of IIIB/IIIC or Geometric imports, though there are compelling reasons to believe that at least some of these objects were manufactured abroad. In light of this evidence, and considering the fact that thousands of beads are regularly found in LBA contexts, it is likely that a large number of beads that were imported to Greece are completely missing from existing import tallies.

The counts for imported faience and glass beads might therefore be over-represented in the PG and underrepresented for the LBA and the Geometric periods, meaning that a multiplier should be applied to even out the difference. But there is no accurate estimate of the number of beads known from LB IIIB/LB IIIC or Geometric Greece, and our knowledge of the relationship between glass imports and locally made products is still developing, so it would be extremely difficult to come up with a reasonably accurate calculation to account for the likely underrepresentation of glass and faience beads in these import counts. Another way to correct for this error is to subtract the total of beads from the import totals for all periods. Since there is little empirical evidence upon which to base suppositions about which beads were or were

---

[36] See evidence presented in Huber 2003, 83–87; while Huber catalogs each bead individually with care and considers its origins, she names many hundreds of *comparanda* from other sites within Greece where beads from Geometric deposits have been discovered, but which are never mentioned by scholars discussing long-distance interaction. Dobiat (1987, 23–24) found that of eye-beads, spread widely around the Mediterranean in the eighth century, 327 of 479 examples were found in Greece.
[37] Nightingale 2009, 508; Higgins in Popham et al. 1980, 217–225.
[38] See Popham et al. 1980, 217–218 regarding Near Eastern comparanda for the Lefkandi beads. For lack of evidence for faience or glass production after IIIB, see Nightingale 2008, 88–89.

TABLE 3.13. *Impact on import quantities if beads are excluded from the counts*[39]

Mainland					
Min. Total imports w/Beads		Min. Total imports w/o Beads		Impact (% change)	
LH IIIB	123	LH IIIB	122	<1	
LH IIIC/SM	82	LH IIIC/SM	82	0	
PG	64	PG	28	56	
G	327	G	302	8	
Crete					
Min. Total imports w/Beads		Min. Total imports w/o Beads		Impact (% change)	
LH IIIB	87	LM IIIB	87	0	
LH IIIC/SM	34	LM IIIC/SM	29	15	
PG	68	PG	49	28	
G	163	G	146	10	

not manufactured or sourced outside of Greece, it makes sense to stop counting beads as de facto imports (Table 3.13).

Therefore, for the analysis in the remainder of this book, I will discount all beads from the import counts given in Chapter 1, as reflected in the minimum import counts given in Table 3.18. This correction has the effect of mitigating the distortion in counts introduced by different archaeological practices of "bead-counting" across the LBA–EIA transition.

Summary

Overall, then, factors of archaeological practice should give us serious reason to pause in a straightforward interpretation of the numbers of identified imports from the IIIB, IIIC, PG, and Geometric periods. Although LBA and EIA archaeologists keep careful track of obvious imports when they find and are able to identify them, there are fundamental differences in the way that the archaeological record is treated across the LBA–EIA transition that make import counts from chronological phases within it difficult to compare directly. Generally speaking, then, problems of archaeological practice are definitely distorting the import record in ways that make raw comparison of the gross number of imports across time highly problematic.

---

[39] Note that I calculate the impact of bead-count reduction here based on the minimum total imports for each period rather than on my "weighted average" figure. That is because the "weighted average" figure is a hypothetical compromise figure from which it is impossible to "add" or "subtract" values based on real counts.

3.4. IS IT LIKELY THAT DIFFERENT RATES OF SURVIVAL OF TRADED ARTIFACTS BASED ON CHANGES IN THE NATURE OF TRADED GOODS OVER TIME MAY ACCOUNT FOR THE PATTERNS IN THE DATA?

Another issue creating uncertainty for the comparison of import counts from different periods is the fact that archaeologically recoverable imports represent an "indirect observable" of an original body of traded goods, which may have changed in composition over time. The imports we have in the archaeological record compose some leftover percentage of the original amount of traded goods circulating, some of which (metals, foodstuffs, organic materials) are bound not to have survived the intervening centuries. So we have some unknown percentage of the original quantity of circulating imports available to count up.

In light of this, we can only meaningfully compare quantities of known imports across cultural phases if we believe that the ratio of total imported goods to surviving imported goods remained more or less consistent across the time periods we are comparing. So if we thought that the "original" set of Mycenaean trade goods and the "original set" of EIA trade goods were the same, we could compare the surviving trade goods effectively, because our indirect observables are likely to represent the same percentage of the original set of traded goods for both periods. However, if we believed that the overall composition of circulating goods changed considerably between the Mycenaean period and the EIA in ways that resulted in a totally different percentage of imports surviving to be observed, then it would be quite difficult to use surviving imports as proxy data for trade volume or intensity, even if they were not distorted by archaeological practice. For instance, if textiles made up most of the traded material in the EIA, while stone seals made up most of the traded material in the LBA, the rate of survival of traded material would be significantly different enough for the two periods to make the quantity of surviving traded goods incomparable without a multiplier of some kind. So for the purpose of comparing the "connectedness" or "intensity" of trade activity over consecutive periods, what matters is getting a sense of how equivalently distorted the datasets are across historical and cultural horizons. As long as the ratio of imported goods to surviving imported goods can be expected to remain more or less consistent across the time periods compared, the indirect observables of surviving imports should be comparable. If, on the other hand, the overall makeup of the body of traded goods changed, it will be harder to compare the indirect observables of surviving goods. In this section, then, I assess the evidence for trade in the LBA and EIA in order to try to determine whether differences in trade over time might be distorting the diachronic patterns in preserved imports in significant ways.

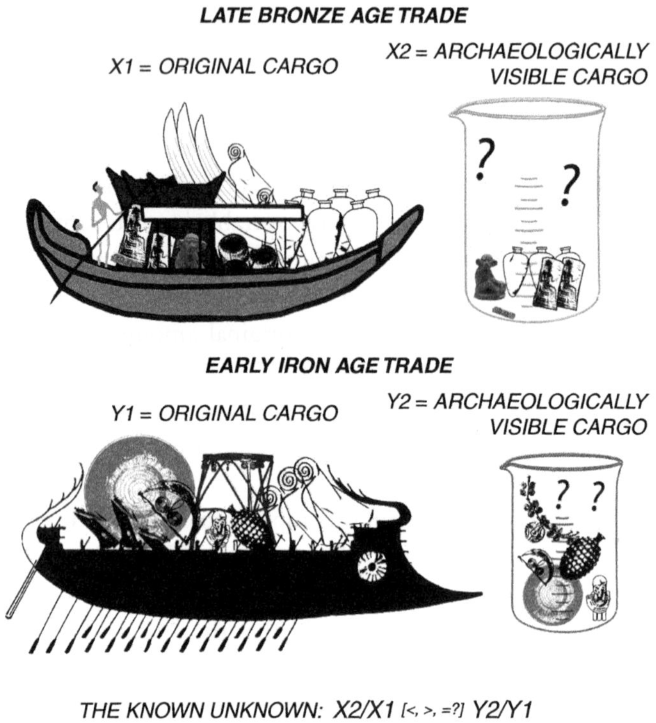

152 COLLAPSE OF THE MYCENAEAN ECONOMY

LATE BRONZE AGE TRADE

X1 = ORIGINAL CARGO   X2 = ARCHAEOLOGICALLY VISIBLE CARGO

EARLY IRON AGE TRADE

Y1 = ORIGINAL CARGO   Y2 = ARCHAEOLOGICALLY VISIBLE CARGO

THE KNOWN UNKNOWN: X2/X1 [<, >, =?] Y2/Y1

Figure 3.6. Visualization of "indirect observables" (by author)

Mycenaean Trade

For the Mycenaean period, evidence from shipwrecks, artistic representations, and textual sources gives us a fair sense of the original assemblage of the goods that circulated in Aegean trade networks. The Uluburun shipwreck at Kaş off the southern coast of Anatolia yielded a rich cargo of objects that was headed from the Near East to the Aegean (though the precise point of origin and final destination are not known with certainty).[40] The finds from the ship include a variety of finished goods and raw materials including copper ingots, tin ingots, pottery from Egypt, Cyprus, Syria-Palestine, and the Aegean, blue glass ingots, Canaanite jewelry, Egyptian scarabs, Mesopotamian cylinder seals, Canaanite bronze weapons, bronze tools, a possibly Italian sword, bronze weights, amber, fishing nets, stone mace heads, ostrich egg shells, elephant and hippopotamus ivory, logs of ebony, and Canaanite jars containing aromatic resin and glass beads.[41] The wreck is dated to the end of the LH IIIA or the beginning of the LH IIIB period. By contrast, the Cape Gelidonya shipwreck, probably datable to either the end of LH IIIB or the beginning of LH IIIC, contained a cargo

---

[40] Pulak 1998; Pulak 2008; Cline and Yasur-Landau 2007, 130–136.
[41] Cline 1994, 100.

of metal objects, including jewelry, weights, tripods, and weapons, as well as bronze ingots.[42] The Point Iria shipwreck, of a Bronze Age vessel dated to the end of the thirteenth century, was carrying primarily Cypriot and Creto-Mycenaean transport vessels.[43]

Another possible source from which to reconstruct the materials traded in the Mycenaean period are the New Kingdom wall paintings inside the tomb of Rekhmire in the necropolis at Egyptian Thebes. Rekhmire was a vizier who served under the kings Tuthmosis III and Amenophis II.[44] The paintings within the tomb depict the vizier in his capacity as registrar of goods brought to the office of the king. These goods included taxable produce from dependents within Egypt as well as tribute brought by foreign visitors. On the southern part of the west wall of the tomb is a depiction of goods being brought to the vizier from Punt, the "princess of Crete and the islands of the Mediterranean," and "the princes of the southern foreign lands, the troglodytes of the extreme south." The Cretan envoy was, at some point in the tomb's history, altered to look more like a Mycenaean.[45] The products depicted as having been brought to Egypt by the Aegean visitor include vessels (pitchers, drinking bowls, amphorae, and lion, bull, and ibex rhyta), a sword, beaded necklaces, oxhide ingots of two colors, a basket of silver rings, and a basket of lapis lazuli. These objects might give us some sense of the sorts of items that the Cretans traded with the Egyptians before LM IIIB. However, since the products were not changed when the traders were altered to look like Mycenaeans, it may be possible that the traded goods represented in the tomb of Rekhmire do not give us much of an idea of the traded material common in the LB IIIB, the period under consideration here. Likewise, the relationship between these images and actual quantities of goods traded is difficult to infer. However, if we momentarily operate under an assumption that the items depicted in this fresco are representative of LBA traded goods, the evidence from this artistic depiction would suggest that ceramics and bulk goods such as agricultural produce and metals formed as significant a portion of traded goods as finished items like swords and necklaces (Table 3.14). The total number of goods that were probably traded as finished goods (rings, necklaces, animal rhyta, open vessels) is about the same as the number of goods that were likely traded as bulk commodities to be transformed into something upon receipt (ingots, a tusk, closed vessels perhaps containing some kind of value-added agricultural product, a basket of lapis lazuli). Likewise, the literary sources discussed in detail in Chapter 1 indicate that raw materials made up a large portion of gifts among kings, thus supporting the impression made by the paintings in the Tomb of Rekhmire.

[42] Bass et al. 1967; Cline 1994, 101; Burns 2010b, 299–300.
[43] Phelps, Lolos, and Vichos 1999.
[44] Hodel-Hoenes 2000, 140; Rehak 1999, 47.
[45] Helck 1979, 51–52. Minoan codpieces were changed into Mycenaean kilts.

TABLE 3.14. *Tribute brought to Egypt by Aegeans in the Tomb of Rekhmire, Thebes*

Imported Finished Good	Number	Imported Commodity	Number
Necklace	2	Tusk	1
Sword	1	Ingot	5
Open Vessel	18	White Cubes	1 basket
Animal Rhyton	5	Closed Vessel	17
Rings	1 basket	Lapis Lazuli	1 basket
Total	**26 + 1 basket**	**Total**	**23 + 2 baskets**

The textual, iconographic and the archaeological evidence suggest that traded goods in the LBA probably consisted of a mixture of raw materials and finished goods. While the raw materials were probably altered beyond recognition once they reached their destination, and perishable goods decayed rapidly after their archaeological deposition, the finished goods are more likely to have survived taphonomic processes and processes of technological or artisinal transformation, meaning that the imports that we have left to count probably represent only a percentage (less than half) of the original quantity of goods that were traded.

Early Iron Age Trade

While our impression of LBA trade is partly filled in by shipwrecks and textual evidence, there is not much written or material evidence to supplement our sketchy knowledge of postpalatial trade. However, some insight into EIA exchange might be gleaned from the evidence of the Homeric poems. The utility of the Homeric evidence for reconstructing EIA culture is the subject of long and acrimonious debate (for this debate, see Chapter 1). For now, I move forward under the relatively uncontroversial assumption that the Homeric poems were probably written down in the eighth century BCE and may reflect the kinds of things that Greeks during the eighth century might have believed to have been circulating among elites in the previous era and/or during their own time.[46] In theory, then, it might be realistic to assume that Homeric heroes in the *Iliad* and *Odyssey* trade things in a way that represents a structural economic tradition dating back to the tenth or ninth centuries. Though this is far from an undeniable certainty, the evidence from Homer is

---

[46] Although even if the poems might give some sense of the kind of items traded by EIA Greeks, they probably emphasize *basileis*-controlled elite exchange rather than commercial exchange (which we only catch brief glimpses of) because of the nature of the subject matter (glimpses especially at *Il.* 7.464–482 and *Od.* 15.459–463).

TABLE 3.15. *Instances of exchange types in the* Iliad *and the* Odyssey

Activity	Instances
bride gift	6
gift exchange	34
honor prize	8
prize (as in a race)	12
ransom	10
"commercial" trade	4

the closest thing we have to a somewhat contemporary literary view of trade, and so it is worth considering cautiously in puzzling out what the "original" trade assemblage from that period might have looked like.

For the sake of argument, let us tentatively imagine that Homeric trade has at least some traits in common with PG and Geometric trade, and that we might gain some insight into the proportion of finished goods and commodities involved in EIA trade by examining traded goods and commodities in the Homeric poems. In Homer, elites traveled and exchanged gifts in a variety of contexts. Much like the LBA materials mentioned in documentary sources and found in shipwrecks, the kinds of goods that these elites exchanged look like a mixture of objects that would survive to be excavated and some that would probably have disappeared from the archaeological record. Characters in Homer traded beads and jewelry,[47] fancy metal vessels (mostly for drinking or mixing wine),[48] gold ingots,[49] belts,[50] wine,[51] clothing,[52] horses,[53] women,[54] and arms.[55] Goods change hand among Homeric *basileis* in contexts including gift exchange, the provision of dowries, the allocation of prizes for athletic prowess, the distribution of booty, and ransom (Table 3.14).

While, as discussed in Chapter 1, much of this Homeric exchange activity could not be described accurately as long-distance or cross-cultural exchange, some maritime trade with foreign individuals or groups does occur. Homer does not recount the relevant transactions in sufficient detail to allow a precise

---

[47] *Od.* 15.459–463; *Od.* 18.290–300.
[48] *Il.* 6.212–236; *Il.* 9.121–161; *Il.* 23.259–271; *Il.* 23.651–653; *Od.* 4.125; *Od.* 4.127–130; *Od.* 4.589–592; *Od.* 4.611–619; *Od.* 8.430–432; *Od.* 9.201–205; *Od.* 13.13–15; *Od.* 15.102–108; *Od.* 16.13.
[49] *Il.* 9.121–161; *Od.* 4.127–130; *Od.* 8.386–397; *Od.* 9.201–205.
[50] *Il.* 6.212–236; *Il.* 7.299–302.
[51] *Il.* 7.464–482; *Od.* 9.164–166; *Od.* 9.201–205.
[52] *Il.* 23.560–563; *Od.* 8.386–397; *Od.* 19.241–243.
[53] *Od.* 4.589–592.
[54] *Il.* 6.212–236; *Il.* 7.299–302; *Od.* 7.7–10.
[55] *Il.* 23.560–563; *Od.* 19.241–243; *Il.* 23.798–800.

quantitative reconstruction of the goods that changed hands, but does give us enough information to reconstruct a general idea of the scale and contents of a "typical" and "international" shipload in the eighth century Greek imagination, and this is enough to see that this imaginary shipload would contrast strongly with the Uluburun ship.

Two representative episodes are the description of the Phoenicians loading their ship full of objects acquired from Ctesius's people in Book 15 of the *Odyssey*[56] and the revelation that the Lemnians frequently ship wine over to Troy to sell to the Achaean armies in *Iliad* Book 7.[57] In both of these Homeric examples of trade, the agents involved appear to be self-interested, nonstate-affiliated entrepreneurs who are carrying specialized cargoes from which they intend to make a profit. In the case of the Lemnians, this is an opportunity to profit from a sought-after commodity not available elsewhere (Lemnian wine). In the case of the Phoenicians, the traders spent a whole year accumulating a shipload of goods that they planned to offload gradually for profit during their onward voyage.

Homer also tells of Greek *basileis* traveling to visit distant lands and exchanging guest gifts with their inhabitants. The items that change hands in these contexts include animals and people as well as objects, 80 percent of which are finished items rather than commodities (Table 3.16). The kind of trade that Hesiod discusses in *Works and Days* might have been different, and more commodity-based, but we remain unsure about whether multitasking farmers participated in anything other than small-scale exchanges with neighbors.

The early Greek evidence is of a different kind (literary) than the evidence from the LBA (archaeological, iconographic, documentary), and this makes direct comparison between the texts difficult. If we are willing to accept the possibility that the Homeric poems give us a reasonable sense of the kinds of things elites in eighth century Greece were interested in acquiring from long-distance contacts, it appears that there were significant differences between the original set of traded goods within the institutions of LBA and later Greek trade.

Summary

We cannot know everything about "original" sets of traded goods from the LBA and EIA, but working with the available evidence gives us some reason to believe that these sets were different. In the LBA and the EIA, trade cargoes included both durable and nondurable materials, both commodities and finished goods. However, the Homeric texts suggest that finished, luxury goods

---

[56] *Od.* 15.530–534, 15.580–581.
[57] *Il.* 7.464–482.

TABLE 3.16. *Traded goods in Homer by category*

Category	Items
Open Vessel	19
Adornment	15
Arms	12
Ingot	8
Textile	6
Tripod	6
Other	4
Closed Vessel	4

represented the majority of traded items during the EIA. Raw and bulk materials like gold talents and wine were integrated into Homeric trade shipments but paled in comparison with the importance of finished goods. On the other hand, it looks like commodities make up a large portion of the material that circulated in the LBA. When we consider the import evidence at the heart of this study, the obvious implication is that, since bulk goods are less visible in the archaeological record, we are probably missing more of the original trade cargoes from the LBA than we are from the EIA.

We should be cautious in approaching this conclusion. The comparison between archaeological and literary cargoes is necessarily fraught with difficulty. On top of that, none of the evidence we have can necessarily be expected to accurately represent "normal" trade shipments from either period, and so it is treacherous to extrapolate general truths from these clearly exceptional examples. Furthermore, we do have evidence, in the form of shipwrecks off the coast of Israel, that commodities did circulate in the Mediterranean during the Geometric period (though ships laden with cargoes of wine may or may not have penetrated the Aegean).[58]

At the same time, the general impression that commodities were not as important in overall trade in the EIA as they were in the LBA is at least worth considering. For the Bronze Age, it is clear that bulk commodities like the ones that sank on the Uluburun, Cape Gelidonya, and Point Iria shipwrecks often reached the Aegean during the LBA. Canaanite storage jars (like those found in the shipwrecks) are represented in the corpus of excavated IIIB imports. If we take these objects to be indicators of sites where ships similar to the Uluburun ship may have landed, it is possible that many metal ingots, ivory tusks, glass ingots, and so forth would have reached the sites where we see imported ceramics as well, suggesting that a large percentage of the original

---

[58] Ballard et al. 2002.

trade assemblage from the LBA did indeed look like what we find on the Uluburun ship and has mostly been lost to time and/or looting.[59]

The characteristics of the imports identified at EIA sites suggest that the picture in this period was probably different. Most of the imports recognized at PG and G sites are finished objects like jewelry or nontransport vessels of faience or metal. Most ceramic imports from Lefkandi come from within Greece rather than from the Near East or Italy, and these are often vessels intended for drinking or mixing wine, perhaps the "poor man's" version of the gold and silver vessels that *basileis* exchange in the Homeric poems. The overall dearth of ceramics imported from outside of Greece, metal ingots, or other indications of bulk exchange at EIA sites could suggest that long-distance trade in commodities decreased after the collapse of the Mycenaean palaces. This supports the impression made by the Homeric poems: that a large proportion of imported goods in the EIA would have been made up of finished luxury goods more likely to survive archaeologically than commodities.

So there is good reason to believe that the "indirect observable" of imports from the LB IIIB period is more likely than the "indirect observable" from the EIA to represent a small portion of long-distance exchange goods originally reaching the Aegean in antiquity. Along with other factors already discussed, including the difficulty associated with counting ceramic and bead imports from the LBA, this analysis pushes us further toward the conclusion that we must be missing a higher percentage of Mycenaean traded goods than EIA ones, meaning that the numbers of imports we compare when we look at raw import counts are not likely to tell us the whole story of quantitative changes in trade volume or intensity over time.

3.5. CONCLUSIONS

The raw import data themselves have probably been distorted by modern archaeological practice (different competencies and strategies in counting imports at sites from different periods), and even if they had not, they probably would not tell anything like the whole story of ancient trade. If, as all the evidence suggests, trade assemblages changed through time, it is difficult to know how and whether this would have affected the ratios between "original" and "surviving" sets of imported goods. Different sets of traded goods could have survived at different rates, and as long as it is impossible to compare the original sets directly, it is difficult to know what these rates are. Caution should

---

[59] Mangou and Ioannou 2000, 207–208: Oxhide ingots from the LBA have been found at some sites that also have other imports, including Kanakia (see Lolos 2002; 2007; 2009a; 2009b; Lolos et al. 2007), Kea, Palaikastro, Phaistos, Tylissos, Nirou Chani, Arkalochori, Agia Triada, Zakros, Gournia, Archanes, Khania, Kommos, Knossos, Mycenae, Poros, Tiryns, Kyme, and Thebes.

be taken when comparing some unknown percentage of one original dataset to another unknown percentage of another original dataset.

There are some indications that the overall quantity of traded goods during LB IIIB was much larger in comparison to EIA quantities than the extant imports suggest (this is especially the case because, in order to be analytically consistent, it is probably best to ignore all imported beads from the PG period, dropping the import counts from PG significantly). As a result, we might read the quantitative decrease in imports after the LB IIIB period as an indication of a precipitous drop off in trade indeed, and the bounce in the Geometric period as less dramatic than it appears to be. But since import data are so deeply problematic, it is necessary to test this theory by looking at what we know about the volumes and distribution of two other datasets, commodities and exports, from early Greece.

FOUR

BRONZE DEPOSITION (AND CIRCULATION?), TRADE IN COMMODITIES, AND EVIDENCE FROM AROUND THE MEDITERRANEAN

IN CHAPTER 3 I SUGGESTED A NUMBER OF REASONS TO BELIEVE THAT we might have a serious problem with our most direct category of evidence for evolution in the scale of long-distance trade over time. While imported objects can provide us with a kind of meager breadcrumb trail for reconstructing possible economic fluctuations, they fall short as a reliable independent metric for trade volume and intensity. Most importantly, because so few of them survive from *any* period between 1300 and 700 BCE, taphonomic distortions make comparison of the quantities of imports involved difficult to rely upon. In order to really understand how the trade economy transformed over the transition between the LBA and the EIA, it is necessary to align the meager record of recognized imported goods with other categories of evidence.

In this chapter I test the quantitative patterns observed in the raw import data – an aggregate decline after 1200 BCE, with recovery coming only in the (probably late) ninth century – against two other categories of evidence that we might expect to fluctuate in tandem with overall scalar change in economic systems: evidence for the import of bulk commodities and exports. There are obstacles to being truly systematic in handling all categories of material from the LBA and EIA, but I present quantitative change when possible. According to a law of cumulative credibility ("if evidence from all approaches converges on a common viewpoint, this creates a strong argument for approximation to reality"), if all of the evidence that we can muster shows a similar pattern as the imports do, we will have a better case for scalar change in economic systems over time.[1]

4.1. LOST COMMODITIES

Identified, finished imported objects provide an insufficient basis upon which to reconstruct the scale of an ancient trade economy. They may even show trends that mislead. In the case of the LBA and the EIA in Greece, there are good reasons to believe that we have a number of actuarial problems when it comes to interpreting the patterns apparent in identifiable imports. Prominent among these reasons is the evidence that traded goods coming into Greece during the EIA may have consisted mostly of finished goods instead of bulk goods, while the opposite was probably true in the LBA, meaning that the ratio of surviving to original traded goods from the EIA might be far higher than the ratio for the LBA data. If that is the case, then directly comparing the indirect observables for the two periods could be highly misleading. If we accept that LBA imports represent the tip of a "trade iceberg" while PG and Geometric imports comprise a larger sample of the original quantity of acquired international goods, we would need to use some kind of multiplier to compare the datasets directly.

In the absence of even a vague sense of the scale of this multiplier, it is impossible to find a coherent way to compare import datasets from the IIIB, IIIC, PG, and Geometric periods with one another. But given the vast number of unknown factors affecting import preservation in the archaeological record, an appropriate multiplier would be difficult to conjure. However, comparing known quantities of materials excavated dating between 1300 and 700 BCE that must have come from abroad might provide some idea of the relative magnitude of commodities reaching Greece. Metals such as tin and electrum as well as ivory and some semiprecious stones do not occur naturally in southern and central Greece, and gold does not occur there in abundance. Likewise, many organic cargoes that we know were being transported in ancient trading vessels are not native to Greece.[2]

These categories of evidence are subject to the same kinds of taphonomic concerns as imported objects themselves. The ones that we excavate are likely to represent only a partial sample of the "source population" of original goods imported to Greece in the past. Some imported commodities, like some finished goods (e.g., textiles), simply do not survive archaeologically in Greece. This is likely true of many of the commodities recovered from the Uluburun shipwreck site and attested in textual sources to have been imported

---

[1] Piggott 1965, 10; Bintliff 2000, 21.
[2] Haldane 1993. See also the evidence for trade in organic materials from the Linear B texts, discussed in Palaima 1991.

to Greece during the Mycenaean period.[3] Other commodities, such as tin bronze, do survive but are subject to reuse and redeposition. This makes it difficult to distinguish the difference between their final depositional context and the context of their acquisition. However, while the direct evidence for trade in commodities is problematic in substantial ways, it does represent another set of material that we can compare with the overall trends in import data. And commodity imports survive in greater quantity than finished imported goods, meaning the patterns that they demonstrate are likely to be more robust and less subject to revision over time, as new sites are discovered and the dataset changes.

Trade in Metals: Tin Bronze

It is often stated that one of the primary drivers of trade in the ancient Mediterranean was the search for metals.[4] The contents of the Uluburun and Cape Gelidonya shipwrecks demonstrate that the raw materials for making bronze as well as bronze objects, perhaps in the form of scrap metal, constituted a considerable proportion of shipboard cargoes during the LBA.[5] Furthermore, the content of the Jn tablets from Pylos demonstrate without a doubt that the Mycenaean palaces had an interest in the working, and distribution of bronze.[6] If bronze formed a key element in a commodity-weighted, directional trade economy during the LBA, and if part of the explanation for a decrease in trade after the end of the LBA is that trade in bulk commodities decreased dramatically, to be replaced with small-scale trade in archaeologically recognizable trinkets, we might expect this to be evident somehow in the amount of metals we encounter when we examine the archaeological record from the LBA and EIA.[7]

In what follows, I show that the overall quantity of bronzes known from the Mycenaean period is far greater than the number known from the IIIC and PG periods, but that published individual bronze objects from the Geometric period dwarf all three. I also consider the nature of the bronze objects found, in order to attempt to get a sense of the raw quantities of bronze involved. While the different quantities of metal we encounter in deposits from periods

---

[3] Examples of such commodities are tin ingots, ebony, and terebinth resin. In some cases we can use scientific techniques to detect these in ceramic containers (Stern et al. 2003; 2008).
[4] Muhly et al. 1977; Muhly 1982; papers in Pare 2000; Sherratt and Sherratt 1993; Sherratt 1994; Sherratt 1998.
[5] Pulak 1998; Bachhuber 2006; Pulak 2000; Bass et al. 1967; Muhly et al. 1977; Bass 1961.
[6] For the Jn tablets and bronzeworking in the Mycenaean palaces, see Killen 1987; Smith 1992–1993; Uchitel 1990; Hiller 1972; Hurst 1968.
[7] The interpretation of this data is complicated by the tendency of depositional practices to change in ways that impact the recoverability of metal artifacts (I. Morris 1989).

with different cultures and traditions are likely to be related to changing depositional practices in some ways, it is nearly impossible to imagine that the magnitude of the changes evident in the data do not have something to do with a contracting trade economy during the period from 1200 to 900 BCE. In any case, we must consider the idea that if cultural traditions and practices changed so dramatically that they are noticeable in major ways in the depositional record of imported metals, that alone will be of help in our effort to track the evolution of culture, society, and the economy over a key period of transition in Greek history. While imperfect, therefore, these data help us to put patterns in archaeologically identifiable imports into perspective.

Imported Metals: A Scientific Note

Putting aside for now issues of deposition and recovery in the archaeology of metals, it is necessary to comment on one further difficulty in calculating the relationship between archaeologically recovered metal objects and the rate of acquisition of mineral resources from abroad. In regard to copper and tin, both of which are required to make tin bronze, this has been a controversial topic. On the one hand, it is certain that tin does not exist within Greece, and would necessarily need to be imported for the manufacture of bronze.[8] On the other hand, while it is presumed that Cyprus and Italy supplied the majority of copper used in Greek bronze artifacts during most of pre- and proto-history, there are copper deposits in Greece at Lavrio in Attica and in the Cyclades, and the degree to which Greek bronze producers sourced copper locally remains a topic of debate. According to the results of some Lead Isotope Analyses (LIA),[9] Mycenaean bronzes, and especially bronzes dating to the LH IIIB period, were made from Lavriotic and Cycladic copper rather than from Cypriot or Sardinian copper, as the presence of Cypriot and Sardinian ingots in palatial deposits would lead us to expect.[10]

[8] The nearest sources of tin being exploited in the LBA are likely to have been either the Zagros mountains in modern Iran or the (much closer) Taurus mountains in Anatolia. While Yener has repeatedly argued that tin was being mined in Bronze Age Taurus, and while there is evidence for the exploitation of these resources, it remains unclear whether they were used in the LBA. For evidence and discussion, see Yener et al. 1991; 1989; Yener 2000; Sayre et al. 2001.

[9] Gale and Stos-Gale pioneered the use of lead isotope analysis as a method by which to source archaeological metal objects in the early 1980s (Gale and Stos-Gale 1982; Gale and Stos-Gale 1986). By generating diagnostic lead isotope fields for Mediterranean ores, and comparing lead isotopes in bronze and copper objects to these characteristic fields, Gale and Stos-Gale were able to state which ore sources matched the metal in archaeological artifacts.

[10] A straightforward breakdown of the distribution of Late Mycenaean bronze objects subjected to lead isotope analysis by Kayafa shows intake in raw metals from outside of Greece during the Late Mycenaean period (18 percent sourced to Cyprus and nine percent to Sardinia). Those scores are roughly double the proportion of nonlocal ores found in any earlier assemblage from the BA Peloponnese, suggesting that there may have been an unusual

Archaeologists and archaeological scientists remain divided regarding the reliability of the results of LIA.[11] Some argue that the confusing signatures are the result of the reuse and recycling of metals,[12] though others have contested this view.[13] Some believe that LIA identifies the level of purity rather than the geographical origin of bronze,[14] so that the entire scientific basis for LIA sourcing of bronze artifacts is deeply flawed and not to be relied upon under any circumstances. As a result of the general confusion and vigorous disagreement that continues to surround LIA, some have concluded that "it is time to realize that there is no unique isotopic fingerprint for Cypriot ore deposits, and thus for Cypriot copper."[15] At the same time, Gale and Stos-Gale continue to stand behind the method, which does seem to be sensitive to different copper ore sources at least in some cases.[16] Given the problematic nature of sourcing

amount of long-distance trade during the Late Mycenaean period. More than half of the assemblage from the Late Mycenaean period comes from copper ore sourced to Lavrio (43 percent) or to the Cyclades (12 percent), so apparently domestic metal sources were also being utilized.

[11] Though initially greeted with great enthusiasm, lead isotope analysis has not proven to be the silver bullet for understanding the ancient metals trade that some had hoped for. Gale and Stos-Gale identified virtually all post-1400 BCE copper oxhide ingots as the products of ores from the Apliki mine in central Cyprus, including "all ingots and fragments from Cyprus itself, Sardinia, Kyme, Mycenae, Bulgaria, Bogazköy, Sarköy, Antalya, Chios, Kommos, Mochlos, Egypt, and the Cape Gelidonya shipwreck" (Gale and Stos-Gale 2012, 71). However, on Cyprus only a handful of analyzed objects tested in the Apliki isotope field, and objects on Sardinia tested in local Sardinian ore ranges (Gale and Stos-Gale 2012, 71, Table 8.1). Scholars have had a hard time accepting that Sardinians would import copper ingots, since there is ample evidence for the local availability and contemporaneous mining of copper (Kassianidou 2001; Kassianidou 2006; Hauptmann 2009, 508).

[12] Budd et al. (1995, 2) suggested that the interpretation of LIA results by Gale and Stos-Gale was flawed because they did not take into adequate consideration the possibility that lead isotope signatures could be affected by the use of recycled or mixed ores, and that copper objects made from mixed ores could carry isotopic signatures that were misleading.

[13] This theory was dismissed by Gale and Stos-Gale (1995), on the grounds that it would require the common practice of precipitating pure copper back out of alloyed bronze objects and subsequent recasting of mixed copper ingots, a process which would destroy the tin content of the bronze alloy. Since tin was probably difficult to obtain, and thus unusually dear, Gale and Stos-Gale deemed this scenario to be unlikely. In addition, the recycling theory might explain the common LIA signature of oxhide ingots, but does not explain the fact that LIA analysis distinguishes among different copper ores within finished objects. If there were a copper *koine*, as Budd et al. suggested, it would be likely that all copper objects would test in the same field as the ingots, which they do not.

[14] Muhly suggests that the LIA signature of Apliki copper as defined by Gale and Stos-Gale relates to the quality and/or purity of the copper instead of its origin. This would explain why the purest copper ingots fall within the Apliki signature, while most bronze artifacts do not. Gale and Stos-Gale have forcefully argued that there is simply no evidence for this (Muhly 2005, 510; Hauptmann 2009; Gale and Stos-Gale 2012).

[15] Muhly 2009, 29, quoting Pernicka 1995, 60.

[16] Kayafa identifies a number of finished objects from Early Mycenaean sites in the Peloponnese as Cypriot in origin (Gale and Stos-Gale 2012, 79; Kayafa 2000, 439, table IX). It may be worth considering the possibility that local lead is contaminating the bronze artifacts tested at places of bronze manufacture. The majority of lead objects from the Peloponnese identify in the Lavrio field. If the same tuyéres, crucibles, and moulds were used to manufacture both

copper, I refrain from comment on this topic in the analysis that follows. I work under the assumption that the production of bronze within Greece would require at least imported tin, and probably some quantity of imported copper as well.[17]

Bronze Quantities and Distribution in Greece, 1300–700 BCE

In what follows I present the evidence, as far as we can reconstruct it, for the presence of tin bronze items in Greece across LBA-EIA transition. As with finished imported goods, there are obstacles to the interpretation of this evidence. And, as with finished imports, we must face the formidable task of gathering the evidence before we even reach the point of interpretation.

In order to assemble a comprehensive dataset of known bronze objects from the LBA and EIA, I began by compiling the results of previous studies for the LBA Peloponnese and the LBA on Crete.[18] For the remainder of the data, I recorded all bronzes mentioned in site publications from all sites contained in the master IIIB – Geometric site catalog I assembled in order to write this book.[19] It is still not possible to claim that the bronze accountings I present here represent a complete record of the relevant evidence. Imported objects are almost uniformly recorded and reported in Aegean contexts when their excavators recognize them; bronzes do not afford the researcher the same luxury. Bronze artifacts from excavations are reported according to widely variable standards of precision. While some sites have produced comprehensive catalogs,[20] this is the exception. Shorter archaeological reports from excavations often record bronze objects in less detail, noting only the presence of metal artifacts in orders of magnitude and making it hard to generate precise

---

lead and bronze artifacts, it is conceivable that some of this lead ended up in local bronzes made of Cypriot copper. This is an attractive possibility, since independent evidence of copper mining at Lavrio is not abundant, while mining of lead and silver is far more likely. Hauptmann suggests a phenomenon something like this (2009, 508–509).

[17] Although less LIA evidence is available for the EIA, some analysis of the Olympia bronzes suggests a copper source in southern Jordan or Israel (Faynan in Wadi Arabah and/or Timna in the Negev) (Kiderlen et al. 2016).

[18] Kayafa 2000; Hakulin 2004; Hakulin 2013.

[19] See S. Murray 2013, 60–65; S. Murray 2015; S. Murray, forthcoming b, for an explanation of the site catalog. The bronze data was extracted as accurately as possible; however, since excavators almost never weigh bronze, it is nearly impossible to assess gross weights of bronze known from different periods, as opposed to rough counts of objects, which are often of diverse sizes. Hakulin (2013) seeks to circumnavigate this issue using estimates, but introducing even more abstraction into an already problematic dataset is not an appealing option (Clarke 2016). As with most of the evidence presented in this book, I press forward despite these difficulties on the assumption that (1) the scale of changes we actually see in the archaeological record are so large that even if they are somewhat distorted our overall picture is dependable and (2) it is better to proceed with analysis with some systematic collection of evidence than with none whatsoever.

[20] For example, Coldstream and Catling 1996 which includes weights of metal artifacts.

counts. Metal artifacts present additional problems of simple accounting. We do not have the resolution of chronological control over many classes of metal artifacts that we have for pottery. Since many metal artifacts are found in tombs with burials dating to multiple periods, in hoards, or in caves with poor stratigraphy it is often difficult to assign particular dates to them. It is also likely that bronze artifacts suffer considerable rates of attrition due to looting and the recycling of metal.

I adopt a variety of strategies to work around these obstacles. In terms of problems with dating and poor reporting, I omitted sites where description of bronze quantities was completely opaque, and only included counts for sites where it was possible to estimate with rough precision a number of bronze objects that seemed likely from their context to belong to one period or another. Thus, the numbers presented represent a minimum possible number of bronzes that *could* date to the periods in question, rather than a maximum likely number. Since the number of total sites from which I could reliably count bronzes (a total of 1,058 site contexts) remains relatively large, it is probable that the numbers concerned give us a reliable sample on which to draw some conclusions about quantities of deposited bronzes from the IIIB to G periods.

As for differential rates of attrition due to looting and recycling, this is certainly a major issue. As with the import data, we can assume that some quantity of metal objects from deposits dating to all periods under consideration here must have been looted, recycled, corroded into nothing, or destroyed in some other fashion. This does not necessarily make diachronic comparison of "indirect observables" problematic when we are trying to evaluate qualitative change in social practice over time. After all, if depositional practices changed so dramatically that they completely distort bronze counts, that must mean people started treating these materials differently, which is a good indication that social practices and perhaps economic institutions also changed. Nonetheless, in evaluating quantitative change in the scale of bronze access and use, it is important to determine whether different proportions of metals from different periods are likely to have survived from antiquity into the present day (that is, variance in the ratio between originally circulating bronze and surviving excavated bronze). If this is the case, our indirect observables for quantitative analysis will not be comparable. The determining factors in deciding whether or not this was true must be (1) the kinds of sites that we have excavated from each period, (2) ancient habits of metal use at the kinds of sites that we have excavated from each period, and (3) ancient habits of metal reuse, purposeful deposition, and recycling during each period.

In terms of the first and second points, we can think of some obvious ways that distortions in the archaeological record would impact our understanding of known bronze ratios. If PG buriers tended to put extraordinary amounts of metals into tombs, while IIIB buriers did not, and tombs dominate the archaeological record for both the IIIB and the PG period, we would be likely to have an overrepresentation of aggregate PG metals compared to IIIB metals. Or, if both PG and IIIB buriers put most of their metals into tombs, and tombs dominated the archaeological record for the PG period but not the IIIB period, we would have a distorted sense of the breadth of bronze distribution among all sites when we compare the IIIB and PG datasets. These are complicated, but important, scenarios to work through if we are to find meaning in raw quantitative measures from the archaeological record.

We can start by thinking about the way that the overall shape of the archaeological record through time shapes our impressions of it. As noted in Chapter 3, the proportion of known sites of each type dating to the IIIB, IIIC, PG, and G periods (that is, the proportion of cemetery to settlement sites) in the total dataset of sites is relatively similar from one period to another, suggesting that the kinds of excavated contexts we are dealing with across the board might be comparable. However, in Chapter 3, I was dealing with the global database – all known sites with archaeological material dating to one of the phases under study in this book. In looking at the distribution of bronze artifacts, it is not reasonable to include sites that have not been excavated or explored enough to have produced the kinds of deposits that might include bronze objects. So here we begin with a smaller set of sites, which may or may not retain an evenness of distribution. What does the sample of sites with available excavation data look like from the point of view of "data demography"? Broadly speaking, it appears as though we do again have a relatively even set of evidence to examine across the board from 1300–700 BCE. For the IIIB, PG, and Geometric periods, the percentage of sites with resolution of publication sufficient to determine bronzes present within an order of magnitude, the ratio of mortuary sites to settlement/sanctuary sites is about 2:1.[21] The only exception to this rule is the IIIC data, in which the ratio is 3:2. That is to say, a larger percentage of IIIC sites with data available were nonmortuary sites.

These are important ratios to keep in mind when examining the data, since we may wish to interpret changes in the quantity of detectable bronze differently depending on how we observe depositional preferences changing over time across different subsets of the archaeological record. Further important considerations that are both complex and challenging from the point of view of middle range theory include the way in which we understand metal counts in relation to habits of recycling and reuse, and in terms of the social values of

---

[21] For the IIIB period, 60 percent of the sites are mortuary while 34 percent are nonmortuary; for the PG period, 62 percent of sites are mortuary while 29 percent are nonmortuary; for the G period, 54 percent of sites are mortuary while 28 percent are nonmortuary. The remainder of sites are those for which it is not really clear whether the artifacts discovered came from a tomb or from a settlement deposit.

TABLE 4.1. *Number of bronzes on the Greek mainland, sites with bronze present at sites with good data, against import counts and period durations*

	Total Sites[22]	w/Bronze Present	Distribution among all Sampled Sites	~No. Bronzes Counted[23]	No. Imports[24]	Duration (yrs.)	~Rate of Deposition (p.a.)
IIIB	514	126	25%	6,600	122–159	~110–125	B:~55 I: ~1.2
IIIC	241	150	62%	2,800	82–109	~125–175	B:~19 I: ~.6
PG	294	110	37%	1,500	32–41	~115–150	B: ~11 I: ~.2
G	401	190	47%	21,300	302–397	~200	B:~107 I: ~1.6

metals within their respective temporal contexts. In general, again, these are issues best considered with the data in hand; we will confront them in due course, in the process of chewing over the evidence.

To start with a basic point, archaeologists have documented fewer bronze objects that date to the IIIC and PG periods than to the IIIB and Geometric ones. Table 4.1 presents the basic data – an approximation of known bronze objects from contexts firmly datable to the periods under study here (with import counts and approximate lengths for reference).

To reiterate, these quantities should be considered imprecise but not insane. They should represent a fair assessment of the order of magnitude of the quantities of bronze objects documented clearly from dated archaeological contexts in mainland Greece. Taken together, the data confirm the idea that bronze was more abundant on the Greek mainland during the final Mycenaean period than it was during the aftermath of the palatial collapse. Nearly twice as many bronze objects are known from the LH IIIB period than from the LH IIIC period, half as many from the PG as from the LH IIIC period, and five times as many from the Geometric period as from the LH IIIB period. However, before we draw any conclusions about patterns of import and commodity movements on the Greek mainland from the raw data in Table 4.1, it is necessary to question the interpretative viability of some aspects of this data.

[22] Indicates the number of site for which it was possible to obtain a rough sense of data. Many sites from all periods were simply never published in sufficient resolution to allow their inclusion in this kind of quantitative study.
[23] To avoid creating an impression of false precision for these numbers I have rounded them to the nearest hundred.
[24] Beads are not included in this count, as explained in Chapter 3.

First, it is important to keep in mind that raw counts of bronzes conceal important differences in the scale of the objects in question. Bronze artifacts from the LBA are typologically quite different from bronze objects recovered in EIA contexts, especially those from the PG. During the Mycenaean period bronze was not usually used to make jewelry, though occasionally bronze decorative attachments for clothing or furniture do appear. The majority of bronzes from the LBA are large objects, especially but not limited to double axes, swords, knives, and other tools. The nature of bronze objects changes in the IIIC period – while large accoutrements such as swords, spearheads, and razors continue to occur in burial contexts and settlements, bronze jewelry becomes more common in mortuary contexts.[25] By the PG period, bronze (with the exception of imported bronze vessels) comes almost exclusively in small packages: we are primarily speaking of tiny pins and fibulae encountered in burial contexts. Larger bronze weapons or tools, bronze sheet, and bronze jewelry do turn up in settlement contexts at some PG sites. We should also keep in mind the indirect evidence for the production of bronze artifacts that exists in the form of molds for casting Cypriot-style rod-tripod legs from the settlement at Lefkandi, which suggests that some sites possessed enough metal to produce sizable bronze artifacts.[26] In the Geometric period, the nature of bronze finds changes again. Although there is some continuity with the PG trend of using bronze rings, pins, and fibulae for self-adornment, a huge number of Geometric bronzes are animal figurines recovered from Greek sanctuaries.[27] Monumental bronze finds appear in the Geometric period in the form of bronze vessels, tripods, and armor, and even the occasional bronze sword or razor, despite the general turn to iron for edge tools and weapons.[28] The bronze fibulae known from some PG tombs develop into truly gargantuan variants by the LG period.[29]

Because of the coarse resolution of publication for the majority of sites with bronze finds, it is not possible to quantify the change in "average magnitude" of bronze finds from these different periods. However, it is important to remember when assessing the change in the scale of the trade economy (that is, how much raw metal was arriving in Greece) that not only are we looking at considerably more bronze objects from the IIIB period than the IIIC and PG

---

[25] The chamber tomb cemetery at Elateia in central Greece contained bronze rings, as did cemeteries excavated in Achaea. For Elateia, see reports in *ArchDelt* starting in 1985; for IIIC burials in Achaea, see Giannopoulos 2008.

[26] Evely 2006, 265–266.

[27] For bronzes deposited at Olympia, see Andrews 1994, who estimates the bronzes from Olympia alone to number roughly 10,000 and account for almost 3,000 kg of bronze.

[28] For a good survey of early Greek bronze production and artifact types, see Bol 1985. For horse figurines in particular, see Zimmermann 1989.

[29] See for example Late Geometric fibulae from Corinth, so big they could not have practically fulfilled their theoretical function in real life (Jacobsthal 1956, 9).

periods, but, especially in comparison with the PG period, the average LBA object probably contains at least 10 times more bronze than the average PG object. The famous bronze cuirass from Dendra (though dated a bit earlier than the thirteenth century) weighs about fifteen kilograms.[30] On a more mundane level, a single Naue Type II sword, common in the Late Mycenaean period, weighed 472 grams.[31] According to the Pylos Jn tablets, hundreds of kilograms of bronze may have been circulating within the territory under Pylian control in the thirteenth century.[32] On the other hand, the total amount of weighed recovered bronze dated to the PG in Knossos' North Cemetery excavations was 1.9 kg, only enough to make about four LBA swords, and less than one percent of the metal on the Uluburun ship.[33] The implication is that most PG bronze objects were small indeed, so the numbers in Table 4.1 most likely underestimate rather than overestimate the difference in the quantity of bulk bronze deposited during these periods. Likewise, the huge bump in consumption of bronze in the G period may not be as dramatic relative to the IIIB period as the numbers suggest, since many of the thousands of G bronzes are relatively small figurines.[34]

Another factor to consider when pondering the meaning of the orders of magnitude apparent in the data is the way in which the number of bronzes deposited in different contexts changes diachronically. During the IIIB period, the deposition of bronze artifacts is spread relatively evenly among mortuary and nonmortuary contexts: 51 percent of bronzes were found in settlement/ sanctuary contexts, and 48 percent in mortuary contexts. This suggests a scenario in which bronze was relatively common – it was used as a grave good, but was also frequently present in settlement contexts, and often abandoned in them.[35] The ratio of burial to nonburial contexts for bronze finds grows in the IIIC period despite the fact that we have data for a remarkably high percentage of IIIC settlement sites. Seventy percent of the bronze documented from this period is found in mortuary contexts. Given the overall distribution of sites from the period, and the outsized representation of bronze in mortuary contexts within that distribution, we might conclude that we are seeing a higher percentage of the overall number of bronze objects that originally circulated in the period purposefully deposited in tombs. Likewise, during

---

[30] You could, therefore, have made over 700 Dendra cuirasses or 22,000 Naue II swords with the ingots from the Uluburun shipwreck. For the cuirass and similar types extending at least to 1350 BCE, King 1970, 294–296.

[31] Weighed example is KNC T201.f7 in Coldstream and Catling 1996.

[32] Calculations of bronze accounting in the Pylos Jn tablets at Ventris and Chadwick 1973, 355–356. The total bronze allotted on the tablets is 801 kg. or enough to make "534,000 arrowheads, or 2300 swords and spears, or 1000 bronze helmets."

[33] Calculated from data in Coldstream and Catling 1996.

[34] An average-sized Geometric animal figurine might have weighed about 200 grams, more than a small PG fibula (perhaps 10 g) but smaller than a large sword or bronze vessel.

[35] Supported by conclusions by Aprile 2013, 434.

TABLE 4.2. *Ratio of mortuary to nonmortuary sites in the sample of excavated sites from which bronze data was collected and distribution of bronzes in mortuary and nonmortuary sites from the IIIB, IIIC, PG, and G periods*

	IIIB	IIIC	PG	G
Ratio of M/NM sites	2:1	3:2	2:1	2:1
Bronze Presence Distribution:				
Settlement/Sanctuary	51%	26%	14%	93%
Mortuary	48%	70%	86%	7%

the PG period, 85 percent of known bronzes come from tombs, and only 14 percent from settlement or sanctuary deposits. The trend reverses strongly in the Geometric period. Although over twice as many bronzes are known from G settlement contexts as the number known from IIIB deposits (~7,000 against ~3,000 from the LBA), and although more bronzes are known from G tombs than from PG tombs, these quantities are totally drowned out by the bronzes that begin to be deposited in sanctuaries in vast quantities (~13,000 of them).

Just as the average size of bronze objects from different periods is important to keep in mind when considering the relationship between excavated bronzes over time relative to an abstract sense of "trade volume," we must think carefully about how bronze finds relate to ancient quantities of circulating bronze.[36] If a community was using all available bronze in funerary rituals, and bronze is more likely to survive and be discovered by archaeologists in mortuary contexts than it is in settlement contexts, then we would be able to record something much closer to the original assemblage of that community's bronze than an assemblage belonging to a community that used bronze in warfare and work. This position assumes that metals used on a battlefield or in a workshop will be broken or lost with some regularity. If we agree with this, we might expect to be missing far more bronze from the IIIB period than from the following IIIC and PG periods. In the Geometric period we have a huge concentration of bronze finds from sanctuaries, but it is also true that bronze becomes relatively common in tombs and in settlements at the same time. The Geometric period appears, like the IIIB period, to have been a time during which bronze was simply a common metal, with many uses, that was encountered on a regular basis (at least among a certain economic class).[37]

---

[36] Complications of extrapolating deposited and excavated metals with originally circulated metals are clearly explained in I. Morris 1989.

[37] It appears that the distribution of metals during the IIIB period was highly concentrated near palatial centers, while bronze distribution during the IIIC and PG period was rather dispersed, with concentration (though not as extreme) during the Geometric period again at sanctuaries. Due to the complicated nature of the spatial distribution of the evidence, I refrain from

So, while interpreting raw data from accumulated bronzes is not straightforward, we can probably conclude, based on the data, that bronze was more abundant in absolute terms in Greece during the LH IIIB period and the Geometric period than it was during the LH IIIC and (especially) the PG period. The precise scale of this change is difficult to assess, but it is hard to imagine a scenario in which the overall quantitative evidence did not line up in broad measure with the evidence from the imports. That is to say, a major decline in the scale of bronze present in the world, concomitant perhaps with a decline in the scale of the trade economy, occurred after the LH IIIB period, with recovery in the Geometric period.

At this juncture, an important question to consider is the following: did residents of LH IIIC Greece continue importing tin and copper, or were they simply recycling metal resources leftover from the IIIB period? If it seemed that recycling was the source of most bronze objects deposited during the IIIC period, then the continued presence of bronze in the archaeological record might be unrelated to any relationship posited between commodity occurrence at sites and trade volumes. Is this likely? There is some evidence that bronze may have been in short supply after the palatial collapse. An unusually large number of hoards are known from the LH IIIB/IIIC transition.[38] The incidence of this practice begins well before the palatial collapse, suggesting that it may have been prompted by a general sense of insecurity rather than a shortage.[39] It is also a localized strategy, concentrated primarily at sites in the Argolid, in Boeotia, and at Athens and Kanakia, perhaps suggesting that there was acute anxiety about bronze supplies particularly near palatial sites that were used to having total control over large quantities of bronze.[40] Finally, the nature of the archaeological record of LH IIIB settlements, many of which were destroyed and thus "sealed" at the end of the LH IIIB period probably resulted in extraordinary preservation of hoards. There is some evidence that recycling may account for the continued abundance of bronze in LH IIIC at sites like Mycenae and Tiryns. Isotope analysis of a IIIC hoard from Mycenae could indicate that bronze objects were made of the same, mostly Lavriotic copper ores, as objects from the IIIB period.[41] Furthermore, some of the Jn

considering these in the current argument: for my purposes here, aggregate quantities are of most pressing interest. However, I will return to this topic in later publications.

[38] Huth 2000, 88; for difficulties associated with precisely dating these hoards, Sherratt 2000, 92, n.22.

[39] Snodgrass 1989, 24; Waldbaum 1978, 72.

[40] Iakovidis 1982, 219. Hoards come from Mycenae (4), Tiryns, Athens, Anthedon, and Orchomenos, among other locations. Regarding the Peloponnese, Kayafa notes that hoarding "is restricted to the end of LH, accounting for about 240 mostly complete bronze objects from Mycenae and Tiryns." See also Evely's recent analysis of metals at Palaikastro which suggests that recycling may have taken place there during IIIC (Evely et al. 2012).

[41] See Kayafa 2000, 441, table XII.

tablets from Pylos may refer to the use of scrap bronze in allotments to smiths and inventories.[42] From the postpalatial period, we have no archaeological evidence for ingots or slags, suggesting that remelting may have been one of the only ways to produce new bronze objects. This may also be evident in the nature of the cargo of the Cape Gelidonya shipwreck, laden with a wide variety of objects that may have been used as scrap bronze for remelting and repair.[43] In any case, it appears that supply networks of copper and tin were not as organized and regularized during the twelfth century as they had been in the IIIB period. On account of this evidence, we should not discount the notion that looting and salvage could have accounted for a fair portion of the bronze supply in the IIIC period. One need only look as far as the early-2000s' epidemic of copper wire theft from construction sites, abandoned buildings, and even fake flower arrangements in small-town cemeteries for a modern instance of what happens when metals become dear in times of social and economic flux.

Against the idea of recycling, it might be argued that areas with negligible quantities of bronze in the IIIB period, such as Achaea, Phokis, and East Lokris can hardly have been depending on nonexistent supplies of salvaged IIIB bronze to make their jewelry and their weapons. But, then again, it might be the case that these areas, which preserve more bronze objects from IIIC deposits than from IIIB deposits, would be the exact areas in which IIIB material was robbed out of tombs in order to enrich the bronze supplies of IIIC inhabitants. Such activity has been documented at twelfth century Kition, on Cyprus.[44]

Another possible explanation for new bronze concentrations in IIIC regions far from the traditional palatial centers (where most bronzes from the IIIB period have been recovered) is that palatial denizens from the Argolid, Boeotia, and Messenia moved en masse to former peripheral regions like Achaea, Phthiotis, and Attica, and brought bronze with them, resulting in an upsurge in bronze deposition in these regions after 1200.[45] But if we assume that bronze

---

[42] Smith 1992–93, 182–183, 194 and 198; Ventris and Chadwick 1973, 357–358 (text no. 257); Chadwick 1976, 141. Chadwick interpreted the tablet Jn 829, which discusses the collection of "temple bronze as points for spears and javelins" as indicating that Pylos was experiencing a metal shortage and that authorities were raiding the temple treasury. See Muhly (1992, 18) for the argument that the tablet refers instead to copper ingots from the sea.

[43] Bass 1961; Bass 1991, 75; Tartaron 2013, 26.

[44] Karageorghis and Kassianidou 1999. Evidence for bronze recycling exists in the form of fourteenth and thirteenth century tombs looted during the twelfth century and the existence of "founder's hoards" at a number of sites across the island. For increased presence of wealth in Achaea and East Lokris in IIIC see Giannopoulos 2008 and Kramer-Hajos 2008, respectively.

[45] For the suggestion that an efflorescence of wealth in the archaeological record of IIIC Achaea is due to an influx of refugees, see Vermeule 1960, 18–19; Papadopoulos 1978–1979, 160; Kolonas 1998, 475. In disagreement with the position is Moschos (2002, 29–30), according to whom "the population remained the same." Moschos also believes that the warrior graves of

becomes abundant in new places because palatial residents took their bronzes with them when they left at the end of the LH IIIB period, it would be difficult to explain the wealth of LH IIIB bronze deposits at palatial sites. The abundance of bronze finds at Tiryns and Mycenae implies that palatial residents of IIIB were not particularly abstemious about removing metal objects from the settlements they were hypothetically about to abandon.[46]

Finally, we should consider the evidence from imports. While imports were common in the Argolid, at Thebes, and probably at Pylos in the IIIB period, other regions appear to gain new access to exogenous objects and materials in LH IIIC. Sites in Achaea and Attica with little evidence of long-distance contacts during the thirteenth century preserve imports from the twelfth. It is unlikely that the newly bronze-rich and newly import-rich regions would overlap so much if increasing acquisition of bronze resources was not part of the new socioeconomic reality for these regions in the IIIC period. Therefore, the simplest explanation for geographic shifts in import and bronze deposition, and for the continued existence of bronze at IIIC sites, is that trade in copper and tin continued to supply Greece during the IIIC period, but that new areas were the focus of this trade. On the other hand, we could also imagine that recycling would have been one strategy used to make up for lost access to trade routes during the transition between the IIIB and IIIC period in places such as Tiryns, Pylos, and Mycenae.[47] Known quantities of bronze from the IIIC period might represent some newly acquired copper and tin resources, and some recycled bronze that originally entered the local economy during the IIIB period.

During the PG period, the number of identified bronzes on the mainland decreases sharply. It is hard not to see in this an echo of the old, well-worn bronze shortage debate. Snodgrass originally argued that the use of bronze in Greece decreased after the LBA because the supply of tin, which must have been brought to Greece from far away to the East or North, was cut off at the end of the Bronze Age, forcing Greeks to find a new metal from which to make their tools and weapons.[48] According to this bronze shortage theory, trade

---

IIIC Achaea probably look exceptionally rich compared with the IIIB burials because the IIIC burials were the last deposited and therefore least disturbed.

[46] Giannopoulos 2008, 255.

[47] Kayafa 2000, 404. For the lack of good evidence for bronze recycling from Nichoria, where chemical analysis has been preformed, see Stos-Gale, Kayafa, and Gale 1999. According to Stos-Gale, Kayafa, and Gale, the logical assumption of bronze recycling after the end of the palatial period does not fit with the patterns apparent in LIA analysis of EIA bronzes from Nichoria. These fit best with a Lavriotic source, and are thus *not* consistent with the idea that different metals from the bronze age were mixed together in an incoherent mélange after the disappearance of the palaces. They conclude (1999, 112) that the amount of recycling in the postpalatial period has been overestimated. The study sampled approximately 25 percent of all copper alloy objects found at Nichoria.

[48] Waldbaum 1982; Muhly et al. 1985; I. Morris 1989, 503.

routes bringing copper and tin to Greece broke down just after some areas of Greece had learned the art of ironworking from Cyprus. When they could no longer obtain copper and tin, Greeks turned their metallurgical attention to forging iron (in places like Euboea where they had learned how to do it) or to the recycling of old Mycenaean bronzes (in places like West Greece where they had not).[49] Bronze became more abundant again when trade with the east was reestablished around 900.[50]

This theory has been controversial. Morris questioned the bronze shortage hypothesis on the grounds that it draws too simple a connection between deliberately deposited metal artifacts and originally circulating quantities of metal.[51] He argued that the prominence of iron in burial assemblages during the EIA reflects new social strategies that were put into place by an emergent elite that used a different metal to set itself apart within society.[52] In this view, the use of iron for tools and jewelry was not the outcome of need generated by the lack of a preferable metal, bronze. Rather, changes in the socially determined meaning of metals led to different types of deliberate deposition, which is what we see in the archaeological record.[53] We might also imagine that as iron became more common in the PG period, demand for bronze would have declined, because metal made from a local ore had replaced many uses of the old exogenous resource. In any case, the notion that tin was in short supply in the EIA has found little support from analyses of bronze objects, which have normal to high tin contents.[54] Snodgrass has now stepped back from his original position, and most scholars have followed suit, questioning just how much access to tin waned.[55]

It is impossible to unravel the bronze shortage dilemma in the current context. However, some clues suggest a lack of access to bronze was not the major determining factor in its decreasing abundance in Greece during the PG period. While many classes of artifact disappear during the EIA, metal objects, including bronze objects, and pottery are still found in abundance.[56] Nine metal objects, most of them bronze, were found in the small area of the settlement excavated at Asine.[57] Bronze is more abundant at Nichoria during the PG phases of that site than it had been at the end of the LBA, and bronzes at Nichoria contain the normal or unusually high amounts of tin and outnumber

---

[49] Snodgrass 1971, 246–249; Snodgrass 1989, 25–26.
[50] Snodgrass 1971, 238.
[51] I. Morris 1989.
[52] I. Morris 1989, 506–508
[53] I. Morris 1989, 507–508; 2000, 208–218.
[54] Rapp et al. 1978; Jones 1980; Catling 1983, 283; Snodgrass 1989; cf. Charalambous et al. 2014 for evidence from Cyprus.
[55] Snodgrass 2000, xxvii–xxix; Lemos 2002, 102–103; Coldstream 2003a, 371; Dickinson 2006, 12, 144–146.
[56] Dickinson 2006, 144.
[57] Wells 1983b, 227, 255, 278.

TABLE 4.3. *Bronze and other metal objects in PG cemeteries*

	Bronze	Iron	Bronze and Iron	Gold	Gold and Iron
Nea Ionia	18	23	0	0	0
Kerameikos	16	14	24	7	0
Agora	4	8	0	0	0
Skoubris	24	8	0	0	0
Velestino	6	4	1	5	0
Tiryns	30	11	15	2	0
Marmariani	5	14	0	1	0
Platykambos	1	4	0	0	0
Krannon	11	1	0	0	0
Argos	27	16	20	9	0
Heraion	1	0	0	0	0
Toumba	28	10	3	34	5
Atalanti	45	0	6	6	0
Skyros	18	1	0	5	0
Homolion	8	5	0	4	0
Palia Perivolia	7	0	0	4	0
Elateia	3	1	0	0	0
Nea Ionia	1	0	3	0	0
Thebes	1	0	0	0	0
Corinth	2	2	0	0	0
Theotokou	5	1	6	2	0
Isthmia	1	0	0	0	0
Halos	1	0	0	0	0
Fiki	2	0	0	0	0
Mycenae	3	0	1	0	0
Asine	0	1	1	0	0
Acropolis S Slope	0	0	1	0	0
Vikiorema	1	0	0	0	0
Elis	25	0	0	0	0
Totals	**294**	**124**	**81**	**79**	**5**
Average per cemetery	**9.6**	**4.4**	**3**	**2.8**	**0.2**

iron objects at a rate of roughly three to one.[58] Likewise, bronze at Lefkandi contains ample amounts of tin.[59] In a sample of tombs from the PG period all over Greece, bronze remains the most common metal deposited in burials, in terms of absolute number of objects tallied (Table 4.3).[60] Iron certainly appears

[58] MacDonald, Coulson, and Rosser 1983, 273–287. Bronzes from DA I: 7, DA I-II: 17, DA II: 32, DA II-III: 5.
[59] Jones 1980, 447–460.
[60] For the opposite view, I. Morris 1989, 505 (summarizing Snodgrass 1980).

during the period, and achieves near parity with bronze in usage for making pins and rings, but the numbers do not support the notion that bronze was impossible to obtain.

These cemeteries are spread around widely, from Thessaly in the north to the deep Peloponnese. There are no cemeteries in which iron is used to the exclusion of bronze, but there are cemeteries in which there is bronze but no iron, a situation that we would not expect to see if the use of iron were a reaction to a shortage of bronze. This makes it unlikely that access to bronze was restricted due to supply issues. While it is true that many of the iron objects in the tombs are far larger than the bronze objects, the point here is not that there was *more* bronze than iron circulating or being deposited during the PG, but simply that both metals continued to be available.

Metallurgical evidence supports the notion that raw metal commodities were in ready supply to PG metal smiths. Tin bronze is used to make decorative objects like rings during the SM and PG period.[61] If tin were in short supply, it might be expected that a copper ring, which would not benefit from the strengthening properties of tin, would do just as good of a job, but we do not see rings made of pure copper.[62] Chemical tests of bronzes from Lefkandi and Nichoria show that there were not only highly variable levels of tin in these artifacts, but that unusually high quantities of lead and iron occurred in them as well, which may suggest that different ores or different combinations of metals were being smelted to create them. All of this points to an active, experimental metallurgical industry not limited to melting down old Mycenaean bronzes pillaged from tombs.[63]

It is true that the previous reasoning must remain speculative. The gross quantitative evidence does not allow us to distinguish with certainty between changes in depositional habits and changes in supply. However, the data does make it look likely that, for whatever reason (supply *or* demand, discursive *or* nondiscursive), bulk copper and tin were not present in Greece in the same quantities as they were during the Mycenaean period. This does not imply that EIA Greeks could not have acquired these quantities of bronze if they had wanted to import them, simply that they were not likely to have been imported in the same volume as they were in the LBA.

The evidence for early Cretan bronze deposition is considerably more difficult to handle than the evidence from the mainland. This is based in part on a scenario in which we are dealing with poor publication records from many of the most important sites, but more so because customs in early Crete

---

[61] Bakhuizen and Kreulen 1976, 43–44.
[62] At Salamis on Cyprus, nails were made without tin, demonstrating at least one case in which discretion was practised among smiths in the allocation of this expensive resource. See Charalambous et al. 2016, 571.
[63] Jones 1980, 455–457.

involved the use and reuse of both tombs and cave sanctuaries over most of the period of interest here, meaning that many bronze artifacts from the island simply cannot be divided up into neat categories for many of the places where metal artifacts are most numerous on the island. Thus, the analysis I present for Crete is much rougher-grained than what is possible for the mainland.

Hakulin has gathered the evidence of bronzes from LBA Crete.[64] The number of total bronze objects she catalogs from the LMIIIA2–B periods is (at 820) much lower than the number published from the mainland,[65] though Hakulin expresses doubts about the quality of the data.[66] She notes that many excavation reports from Crete are incomplete with regard to more quotidian bronze artifacts, especially since many major sites on Crete were excavated early in the twentieth century, when data collection was not comprehensive, and since many finds are in private collections (for example, the Mitsotakis collection) and are thus not accessible to researchers.[67] However, Hakulin estimates that her databases comprise 80–90 percent of all known bronze objects on Crete, which is likely to be a reasonably representative sample, all things considered.[68]

From a regional perspective bronze finds are most plentiful in West Crete, probably because the excavation of the cemetery at Armeni has yielded plentiful and well-recorded artifact data, and dates to the LM IIIB period.[69] In central Crete, bronze objects occur in the hundreds at Knossos during the Final Palatial period, but the numbers drop off precipitously afterwards.[70] Otherwise, bronze finds dated to the IIIB/C periods are most plentiful in the sites that have been excavated carefully and relatively recently, like Chania (thirty-nine finds) in the west, Kommos (seventeen finds) in the Mesara, and Palaikastro (thirty-one objects) in the far east.[71]

It is likely that the quantities of known bronze objects from central Crete in the IIIB period will swell once excavations from Poros-Katsambas are published in full.[72] At Poros-Katsambas, numerous signs of metalworking,

---

[64] Hakulin 2004; Hakulin 2013.
[65] The smaller number of bronze objects remains unimposing even if we consider the fact that Crete represents a smaller geographical unit and a smaller number of total sites than the mainland. The total number of copper-based objects from the LM IIIA2-B periods on Crete represents about 0.08 objects/km^2 against 0.14 objects/km^2, from the Peloponnese in LH IIIA-B.
[66] Hakulin 2013, 13–15.
[67] Hakulin 2013, 14.
[68] Hakulin 2013, 15.
[69] Andreadaki–Vlasaki 1988; 1991–1993; 1994–1996; 1999; 2002.
[70] See Hakulin 2013, 91, 109 (over 400 bronze finds from the Knossos region in the Final Palatial Period compared with only 59 from the postpalatial period).
[71] Hakulin 2013, 99–117.
[72] Hakulin does not include this site because most of its material still awaits full publication (Hakulin 2013, 40).

including both ingots and pieces of finished and working bronzes, have been found.[73] The metalworking areas of the site date from MM II–LM IIIB, but the most intense activity appears to belong to the Neopalatial period. From the LM IIIB period, evidence for metalworking is attested, but the quantities of metal reported diminish considerably, and the lack of ingots has led the excavators to suggest that the postpalatial craftsmen worked with scrap instead of with raw materials.[74] The quantities of metal from Poros-Katsambas are likely to rival those from Chania, Kommos, and Knossos, and to place the harbor among the select sites from LM IIIB Crete with any significant number of recorded bronze goods. Probably not coincidentally, there is evidence to support the notion that metal was worked at Poros-Katsambas, Kommos,[75] and Chania[76] and many of the metal finds from these sites are probably byproducts of these industries (scraps, wires, strips, globules, and so forth).[77]

Hakulin shies away from attempting to calculate bronze usage specifically from the IIIC period, citing the difficulty of dealing with the publication record.[78] However, it is likely that many of the artifacts generically dated to the postpalatial period (for instance, some of the thirty-two bronzes at the Diktaean Cave) really belong to IIIC. The same is likely to be true of many of the artifacts found at other sanctuaries such as Kato Syme,[79] and in tombs at Vrokastro and at Knossos.[80] At Chania, a total of twenty bronze objects come from the LM IIIC settlement.[81] Here, IIIC bronzes were frequently found together with slag and crucibles and, in one exceptional case, with an ivory balance scale, so metals probably continued to circulate in IIIC Chania.[82] Lead isotope analysis of the bronzes from IIIC Chania traced the copper ores utilized

---

[73] Dimopoulou 1997, 434.
[74] Dimopoulou-Rethemiotaki 2004, 370; Dimopoulou 2012, 139–140.
[75] Blitzer 1995, 500, 530; Knapp and Cherry 1994, 139; Blitzer and Watrous in Shaw and Shaw 1985, 16–17.
[76] Hallager and Hallager 2003, 269.
[77] This may be a reminder that the evidence is probably not reliable in a number of ways. Detritus might be more likely to survive over time than large goods of value, and the concentration of bronze finds at these industrial sites could suggest only that the sorts of bronze items that are more likely to be recoverable in the archaeological record are abundant here, rather than that these sites alone had access to extraordinary quantities of bronze to begin with.
[78] Hakulin 2013, 11.
[79] Schürmann 1996, 14.
[80] Hall 1914, 135–136, 148 (Karakovilia chamber tomb at Vrokastro); Coldstream and Hood 1968, 205–206 (tomb at Agios Ioannis with bronze pins and bronze sheet).
[81] Hallager and Hallager 2000. Bronzes from IIIC are as follows: Building 1, Room I (p. 42) two sheets, one tweezers, one blade (also piece of slag, ivory balance); Building 1, Space P (p. 47) nail (also one lead tube); Building 1, Room K/H (p. 56) sheet fragments (also a crucible); Building 1, Room O (p. 81) two strips, one nail, one knife, one small round piece (also slag and a crucible); Building 2, Room A (pp. 91–92) two small triangles, earring; Building 2, Space A-D (p. 99) bronze rod; Rubbish area North (p. 105) two hooks, nail, arrowhead, fibula.
[82] Brun-Lundgren and Wiman in Hallager and Hallager 2000, 180.

to Sardinia, suggesting that trade between Crete and the central Mediterranean continued into LM IIIC.[83] Otherwise, there is not much left at Kommos during this period, and Poros-Katsambas also appears to have gone out of use during IIIC, so Chania and Palaikastro (where there is also ample evidence for post-IIIB metalworking) may have been left standing as the major metal importing center in Crete after the Mycenaean collapse.[84] The site of Karfi was founded in the LM IIIC period, and so some of the bronze from this site (almost 100 bronze objects) may need to be filed under this heading.[85] Recent excavation at Chalasmenos turned up at least one bronze fibula,[86] and bronzes from the period (including bronze items in tombs at Orthi Petra, Mouliana, and Praisos[87] and the Late Minoan tombs at Knossos)[88] are found throughout the island. Even the precipitous cliff settlement at Monastiraki Katalimata, perched on a high ledge above the mouth of the Cha gorge, had some sort of access to metals. Excavations there revealed a bronze pin and a bronze knife in the LM IIIC buildings.[89] On the other hand, IIIC Kavousi appears to have depended almost entirely on stone tools – only one stratified metal find exists from the site.[90] Regardless of these glimpses into the evidence for IIIC Crete, and despite Hakulin's efforts, the resolution and completeness of the data is poor for the island at present and so not much can be said about the overall bronze distribution on the island after LM IIIB with certainty.

From the PG and G periods, the Cretan data continues to be poor in resolution. Most bronze objects come from tombs or cave sanctuaries with long periods of use, where distinguishing between PG and G deposition often proves to be impossible. In addition, many publications are of less than optimal quality, since the relevant sites were excavated in a different era of standards and expectations.[91] It is difficult to compare the evidence for commodities to the patterns in finished imported goods, since much of the resolution of this evidence is so poor. The best published evidence for metals use in the PG–G period is from the Knossos Cemeteries, and it may be that the large number of metals known from Knossos is the result of the fact that tombs from this site are

---

[83] Hallager and Hallager 2000, 179.
[84] Dimopoulou 1997, 434; Dimopoulou-Rethemiotaki 2004, 363–380: Hemingway and Harrison 1996; though see Evely, Hein, and Nodarou 2012 for evidence that the bronze generated at postpalatial Palaikastro was made from recycling.
[85] Ksipharas 2004, 212–213; Wallace 2010, 126.
[86] Tsipopoulou and Nowicki 2003, 575.
[87] Kanta 2005, 701; Kanta 2003, 180–182; Prent 2006, 119.
[88] Coldstream and Catling 1996.
[89] Nowicki 2008, 63.
[90] Day, Klein, and Turner 2009. Most of the buildings so far published from Vronda contained at least a few examples of ground stone or chipped stone tools, but the one scrap of lead is the only piece of metal recovered from a good context.
[91] See comments at Ksipharas 2004, 331; Wallace 2010, 286. For difficulty in dating bronze figurines, see Naumann 1976, 11–12; Verlinden 1984, 164–165; Pilali-Papasteriou 1985, 1.

the ones that have been most carefully excavated and thoroughly published.[92] There must be some bronzes from the PG and Geometric period in the cave sanctuaries on Mts. Dikte and Ida, but because of the nature of the deposits we cannot figure out which objects were deposited in which period.[93] Thus, the overarching spatial patterns for Crete are nearly impossible to assess, even at a rough resolution attempted for the mainland data.

However, at a certain resolution, it is possible to generalize about access to metals in PG Crete. The excavated tombs at Knossos certainly display a level of wealth in metals that was unknown even to the relatively prosperous residents of Lefkandi: the approximate total weight of bronze objects from PG graves in the Knossos area is about 7.6 kilograms, about the same as the quantity of bronze found in contemporary burials in Athens (c. 8.8 kg) and Lefkandi (c. 7 kg).[94] Compared to the amount of bronze represented on the Uluburun ship (11 tons) these quantities are tiny, but they still amount to something. In the G period, an increase in the acquisition of metals is anecdotally apparent in the wealth deposited in rich tombs at sites like Knossos and Eleutherna, and in cave sanctuary deposits throughout the island.[95]

Summary of Bronze Evidence

Patterns in metal distribution and use, then, appear to change dramatically through early Greek history. After a IIIB period during which copper-based metals were circulating in relatively large quantities on the mainland and more limited quantities on Crete, there may have been fewer bronze objects circulating in the aggregate in the IIIC period. During the PG period, the bronze objects that we have found are relatively small in number and tiny, representing a small fraction of the quantity of metal known from the IIIB period. Recovery

---

[92] Catling and Coldstream 2006; the total number of published metal objects from these tombs is well into the quadruple digits.

[93] Original publication of the Vrokastro tombs is in Hall 1914.

[94] Quantities calculated based on data in the publications for these cemeteries; the total weight is approximate. Since weights are not published for objects excavated from tombs at Athens and at Lefkandi, I used the weights of similar objects from the Knossian tombs to generate an estimate for the total weight of the objects recovered from the mainland tombs. For example, the average weight of a bronze fibula from a PG tomb in the Knossos North Cemetery weighed approximately ten grams, and this number was applied to all fibulae in the Athenian burials, and so on. For further details, see full analysis in S. Murray 2013, 87–92.

[95] As Prent (2006, 224) states, the record is slight for Cretan sanctuaries in the tenth and ninth centuries, with few votive objects that clearly date to this period. On the other hand, by the ninth and eighth centuries bronze shields and bowls with relief figurative decoration were being manufactured on the island (Markoe 1985; Prent 2006, 233–234), finds of metal in tombs become more abundant throughout the island, and local gold workshops are proposed to have entered the scene as well (Boardman 1967, 63; Coldstream 2003a, 100). See Catling in Catling and Coldstream 1996, 543–574 for bronzes in the Knossos North Cemeteries, which appear to be largely PGB–Orientalizing in date.

comes with a bang in the Geometric period, when the quantity of bronze objects skyrockets, although we should keep in mind that these numbers are probably inflated by the purposeful deposition in sanctuaries of thousands of small bronze figurines. On Crete, sparse bronze distribution in IIIB gives way to even sparser bronze distribution in IIIC and then proliferation in the PG and Geometric periods, though caution is necessary in interpreting this evidence.

It is true that the schematic picture of fluctuations in bronze in the archaeological record is based upon calculations requiring many assumptions about the relationship of circulating metal to recovered artifacts (whether much bronze survives archaeologically) and of burial goods to goods in circulation (how much of a group's bronze resources end up in tombs where they are likely to be recovered by archaeologists), but it would be difficult indeed to find a way to interpret these data in a way that does not suggest strongly that ships laden with large amounts of copper and tin were not regularly landing in Greece during the earlier parts of the EIA.

Comparison to Other Commodities

While debate about the purported decrease in the quantity of bronze circulating in Greece during the LBA has long stood at the center of discussion about the LBA–EIA transition and may tell us something about the volume of commodities moving into Greece over time, a brief survey of the evidence for Greek consumption of other commodities from abroad is worth considering. The comparison is not an easy one to make because our basis for documenting trade relationships is far more extensive for the IIIB period.[96] However, even without appealing to textual evidence, we can establish that copper and tin were not the only commodities arriving in Greece in smaller numbers during the IIIC and PG periods.

There is ample evidence for a bustling maritime trade in nonmetallic raw materials in the thirteenth century Mediterranean, and compelling reason to believe that considerable quantities of these raw materials were imported by Greeks in the LBA.[97] The most direct evidence for Greek involvement in commodities trade comes from the Uluburun ship, discussed already in Chapter 3. The ship sank off the south coast of Turkey, carrying what was apparently a large cargo of goods, probably comprising a diplomatic gift, though the exact purpose and nature of the shipment is debated. Also debated

---

[96] Textual evidence for the import of commodities from the wider Mediterranean into Greece includes the Pylos Jn tablets, but also others. Linear B tablets from Pylos and Knossos that refer to Cypriot commodities are discussed in Aura-Jorro 1985, 405; Palaima 1991: 280–281; Cline 1994, 130; Shelmerdine 1998, 295). Other tablets from Knossos may refer to Phoenician spices (KN Bg 834, 992, 1021).

[97] For the most relevant general discussion, a see Sherratt and Sherratt 1991, 370–373; Bass 1997a; Bass 1998; Leonard 1998.

are the start and end points for the voyage, though the fact that at least one Mycenaean was a participant in the voyage is likely because a Mycenaean drinking set was among the finds.[98] Along with a large quantity of copper and tin ingots, the cargo included other commodities. Raw materials represented in the cargo included silver ingots, blue glass ingots, hippopotamus and elephant ivory, tortoise shell, ebony logs, scrap gold and silver jewelry, aromatic resin, oils, fruits, nuts, and spices. Also present in the cargo was a transport jar full of glass beads. Among organic cargoes, sampling of the remains from the Uluburun ship specifically demonstrated the presence on the ship of almonds, acorns, pine nuts, pine cone fragments, wild pistachio nutlets, olives and olive stones (2,500 of which are likely to be from Timna in the Negev desert),[99] pomegranate and fig seeds, two types of grape seeds, coriander, nigella, and sumac seeds.[100] One hundred and twenty Canaanite jars discovered in the sunken wreck were filled with terebinth resin, representing about a metric ton of the material, probably carried in liquid form.[101]

The Uluburun ship, then, provides evidence that substantial commodities, organic and inorganic, were moving around the Mediterranean during the LBA. It is not easy to discern how frequently or in what volumes the Mycenaeans were involved in importing these commodities. Certainly the presence of copper oxhide ingots (and rarely, tin ingots) in Mycenaean deposits demonstrates that ships with this kind of cargo did occasionally call at Mycenaean ports.[102] Likewise, Canaanite Jars that may (like the jars discovered in the Uluburun wreck) have contained terebinth resin, exotic olives, or other organic cargoes, are prominent among known imports from the IIIB period.[103] Many of the organic products identified in the Uluburun assemblage represent crops available and abundant in Greece, such as pistachios, almonds, pomegranates, and figs, but we have little archaeological data which would allow us to identify the presence of exotic organics such as cardamom and nigella at Mycenaean sites.

[98] Bachhuber 2006.
[99] Haldane 1993, 354.
[100] Haldane 1993, 352.
[101] Haldane 1993, 352–353; Mills and White 1989; Hairfield and Hairfield 1990.
[102] Copper ingots are known from a number of LBA sites (Mycenae (one from the acropolis and twelve from the Poros Wall Hoard), Tiryns, Thebes, and now Kanakia on Salamis) as well as from a shipwreck off the north coast of Euboea. Only one or two tin ingots are known from the LBA, and both come from Crete: the tin ingot from Mochlos (Soles 2008, 154) is the best-documented example. Likewise, a copper oxhide ingot in hoard 10 at Mochlos was clearly used in a way that may indicate ritual connotations. So far as I know the only other tin ingot found from a site in Greece or Crete was uncovered in an LM IB context during excavations at Gournia in 2012 and is not fully published as of 2016 (www.gournia.org/annual-reports.php). Preliminary reports suggest that this ingot was found in the palace (room 15) next to a room with evidence of metallurgy ("70 pieces of scrap copper or copper alloy, and three pieces of iron slag or bloom.").
[103] At Menidi, Tiryns, Pylos, Mycenae, and perhaps Dimini (Rutter 2014, table 3).

We are on better footing when it comes to the presence of exogenous raw materials like ivory, blue glass paste, and semiprecious stones into Greece in the IIIB period.[104] As discussed already in Chapter 3, we have little systematic information about the total number of beads in the Mycenaean world, or how many of those represent imported beads, beads manufactured locally but made of imported materials, and beads made locally out of local materials, respectively. However, we can say that the number of beads from Mycenaean deposits may rival the number of stars in the sky; and it is likely that at least some of them were imported from glass production centers of Egypt,[105] or made from imported blue glass paste ingots like the ones preserved in the Uluburun wreck.

Likewise, evidence for the manufacture of products made from or integrating worked pieces of ivory, both elephant and hippopotamus, have been discovered in extraordinary quantities in IIIB deposits.[106] Since neither animal was native to mainland Greece in the Bronze Age, this ivory must have been imported. Palatial interest in the acquisition and management of ivory is attested in the Linear B tablets.[107] Although few whole tusks have been found in Greece, it is apparent from the "ingot"-sized pieces recovered at the workshops at Mycenae that ivory did come into Greece as a raw material in the IIIB period. Major craft workshops have been identified within the immediate vicinity of IIIB palatial sites themselves, at Mycenae and Thebes, where value-added products such as furniture and jewelry that integrate ivory and semi-precious stones were manufactured.[108]

As far as quantities go, the workshops at Mycenae have produced "tens of thousands" of pieces of ivory, and the same is probably true of the workshops at Thebes.[109] Likewise, unusual quantities of ivory come from the chamber

---

[104] Desborough 1972, 15.
[105] Rehren and Pusch 2005, 1758.
[106] Tournavitou 1992; Tournavitou 1995; Symeonoglou 1973, 44.
[107] Mentioned in the Ta series from Pylos and in PY Ra 984 and PY Vq 02 (482) in connection with a variety of tables, footstools, and chairs. Ivory is used in combination with stone, ebony in other objects, as an unworked raw material. Two of the Knossos "chariot tablets" attest that ivory was used in the construction of chariots and bridles, probably stained red in some cases. See Lynn 1988, 158–159. As far as the quantities involved are concerned, tablet KN Og 7504 contains signs that indicate "fractional quantities used by Mycenaean scribes to denote larger quantities of agricultural and industrial commodities, measured by weight and bulk ... This suggests that ivory was imported into Mycenaean Greece in bulk form and in not inconsequential quantity" (Lynn 1988, 164–165). For a recent discussion of the Linear B evidence for ivory working see Luján Martínez and Bernabé 2012. For further discussion of the fact that ivory was brought into the Mycenaean mainland and then worked to suit local demand, see Kryszkowska 1992.
[108] Lynn 1988, 168. For full publication of the Ivory Houses at Mycenae, Tournavitou 1995.
[109] Tournavitou 1992; 1995; workshops in Thebes, Voutsaki 2001; ivory specifically in context at the Kadmeion, Burns 2010b, 136–137. Ivory was also recovered from excavations at Thebes Thepsiadou street (Andrikou 1995, 292).

tombs at Spata and Menidi in Attica.[110] Smaller quantities of ivory finds are known widely from IIIB contexts, especially burials.[111] Given all the evidence we can be relatively confident that ivory as a raw material reached Greece in quantity and with some regularity in the Mycenaean period.[112]

During the IIIC period, ivory is present in smaller quantities. No single deposit on the scale of finds we have at IIIB sites like Mycenae, Spata, Menidi, or Thebes has been discovered from the twelfth and eleventh centuries. Ivory does appear in a number of wealthy tombs from the twelfth century[113] and occasionally in settlement deposits.[114] Evidence for other commodity imports during the IIIC period is thin on the ground. Apart from a few Canaanite jar sherds from IIIC early contexts, which may or may not represent kickups from earlier IIIB deposits, there is no direct evidence that organic cargoes reached Greece in the twelfth century whatsoever, but this may simply be because the evidence is limited. On the other hand, it is apparent that at least some inorganic commodities are likely to have continued circulating on both Crete and the mainland during this period, in the form of, for example, semiprecious stone and gold objects.

The quantity of ivory recovered from PG deposits is negligible. Ivory is "extraordinarily rare" in PG contexts.[115] Maybe a few dozen objects are known from the mainland,[116] and a similar number can be firmly dated to the Cretan PG.[117] The only gold artifacts known from mainland Greece, outside of the cemeteries at Lefkandi and on Skyros are thin wire rings or hoops. A couple of these are known from EPG and MPG tombs in Athens[118] as well as from LPG tombs in the Argolid, Atalanti, and sites in Thessaly.[119] The

[110] For Spata, see Grammenos 1992; For Menidi, see *Deutsches Archäologischen Institute* 1880.
[111] To name only a few examples, IIIB ivory finds come also from Thorikos (Privitera Bozza 2013, 133–140); the Athenian Agora (Immerwahr 1971, 106–107, 151, 166–167, 177, 189, 208, 220), Kalapodi Kokkalia (Dakoronia and Dimaki 1998, 394–395) as well as many sites in the Peloponnese and on Crete.
[112] See Burns 2010b for the consumption of ivories by the Bronze Age elite.
[113] Ivory comes from tombs in Lamia (Stamoudi 1994, 301–305), Agios Elias (Mastrokosta 1966, 203–210), Agnanti (Spyropoulos 1970, 235–237), Kalapodi (Dakoronia and Dimaki 1998, 394–395), and Elateia, among others.
[114] Thebes Threpsiadis street: Andrikou 1995, 290–294. In particular, at the cemetery at Perati, where most of the imports from this period have been discovered, over fifty ivory objects were deposited.
[115] Desborough 1972, 298, n.5
[116] Lemos 2002, 108. A small number of iron pins with ivory heads or globes are known from prosperous communities such as Lefkandi and Athens. Other ivory scraps come from the Lefkandi cemeteries.
[117] See a good recent summary of Cretan ivories from the PG period in Evely 1996.
[118] Lemos 2002,128; Kübler 1943, 32, pl. 39; Brouskari 1980, 24.
[119] Lemos 2002, 129. Two are known from Tiryns (Verdelis 1963, 30) and fewer than a dozen from Argos. Additional gold wire rings or spirals come from cemeteries in Atalanti (Dakoronia 1985, 165–167), from Theotokou (Chatziangelakis 1982, 230), Pherai, Marmariani (Heurtley and Skeat 1930–1931, 33–34), and Homolion (Theocharis 1961–1962, 174). These are mostly associated with female and child burials.

overall quantity of both gold artifacts and the aggregate quantity of gold known from PG contexts on both Crete and the mainland is small, even when the slightly more complex and numerous gold objects from the Lefkandi cemeteries are taken into account.[120] The same is true for semiprecious stones; they are found in a sufficiently small number of PG deposits that they are typically presumed to be "survivals" or recycled objects from Mycenaean or Minoan times.[121] I have already discussed the extraordinary rarity of faience and glass beads from Greece during the PG period.[122] Likewise any substantial evidence for a trade in organic materials is not forthcoming, with the exception of the Phoenician transport vessels found at Kommos which may or may not have ever seen their goods filter into circulation on Crete itself.[123] A few sites like Lefkandi, Knossos, Argos, and Athens clearly possess some measure of these kinds of resources, but not in the quantities that were evidently circulating in the LBA.

In the Geometric period things change, though not in straightforward ways. As for durable commodities, ivory again shows up in the form of tens of thousands of objects on the mainland,[124] particularly at sanctuaries – to the extent that Winter could argue for local schools of resident foreigners producing ivory in the eighth century at Athens, Delphi, and Perachora.[125] Likewise, excavators at the the sanctuary of Artemis Orthia in Sparta turned up hundreds of ivory objects. Many of these demonstrate considerable eastern influence. Most were probably deposited toward the end of the eighth century BCE.[126] Ivory from mainland burials is not common, even at Lefkandi. On Crete ivories that can be dated from the Geometric period are "scarce and ordinary"[127] although finds from the Idaean cave, probably either derived from eastern models or imported from Syria-Palestine and Phoenicia, number almost into

---

[120] For full discussion of gold from Lefkandi, see Lemos 2002, 129–133. In addition, comments at Popham et al. 1980, 217–218: "For the bulk of the PG period no gold is recorded, and this seems to be the rule throughout Greece."

[121] For example, Evely 1996, 623.

[122] Full discussion is in Chapter 3. Even in the well-furnished Knossos North Cemetery tombs hardly a dozen faience beads have turned up (Webb in Coldstream and Catling 1996). No Phoenician vessels are known from Cretan sites outside of Kommos from the PG period.

[123] Rutter 2006, 677 (as evidence of a carry trade, with their contents recanted and sent onward from Kommos in different containers).

[124] Kourou 2015, 220.

[125] Winter 1976. Ivory that appears in Greece in the eighth century is almost exclusively elephant ivory, with no hippopotamus products represented (Gazon-Bizollon 2007; Fischer 2007).

[126] Kopanias 2009. Dawkins (1929; 1906–1907) originally dated the finds to the tenth–eighth centuries, but others (Kunze-Goette 1933; Matz 1950; Spartz 1962) contest this early date on stylistic grounds. Kopanias insists that a late eighth century date is probably most accurate for the majority of the finds.

[127] Evely 1996: A few pins from the Knossos region and at Psychro cave (extending into G), one or two from Prinias; seven handles at the Knossos North Cemetery; one each from the Idaean cave, Psychro cave, and Liopetri (this may be an heirloom).

the hundreds.[128] Most ivories[129] from Geometric Crete are indeed known from the spectacular cache of such material from the Idaean cave, to the extent that some have suggested that ivories were specifically directed to the cave through some ritual or social mechanism.[130]

Faience and glass begin to turn up in greater numbers in the Geometric period.[131] At Lefkandi Toumba burials dated to the ninth century (local LPG/SPG) contain jewelry as often as they do not.[132] Likewise, faience beads are not unusual finds from the EG period onwards in the cemeteries of Athens.[133] Faience beads appear in larger numbers in tombs excavated from Geometric Crete: beads and amulets are known from Knossos, Aphrati, Amnisos, Eleutherna, Gortyn, Kavousi, Kommos, Palaikastro, Phaistos, Praisos, Prinias, Vrokastro, and the Idaean, Inatos, and Diktaean Caves.[134] To quote Stampolidis and Kotsonas (2006, 345), "these artefacts are not rare." Other precious materials do occur in some quantity during the Geometric period, for example in the wealthy burials at Eleutherna and Knossos, but again are difficult to date with much certainty to the period between 900 and 700 BCE.[135]

Gold, which is vanishingly rare at Greek sites dating to the PG, is found in greater quantity again near the end of the tenth century and continues to be common in deposits throughout the ninth and eighth centuries.[136] At Lefkandi, "the use of gold starts up again and continues unabated" until the abandonment of the cemeteries around 825 BCE.[137] During the final phase of the cemetery, especially beginning around 860, gold is "amazingly plentiful" and considerably complex, employing techniques such as granulation, composite sheeting, and the incorporation of amber (another indication of a revival of robust trade in a variety of directions).[138] Many of these objects have close

---

[128] Sakellarakis 2013, 172–174.
[129] For general discussions of ivory found in early Crete, see Hoffman 1997, 53–65; more recent studies and discoveries include Evely 1996 (tombs 219 and 292) and Stampolidis 1998, 271–272. Kopanias (2009, 129–130) has argued that "craftsmen trained in an Oriental or Orientalizing workshop worked as ivory carvers at the Idaean Cave at some time during the third quarter of the eighth century BC." He surmises some of these craftsmen moved to the Artemis Orthia sanctuary in Lakonia during the late eighth century.
[130] Stampolidis and Kotsonas 2006, 346.
[131] Webb in Coldstream and Catling 1996.
[132] Popham et al. 1980, 218.
[133] Coldstream 2003a, 4.
[134] Webb in Coldstream and Catling 1996, 609–610.
[135] Four ivory carved heads from Eleutherna, for instance, might be either Geometric or Archaic; the context is not conclusive (Stampolidis 1992).
[136] For a detailed study of gold bands from eighth century Greece, see Ohly 1953. To my knowledge a thorough study of gold artifacts from the Geometric period has not been attempted, a fact which may in and of itself suggest that the quantities involved have deterred researchers.
[137] Popham et al. 1980, 218.
[138] Popham et al. 1980, 218–222.

parallels in contemporary Athens,[139] Eretria,[140] and Skyros,[141] and all look inspired by Cypriot models. The most aggressive acquisitors of gold in the Geometric period appear to have been the workshops in Athens and Attica. The earliest gold finds (two, possibly Cypriot finger rings) in Athens (after a hiatus starting around 1050 BCE) come from a tomb in the Kerameikos.[142] By the MG period gold is attested from burials throughout Greece in quantities that dwarf those recovered by archaeologists from the PG period.[143] We cannot necessarily assume that the rate of recovery of this precious metal tracks closely with ancient quantities in circulation, but it is hard to imagine scenarios in which the sizable changes in quantitative evidence from the PG to the Geometric period do not give us at least some meaningful clue to the overall quantities of gold present in mainland Greece before and after the ninth century.

On Crete, gold jewelry becomes plentiful enough in the Geometric period that the notional presence of a Syrian goldsmith in Knossos around 800 BCE is deeply rooted in EIA scholarship.[144] Since no granulation or filigree is known from Greece between the eleventh and ninth centuries, that individual or workshop is credited with reintroducing these techniques to the island in the eighth century.[145] A group of gold artifacts, sometimes considered a "hoard," comes from the Tekke tomb at Knossos, echoing the eighth century explosion of gold finds in Athens and at Lefkandi on the mainland.[146] Once again, the impression the evidence leaves is of a major increase in the access to and expression of wealth in exotic materials after the PG period.

[139] Kübler 1954, 158; Stavropoulos 1965, 78, pl. 44a; Droop 1905–1906, 91 (at least ten similar bands from Dipylon graves in the National Museum); Schlörb-Vierneisel 1966, beilagen 13.
[140] Bérard 1970, 21, 35–45, color pl. 2.
[141] Sapouna-Sakellarakis 1986.
[142] Coldstream 2003a, 9; Cypriot comparanda cited.
[143] Gold is not rare in eighth century mortuary contexts at major sites, certainly around Athens (where it was dicovered in excavations that are relatively widely distributed throughout the region, for example in excavations under the Theseion (Alexandri 1968, 79–80), on the NW slope of the acropolis (Dörpfeld 1897, 478) at Odos Kavalotti (Stavropoulos 1965, 75–80), on Vouliagmeni boulevard (Alexandri 1972, 165–176)) and on Skyros (Sapouna-Sakellaraki 2000, 316; Papadimitriu 1936, 228–234; Luce and Blegen 1939, 131), but there are also gold finds from minor or less-extensively explored sites like Megara (Nikopoulou 1972, 101–102), Spata (Philadelpheus 1923, 131–138), Anavyssos (Verdelis and Davaras 1968, 97–98), Argos (Pappi 2012, 32–33), Nafplio (Charitonidis 1956), Neochorakion, Klenia (Charitonidis 1955) and dozens of other sites. See also Ohly's collection of data on gold bands (Ohly 1953).
[144] For example, Dunbabin 1957, 40–43; Boardman 1967; Coldstream 1993, 98–100.
[145] Stampolidis and Kotsonas 2006, 349; Hoffman 1997, 213–243.
[146] In the Tekke tomb at Knossos, gold finds were encountered in the dromos and chamber of the tomb; in addition, deposits near the door and doorjamb revealed two pots full of gold and silver jewelry in addition to ingots. Hoffman 1997, 191–197; Boardman 2005. See also discussion of wealth in Iron Age tombs at Knossos in Kotsonas 2002; 2006.

Evidence for the import of agricultural commodities into Crete, in the form of Phoenician jars, continues into the Geometric period. No comparable evidence exists on the mainland. Indeed, long-distance ceramic imports, with the exception of a few Cypriot vessels (mostly jugs and juglets) from Crete, have not been documented from Geometric Crete, in spite of the fact that pottery from the Greek mainland and Cyclades are imported to Crete in this period. The development on Crete of a local Cypro-Cretan style suggests that interactions between the two islands in the Geometric period were intense, despite the low number of ceramic imports. Deepwater shipwrecks off the coast of Ashkelon in the Levant suggest that wine was circulating in the Mediterranean by the eighth century, but the degree to which this commodities trade reached the Greek world is not clear.[147] A lack of imported commodity containers from Geometric deposits need not obviate the possibility that commodity imports reached Greece during a period that preserves a wide array of other evidence for a bustling international trade economy. Archaeologically invisible agricultural commodities are difficult to account for. However, to the extent that the evidence can assist us, we can only say for certain that commodity imports in the Geometric period included ample quantities of gold, faience/glass, metal resources required for bronze-making, ivory, and semiprecious stones.

4.2. AN EXPORT ECONOMY? EVIDENCE FROM AROUND THE MEDITERRANEAN

At this point in the argument, it has already been relatively firmly established that fewer imports and less evidence for imported commodities are documented from deposits dating to the periods directly following the Mycenaean collapse, with significant recovery beginning sometime in the late ninth or eighth centuries. This conclusion is not meaningless, but a deep inquiry into the numbers has often shown that confidently orienting an intellectual conclusion around a body of archaeological evidence that is as subject to distortion as fancy imported goods and metal objects is likely to be fraught with interpretive problems. It thus makes sense to gather as much additional evidence as possible in order to flesh these patterns out. An obvious place we might wish to look in our quest to find meaning in the patterns of import deposition and commodity presence from the domestic archaeological material in Greece is the opposite side of the "trade equation": the diaspora of Greek artifacts encountered outside of the Greek cultural sphere. It is reasonable to expect that a bustling Greek institution of long-distance trade would be likely to leave some kind of residue in the lands of the peoples with whom the Greeks traded,

---

[147] Ballard et al. 2002.

and that quantities of that residue might fluctuate according to the intensity of trade in different periods. Thus, export quantities can help us to get a sense of change in the intensity of long-distance trade over time, and to help us assess the validity of patterns in the rest of the evidence that we have observed so far. Aligning the import data and evidence from commodities with the data from exports will help to determine whether trade really did collapse, or whether the evidence is letting us down in important ways.

The Export Evidence

While gathering evidence for imported exotica is challenging, looking at exports in a systematic way across the vast spaces and times of the Mediterranean presents problems that are in many senses completely insuperable. Aegean societies in prehistory were more often than not involved in relationships with states and peoples in the Syro-Palestinian littoral. Due to political instability the history of archaeological work in this region cannot be counted on to have produced an even record of remains. For instance, there is a great deal of Mycenaean pottery known from the area within modern Israel, but this may be partly due to a long record of intensive archaeological work here, rather than because Greeks had especially intense trade relations with the region in the past. On the other hand, Lebanon has been a more difficult place to work, and consequently produces fewer dots on a distribution map. North Cyprus is poorly represented because archaeologists have not been able to work there since the 1970s, even though it is clearly an important region with much to tell us about Greek interactions with the wider world throughout the period. Excavation in Italy has, for obvious reasons, presented fewer challenges during the majority of the twentieth century. Thus, many hazards exist in the interpretation of export distributions.

In addition to the differential rates of recovery of materials encountered in a politically complex modern environment, there are other complexities associated with assembling export data. First, there is the problem of awareness. Archaeologists working in countries throughout the Mediterranean may or may or may not be trained to recognize Greek imports. For example, while hundreds of Euboean sherds have been found in Geometric contexts in Italy in the last forty years, none had been identified before that, surely an example of a change in the literacy of Italian archaeologists in reading Greek imported pottery.[148] There is also the problem of handling "local imitations." Vessels that look like they may have been imported from Greece may in fact be local imitations of a known style of pottery. These imitations can sometimes be identified by macroscopic fabric analysis, but are often difficult to distinguish

---

[148] Fletcher 2007, 45; Coldstream 1968, 164–165.

TABLE 4.4. *Sites in Mediterranean regions where Greek pottery has been discovered*[149]

Region	<10	10–50	50–100	100–500	500+	Total Sites	Approximate Quantity
IIIB							
Anatolia	17	3	1	1	2	24	~1,500
Cyprus	41	24	2	3	3	73	~3,300
Levant	45	18	6	6	0	75	~2,500
Egypt	23	1	1	1	1	27	~1,000
Italy	35	6	2	5	1	49	~1,300
Total	**161**	**52**	**12**	**16**	**7**	**248**	**~9,600**
IIIC[150]							
Anatolia	5	3	1	3	0	12	~500
Cyprus	5	5	1	1	2	14	~1,500
Levant	12	2	2	0	0	16	~200
Egypt	0	0	0	0	0	0	~0[151]
Italy	50	6	2	6	2	66	~1,500
Total	**72**	**16**	**6**	**10**	**4**	**108**	**~3,700**
PG[152]							
Anatolia							?
Cyprus	1	0	0	0	0	1	~5
Levant	6	2	0	0	0	8	~100
Egypt	0	0	0	0	0	0	0
Italy	0	0	0	0	0	0	0
Total	**7**	**2**	**0**	**0**	**0**	**9**	**~105**

(continued)

---

[149] van Wijngaarten 2012 for the IIIB period; especially from the tables in catalogue I.

[150] van Wijngaarden 2012 and Vagnetti 1999, who suggests that the number of Italian sherds with Mycenaean characteristics from Italy is considerably lower than most estimates, because at least half of the sherds are probably local imitations. This conclusion is supported by other studies (including Guglielmino et al. 2010; Vagnetti et al. 2009; Tanasi 2005). Thus, the number presented here is lower than many might assume for IIIC Mycenaean imports in Italy. In general, For IIIC pottery found outside of Greece, there remains significant debate about the ratios of locally produced imitations to imports on Cyprus, along the southern Levantine coast, in Cilicia, and in Italy. The growing body of scholarship on this topic makes it seem likely that our picture will continue to change rapidly in the coming years. See, among others, Ben-Shlomo 2006; Killebrew and Lehmann 2013; Killebrew 2000; Vagnetti and Jones 1988; Vagnetti 1998; Vagnetti 1999; Jones et al. 2005; Tanasi 2005; Vagnetti et al. 2009; Mountjoy 2011; Mountjoy and Mommsen 2001; Badre et al. 2005; D'Agata et al. 2005; Mommsen and Sjöberg 2007; Zuckerman et al. 2009. It should be kept in mind, then, that the numbers presented here for the IIIC period may be too high. Regardless, the error is probably not so great that it elides the major differences in scale between known exports from the IIIB period OR known exports from the PG and Geometric periods.

[151] While there are Aegeanizing vessels found at various sites extending down the Nile Delta, these were manufactured in Cyprus (see Mountjoy 2011; Mommsen et al. 2011; Mühlenbruch et al. 2009; Mühlenbruch and Mommsen 2011).

[152] Export data from the PG period based on appendix II in Lemos 2002, augmented by data in Luke 2003; Gjerstad 1977; Saltz 1978. Helpfully discussed in Waldbaum 1994.

TABLE 4.4. *(continued)*

Region	<10	10–50	50–100	100–500	500+	Total Sites	Approximate Quantity
G							
Anatolia							?
Cyprus	11	1	1	0	0	13	~100
Levant	21	2	3	2	0	28	~750
Egypt	0	0	0	0	0	0	0
Italy	30	18	4	2	0	55	~1,500
Total	62	21	8	4	0	96	~2,350

from imports without more expensive and time-consuming petrographic or NAA analysis. In addition, sorting out chronological equivalencies across a complicated array of local ceramic sequences presents serious challenges. Thus, establishing a "complete" or "authoritative" catalog of Greek exports would be the project of many years, and is well outside the scope of the current project. That said, a sizeable body of previous work has gathered much of the evidence for LBA and EIA exports from Greece, and concatenating previous studies here should provide accurate impressions on the level of an "order of magnitude."[153]

4.2.1 The IIIB Period

Mycenaean or Mycenaean-style pottery dating to the fourteenth and thirteenth centuries has been excavated at sites in the Levant, Anatolia, Cyprus, Egypt, and Italy.[154] While the geographical distribution of Mycenaean sherds is wide, the number of sites producing large quantities of Mycenaean sherds (more than five hundred) is limited.[155] Smaller quantities of Mycenaean pottery appear to

---

[153] Important studies of LBA ceramic exports include van Wijngaarden 2002; Leonard 1994; Vianello 2005; Fisher 1988. For the Protogeometric period, Lemos (2002) includes a small summary of exported PG material in Appendix 2. These data have been updated according to recent finds mentioned in Maier, Fantalkin, and Zukerman 2009. For the Geometric period, evidence for Greek pottery in the Levant is gathered in Saltz's unpublished PhD dissertation, and summarized also at various levels of resolution in: Luke 2003; Wallace 2010, 205–206; Jones 2000. Evidence for Italy in the eighth century is provided by Fletcher 2007, though the data he presents is somewhat difficult to parse due to the fact that it is presented almost entirely in pie charts, maps, and bar graphs that do not always make clear important divisions within it.

[154] Some important publications are van Wijngaarden 2002; Vagnetti et al. 2009; Fisher 1988; Kelder 2009; Hankey 1981; Mountjoy 1998.

[155] van Wijngaarden 2002, 71: "Mycenaean pottery was fairly common at Ugarit: it has been found in all excavated parts of Ras-Shamra and Minet el-Beida and it occurs in different types of contexts."

have been distributed further "down-the-line" through regional exchange networks.[156] Almost all of the Mycenaean decorated fineware that has been analyzed can be traced to a clay source somewhere in the Argolid.[157] However, the participation of Mycenaeans themselves in bringing this pottery to the East and West remains a topic of debate. There is ample evidence, from the lack of direct mention of Levantine toponyms in Linear B texts, to the co-occurrence of vast quantities of Cypriot pottery at sites with Mycenaean pottery, to the presence of Cypro-Minoan marks on Aegean pottery in the Mediterranean, that Cypriot traders may have served as middleman.[158]

Late Mycenaean pottery found throughout the Mediterranean consists primarily of decorated fineware, although coarseware stirrup jars, perhaps from Crete, also appear in the corpus of finds from the Levant and from Cyprus.[159] The distribution of vessel types varies from site to site, though closed vessels are more common overall. Coastal sites in the Levant with abundant Mycenaean pottery, such as Tell Abu Hawam and Ashdod, turned up a range of vessels, including open vessels for dining and drinking and closed vessels for storage, while inland sites with few Mycenaean imports contain a limited assemblage, mostly storage vessels like stirrup jars. At a few sites, notably Ugarit, vessels that may have been used in ritual practice are present along with Mycenaean figurines, although the representation of Mycenaean material as a function of the overall assemblage at Ugarit is quite small (and is notably lower than the proportion of Cypriot wares at the port). The reverse is true at Sarepta, in Phoenicia.[160]

Both the Levantine and Cypriot assemblages of Mycenaean pottery are notable for the presence of certain "specialized" shapes (both open and closed) that are found frequently in the east but rarely in mainland Greece. These may have been produced specifically for consumption in an overseas market, but we cannot be sure about this without further study.[161]

---

[156] van Wijngaarden 2002, 261; Marazzi 1988, 6–7.
[157] Leonard et al. 1993.
[158] For discussions of a Cypriot role in the movement of Mycenaean pottery, see Hirschfeld 1992; 1993; 2004. For Cypriot marks on Canaanite jars, see Hirschfeld's work, as well as Cross and Stager 2006; Yasur-Landau and Goren 2004.
[159] Catling et al. 1980, 92–93; Day and Haskell 1995; Haskell 2011; Pratt 2016. Coarse ware TSJs have been discovered at many sites on Cyprus, but only a few coastal sites in the Levant (Leonard 1994, 46–47). Some similar vessels have been found in Italy at Broglio di Trebisacce and Scoglio del Tonno (van Wijngaarden 2002, 262).
[160] Bell 2006, 60. Sarepta might have been directly in contact with Aegean suppliers, while Cypriots may have served as merchants bringing Mycenaean material to Ugarit.
[161] Examples of these specialized vessels include piriform jars, amphoroid kraters, and chalices. Sherratt 1981, 183; 1999, 182–184; Jones 1986, 599–600. Another intriguing feature of the evidence is the fact that Canaanite assemblages, whether consisting of open vessels, closed vessels, or a combination, do not resemble Mycenaean assemblages, indicating that rituals such as drinking and feasting were not replicated along with the pottery there (Yasur-Landau 2010, 196).

194 COLLAPSE OF THE MYCENAEAN ECONOMY

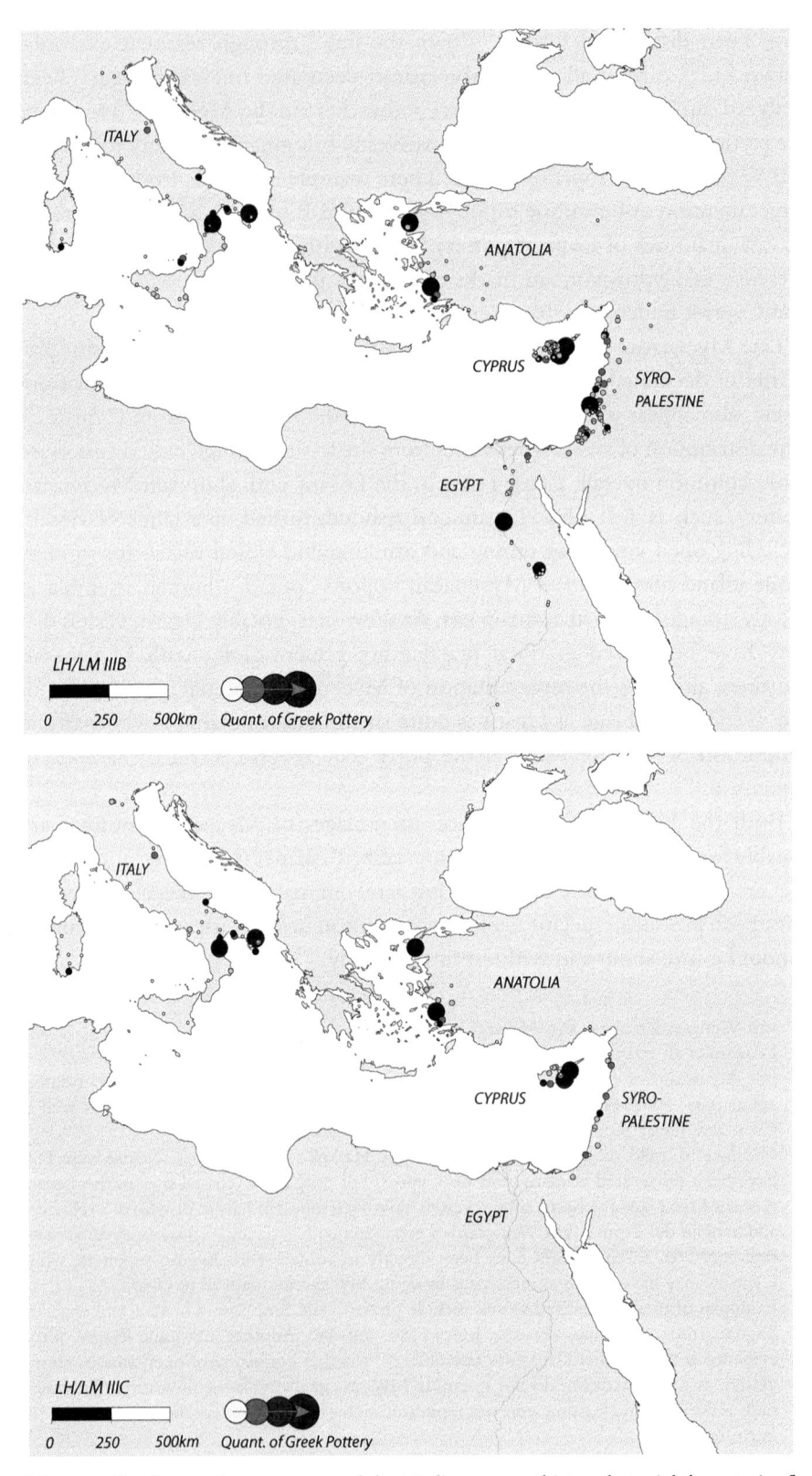

Map 4.1. Greek ceramic exports around the Mediterranean, thirteenth to eighth centuries (by author)

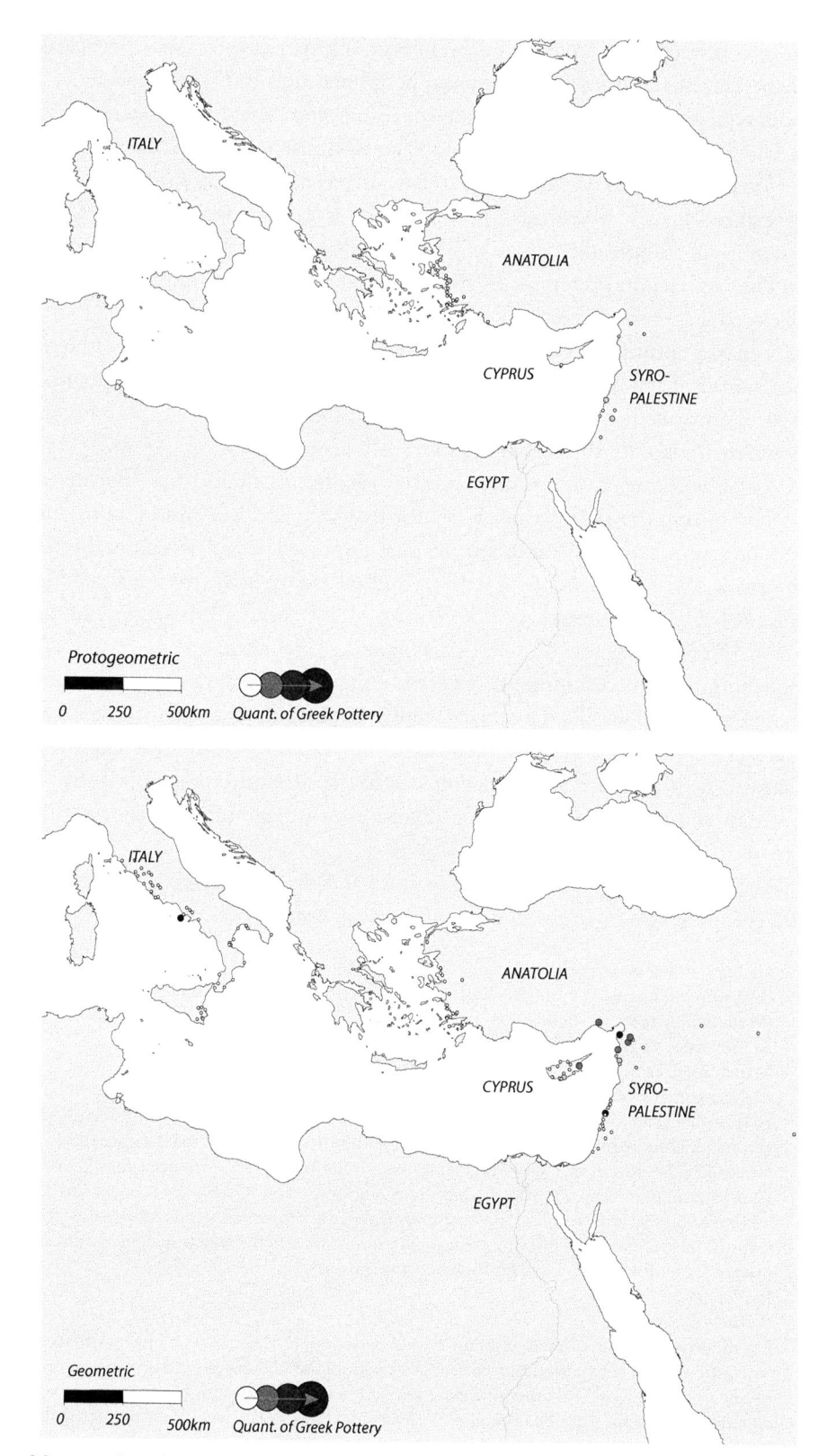

Map 4.1. (cont.)

In contrast to the situation in the Levant, a broad array of open and closed shapes appears at primary centers and peripheral sites in Cyprus and Italy. In both regions, almost all sites with Mycenaean pottery that have been identified are coastal. While the Cypriot assemblage is similar in type to the Levantine material, Italian sites do not appear to have been a destination for the export of specialized shapes. Mycenaean pottery found in Italy reflects a typical Greek assemblage, comprising a range of both closed and open shapes.

The Mycenaean pottery in Egypt stands out for its monotonous assemblage of closed shapes, almost entirely small, fineware stirrup jars and pilgrim flasks.[162] Mycenaean pottery in Egypt is associated with elite settlement contexts, although occasionally it appears in mortuary contexts.[163] Finds are known in quantity from Tell el-Amarna and Deir el-Medina, but apparently made their way up and down the Nile until the end of the thirteenth century.[164]

As far as the economic underpinnings for the distribution of Mycenaean pottery during the IIIB period, it is clear that we need to consider numerous variables when approaching this topic. First, exported storage jars point directly toward a Mycenaean value-added agricultural export industry. Perfumed oil was probably an important component of this,[165] although the export of raw olives,[166] textiles, octopi,[167] and other materials (including fine pottery) could have complemented shipments. There is compelling evidence to suggest that these kinds of value-added materials were produced under palatial control, and therefore could have been an element of an economy geared for export.[168] Linear B texts demonstrate special interest in the administration and control of oil, and we find evidence for the production or storage of it at major palatial sites like Thebes and Mycenae.

Recent work on transport jars has shed valuable light on the geography of the complex system of production and circulation of perfumed oil.[169] West

---

[162] Hankey 1981; Podzuweit 1994, 466; Kelder 2009, 341; van Wijngaarten 2011. cf. the depiction of stirrup jars on the wall paintings of the tomb of Ramesses III at Thebes (Wachsmann 1987, pl. 59; Hankey 1995, 123).

[163] Kelder 2009, 340–342; Bell 1982; Warren and Hankey 1989.

[164] Maran 2005, 427–428.

[165] Melena argues that Mycenaean oil was used primarily for perfume manufacturing (Melena 1983) rather than for eating. He suggests that olives themselves were also used primarily as a raw material in manufacturing contexts (Shelmerdine 1985; Leonard 1981) rather than as a foodstuff. The notion that oils were being specifically treated and produced for export to Cyprus is supported by a Linear B tablet from Knossos, tablet KN Fh 369, concerning the boiling of oil that is *a-ra-si-jo*, Alasiyan, presumably either from or intended for transport to Cyprus. In addition, *ku-pi-ri-jo* might in some cases be used in the tablets designate a normal market for perfumed oils (see Himmelhoch 1990, 93–98).

[166] Kelder 2009.

[167] Rutter 1992, 63–64.

[168] On the Mycenaean perfumed oil industry, see Foster 1974; Melena 1983; Phappas 2010.

[169] Scientific analysis of exported Mycenaean pottery from the LBA has shown that the majority of fineware stirrup jars and other fine closed vessels found in the eastern Mediterranean were manufactured in the Argolid. Because of this evidence, scholars have long suspected that

Crete and central Crete produced quantities of some liquid and exported this liquid, in TSJs, to mainland sites, "with only a [small amount] sent to other regions of Crete and only a tiny trickle beyond the Aegean."[170] Kommos, Knossos, and Chania were participants in this system. Mainland sites did not manufacture many TSJs, but Mycenae, Tiryns, and Thebes were supplied with whatever liquid they contained from west and central Crete. Fineware stirrup jars from the Argolid and from East Crete have been found in the East Mediterranean. Synthesizing this evidence, Haskell argues that Cretan transport stirrup jars were filled with local oil-based products on Crete, and then sent to the mainland, where their contents were (a) recanted and/or modified and then shipped onward to eastern markets in their new Argolic perfume containers and/or (b) used to treat exportable textiles.[171] This dovetails obliquely with the snippet of evidence for directed interregional movement of trade goods glimpsed in tablet MY X 508, which records cloth sent to Thebes from Mycenae[172] and suggests that Cretan and Mycenaean oil and export industries were surprisingly complex and certainly could have been geared toward participation in an active commodities market.

Although there is also evidence that Mycenaean palatial institutions were concerned with the manufacture of elite crafts, such as fine furniture and jewelry, for the IIIB period we do not have compelling evidence that these crafts were intended for export.[173] On the other hand, although most ceramic production appears to have been outside of the purview of Mycenaean palatial control,[174] Mycenaean decorated fineware pottery appears outside of Greece in large quantities. Given the presence of fine Mycenaean decorated pottery in addition to transport vessels of various kinds around the Mediterranean, we could consider the possibility that the high quality drinking and eating vessels represented in the Mycenaean ceramic repertoire themselves represented a desirable commodity on the international market. This is an especially compelling notion given the comparatively low quality of local ceramics in Cyprus, Italy, and the Levant during the LBA.[175] The general consensus among scholars is that individuals at both Levantine and Cypriot sites were consumers of Mycenaean goods which took on special significance because they were brought from afar, and were monopolized by

---

Tiryns and Mycenae were preferentially involved in sending perfumed oil or other sought-after liquids from Greece to the east (Killen 1985, 269; Shelmerdine 1985, 89, 150).

[170] Haskell 2011a, 123. For an argument that the jars may have been sent from Crete to the Argolid and to Thebes as tribute, see Haskell 1981, 220; Maran 2005, 428.
[171] Haskell 2011b, 128.
[172] Palaima 1991, 276–277; Killen 2008, 187–188.
[173] Or in any case, there is no apparent evidence to this effect in the Linear B texts, nor has luxury furniture of clearly Mycenaean manufacture been listed among possible IIIB exports.
[174] See especially Galaty 1999; Whitelaw 2001b; Knappet 2001.
[175] van Wijngaarten 2002.

certain segments of society.[176] Although some Mycenaean pictorial kraters and storage jars appear in Cypriot and Levantine tombs,[177] the majority of Mycenaean pottery from around the Mediterranean was discovered in settlement contexts and is often interpreted as an accessory for elite activities.[178]

Alternatively, these assemblages could represent a mobile population of Mycenaeans who liked to have their normal ceramic wares with them during maritime voyages, as might be indicated by the Mycenaean drinking assemblage on the Uluburun ship. Did Mycenaeans themselves carry finewares with them in their travels, or were these objects really exchanged with individuals and communities around the Mediterranean? Debate continues about whether most of the local Mycenaean-style pottery found in Italy was imported or locally made, and whether these ceramic finds imply a major Mycenaean presence in the area instead of active exchange networks.[179]

In Anatolia, there is clear evidence for at least one Mycenaean colony at Miletus, but scholars have not come to a consensus regarding the difference between Mycenaeanization among local groups and colonial Mycenaean endeavors in western Asia Minor.[180] Mountjoy delineated two general zones of Mycenaean engagement here, including an "Upper Interface" in the NE Aegean and a second zone of interaction in the Dodecanese and Rhodes,[181] but the exact nature of Mycenaean trade, acculturation, or colonization in Anatolia in either of these zones remains out of focus. Patterns vary among different sites, making generalizations about Mycenaean export practices in Anatolia difficult. For instance, while on Rhodes Mycenaean tablewares dominate the assemblage, and while the finds from some tombs make it appear that Mycenaean burial customs might have been in operation on the island, Mycenaean pottery at Iasos is mostly made locally and occurs in a variety of shapes and contexts.[182] Suffice it to say that there was probably a significant Mycenaean presence in

---

[176] Sherratt and Sherratt 1991, 372; Watrous 1992, 178–183; Knapp and Cherry 1994, 44–46; Steel 1998, 296; van Wijngaarden 2002, 23: "I consider the bulk of Mycenaean pots in overseas areas to be the result of exchange processes."

[177] Levantine tombs often contain storage vessels that might be associated with the oils required for local funerary rituals (Kinet 1981, 146–147; Salles 1995, 176).

[178] In Italy, locally produced LH IIIB pottery appears alongside imported materials at a number of sites, especially in Apulia (Jones and Vagnetti 1991, 132–133, 140). Storage vessels come from a variety of contexts, suggesting that whatever bulk goods were being exported from Greece had a different social and economic function than did decorated finewares.

[179] Blake 2008; Vagnetti 1999, 194; Vagnetti 1993, 152; Bietti Sestieri 1988, 30. Some have argued that the Mycenaeans operated a major trade network encompassing the Tyrhennian and Adriatic seas: Smith 1987; Marazzi and Tusa 2005, 604; Merkouri 2005, 612.

[180] For Miletus in the LBA, see Niemeier 2009. For some discussion and debate on the topic of local consumption versus colonization for the LBA in general, see Knappett and Nikolakopoulou 2008, 37–39; Davis and Gorogianni 2008, 339; Melas 2009, 70–71. For specific examples of sites in Rhodes, see Marketou 2009. For Iasos, Benzi 2005, 206.

[181] Mountjoy 1998.

[182] Eerbeek 2015; Karantzli 2009, 356–359; Benzi 2005, 206.

Anatolia in the IIIB period, and this presence is likely to have comprised groups of Mycenaeans settling along the coast as well as some kind of system for the distribution or exchange of finewares and commodities among and with local communities.[183] Little material with Mycenaean characteristics is found in Central Anatolia, Cilicia, or SE Anatolia.[184]

4.2.2 *The IIIC Period*

The distribution of Mycenaean pottery in the Mediterranean decreases in the aggregate during the IIIC period. In Egypt, IIIC pottery is not present. A significant quantity of Mycenaean-style pottery continues to characterize the assemblages of sites in Italy, Cyprus, and the Levant in the IIIC period, although the differences in magnitude between locally made Aegean-style wares and actual imports remains a subject of debate.[185] On Cyprus, Mycenaean imports dated to the IIIB period likewise appear to be replaced in the IIIC:1a period by an ensemble of locally made Mycenaean wares,[186] though Cretan TSJs from 12th century Cypriot deposits have been recognized.[187] Evidence for a newly important Mycenaean presence on Cyprus is apparent in the appearance of a variety of "Mycenaean behavioral patterns"[188] in addition to locally produced Mycenaean pottery. There is much evidence to suggest that this evidence is the result of migration, although not everyone is in agreement about this.[189]

Across the sea in the Levant, those making Aegean-style pottery on Cyprus were circulating wares to sites in Phoenicia and Syria.[190] In Israel, LH IIIC pottery occurs primarily in the southern coastal plain, and also in the Egyptian garrisons in the north. The Aegean-style pottery in the north has been shown by NAA to have been produced on Cyprus.[191] Closed vessels continue to dominate most assemblages, though open vessels are also present. The implication is that vessels (and their contents) were no longer available from the Argolid; Cypriots did their best to replace these goods to continue filling a Levantine demand for them during the twelfth century.[192] In the Canaanite territories, however, at sites such as Ashdod, Ashkelon, and Tel Miqne, locals produced

---

[183] For discussion of Mycenaean objects of Mycenaean origin at Iasos, Miletus, Ephesus, Kolophon, and Klazomenai, see Mee 1998, 138–141.
[184] Kozal 2015, 698.
[185] See, for example, Blake 2008.
[186] Yasur-Landau 2010, 140; Cline 1994, 61–62.
[187] Maran 2005, 416; also see Courtois 1978, 163–167; Haskell 1981, 140–142; Karageorghis and Demas 1988, 137 and pl. 96.
[188] Yasur-Landau 2010, 140–148.
[189] Review in Knapp and Manning 2016, 133–134.
[190] Yasur-Landau 2010, 189.
[191] van Wijngaarden 2002, 262.
[192] D'Agata et al. 2005; Yasur-Landau 2010, 203–204.

their own versions of Aegean-derived pottery.[193] Yasur-Landau (2010) has argued persuasively that the "deep change" in the archaeological record apparent in thirteenth century Philistia is likely to represent the arrival of a group of refugee Mycenaeans, perhaps utilizing a route through Tarsus and the Amuq plain.[194]

At many sites in Italy, in SW Sicily and Apulia, but also along the north Adriatic coast, Mycenaean-style pottery continues to appear in significant quantities in the twelfth century.[195] Whereas IIIB pottery in Italy had typological connections to Rhodes, Crete, and the Argolid, the pottery of the IIIC period is typologically similar to the pottery from Mycenaean sites in the Patras/Kefallenia region, or from Achaea in general.[196] By the end of the period, most of the Aegean-type pottery in the region appears to have been locally produced. The increasing presence of local imitations of Mycenaean pottery at IIIC sites, as well as the evidence for depopulation within west Greece during the twelfth century, may suggest that some Greeks in the IIIC period relocated to Italy after the palatial collapse. Others have suggested that the local imitations indicate the presence of Mycenaean migrant potters rather than colonists.[197] According to this theory, potters would have fled Greece as demand for their wares diminished in the wake of social disintegration to find greener pastures to the west.[198] Regardless of the circumstances of its production, its depositional context suggests that IIIC pottery in Italy is usually considered to have continued to serve as a luxury marking out elite groups.[199]

In Anatolia, habitation continues in Miletus into either IIIC Early or Late[200] and IIIC pottery continues to be found along the Anatolian coast and in the NE

---

[193] For a systematic study of this IIIC pottery, see Dothan and Zuckerman 2004.

[194] This is a vigorous and well-founded argument. The sudden appearance of LH IIIC-type pottery and loomweights (see Rahmstorf 2005) in Tell Ta'yinat, Çatal Hüyük and Tarsus supports the idea that Greek people could have migrated to the Levant and Cyprus via a combination of land and sea routes. See Haines 1971; Janeway 2006–2007, 131; Pruss 2002. For a critical view, Middleton 2015.

[195] Fisher 1988, 126; Vianello 2005, 88–89. Detailed work on a few different sites, Tanasi 2004a; Tanasi 2004b; Tanasi 2007; Tanasi 2008.

[196] Fisher 1988, 127–128. An exception is the octopus stirrup jar.

[197] Although most accept that the archaeological record of Scoglio del Tonno shows signs of the presence of Mycenaean settlers (Webster 1996, 140–141; Vagnetti 1999, 148–149).

[198] Vagnetti 1999, 148–149. There is some evidence for the technological transmission of techniques for bronzeworking from east to west (Vagnetti and Jones 1991, 140), and new production of faience object occurs in the twelfth century. The site of Frattesina, which contained evidence of industrial activity including glassmaking and metalworking from the twelfth through the eighth century, may have become one node in a new western trade network that rose to prominence when troubles roiled the eastern Mediterranean (though we cannot assume that the central Mediterranean was not likewise roiled).

[199] Vianello 2005, 85.

[200] Early according to Mountjoy 2004 but Late according to Schachermeyr; Niemeier and Niemeier 1997, 205–206.

Aegean islands in significant quantities.[201] Recent work at a number of sites along the Anatolian coast and the hinterland of western Anatolia has likewise suggested that the presence of Mycenaean culture strengthened rather than weakened in the IIIC period, although the evidence from these sites might again be likely to indicate diplomatic, military, or migratory connections rather than economic ones.[202] Much of the IIIC Mycenaean-style pottery in Anatolia, as on Cyprus and in the Canaanite Pentapolis, appears to have been locally produced rather than imported.[203]

4.2.3 The PG Period

During the Protogeometric period there is little evidence for the export of value added goods or other commodities from Greece to either the east or the west. The quantity of known PG pottery outside of Greece from this period is small, perhaps one hundred total sherds, and the extent of its distribution is limited. The range of shapes discovered is likewise small: most vessels are open shapes, especially the skyphos, although a few amphorae round out the assemblage,[204] indicating that exported Greek bulk goods may have traveled around the Mediterranean in limited quantities at this time.[205] Most imported Greek pottery from the Levant has been identified as Euboean, Attic, or Cycladic in origin, although at least two Argive deep bowls are represented. The contexts of use in the Levant are unfortunately mostly disturbed; all Greek imports from this period come from settlement contexts rather than from mortuary ones.

Only one site on Cyprus, an apparently elite cemetery at Amathus in the south, has turned up PG Greek pottery (two LPG skyphoi and a cup).[206] Pottery in the PG style has been found in Anatolia and PG Greek imports

---

[201] For an up-to-date treatment of IIIC on the Anatolian coast, see Mountjoy 2015. IIIC material is known from the Dodecanesian islands of Kos, Kalymnos, Astypalaia, Miletus, and Chios as well as Rhodes. On the Anatolian coast, sites with IIIC pottery include Liman Tepe (Erkanal 2008), Bakla Tepe (Özkan and Erkanal 1999, 14–17), Bademgediği Tepe (Meriç and Mountjoy 2002), Kadıkalesi (Akdeniz 2007), Pilavtepe (Benter 2009), and Çine Tepecik (Günel 2008; 2010).

[202] See recent publication of IIIC Mycenaean material from the inland sites of Bademgediği Tepe (Meriç and Öz 2015) and Çine-Tepecik (Günel 2015), to add to known IIIC Anatolian sites on the coast such as Liman Tepe (Mangaloğlu-Votruba 2015).

[203] Mountjoy 2015, 42; Mangaloğlu-Votruba 2015, 661.

[204] Including a tenth century Attic amphora from Çatal Hüyük (Saltz 1978, 81).

[205] Based on the repertoire of shapes exported in the PG period, it seems apparent that whatever liquids were being exported from Greece in the IIIB period no longer traveled from west to east in the PG. Based on the small faience vessels found in small numbers at Lefkandi and Knossos, a flow of unguents in the opposite direction is possible. See comments in Luke 2003, 41; Coldstream 1998, 354.

[206] Coldstream 1995.

of open vessels have been found in small numbers in MPG levels at Miletus as well as in PG deposits from Asarlik, Dirmil, Smyrna, Ephesus, and Klaros.[207] A close connection between Athens and Miletus in the PG period is especially apparent.[208] As was the case with IIIB and IIIC material, sorting out local production from exchanged objects represents a continuing challenge.[209] Looking to the west, only a few "genuinely PG" sherds have been identified in South Italy, although it is notable that local Iapygian wares developed a distinctive pseudo-Greek Geometric style during the period.[210]

As for a mechanism for the exchange we do have, there are probably only three sensible possibilities. The first would involve Greek individuals sailing to the Levant with personal drinking sets. The second would presume that Phoenician or Cypriot merchants occasionally visited ports in Greece, and acquired either passengers or ceramics during their stay. The notion that Greek goods traveled with Cypriot or Phoenician merchants is supported by the fact that Cypriot pottery is found in many of the same contexts as PG Greek pottery in the Levant.[211] Finally, Greeks could have been exchanging textiles or some other archaeologically invisible goods or commodities that we cannot detect in the archaeological record. While we should keep in mind the fact that we are likely missing some of the picture, as we always are when we interpret the archaeological record, decline in the frequency of Greek overseas interactions during the eleventh century seems like a reasonable conclusion to draw based on the evidence.[212]

---

[207] Krumme 2015, 585; Mitchell 1989/1990, 99, fig. 20; Vaessen 2015, 825; Catling 1998; Lemos 2007c. Local sites that have turned up cups and skyphoi with stylistic similarities to Attic examples are Dirmil and Teichiussa (Boysal 1969, 31; Bulba 2010, no. Sk1; Voigtländer 2004, pl. 158). Mainland pottery is also found on Samos and Lesbos.

[208] Desborough 1972, 180.

[209] At Troy, scientific analysis has shown that PG pottery is a local product, not an imported good (Aslan, Kealhoffer, and Grave 2014; discussion of PG Troy in Aslan and Hnila 2015). However, many of the amphorae from the PG period have similar profiles to those from Lefkandi and Athens.

[210] For the presence of a small number of PG sherds in Italy, see Snodgrass 1971, 85–86, n. 60; Benton 1953, 327, n. 491. For the Iapygians and their local pottery styles, as well as hypothetical continuation of Greek presence in Apulia through the LBA–EIA transition, see Coldstream 2003a, 222. At least one Cycladic PG piece has been claimed from Satyrion. For evidence of eleventh century influence and contacts between Greece and the west from Malta and Sicily, see Tanasi 2010a; Tanasi 2010b.

[211] This is true of the earliest known PG sherd from Tell Es-Safi/Gath (Maier, Fantalkin, and Zukerman 2009); Tel-Afis (Bonatz 1998, 2014–2015); the PG amphora from Çatal Hüyük (Saltz 1978, 77–83); Ras el-Bassit (Saltz 1978, 73). Phoenicians and Cypriots were obviously also present from an early date at Tyre.

[212] Although one possibility is that the archaeological record, in which ceramics are prominent, is not accurately representing interaction in this period. If western Greeks were trading something other than ceramics with Italians frequently during this period, it may be difficult to find evidence for this exchange.

4.2.4 The Geometric Period

Greek imports dated to the Geometric period have been discovered at sites in some regions of the Mediterranean. As in the PG period, there are local Geometric ceramic styles in Anatolia that closely resemble Greek examples, and it can be difficult to sort local imitations from imports, but certainly at least some of these objects represent imports from East Greece, Attica, and the Cyclades.[213] Levantine imports grow in number in the ninth and eighth centuries[214] and Greek imports are commonly encountered at sites in Apulia, SW Sicily, and Etruria in deposits dated to the eighth century. Evidence from Huelva in Spain shows that Greek pottery was moving even further to the west in the first half of the ninth century.[215] In Cyprus Greek Geometric imports are known from over a dozen sites, mostly elite burials.[216]

Greek imports present in the Levant during the Geometric period include open drinking vessels, especially the PSC skyphos but also kotylae and kraters, sourced from Euboea, Attica, and the Cyclades.[217] A small fraction of closed shapes, including at least one amphora, an amphoriskos, and an aryballos, have also been discovered along the Levantine littoral. As Luke points out, the highly limited range of imported Greek shapes contrasts sharply with the much fuller array of Phoenician and Cypriot wares at presumed emporia such as Al Mina.[218] In the Levant, Geometric pottery is discovered either at major sites or at sites likely to have been sea or river ports, though the number of sites with Geometric imports present is relatively small, only about two dozen.

Intrasite contexts of use for this pottery have usually been described as "elite."[219] As opposed to imported Greek wares in the Levant, all Greek imports in Cyprus come from cemetery deposits, specifically from tombs identified as elite or royal.[220] As Crielaard has discussed, Geometric imports

---

[213] For imports at Ephesus, Miletus, and Bodrum, see brief summary in Coldstream 2003a, 246.
[214] The most comprehensive treatment of Greek Geometric pottery in the east is Saltz 1978. Summaries of same include Luke 2003; Coldstream 1998; Gjerstad 1977.
[215] Finds from a sample of about 8,000 potsherds from Huelva included 3,233 Phoenician jars, 4,703 indigenous vessels, thirty-three Greek sherds, thirty from Sardinia, eight from Cyprus, and two from Villanovan Italy. The Greek vessels included nine early eighth century Attic amphorae and ninth century Euboean skyphoi. Other exotic goods at the site included agate, amber, glass, ostrich eggs, an elephant tusk, and 2.23 kg of worked ivory artifacts. There was also evidence for ironworking on the site. For summary, see González de Canales, Serrano, and Llompart 2006.
[216] For a summary of Greek Geometric finds in Cyprus, see Coldstream 1998; Luke 2003, 42–44.
[217] Recent work (Vacek 2014) has shown that pottery from Al-Mina was indeed not locally produced but made in Euboea, though it remains impossible to pin down a particular locality of production within the island.
[218] Luke 2003, 41.
[219] Including royal sanctuaries or temples, palaces, public buildings, and elite zones.
[220] This is almost certainly, to some degree, a factor of excavation history, since settlements are more common in the IA archaeological record in the Levant and tombs more common in Cyprus.

in Cyprus are the same in type and distribution as those in the Levant and drinking cups feature prominently in both assemblages.[221] These assemblages include complete dining sets from royal tombs at Salamis, Amathus, and Kourion.[222] Most imports are Euboean, though a few Attic and Cycladic specimens have been published.[223] Cypriots occasionally imitate Greek pottery, especially PSC skyphoi, but only at a few sites, ones that possess no imported material.[224]

Geometric Anatolia presents difficulties for the estimation of economic engagement across the Aegean sea. A common assumption is that Greek ceramics appearing in Anatolian contexts from the ninth and eighth centuries represent the "Ionian migration" that involved Greeks traveling across the Aegean as groups of migrants, rather than exchange *sensu stricto*. Nonetheless, the idea of an Ionian migration has lately come under fire,[225] mostly due to the postcolonial turn in archaeology and related refinements in the way that archaeologists conceptualize the movement of peoples.[226] It is not possible to wade into these discussions in the current context. Suffice it to say that a variety of mechanisms and activities likely account for the existence of Greek pottery in Anatolia during the Geometric period.

In Italy, the range of Geometric imports echoes what is known from Cyprus and the Levant. Greek imports from Euboea do not begin to appear in the Italian archaeological record until MG, or about 800 BCE, at the same time as imports of Levantine origin (scarabs, amulets) and at the same sites (Veii and Cumae).[227] By 780/770 the Levantines and Euboeans had established a colony at Pithekoussai, and with them arrived considerable quantities of Greek pottery. Euboean and Cycladic imports are well-represented among eighth century Italian imports; over half of these are drinking cups, kraters, or pouring vessels, although aryballoi are present as well. Although the earliest Euboean material appears in southern Etruria and Latium (Veii, Tarquinia, Rome,

---

[221] Crielaard 1999. For catalogs and discussions of Greek imports on Cyprus, see Gjerstad 1977; Wriedt Sørensen 1988; Luke 2003, 42–43; Coldstream 1998.
[222] From Salamis Tomb I, Amathus Tomb 194, and a tomb at Kourion (Coldstream 1988, 35).
[223] Lemos and Hatcher 1991; Coldstream 2001, 229; Gjerstad 1977, nos. 28–47 and 49–50.
[224] Crielaard 1999, 275. This is an interesting contrast to local imitations of Mycenaean pottery, which are usually found at the same sites where least a few instances of *bona fide* Mycenaean imports are attested as well.
[225] Lemos 2007c; Crielaard 2009.
[226] Examples at van Dommelen 1997; van Dommelen 2002; Malkin 2002; Knapp 2008.
[227] The earliest post-BA Levantine import found in Italy is a scarab from Veii dating to the beginning of the eighth century (Hölbl 1979, cat. 36). Scarabs continue to appear at other Etruscan sites such as Veii and Torre Galli in Calabria and Cumae in the bay of Naples. The distribution of Levantine imports in eighth century Italy does not align closely with the distribution of Greek imports, appearing primarily in southern Etruria. Greek trade in the west may therefore not have been mediated through Cypriot middlemen (cf. Fletcher 2007, 45; for another view, S. Morris and Papadopoulos 1998).

Narce), by the mid-eighth century it is distributed across southern Apulia, Campania, and western Sicily.[228]

Also reaching Italy in the eighth century were Corinthian drinking sets, aryballoi,[229] pyxides, kraters, and transport amphorae.[230] Whereas the earliest Euboean and Levantine imports appear at Veii and Cumae, the earliest Corinthian skyphoi and oinochoai show up in Salento, in South Apulia. Early material is also found at Incoronata, Pontecagnano, Pithekoussai, and Veii (together with the earliest Euboean and Levantine material).[231] Euboean pottery was always limited in its range of distribution, but eighth century Corinthian pottery is found widely across the entire peninsula, in Sicily, and in southern Sardinia. This is not surprising, considering the fact that the earliest Corinthian colonies in Italy began in the late eighth century.[232] By this time, it is apparent from the corpus of Corinthian imports in Italy that the Corinthians were in the business of exporting perfumed oil in Corinthian aryballoi, in addition to their colonial ventures.[233]

Have we come, then, full circle? From a Mycenaean assemblage that suggests Mycenaeans either traveling with or exchanging their drinking cups and marketing perfumed oil in specialized containers, we have gone through eras of apparent migration and stagnation to return to a strikingly similar picture that suggests Corinthians and Euboeans either traveling with or exchanging their drinking cups and marketing perfumed oil in specialized containers. Of course we should be cautious in approaching the complex evidence so obtusely. Indeed, there are notable differences between the two bodies of evidence that should not be overlooked. While Mycenaean ceramic exports may have been related to trade in liquid contents of stirrup jars around the Mediterranean, the Geometric ceramics from the east, and their archaeological circumstances of discovery, make it look like Greeks interacted with Cypriots and Levantines in bibulous symposia, rather than in the context of trade or exchange of value-added goods. Geometric trade in perfumed oil, apparently driven by

---

[228] See Fletcher 2007, 46, fig. 46; Coldstream 1968, 369–370; Tandy 1997.

[229] It is often difficult to distinguish Corinthian imports from imitations made locally. Some colonies may have imported Corinthian clay to coat aryballoi (Neeft 1987, 59, 367; Scheibler 1983, 180).

[230] Fletcher 2007, 47.

[231] Fletcher 2007, 47.

[232] See Salmon 1984, 62–63. There are a small number of Attic skyphoi from late eighth century deposits in Italy (Veii, Salento, and perhaps Canale in Calabria); Fletcher 2007, 51.

[233] S. Morris and Papadopoulos 1998, 253; Salmon 1984, 117. Fletcher notes that the Corinthians became active in Illyria, at Vitsa, at the same time that their perfumed oil industry appears to have blossomed (Fletcher 2007, 54). Pliny claims that this area boasted the best native plants for perfuming oil (*HN* 13.5). A small quantity of Achaean pottery, especially kantharoi, may be present in some deposits dating to the end of the eighth century, but it is not yet possible to verify this due to the confusing nature of the relevant deposits at Sybaris and Francavilla Marittima (Papadopoulos 2001, 438).

TABLE 4.5. *Summary of evidence from exports, IIIB-G periods*

Region	IIIB Context	IIIB Shapes	IIIC Context	IIIC Shapes	PG Context	PG Shapes	G Context	G Shapes
Levant	Coastal centers (dining wares), inland sites (storage vessels)	Special dining wares, ritual vessels, and storage vessels	Southern Levant esp.	All shapes including cooking pots	Coastal sites/Ports; settlement	Drinking cups; a few amphorae	Ports and central places; settlement	Drinking cups; a few amphorae
Cyprus	Coastal centers, elite dining; some tombs	Special dining wares and storage vessels for eastern markets	Coastal centers; local production	All shapes, including cooking pots	Amathus; elite tombs; imitations elsewhere	All cups	Ports and central places; elite tombs	Drinking and dining sets
Italy	Coastal centers, maritime exchange operators, some tombs	storage wares typical of mainland, some open shapes, especially drinking vessels	Coastal Apulia; Veneto?; settlements; widely distributed but some elite use	Closed and open shapes; often alongside local imitations	Maybe a handful of sherds in south Apulia	?	A wide variety; colonies, local uses in settlements/cemeteries	Dining and drinking sets; aryballoi

(continued)

206

Anatolia	Coastal and inland sites of W. Anatolia, widely distributed	Closed and open shapes; local imitations	Coastal and inland sites of W. Anatolia; widely distributed	Closed and open shapes; local imitations	A few coastal sites and sanctuaries	Skyphoi and amphorae	Coastal sites: Ionian migration?	Wide range
Egypt	Tombs and elite settlement contexts only	closed storage/transport vessels almost exclusively						
Production Center	Argolid, Crete, Rhodes, some locally made in Italy	Locally made in Italy, Cyprus, Levant; Italian imports from Achaea			Euboea, Argolid		Euboea, Corinth, Attica	
Quantity	~9,600	~3,700			~150		~2,350	

Corinthians, looks to the west instead. In some ways this looks like an inverted circle, then, with similar patterns in place that are mixed up geographically.

Whatever we make of the comparison and contrast of export evidence from the thirteenth and eighth centuries, we can at least conclude that after a long period during which exports from Greece are either absent or largely archaeologically invisible from both east and west, the eighth century sees an increase in such material. The quantitative evidence of Greek exports to the wider Mediterranean bears out the idea of a rhythm of decline and recovery, with movements of peoples comprising the majority of Greek activities abroad after the Mycenaean collapse, a major break in any substantial such ventures in the PG period, and a reestablishment of relationships in the east and west in the ninth and eighth centuries, on both old and new ground.

4.3. CONCLUSIONS

During the LBA, commodities probably made up a sizable fraction of exogenous goods that Greeks imported. We find relatively large quantities of relatively large objects made from bronze, ivory, gold, and glass at both cemetery sites and settlement sites, especially on the Greek mainland. A diverse array of corroborating evidence – from the cargoes of sunken ships at Uluburun and Gelidonya, to the prominent position of transport jars within the LBA import and export repertoire, to the quantities of glass, faience, and ivory present at IIIB sites – indicates that the acquisition of raw materials, rather than finished goods, drove LBA trade.

During the IIIC period and beyond, evidence for major trade in commodities is not as robustly evident. It is clear that bronze, and the raw materials needed to produce it, continued to be available to Greeks through the end of the Bronze Age and during the EIA, but the numbers of artifacts apparent in the archaeological record suggest an overall decline in the intake of copper and tin by Greeks after 1200 BCE. The tiny size and small number of bronzes from the PG period especially point toward (though do not prove) a low point in the acquisition of commodities during this period. Likewise, there is an across-the-board decline in the use of other imported materials, such glass and ivory, in the IIIC period that continues in the PG period. Evidence for the import of agricultural commodities from long-distance trading partners from the eleventh and tenth centuries is largely absent, except for the Phoenician jars at Kommos that come from the end of the tenth century.

In the Geometric period, as the number of identified imports rebounds over the course of the ninth and eighth centuries, so does the evidence for commodity imports. The quantity of bronze objects recovered from Greek deposits dated to the eighth century dwarfs anything from the Bronze Age itself, though it should be kept in mind that the average-sized bronze votive statue would not contain the same quantity of metal as an LBA sword (though a bronze cauldron or large votive fibula probably would contain more). The acquisition of metals, ivory, and faience probably rebounded during this period as well, although there is as yet not much evidence that agricultural goods played much of a role in the Geometric Greek trade economy.

The export evidence is also helpful in reinforcing the overall decline and then recovery in long-distance exchange over the transition from the thirteenth to the eighth century. Mycenaean exports are found in large numbers around the Mediterranean from sites dated to the IIIB period. Many of the IIIC imports known from Italy and the Near East are locally produced imitations, perhaps to be associated with emigrating Greeks at this time rather than exchange. PG exports are vanishingly rare (even more so than we would expect them to be based on the import evidence), and consist mostly of open cups, as opposed to the exported closed shapes common in the Mycenaean evidence. By the eighth century, Greek exports are more common again, but do not reach the numbers known from the IIIB period – and consist of different sorts of objects, mostly vessels for feasting or drinking.

It is a rare occasion in archaeology when the data line up to support one conclusion. In assessing change in the Greek trade economy over time, however, we have happened upon one such instance. Thus far, I have interrogated a number of lines of evidence: what texts we have, the most direct category of evidence for trade (imported objects), indirect evidence for trade in the form of imported commodities, and objects exported from Greece to the broader Mediterranean. While taken individually each would fail to convince a skeptic, these lines of evidence are univocal in their eloquent expression of a major scalar decline in Greek exchanges with the wider Mediterranean after the end of the IIIB period and a subsequent recovery in the Geometric period. In the following two chapters, it remains to flesh out the nuances and details that help us to place the human and historical element within this largely metrical and quantitative story.

FIVE

DEMOGRAPHIC AND DOMESTIC ECONOMIC CHANGE IN EARLY GREECE: FACTORS OF SUPPLY AND DEMAND

ALL FINGERS ON OUR DETECTIVE GLOVE THUS FAR POINT IN A SINGLE direction: in the aggregate, the story of the Greek trade economy over the LBA–EIA transition is one of decline soon after 1200 BCE, a long period of stagnation, and eventual recovery in the ninth and eighth centuries. The quantitative changes in import data, in the evidence for trade in commodities, and in the export evidence from the LBA to the Geometric periods show that Greeks probably had less contact with their neighbors around the Mediterranean in the IIIC and PG periods in the aggregate than they did in the IIIB and the Geometric periods. This might lead us to conclude that Greece truly was "in the dark" and cut off from the wider Mediterranean during the period between the Mycenaean collapse and the eighth century BCE. However, in this chapter, I consider a final variable that we must take into account before drawing any conclusions about economic change based on the numbers presented in the previous chapters. I examine how an apparent decline in trade volume after the collapse of Mycenaean society looks if demographic change, and its likely impact on the scale and structure of the economy as a whole, is taken into account.

The lower import quantities from the PG have most commonly been viewed as a direct reflection of a decrease in the robustness or existence of Mediterranean trade routes after the collapse of the Mycenaean palaces. However, most people also think that the population of the Greek world decreased dramatically after LB IIIB (though this is still a controversial topic).[1] If there was significant demographic change after IIIB, this must be taken into account when assessing changes in archaeological quantities through time, because "population trends and the economy are locked into dynamic interrelationships that affect ... the wealth or poverty of society itself."[2] The size of a population will therefore directly influence patterns of consumption and production. If the number of imports declined in proportion to the population, it might indicate not that Aegean trade routes fell out of use during the EIA, but that it was the economy in general that contracted, squelching Greeks' purchasing power and simplifying productive organization in ways that made interaction and exchange more difficult, and less of a priority. If this were the case, a decline in imported goods and commodities in Greece during the postpalatial period would have been the result of demand-side, rather than supply-side, factors: the aggregate quantity of traded objects and materials decreased because there were fewer people around who could produce them, could afford to purchase them, and/or had the need and desire to use them. In this chapter I will argue that it was in fact demographic change, rather than changes or interruptions of trade routes, that explains the quantitative changes that we see in the evidence the best.

5.1. ESTIMATING THE POPULATION OF EARLY GREECE

Is it important to know the population of prehistoric Greece? If so, why and how would this knowledge impact our interpretation of the prehistoric economy? In the same vein that I maintain the importance of knowing "how much" trade declined after the Bronze Age, I also believe that we must put this information into a demographic context in order to truly understand its meaning. In this section I discuss the rationale for including a chapter on demography in this book, and provide a brief review of standard methods in the study of ancient populations.[3] I break down the kinds of evidence available, and lay out the basic picture of population change we have for early Greece. Weighing all the evidence, I argue that a population decline of about 40–60 percent between the late thirteenth and late eleventh century is likely, with steady growth after that.

Why Demography?

Though I will argue that demography played a particularly important role in the processes that defined the Greek Bronze/Iron Age transition, a sense of

---

[1] Some beats in the debate: Snodgrass 1971, 367; Desborough 1972, 18; Dietz 1982, 102; Papadopoulos 1996, 254; Tandy 1997, 20; I. Morris 1997b, 540; Walløe 1999; Dickinson 2006, 88, 93–98; I. Morris 2006.
[2] Abernathy 2002, 69.
[3] For a full explanation of demographic methods and approaches, see S. Murray 2013, 98–145.

population change through time is important in any comparative, historical, economic study. The size, density, and composition of a population will have an effect on almost every aspect of its functioning, and it is difficult to understand social processes without at least a crude grasp of these figures. As Scheidel puts it, "demography is much more than just numbers, and relevant to much of what we seek to know and understand about the distant past."[4]

In addition to being generally instrumental in reconstructing past economies, demographic trends are particularly important in the study of the LBA–EIA economy because of the ongoing debate about the role trade played in sociopolitical processes at the end of the Bronze Age. This debate is reviewed in full in the Introduction to this book, but it is worth restating here. The notion that trade was disrupted around 1200 BCE has been central to many explanations of the Bronze Age collapse. According to this position, the Bronze Age palatial elite was meant to have been able to support its authority in part because of the elite's preferential access to luxury goods from exotic lands, which allowed them to claim special status vis-à-vis the rest of the population.[5] Thus, trade routes must, at least to some extent, have underpinned the hierarchy and structure of society in the LBA. A complete breakdown in trade routes would therefore have caused significant changes in the ability of states to function and thus in the way that communities and power were organized.[6]

This argument rests in part on a straightforward interpretation of imports, which become less common in Greece after 1200 BCE, as we have seen. Most people explain the observed decrease in imports in Greece after the Mycenaean collapse as a symptom of a general slackening in Mediterranean trade networks, or even a total disruption, at this time. However, identifying a decrease in import quantities does not in itself prove that the Greeks had less access to a system of Mediterranean trade in the IIIC and PG periods. An observed pattern can often arise from a variety of different circumstances, and so it is always important to sort out different possible causes for the observed patterns before coming to a conclusion. While a disruption of trade routes is *one* possible cause for a decreased number of imports, other scenarios could have led to the same outcome. One likely alternative explanation is demographic change.

If we were to correlate the decrease in imported objects from the Late Mycenaean period with a decrease in access to trade (that is, if we focus on

---

[4] Scheidel 2009, 134.
[5] Prestige goods in the LBA were not used as moveable, convertible wealth, but were instead symbolically important nonfungible objects that cemented alliances with other elites, both within and outside of the Aegean (Bennet 2007, 201; Nakassis 2007, 133).
[6] Dickinson 2006, 207; Sherratt and Sherratt (1991, 364) summarize the main features that, in their analysis, distinguish the LBA from the EIA.

supply side issues), this could strongly imply a direct causal connection between a decrease in import numbers and the Mycenaean collapse. There are various scenarios of causality that could be read into this hypothesis. One possible scenario is that the demise of Mycenaean palatial institutions, which may have had some primacy in managing long-distance trade, caused a decrease in trade. Another possibility would be that a disruption of trade routes played some part in causing the social hierarchy of Mycenaean culture (which relied on imports for creating social difference) to collapse and brought on the end of the Aegean Bronze Age.[7] If we accept this scenario, we then would conclude that a supply-side crisis in palatial access to exogenous goods was a major factor in the events that led to the end of Mycenaean society. In either case, a change in import deposition is causally linked (as either a consequence or catalyst) in a direct way with the Mycenaean collapse.

However, I wish to focus more closely on the question of demand, and to argue that the patterns in import totals, apparent commodity acquisition, and export totals are *epiphenomena* of a decrease in the quantity of people living and working in Greece after the events that precipitated the end of the Mycenaean palatial system. This is an important move from the point of view of reconstructing the causal chain of ancient social processes, so I will take a moment to clarify it here. If it is likely that import totals correlate well with population levels in a way that makes it clear that trade was never "disrupted" as a supply side argument would suggest, the possibility that the disruption in trade routes played a role in, or had much structural connection to, the collapse of the Mycenaean palace societies must be reconsidered. In this interpretation, patterns in the number of import totals would be best understood as a correlate of population fluctuation, rather than a cause or effect of social phenomena. This would, in turn, suggest that trade was not a factor in the social changes associated with the end of Mycenaean civilization, and that we should seek different explanations for those social changes besides the breakdown of trade.[8] Finally, this line of reasoning would suggest that the key issues that we should focus on when we are trying to unravel the economic nature of the LBA–EIA transition are the cadence and causes of depopulation in the IIIC period. We might also need to re-think our understanding of the way in which Mycenaean elites cultivated power during the LBA, and the power structures surrounding LBA trade.

Determining the relationship between patterns in imports, exports, commodities, population patterns, and trade networks in the prehistoric Mediterranean therefore has considerable implications for the study of the LBA–EIA transition in general. For my argument, determining the size of

---

[7] See comments and bibliography in the Introduction to this book.
[8] Jung 2016 has recently suggested a Marxian reading, and reviews other theories. See also Cline 2014.

the population will help me to find the best explanation for the patterns in the evidence laid out in the preceding chapters. In what follows, I seek to distinguish between two possibilities – whether imports declined in number because of disrupted trade routes, or whether imports declined in number because of depopulation and overall economic contraction.

Estimating Population from Archaeological Evidence
In order to conduct an analysis of the relationships among import tallies, trade, and population change, it is first necessary to get some idea of the size of the population of Greece. Demography in prehistoric populations is a complicated and controversial topic, and so I review the nature of the evidence before arriving at some tentative estimates about the Greek population.

The first step in formal demography is to describe the population.[9] Demographers usually describe populations in consultation with data from a direct measure, such as a census. Palaeodemographers, on the other hand, do not have direct access to the populations they are interested in describing. It is therefore necessary to use proxy data to describe any hypothetical archaeological population. Proxy data are by definition indirect measures rather than explicit ones, and their interpretation can be problematic.[10] In archaeology, the primary categories of proxy data are burials, settlements/structures, and ceramic evidence from surveys. Burials can be added up and assumed to represent some percentage of a total community,[11] settlement size can be extrapolated out into figures based on assumed occupation per hectare,[12] and the evaluation of the density of surface pottery can indicate fluctuation in site distribution and agricultural intensification over time.[13]

However, while all three types of archaeological evidence provide information about past populations, each category is considerably flawed as far as its potential for producing even roughly accurate estimates for overall population size. Archaeologically visible burial can be limited to certain sectors of the population, skeletons rarely survive in good stead in acidic Greek soils (hindering attempts to model age and sex ratios), and cemeteries may or may not be thoroughly excavated, even when found unlooted.[14] Therefore, even though it is clear that we have excavated more cemeteries from the IIIB and

---

[9] Sbonias 2000a, 1.
[10] Chapman 2000, 65: "Proxy data generally provide limited information for their problem, generally qualitative or semi-qualitative rather than fully quantitative."
[11] Alden 1981; Francovich and Gruspier 2000.
[12] Evans 1928, 563–564; Whitelaw 2004.
[13] Schofield 1991; Bintliff 2000; Sbonias 2000b; Osborne 2006; Corvisier 2008.
[14] For an example of an attempt to model BA Greek population from burial evidence see Alden 1981; negatively reviewed in Cherry 1984. For problems with estimating the population from burial evidence (and some defence of statistical methods of doing so), see Petersen 1975; Bocquet-Appel and Masset 1982; I. Morris 1987; Roth 1992, 186; Fracovich and Gruspier 2000 (esp. 255); Hoppa 2002.

G periods (IIIB = ~450; G = ~332) and as compared to the IIIC and PG periods (IIIC = ~205; PG = ~245), it is difficult to interpret this data where population fluctuations are concerned. The situation for our period is even further exacerbated by the fact that most Bronze Age burials are multiple, while most from the EIA contain only a single individual.

Another way to get a rough idea of the size of a population is to use excavated or estimated settlement size coupled with assumed or inferred density of habitation. As in the case of burial evidence, the size and number of buildings in a settlement that is fully excavated, or the assumed or inferred extent of settlements that are only partially excavated, are indirect proxies for an original population. While archaeologists have used a variety of methods to deduce population from settlement sizes, these have proven as problematic as burial evidence for generating convincing estimates. Efforts to create universal models of population based on normal human tolerances have been criticized for ignoring important variation in psychological attitudes and approaches to space across cultures.[15] Furthermore, archaeological approaches based on this method have been criticized because they ignore the variable, culturally dependent relationship between individuals and required/preferred living space.[16] An alternative is to "build up a culture-specific occupation density assessment,"[17] but this requires the existence of well-excavated settlements, not to mention information about how people share space, which can be unforthcoming for prehistoric societies.[18] Perhaps as a result of these difficulties, Aegean archaeologists are generally hesitant to make population estimates for individual settlements, preferring to limit themselves to qualitative descriptions of periodic settlement sizes or settlement patterns that they perceive to be larger or smaller, denser or sparser than in the preceding and following eras.[19] When archaeologists do estimate population size for individual sites, these vary dramatically. Whitelaw settles on a figure of 14,000–18,000 for Neopalatial

---

[15] Naroll 1962; Fletcher 1995; Criticisms at Whitelaw 2001a; Whitelaw 2004.
[16] Whitelaw 2001a; Whitelaw 2004, 152.
[17] Whitelaw 2001b, 63. On this principle, he has estimated the size of some Mycenaean settlements using analogy with the well-documented site of Pavlopetri, where the evidence suggests that the settlement density was c. 200 person/ha.
[18] See Clinton 2013 for the suggestion that the Minoans had different ideas about public and private space than twenty-first century Americans.
[19] To choose just one of many examples, Foxhall (1995, 249) states that "[t]here is clear evidence for nucleated communities, though they are usually different from palace centers and not normally as large as later *poleis* (though Lefkandi is hardly insignificant in size in this period, even in comparison with some later poleis.)" Reticence to identify settlement sizes is in opposition to Renfrew's early appeal that attention to settlement size and patterning must "form the starting point for any investigation of a prehistoric culture or society" (Renfrew 1972, 225). In *The Emergence of Civilization* Renfrew calculated the populations of the regions of Greece for which there was reliable data at the time. These figures have been reconsidered and somewhat reevaluated by Cherry (2005), Branigan (2001), and Whitelaw (2001a; 2004). See also Carothers and MacDonald 1979.

Knossos, but previous estimates have put the figure as high as 100,000.[20] Bennet proposes 6,400 for the population of Mycenae (circa 32 ha at 200 people/ha),[21] but French suspects that this figure may be too high. According to this logic, the population of Pylos (at 15 ha) would only be 3,000.[22]

For the EIA, the reliability and quantity of settlement data is worse. Despite the progress archaeologists have made in exploring material record of the EIA during recent decades, we still lack a good sense of "normal" settlement structure or size for the earlier part of the period.[23] It is therefore no surprise that calculations of EIA settlement sizes have varied widely. The evidence suggests that these were rarely larger than hamlets or villages, though acknowledging this does not bring us any closer to a sense of the absolute population of EIA Greece.[24]

Finally, ceramic frequency data drawn from regional intensive and extensive surveys is another proxy that could potentially be used to make estimates about the population of prehistoric Greece.[25] However, these datasets are difficult to interpret.[26] Cultural attributes of the "subject population" such as settlement pattern (centralized versus dispersed), agricultural regime (intensive versus pastoral), and rate of artifact discard (frequent versus infrequent) can all affect the archaeological visibility of a given group.[27] It is generally thought to be unlikely that ceramics collected during intensive survey accurately reflect the original "parent" population of either ceramics or of the people who made and

---

[20] Evans 1928, 563–564; Whitelaw 2004, 153 and 149, Figure 10.1. Few believe that Evans's figure of 100,000 has much to recommend it.

[21] Bennet 2007, 186–187. See also Firth 1995.

[22] Chadwick 1988, 76; Bennet and Shelmerdine 2001, 136; Whitelaw 2001b, 63; Bennet 2007, 187.

[23] Lemos 2002, 149–150.

[24] See full analysis of the value of settlement evidence for estimating EIA population at S. Murray 2013, 109–119. For perhaps the best existing analysis of an EIA village, its layout, and population see Rückl 2008, according to which EIA Mitrou would have sheltered only 25–75 souls. Population densities "as low as twelve and as high as fifty inhabitants per hectare have been proposed" for PG and EG settlements (Hall 2007, 73). These figures "would yield anything from 540–2,250 inhabitants for Eretria or from 90–375 inhabitants for Zagora." At the high end, Athens may have been home to about 7,000 people (I. Morris 1987, 101).

[25] Sbonias 2000a, 11.

[26] Though it is possible to use survey data to determine absolute figures, the nature of the data makes it much more amenable for comparing change over time than for arriving at aggregate demographic estimates. Sbonias (2000a, 8) suggests a complex multistep process for determining absolute population figures from survey evidence as follows: "(i) consider the size of the sites, (ii) discuss the contemporaneity of sites, evaluate missing sites, (iii) separate permanent settlements from other sites, and produce a list of number of sites in each functional category for each period, (iv) accept a figure of people per settlement category, (v) multiply by the number of sites." This is essentially the prescription used by Bintliff (1997) to estimate the absolute population of Boeotia, but with much more supplementary historical data than is available for the prehistoric period.

[27] Bintliff, Howard, and Snodgrass 1999, 165.

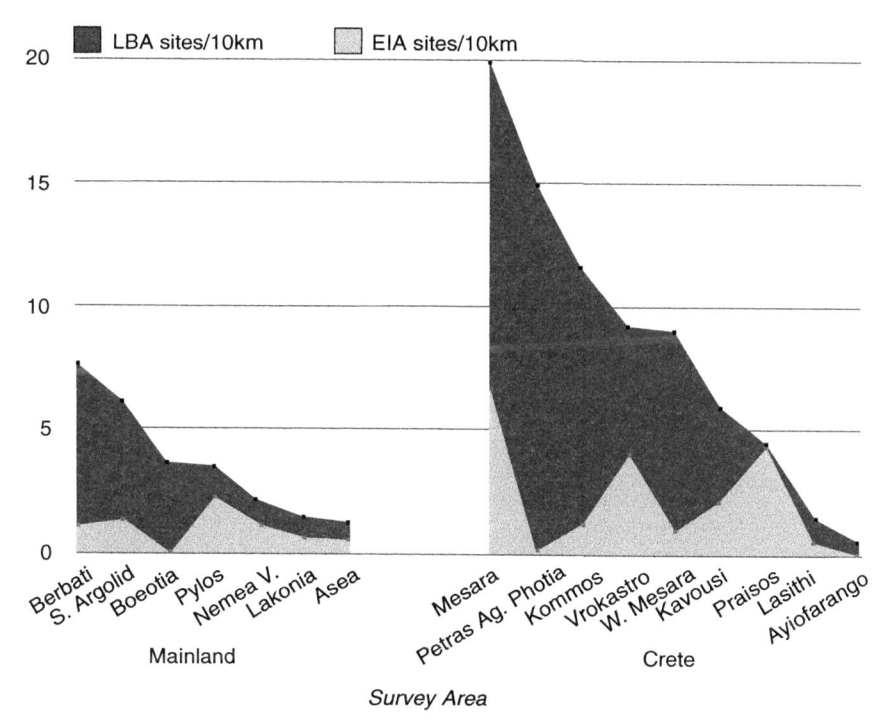

Figure 5.1. LBA and EIA sites from surveys in Greece (by author)

used those ceramics.[28] Due to limitations of space, it is not possible to rehearse all of the methodological and interpretative problems with surface survey in the current context, because they are legion.[29]

For the current discussion, the most relevant problem with survey data is the fact that almost every regional survey in Greece has recovered less PG pottery than LBA pottery, creating the impression that in the Iron Age landscape of Greece, "people were obliged to go about calling aloud in the hopes of meeting somebody else, as whales are said to do."[30] Results from extensive survey in Messenia suggested that "the Dark Age population was … 10% of what it was in LH IIIB."[31] In the Southern Argolid survey there was one definite PG site found, compared with twenty-seven confirmed LH sites.[32] Figure 5.1 summarizes the

[28] Though see Sbonias 2000b for evidence that it does, at least sometimes. For factors affecting the rate of recovery of ceramics in archaeological survey, despite recent methodological advances see Bintliff, Howard, and Snodgrass 1999 (165: collected sherds "represent the tip of a giant iceberg of many thousands of small and ephemeral occupation and activity foci, shifting within small areas of landscape, across the millennia of farming prehistory."); Bintliff, Howard, and Snodgrass 2000; Mee and Cavanagh 2000; Schon 2000; Thompson 2000. More recently Given 2004; Terrenato 2004; Osborne 2006; Tartaron et al. 2006.

[29] See S. Murray 2013, 121–123.

[30] Alden 1981, 4. Although see Maps 5.1–6 for evidence that this may not have been the case for many regions of Greece.

[31] Hall 2007, 59.

[32] Jameson et al. 1994, 236 (figs. 4.16, 4.17). Reports from the Kythera survey project report a total of zero sherds dating from the postpalatial period to the Geometric (Kiriatzi and Broodbank, n.d.).

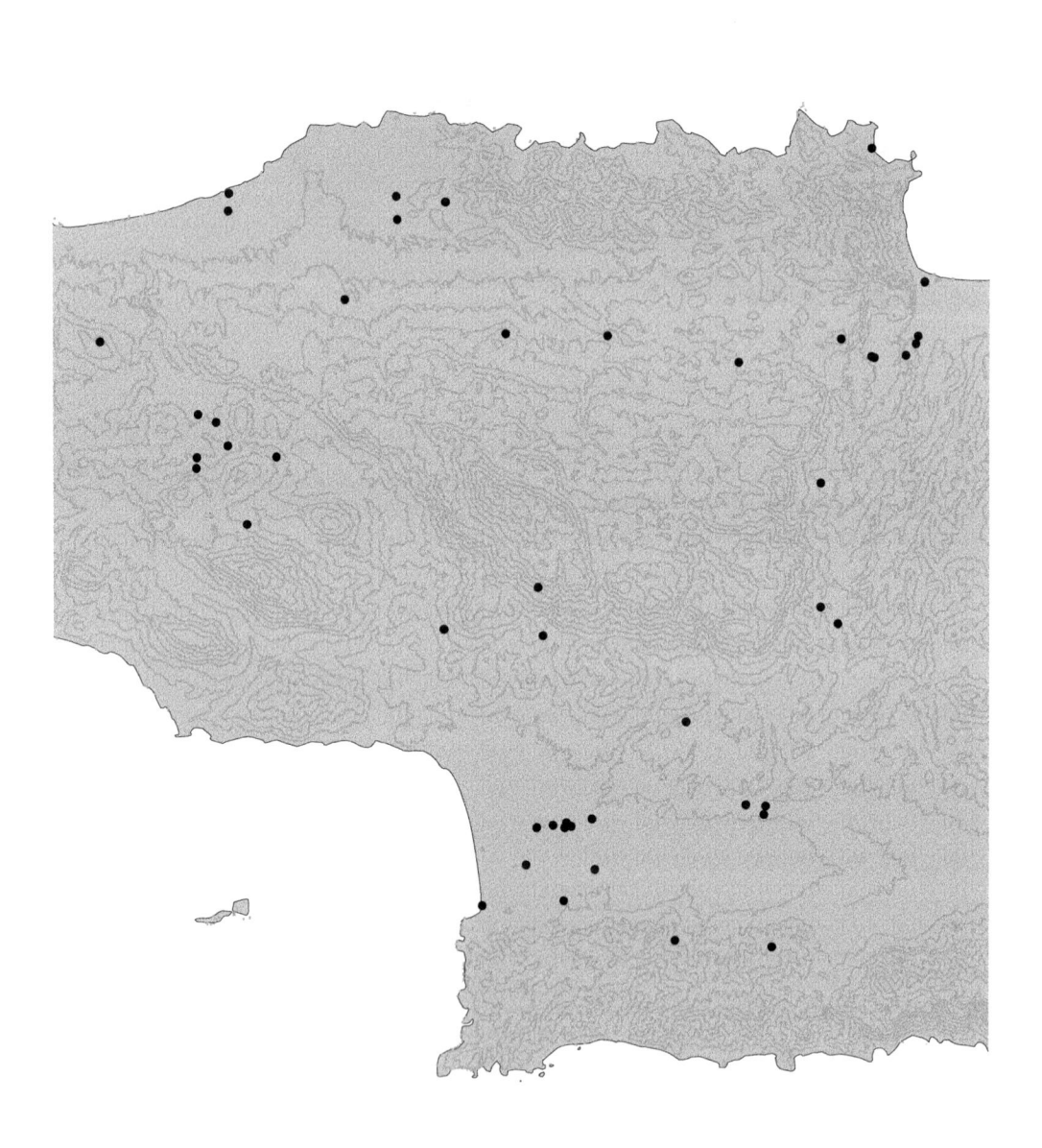

Map 5.1. Distribution of Protogeometric sites in central Crete (by author)

DEMOGRAPHIC AND DOMESTIC ECONOMIC CHANGE 219

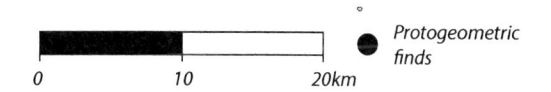

LIBYAN SEA

Map 5.1. (cont.)

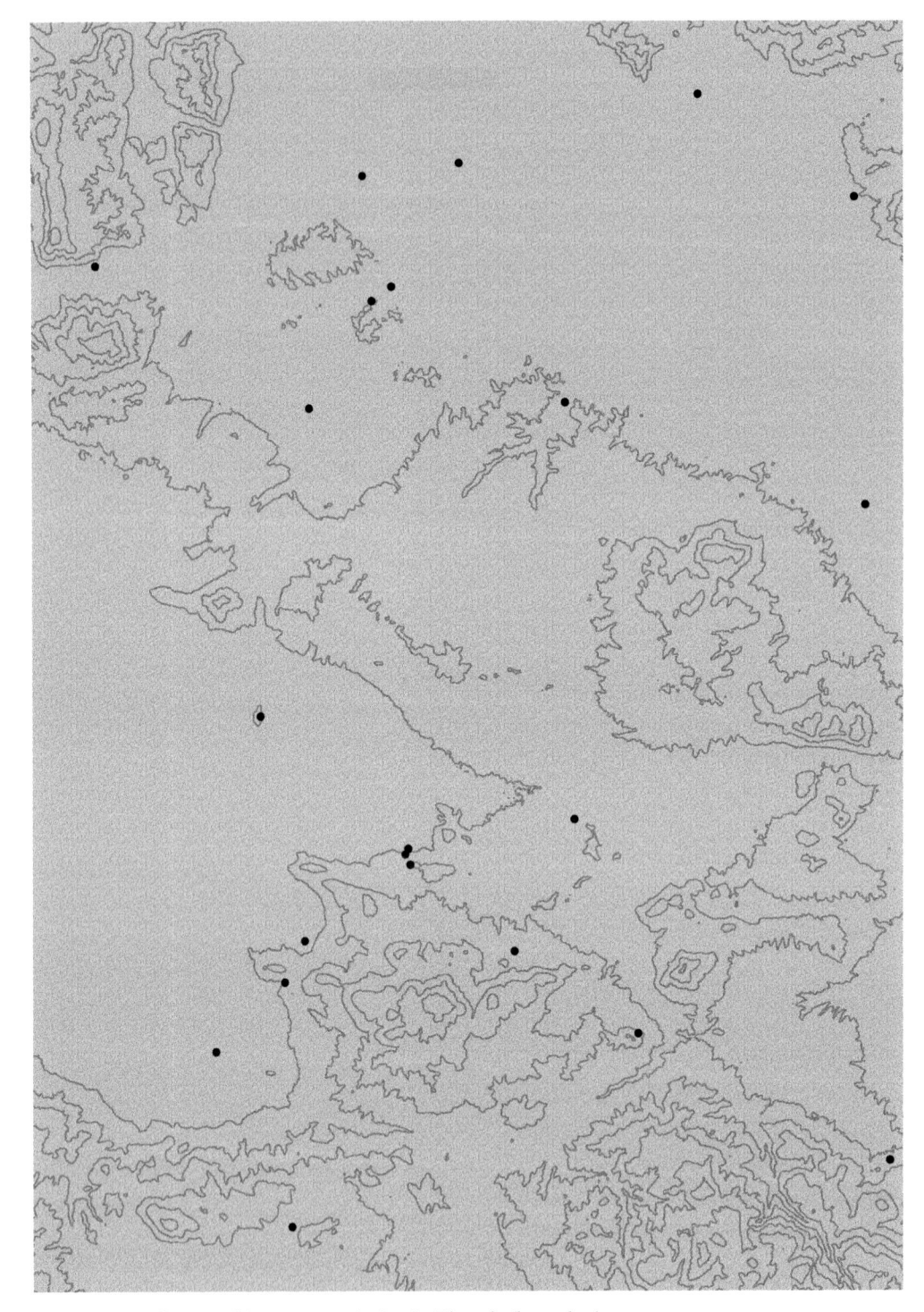

Map 5.2. Distribution of Protogeometric sites in Thessaly (by author)

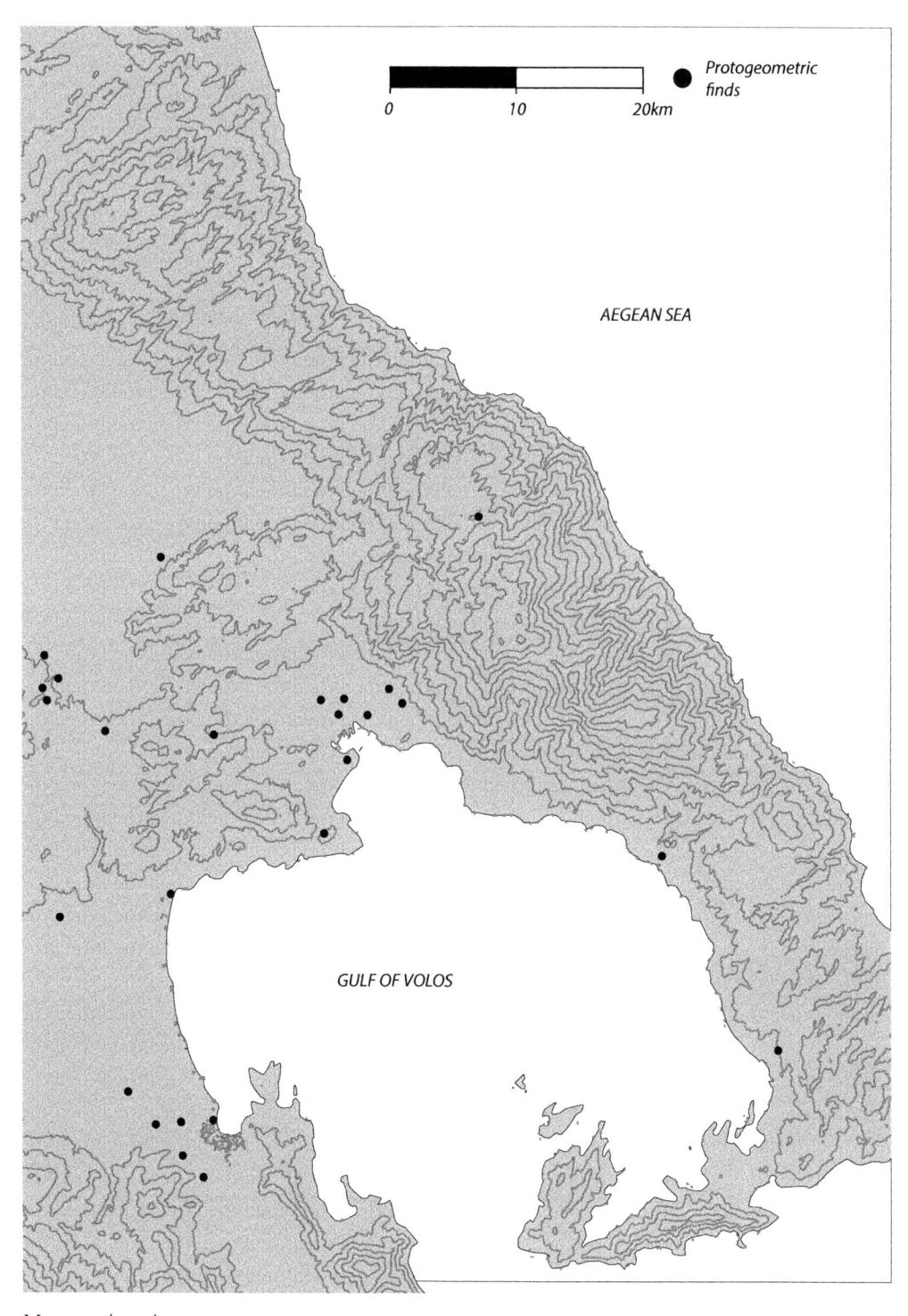

Map 5.2. (cont.)

222   COLLAPSE OF THE MYCENAEAN ECONOMY

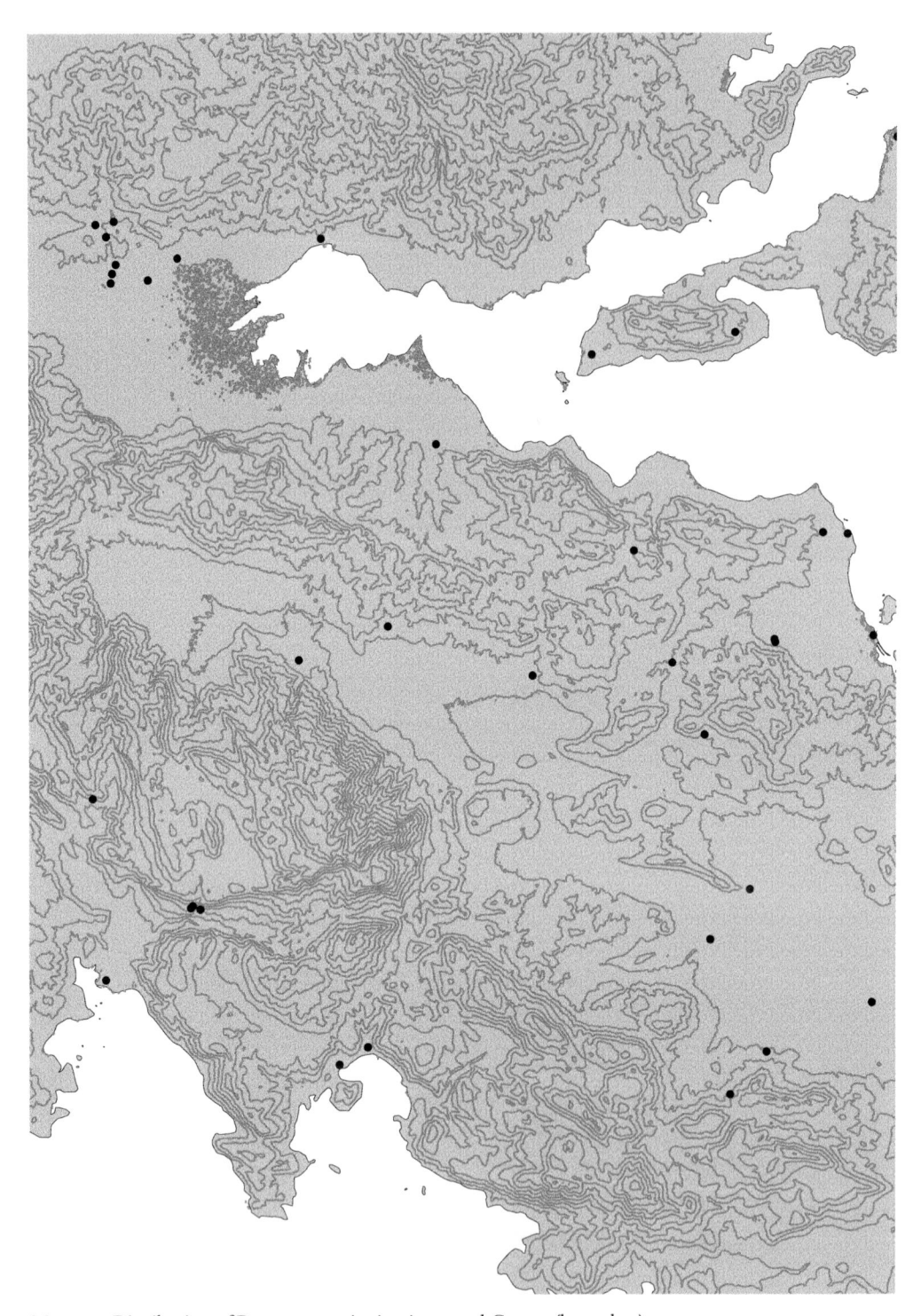

Map 5.3. Distribution of Protogeometric sites in central Greece (by author)

DEMOGRAPHIC AND DOMESTIC ECONOMIC CHANGE 223

AEGEAN SEA

EUBOEAN GULF

Protogeometric finds

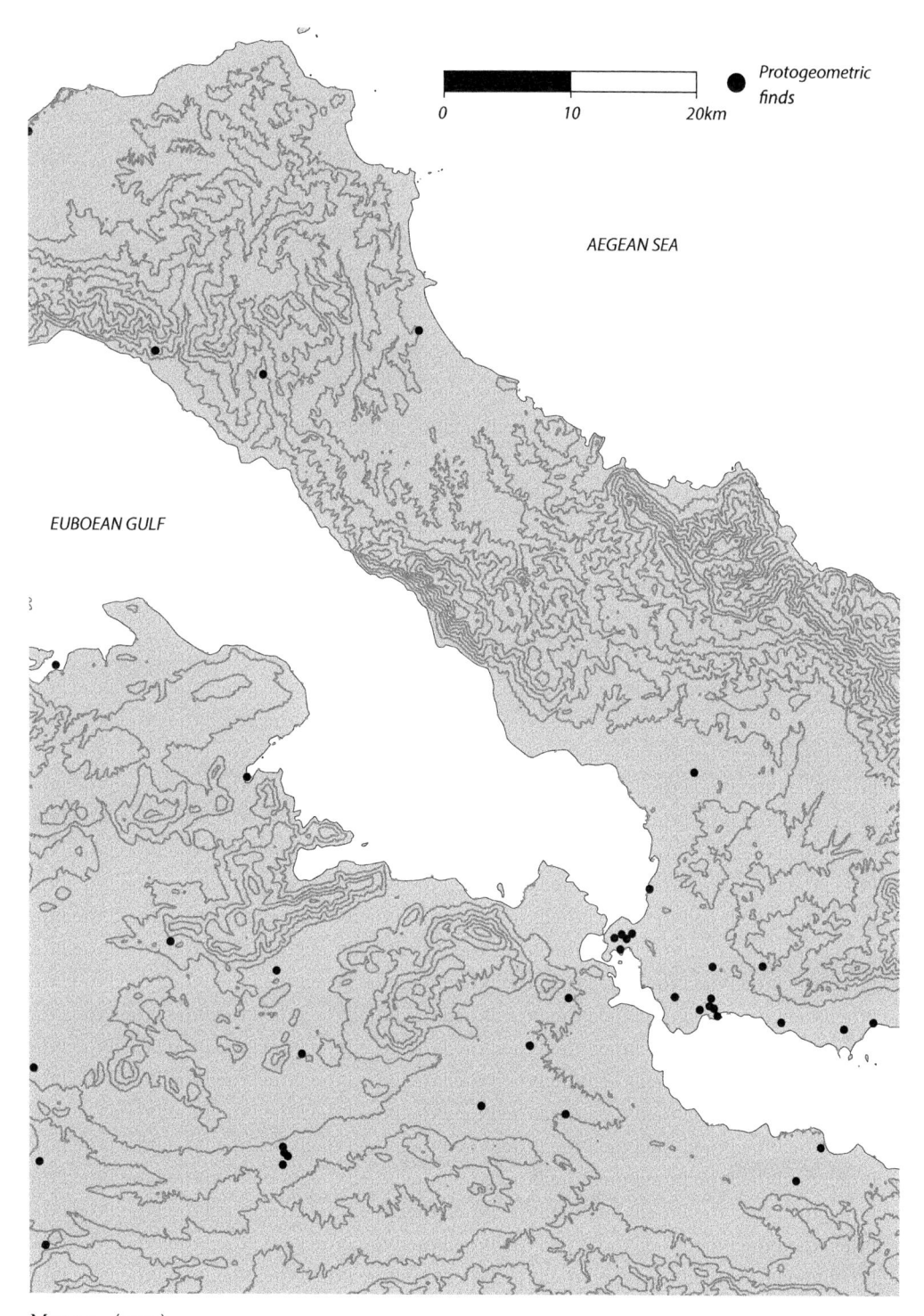

Map 5.3. (cont.)

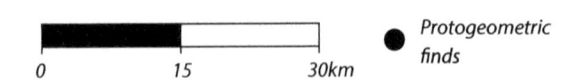

Map 5.4. Distribution of Protogeometric sites in the southern Peloponnese (by author)

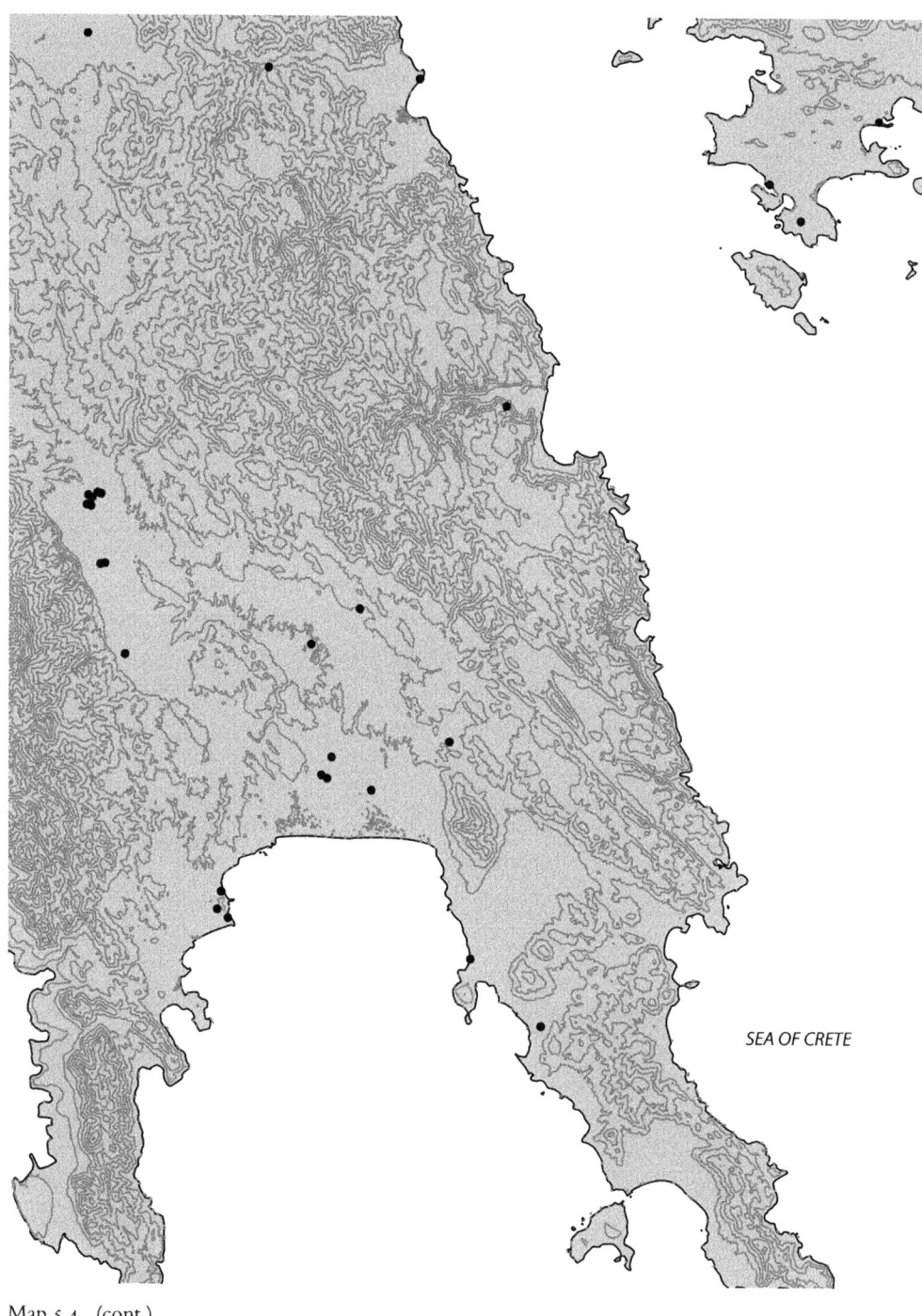

DEMOGRAPHIC AND DOMESTIC ECONOMIC CHANGE 225

Map 5.4. (cont.)

SEA OF CRETE

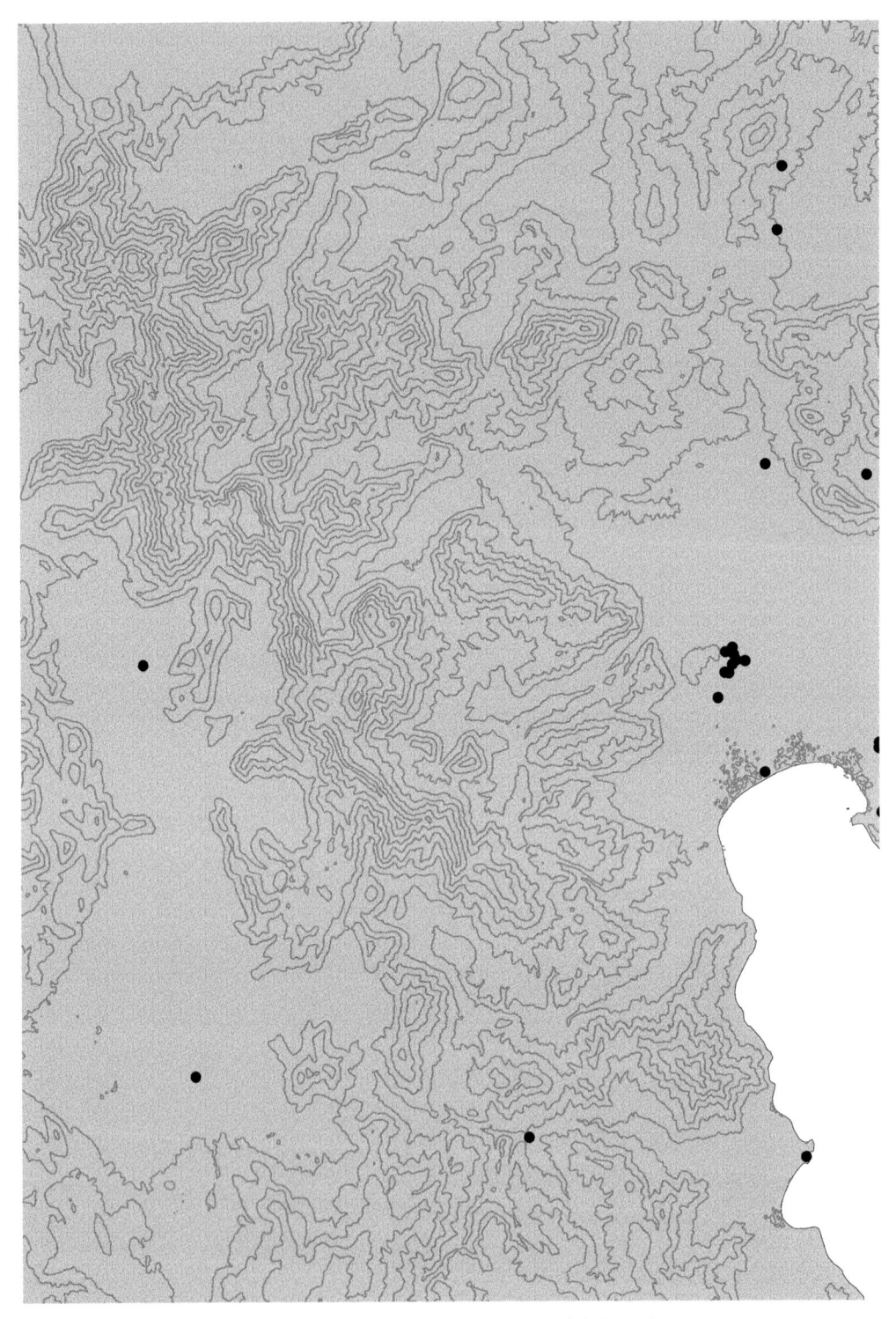

Map 5.5. Distribution of Protogeometric sites in the northern Argolid (by author)

DEMOGRAPHIC AND DOMESTIC ECONOMIC CHANGE 227

Protogeometric finds

SARONIC GULF

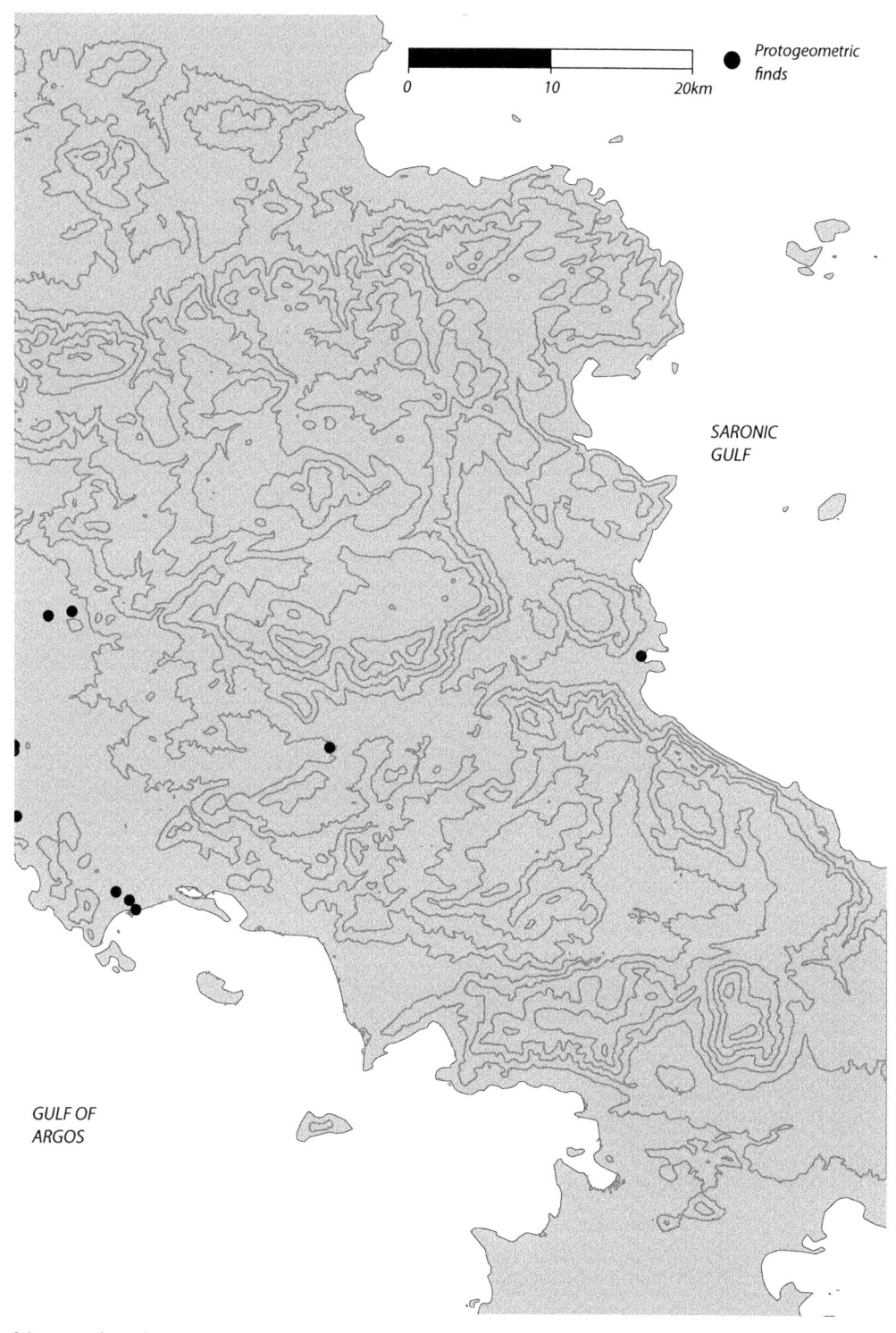

GULF OF ARGOS

Map 5.5. (cont.)

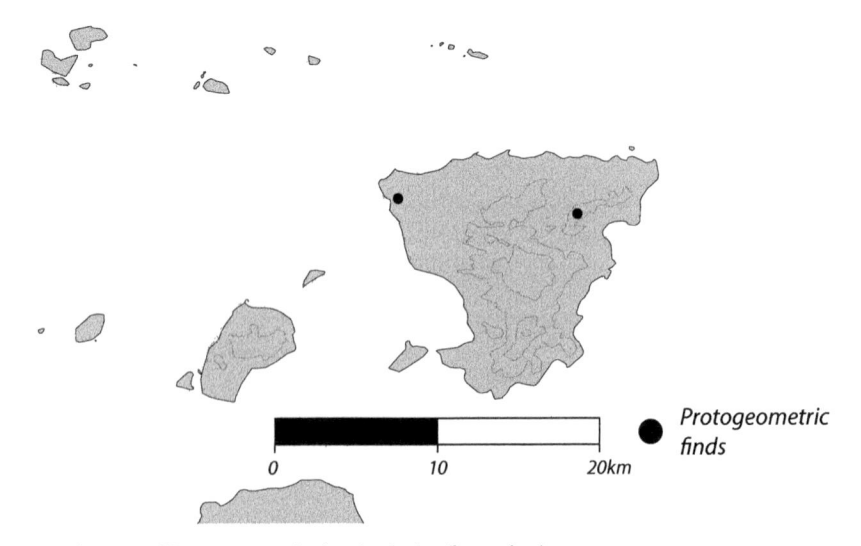

Map 5.6. Distribution of Protogeometric sites in Attica (by author)

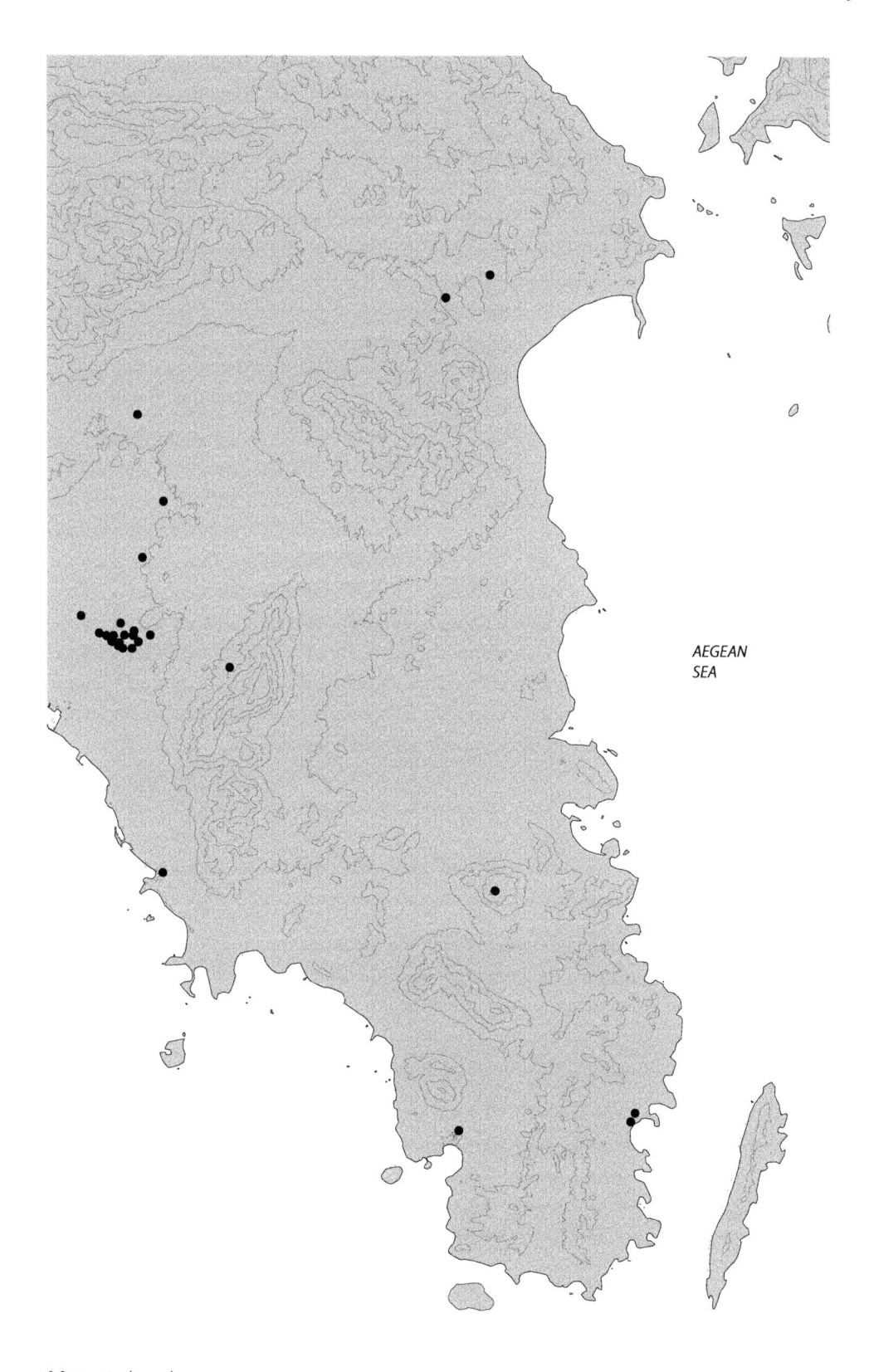

Map 5.6. (cont.)

results from a number of Mediterranean surveys. Is the under-representation of the EIA in surveys evidence of severe depopulation? This is one possibility. The low profile of Protogeometric pottery in surveys could be an accurate index of population size and density (fewer pots = fewer people).

However, there are other possible scenarios.[33] We could conjecture that PG Greeks lived in temporary dwellings and moved around so much that their sites are simply too small and dispersed to leave much of a ceramic signature in the kinds of areas (low-lying agricultural fields) that tend to be represented by intensive survey tracts.[34] Any combination of poor survival and recognition rates of PG pottery and a dispersed settlement pattern might explain our inability to "find" the EIA in the Greek landscape. That is to say, the record that we have of PG in the survey evidence could be the result of distortions on a variety of levels. Protogeometric pottery may not survive because of taphonomic factors, or it may survive in ways that go unnoticed by archaeologists, or it may never have existed. Protogeometric people were sparse and discarded ceramics at rates equal to their predecessors and successors, or they were plentiful but did not use or discard much pottery, or they were plentiful and discarded pottery in ways that are difficult for us to perceive. It is a classic case of equifinality – whatever the mechanisms involved, the end result is that we are left with little PG material. In short, there are many reasons to believe that the record of intensive survey data, especially that from the period between the thirteenth and eighth century BCE, is deeply problematic for reconstructing accurate population figures with any confidence.

Absolute Population

In summary, the evidence suggests that neither mortuary, nor settlement, nor survey evidence will give us much of a firm basis from which to accurately estimate

(1) the population of Greece during the Mycenaean period
(2) the population of Greece right after the fall of the palaces

or

(3) the population of Greece during the EIA.

A bleak outlook indeed![35] In this scenario, it is difficult to imagine that we will ever have even a viable starting point from which to compare populations across time periods, or to achieve the goal of this chapter, which is to calculate roughly accurate diachronic values for imports per capita. However, although we may not be able to be precise in describing prehistoric populations over

---

[33] Rutter 1983; Foxhall 1995, 249 n. 46; I. Morris 2007, 218.
[34] Corvisier 2008, 33.
[35] See comments at Cherry 2005, 9.

time, it is still possible to use the data that we have to approximate a generally accurate impression of early populations. I try my best to do this using the same "cumulative credibility" strategy evoked in Chapter 4, relying again on the assumption that "if evidence from all approaches converges on a common viewpoint, this creates a strong argument for approximation to reality in reconstructing past population levels."[36]

In this section I briefly summarize current views held by scholars regarding the scale and chronology of demographic change in Greece, present a tentative model for population change, then set this view against a background of some estimates based on a sample of archaeological evidence. The most likely scenario, taking into account informed opinion, statistical models, and the archaeological material overall, suggests that there was a decline in population after 1200 BCE followed by sustained low habitation levels until the eighth century, when steady growth that would continue into the Classical period began in earnest. I propose that there were something like 600,000 people in the core areas of Greece in the Bronze Age and that this number dwindled to a nadir of about 330,000 in the EIA.

Past and Current Views on EIA Population Change

In one of the earliest synthetic studies of the EIA in Greece, Snodgrass began his description of the period by positing "a fall in population that is certainly detectable and that may have been devastating."[37] In one of the most recent synthetic works on the EIA, Dickinson more equivocally states, "[a] major and surely highly significant shift in the distribution of population was clearly taking place, and the total population shrank markedly in some regions (for example, Messenia)."[38] Most people agree that civilization in LBA represented a relative peak of settlement density and intensive land use in Greece,[39] but that there were many fewer people around during the eleventh through ninth centuries.[40]

At the same time, the scale of population change remains controversial. Snodgrass's figures suggested that there was a severe population decline.[41] From a straightforward reading of the evidence he hypothesized that there were 75 percent fewer people in Greece during the eleventh century than there had been 200 years prior.[42] Desborough, in turn, believed that there was a 90 percent decrease in population by the end of the twelfth century.[43]

---

[36] See n. 1, Chapter 4 in this book.
[37] Snodgrass 1971, 365.
[38] Dickinson 2006, 486.
[39] Scheidel 2003, 120; Whitelaw 2004; Bennet 2007, 186–187; Voutsaki 2010, 605.
[40] Hall 2007, 59.
[41] Snodgrass 1971, 364–367.
[42] Snodgrass 1971, 367: Greece "lost over three-quarters of its population."
[43] Desborough 1972, 18.

Both these estimates were based on a drop in the number of known sites, which probably overestimated the scale of decline. Indeed, I. Morris has since demonstrated that such a swift drop would have been exceptional indeed, requiring us to imagine a "catastrophic" change in mortality.[44] Scheidel suggested that the raw archaeological data should be tempered in ways that do not require us to adopt "bizarre saltationist"[45] models for reconstructing ancient demographic change. Still, I. Morris argues that the evidence we have points mostly toward a relatively dramatic decline in the number of inhabitants in Greece after 1200 BCE, with recovery only slowly beginning in the tenth century.[46] Tandy and Dickinson follow the same basic figures.[47] Most recent estimates put the decline in population at about one-half to two-thirds.[48]

However, some scholars[49] deny that there was drastic depopulation in the EIA because they think we have fundamentally misunderstood the evidence. Foxhall argues that PG pottery is not often recognized by archaeologists, and that although Greek communities were "rattled" around 1150, they "survived and ... continued to produce much the same things in many of the same ways" (though she admits that political units "may sometimes have differed in scale").[50] Papadopoulos takes a harder line, suggesting that the Dark Age is an imaginative figment of Eurocentric schools of thought emanating from an old-fashioned university cabal at Cambridge.[51] He states, "[t]he concept of a Dark Age is more of a modern scholarly construction than one based on solid archaeological evidence."[52] Papadopoulos denies the existence of the era of decline and stagnation described by Snodgrass, et al., and in particular suggests that the "intimations of poverty and the depopulation of the landscape inherent in the traditional view of the period are based on a certain reading of the archaeological record, relying on historical exceptionalism."[53] His position is that decentralization, rather than depopulation, can account for the differences between LBA and PG settlement tallies from surveys, though Dickinson points out that the evidence from the surviving settlements does not support this.[54] Mazarakis Ainian suggests that the known EIA buildings with stone socles were derived from other, flimsier buildings made "entirely of perishable materials" meaning that most EIA buildings do not survive in the

---

[44] I. Morris 2007, 216: "[W]e should demand strong evidence before accepting this."
[45] Scheidel 2003, 124.
[46] I. Morris 2007, 235.
[47] Tandy 1997, 20; Dickinson 2006, 93.
[48] I. Morris 1987, 146; Tandy 1997, 20; I. Morris 2005; I. Morris 2006; I. Morris 2007, 218.
[49] I. Morris 2006; see also, Chapter 1.
[50] Foxhall 1995, 249.
[51] Papadopoulos 1993 on work by Snodgrass, I. Morris (1987) and Whitley (1991a).
[52] Papadopoulos 1996, 254.
[53] Papadopoulos 1996, 254.
[54] Dickinson 2006, 88.

archaeological record at all.⁵⁵ Similar arguments, suggesting that the depopulation of EIA Greece is an illusion, are not uncommon.⁵⁶

It is difficult to evaluate the claims about relative population levels that are made by these dissenting scholars because they avoid quantification in a way that makes their arguments impossible to compare to those put forward in clear terms by Snodgrass. Furthermore, although they do raise credible concerns about the way in which EIA material has been interpreted, scholars that dissent from the prevailing depopulation orthodoxy do not do a good job of providing a convincing alternative scenario that would explain the observable changes in the archaeological record. Any position that denies a significant depopulation after the Bronze Age presumably works under the assumption that there was steady growth from circa 1600 BCE to the Classical period. In order to convincingly demonstrate steady demographic and economic growth for this stretch of time, it would first be necessary to present a convincing explanation for the relative impoverishment of the archaeological record from 1200–900 BCE that does a better job of accounting for the evidence than demographic and economic collapse.

In the absence of such an explanation, it remains true that, given the premodern context, demographic change caused by endogenous or climatic factors is the most economical and probabilistic explanation for the rapid changes in political structure and social conditions that are evident in Greece between 1400 and 700 BCE.⁵⁷ An appraisal of early Greek history that denies any decrease in population after 1200 must therefore demonstrate thoroughgoing and robust evidence and possess great explanatory power before it gains general acceptance. To date such an appraisal has not yet been presented. Therefore, I assume substantial population decline after 1200 BCE,⁵⁸ with growth thereafter, continuing into the eighth century and beyond.

Model and Estimates

Given this schematic scenario of relative population change, is it possible to produce some believable numbers for the absolute population of Greece during the LB IIIB, IIIC, and PG periods? The first step in this process is to find a benchmark population, some "known" absolute population from which to begin calculating. Since we have no such figure from prehistoric Greece, the best, most proximate benchmark for population estimates comes from Classical

---

[55] Mazarakis-Ainian 1997, 100.
[56] Summary at Dickinson 2006, 93–97.
[57] Scheidel 2003, 121; Sallares 2007, 50–51.
[58] Scheidel 2003, 120.

TABLE 5.1. *Proposed population growth and growth rates in the EIA*

	1000 BCE	900 BCE	800 BCE	700 BCE
.25	440,000	560,000	720,000	930,000
.3	330,000	445,000	600,000	800,000
.35	240,000	340,000	480,000	680,000
.4	180,000	270,000	400,000	600,000
.45	130,000	200,000	320,000	500,000

Greece.[59] Greek historians have used various documentary sources to produce estimates of the population of the Greek world. The generally accepted estimate puts the population of the Greek mainland and parts of the Aegean islands at two to three million inhabitants during the Classical period (480–323 BCE).[60] This may be overly conservative. Something closer to a minimum of four million people, including slaves, in the Greek mainland by the end of the fourth century has lately gained favor as an estimate.[61] Hansen's work on Greek demography stems from a detailed and thorough study of the evidence, and his calculations are compelling because they are based on sources that are largely independent of literary accounts.[62] However, since Classical Greek "polis culture" probably covered a much larger area than the Mycenaean and EIA heartlands and since slave populations may inflate Hansen's total in ways that might obscure natural growth patterns, I settle on the more conservative figure of two million people in the fourth century.[63]

Scheidel argues persuasively that "it is unlikely that the mean growth rate deviated significantly from a range of between perhaps 0.25 and 0.45 percent per year"[64] between 1000 BCE and the fourth century. A range of these possible growth rates would give Table 5.1's diachronic growth scenarios, assuming steady, that is, noncyclical, patterns for the EIA.

The ranges in Table 5.1 which assume a relatively rapid growth rate and a beginning population of fewer than 200,000 people in the EIA are probably wrong, and even the higher starting population estimate of 440,000 for 1000 BCE may be too low. If growth rates vacillated considerably over time, starting out slowly in the tenth and ninth centuries and accelerating after 800 BCE, EIA Greece could have been home to over 500,000 people. Given the general

---

[59] Scheidel 2003, 122.
[60] Beloch 1886; Ruschenbusch 1999; Corvisier and Suder 2000, 32–34; Scheidel 2003, 122.
[61] Hansen 2006; Hansen 2008, 259.
[62] Though he does use literary sources extensively in inferring the accuracy of his estimates, he tends to assume that they are exaggerated. See Hunt 2007 for a critical review (to which Hansen (2008) responds).
[63] Following Scheidel 2003, 122.
[64] Scheidel 2003, 123.

uncertainty about finer-grained changes in growth rates during the tenth to eighth centuries, it may be prudent to assume a middling growth rate of 0.3 percent over the early part of the EIA and a maximum possible population of around 330,000 in 1000 BCE.

For the LBA, Renfrew estimated a total population of about one million people.[65] He based this figure on a generalizing model, made before much intensive survey data from the region was published.[66] As noted, work based on this archaeological evidence is flawed, but it is worth considering calculations based on this evidence as a general check of the plausibility of a Scheidelian growth model.[67] Whitelaw's work has much to recommend it, but it focuses on Crete in particular and focuses more on individual settlements and polities than on aggregate figures.[68] Branigan and Cherry each provide more general estimates, but also focus mostly on Crete.[69] Their estimates for total population are slightly lower than Renfrew's, but the idea that Mycenaean Greece could not have supported more than one million people remains standard.

It is appropriate to reevaluate Renfrew's figure of one million in light of current evidence. A recent overall summary of LBA settlement patterns states that "Minoan and Mycenaean states were relatively small, with territories of about 1,500 square km and central settlements of 20–100 hectares."[70] It is not clear how many Mycenaean states or (if there was only one Mycenaean state) how many political subunits of the Mycenaean state there were. On the mainland, we can say confidently that there was at least one political unit in the Argolid, one each in Messenia, Lakonia, Corinth, Athens, Thebes, Orchomenos, and Dimini. On Crete, Mycenaean states may have been centered at Chania, somewhere in the Mesara, at Palaikastro, and at Knossos. Thus there is clear evidence that something in the vicinity of twelve palace-centered states existed in the LBA. We might also consider that, given the density of Mycenaean remains in Achaea, there might have been a palatial center somewhere in or around the modern Greek city of Patras. In addition, recent excavations at Kanakia on Salamis suggest the existence of a possibly palatial settlement here that must have been quite important, and there is sure to have been some kind of Mycenaean presence in both central-east and central Crete. If we assume that approximately fifteen palace centers served as the foci of the main LBA

---

[65] Renfrew 1972, 240–244.
[66] Cherry 2005.
[67] Pessimistically, Bintliff 2000, 22; against this radical opinion, Cherry 2005, 10.
[68] Whitelaw (2001a; 2004) focused on Crete in particular, though 2001a gives estimates on the size of select Mainland urban centers.
[69] Branigan 2001; Cherry 2005.
[70] Nakassis, Galaty, and Parkinson 2011a, 240.

TABLE 5.2. *Range of "Urban/Polity" Population in Bronze Age centers*

Average Area per Central Settlement	Total Size (ha)	Population: (low 12–50 people/ha)	Population: (medium 50–100 people/ha)	Population: (high 100–300 people/ha)
20	300	3,600–15,000	15,000–30,000	30,000–90,000
50	750	9,000–37,500	37,500–75,000	75,000–225,000
70	1050	12,600–52,500	52,500–105,000	105,000–315,000
100	1500	18,000–75,000	75,000–150,000	150,000–450,000

polities, it is possible to provide a range of possible urban population estimates for the mainland and Crete:[71]

Current estimates for the density of occupation at LBA palace centers and their urban surroundings are in the higher range, and something like 200 people per hectare may be a good average. A mean urban size in the middle of the ranges given previously (60 ha) and an assumed urban density of 200 persons/hectare gives a rough estimate of 180,000 urban dwellers in all of Mycenaean Greece.[72] Converting this total number of urban-center dwellers to overall population requires having some sense of the ratio of urban to rural settlement, that is, the proportion of individuals living in the palatial centers and the people living in smaller towns or in the countryside. The ratio of identified urban sites to sites that are known only from surface artifacts (for IIIB the numbers break down to 284 sites and 592 artifact scatters, or about a 1:2 ratio of urban to rural sites) might give us a good sense of the breakdown between those who dwell in the hinterland and those who lived in settlements. I chose a ratio of 1:2.5 of urban to rural occupants, on the assumption that a sizable portion of people who live outside of town centers must be completely invisible archaeologically.[73] This would suggest a general figure of 600,000 people in Greece, much lower than Renfrew and others posit, but in line with the statistical models suggested by Scheidel.[74]

---

[71] Palaces cited in Nakassis, Galaty, and Parkinson 2011a, 241 fig.18.1: Pylos, Sparta, Mycenae, Tiryns, Athens, Thebes, Orchomenos, Iolkos, Chania, Phaistos, Knossos, Malia, Gournia, Zakros, and Palaikastro.

[72] Though 60 hectares per palace is probably too high, there were probably more than fifteen palace centers, so I accept 180,000 as a fair enough estimate of the number of urban dwellers.

[73] Bintliff 2000, 22. Seventy percent of the population lived in urban settlements in Classical Greece, but " ... the reverse would be true in the Bronze Age, when we would suggest that a majority of the population lived in small to medium sites that are subject to under-representation even with intensive survey." For the population of Messenia, Bennet and Shelmerdine 2001, 136; Whitelaw 2001b, 63; Bennet 2007, 187. Ratio in Crete: Branigan 2001.

[74] Scheidel (2003, 123) suggests a cumulative long-term growth rate of 0.15 to 0.2 percent from the LBA to the fourth century, which would accommodate a LBA population of around 500,000–700,000.

Accepting a figure of 600,000 people for the LBA and 330,000 for the beginning of the EIA would imply one of two basic scenarios for demographic patterns. On the one hand, there could have been a drastic depopulation directly after the fall of the palaces (of around 75 percent) and steady growth at 0.3 percent for two centuries, reaching a level of 330,000 by the beginning of the tenth century. Alternatively, slower decline is possible, with losses of 50 percent of the population slowly accumulating over two centuries, and bottoming out in 1000 BCE. Another possibility is that population declined drastically right after the palatial collapse and was stagnant through the twelfth and eleventh centuries before beginning to grow quickly in the tenth century. Since the sequence of population change is not clear, I assume that the population in the middle of IIIC and the middle of PG may have been about the same, since these points would come on either side of a proposed 1000 BCE nadir. That said, a slightly higher or lower figure for either period is possible, depending on the rate of population change after the palatial collapse and the rate of growth after 1000 BCE.

In any case, a combination of models and studies of urbanism suggests that a decrease in population of around 40–60 percent between the thirteenth and tenth centuries is plausible. A brief examination of other archaeological evidence supports this. While there are many new sites on Crete that appear right after LB IIIB, these are on the whole much smaller than their predecessors. Likewise, the few sites on the mainland with continued habitation after the end of the palatial period shrink considerably, with a few exceptions.[75] Overall, the number of all settlement sites that I have been able to identify shrinks to about one third, from 296 in the IIIB, to 134 in IIIC, to 90 in the PG.

According to these figures, then, an estimate of 250,000 to 350,000 people in the PG does not seem unreasonable. If there were about 100 settlements, and an average of 1,000 people per settlement (accounting for both tiny hamlets like Mitrou and larger settlements like Athens and Knossos), we would have 100,000 people living in settlements in the PG period. If the population were as urban as it had been in the LBA (with one urban dweller for every 2.5 rural dwellers), the total population could be something like 250,000. However, if the population were considerably more rural in the PG, as some have argued, a figure of up to 350,000 is not impossible to imagine.

Combining these various strands of reasoning, I therefore settle on figures of about 500,000–700,000 people in Mycenaean Greece, and figures of 250,000–350,000 people on average during the postpalatial periods, depending on the rate of decline and growth between 1200 and 900 BCE, with probable variation in changes both regionally and over time. Assuming

[75] Hall 2007, 60.

a reasonable growth rate during the EIA, a population of the same approximate size as the LBA figure had likely been re-established, if not slightly outstripped, by the end of the Geometric period. These numbers are likely to be imprecise, but not insane.

5.2. POPULATION AND THE ECONOMY

Archaeological reasoning involves trying to take all of the evidence into account when coming up with an argument about the way things happened in the past. When the evidence indicates a pattern that diverges from prevailing opinion about the way things happened, it is important to try to explain the dissonance between consensus and evidence. I have argued that the population of Greece was between 500,000 and 700,000 during the final periods of the LBA, decreased to 250,000–350,000 by about 1000 BCE, and grew steadily after that. Comparing these demographic changes with the number of imports known from ancient Greece shows that imports were extremely rare at all periods, but that import totals track population change with some fidelity. I summarize the data in Table 5.3.

There is variation in the patterns, depending (as usual) on preferred chronological breakdown of the period between 1300 and 700 BCE. But, an overall decline in import and bronze deposition after the end of the IIIB period, commensurate with the decline in population, is clear. Imports continue to track population size, roughly, in the PG period and increase only during the general period of growth that accompanied the LPG and the Geometric periods. It is not surprising that smaller populations of human beings, and smaller numbers of sites overall, would produce smaller quantities of material. The notion that quantities of particular categories of material evidence are a direct reflection of population size is, however, not necessarily borne out by our additional categories of evidence. The number of bronzes deposited from period to period, for instance, while still supporting a notional decline of deposition rates in tandem with a shrinking population after 1200 BCE, shows unexpectedly low numbers of bronzes for the PG period, and unexpectedly high numbers for the Geometric period. We can think of some ways to account for this given our knowledge of social practice during the PG and G periods. The unexpectedly low number of bronzes from the PG period might be accounted for by the decreasing popularity of this metal as a signifier of social class amongst EIA Greeks, and the unexpectedly high number of bronzes from the Geometric period as a reflection of a new habit of purposeful deposition of tiny bronze figurines in sanctuaries, where they are likely to make their way into the archaeological record. Nonetheless, within a margin of error, both the import evidence and the bronze evidence suggest we might be able to align quantitative change in trade volume directly with population growth and decline.

TABLE 5.3 *Change in population vs. change in various categories of material evidence*

Change in Population versus Change in Imports, IIIB-G

Period	Population (avg.)	Δ (Population)	Min. Objects[76]	~Population Totals	~Object Totals
IIIB	600,000	–	209	y	x
IIIC	300,000	−100%	111	y/2	x/2
PG	300,000	–	77	y/2	x/3
G	800,000	+130%	448	1.3y	2.5x

Change in Population versus Change in Imports, IIIB-G (scaled to reflect approximate length of periods according to a mainland traditional chronology)

IIIB	600,000	–	334	y	x
IIIC	300,000	−100%	178	y/2	x/2
PG	300,000	–	103	y/2	x/3
G	800,000	+130%	448	1.3y	1.3x

Change in Population versus Change in Imports, IIIB-G (scaled to reflect approximate length of periods according to a mainland low chronology)

IIIB	600,000	–	380	y	x
IIIC	300,000	−100%	127	y/2	x/3
PG	300,000	–	134	y/2	x/3
G	800,000	+130%	448	1.3y	1.2x

Change in Population versus Change in Bronze Quantities, IIIB-G

IIIB	600,000	–	6,600	y	x
IIIC	300,000	−100%	2,800	y/2	x/2
PG	300,000	–	1,500	y/2	x/5
G	800,000	+130%	21,300	1.3y	3.5x

Change in Population versus Change in Bronze Quantities, IIIB-G (scaled to reflect approximate length of periods according to a traditional chronology)

IIIB	600,000	–	10,560	y	x
IIIC	300,000	−100%	4,480	y/2	x/2
PG	300,000	–	2,000	y/2	x/5
G	800,000	+130%	21,300	1.3y	2x

Change in Population versus Change in Export Quantities, IIIB-G

IIIB	600,000	–	9,600	y	x
IIIC	300,000	−100%	3,700	y/2	x/2
PG	300,000	–	100	y/2	x/100
G	800,000	+130%	2,350	1.3y	x/5

Taking into account the export evidence complicates matters and leads us to fresh questions about quantities in the archaeological record (as if the reader will not have had enough of these by now!). The relationship between LB IIIB

---

[76] Figures given for imports in this chapter do not include imported beads, given the problems associated with comparing their quantity from the Bronze and Iron Ages (see Chapter 3).

exports and LB IIIC exports does support an alignment between gross quantitative change and population (the number of bronzes declines by about half after the IIIB period) but things in the EIA look difficult to align with population in any meaningful way. The number of known exports from the PG period is vanishingly tiny, and clearly does not track overall population decline. The data for the Geometric period is perhaps most surprising. Based on all other indicators, if quantitative evidence tracked perfectly with the overall scale of the economy, we would expect export quantities from the G period to be far higher. During the eighth century, when we have so much evidence for a booming population and import economy, Greek exports are surprisingly uncommon abroad.

How we interpret this evidence will depend upon how we choose to conceptualize the complex relationship between demography and trade economies. How should we imagine demography and trade interacting? The argument that fluctuation in domestic demand best explains the archaeological record finds a great deal of support from both logical and empirical perspectives, and so while there are other ways that we could proceed, I will focus on the possible implication of low population levels for the scale of a trade economy. In order to participate in a long-distance trade economy, any hypothetical community must not only have access to trade networks, but also the means to acquire goods that circulate via those trade networks. Greece during all phases of the LBA and EIA had access to trade networks – imported objects do turn up in Greece in numbers commensurate with the small population of the period and metals made of imported materials do too.

But is it likely that the small population of Protogeometric Greece was well positioned to participate actively in these long-distance trade networks? To answer this question, we must take into account the broader economic framework within which trade operates. Any economic system contains a number of different parts, often conceptualized as elements of three different subsystems: production, circulation, and consumption. In order to participate in an exchange economy, a community ought to be producing goods or materials of some kind in surplus in order to exchange for incoming objects or materials. The larger the size of a population, the greater the quantity of human capital available to produce fungible materials such as agricultural surplus and value-added goods that could be fed into an active exchange economy. Thus, we might expect that in the aggregate, periods of peak demography would naturally encompass times of increased exchange volume.

Does this necessarily mean that there is a linear relationship between scalar change in trade and scalar change in population? As the evidence shows, this is not the case. Demographic change is likely to be accompanied by complex transformations in social and economic structure, as changing ratios of capital and labor, for instance, alter the basic calculations of everyday life.[77] Likewise, the disintegration of complex societies, which in the Greek LBA example was apparently accompanied by demographic decline, will also change a variety of the underlying factors determining the quality of trade systems: the peer-polity relationships between trading partners, the organizational stability underpinning reliably revisitable ports, the incentives/coercive forces compelling specialized artisans to continue production, peaceful conditions encouraging trust-based relationships among trading partners, and so forth. Given all of the complex factors playing into the shaping of economies, and trade economies in particular, we cannot necessarily pin down the exact relationship between population and scalar change in trade during this period.

However, we can get some glimpses of the transformations within the overall domestic Greek economy from the LBA–EIA transition. It is apparent from the domestic evidence for production and the evidence of the exports that the Mycenaean system for transforming agricultural goods into value-added products like perfumed oil at scale was key in enabling their participation in a long-distance economy. To maintain this kind of system, the Mycenaeans apparently depended to some degree on attached labor and slaves,[78] part of a heterogeneous division of work whereby the population was divided into many categories along a chain of production that was geographically and socially dispersed.[79] This economic structure had many moving parts that enabled Mycenaean states to muster considerable capital and acquire exogenous materials like bronze, glass, ivory, and gold in quantity. The archaeological evidence from the IIIB period contains large-scale production facilities, and other intimations of labor concentration and organization that support this view.[80]

---

[77] See Donlan's analysis (1989b; 1997, 654–657) of the ratio of land versus labor in EIA Greece and the impact of demographic growth in the eighth century. For larger communities becoming more complex as a matter of survival and progress, see Carneiro 1970, 239; Johnson 1982.

[78] On the transformation of staple commodities into other kinds of goods through institutionally supported artisanal labor see Nakassis, Galaty, and Parkinson 2011b, 181. On the organization of labor for production in the Mycenaean period see Schon 2007; On the production of textiles at Knossos, Killen 1984. On workshops in the Mycenaean world, see Shelmerdine 1997. For the concentration of production at elite centers, Voutsaki 2001.

[79] The complexity of the production system, and the diversity of roles within it are made especially evident in the insights produced by Nakassis's (2013) prosopographic analysis of the Linear B tablets.

[80] At Knossos, the palace claimed dominion over the wool on a total flock of around 100,000 sheep. This wool, once harvested, was redistributed to groups of female textile manufacturing groups (a total of 500 women is recorded, though there are likely to have been up to twice as many), to whom the palace owed rations. The textiles produced by these workers eventually arrived at the palace for "finishing" before being sent out somewhere else (to *xenoi*), probably for exchange. Knossos controlled a large number of flocks, which produced an estimate of 30–50 tons of wool per year (Killen 1984, 50; Burke 2010, 83). Impressive installations for

Though the evidence is limited, the overall picture of the domestic economy after the end of the IIIB period is overwhelmingly one of considerable change on all possible axes. There is no evidence that production of luxury goods continued after the fall of the palaces, and industries for the production of more common products (textiles, ceramics, bronze) were simplified and probably were not produced for the purpose of exchange.[81] There is little in the material record (with the possible exception of industrial activity in the lower citadel at IIIC Tiryns)[82] to show that attached labor was common after the collapse of palatial administration, although in the absence of texts, this might be difficult to assess. The archaeological evidence is clearer when it comes to the organization of craft activities. Nucleated production appears to have been commonplace in IIIB, when many sites did not produce their own pottery or textiles, indicating that production was not fully dispersed. On the other hand, the archaeological record for the IIIC period features a greater deal of homogeneity.[83] More excavated sites have some evidence of small-scale craft or agricultural production. Like evidence for production, the import corpus and the known bronzes from the IIIC period are more evenly dispersed throughout Greece than they were in the IIIB period.[84]

All of this appears to underscore a major change in the organization of both production and trade after the end of the palatial economies, involving the

major industrial manufacture probably include (but are not limited to) the Ivory Houses and other intimations of production at Mycenae (Tournavitou 1995; Sjoberg 2004, 57: "If the archaeological record is anything to go by, most of the craft production was concentrated to the second part of the LH IIIB period. The period has left traces of metal-working (cf. Killen 1987), jewelry and ivory production. Large-scale storage facilities indicating a centralized, redistributive economy cannot be associated with the LH IIIB1 period and the same pattern emerges for the second part of LH IIIB period."; Taylour 1981, 40; Thomatos 2006, 185; Iakovidis 1983a, 64; Hiesel 1990, 188). For productive facilities beyond Mycenae, see chart in Voutsaki 2010, 102 (table 5.4). Excavations at Mycenae's Petsas house (Shelton 2010) and work at Berbati (Åkerström 1968) likewise suggest the existence of palatially directed craft industries. There is plenty of evidence for metal production at both Tiryns (Brysbaert and Vetters 2010; Sjoberg 2004, 64; Rahmstorf 2008, 296) and Poros-Katsambas on Crete (Dimopoulou-Rethemiotaki 2004; Dimopoulou 1997, 434–436). A new Mycenaean production center is coming to light at Kontopigadi in Attica (Kaza-Papageorgiou et al. 2011).

[81] We know of no single large-scale production facility from the IIIC period that compares to the evidence from IIIB. Evidence for production continues to appear, but in the IIIC period it is far more dispersed than it was in the IIIB, occurring at a greater percentage of sites overall (see S. Murray forthcoming c), but all of these installations look small in scale. For industrial activity at IIIC sites see Rahmstorf 2008, 316 for Tiryns; Sjoberg 2001, 49–51 for Asine; Evely 2006, 265, 282 for Lefkandi; Alram-Stern 2007 for Aigeira; Hallager and Hallager 2000 175–193 for Chania; Glowacki and Klein 2011, 454 for Kavousi.

[82] Kilian 1981, 155; Kilian 1978, 459; Kilian 1979, 383; Kilian 1984; cf. Rahmstorf 2008.

[83] See argument in S. Murray forthcoming c for detailed proportion of known sites to presence of evidence for industry.

[84] According to the site database I assembled, there is evidence for *some* kind of industrial production from 35 percent of IIIC sites, against 15 percent of IIIB ones.

relatively "neat decomposition" of a complex society from a confederate, formal state into its constituent parts, each comprising an independent and largely self-sufficient unit.[85] small communities producing small quantities of capital each had an equal share in a fragmented world of long-distance trade: Achaea was still actively connected as a producer and consumer of finished goods with the west/Italy, Attica continued contacts of some kind with the east (perhaps thanks to mineral resources), and Crete was engaged with both at once. I will consider the possible mechanisms for these contacts in the next chapter. Regardless of how IIIC exchanges took place, the patterns of production and consumption are both evocative of a smaller, less-unified economic system, exactly what we would expect to see during a period of severe depopulation.[86]

The scale and degree of concentration of craft production remained limited during the twelfth to ninth centuries, and we do not see much change in the evidence for domestic economies between the IIIC and PG periods; in both periods there are signs of household production at an unusually large percentage of sites, but few apparent industrial facilities at scales comparable to those known from the IIIB period.[87] Given the demographic stagnation across this transition, we might not be surprised by the lack of development in apparent economic complexity between 1150 and 1050. While the domestic scene does not present clear differences, the quantity of exports known from the PG period is far lower than from the IIIC period, suggesting more economic dynamism between IIIC and PG than an initial survey of the evidence reveals. We could account for this dynamism in a few ways. First, it is now widely believed that the IIIC period was a time of uncontrolled migration, and that post-Mycenaean Greeks moved abroad in large numbers during the early twelfth century, taking with them their ceramic traditions.[88] The quantitative evidence for exports from IIIC might therefore *not* represent a system of production geared up for export, but rather a movement of individuals. In this case, the "export data" for this period might be a combination of actually-exported and "export-imitating" domestically-produced wares, as is almost certainly the case from IIIB/C Italy and the Philistine territories. So, exports in the IIIC period may not all be representative surrogates of two-way long-distance exchange. On the other hand, the number of PG imports is unexpectedly low, and so even a dramatic adjustment of the IIIC numbers that took into account the movement of people in the twelfth century would probably not bring PG and IIIC export quantities into alignment. Since almost

---

[85] Tainter 1988, 23–24.
[86] Tainter 1988, 41.
[87] See S. Murray, forthcoming c. Ceramic production in the Agora at Athens may have occurred on a large scale (Papadopoulos 2003).
[88] Evidence summarized in Yasur-Landau 2010.

all exports from all of early Greek history consist of pottery, we must assume that PG *ceramics* were not being exported, either for their own value or the value of contents, in the same quantities as IIIC ceramics or IIIB ones.

A substantive change in economic institutions is a likely explanation for this. A possibility we may consider is that Greeks were exporting something other than ceramics or goods contained in ceramics during the PG period. Given the low apparent population levels, and the large labor inputs required to create agricultural surplus in a harsh Mediterranean environment, bulk agricultural goods like olive oil or wheat are not a likely candidate. A small population of herders with large stock holdings (as the Homeric poems suggest might have existed in early Greece) could notionally have made a reputation as exporters of animal products, value-added goods like textiles made from animal products, or even of animals themselves.[89] We know from fictional episodes like the shipment of a hecatomb of cattle to Chryse in book one of the *Iliad* that moving large herds of animals around for exchange was possible, though it would be hard to track this archaeologically.[90] Given biblical evidence that purportedly refers to contemporary trade in the Near East, we might also consider the notion that the purchase and sale of human labor accounts for some of the Greek wealth in the tenth through eighth centuries.[91] Finally, the idea that "early adopters" of iron production were profiting from trade in ores or finished metal products in the Protogeometric period is attractive, and will be discussed further in Chapter 6.

Whatever structural changes in the economy we want to tentatively reconstruct to explain the low number of exports compared to all other economic indicators from the PG and Geometric periods, it is relatively clear that the productive economy was simpler, and structured differently, across the board in the Protogeometric and Geometric periods than it was in the Late Bronze Age. Some indication of the decrease in economic complexity after the end of the palatial period may be provided by the fact that the number of occupational names and titles in the Homeric texts is a small sample of the extensive repertoire preserved in the Linear B documents. While Morpurgo-Davies counts different specialized occupations in Linear B, only 40 seem to have continued on to Homeric times.[92] *Kerameus* and *chalkeis* survived, but words for workers such as shipbuilders, wheelwrights, and unguent boilers fell out of the

---

[89] For large herds of animals in the *Iliad* and *Odyssey*, *Il.* 220–222; *Od.* 96–99. For the idea of moving an entire man's possessions and people over long distances, *Od.* 4.174–177.

[90] *Il.* 1.304–317.

[91] Joel 3:6: "You [Tyre and Sidon] have sold the people of Judah and Jerusalem to the Greeks in order to remove them far from their own border." At Ezekiel 27:13 Javan (Greece), Tubal, and Meshech "bartered human lives and vessels of bronze for your merchandise"; see also Amos 1:9–10 for further evidence of Tyre as a trafficker of human slaves. Slave trading is one of the Taphians' activities in the *Odyssey* (14.450–452; 15.427).

[92] Morpurgo Davies 1979, 99–102, 102–105.

language. Presumably, this shrinking of the lexical range of artisanal categorization reflects a narrowing of economic range. Though the loss of lexical range does not necessarily imply the loss of some professions,[93] the implication could likely be that the organization of craft production shifted toward a more modest range of goods produced by a less specialized body of craftspeople.[94] Thus, we can probably conclude that "the craft sphere was [simple] compared to the Bronze Age."[95]

I suggest that all of this evidence is consistent with a scenario of Early Iron Age economy in which a small local population, organized according to relatively uncomplicated *oikos*-centered institutions was unlikely to have been able to manufacture goods or commodities on the same scale of production or level of artisanal sophistication as a large and complex, organized population, and therefore did not participate in long-distance exchange networks in gross quantitative measure with the Mycenaean polities of the LBA. However, it is also true that trade probably continued through the demographic decline in a measure appropriate to the new demographic realities. In this light, we should not be surprised that the scale of trade in the aggregate did decline after the end of the LBA. Does this imply that population size has a determinant impact on the nature of economic structures? Not necessarily; it is interesting to see, for example, that when the economy and population began to recover in the ninth and especially eighth centuries, the prevailing model of long-distance interaction did not revert suddenly back to an LBA one in straightforward ways. In the Geometric period, craft production shows some signs of development, but not in the way that a study of LBA crafts would push us to anticipate. While there are a few indications of the production of luxury goods attached to some social elite[96] and of ceramic production in worksites like the Athenian Agora[97] the sort of large manufacturing installations apparent in the archaeological record from the IIIB period have not yet come to light from the Geometric period (though by the Archaic period the picture changes dramatically). The primary evidence for Geometric production does not come from ceramic workshops, or installations for the production

---

[93] For instance, something must have been known about shipbuilding (Wedde 1998) and chariot-construction in the EIA: *Il.* 4.485–7.
[94] Crielaard 2011, 96.
[95] Donlan 1997, 651.
[96] Gold workshops presided over by Phoenician smiths have been proposed for both Athenian (Higgins 1969, 145–146) and Cretan (Higgins 1969, 150) assemblages. Gold was also being produced by an artisan in Eretria (Themelis 1983); this may or may not have been associated with the Daphnephoros temple. Gold workshops are also discussed at Hoffman 1997, 234–235; Kotsonas 2006.
[97] Papadopoulos 2003 (21–27), for ceramic production from the Agora dated to the PG–G periods; Further indication of developed/late PG ceramic workshops comes from Wells A 20:5 (60–66) in the Areopagus valley and K 12:1 (67–73) (Papadopoulos 2003, 77–84).

of fancy luxury goods attached to elite settlements, but rather from evidence of the production of bronze or iron artifacts at sanctuaries.[98] There are many implications of this phenomenon, but for the purposes of distinguishing change in the archaeological record of the domestic economy the main point is that overlap with the context of the productive economy with earlier periods is not immediately obvious.

5.3. CONCLUSION

In this chapter I have considered the relationship between aggregate and per capita change in the data for long-distance trade from early Greece. While there is a relatively steep drop in the aggregate number of imported objects in Greece after the thirteenth century, and a rise again in the Geometric period, controlling this for population decline and growth makes fluctuation in the quantitative evidence look like less of a phenomenon of its own significance, and more like the natural outcome of population decline and growth. That is to say, if we take demographic change into account, it looks like patterns in the remaining number of known material categories of evidence for long-distance exchange correlate relatively closely with demography. The data show that figures of imports per capita remain steady (within a margin of error, at a low level) over time. Considering all of the evidence suggests that it was the population rather than the intensity of Greeks' interactions with the rest of the Mediterranean that declined between 1200 and 900 BCE. I therefore reject the notion that regular long-distant contact was absent or even much-diminished at any juncture of early Greek history, even when people living in Greece were materially at their poorest. At the same time, adding in the evidence of exports muddies the picture, and makes the formulation of a direct, linear relationship between the size of the population, the organization of the economy, and the nature of long-distance exchange difficult to sustain. Notwithstanding the fact that the interplay of imports, trade, society, and economy in Early Greece was highly complex and remains poorly understood, there are clear signs of demographic changes across this period that must have had far-reaching impacts on the economy, and may explain at least some of the aggregate quantitative change we observe in the archaeological record.

---

[98] For bronze production in Geometric sanctuaries, see Kilian 1983b (Philia); Felsch 1983 (Kalapodi); Kyrieleis 2002 (Olympia); Rolley 1977, 131–146 (Delphi, with general discussion). For debris from the production of iron and gold at the Apollo Daphnephoros sanctuary at Eretria, Verdan 2013, 145–153. While some metal production is known outside of sanctuaries, this is rare. For workshops in sanctuaries generally, see Morgan 1990, 35–39.

SIX

SNAPSHOTS OF A TRADE SYSTEM IN FLUX

The majority of this book has been concerned with establishing a firm quantitative basis for our understanding of how much the Greek trade economy changed over the course of the LBA–EIA transition. The numbers show a few nearly incontrovertible conclusions. First, a significant decline in the absolute scale of exchange economy in the twelfth through tenth centuries is clear; having arrayed several categories of evidence, I see no good reason to doubt that contraction was a characteristic of the domestic economy in Greece during this period. The observable decline in aggregate exchange between Greeks and others around the Mediterranean probably had little to do with a notional "severance of ties" or a cessation of pan-Mediterranean commerce, but was the result of the impact demographic collapse had on domestic demand and purchasing power, to the extent that these concepts can be brought to bear on a premodern economy. On the assumption that the commodities trade made up a major part of the LBA exchange economy, it may also be likely that the increasing use of iron for tools and weapons decreased Greek demand for copper and tin, which could have dampened the exchange economy. The evidence for recovery in long-distance exchange in the ninth and especially eighth centuries reveals some new patterns not apparent in the evidence from the LBA. Among these are an altered balance between imported and exported objects and more clearly apparent mobility of individuals. In this chapter, I attempt to provide a thicker, and necessarily more speculative, summary of the changes outlined quantitatively in previous chapters, and seek to elucidate the overall picture with representative vignettes from moments and sites that seem to me to be key in understanding the overall transition.

6.1. THE LATE BRONZE AGE: PALACES, AUTHORITY, CRAFTSMEN, AND TRADE

The traditional model of Mycenaean statehood, though recently criticized along several axes, continues to perform adequately as a lens through which to view long-distance trade and exchange.[1] According to this model, the major driver of demand for imported commodities and luxuries during the palatial period were palatial institutions.[2] Most of the imported finished goods, and most exotic commodities, encountered in LH/M IIIB contexts come from palatial sites. There is surprisingly little concrete evidence for redistribution of these commodities and objects to members of the wider community.[3] While it is tempting to attribute this to research bias, I see little reason to suspect that the distribution is skewed or unrepresentative. The data in this study comes from excavation reports representing more than five hundred known IIIB sites from all over the Mycenaean world, including the results of many rescue excavations, which presumably have a greater chance of making unexpected finds at nonpalatial centers than major excavations funded by university research programs. Given that it is evident in such a large sample of evidence, the pattern of overrepresentation of imports at palatial sites should surely be taken seriously. We can probably assume that it is replicating ancient patterns with some fidelity.

The concentration of exotic goods near palatial centers, while a clear pattern, does not have much explanatory power. Did palatial entities control and actively participate in the administration of trade on the ground (that is, sending out and receiving shipments, manning vessels, and coordinating supplies to meet demand), or were they simply customers and producers, generating inputs of supply and demand for a preexisting or externally administered system of exchange?[4] If the Mycenaeans actively sought imported commodities and objects, as it appears that they did, what was their social value? These are questions that have been considered with sophistication in existing scholarship.[5] Here, I seek to address them within a square frame of data.

---

[1] Cline 2010; Manning and Hulin 2005; Dickinson 2006, 196–197; Bennet 2007; Sherratt 2010; Galaty, Thomas, and Parkinson 2014.
[2] Especially articulated in Dickinson 2006, 196–197; Sherratt 2010; Kardulias 2010; Cline 2010; cf. Renfrew 1975.
[3] For the idea that we should expect this, see Cline 2010, 163.
[4] Galaty and Parkinson 1999; Parkinson and Galaty 2010; Parkinson, Nakassis and Galaty 2013; Nakassis forthcoming.
[5] Burns 2010b; see also recent approaches in, and cited by, Galaty, Thomas, and Parkinson 2014.

If we look carefully at the nature and origin of the imports known from the IIIB world, it is obvious that the answers to these questions are neither simple nor uniform throughout the Mycenaean world. The palatial states, their agents, and other Mycenaeans were neither passive customers and suppliers within a system over which they had no specific political stake or control, nor were they impresarios orchestrating the system.[6]

Imports at Mycenaean sites share some characteristics. Canaanite jars, presumably intended to deliver an agricultural product (terebinth resin and/or wine, if the results of analysis from Uluburun can be extrapolated to Canaanite jars in general) occur at Tiryns and Mycenae, as well as a few other sites throughout the mainland and on Crete, as do Mitannian seals, copper oxhide ingots, Egyptian cartouches/scarabs, and faience vessels. At rough resolution, these finds might lead us to believe the usual interpretation that imports in the Mycenaean period were primarily used by Mycenaean palatial elites to legitimate their authority and express their privileged status through conspicuous displays. A closer look at the evidence shows that this premise is not unimpeachable.

Let us first consider the context and function of imports. At Mycenae, imported commodities like bronze and ivory appear to have been valued most highly as raw materials that could be transformed into craft products including furniture, jewelry, and weapons.[7] Finished imported objects from Mycenae are, however, remarkably humble in nature: inconspicuous small faience vessels or wall brackets hardly seem like the kinds of objects that a leader would use to impress power and influence upon his followers. Moreover, the depositional context of these objects does not obviously support the notion that these imports were usually used for that purpose. Instead, they are most frequently recovered from areas used for storage or manufacturing, or in cult spaces. While it remains possible that the possession of composite crafts containing exotic materials and/or the consumption or use of special foods/substances (whatever was contained in Canaanite jars) distinguished elevated members of society from the general populace,[8] imported finished goods do not seem to have served this purpose. Objects associated with workshops are unlikely to have been displayed in the public sphere in a way that would allow differentiation between elite and commoner. Likewise, access to Mycenaean

---

[6] Chadwick 1976, 158; Sherratt and Sherratt 1993; Wallace 2010, 171. For work suggesting a multi-tiered system with the palatial economies representing one aspect of the production and exchange market, see I. Morris 1986; Halstead 1988; Halstead 1992; Hruby 2013; Knappett 2001; Whitelaw 2001b; Nakassis 2013.
[7] At the sites where imports are most commonly encountered, Mycenae, Thebes, and Tiryns, they are closely associated with cult areas or with areas that are dedicated to the manufacturing of special composite goods, which may or may not have eventually served as accoutrements to power amongst some unknown group of Mycenaean officials.
[8] Following Burns 2010b.

cult areas, located within palatial complexes, is likely to have been restricted, and so it is unclear how imports used in cult activities could have contributed to elite legitimation.

Likewise, at Thebes the cache of cylinder seals that comprises the majority of exotica found at the site comes from a palatial workshop, rich in ivory and other imported raw materials. According to most, these seals were of interest to the Theban palace because of their value as raw material rather than because they could be used as talismans of international cosmopolitanism. If imported objects were being used as signs of elite legitimation, it does not follow that they would occur primarily in areas of the site not particularly suited for public display, like workshops and sanctuaries, as they do at Mycenae and Thebes.

At Tiryns, the evidence may clarify what is going on with this unexpected local distribution of finished imported goods. Recent discoveries in the lower citadel and admirably incisive analysis of them have revealed the presence of foreign practices, and probably Cypriot workmen, at the site in the IIIB period.[9] These Cypriots evidently produced value-added crafts within the confines of the lower citadel, practicing their trade in a foreign context but retaining various beliefs and traditions brought from their homeland.[10] These beliefs and traditions evidently entailed the use of special functional and ritual artifacts, which we can easily imagine might have made a foreign environment more comfortable to someone far from home.[11]

We might reconstruct, then, a similar function of finished imported goods at Mycenae and Thebes had something to do with the presence of exogenous people or ritual practice, on the one hand, or the presence of individuals practicing crafts using exogenous materials, on the other. If we accept this, what becomes evident is a clear divide between the functional meaning of imported bulk materials, either contained in ceramic vessels or occurring in ingot form, and that of finished imported objects. Thus, although our best evidence for the use of imports in palatial Mycenaean contexts suggests that these imports had something to do with a palatial economy, the notion that palatial elites were interested in self-aggrandizing displays of exotica is not borne out by the context or apparent use of these artifacts. There is simply no compelling reason, based on the intrasite distribution of imported, finished objects at thirteenth century Mycenae, Tiryns, and Thebes, to believe that these objects were particularly valued by palatial elites as recognizable exotica that could create social power.

At the same time, there is an overwhelming concentration of finished imported goods and imported commodities at important Mycenaean centers

---

[9] Brysbaert and Vetters 2013; Maran 2004; 2006; Cohen et al. 2010; Brysbaert 2013.
[10] Cohen, Maran, and Vetters 2010, 17.
[11] Maran 2004; Cohen, Maran, and Vetters 2010; Vetters 2011; Brysbaert and Vetters 2013.

in the thirteenth century, with surprisingly little "redistribution" out the spokes of the settlement hierarchy:[12] imports have been recovered from only forty-one of over 500 sites. This might serve as further evidence that finished imported goods were small talismanic tokens, not seen as inherently valuable by the Mycenaeans, and thus of no use in cementing alliances or ingratiating followers.

If we assume that finished imported goods held little to no interest for the Mycenaeans, this would also make sense of a question that has perplexed scholars for years: why, if the Mycenaeans were so heavily involved in exchange systems, are there so few imports in the archaeological record from the LBA? While this question has mostly been left unanswered, I suggest that part of the answer is that the Mycenaeans were not engaged in trade because they wanted to acquire finished imported objects, but because they were interested in acquiring commodities such as gold, tin, copper, and ivory.[13] Objects made of these materials are much harder to "count" in the archaeological record, so we have a more difficult time making catalogs of them for scholars to have debates over, but this does not mean that they are not there in remarkable abundance (as discussed in Chapter 4).

Furthermore, I wish to press the related point that the existence of a large number of imported, finished objects is not a prerequisite for reconstructing a lively market of intercultural exchange. We can "check" expected archaeological outcomes of minimalist and maximalist approaches to LBA trade, and their likely material outcomes, against evidence from the Hittite empire, where textual records are more eloquent than Mycenaean ones when it comes to the topic of long-distance trade. Most of the texts that enlighten the participation of the Hittite kings in royal gift exchange (see Chapter 1 for a summary of this institution) come from the site of Hattuša, the sprawling imperial Hittite capital in central Anatolia. According to these texts, the Egyptian and Hittite kings had close diplomatic ties in the thirteenth century. After Hattusili III usurped the Hittite throne, a peace treaty with Ramesses and Egypt was negotiated and signed in 1259. About ten years later the Egyptian king married one of Hattusili's daughters. The need to make arrangements for both the treaty and the wedding precipitated frequent correspondence between the two kings, correspondence that was often accompanied by greeting gifts.[14]

Despite this textually-attested close relationship, material evidence for the relationship between Hatti and Egypt is surprisingly scanty. Egyptian imports at

---

[12] See also Voutsaki 2010, 102. For the idea of redistribution of exotic items and materials as a political and social strategy, Aprile 2013, 434–435; Pullen 2013, 440.
[13] A well-established idea, see Dickinson 2006, 196–197; Sherratt 2010.
[14] Genz 2011, 318.

Hattuša are limited to a fragment of a small stele,[15] and an Egyptian alabaster vase and lid[16] from Büyükkale, an Egyptian axe from temple 26 in the Upper City,[17] and a small frit sphinx.[18] Outside of the capital, at the nearby royal residences of Ortaköy-Şapinuwa and Alaca Höyük, a small bronze plaque,[19] a gold hair ring,[20] and a couple of Egyptian amulets[21] have been recovered.[22] The number of Egyptian finds is smaller than we would expect it to be, considering the extensive correspondence that changed hands between the Egyptian and Hittite kings in the same way that the small number of exotica recovered from sites like Mycenae and Tiryns contrasts with scholars' impression of the Mycenaeans as participants in Mediterranean diplomatic and economic networks.

Imported objects from other Great Kingdoms with which the Hittites corresponded are likewise scarce. Several cylinder seals from Cyprus have been found at Hattuša and at Alaca Höyük.[23] A fragment of an oxhide ingot at Hattuša may be from Cyprus as well.[24] Other Cypriot finds in Central Anatolia are limited to a milk bowl and a gold funnel from Maşat Höyük.[25] From the Hittite capital two Mitannian cylinder seals dating to the 13th century are also attested.[26] Mycenaean objects are equally limited in number – a few imported ceramics have recently been identified at Boğazköy[27] and at Kuşakli-Sarissa[28] to go along with the well-known imports from Maşat Höyük.[29] Otherwise, Mycenaean imports include a sword of disputed origin and a bronze belt that might be Mycenaean or Mycenaean-influenced.[30]

Whatever the extent or intensity of gift exchange or commercial exchange that once existed between Hatti, Egypt, Assyria, Ahhiyawa, and Alašiya, it appears to have left a minimal material footprint. The archaeological evidence from Central Anatolia aligns nicely with the Mycenaean evidence. Like

[15] Boehmer 1972, 208; de Vos 2002, 46.
[16] Boehmer 1972, 211; de Vos 2002, 46.
[17] Neve 1993, 29 and fig. 70; de Vos 2002, 46.
[18] Boehmer 1972, 179–180; Cline 1991, 134.
[19] Süel and Süel 2000, 323. This was possibly part of the revetment for a wooden statue.
[20] Süel 1998, 45–46; de Vos 2002, 46.
[21] de Vos 2002, 46.
[22] See Genz (2011, 319) for the idea that the amulets might be indicative of the use of Egyptian magical or medical practices in the Anatolian capital rather than as trappings of kingly legitimation.
[23] Boehmer and Güterbock 1987, 108–109.
[24] Müller-Karpe 1980, 303–304.
[25] Özgüç 1978, 66; Özgüç 1982, 115; Todd 2001, 210; Kozal 2003, 69.
[26] Boehmer and Güterbock 1987, 108.
[27] Hawkins 1998, 8–9.
[28] Mielke 2004a, 26; Mielke 2004b, 155–157.
[29] Özgüç 1978, 66; Özgüç 1982, 102–103; Mee 1978, 132–133; Mee 1998, 141; Cline 1994, 68; Kozal 2003, 68.
[30] Müller-Karpe 1994, 434–439; Cline 1996; Boehmer 1972, 70–71; Cline 1994, 68.

imports in the Hittite world, imported objects are surprisingly few in number in the Mycenaean heartland, despite our expectation that the Greeks were actively involved in bustling long-distance trade during the period. Most of the imports that we can identify from Egypt, Mesopotamia, Cyprus, and other areas have similar spatial and typological distributions. They are concentrated in and near centers of political and economic power and as often as not, they are not the kinds of things we might expect to provide elite legitimation, and may suggest the presence of unusual ritual practices instead.

The implication is that Hittite and Mycenaean rulers may not have cared so much for imported objects as the scholarship, largely drawing on anthropological models, would lead us to believe. In many cases, we might instead imagine that those responsible for acquiring or transporting the imported objects we find in palatial contexts were not the *wanax* and his associates, but other individuals that were not necessarily engaged in long-distance gift-exchange in straightforward ways. That said, it is clear that imports and imported commodities are concentrated at palatial centers. This brings us to the question of how much agency the palatial institutions had in LBA exchange. Were the Mycenaeans simply "good customers" to whom third-party traders returned again and again? Or did the palaces control trade in some sense?

The first problem for the proposition that the "Mycenaeans controlled trade" seems to be with the fundamental notion of how the Mycenaean world was organized. It is by no means certain there was a single entity overseeing the long-distance acquisition and distribution of commodities and finished goods for the Mycenaean world, although there is some evidence that the main inputs and outputs went through the Argolid.[31] While we should probably assume that some Mycenaean leaders did at times engage in gift exchange interactions with the Near East, a scenario in which all trade going into or out of Greece had to pass through this mechanism seems unlikely. Concentrations of ceramic imports within Greece, in particular at Kommos, echo the quantities of Canaanite Jars at independent commercial hubs like Ugarit, and confirm that there were probably multiple modalities of trade during this period. These would have included directional trade to palatial centers, an independent carry trade with stopovers at cosmopolitan ports, and small-scale exchanges by merchants supplying the needs of individuals. The evidence for a central Cypriot role in the LBA economy, and in bringing objects and technologies to the Aegean, should give final notice to any naïve sense of a palatial exchange economy that somehow dominated all intakes and outgoing shipments in a world as fragmented and many-faceted as the LBA Mediterranean.[32]

---

[31] Including concentration of imports in IIIB Argolid; concentration of bronzes (Kayafa 2000, 404); apparent domination of clays from the Argolid in Mycenaean pottery outside Greece (Killen 1985, 269; Shelmerdine 1985, 89, 150).

[32] See a strongly stated version of this view in Chadwick 1976, 158.

In this sense, we can tentatively reconstruct a trade system in which Mycenaean leaders at major sites represented consumers in a market with sophisticated institutions in place to govern long-distance exchange. One or more central leaders may have exercised some control or administration over exchange relations with the Near East, insofar as these leaders are understood to have possessed the ability, through coercive force and institutional structures, to mobilize individuals, build ships, and command taxes. However, we do not have much basis to conclude that the concentration of imports at major palatial sites is a sign that these palaces controlled exchange, except in the minimal way in which any consumer has some level of control, through the mechanism of demand.

In light of recent reevaluations of the Mycenaean state, we might think of Mycenaeans in this system not as interchangeable bureaucrats, but as individuals seeking to engage with an existing long-distance exchange market at a variety of resolutions,[33] from Mycenaean leaders seeking trading partners and diplomatic exchanges as both an economic and political strategy, to workshops employing Cypriots in order to generate the value-added crafts, to sailors risking the uncertainty of the wider world to seek profit in trade. Mycenaeans at various levels of society interacted with trading partners both east and west, not limiting themselves to engagement with palatial peer-polities in the Near East, but also pursuing commercial interests in Italy, perhaps as part of a quest for metals,[34] or in an attempt to expand the scope of their territory.[35] In a complex world of porous boundaries and many scales of interactions, the Mycenaean state did not have a monopoly on long-distance trade, but was a player on a diverse stage of commerce and interaction.[36]

6.2. THE KING IS DEAD: EXCHANGE AND INSTABILITY IN THE POSTPALATIAL PERIOD

> "All who handle the oar,
> The mariners,
> All the pilots of the sea
> Will come down from their ships and stand on the shore.
> They will make their voice heard because of you;
> They will cry bitterly and cast dust on their heads;
> They will roll about in ashes ... "
>
> *-Ezekiel 26: 29–30*

---

[33] Shelmerdine 2011; Parkinson, Nakassis and Galaty 2013; Garfinkle 2012; Nakassis forthcoming; objection at Bennet 2007, 191.

[34] Dickinson 1977, 101; Bietti Sestieri 1988; Gras 1985, 57–97.

[35] See also comments at Papadopoulos 2001, 441–442; Ridgway 1992, 3–8; Malkin 1998, 10–14. On the other hand, Taylour noted Scoglio del Tonno as a possible colony in 1958 – he speculated that the motivation for the settlement was not the search for metals, but murex dye for textiles (Taylour 1958, 128–131).

[36] See Knapp 1991, 52; comments on Uluburun as independent of palaces: Dickinson 2006, 34; Shelmerdine 2013, 451; contribution of Tartaron 2013.

During the IIIC period we see clear evidence that the state, which may or may not have controlled but certainty stimulated long-distance exchange in the IIIB period, disintegrated. While the collapse of complex societies that took place in semi slow-motion in the twelfth century must have caused much lamenting amongst merchants and long-distance traders, at least partially shattering the economic system to which they had become accustomed, long-distance trade continued to operate in the Mediterranean during the twelfth century. In the IIIC period, imports and exports continue to be deposited in the material record apace, if we take demographic decline into account, although in this period of increasing mobility of peoples and military unrest, it becomes difficult to distinguish between patterns in the evidence that are due to the mobility of people and patterns that represent commercial or gift exchange (although as I have emphasized throughout this book, that is never a simple process). Patterns in the deposition of imports and exports in IIIC Greece look completely different than they did in the thirteenth century. IIIC Imports are more heterogeneous and are deposited roughly evenly in mortuary and settlement contexts spread relatively widely throughout Greece, rather than being concentrated in palatial centers. The use of imported amulets and ritual objects in IIIC mortuary contexts is a newly dominant feature of the import corpus, and may suggest that behaviors surrounding exotica in the Mycenaean world were changing during this period in thoroughgoing ways. What can we say about the cultural context of long-distance trade in the postpalatial, postapocalyptic world of the twelfth century? In order to understand this period, I believe that we must first come to terms with its chaotic and unstable nature.

Mediterranean political order changed in thoroughgoing ways in the early part of the twelfth century, and it is reasonable to expect, based on the maritime nature of the disturbances that contributed to these circumstances, that trade overseas should have undergone changes simultaneously. With the collapse of the Hittite empire, the weakening of Egypt, the apparent florescence of Cyprus, and the demise of Ugarit in the twelfth century, dramatic upheavals in trade systems would not have been easy to avoid. With the disintegration of states and the laws and guarantees that they provided merchants and traders, sailing in the Eastern Mediterranean would have become intolerably risky for some.[37] We catch a glimpse of the kinds of hazards traders and merchants would have confronted thanks to the testimony of the final accounts from Ugarit – they describe starving merchants and burning villages – and from Tudhaliya III's campaigns – describing sea battles and pursuits onto adjacent

---

[37] For the kinds of risks that merchants probably faced we can rely upon Near Eastern texts explicitly spelling out punishments for the harassment or murder of merchants and assurances against the unmitigated disaster of losing a cargo. See Monroe 2009, 98–99, 173–180; Monroe 2015, 28–30.

shores.[38] The old order of palatial administration and the structuring formal institutions that went along with it had fallen to pieces, or were in the process of doing so. The causes remain unclear, but may have included natural disasters, climate change, and social unrest. The eventual result seems to have been a period of unchecked migrations and internal displacement.[39] The fundamental question we must face when trying to understand anything about IIIC Greece is how people who dwelt in the shadow of the ruins of the Mycenaean world are likely to have dealt with this kind of environment.

It is apparent that strategies varied geographically. In the Argolid, residents of Tiryns attempted to cling to the old order, to perpetuate and reify ideologies and traditions on which the old authorities relied.[40] In Achaea, which may never have had a palatial elite to begin with, a newly unfettered warrior class rose to prominence, and was perhaps able to forge strong links with Italy, which supplied the region with ample quantities of bronze in the form of both finished objects and raw materials.[41] We can imagine that, in the absence of the mature palatial political institutions of the Mycenaean period, the dismembered smaller units of Greek communities would have been newly squared as peer-polity interaction partners with the similarly sized communities in Italy during the IIIC period.

The chaotic nature of the IIIC period must have made long-distance exchange in the Eastern Mediterranean more complicated and far riskier.[42] Supply of particular categories of material like ivory and lapis lazuli would have decreased because of military and political instability in the source countries. Notwithstanding these challenges, it is clear that exchange continued. How and why did IIIC participants in long-distance exchange manage to navigate the newly chaotic world of the twelfth century? In order to get a sense of the mechanisms that allowed trade to continue even when the palaces and empires that had obviously been so involved in it had ceased to exist, it is helpful to turn again to documentary evidence from Ugarit (see Chapter 1). This evidence

---

[38] But any true time of complete chaos must not have lasted for long, judging from the continuity and flourishing of the twelfth century Levantine and Cypriot copper industries (Negbi 1991, 228), of Cypro-Cretan trade (Muhly 1998, 323; see also Knapp 1998; Knapp 1986; discussion in Voskos and Knapp 2008), and the clear continuity of ship-building and seafaring traditions through the twelfth and eleventh centuries (Wedde 1998; Yasur-Landau 2010, 104–106); for possible maritime migrations during this period, see Yasur-Landau 2010; Leriou 2002; Leriou 2007.

[39] Cline 2014; Knapp and Manning 2016 review the possible precipitants of the collapse.

[40] Maran 2004; Maran 2006; Brysbaert and Vetters 2010; Cohen, Maran and Vetters 2010; Vetters 2011; Rahmstorf 2008.

[41] For recent assembly of data on IIIC Achaea, see Giannopoulos 2008; Deger-Jalkotzy 2006.

[42] I. Morris's (2013, 32) suggestion that the most frightening words in the English language are not "I'm from the government and I'm here to help," but "there is no government and I'm here to kill you," is relevant.

includes records of the operations of merchants trading in tin and copper, by way of both overland and maritime routes.[43] Among the named merchants working in Ugarit were Rapanu, Yabninu, Rasap-abu, and Urtenu. Analysis of letters from the houses of these merchants has shown that, while they engaged in interactions with kings and palaces, they were not endowed by them, but acted as principals, buying and selling on their own accounts and at their own risk.[44] The merchants' objectives were to accumulate capital for themselves by dealing in services (taking commissions to facilitate transactions) and goods. Yabninu, who also served in the military, had explicit trade relations with Arwad, Byblos, Sidon, Akko, Ashdod, Ashkelon, and Cyprus. Documents discovered in his home attest to active engagement in the trade of bronze, hammers, cloth, and mules with the Hittites and the Egyptians. Rasap-abu, also a soldier, served as a notary at Ugarit, keeping accounts for tin, copper, and bronze vessels. In Urtenu's house, a letter (RS 94.2530) addressed to Ammurapi of Ugarit from a Hittite king read addressed the problem that Ahhiyawan ships were awaiting supplies of copper in the land of Lukka.[45] These texts give an impression of an active community of merchants who acted as intermediaries for the state and gain-seeking individuals operating their own trade firms.[46] Thus, while scholars have traditionally viewed trade as an appendage of the palace[47] there is increasing evidence that there were instead traders acting on their own to facilitate palatial trade for their own profit as well as to fulfill market demand.[48] As Snodgrass has suggested, the "removal of [palace-centered importation and redistribution of metals] was bound to lead to urgent adjustment and improvisation"[49] and it is likely that individuals such as Urtenu et al. would have improvised and adjusted accordingly in the twelfth century.

We should imagine in light of this evidence that the Mediterranean Bronze Age world was equipped with traders who possessed enough power and capital to "disintermediate the state" and carry on with their commercial activities regardless of the political situation.[50] The powerful state entities in the LBA

---

[43] Bell 2012, 181.
[44] Bell 2012, 183: RS 11.795 accounts for the delivery of twenty talents of tin and two talents of iron.
[45] Bell 2012, 184.
[46] Monroe 2009, 240.
[47] Liverani 1997, 562.
[48] Bell (2012, 187) compares the demise of palatial states at the end of the LBA to the fall of the Soviet Union: "Despite the lack of living experience of a free market system, and the fact that arguably Tsarist Russia had been more feudal than capitalist, individual entrepreneurs were nevertheless ready to step into the void represented by the collapse of the Soviet Union."
[49] Snodgrass 1989, 25.
[50] Compatible with Liverani's (1987, 69–70) views on the topic: "At the moment of the collapse, the merchants were in a position to survive without the Palace organization, and to continue their personal activities in a different framework."; also discussed in Liverani 1978, 191–198.

Aegean and in the Near East were important partners in trade in the IIIB period, but must not have been solely responsible for marshalling the capital, infrastructure, and manpower necessary to undertake long-distance commercial shipping.[51] If they had been, their demise would surely have precipitated a period lacking in much evidence of any long-distance trade. Instead, trade continued after the end of the palace institutions, meaning that it must have served the purposes of, but was not integrated into the operations of, palatial polities. Traders continued to visit Greece as long as there was sufficient demand for their wares, and provided that the communities they visited were able to proffer something valuable in return.

We can see this clearly in many subsets of the import evidence from the IIIC period. In Tiryns, where the old Mycenaean symbolic and political order was adhered to, at least to some degree, in the twelfth century, the import record shows little change from the preceding IIIB period: imported objects are located in the same areas of the lower citadel as they had been during the thirteenth century, and include Canaanite Jars (which may be kickups) along with items (accoutrements for opium smoking, a ritually deposited armor scale) that suggest the continued presence of Cypriot resident craftsmen, specifically metalworkers.[52] A similar find of a single armor scale might lead us to the same conclusion about IIIC Kanakia on Salamis.[53] In Achaea, imports become more abundant during the twelfth century, and are relatively widely distributed in mortuary contexts, usually associated with what have been categorized as "warrior burials," a pattern that we see at Knossos and in Lokris as well. Who are the warriors buried in these tombs, and how did they acquire the imports buried with them? The prominence of Cypriot imports in this period suggests that perhaps it was Cypriot intermediaries who perpetuated a carry trade to receptive markets during the twelfth century, though agency is difficult to assign in a period for which we still possess such limited cultural understanding.[54]

It is at Perati that we can get perhaps get the best glimpse of the social roles of innovative and independent merchants most clearly.[55] The majority of IIIC imports on the Greek mainland come from Perati, and this concentration has often been noted and taken as evidence for continuing contact between elites of mainland Greece and the eastern Mediterranean during the twelfth century. But this conclusion is hardly helpful in reconstructing postpalatial long-distance

---

[51] This was almost certainly not the case for the better-documented Near Eastern states, as Monroe (Monroe 2009; Monroe 2015, 23–30) has shown.
[52] Maran 2004; Brysbaert and Vetters 2010; Vetters 2011.
[53] Georganas 2010. Armor scales discovered at Mycenae, albeit in less enlightening depositional contexts, suggest that Cypriots could have been present there too.
[54] Fisher 1988, 90–191.
[55] Iakovidis 1969–1970.

interaction.[56] A closer look at the imports in the cemetery suggests that the import record in Perati is not compatible with the idea that this cemetery straightforwardly represents a well-connected elite prospering in the palatial aftermath. Imports are found in tombs of all shapes and sizes in the cemetery, and with burials that are wealthy in every sense and burials that contain few other offerings besides the imported objects. In addition, many of the imports that we find at Perati are not of great inherent value, for instance stone weights and faience figurines. I have argued elsewhere that these objects may have served as familiar objects or good luck charms for those bold enough to travel overseas during tumultuous times.[57] The site was apparently newly established in LH IIIC Early and the question of where the inhabitants came from remains a mystery, but most assume their presence at the site had to do with the desire the exploit the metal resources of southern Attica. The possibility that these were once resident craftsmen in Mycenaean palaces before the collapse, who fled during the chaos to make a new foundation in east Attica, but continued to parlay their contacts abroad into some kind of continued long-distance exchange during the first half of the twelfth century, should be considered a possibility.

However, we want to interpret the import evidence at Perati, it is clear that the patterns and use of imports that are evidence in the IIIC period are reflective of just the kind of diversity of strategies we might expect to be pursued by enterprising individuals living during a time when political power and stability dissolved. We could interpret the more dispersed pattern of imports and their geographical shifts from the Mycenaean centers of the Argolid and Boeotia to the West (Achaea) and the East (Perati) in LH IIIC as the result of the dissolution of the primary trade institutions that dominated long-distance exchange during the previous period.[58] The role of organized states in long-distance exchange appears to have been minimal in the IIIC period, and new patterns in the archaeological record naturally follow this institutional change.

6.3. DARK DAYS IN PG GREECE?

I have argued in Chapter 5 that the key to understanding the dynamics of long-distance exchange during the Protogeometric period is to accept the robust archaeological evidence that we are dealing with an era of overall demographic stagnation, low population, and a simplified economy. This fact must come

---

[56] Iakovidis 1980, 11; Desborough 1964, 69–70; Skon–Jedele 1994, 3–5; Dickinson 2006, 185; Muhly 2003, 26; Thomatos 2006, 178; Lewartowski 1989, 75.

[57] Stampolidis 1998 (109–111, 124–125) argues that tradesmen, craftsmen, artists, musicians, and healers probably would have been more likely to travel during times of war than of peace.

[58] Borgna 2013; Negbi 2005, with summary of literature prior to that date.

first when we consider trade in PG Greece, as a trade economy must flow from some kind of inputs to the system – the extraction and refinement of raw materials, input of human labor at scale, complex and surplus-geared production lines, or participation in diplomatic exchange networks. In the IIIB period, value-added exports seem to have fed the Mycenaean participation in long-distance trade. In the IIIC period, the continued export of stirrup jars may have perpetuated some kind of long-distance exchange networks, while local resident merchants may have continued trading raw materials from east Attica, and Achaean warriors engaged in diplomatic exchanges with new peer polities in the west. What inputs to an exchange system could PG Greeks have mustered? Though the recent trend has been to focus on the "positive" aspects of collapse, I do not think we should so flippantly dismiss the importance or economic implications of the disruptive events that took place at the end of the LBA. This does not necessarily imply that life had to have been nasty, brutish, and short for everyone in the centuries that followed. Once the crisis of the IIIC period passed, it is likely that land and resources might have been extraordinarily plentiful, and life relatively good, for those left behind in Greece.[59] However, this does not elide the fact that this was a time of stagnation from a macroeconomic viewpoint, and this can only have had an impact on the total scale of interactions between Greece and the wider world.

First, let us consider the mounting evidence that significant quantities of the population of Greece either died or emigrated after the IIIB period.[60] The scale of this depopulation was considerable, and may have wiped out half of the entire population by the time the eleventh century was over. We must imagine that its causes – whether they were internal instability, agricultural or environmental disaster, or something else that we cannot detect in the archaeological record – were highly compelling, because they apparently motivated large numbers of people to move away from their homeland and take their chances elsewhere. In a world of general instability, this is not likely to have been a decision easily taken. The goal of this book is not to delve deeply into the mindsets and traumas of the emigrants that apparently left Greece in large numbers in the IIIC period, but to appreciate the economic impact that the depopulations and destructions that afflicted Greece in the twelfth century had domestically.

As I have shown in the foregoing chapters, all of the quantitative evidence that we can muster points to a severe contraction of the Greek economy

---

[59] As has been suggested for the period following the Black Death in early modern Europe: Allen 2001; Clark 2005; Pamuk 2007. Peasants looked back on this time as a "golden age"(Braudel 1981, 194–195).
[60] See Yasur-Landau 2010, but also Mühlenbruch's recent work on the topic (Mühlenbruch 2009; 2013) and the evidence presented here in Chapter 5.

after the early twelfth century. The absolute volume of traded goods and commodities coming into Greece almost certainly reached a nadir at this time, continuing to stagnate after an already low point in the twelfth century, there are few signs of complex productive economies beyond the household level, and exports from Greece are almost nonexistent. Many have argued that these indicators should lead us to believe that Greece was "cut off" from the rest of the world during this period,[61] while others have argued that the presence of some imports shows instead that the trade economy never declined at all.[62] Neither statement does justice to the evidence.

Let us begin with the proposition that Greece did not have access to long-distance markets in the PG period. Although traveling abroad during the PG period is unlikely to have been free of hazards,[63] some Greeks did acquire exotica during this period, and the number of such objects known aligns quite well, on a per-capita basis, with the number of such objects known from the IIIB and IIIC periods. The question of whether or not Greeks had access to commodities from outside of Greece in the PG period has normally been tied up with the issue of the transition from bronze to iron as a "working metal" at the end of the IIIC period.[64] While many used to believe that it was necessity (lack of access to copper and tin) that precipitated this change, it now looks more like the adoption of iron was not motivated by a bronze shortage.[65] Overall, in a sample of tombs from the PG period all over Greece, bronze remains the most frequently encountered metal in burial deposits (see Tables 4.3 and 6.1)[66] and plenty of other evidence bears out the notion that Greeks probably had access to both tin and bronze, that is, were not "cut off" from access to these commodities.[67] Iron certainly appears during the period, and achieves near parity with bronze as a component

---

[61] For example, Skon-Jedele 1994, 3; Coldstream 1998, 1; Boardman 1999, 40; Heymans and van Wijngaarden 2009, 124–136; Kourou 2015, 216.

[62] For example, S. Morris 1992, 102; Papadopoulos 1996, 254–255; Osborne 1996a, 35, 41 ("Greece was not ... impoverished.");

[63] On the notion that going to go out trading was not safe in the PG period, see Knapp 2008, 26.

[64] Snodgrass 2000, 213–295; Snodgrass 1980a; Dickinson 2006, 146–150.

[65] Original argument put forth in Snodgrass 1971; Refuted by I. Morris 1989; alternative model suggested in I. Morris 2000. Lack of evidence for a tin shorage summarized in Walbaum 1999, 29; see also arguments for bronze to iron transition in Wertime 1982; Wertime 1983; Sherratt and Sherratt 1993.

[66] Based on catalogues of PG metal finds in Lemos 2002, supplemented by Eder 2001c, Eder 2006, and Choremis 1973.

[67] Despite the fact that bronze finds are not abundant, there is no reason to believe that Greeks could not acquire bronze when they had the means to do so. On the contrary, while many classes of artifact disappear from the archaeological record of the EIA, metals and pottery are still present. See Chapter 4. See discussion at Dickinson 2006, 144.

TABLE 6.1. *Metal use in a sample of regional groupings of EPG-LPG tombs in Greece*

	Total Bronze	Total Iron	Total Gold
Attica	38	70	7
Argolid	63	65	6
Euboea	84	77	91
Thessaly	41	16	12
Central Greece Interior	49	7	6
Skyros	18	1	5
W. Pelop.	58	4	0

ingredient in rings and pins, but the numbers do not support the notion that bronze was unusually scarce on a per capita level.

If bronze did not decrease in availability during the PG period, then how can we account for the adoption of iron for items like pins, fibula, and rings?[68] I. Morris's model of selective metal use according to local preference has been influential. He argued that people in the PG period chose to use iron instead of bronze in their burials because they sought to distance themselves from their bronze-wielding ancestors, though he admitted that a shortage of bronze of some kind could have helped this process along.[69] Other ideas include a price difference: because iron was cheaper than bronze, it became more popular because iron tools achieved the same piercing and stabbing results as the more expensive bronze ones.[70]

I suggest something like a middle route between these hypotheses. Instead of arguing that the adoption of iron was based purely on either ideology or necessity, I propose that the small quantities of bronze present in EIA deposits reflect a lack of something like purchasing power. In a deeply contracted and simplified economy, the capability of purchasing things on a long-distance exchange market was unlikely to have been widespread. Again, in bringing this point to the center of the bronze/iron debate, I seek to reorient our notions of fluctuations in long-distance commerce around the notion of a total economic fact, rather than focusing in particular on supply-side changes. Given the

---

[68] See Wertime (1982; 1983) for the idea that a fuel shortage led to the change; S. Sherratt (1994) that Cypriot commercial strategies do instead.
[69] I. Morris 2000, 218.
[70] Originally proposed by Childe 1942, 183 and quoted at Snodgrass 1971, 239; Snodgrass 1989, 30. This idea has been criticized by scholars arguing that it does not fit the evidence well: iron appears to have remained relatively valuable into the eighth century (I. Morris 1989; Pleiner 1969).

apparent lack of material abundance among Greek communities during the PG period, it is not difficult to imagine why the development of locally available metal resources, and technologies that could enhance the exploitation of these resources, might have become a priority.[71] This would have given communities with access to iron ore a powerful incentive to develop some kind of iron industry.[72]

In sum, while Greeks may have struggled to muster the economic capability to participate in long-distance exchange with frequency, mobility and trade continued throughout the EIA in the Mediterranean, and the idea that Greece, at the center of the great middle sea, would have been bypassed entirely is implausible.[73] The economy of most Greek communities during the PG period was simply not scaled toward the production of surplus for export, and thus would not likely have been in a position to participate enthusiastically in long-distance exchange networks.

In terms of the context of exchange within society, it is apparent is that the social dynamics of the trade institutions that arose in the Protogeometric period look quite different from those apparent in both final stages of the LBA. Finished metal vessels and jewelry figure prominently in the catalog of eleventh and tenth century imports in Greece, a clear change from the Canaanite Jars and bronze ingots that represent the archaeological correlate of Mycenaean trade. From the depositional context of exotica, known mostly from otherwise wealthy cemetery contexts, we deduce that the consumption of exotica was the purchase of a small cross-section of society,[74] but one that was demographically diverse, including men, women, and children, both on Crete and on the mainland.[75] Nonlocal objects may have served as material constituents of relationships between individuals, or may have indicated nonlocal ritual or supernatural beliefs that had been "acquired" along with small talismans or tokens. Sometimes exotica appear to be heirlooms, and may have been passed

---

[71] Most iron in early Greece is assumed to be locally procured and produced, although imported ingots/billets of iron are known from Delphi in an eighth–sixth century context (Perdrizet 1908, 213–214) and at Naukratis (Petrie 1886, 39). Knowledge of iron production in the eighth century is attested in the *Odyssey* (9.391–395).

[72] The best iron sources in mainland Greece are located in Euboea and around Atalanti on the Euboean gulf, and on Crete (Markoe 1998, 237) near sites where gold instead of iron became an important status indicator (Varoufakis 1982, 317); for Euboea the richness of iron deposits is attested in Strabo (*Geographica* 10.1.9). See additional discussion of the region in Lemos 2002; Kourou 1990.

[73] Evidence for continuing trade: some Sardinian hoards with ingots and Cypriot artifacts from Sardinia in EIA contexts (Lo Schiavo 2003, 156; Stampolidis 2003, 44); Sicels arriving in Sicily in the tenth/ninth centuries (Panvini 2003, 132); Fibulae with Syro-Palestinian influence (Panvini 1997, 497–498; 1997–1998, 37–39).

[74] Catling 1996 (565) for vases from Knossos as "personal gifts."

[75] The association between wealthy tombs and restricted circulation is well-established and fits with the evidence presented in Chapter 2.

down through families[76] or exchange networks many times before finally being deposited in burials.[77] Likewise, the few exported objects that we have from the PG period look like an indication of Greeks traveling around, carrying individualized drinking cups with them, perhaps forging personal relationships with strangers across the Mediterranean.[78]

On Crete elite culture is apparent in the tombs at Knossos,[79] but the deposition of imported ivories and bronzes in sacred caves is not explained by the textual evidence, and may presage the Geometric distribution of wealth and exotica in sanctuaries on the mainland in the eighth century. Signs of persistent contacts between Crete, Cyprus, and the west in the Protogeometric period seem to suggest that the more complex depositional pattern of imports on the island is probably related to the relatively certain truth that some Cretans had a more robust and diverse experience of the wider world in the ninth century than most mainlanders did.[80]

We could interpret the new pattern of import deposition in wealthy individual burials (rather than in palatial settlements) as indicative of a turn more toward "Homeric" trade institutions in tenth century Greece. However, Homer's presentation of gift exchange only gives us an ideal form of trade based

---

[76] Given the social importance of Homeric gifts within an *oikos* or lineage, we could imagine that these kinds of objects were used as grave goods for prominent members of the kin group. The only material goods placed (alongside sacrificial horses, dogs, and Trojans) on Patrokles' funeral pyre were "two-handled jars of oil and honey" (*Il.* 23.170–177). His cremated bones were buried in a golden urn of unknown provenience (*Il.* 23.243–244; *Il.* 23.252–253). Other valuable items from Patrokles' estate are given away during the funeral games, suggesting another mechanism through which heirlooms might have circulated through time and space (*Il.* 23.740–747). For strong ties of kin and family in the Homeric epics, see Finley 1954, 74–107.

[77] The Sidonian vessel Telemachus acquires in Sparta might be a good example of this (*Od.* 4.615–619; *Od.* 15.99–129).

[78] Maier, Fantalkin, and Zukerman, 2009 73–74. These may have been "valued" exports for their own inherent value. Or, they might represent Greeks traveling with their personal drinking and feasting gear. The notion that a drinking vessel might be something of great personal significance that could be taken on a long journey is supported by the Mycenaean drinking assemblage found on the Uluburun ship. One thinks also of the inscribed MG skyphos from the sanctuary of Apollo at Eretria (Papadopoulos 2011; Kenzelmann Pfyffer 2005; Theurillat 2007) that is possibly written in semitic, or the assemblage of inscribed Cretan drinking cups from the eighth/seventh century Temple B at Kommos (Csapo et al. 2000). The personal relationship between individuals and their drinking cups might be implied by the appearance of playful hexameter in some of their earliest iterations, for example the cup of Nestor (Powell 2009, 239) and the Dipylon oinochoe (Powell 1991, 159) as well as new finds from Methone (Besios, Tzifopoulos, and Kotsonas 2012). See also Knodell 2013, 304–315, esp. 312, table 8.3. A possible LBA precursor might be the Cypriot White Slip bowls known from a few sites in the Aegean.

[79] Kotsonas 2006, 159–162.

[80] Snodgrass 2000, 340. In addition, Odysseus's adoption of a Cretan persona during his masquerades could suggest that Cretans were more frequent adventurers abroad than a normal basileus might be in early Greece. Odysseus lies about being a Cretan to Athena (*Od.* 13.256–286), Eumaeus (*Od.* 14.191–359), and Penelope (*Od.* 19.165–202, 221–248, 262–307, and 336–342).

upon one perspective. We might also see echoes of the dastardly merchants he describes in the Phoenician carry trade apparent at the end of the tenth century at Kommos and the "trinkets" deposited in Protogeometric tombs. But in general a Homeric model of trade does not fit all of our evidence neatly, as we would expect from a body of poetry that does not necessarily reflect the complex realities of the "real" Protogeometric world.

What does come through clearly from both the texts and the PG archaeological record is that the extravagant gifts attested in the LBA royal correspondence were far greater in scale than what flights of Homeric fantasy could come up with. Both sets of evidence likewise show that the mechanisms of trade could not have been the same in the two periods because the technology (writing) that tied LBA trading relationships together did not exist in Greece between the twelfth and eighth centuries. Evidence for sealing or other practices that would have enabled transshipping by delegates or personal proxies is lacking for the eleventh and tenth centuries.[81] In the Protogeometric period, individual fortune seekers were obliged to take upon themselves both the risks and the potential rewards of adventures across the watery ways (as Hesiod's *Works and Days* suggests). Despite the actions of these individuals, it looks unlikely that Greeks were active in long-distance exchanges, at least commercial ones, in the eleventh and tenth centuries. This was not because they had no contact with the outside world, but because their local economies endured crises that made production at a scale conducive to reciprocal exchange or the export of agricultural commodities difficult to sustain.

6.4. THE FUTURE EMERGENT IN GEOMETRIC GREECE

The story of the Geometric period in Greece appears to be one of the reemergence of complex society against a background of overall economic growth after a period of severe demographic disaster and stagnation in the eleventh and tenth centuries.[82] Tainter and others have identified the prominent role of religion and ceremony in establishing the legitimacy of some kind of higher authority during the process of knitting together kin and tribal groups into a new, bigger institution when complex societies are formed or reformed.[83] Another strand of state development is the universal recognition of some sort of symbolic center, which does not necessarily coincide with the

---

[81] Papadopoulos (1994) argues that a few pot marks (mostly from the Athenian Agora) represent evidence for a continuous tradition in this area between the Mycenaean and historical period.
[82] I. Morris 2005; 2007; some points contested in subsequent publications by others, including Papadopoulos 2014.
[83] Netting 1972, 233–234; Claessen 1978, 557; Tainter 1988, 27–28: "sacred legitimization provides a binding framework until real vehicles of power have been consolidated."

physical center of the region encompassed by the state, but which symbolizes the authority of the greater unit.[84] The record of imported goods and objects from Geometric Greece supports the notion that part of the process of the reestablishment of complex society during the eighth century took place along these lines.

When complex societies come into existence, a major part of the process is the bonding together of smaller units, with individual sets of interests, under one larger state umbrella. The mechanisms for this process in early Greece are complex and have been the topic of much discussion.[85] This is neither the time nor the place to reprise the merits and drawbacks of all sides of this argument. The most relevant issue and the one I wish to address here is that a normal mechanism whereby competing local interests are subsumed under a single authority during periods of rising social complexity is the association of the authority (be it an institution or an individual) with the supernatural. In many historically attested cases, this link took place at the level of the individual – through a universal rally to the cause of a kingship believed to be sanctioned by divine right. In Greece, godlike kings were never really accepted.[86] However, both the development of central authority within individual city-states and the idea of Panhellenic collectivity among all Greeks are connected to the development of religious sanctuaries.[87] Along these lines, it is fascinating to see that the evidence from the early Greek economy shows that these sanctuaries began to accrue many of the kinds of materials and objects that had been distributed among (mostly) elite graves during the preceding PG period.[88] Bronze objects and exotic materials like ivory are concentrated in sanctuary deposits (Chapter 4), and so are finished imported goods of a variety of categories (Chapter 2). Some of the dedications at sanctuaries could represent the symbolic redistribution of wealth from individual *oikoi* to the religious authority of the nascent state, as wealth moves from tombs to sanctuaries. Some imported dedications, like ivory horse-tack, elaborately-decorated bronze cauldrons, and tripod stands are explicitly associated with élite lifestyles in early Greek

---

[84] Shils 1975, 3; Bell 1997; for Greece, see Morgan 2003, 107–110.

[85] On state formation in the early first millennium in Greece, Snodgrass 1980b, 27–28 and 85–86; Snodgrass 1985; Snodgrass 1993; Morgan 2003; Coldstream 1984; I. Morris 1991, 41–42; de Polignac 1995; Malkin 1987; Foxhall 1995; Morgan 1990; S. Morris 1992; 1997, 64–65; Schapp-Gourbellion 2002; Prent 2006 (for Crete); Knodell 2013.

[86] Aristotle (*Pol.* 1285a-b); see discussion at Drews 1984, 10–97.

[87] Especially apparent in Morgan's work (Morgan 1990; 1996; 1997; 2003) and in de Polignac's (de Polignac 1995; de Polignac 1996) thesis, now widely accepted.

[88] Morgan 1993, 19; Snodgrass 1980a, 52–54; Coldstream 2003a, 355–358. It is perhaps no coincidence that most of our evidence for permanent eighth century production facilities comes from sanctuaries, suggesting that entire economic geographies changed along with depositional practices of exotica and nonlocal commodities in the Geometric period. Metalworking installations may have been set up by the sanctuary authorities or by enterprising individuals who recognized that pilgrims seeking to purchase votives would provide a ready market (Morgan 1990, 35–39).

literature. As Herodotus suggests, lavish donations from foreign kings might be responsible for some other votive exotica.[89] But not all of the evidence, including the inherently low value of votives like faience scarabs, and their distribution at many local (nonoracular) sanctuaries, fits this model well. Instead, these offerings, found at coastal sanctuaries at Perachora, Eretria, and Aegina, may be from passing or returning sailors.[90] In other words, as was the case in all periods under study here, it is unlikely that the wide variety of kinds and geographical contexts of these objects can all be explained by a single mechanism.

Another compelling feature of exchange and economy during the Geometric period is the likely presence of resident nonnative craftsmen working to fill the demand for fancy goods that apparently rose throughout the ninth and eighth centuries.[91] The best evidence for these resident craftsmen comes from Crete.[92] At some point in the eighth century, local Cypro-Phoenician Black-on-Red juglets were being manufactured in the context of a perfume or unguent factory near Knossos, and it has been suggested that Near Easterners were involved.[93] Likewise Sakellarakis has suggested that ivory coming into the island from the Near East was also worked by either itinerant or established Levantine craftsmen, who then trained locals in their areas of expertise.[94] An eighth century limestone sculpture from Amnisos may have been made by a North Syrian sculptor.[95] Boardman has argued that several eighth and seventh century graves at Aphrati have their closest parallels in Karkemish, a Neo-Assyrian site on the modern Turkish/Syrian border.[96]

---

[89] Hdt. 1.14; 1.45–55; 2.159.3, 3.180–3; 3.47.3; 4.162. The presence of non-Greeks visiting and living in Geometric Greece has been long suggested and now seems almost sure (Dunbabin 1957; Burkert 1992; S. Morris 1992; Hoffman 1997). We need only to look across the Aegean to Samos for evidence that visiting foreigners often made a habit of offering votives from their homes to gods at major sanctuaries (see discussions at Gunter 2009, 150–151; Simon 1986; Morgan 1990, 229).

[90] For example, Hdt. 4.152.

[91] See S. Morris 1992; Hoffman 1997, Coldstream 1993, 99–100; Kurtz and Boardman 1971, 174.

[92] Dunbabin 1957; Boardman 1973, 56–62; Boardman 2005.

[93] See Kotsonas 2012 for B-o-R jugs in Crete; Coldstream 1982, 268–269; Critiques of the idea that this factory was run by resident foreigners at Frankenstein 1979, 276; Bisi 1987; Jones 1993; Hoffman 1997, 176–185.

[94] Barnett 1948, 6; Sakellarakis 1993, 361; Sakellarakis 1992, 116–117. Criticisms of the view include Frankenstein 1979, 273–274; Hoffman 1997, 157–159.

[95] Prent 2006, 235.

[96] The burials are cremation urns placed in stone dishes with terracotta basin covers (Boardman 1970, 18–23; Boardman 1980, 60; Kurtz and Boardman 1971, 173). Stampolidis has argued that Phoenicians were buried at Eleutherna in the seventh century, as suggested by the presence of stone *cippi* in their funerary assemblages. Further *cippi* are known from Heraklion and Knossos (Stampolidis and Karetsou 1998, 276). For thoughts on the relationship between locals and others in Cretan material culture see Ksipharas 2004, 96–98; Coldstream 1994, 118; Stampolidis 1998, 109–111, 124–125.

So the increase of imported objects and imported commodities in Greece during the eighth century is not solely attributable to an increase of exchange in a strictly transactional, commercial sense. This also looks like an era characterized by regular movements of people and technologies, connecting the world through complex networks that we are only beginning to understand.[97] Could these networks have been slowly built up over time from the sparse ties that remained between those who had fled Greece during the twelfth century crisis and their ancestors, which intensified as the economy and population recovered over the ninth and eighth centuries? We cannot hope to prove or disprove such a statement. But when we consider the nature of the apparent reinvigoration of exchange networks between Greeks and foreigners during the ninth century, we should not overlook the logistics of how and why this occurred.

During the Mycenaean period, it is apparent that commodities were being produced domestically and traded abroad; a clear export trade, probably in value-added agricultural goods like perfumed oil, existed in tandem with the acquisition of significant quantities of raw glass, copper, tin, ivory, and gold (see Figure 4.1). In the Geometric period, the economic growth apparent in all categories of the material record did not apparently include much of a revival of agricultural exports. Or, if it did, there is little evidence thereof in the archaeological record, suggesting that whatever export economy was present in Greece in the eighth century must have taken place along different lines than it had in the thirteenth. Geometric exports from Greece, while relatively abundant compared to Protogeometric ones, consist mostly of drinking cups, and are far fewer in number than Mycenaean ones. We could imagine that Greeks were exporting large quantities of archaeologically invisible commodities like textiles or livestock, that they did export wine and oil in coarseware jars that have gone unrecognized in the archaeological record, or that Greek ceramics were themselves great value and fetched enough of a price to account for increasing quantities of exotic materials reaching Greece. The increase of population during the period would have yielded new opportunities for production at scale, making surpluses possible in ways that would not have been available to a tiny PG population. But the export evidence does not show much reason to believe that value-added or agricultural exports were the basis of Greek interactions around the Mediterranean.

In this respect we could return once again to a Homeric model. Despite the intellectually weak position of explaining everything in the archaeological record based on the Homeric poems, the notion of a universal Mediterranean

[97] For an application of network theories to the early Greek world, see Malkin 2011; more specifically for Greece in the EIA, in the Euboean gulf specifically, Knodell 2013 and Kotsonas 2015. For networks in the Aegean LBA, see Knappett 2011; Kramer-Hajos 2016.

elite culture, which involved the sharing of guest gifts and commensality, is apparent in the archaeological record for the Geometric period. There are many signs of connections between Greek and other Mediterranean political leaders in the Geometric period, including the pottery exports from Greece already mentioned. But none of these vestigial connections speak as loudly to the kinds of shared personal convictions and connections as the appearance of some common sets of artifactual assemblages.[98] Good examples are the identical sets of andirons and *obeloi* (spits) discovered in a series of Geometric tombs from such widely separated locations as Etruria,[99] Argos, Crete, and Cyprus.[100] However we define the spits (as imports, ingots, or early forms of money) the uniform assemblages of objects that represented wealth and personal connections with long-distance peers must suggest close social affinities and shared notions of commensality between the elite of the Peloponnese, Italy, Crete, and Cyprus in the eighth century, at a level that is

---

[98] Crielaard 1998.

[99] For the Etruscan Tombs, see D'Agostino 1977, 18–20; D'Agostino 1990, 9–13; D'Agostino and Gastaldi 1988, 76. The iron spits appear in Etruria at about the same time they begin to be found in Greek contexts and appear to be influenced by Greek types (see Haarer 2000, 194–195). Etruscans also later began imitating iron spits in bronze. Could Greeks have been carrying iron to Etruria in exchange for bronze during this period? The suggestion is possibly bolstered by *Od.* 1.169–174 in which Mentes travels to Temese (perhaps Bruttium, or else Tamassos in Cyprus) to acquire copper, bearing iron.

[100] For a summary of the Cypro-Geometric spits, see Haarer 2000, 12. About a dozen spit fragments are also known from Pyre 13 at the Lefkandi Toumba cemetery, dated to the SPG I period (Popham et al. 1982, 229, 240). For good analysis of these assemblages, Tandy 1997, 155–165. I briefly rehearse the main points here. In the Palaepaphos tomb from Cyprus, a set of andirons was uncovered in a so-called "warrior's" tomb during excavations in 1960 (Karageorghis 1983, 158, 162, Nos. 56 and 76); contents included Attic/Euboean skyphoi, and bronze and iron equipment for two horses, one of which was found associated with the burial. The andirons terminate in the prow and stern of a ship, making them completely indistinguishable from a set from the same date discovered in Argos, in a tomb also containing 12 skewers or *obeloi* of iron (Courbin 1957, 369; Courbin 1974, 136). Similar andirons found in other contexts in Etruria and in Crete were, like the Palaepaphos burial, accompanied by groups of 12–18 iron *obeloi*. In 1976, when the richest "Royal" tomb at the site of Salamis was excavated, another set of navicular iron andirons was discovered. Tomb 79 contained ornate furniture decorated with silver and ivory, over 200 ceramic vessels, some coated in tin bronze horse trappings, bronze and iron weapons, and an iron tripod stand, as well as evidence of seafood offerings, birds, and murex shells (Karageorghis 1973, 76; Rupp 1988, 129–134). The Salaminian fire-dogs were accompanied by eighteen iron skewers, bound together by iron rings (Karageorghis 1972, 172). Another set of navicular fire-dogs comes from an LG tomb at Kavousi on Crete, along with iron spits of an undetermined number, and spits are found in Knossian tombs in the Geometric period (Catling and Coldstream 1996, 223; Tomb 219.f131). Another set of navicular firedogs as well as two kinds of spits and a double axe come from tomb A1K1 at Eleutherna (from the early seventh century, nicely illustrated at Stampolidis 2008, 117); see also axes with spits at Patriki (Boardman 1971, 7, pl. Γ) and Argos (Courbin 1957, 322–386). Recently another broken set, along with an iron knife, was discovered at Eltyna on Crete (Egglezou 2007, 182).

usually difficult to prove archaeologically.[101] The combination of what can be nicely conceptualized as sets of barbeque equipment immediately calls to mind the Homeric feast: a knife or axe to kill the unlucky animal, a spit to skewer the meat, and firedogs on which to place a hot iron spit. This material is deeply resonant of feasting scenes from the *Iliad* and *Odyssey*.[102] The association of iron spits and navicular firedogs with wealthy, apparently often warrioresque, cosmopolitan elites in the Geometric period might lead us to some conclusions about the sources of imported material in this period.[103] Specific episodes in the Homeric poems (for example, 23.740–749; *Od.* 4. 615–619; *Od.* 15.99–129) suggest that objects like the bronze bowls we find in sanctuaries, or ivory horse-trappings, were the kinds of things that eighth century elites would pass around through gift-exchange networks, so the Homeric model is persuasive in explaining some of our evidence.[104]

We could therefore reconstruct the Geometric period along the lines of a straightforwardly Homeric model, in which status was acquired regionally by a semi-hereditary elite displaying the virtues of martial valor, extraordinary intelligence, and good looks, who then parlayed local importance into adventures abroad where gift-exchange relationships that served as conduits for the acquisition of reifying exotica were secured. If the population estimates provided in Chapter 5 are accepted, it seems likely that the swinging pendulum of the land-to-labor availability ratio would have moved toward favoring landowners in the Geometric period, allowing the rise of a class of exploitative elite that could not get a real foothold on wealth in the Protogeometric period.

[101] The *obeloi* are only one subset of the material evidence that could be called upon to witness such a shared elite culture. Sakellarakis has recently argued that some of the ivory objects in the Idaean cave were one part of a throne much like the one found in the wealthy burial at Cypriot Salamis, a parallel that would support the increasingly clear connections between Cypriot and Greek elites (like the individual buried in the Lefkandi *heroon*) that is emerging (Sakellarakis 1992, 115; Sakellarakis 2006). One could also cite here the discovery of a possible goldsmith's hoard in Eretria, maybe suggesting (along with the *obeloi*) shared "premonetary practices" between Greece and the East in the period (Verdan 2015, 189). Also at Eretria (Huber 2003, 103) and at a variety of other sites in PG and Geometric Greece with clear eastern and western contacts (such as Eleutherna, see Yalouri 1994). The existence of 2–3 cm clay balls of the type used in Cyprus (see Vetters 2011) to measure metals in an economic context points in the same direction. The argument here does not line up with Duplouy's (2006) position that elites did not gain high status or define themselves through the construction of a long-distance inter-aristocratic *koine* but rather engaged in hierarchical gamesmanship only within the community.

[102] It is probably not incidental that the iron handles of the spits resemble the ends of oars. The vision of a dozen spits arranged perpendicularly along the axis of the firedogs, must have resembled an oared ship sailing over the dark embers of the fire (and might have reduplicated the aesthetics of depictions of ships in Geometric vase-paintings). For a feast in Homer mentioning spits, see *Il.* 9.205–214.

[103] On correlation between spits and warrior burials, see Tandy 1997, 163–165. On the function of firedogs as burial goods, see Courbin 1957, 378; Karageorghis 1963, 292–294; Deonna 1959; Boardman 1971, 8.

[104] Crielaard 2015, 355–363.

These new men of leisure took their fortunes and built relationships with their new peers abroad. Such a model fits nicely with the Homeric evidence, but ultimately it does not have much explanatory power, since it fails to account for the complex relationship between the Homeric poems and the real world (see Chapter 1), and falls back on the usual crutch of using the simplified world of Homer to bail out a confusing archaeological record.

Thinking more carefully about the evidence, if we assume that some of the iron spits and firedogs found in Greek graves were manufactured in Greece, it could lead us to conclude that an expanding Greek economy, owing at least some of its growth to demographic change, began producing iron for export in quantity in the eighth century, and that iron formed the basis of the Greek exchange economy in the Geometric period. This possibility is supported by the physical characteristics and geographical distribution of the iron spits, many of which come from Greek burials or sanctuaries. Only good iron could be made into spits, so if some spits are Greek, Greek iron must have been good and thus perhaps worthy of export.[105] Eighth century communities that seem to have flourished most on the mainland were located in and around the Euboean gulf, where evidence for local iron ore exploitation from EIA Greece is strongest, and on Crete, where iron ores are abundant.[106] The apparent spread of ironworking within Greece during the eighth century, for which there is evidence around the southern Aegean, shows that Greeks were actively intensifying production of this valuable metal.[107] The absence of expected export quantities from the Geometric period is one of the major missing pieces of the evidentiary puzzle I have presented in this book; perhaps better analytical work on the origin of iron artifacts around the EIA Mediterranean could fill a gap here.[108]

[105] See work by Crew 1991, 32–33. See Åstrom et al. 1986 for the high value of good iron during the EIA.

[106] For the evidence of iron ore exploitation in early Greece, see Markoe 1998, 234–235, 235–237; Backe-Forsberg et al. 2000–2001, 31–34; MacDonald et al.1983, 184. For exploitation of iron in Euboea especially, see Knodell 2013, 248–250. In order to make a long spit of iron, high quality material is required (Crew 1991). The notion that spits constituted the earliest form of exchange unit among Greeks is supported by the tale of Pheidon, said to have gathered up excess spits once coinage had taken their place in order to dedicate them at the Argive Heraion (attested in the *Etymologicum Magnum* 3.613.13), where a large iron "spit-wad" was excavated (Courbin 1983).

[107] Ironworking is attested at Asine, Oropos, Eretria, a few Laconian sites, Kommos, Knossos, Kephala on Skiathos, and the Greek colony at Pithekoussai. See Risberg 1995, 129; Bassiakos 1988; Sackett 1992, 366–368; Shaw 1984, 283; Ridgway 1992, 91–93; Doonan and Mazarakis Ainian 2007; Mazarakis Ainian 2012, 61. For ore resources in Greece, see Bakhuizen 1976; 1977; S. Morris 1992, 131–132; Muhly 2008 (a skeptical view).

[108] Other sources of wealth besides export for Greeks in the EIA could (if we peer forward in history) include piracy, mercenary labor, or slave trading. Passages in the Bible state that King David hired Greek-speaking mercenaries from Crete in the 10th century (Cartledge 1987, 315; evidence is from the Biblical texts, specifically II Samuel 20.23 and I Kings 1.38). The earliest Greek word for mercenary is *epikouros*, similar to the Mycenaean *e-pi-ko-wo*

6.5. CONCLUSIONS

However Geometric Greeks were able to acquire new wealth during the eighth century (and these ways are almost certain to have been complex, multifaceted, and under-evident in the archaeological evidence),[109] the key concept I wish to emphasize is that every metric shows strong economic growth in the Geometric period. But the new economic engagement of the eighth century did not mirror the embodiment of the trade economy of the IIIB period particularly closely. The ratios of imports and exports from the PG and Geometric periods are dramatically different than the ones from the thirteenth and twelfth centuries, suggesting that we are dealing with an altogether different economic model, with new institutions to go along with it. Geometric Greeks seem likely to have been exchanging raw or value-added materials on Mediterranean markets of a different kind than the Mycenaeans did, and direct (that is, face-to-face) gift exchanges or personal relationships look like they might have played a more important part in Geometric interactions than they did in LBA ones. Depositional contexts in Greece likewise show that exotica were used differently within society during the post-IIIB period than they had during the thirteenth century, although some vicissitudes of our archaeological contexts make it hard to know whether the patterns are meaningful.

On the other hand, there are also a number of compelling signs of continuity in the evidence. The presence of resident foreign craftsmen, and their close relationship with the presence of exotica in the archaeological record is a common thread that binds the evidence from the LBA to the Geometric period (and beyond) and speaks to an enduringly cosmopolitan nature of life, not entirely to be unexpected for a maritime world like Greece. There is convincing evidence from Crete that this presence may have been a feature of the domestic craft economy throughout the EIA, so that we may indeed have a band of uninterrupted continuity from the IIIB to the G period in the form of artisanal diversity within Greece. However, it is notoriously difficult to read any kind of ethnicity or cultural affiliation from the archaeological record, so we must approach this conclusion with due caution. In general we can probably conclude that thoroughgoing travel and mobility, on the part of artists or craftspeople especially but probably of others besides, was a common characteristic of the Aegean world across the LBA–EIA transition.

(Lavelle 1997, 232) although the use of the word in the Homeric poems is limited to the description of Trojan allies (Lavelle 1997, 229–235). According to Herodotus (2.152–4), Ionians fought for the Pharaoh Psammetichus around 664 BCE. For Greek mercenaries generally, see Trundle 2004.

[109] Papadopoulos 2001, 382.

The process of reading religious, superstitious or ritual practice from the archaeological record is as fraught as determining ethnicity from material remains. Yet the role of such practice in explaining the deposition of exotica in Greece throughout the LBA–EIA transition demands consideration. The similarity between the imported objects deposited in the twelfth century cemetery of Perati and the commonest categories of imported exotica from the PG and Geometric periods is striking. Figurines (of Egyptian gods and mythological figures) and amulets (scarabs and a wide variety of others) are not prominent (and are nearly nonexistent) in the import corpus from the entire LBA (not just the IIIB period). Yet starting in the twelfth century a crescendoing thread of such artifacts winds its way through the archaeological evidence. This is only one note in a cacophonous fugue that cries out across the qualitative and quantitative dataset – the twelfth century (not the PG period) appears to be the era of most dramatic change and transformation in a whole variety of evidentiary categories (including the shift from inhumation to cremation), even though its cultural attributes continue to echo the Mycenaean past in important ways. It is regrettable that this phase has, until the twenty-first century, been treated as a cultural "dead end" or "twilight" instead of an exciting era of transformation, because it is clear that many of the keys to unlocking the story of early Greek history must be found in the twelfth century.

In light of apparently ritual meaning of the figurines and amulets, probably intended to guarantee provision of something good in the afterlife, deposited in tombs at Perati and in later cemeteries and sanctuaries, I would venture to speculate that these are signaling the beginning of a period in which nonlocal ritual practices involving the deposition of such amulets and figurines form part of the normal socioreligious landscape of the Greek world. Whether the depositors are Greeks returning from mercantile voyages abroad, Phoenician sailors dedicating scarabs at sanctuaries and hoping for a safe trip, non-Greeks living and working in Crete, or local elites who have picked up new ritual practices from their peers around the Mediterranean is largely impossible to discern from the archaeological record. There seems likely to be a connection between the appearance of these objects in the archaeological record, a time of extraordinary migration and movements of peoples, and an era in which the world seemed especially frightening and risky, where good luck was in short supply. But the largely ritual context or function of many post twelfth century exotica calls into question the usual idea that these items serve only to "confer power" onto the elite,[110] a simplistic formula which has been correctly problematized in recent literature.[111]

---

[110] Sherratt 1998, 294.
[111] Heymans and van Wijngaarden 2009; Brysbaert and Vetters 2013; Arrington 2016.

Does this represent a new feature of the postpalatial environment? The answer is not clear, but may be negative. In the Mycenaean palatial period, for which the link between elites, exotica, and power is seen as so important that the interruption of trade routes or their monopolization by the palace has been blamed for the toppling of the entire system, finished imported goods seem to have little to do with elites, while being concentrated at palatial centers.[112] Superstition, ritual, and nonlocal belief systems probably account best for the deposition of Egyptian plaques and Syro-Palestinian armor scales in foundation deposits at Mycenae and Tiryns; other imports seem to be valued as commodities, to be integrated into local craft practice, rather than exotica proper, or to have been the possessions of palatial craftspeople. We lack detailed evidence about how Mycenaean religion worked, but we should consider the possibility that shrines within Mycenaean palaces served the same function within a community as Greek sanctuaries in the Geometric period did – and therefore that the concentration of imported *exotica* in these religious contexts represents a kind of continuity from the LBA to the EIA.

In sum, the association of a sizable portion of known imports with some kind of ritual context, mortuary or otherwise, holds true across the dataset. In this regard, it is also fascinating to observe the fact that bronzeworkers may have been associated with sanctuaries, or at least attached to religious offices or officials, in both the Geometric period and the LBA.[113] If there is a major strand of continuity that both upsets old notions of exotica as signs of elite privilege or self-fashioning and the relationship between trade and imports, it is the consistent affiliation of imports with ritual contexts. The possible implication is that imported exotica in the early Greek world served more to provide individuals with an unseen superstitious advantage rather than a purely socio-political one, and that spiritual authorities, rather than political or economic ones, were at the center of early Greek cosmopolitanism.

---

[112] On analogy with Geometric imports at sanctuaries, it is possible that these objects were dedicated to local gods by visiting dignitaries, or by Mycenaeans returning home from long voyages. This possibility has not been explored in the literature.

[113] For the latter, there might be evidence for this in the Jn tablets from Pylos, which list *ka-ke-we po-ti-ni-ja-we-jo*, possibly to be translated as "bronzeworkers belonging to the lady/goddess." The Jn tablets deal with the distribution of bronze in general; some from the periphery to the central authority and some from the central authority to the individual bronzeworkers. See discussion in Uchitel 1990; Milani 1998; comments at Hiller 1988, 62.

CONCLUSIONS

IMPORTS AND ECONOMY, CRISIS AND RESILIENCE, BRONZE AGE AND IRON AGE

I WROTE THIS BOOK IN ORDER TO CONTRIBUTE TO THE STATE OF knowledge about the degree of change, both scalar and institutional, that characterized the Bronze to Iron Age transition in the Aegean. In part, I aimed to do this by correcting a deficiency in scholarship on the early history of the Greek trade economy. Existing accounts of the way that the long-distance exchange economy transformed after the collapse of the Mycenaean palaces around 1200 BCE do not do an adequate job of accounting for the complexities involved in interpreting the surviving archaeological evidence. These studies are characterized by an undue focus on imports (recognizable, finished objects identified with a foreign production center) which have too often and too uncritically been taken to be a good proxy for intensity or magnitude of trade relations. According to this view, a decrease in the number of observed imports from the period after the demise of the palatial administration was taken to indicate that there was a decrease in the volume or intensity of trade during the Greek EIA, followed by more imports in the Geometric period, which was taken as self-standing evidence that there was "more trade" in the eighth century. This is a highly reductive notion that I reject on the basis of an unprecedentedly thorough interrogation into the actual meaning of import counts and a comparison of these counts with other potential proxies for trade volume and intensity. Second, most previous studies of trade tend to lean back on textual evidence that is used to "explain" the archaeological record, something that I showed in Chapter 1 is a risky proposition, unlikely to provide reliable answers to historical questions. Over the course of the book, I largely eschewed the use of textual evidence, as I sought to muster a rich, multifaceted array of archaeological material in order to show that, treated properly, even mute stones can ring out with remarkable eloquence regarding the Mycenaean collapse and its economic aftermath.

Methodologically, then, my goal in putting together this project was to pull off the scholarly white gloves and to aggressively engage with the merits and drawbacks of an import-based, textually dependent approach to ancient trade systems and to determine what, if anything, archaeologically visible imports really tell us about change in trade. More substantively, I aimed to answer a fundamental question about the nature of the transition between the LBA and EIA economies of Greece: what changed, and by how much, in evidence we have for engagement with the outside world over a period of major economic and political dynamism? The advances I have made here are, in the end, a combination of empirical strides in the arena of ancient trade and methodological revelations about the importance of contextualizing all synthetic arguments about the past within a comprehensive dataset.

Overall, I have shown that Greece was never particularly isolated from the wider Mediterranean, but that trade and the economy changed in a variety of ways over the period from 1300 to 700 BCE The story the archaeological record tells fits best with a "collapse and regeneration" model of historical development as originally posited by Snodgrass in the 1970s. For Greek history, there are two major implications. First, the economic developments I observe are likely to be related to deep and broad changes in social and political realities. The notion of post-Mycenaean Greece as a time of crisis, when much of life was consumed with a fight for survival, and during which institutions that would later become evident as the building blocks of historical Greece formed, seems to fit well with the evidence. Greeks living and dying in the twelfth and eleventh centuries were confronted with a world that bore little resemblance to the world of those living under palatial institutions in the fourteenth and thirteenth. By the eighth century, when growth resumed, Greeks constructed a new social order in a way that is characteristic of those building complex societies out of scratch, rather than reconstructing or building upon an immediate predecessor.

The evidence in this book contradicts some common notions about the intensity of trade in early Greek history. The first is the, often implied if rarely stated, straightforward understanding of the relationship between number of imports and *volume* or *intensity* of trade. Another is the notion that prevailing political elites at the administrative centers of LBA states controlled long-distance connections and curated a fetish for imported exotica. A third is the idea that Greece was ever really significantly cut off from long-distance trade interactions. There is little compelling reason to believe, as most do, that issues of supply rather than fluctuating demand and purchasing power based on demographic change account for the decrease in imported commodities and objects that is evident during the postpalatial periods of Greek history. Here, I have attempted to show that it was a weak domestic economy, rather than supply-side issues preventing Mediterranean interaction, that best accounts for the apparent decline in exotica of all kinds in the archaeological record of the twelfth and eleventh centuries.

To close, I summarize a few of the implications of the work:

1. IMPORTS AND EXCHANGE

The small density of imports within the artifact assemblages from Early Greece suggest that few people in Late Mycenaean, Protogeometric, or Geometric Greece ever had any interest in finished, imported objects. Even at the sites where imports show up in exceptional numbers, the overall "intensity" of trade that import tallies suggest is low indeed. Many imports seem not to be explicitly tied to any kind of recognizable commercial or even political exchange, but instead represent the material correlates of nonlocal ritual or cultural practice in Greece. Surely, as this wrinkle suggests, number of imports do not tell the whole story of exchange systems, whether they were economic, social, or political in nature.

Does an inconspicuous record of imported objects prove that there was not much long-distance trade going on at all in early Greece? That would be an overly facile reading of the evidence. In assessing patterns in the archaeological record we must be aware that data like import counts only provides a proxy, a sample used to construct interpretations. The tiny quantities of finished imported goods that find their way into the archaeological record are likely to (mis-)represent a much-diminished carapace of the original volume of "traded goods," loosely defined. There are a number of "known unknowns." Many imported cargoes may have been made of perishable materials that are unlikely to survive archaeologically. Others were transformed by Greeks after their initial acquisition, making them hard to identify or date correctly. Looters have dug up still more, so that they do not survive to be analyzed by archaeologists. More important than interrogating the low absolute volume of imports is determining the relationship between the volume of surviving imports and the intensity of trade in the distant past. Does a small number of recorded imports translate into low intensity trade in obvious ways? The answer to this question should be made in reference to all of the other available evidence, as I have arrayed it in the chapters of this book. Most of the strong indicators for a significant long-distance trade economy do suggest what the imports fail to confirm: the scale of exchange was robust in the LBA, with decline after the thirteenth century and recovery in the Geometric period.

TABLE 7.1. *Summary of evidence for trade in the Aegean*

	Late Bronze Age	Postpalatial	Protogeometric	Geometric
Shipwrecks	Confirm trade (Gelidonya, Uluburun)	Confirm trade, but perhaps only local (Point Iria, Modi)[1]	None	Confirm but not necessarily in Greece[2]
Texts	Near Eastern texts confirm trade, but no trade with other major Bronze Age kingdoms evident in Linear B texts	Near Eastern texts confirm trade, but not explicitly with the Aegean	Homeric texts indicate trade, but applicability throughout period questionable; Some Biblical evidence confirms continued tradition of gift exchange among elites[3]	Homeric texts indicate trade; Historical sources retroject colonization and movements of people into the period
Imports	Few imports, much imported material	Few imports, some imported material	Few imports, some imported material	Few imports, much imported material
Exports	Exports confirmed in considerable numbers	Exports confirmed, but fewer than LBA	Exports confirmed in tiny numbers, and only after c. 950	Exports confirmed in small numbers
Collateral	General wealth, large settlements, investment in monumental architecture, social complexity	Few major monuments, getting poorer, but social complexity remains	Generally impoverished, few major monuments, some social complexity	Growth and state formation, emphasis of wealth in sanctuaries

The apparent conclusion is that although imports may be an indicator of trade, they are not a reliable source from which to draw conclusions about volume or intensity of trade. In other words, the number of imports at a site or in a region is not likely to be a good indicator of the amount of trade "that happened" there.

From a methodological point of view, the major implications of the book are significant, both for the study of trade and for the way in which we go about reconstructing the history of prehistoric periods in general. While imports

---

[1] Recent work at Modi off the coast of Attica has revealed the wreck of an LH IIIC "merchantman" carrying transport vessels. Thirty vessels have been lifted, but these have not yet been published in detail (Konsolaki-Giannopoulou 2007).

[2] A Geometric-period shipwreck containing a cargo of wine has been excavated on the Syro-Palestinian coast (Ballard et al. 2002; Foxhall 1998).

[3] For example, 2 Kings 12–13 (and generally Nam 2012).

might tell us about the way in which trade systems may have been structured in the ancient past, they cannot stand alone as indices to the "amount" of trade that occurred within any particular period. Economic systems, including trade systems, are far too complex to be defined by a dataset consisting of objects that are ambiguously related to the "target population" of originally traded goods. Even if surviving imports happen to represent a fair sample of goods that were traded in a given period, we cannot determine what they tell us about anything unless we immerse them in a much larger nexus of data that helps us to sort out patterns that are likely to be meaningful from spurious variation in a material record that is aggressively contingent.

2. TRADE AND POLITICS

Scholarly understanding of the cadence of trade across the LBA–EIA transition has long presupposed an interdependence between palatial polities and long-distance Mediterranean trade routes: the palaces controlled and/or administered trade and its interruption upset the political balance. Neither side of this proposition can be sustained, based on the evidence. If the palaces controlled long-distance maritime trade routes in the IIIB period, and the palaces ceased to exist after the IIIB period, we would expect to see a complete disappearance of nonheirloom imported objects (imported objects that were manufactured after 1200) from the archaeological record after IIIB, rather than a decrease in these objects. One thing we can say about the quantitative patterns is that they do not sustain this point of view. First, imported objects do not occur in the contexts we would expect them to if they were being used in the manner suggested by the current model. Second, these objects appear in many cases to be associated with workshops and cult spaces rather than with the displaymaking of political leaders.

Likewise, if the downfall of the Mycenaean palaces were somehow tied to a collapse of Mediterranean trade routes, this should be evident in the pattern we see in the imports. But imports continue to appear in the archaeological record in Greece at similar per capita rates well after the palatial collapse took place, undermining the notion that long-distance trade was dependent upon these polities. All of the evidence suggests a restructuring of trade, which was largely in the hands of independent intermediaries, rather than a disruption of trade, in the twelfth century. We have been uncritically conflating the presence of imported goods at palaces with the notion that palaces controlled or depended upon trade for too long; this should be reconsidered.

3. TRADE AND DARKNESS

Most narratives of exchange and interaction over the LBA–EIA transition assume some fluctuation of access to trade networks during the period, specifically a severance or interruption of such networks in the "Dark Age" of the eleventh and tenth centuries BCE. But the most efficient explanation for the quantitative trends apparent in the evidence is that the domestic Greek economy became smaller and simpler after the end of the LBA, and that this contraction caused major changes to the structure and capabilities of the domestic economy in ways that had implications for long-distance exchange. In other words, there was not so much a crisis in supply as diminishing demand, with imports tracking relatively closely with demographic trends. That said, with depopulation came thoroughgoing adjustments to the economic system as a whole. We can see a variety of axes along which exchange systems suffered seismic shifts after the LBA: the types of commodities and objects exchanged, the function and context of those exchanges, and the way in which human movement and exchange overlapped. While Geometric trade institutions and habits have some fascinating similarities with Mycenaean ones, for the most part, the overall *kosmos* of evidence for exchange systems presented in this book looks quite different in the eighth century than it did in the thirteenth. But there is no reason to believe that Greece was ever "cut off" in a meaningful way from the wider Mediterranean.

4. EX(CHANGE) AND CONTINUITY

So, while trade routes never ceased actively functioning at any point in early Mediterranean history, trade institutions (and probably the economy and society of Greece as a whole) changed dramatically between 1200 and 700 BCE. In emphatically restating all of the evidence for changes after the LBA, I do not mean to say that there are not aspects of continuity in the way that people would have lived their lives, created meaning, and negotiated a natural world that had, after all, the same basic characteristics as it had in 1300 BCE. We can identify plenty of strands of continuity between the LBA and the EIA. Agriculture remained at the heart of the economy; it is unlikely that the lifting of a relatively light Mycenaean tax burden would have made much of a difference in the life of the average farmer. In a place like Greece, where life has always had a maritime focus, the mobility of people, ideas, and traditions was an ever-present reality. But we must assume that the disruptions and resulting population changes that occurred over the course of the twelfth century must have impacted the daily calculations of risk and material investment of all Greeks in serious ways, and that life in this period presented severe challenges to the effort to merely survive. Whatever precipitated it, the economic decline of the postpalatial world seems to have set in motion a long process of crisis and recovery; a process which reformed the social order dramatically. One implication is that it is almost certainly the twelfth century world of the IIIC period that holds the key to understanding the LBA–EIA transition more than the presumed "new beginning" of the PG period. Though it has long been seen as the dead end of Mycenaean BA culture, it looks increasingly like a period that deserves more attention than it has gotten so far in studies seeking to understand the institutional history of early Greece. This is bad news for Greek historians who will have to stretch back further in time to find the beginning of their narratives, but good news for scholars seeking fresh ground for new revelations about cultural history.

WORKS CITED

Note: Journal abbreviations used are in accordance with the conventions of the *American Journal of Archaeology*.

Abernathy, V. 2002. "Population Dynamics: Poverty, Inequality, and Self-Regulating Fertility Rates." *Population and Environment* 24.1: 69–96.

Agresti, A. and B. Coull. 1998. "Approximate Is Better than 'Exact' for Interval Estimation of Binomial Proportions." *The American Statistician* 52.2: 119–126.

Akdeniz, E. 2007. "Kadıkalesi Kazısı Miken Buluntarı." *Ege Üniversitesi Arkeoloji Dergisi IX*: 35–70.

Åkerström, Å. 1968. "A Mycenaean Potter's Factory at Berbati Near Mycenae." In *Atti e Memorie del I Congresso Internazionale di Micenologia, Roma, 27 settembre–3 ottobre 1967*, 48–53. Incunabula Graeca 25. Rome: Edizioni dell'Ateneo.

Akkermans, P. and G. Schwartz. 2003. *The Archaeology of Syria: From Complex Hunter Gatherers to Early Urban Societies (ca. 16,000–300 BC)*. Cambridge: Cambridge University Press.

Alden, M. 1981. *Bronze Age Population Fluctuations in the Argolid from the Evidence of Mycenaean Tombs*. Göteborg: P. Åström.

Alexandri, O. 1968. "Ερυσίχθονος καὶ Νηλέως." *ArchDelt* 22 B1 Chr: 79–83.

———. 1972. "Γεωμετρικὶ τάφοι εἰς περιοχὴν Κυνοσάργους." *AAA* 5.2: 165–175.

Allen, R. 2001. "The Great Divergence in European Wages and Prices from the Middle Ages to the First World War." *Explorations in Economic History* 38: 411–448.

Allen, T. 1921. *The Homeric Catalogue of Ships*. Oxford: Clarendon Press.

Alram-Stern, E. 2007. "Characteristic Small Finds of LH IIIC from Aigeira and their Context." In *LH IIIC Chronology and Synchronisms II: LH IIIC Middle*, edited by S. Deger-Jalkotzy and M. Zavadil, 15–26. Veröffentlichungen der Mykenischen Kommission 30. Vienna: Verlag der Österreichischen Akademie der Wissenschaften.

Alušik, T. 2007. *Defensive Architecture of Prehistoric Crete*. Oxford: Archaeopress.

Ammerman, A. 1992. "Taking Stock of Quantitative Archaeology." *Annual Review of Archaeology* 21: 231–255.

Andreadaki-Vlasaki, M. 1988. "Νόμος Χανίων, Μινωική Νεκρόπολη." *Κριτική Εστία* 2: 278.

———. 1991–1993. "Νόμος Χανίων, Επαρχία Κυδωνίας, Πόλη Χανίων, Μινωική Νεκρόπολη: Νάος Αποστολών Πετρού και Παυλού (ισόπεδο Μαζάλη)": *Κριτική Εστία* 4: 207.

———. 1994–1996. "Νόμος Χανίων, Επαρχία Κυδωνίας, Πόλη Χανίων, Μινωική και κλασική Νεκρόπολη. Οικοπ. Κληπονομών Μανωλικάκη." *Κριτική Εστία* 9: 196.

———. 1999. "Νόμος Χανίων, Επαρχία Κυδωνίας, Πόλη Χανίων, Μινωική και κλασική Νεκρόπολη. Οικόπεδο

Κ. Ροβιθάκη." *Κριτική Εστία* 7: 143–149.

2002. "Νόμος Χανίων, Επαρχία Κυδονίας, Πόλη Χανίων, Μινωική και κλασική Νεκροπόλη." *Κριτική Εστία* 9: 233.

Andrewes, A. 1961. "Phratries in Homer." *Hermes* 89: 129–140.

1967. *The Greeks*. London: Knopf.

Andrews, T. 1994. "Bronzecasting at Geometric Period Olympia and Early Greek Metal Sources." Ph.D. dissertation, Brandeis University.

Andrikou, E. 1995. "Συμβολή οδών Λ. Μπέλλου και Ι. Θρεψιάδου (οικόπεδο Δημοτικού Συνεδριακού Κέντρου (ΔΣΚ) δήμου Θηβών Ο.Τ. 377)." *ArchDelt* 49 B1 *Chr*: 290–294.

Antonaccio, C. 1995. *An Archaeology of Ancestors: Tomb Cult and Hero Cult in Early Greece*. Lanham, MD: Rowman & Littlefield.

2002. "Warriors, Traders, Ancestors: The 'Heroes' of Lefkandi." In *Images of Ancestors*, edited by E. Hotje, 13–42. Aarhus: Aarhus University Press.

Aprile, J. 2013. "The New Political Economy of Nichoria: Using Intrasite Distributional Data to Investigate Regional Institutions." *AJA* 117.3: 429–436.

Aravantinos, V. 1991. "The Mycenaean Inscribed Sealings from Thebes: Problems of Content and Function." In *Aegean Seals, Sealings, and Administration*, edited by T. Palaima, 149–174. Aegaeum 5. Liège: Université de Liège.

Aravantinos, V., L. Godart, and A. Sacconi, eds. 2001. *Thèbes: fouilles de la Cadmée*. Pisa: Istituti editoriali e poligrafici internazionali.

Arrington, N. 2016. "Talismanic Practice at Lefkandi: Trinkets, Burials, and Belief in the Early Iron Age." *CCJ* 62: 1–30.

Artzy, M. 1998. "Routes, Trade, Boats, and 'Nomads of the Sea'." In *Mediterranean Peoples in Transition: Thirteenth to Early Tenth Centuries BCE*, edited by S. Gitin, A. Mazar, and E. Stern, 439–448. Jerusalem: Israel Exploration Society.

2005. "*Emporia* on the Carmel Coast? Tel Akko, Tell Abu Hawam, and Tel Nami of the Late Bronze Age." In *Emporia. Aegeans in the Central and Eastern Mediterranean*, edited by R. Laffineur and E. Greco, 355–361. Aegaeum 25. Liège: Université de Liège.

Aruz, J. 1997. "Cypriot and 'Cypro-Aegean' Seals." In *De Chypre à la Bactriane, les sceaux du Proche-Orient ancien*, edited by A. Caubet, 271–288. Paris: Musée du Louvre.

Aslan, C. and P. Hnila. 2015. "Migration and Interaction at Troy from the End of the Late Bronze Age to the Iron Age." In *NOSTOI: Indigenous Culture, Migration, + Integration in the Aegean Islands + Western Anatolia during the Late Bronze + Early Iron Ages*, edited by N. Stampolidis, Ç. Maner, and K. Kopanias, 185–209. Istanbul: Koç University Press.

Aslan, C., L. Kealhofer, and P. Grave. 2014. "The Early Iron Age at Troy Reconsidered." *OJA* 33.3: 275–312.

Astour, M. 1972. "The Merchant Class of Ugarit." In *Gesellschaftsklassen im Alten Zweistromland und in den angrenzenden Gebieten*, edited by D. Edzard, 12–26. Munich: Verlag der Bayerischen Akademie der Wissenschaften.

Åström, P. 1996. "Hala Sultan Tekke – A Late Cypriote Harbour Town." In *Late Bronze Age Settlement in Cyprus: Function and Settlement*, edited by P. Åström and E. Herscher, 9–14. Jonsered: Paul Åströms Förlag.

Åström, P. et al., 1986. "Iron Artifacts form Swedish Excavations on Cyprus." *OpAth* 16.3: 27–41.

Auberson, P. and K. Schefold. 1972. *Führer durch Eretria*. Bern: Francke.

Aura-Jorro, F., and F. Adrados. 1985. *Diccionario Griego-español, Anejo I:*

Diccionario micénico 1. Madrid: Consejo Superior de Investigaciones Científicas.

Avruch, K. 2000. "Reciprocity, Equality, and Status-Anxiety in the Amarna Letters." In *Amarna Diplomacy: The Beginnings of International Relations*, edited by R. Cohen and R. Westerbrook, 154–164. Baltimore: Johns Hopkins University Press.

Bachhuber, C. 2006. "Aegean Interest on the Uluburun Ship." *AJA* 110.3: 345–363.

Bachvarova, M. 2009. "Hittite and Greek Perspectives on Travelling Poets, Texts, and Festivals." In *Wandering Poets in Ancient Greek Culture*, edited by R. Hunter and I. Rutherford, 23–45. Cambridge: Cambridge University Press.

———. 2016. *From Hittite to Homer: The Anatolian Background of Ancient Greek Epic*. Cambridge: Cambridge University Press.

Backe-Forsberg, Y., C. Risberg, and Y. Bassiakos. 2000–2001. "Metal-Working at Asine." *OpAth* 25.6: 25–34.

Badre, L., M.-L. Boileau, R. Jung, and H. Mommsen. 2005. "The Provenance of Aegean- and Syrian-Type Pottery Found at Tell Kazel (Syria)." *Ägypten und Levante* 15: 15–47.

Bakhuizen, S. 1977. "Greek Steel." *WorldArch* 9.2: 220–234.

Bakhuizen, S. and R. Kreulen. 1976. *Chalkis in Euboea, Iron and Chalkidians Abroad. Chalkidian Studies III*. Leiden: Brill.

Ballard, R. et al., 2002. "Iron Age Shipwrecks in Deep Water Off Ashkelon, Israel." *AJA* 106: 151–168.

Banou, E. 2002. "Κνωσός. Αμπελόκηποι." *Κρητική Εστία* 9: 307–314.

Barker, G. and R. Hodges, eds. 1981. *Archaeology and Italian Society. Prehistoric, Roman, and Medieval Studies. Papers in Italian Archaeology II*. Oxford: Archaeopress.

Barnett, R. 1948. "Early Greek and Oriental Ivories." *JHS* 68: 1–25.

Bass, G. 1991. "Evidence of Trade from Bronze Age Shipwrecks." In *Bronze Age Trade in the Mediterranean*, edited by N. Gale, 69–82. Göteborg: P Åströms Förlag.

———. 1997a. "Prolegomena to a Study of Maritime Traffic in Raw Materials in the Fourteenth and Thirteenth Centuries BC." In *TEXNH: Craftsmen, Craftswomen and Craftsmanship in the Aegean Bronze Age*, edited by R. Laffineur and P. Betancourt, 153–170. Aegaeum 16.1. Liège: Université de Liège.

———. 1997b. "Beneath the Wine Dark Sea: Nautical Archaeology and the Phoenicians of the *Odyssey*." In *Greeks and Barbarians. Essays on the Interactions between Greeks and Non-Greeks in Antiquity and the Consequences for Eurocentrism*, edited by J. Coleman and C. Walz, 71–101. Bethesda, MD: CDL Press.

———. 1998. "Sailing between the Aegean and the Orient in the Second Millennium BC." In *The Aegean and the Orient in the Second Millennium*, edited by E. Cline and D. Harris-Cline, 183–189. Aegaeum 18. Liège: Université de Liège.

Bass, G., et al., 1967. "Cape Gelidonya: A Bronze Age Shipwreck." *TAPA* 57: 1–77.

Bassiakos, Y. 1988. "Ancient Iron Metallurgy in Laconia." In *New Aspects of Archaeological Science in Greece*, edited by R. Jones and H. Catling, 55–58. Athens: British School at Athens.

Baumbach, L. 1983. "An Examination of the Evidence for a State of Emergency at Pylos c. 1200 BC from the Linear B Tablets." In *Res Mycenaeae*, edited by A. Heubeck and G. Neumann,

28–40. Göttingen: Vandenhoeck and Ruprecht.

Beaufils, K. 2000. "Beyond the Argo-Polis. A Social Archaeology of the Argolid in the 6th and 5th centuries BCE." Ph.D. dissertation, University College London.

Beazley, J. and M. Robertson. 1926. "Early Greek Art." In *The Cambridge Ancient History* IV, 579–610. Cambridge: Cambridge University Press.

Beckman, G. 1995. *Hittite Diplomatic Texts*, edited by H. Hoffner. Atlanta, GA: Scholars Press.

———. 1996. "Hittite Documents from Hattusa." In *Sources for the History of Cyprus II: Near Eastern and Aegean Texts from the Third to the First Millennia BC*, edited by B. Knapp, 31–35. Altamont, NY: Greece and Cyprus research center.

Beckman, G., T. Bryce, and E. Cline, eds. 2011. *The Ahhiyawa Texts*. Atlanta, GA: Scholars Press.

Bell. C. 1997. *Ritual: Perspectives and Dimensions*. Oxford: Oxford University Press.

———. 2006. *The Evolution of Long Distance Trading Relationships across the LBA/Iron Age Transition on the Northern Levantine Coast*. Oxford: Archaeopress.

———. 2009. "Continuity and Change: The Divergent Destinies of Late Bronze Age Ports in Syria and Lebanon across the LBA/Iron Age Transition." In *Forces of Transformation*, edited by G. Bachhuber and G. Roberts, 30–38. Oxford: Oxbow.

———. 2012. "The Merchants of Ugarit: Oligarchs of the Late Bronze Age Trade in Metals." In *Eastern Mediterranean Metallurgy and Metalworking in the Second Millennium BC*, edited by V. Kassianidou and G. Papasavvas, 180–187. Oxford: Oxbow.

Bell, M. 1982. "Mycenaean Pottery at Amarna." *Newsletter of the American Research Center in Egypt* 99.100: 10.

Bellina, B. 2003. "Beads, Social Exchange, and Interaction between India and South East Asia." *Antiquity* 78: 285–297.

Beloch, K. 1886. *Die Bevölkerung der griechisch-römischen Welt*. Leipzig: Duncker & Humblot.

Ben-Shlomo, D. 1997. "Homer and the Bronze Age." In *A New Companion to Homer*, edited by I. Morris and B. Powell, 511–534. Leiden: Brill.

———. 2006. *Decorated Philistine Pottery: An Archaeological and Archaeometric Study*. Oxford: Archaeopress.

Bennet, J. 2007. "The Aegean Bronze Age." In *The Cambridge Economic History of the Greco-Roman World*, edited by I. Morris, R. Saller, and W. Scheidel, 175–210. Cambridge: Cambridge University Press.

———. 2008. "Palace TM: Speculations on Palatial Production in Mycenaean Greece with (some) reference to Glass." In *Vitreous Materials in the Late Bronze Age Aegean*, edited by C. Jackson and E. Wagner, 151–172. Oxford: Oxbow.

Bennet, J. and C. Shelmerdine. 2001. "Not the Palace of Nestor: The Development of the 'Lower Town' and Other Non-Palatial Settlements in LBA Messenia." In *Urbanism in the Aegean Bronze Age*, edited by K. Branigan, 135–140. Sheffield Studies in Aegean Archaeology 4. London and New York: Sheffield Academic Press.

Benter, M. 2009. "Das mykenische Kammergrab vom Pilavtepe." in *Die Karer und die Anderen*, edited by F. Rumscheid, 349–358. Bonn: Habelt.

Benton, S. 1953. "Further Excavations at Aetos." *BSA* 48: 255–358.

Benzi, M. 2005. "Mycenaeans at Iasos? A Reassessment of Doro Levi's Excavations." In *Emporia: Aegeans in the Central and Eastern Mediterranean*, edited by R. Laffineur and E. Greco,

205–215. *Aegaeum* 25. Liège: Université de Liège.

Béquignon, Y. 1937. *Recherches archéologiques à Phères de Thessalie*. Paris: Société d'Édition Les Belles lettres.

Bérard, C. 1970. *Fouilles et Recherches, L'Hérôon à la porte de l'ouest. Eretria III*. Zürich: Éditions Francke Berne.

——— 1982. "Le premier temple de la cité grecque." *Antike Kunst* 25: 90–92.

Besios, M., Y. Tzifopoulos, and A. Kotsonas. 2012. *ΜεθώνηI: Επιγραφές, χαράγματα και εμπορικά σύμβολα στη Γεωμετρική και Αρχαϊκή κεραμική από το "Υπόγειο."* Thessaloniki: Centre for the Greek Language.

Betelli, M. 2011. "Interaction and Acculturation: The Aegean and the Central Mediterranean in the Late Bronze Age." In *Der Orient und die Anfänge Europas*, edited by H. Matthäus, N. Oettinger, and S. Schröder, 109–126. Wiesbaden: Harrassowitz Verlag.

Bettelli, M. 2000. "La punta di lancia dalla tomba 6 di Eretria: una riconsiderazione." In *Romolo, Remo e la fondazione della città*, edited by A. Carandini and E. Cappelli, 346–348. Rome: Museo Nazionale Romano.

Bietti-Sestieri, A. 1988. "The Mycenaean Connection and Its Impact on the Central Mediterranean Societies." *DialArch* 6.1 (3rd ser.): 23–51.

Bikai, P. 2000. "Phoenician Ceramics from the Greek Sanctuary." In *Kommos IV: The Greek Sanctuary. Part I*, edited by J. Shaw and M. Shaw, 302–312. Princeton, NJ: Princeton University Press.

Binford, S. and L. Binford. 1966. "A Preliminary Analysis of Functional Variability in the Mousterian of Levallois Facies." *American Anthropologist* 68: 238–295.

Bintliff, J. 1997. "Further Considerations on the Population of Ancient Boeotia." In *Recent Research on the History and Archaeology of Central Greece*, edited by J. Bintliff, 231–252. Oxford: Archaeopress.

——— 2000. "Regional Field Surveys and Population Cycles." In *Reconstructing Past Population Trends in Mediterranean Europe*, edited by J. Bintliff and K. Sbonias, 21–34. *The Archaeology of Mediterranean Landscapes* 1. Oxford: Oxbow.

Bintliff, J., P. Howard, and A. Snodgrass. 1999. "The Hidden Landscape of Prehistoric Greece." *JMA* 12.2: 139–168.

——— 2000. "Rejoinder." *JMA* 13.1: 116–123.

Bisi, A. 1987. "Ateliers phéniciens dans le monde égéen." In *Phoenicians and the East Mediterranean in the First Millennium BC*, edited by E. Lipinski, 225–237. Leuven: Peeters.

Blake, E. 2008. "The Mycenaeans in Italy: A Minimalist Position." *PBSR* 76: 1–34.

Blandin, B. 2007. *Les Pratiques Funéraires d'Époque Géometrique à Érétrie. Eretria XVII*. Bern: Francke.

Blegen, C. 1937a. *Prosymna, the Helladic Settlement Preceding the Argive Heraeum*. Cambridge: Cambridge University Press.

——— 1937b. "Post-Mycenaean Deposits in Chamber-Tombs." *ArchEph* 1937: 377–390.

——— 1962. "The Principal Homeric Sites." In *A Companion to Homer*, edited by A. Wace and F. Stubbings, 362–430. New York: St. Maartens.

Blench, R. 1982. "The Silent Trade: An Igala Version." *Cambridge Anthropology* 7: 59–61.

Blitzer, H. 1995. "Minoan Implements and Industries." In *Kommos I: The Kommos Region and Houses of the Minoan Town*, edited by J. Shaw and M. Shaw, 403–535. Princeton, NJ: Princeton University Press.

Bloch, M. and J. Parry. 1989. *Money and the Morality of Exchange*. Cambridge: Cambridge University Press.

Boardman, J. 1967. "The Khaniale Tekke Tombs, II." *BSA* 62: 57–75.

———. 1970. "Orientalen auf Kreta." In *Dädalische Kunst auf Kreta im 7. Jahrhundert v. Chr*, 14–25. Mainz am Rhein: Verlag P. von Zabern.

———. 1971. "Ship Firedogs and Other Metalwork from Kavousi." *CretChron* 23: 5–8.

———. 1980. *The Greeks Overseas, Their Early Colonies and Trade*. 2nd ed. London: Thames and Hudson.

———. 1990. "Al Mina and History." *OJA* 9: 169–189.

———. 1999. *The Greeks Overseas*. 4th ed. London: Thames and Hudson.

———. 2002. "Al Mina: The Study of a Site." *Ancient West and East* 1: 315–331.

———. 2005. "The Knossos Tekke Jewelry Hoards." In *Megalai Nesoi: studi dedicati a Giovanni Rizza per il suo ottantesimo compleanno*, edited by R. Patane, 163–166. Catania: Consiglio nazionale delle ricerche I.B.A.M.

Bocquet-Appel, J.-P. and C. Masset. 1982. "Farewell to Palaeodemography." *Journal of Human Evolution* 11: 321–333.

Boehmer, R. 1972. *Die Kleinfunde von Boğazköy aus den Grabungskampagnen 1931–1939 und 1952–1969*. Berlin: Mann.

Boehmer, R. and H. Güterbock. 1987. *Glyptik aus dem Stadtgebiet von Boğazköy: Grabungskampagnen 1931–1939, 1952–1978*. Berlin: Mann.

Bohannon, P. and G. Dalton, eds. 1962. *Markets in Africa*. Evanston, IL: Northwestern University Press.

Bol, P. 1985. *Antike Bronzetechnik: Kunst und Handwerk antiker Erzbildner*. Munich: Beck.

Bonatz, D. 1998. "Imported Pottery." In *Tell Afis, Siria: scavi sull'acropoli 1988–1992*, edited by S. Cecchini and S. Mazzoni, 211–228. Pisa: ETS.

Bordreuil, P. and D. Pardee. 1989. *La trouvaille épigraphique de l'Ougarit, 1, Concordance. Ras Shamra-Ougarit* 5.1. Paris: ERC.

Borgna, E. 2013. "Di periferia in periferia. Italia e Mediterraneo orientale ai tempi della koinè metallurgica: una proposta di lettura diacronica." *Rivista di Scienze Preistoriche* LXIII: 125–153.

Botsford, G. 1922. *Hellenic History*. New York: Macmillan.

Bouzek, J. 1985. *The Aegean, Anatolia, and Europe: Cultural Inter-Relations in the Second Millennium BC*. Göteborg: Paul Åströms Förlag.

———. 1996. "Mycenaean Greece and Minoan Crete: The Problem of Migrations." *Cretan Studies* 5: 85–90.

———. 1997. *Greece, Anatolia, and Europe: Cultural Interrelations during the Early Iron Age*. Jonsered: Paul Åströms Förlag.

Boysal, Y. 1969. *Katalog der Vasen im Museum im Bodum, 1. Mykenisch-protogeometrisch*. Ankara: Dil ve Tarih-Coğrafya Fakültesi.

Branigan, K. 1988. "Some Observations on State Formation in Crete." In *Problems in Prehistory*, edited by E. French and K. Wardle, 63–71. Bristol: Bristol Classical Press.

———. 2001. "Aspects of Minoan Urbanism." In *Urbanism in the Aegean Bronze Age*, edited by K. Branigan, 38–50. Sheffield Studies in Aegean Archaeology 4. Sheffield: Sheffield Academic Press.

Braudel, F. 1981. *Civilization and Capitalism, 15th-18th Century I: The Structures of Everyday Life*. New York: Harper and Row.

Braun-Holzinger, E. and E. Rehm. 2005. *Orientalischer Import in Griechenland im frühen 1. Jahrtausend v. Chr*. Münster: Ugarit-Verlag.

Bravo, B. 1977. "Remarques sur les assises sociales, les forms d'organisation et la terminologie du commerce maritime à l'époque archaïque." *Dialogues d'histoire ancienne* 3.1: 1–59.

Brock, J. 1957. *Fortetsa: Early Greek Tombs Near Knossos. BSA Supplements* 2. Cambridge: Cambridge University Press.

Brody, A. 1998. *Each Man Cried Out to His God: The Specialized Religion of Canaanite and Phoenician Seafarers.* Atlanta, GA: Scholars Press.

Broodbank, C. 2013. *The Making of the Middle Sea: A History of the Mediterranean from the Beginning to the Emergence of the Classical World.* Oxford and New York: Oxford University Press.

Brouskari, M. 1980. "A Dark Age Cemetery in Erechtheion Street, Athens." *BSA* 75: 13–31.

Brunton, R. 1971. "Cargo Cults and Systems of Exchange in Melanesia." *Mankind* 8: 115–128.

Bryce, T. 1998. *The Kingdom of the Hittites.* Oxford: Oxford University Press.

― 2002. *Life and Society in the Hittite World.* Oxford: Oxford University Press.

― 2003. "Relations between Hatti and Ahhiyawa in the Last Decades of the Bronze Age." In *Hittite Studies in Honor of Harry A. Hoffner Jr. on the Occasion of His 65th Birthday*, edited by G. Beckman, R. Beal, and G. McMahon, 59–72. Winona Lake, IN: Eisenbrauns.

― 2011. "Ahhiyawa." In *The Routledge Handbook of the Peoples and Places of Ancient Western Asia: From the Early Bronze Age to the Fall of the Persian Empire*, edited by T. Bryce, 10–11. London and New York: Routledge.

Brysbaert, A. 2013. "The Chicken or the Egg? International Contacts Viewed through a Technological Lens at Late Bronze Age Tiryns, Greece." *OJA* 32.3: 233–256.

Brysbaert, A. and M. Vetters. 2010. "Practicing Identity: A Crafty Ideal?" *Mediterranean Archaeology and Archaeometry* 10.2: 25–43.

― 2013. "A Moving Story about Exotica: Objects' Long-Distance Production Chains and Associated Identities at Tiryns, Greece." *OpAth* 6: 175–210.

Budd, P., A. Pollard, B. Scaife, and R. Thomas. 1995. "Oxhide Ingots Recycling and the Mediterranean Metals Trade." *JMA* 8.1: 1–32.

Bulba, M. 2010. *Geometrische Keramik Kariens, Peleus.* Mainz: Rutzen.

Bulle, H. 1907. *Orchomenos I.* Munich: Bayerische Akademie der Wissenschaften.

Burke, B. 2010. *From Minos to Midas: Ancient Cloth Production in the Aegean and Anatolia.* Oxford: Oxbow.

Burkert, W. 1992. *The Orientalizing Revolution.* Cambridge, MA: Harvard University Press.

Burn, A. 1936. *The World of Hesiod: A Study of the Greek Middle Ages c. 900–700 B.C.* London: K. Paul, Trench, Trubner, & Co.

Burns, B. 1999. "Import Consumption in the Bronze Age Argolid (Greece): Effects of Mediterranean Trade on Mycenaean Society." Ph. D. dissertation, University of Michigan.

― 2010a. "Trade." In *The Oxford Handbook of the Bronze Age Aegean*, edited by E. Cline, 291–304. Oxford: Oxford University Press.

― 2010b. *Mycenaean Greece, Mediterranean Commerce, and the Formation of Identity.* Cambridge: Cambridge University Press.

― 2011. "Context and Distance: Associations of Egyptian Objects and Style at Mycenae." In *Intercultural Contacts in the Ancient Mediterranean*, edited by K. Duistermaat and I. Regulski, 253–266. Leuven: Peeters.

Cadogan, G. 1973. "Patterns in the Distribution of Mycenaean Pottery in the East Mediterranean." In *Acts of the International Archaeological Symposium "The Mycenaeans in the Eastern Mediterranean,"* edited by

V. Karageorghis, 166–174. Nicosia: Dept. of Antiquities, Cyprus.
Calder, W. 1984. "Gold for Bronze: *Iliad* 6.232–36." In *Studies Presented to Sterling Dow on His Eightieth Birthday*, edited by S. Dow and A. Boegehold, 31–35. GRBS Monograph 10. Durham, NC: Duke University.
Callaghan, P. and A. Johnston. 2000. "The Pottery from the Greek Temples at Kommos." In *Kommos IV: The Greek Sanctuary*, edited by J. Shaw and M. Shaw, 210–301. Princeton, NJ: Princeton University Press.
Calligas, P. 1987. "Η Ελλάδα κατά την πρώιμη Εποχή του Σιδήρου." *Annals of Anthropology and Archaeology* 2: 17–21.
——— 1988. "Hero-Cult in Early Iron Age Greece." In *Early Greek Cult Practice*, edited by R. Hägg, N. Marinatos, and G. Nordquist, 229–34. Stockholm: Swedish Institute at Athens.
Cambitoglou, A. et al., 1971. *Zagora I*. Sydney: Sydney University Press for the Australian Academy of the Humanities
Caminos, R. 1954. *Late Egyptian Miscellanies*. London: Oxford University Press.
Carlier, P. 1984. *La royauté en Grèce avant Alexandre*. Strasbourg: AECR.
——— 1991. "La procédure de décision politique du monde mycénien a l'époque archaïque." In *La transizione dal Miceneo all'Alto Arcaismo: dal palazzo alla città*, edited by D. Musti, A. Sacconi, L. Rocchetti, M. Rocchi, E. Scafa, L. Sportiello, and M. Giannotta, 85–95. Rome: Consiglio nazionale delle ricerche.
Carneiro, R. 1970. "A Theory of the Origin of the State." *Science* 169: 733–748.
Carothers, J. and W. McDonald. 1979. "Size and Distribution of the Population in Late Bronze Age Messenia." *JFA* 6.4: 433–154.
Carter, J. 1998. "Egyptian Bronze Jugs from Crete and Lefkandi." *JHS* 118: 172–177.
Cartledge, P. 1983. "Trade and Politics Revisited: Archaic Greece." In *Trade in the Ancient Economy*, edited by P. Garnsey, K. Hopkins, and C. Whittaker, 1–15. Berkeley: University of California Press.
——— 1987. *Agesilaos and the Crisis of Sparta*. London: Duckworth.
Catapoti, D. 2005. "From Power to Paradigm: Rethinking the Emergence of the 'Palatial Phenomenon' in Bronze Age Crete." Ph.D. dissertation, University of Sheffield.
Catling, H. 1979. "Knossos, 1978." *AR* 25: 43–58.
——— 1980. "Objects of Bronze, Iron, and Lead." In *Lefkandi I: The Iron Age Settlement: The Cemeteries*, edited by M. Popham, H. Sackett, and P. Themelis, 231–264. London: Thames and Hudson.
——— 1983. "The small finds." In *Excavations at Nichoria in South West Greece III: Dark Age and Byzantine Occupation*, edited by W. McDonald, W. Coulson, and J. Rosser, 273–287. Minneapolis: University of Minnesota Press.
——— 1996. "The Dark Age and Later Bronzes." In *Knossos North Cemetery: Early Greek Tombs*, vol. 2, edited by J. Coldstream and H. Catling, 543–574. London: British School at Athens.
——— 1998. "Exports of Attic Protogeometric Pottery and Their Identification by Non-Analytical Means." *BSA* 93: 365–378.
Catling, H., J. Cherry, R. Jones, and J. Killen. 1980. "The Linear B Inscribed Stirrup Jars and West Crete." *BSA* 75: 49–113.
Cavanagh, W. and C. Mee. 1998. *A Private Place: Death in Mycenaean Greece*. Jonsered: Paul Åströms Förlag.
——— 2009. "Perati kai Pera Pera." In *Δώρον. Τιμητικός τομός για τον καθηγητή Σπύρο Ιακωβίδη*, edited by D. Danielidou, 169–189. Athens: Academy of Athens.

Chadwick, J. 1956. "The Greek Dialects and Greek Prehistory." *GaR* n.s. 3: 38–50.

1976. *The Mycenaean World*. Cambridge: Cambridge University Press.

1987. *Linear B and Related Scripts*. Berkeley: University of California Press.

1988. "The Women of Pylos." In *Texts, Tablets and Scribes: Studies in Mycenaean Epigraphy Offered to Emmett L. Bennett Jr.*, edited by J.-P. Olivier and T. Palaima, 43–95. Salamanca: Ed. Universidad de Salamanca.

1990. "The Descent of Greek Epic." *JHS* 110: 174–177.

Chadwick, J. et al., 1986–1998. *Corpus of Mycenaean Inscriptions from Knossos I-IV. Incunabula Graeca*. Rome and Cambridge: Cambridge University Press and Edizioni dell'Ateneo.

Chapman, J. 2000. "Archaeological Proxy-Data for Demographic Reconstructions: Facts, Factoids, or Fiction?" In *Reconstructing Past Population Trends in Mediterranean Europe (3000–1800 BCE)*, edited by J. Bintliff and K. Sbonias, 65–76. Oxford: Oxbow.

Charalambous, A. 2016. "A Diachronic Study of Cypriot Copper Alloy Artefacts." *JASR* 7: 566–573.

Charalambous, A., V. Kassianidou, and G. Papasavvas. 2014. "A Compositional Study of Cypriot Bronzes Dating to the Early Iron Age Using Portable X-Ray Flourescence Spectrometry." *JAS* 46: 205–216.

Charbonnet, A. 1986. "Le dieu aux lions d'Érétrie." *AION* 8: 117–173.

Charitonidis, S. 1955. "A Geometric Grave at Clenia in Corinthia." *AJA* 59.2: 125–128.

1956. "Ἀνασκαφαί ἐν Ναυπλία." *Prakt* 1953: 191–204.

Chase-Dunn, C. and T. Hall. 1991. *Core-Periphery Relations in the Precapitalist Worlds*. Boulder, CO: Westview Press.

Chatziangelakis, L. 1982. "Θεοτόκου." *ArchDelt* 37 *Chr* B2: 230.

Cherry, J. 1984. Review of *Bronze Age Population Fluctuations in the Argolid from the Evidence of Mycenaean Tombs*, by M. Alden. *Biblioteca Orientalis* 41.1–2: 196–199.

1986. "Polities and Palaces: Some Problems in Minoan State Formation." In *Peer Polity Interaction and Socio-Political Change*, edited by C. Renfrew and J. Cherry, 19–45. Cambridge: Cambridge University Press.

2005. "Chapter 14 Revisited: Sites, Settlement, and Population in the Prehistoric Aegean since the Emergence of Civilization." In *The Emergence of Civilization Revisited*, edited by J. Barrett and P. Halstead, 1–20. Oxford: Oxbow.

2010. "Sorting Out Crete's Prepalatial Off-Island Interactions." In *Archaic State Interaction: The Eastern Mediterranean in the Bronze Age*, edited by W. Parkinson and M. Galaty, 107–140. Santa Fe, NM: School for Advanced Research Press.

Childe, V. 1942. *What Happened in History*. Harmondsworth: Penguin.

Choremis, A. 1973. "Μυκιναϊκοί και πρωτογεωμετρικοί τάφοι εις Καρποφόραν Μεσσηνίας." *ArchEph* 1973: 25–74.

Cipolla, C. 1970. "The Economic Decline of Italy." In *The Economic Decline of Empires*, edited by C. Cipolla, 1–15. London: Methuen.

Claessen, H. 1978. "The Early State: A Structural Approach." In *The Early State*, edited by H. Claessen and P. Skalnik, 533–596. The Hague: Mouton.

Clark, G. 2005. "The Condition of the Working Class in England, 1209–2008." *Journal of Political Economy* 113: 1307–1340.

Clarke, C. 2016. Review of *Metals in LBA Minoan and Mycenaean Societies on Crete. A Quantitative Approach*, by L. Hakulin. *BMCR* 2016.05.04.

Clarke, D. 1968. *Analytical Archaeology*. London: Methuen.

———. 1973. "The Loss of Innocence." *Antiquity* 47: 6–18.

Cline, E. 1990. "An Unpublished Amenhotep III Faience Plaque from Mycenae." *BASOR* 110.2: 200–212.

———. 1991. "Hittite Objects in the Bronze Age Aegean." *AnatSt* 41: 133–143.

———. 1994. *Sailing the Wine-Dark Sea: International Trade and the Late Bronze Age Aegean*. BAR International Series 591. Oxford: Archaeopress.

———. 1996. "Assuwa and the Achaeans: The 'Mycenaean' Sword at Hattušas and Its Possible Implications." *BSA* 91: 137–151.

———. 1997. "A Wrinkle in Time: Orientalia and the Mycenaean Occupation(s) of Crete." In *Ancient Egypt, the Aegean, and the Near East*, edited by J. Phillips, 163–167. San Antonio, TX: Van Siclen Books.

———. 2010. "Bronze Age Interaction between the Aegean and the Eastern Mediterranean Revisited: Mainstream, Periphery, or Margin?" In *Archaic State Interaction: The Eastern Mediterranean in the Bronze Age*, edited by W. Parkinson and M. Galaty, 161–180. Santa Fe, NM: School for Advanced Research Press.

———. 2014. *1177: The Year Civilization Collapsed*. Princeton, NJ: Princeton University Press.

Cline, E. and A. Yasur-Landau. 2007. "Musings from a Distant Shore: The Nature and Destination of the Uluburun Ship and Its Cargo." *TelAviv* 34.2: 125–141.

Clinton, M. 2013. "Access and Circulation Pattern Analysis in Neopalatial Architecture on Crete: A Methodology for Identifying Private Spaces." Ph.D. dissertation, University of Pennsylvania.

Cohen, C., J. Maran, and M. Vetters. 2010. "An Ivory Rod with a Cuneiform Inscription, Most Probably Ugaritic, from a Final Palatial Workshop in the Lower Citadel at Tiryns." *AA* 2010/2: 1–22.

Coldstream, J. 1963. "Five Tombs at Knossos," *BSA* 58: 30–43.

———. 1968. *Greek Geometric Pottery: A survey of Ten Local Styles and Their Chronology*. London: Methuen.

———. 1983. "The Meaning of Regional Styles in the Eighth Century B.C." in *The Greek Renaissance of the Eighth Century B.C. Tradition and Innovation*, edited by R. Hägg, 17–25. Stockholm: Lund.

———. 1982. "Greeks and Phoenicians in the Aegean." In *Phönizier im Westen*, edited by H. Niemeyer, 261–275. Madrider Beiträge 8. Mainz am Rhein: Zabern.

———. 1984. "Cypriaca and Cretocypriaca from the North Cemetery at Knossos." *RDAC* 1984: 122–137.

———. 1988. "Early Greek Visitors to Cyprus and the Eastern Mediterranean." In *Cyprus and the East Mediterranean in the Iron Age*, edited by V. Tatton-Brown, 90–96. London: British Museum.

———. 1991. "Knossos: An Urban Nucleus in the Dark Age?" In *La transizione dal Miceneo all'Alto Arcaismo: dal palazzo alla città*, edited by D. Musti et al., 287–300. Rome: Consiglio nazionale delle ricerche.

———. 1993. "Mixed Marriages at the Frontiers of the Early Greek World." *OJA* 12.1: 89–107.

———. 1994. "Urns with Lids: The Visible Face of the Knossian "Dark Age."" In *Knossos, a Labyrinth of History: Papers Presented in Honour of S. Hood*, edited by D. Evely, H. Hughes-Brock, and N. Momigliano, 105–121. Athens: British School at Athens.

1995. "Greek Geometric and Archaic Imports from the Tombs of Amathus II." *RDAC* 1995: 199.

1996. "Knossos and Lefkandi: The Attic Connections." In *Minotaur and Centaur: Studies in the Archaeology of Crete and Euboea Presented to Mervyn Popham*, edited by D. Evely, I. Lemos, and S. Sherratt, 133–145. Oxford: Tempus Reparatum.

1998. "The First Exchanges between Euboeans and Phoenicians: Who Took the Initiative?" In *Mediterranean Peoples in Transition*, edited by S. Gitin, A. Mazar, and E. Stern, 353–360. Jerusalem: Israel Exploration Society.

2001. "Greek Geometric Pottery in Italy and Cyprus: Contrasts and Comparisons." In *Italy and Cyprus in Antiquity 1500–450 BC*, edited by L. Bonfante and V. Karageorghis, 227–238. Nicosia: Costakis and Leto Severis Foundation.

2002. "Knossos: 'Geometric' Tombs Excavated by D.G. Hogarth, 1900." *BSA* 97: 201–216.

2003a. *Geometric Greece*. 2nd ed. London: Methuen.

2003b. "Some Aegean Reactions to the Chronological Debate in the Southern Levant." *TelAviv* 30.2: 253–254.

2006. "Knossos in Early Greek Times." In *From Mycenae to Homer*, edited by S. Deger-Jalkotzy and I. Lemos, 581–596. Edinburgh: University of Edinburgh.

Coldstream, J., P. Callaghan, and J. Musgrave. 1981. "Knossos: An Early Greek Tomb on Lower Gypsadhes Hill." *BSA* 76: 141–165.

Coldstream, J. and H. Catling, eds. 1996. *Knossos North Cemetery. Early Greek Tombs Volumes I and II*. B.S.A. S.V. 28. London: British School at Athens.

Coldstream, J. and M. Hood. 1968. "A Late Minoan Tomb at Agios Ioannis Near Knossos." *BSA* 63: 205–218.

Collins, M. 1975. "Sources of Bias in Processual Data: An Appraisal." In *Sampling in Archaeology*, edited by J. Mueller, 26–32. Tucson: University of Arizona Press.

Cook, V. 1988. "Cyprus and the Outside World during the Transition from the Bronze Age to the Iron Age." *OpAth* 17: 13–32.

Corvisier, J.-N. 2008. "Assessment of Land Surveys in Greece: Contributions and Limitations." In *Recent Advances in Palaeodemography*, edited by J.-P. Bocquet-Appel, 31–61. Dordrecht: Springer.

Corvisier, J.-N. and W. Suder. 2000. *La population de l'antiquité classique*. Paris: Presses universitaires de France.

Costin, C. 1991. "Craft Specialization: Issues in Defining, Documenting, and Explaining the Organization of Production." *Journal of Archaeological Method and Theory* 3: 1–56.

Coulsen, W. 1990. *The Greek Dark Ages. A Review of the Evidence and Suggestions for Further Research*. Athens.

Courbin, P. 1957. "Une Tombe Geometrique d'Argos." *BCH* 81: 322–386.

1959. "Valeur Comparée du Fer et de L'Argent lors de l'introduction du monnayage." *Annales Economies Societes Civilisations* 14.2: 209–233.

1974. *Tombes Géometriques d'Argos I (1952–1958)*. Paris: Vrin.

1983. "Obeloi d'Argolide et d'ailleurs." In *The Greek Renaissance of the Eighth Century BC: Tradition and Innovation*, edited by R. Hägg, 149–163. Stockholm: Swedish Institute at Athens.

Courtois, J.-C. 1978. "Corpus céramique de Ras Shamra-Ugarit, niveaux historiques d'Ugarit: Bronze Moyen et Bronze Récent." *Ugaritica* 7: 131–370.

1990. "Poids, prix, taxes et salaires à Ougarit (Syrie) au IIe millénaire." In *Res Orientales II. Prix, salaires, poids et mesures*, edited by R. Gyselen, 119–127. Paris: Groupe pour l'Étude de la Civilisation du Moyen-Orient.

Crew, P. 1991. "The Experimental Production of Prehistoric Bar Iron." *Historical Metallurgy* 15.1: 21–36.

Crielaard, J.-P. 1992. "How the West Was Won: Euboeans vs. Phoenicians." *HBA* 19/20: 235–260.

———. 1995. "Homer, History, and Archaeology." In *Homeric Questions*, edited by J. P. Crielaard, 201–288. Amsterdam: J.C. Gieben.

———. 1998. "Surfing on the Mediterranean Web: Cypriot Long-Distance Communications during the Eleventh and Tenth Centuries BC." In *Eastern Mediterranean: Cyprus-Dodecanese-Crete, 16th–6th Centuries BC*, edited by V. Karageorghis and N. Stampolidis, 187–204. Heraklion: University of Crete.

———. 1999. "Production, Circulation, and Consumption of Early Iron Age Greek Pottery (Eleventh to Seventh Centuries BC)." In *The Complex Past of Pottery: Production, Circulation, and Consumption of Mycenaean and Greek Pottery (Sixteenth to Early Fifth Centuries BC)*, edited by J.-P. Crielaard, V. Stissi, and G. van Wijngaarden, 49–81. Amsterdam: J.C. Gieben.

———. 2000. "Homeric and Mycenaean Long-Distance Contact: Discrepancies in the Evidence." *BABesch* 75: 51–63.

———. 2006. "Basileis at Sea: Elites and External Contacts in the Euboean Gulf Region from the End of the Bronze Age to the Beginning of the Iron Age." In *Ancient Greece from the Mycenaean Palaces to the Age of Homer*, edited by S. Deger-Jalkotzy and I. Lemos, 271–297. *Edinburgh Leventis Studies* 3. Edinburgh: Edinburgh University Press.

———. 2009. "The Ionians in the Archaic Period: Shifting Identities in a Changing World." In *Ethnic Constructs in Antiquity: The Role of Power and Tradition*, edited by T. Derks and N. Roymans, 37–84. Amsterdam: Amsterdam University Press.

———. 2011. "The Wanax to Basileus Model Reconsidered: Authority and Ideology after the Collapse of the Mycenaean Palaces." In *The Dark Ages Revisited*, edited by A. Mazarakis Ainian, 83–112. Volos: University of Thessaly.

———. 2015. "Powerful Things in Motion: A Biographical Approach to Eastern Elite Goods in Greek Sanctuaries." In *Sanctuaries and the Power of Consumption*, edited by E. Kistler, B. Öhlinger, M. Mohr, and M. Hoernes, 351–372. *Philippika* 92. Wiesbaden: Harrassowitz Verlag.

Cross, F. and L. Stager. 2006. "Cypro-Minoan Inscriptions Found in Ashkelon." *Israel Exploration Journal* 56.2: 129–159.

Csapo, E., A. Johnston, and D. Geagan. 2000. "The Iron Age Inscriptions." In *Kommos IV: The Greek Sanctuary*, edited by J. Shaw and M. Shaw, 101–134. Princeton, NJ: Princeton University Press.

Cultraro, M. 2005. "The LH IIIC Period in Arcadia and Imports from Southern Italy." In *Ancient Arcadia*, edited by E. Østby, 17–33. Athens: The Norwegian Institute at Athens.

Dabney, M. 1996. "Jewellery and Seals." In *Kommos I: The Kommos Region and Houses of the Minoan Town. Part 2: The Minoan Hilltop and Hillside Houses*, edited by J. Shaw and M. Shaw, 263–269. Princeton, NJ: Princeton University Press.

D'Agata, A., Y. Goren, H. Mommsen, A. Schwadt, and A. Yasur-Landau. 2005. "Imported Pottery of LH IIIC Style from Israel: Style, Provenance, and Chronology." In *Emporia: Aegeans in the Central and Eastern Mediterranean*, edited by R. Laffineur and E. Greco, 371–379. *Aegaeum* 25. Liège: Université de Liège.

D'Agostino, B. 1977. "Tombe "Principesche" Dell'Orientalizzante Antico da Pontecagnano." *MonAnt* 49: 9–110.

———. 1990. "Military Organization and Social Structure in Archaic Etruria." In *The Greek City from Homer to Alexander*, edited by O. Murray and S. Price, 59–82. Oxford: Clarendon.

D'Agostino, B. and P. Gastaldi. 1988. *Pontecagnano II. La necropoli del Picentino*. Naples: Istituto universitario orientale.

Dakoronia, F. 1985. "Αταλάντη, Οικόπεδο Ν. Καραγιώργου." *ArchDelt* 40 Chr 165–167.

———. 2006. "Early Iron Age Burials in East Lokris." In *Ancient Greece from the Mycenaean Palaces to the Age of Homer*, edited by S. Deger-Jalkotzy and I. Lemos, 483–504. *Edinburgh Leventis Studies* 3. Edinburgh: Edinburgh University Press.

———. 2007. "Rare Burial Gifts from Mycenaean Chamber Tombs in NE Phokis." In *Keimelion: Elitenbildung und Elitarer Konsum von der Mykenischen Palastzeit bis zur Homerischen Epoche*, edited by E. Alram-Stern and G. Nightingale, 59–64. Vienna: Verlag der Österreichischen Akademie der Wissenschaften.

Dakoronia, F. and S. Dimaki. 1998. "Καλαπόδι Οικόπεδα Α. Δαλιάνη – Α. Μπακανδρίτσου." *ArchDelt* 53 B2 Chr: 394–395.

Dalby, A. 1995. "The Iliad, the Odyssey, and Their Audiences." *CQ* 45.2: 269–279.

Dalton, G., ed. 1968. *Primitive, Archaic, and Modern Economies: Essays of Karl Polanyi*. Garden City, NY: Anchor Books.

———. 1975. "Karl Polanyi's Analysis of Long Distance Trade and His Wider Paradigm." In *Ancient Civilization and Trade*, edited by J. Sabloff and C. Lamberg-Karlovsky, 63–132. Albuquerque: University of New Mexico Press.

Darque, P. 2005. *L'Habitat Mycénien. Formes et Fonctions de l'Espace Bâti en Grèce Continentale à la Fin du IIe Millénaire avant J.-C.* Athens: French School at Athens.

Davis, J. and E. Gorogianni. 2008. "Potsherds from the Edge: The Construction of Identities and the Limits of Minoanized Areas in the Aegean." In *Horizon. A Colloquium on the Prehistory of the Cyclades*, edited by N. Brodie, J. Doole, G. Gavalas, and C. Renfrew, 339–348. Oxford: Oxbow.

Dawkins, R. 1906–1907. "The Sanctuary of Artemis Orthia." *BSA* 13: 44–108.

———. 1929. *The Sanctuary of Artemis Orthia at Sparta*. JHS Supplement 5. London: Macmillan.

Day, P. and H. Haskell. 1995. "Transport Stirrup Jars from Thebes as Evidence for Trade in the Late Bronze Age III." In *Trade and Production in Premonetary Greece: Aspects of Trade*, edited by C. Gillis, C. Risberg, and B. Sjöberg, 125–128. Jonsered: Paul Åström Förlag.

Day, P., N. Klein, and L. Turner. 2009. *Kavousi IIA: The Late Minoan IIIC Settlement at Vronda. The Buildings on the Summit*. Philadelphia: INSTAP.

Deger-Jalkotzy, S. 1983. *Griechenland, die Ägäis und die Levante wahrend die 'Dark Ages'*. Vienna: Österreichische Akademie der Wissenschaften.

———. 1988. "Diskontinuität und Kontinuität: Askpekte politischer und sozialer Organization in mykenischer Zeit und in der Welt der homerischen Epen." In *La transizione dal Miceneo all'Alto Arcaismo: dal palazzo alla città*, edited by D. Musti et al., 53–66. Rome: Consiglio nazionale delle ricerche.

———. 1991. "Die Erforschung des Zusammenbruchs der sogenannten mykenischen Kultur und der sogenannten dunklen Jahrhunderte."

In *Zweihundert Jahre Homer-Forschung: Rückblick und Ausblick*, edited by J. Latacz, 127–154. Stuttgart: Teubner.

1994. "The Post-Palatial Period of Greece: An Aegean Prelude to the 11th Century BC in Cyprus." In *Cyprus in the 11th Century BC*, edited by V. Karageorghis, 11–30. Nicosia: A.G. Leventis Foundation.

1998a. "The Last Mycenaeans and Their Successors Updated." In *Mediterranean Peoples in Transition*, edited by S. Gitin, A. Mazar, and E. Stern, 114–128. Jerusalem: Israel Exploration Society.

1998b. "The Aegean Islands and the Breakdown of the Mycenaean Palaces around 1200 BC." In *Eastern Mediterranean: Cyprus-Dodecanese-Crete*, edited by V. Karageorghis and N. Stampolidis, 105–120. Athens: University of Crete and A.G. Leventis Foundation.

2002. "Innerägäische Bezeihungen und auswärtige Kontakte des mykenischen Griechenland in nachpalatialer Zeit." In *Die nahöstlichen Kulturen und Griechenland an der Wende vom 2. Zum 1. Jahrtausend v. Chr. Kontinuität und Wandel von Strukturen und Mechanismen kultureller Interaktion*, edited by E. Braun–Holzinger and H. Matthäus, 47–74. Möhnesee: Bibliopolis.

2006. "Late Mycenaean Warrior Tombs." In *Ancient Greece: From the Mycenaean Palaces to the Age of Homer*, edited by S. Deger-Jalkotzy and I. Lemos, 151–180. *Edinburgh Leventis Series* 3. Edinburgh: Edinburgh University Press.

2008. "Decline, Destruction, Aftermath." In *The Cambridge Companion to the Aegean Bronze Age*, edited by C. Shelmerdine, 387–415. Cambridge: Cambridge University Press.

Deger-Jalkotzy, S. and A. Bächle, eds. 2009. *LH IIIC Chronology and Synchronisms III: LH IIIC Late and the Transition to the Early Iron Age.* Vienna: Österreichische Akademie der Wissenschaften.

Deger-Jalkotzy, S. and I. Lemos, eds. 2006. *Ancient Greece: From the Mycenaean Palaces to the Age of Homer. Edinburgh Leventis Series* 3. Edinburgh: University of Edinburgh Press.

Deonna, W. 1959. "Haches, broches, et chenets dans une tombe géométrique d'Argos." *BCH* 83: 247–252.

de Polignac, F. 1995. *Cults, Territory, and the Origins of the Greek City State.* Translated by J. Lloyd. Chicago: University of Chicago Press.

1996. "Offrandes, mémoire et competition ritualisée dans les sanctuaires grecs à l'époque géométrique." In *Religion and Power in the Ancient Greek World*, edited by P. Hellström and B. Alroth, 59–66. Uppsala: Acta Universitatis Upsaliensis.

Desborough, V. 1952. *Protogeometric Pottery.* Oxford: Clarendon.

1964. *The Last Mycenaeans and Their Successors: An Archaeological Survey c. 1200–1000 B.C.* Oxford: Clarendon Press.

1972. *The Greek Dark Ages.* New York: St. Martin's.

de Ste. Croix, G. 1981. *The Class Struggle in the Ancient World.* London: Duckworth.

Deutsches Archäologischen Institut, ed. 1880. *Das Kuppelgrab bei Menidi.* Athens: Karl Wilberg.

de Vos, J. 2002. "À propos de Aegyptiaca d'Asie mineure datés du IIe millénaire av. J.-C." *Hethitica* 15: 43–63.

Dialismas, A. 2004. "The Aegean Melting Pot: History and Archaeology for Historians and Prehistorians." In *Archaeology and Ancient History*, edited by E. Sauer, 62–75. London and New York: Routledge.

Dickinson, O. 1977. *The Origins of Mycenaean Civilization.* Göteborg: P. Åström Förlag.

1986. "Homer, the Poet of the Dark Age." *GaR* 33: 20–37.

1994. *The Aegean Bronze Age.* Cambridge: Cambridge University Press.

2006. *The Aegean from Bronze Age to Iron Age: Continuity and Change between the Twelfth and Eighth Centuries BC.* London and New York: Routledge.

2009. "Social Development in the Postpalatial Period in the Aegean." In *From the Aegean to the Adriatic: Social Organizations, Modes of Exchange, and Interaction in Postpalatial Times (12th–11th BC)*, edited E. Borgna and P. Cassola Guida, 11–20. Rome: Quasar.

Dietz, S. 1982. *Asine II. Results of the Excavations East of the Acropolis 1970–1974. Fasc. 1: General Stratigraphical Analysis and Architectural Remains.* Stockholm: Swedish Institute at Athens.

Dimopoulou, N. 1997. "Workshops and Craftsmen in the Harbour-Town of Knossos at Poros-Katsambas." In *TEXNH. Craftsmen, Craftswomen and Craftsmanship in the Aegean Bronze Age, Vol. II*, edited by R. Laffineur and P. Betancourt, 433–438. Aegaeum 16. Liège: Université de Liège.

2012. "Metallurgy and Metalworking in the Harbor Town of Knossos at Poros-Katsambas." In *Eastern Mediterranean Metallurgy and Metalwork in the Second Millenium BC*, edited by V. Kassianidou and G. Papasavvas, 135–141. Oxford: Oxbow.

Dimopoulou-Rethemiotaki, N. 2004. "Το επίνειο της Κνωσού στον Πόρο-Κατσαμπά." In *Knossos: Palace, City, State*, edited by G. Cadogan, E. Hatzaki, and A. Vasilakis, 363–380. British School at Athens Studies 12. London: British School at Athens.

Dobiat, C. 1987. "Perlen mit konzentrischen Ringen." In *Glasperlen der Vorrömischen Eisenzeit II*, edited by T. Haevernick, O.-H. Frey, M. Zepezauer, and K. Kunter, 15–25. Mainz am Rein: von Zabern.

van Dommelen, P. 1997. "Colonial Constructs: Colonialism and Archaeology in the Mediterranean." *WorldArch* 28: 305–323.

2002. "Ambiguous Matters: Colonialism and Local Identities in Punic Sardinia." In *The Archaeology of Colonialism*, edited by C. Lyons and J. Papadopoulos, 121–147. Los Angeles: Getty Research Institute.

Donlan, W. 1981. "Scale, Value, and Function in the Homeric Economy." *AJAH* 6: 101–117.

1989a. "The Unequal Exchange between Glaucus and Diomedes in Light of the Homeric Gift Economy." *Phoenix* 43: 1–15.

1989b. "Homeric Temenos and the Land Economy of the Dark Age." *MusHelv* 46: 129–145.

1997. "The Homeric Economy." In *A New Companion to Homer*, edited by I. Morris and B. Powell, 649–667. Leiden: Brill.

Doonan, R. and A. Mazarakis Ainian. 2007. "Forging Identity in Early Iron Age Greece: Implications of the Metalworking Evidence from Oropos." In *Oropos and Euboea in the Early Iron Age*, edited by A. Mazarakis Ainian, 361–378. Volos: University of Thessaly.

Dörpfeld, W. 1897. "Funde." *AM* 22: 476–480.

Dothan, T. and A. Zukerman. 2004. "A Preliminary Study of the Mycenaean IIIC:1 Pottery Assemblages from Tel Miqne-Keron and Ashdod." *BASOR* 333: 1–54.

Drews, R. 1984. *Basileus: The Evidence for Kingship in Geometric Greece.* New Haven, CT and London: Yale University Press.

Driessen, J. 1990. *An Early Destruction in the Mycenaean Palace at Knossos: A New*

Interpretation of the Excavation Field-Notes of the South-East Area of the West Wing. Leuven: Katholieke Universiteit Leuven.

———. 2000. *The Scribes of the Room of the Chariot Tablets*. Salamanca: Ediciones Universidad de Salamanca.

Droop, J. 1905–1906. "Dipylon Vases from the Kynosarges Site." *BSA* 12: 82–92

Druckman, D. and S. Güner. 2000. "A Social-Psychological Analysis of Amarna Diplomacy." In *Amarna Diplomacy: The Beginnings of International Relations*, edited by R. Cohen and R. Westbrook, 174–188. Baltimore, MD: Johns Hopkins University Press.

Dunbabin, T. 1957. *The Greeks and Their Eastern Neighbors*. London: Society for the Promotion of Hellenic Studies.

Duplouy, A. 2006. *Le Prestige des Élites: Recherches sur les modes de reconnaissance sociale en Grèce entre les Xe et Ve siècles avant J.-C.* Paris: Les Belles Lettres.

Dussaud, R. 1940. "Coupe de Bronze Chypro-Phénicienne Trouvée en Gréce." *BSA* 37: 92–95.

Earle, T. 1982. "Prehistoric Economies and the Archaeology of Exchange." In *Exchange Systems in Prehistory*, edited by J. Ericson and T. Earle, 213–232. New York: Academic Press.

———. 2002. *Bronze Age Economics: The Beginnings of Political Economies*. Boulder, CO: Westview Press.

Ebeling, E. 1927. *Keilschrifttexte aus Assur juristischen Inhalts*. Leipzig: J.C. Hinrichs.

Eckholm, K. 1980. "On the Limits of Civilization: The Structure and Dynamics of Global Systems." *Dialectical Anthropology* 5: 155–166.

Eckstein, F. 1974. *Handwerk: Die Aussagen des frühgriechischen Epos. Archaeologica Homerica* 2. Göttingen: Vandenhoeck und Ruprecht.

Eder, B. 2001a. "Continuity of Bronze Age Cult at Olympia? The Evidence of the Late Bronze and Early Iron Age Pottery." In *Potnia: Deities and Religion in the Aegean Bronze Age*, edited by R. Laffineur and R. Hägg, 201–212. *Aegaeum* 22. Liège: Université de Liège.

———. 2001b. "Die Anfänge von Elis und Olympia: zur Siedlungsgeschichte der Landschaft Elis am Übergang von der Spätbronze- zur Früheisenzeit." In *Forschungen in der Peloponnes*, edited by V. Mitsopoulos-Leon, 233–243. Athens: Österreichisches Archäologisches Institut.

———. 2001c. *Die Submykenischen und Protogeometrischen Gräber von Elis*. Athens: Archaeological Society of Athens.

———. 2004. "Im Reich des Augeias: Elis und Olympia zwischen 1200 und 700 c. Chr." *Anzeiger der philosophisch-historischen Klasse der Österreichischen Akademie der Wissenschaften Wien*: 89–121.

———. 2006. "The World of Telemachus: Western Greece 1200–700 BC." In *Ancient Greece: From the Mycenaean Palaces to the Age of Homer*, edited by S. Deger-Jalkotzy and I. Lemos, 549–580. Edinburgh Leventis Studies 3. Edinburgh: Edinburgh University Press.

Eder, B. and R. Jung. 2005. "On the Character of Social Relations between Greece and Italy in the 12th/11th cent. BC." In *Emporia: Aegeans in the Central and Eastern Mediterranean*, edited by R. Laffineur and E. Greco, 485–496. *Aegaeum* 25. Liège: Université de Liège.

Edwards, A. 2004. *Hesiod's Ascra*. Berkeley: University of California Press.

Eerbeek, J. 2015. "The 'Mycenaeans' in the Southeast Aegean Revisited: An Inter-Regional Comparison." In *NOSTOI: Indigenous Culture, Migration + Integration in the Aegean*

Islands + Western Anatolia during the Late Bronze + Early Iron Ages, edited by N. Stampolidis, Ç. Maner, and K. Kopanias, 289–310. Istanbul: Koç University Press.

Egetmeyer, M. 2013. "From the Cypro-Minoan to the Cypro-Greek Syllabaries: Linguistic Remarks on the Script Reform." In *Syllabic Writing on Cyprus and Its Context*, edited by P. Steele, 107–132. Cambridge: Cambridge University Press.

Englezou, M. and G. Rethemiotakis. 2007. "Το Γεωμετρικό νεκροταφείο της Έλτυνας στους Κουνάβους Ηρακλείου." In *Kreta in der geometrischen und archaischen Zeit*, edited by W.-D. Niemeier, O. Pilz, and I. Kaiser, 157–186. Munich: Hirmer Verlag.

Erkanal, H. 2008. "*Liman Tepe: New Lights on Prehistoric Aegean Cultures.*" In *The Aegean in the Neolithic, Chalcolithic, and Early Bronze Age*, edited by H. Erkanal et al., 179–190. Ankara: Ankara University Press.

Evans, A. 1925. "The Early Nilotic, Libyan, and Egyptian Relations with Minoan Crete." *The Journal of the Royal Anthropological Institute of Great Britain and Ireland* 55: 199–228.

——— 1928. *The Palace of Minos at Knossos 2*. London and New York: Macmillan.

Evely, D. 1996. "Other Materials." In *Knossos North Cemetery*, edited by J. Coldstream and H. Catling, 621–639. London: British School at Athens.

——— 2006. "The Small Finds." In *Lefkandi IV: The Bronze Age, The Late Helladic IIIC Settlement at Xeropolis*, edited by D. Evely, 265–302. Athens: British School at Athens.

Evely, D., A. Hein, and E. Nodarou. 2012. "Crucibles from Palaikastro, East Crete: Insights into Metallurgical Technology in the Aegean Late Bronze Age." *JAS* 39.6: 1821–1836.

Falkenstein, A. 1964. "Zu den Siegelzylindern aus Theben." *Kadmos* 3/1: 108–109.

Fantalkin, A. 2006. "Identity in the Making: Greeks in the Eastern Mediterranean during the Iron Age." In *Naukratis: Greek Diversity in Egypt*, edited by A. Villing and U. Schlotzhause, 199–208. London: British Museum.

Fantalkin, A., I. Finkelstein, and E. Piasetzky. 2015. "Late Helladic to Middle Geometric Aegean and Contemporary Cypriot Chronologies: A Radiocarbon View from the Levant." *BASOR* 373: 25–48.

Feldman, M. 2014. *Communities of Style: Portable Luxury Arts, Identity, and Collective Memory in the Iron Age Levant*. Chicago and London: University of Chicago Press.

Felsch, R. 1983. "Zur Chronologie und zum Stil geometrischen Bronzen aus Kalapodi." In *The Greek Renaissance of the Eighth Century BC: Tradition and Innovation*, edited by R. Hägg, 123–129. Skrifter utgivna av Svenska Institutet i Athen. Series 4, 30. Lund: Paul Åströms Förlag.

Ferrara, S. 2012. *Cypro-Minoan Inscriptions. Volume I: Analysis*. Oxford: Oxford University Press.

Feuer, B. 1983. *The Northern Mycenaean Border in Thessaly*. BAR International Series 176. Oxford: Archaeopress.

Finley, M. 1954. *The World of Odysseus*. New York: Viking Press.

——— 1957. "The Mycenaean Tablets and Economic History." *Economic History Review* 10: 128–141.

——— 1968. "The Alienability of Land in Ancient Greece." *Eirene* 7: 25–32.

——— 1970. *Early Greece: The Bronze and Archaic Ages*. New York: Norton.

——— 1981. *Economy and Society in Ancient Greece*. London: Chatto and Windus.

Firth, R. 1995. "Estimating the Population of Crete during LMIIIA/B." *Minos* 29–55.

Fisher, E. 1988. "A Comparison of Mycenaean Pottery from Apulia with Mycenaean Pottery from Western Greece." Ph.D. dissertation, University of Minnesota.

——— 2007. *Ägyptische und ägyptisierende Elfbeine aus Megiddo und Laschisch: Inschriftenfunder, Flaschen, Löffel.* Münster: Ugarit-Verlag.

Fletcher, N. 2007. *Patterns of Imports in Iron Age Italy.* BAR International Series 1732. Oxford: Archaeopress.

Fletcher, R. 1995. *The Limits of Settlement Growth.* Cambridge: Cambridge University Press.

Foster, E. 1974. "The Manufacture and Trade of Mycenaean Perfumed Oil." Ph.D. dissertation, Duke University.

Foster, K. 1979. *Aegean Faience of the Bronze Age.* New Haven, CT: Yale University Press.

Foxhall, L. 1995. "Bronze to Iron: Agricultural Systems and Political Structures in Late Bronze Age and Early Iron Age Greece." *BSA* 90: 239–250.

——— 1998. "Cargoes of the Heart's Desire: The Character of Trade in the Archaic Mediterranean World." In *Archaic Greece: New Approaches and New Evidence*, edited by H. van Wees, 295–309. London: Duckworth.

Francovich, R. and K. Gruspier. 2000. "Relating Cemetery Studies to Regional Survey: Rocca San Silvestro, A Case Study." In *Reconstructing Past Population Trends in Mediterranean Europe*, edited by J. Bintliff and K. Sbonias, 249–258. The Archaeology of Mediterranean Landscapes 1. Oxford: Oxbow.

Frankenstein, S. 1979. "The Phoenicians in the Far West: A Function of Neo-Assyrian Imperialism." In *Power and Propaganda. A Symposium on Ancient Empires*, edited by M. Larsen, 263–294. Copenhagen: Akademisk Förlag.

French, E. 1981. "Cult Places at Mycenae." In *Sanctuaries and Cults in the Bronze Age Aegean*, edited by R. Hägg and N. Marinatos, 41–48. SkrAth, 4° 28. Stockholm: Paul Åströms Förlag.

French, E. and P. Stockhammer. 2009. "Mycenae and Tiryns: The Pottery of the Second Half of the Thirteenth Century BC – Contexts and Definitions." *BSA* 104: 175–232.

Freydank, H. 1979. "Eine mittelassyrische Urkunde (*KAJ* 249) über den Metallhandel." *Altorientalische Forschungen* 6: 269–271.

Fürtwangler, A. 1890. *Die Bronzen und die übrigen kleineren funde. Olympia IV.* Berlin: Asher & Co.

Gachet-Bizollon, J. 2007. *Les ivoires d'Ougarit et l'art des ivoiriers du Levant au Bronze Récent.* Ras Shamra-Ougarit 16. Paris: ERC.

Galaty, M. 1999. *Nestor's Wine Cups: Investigating Ceramic Manufacture and Exchange in a Late Bronze Age "Mycenaean" State.* BAR International Series 766. Oxford: J. & E. Hedges.

——— 2011. "World-Systems Analysis and Anthropology: A New Détante?" *Reviews in Anthropology* 40.1: 3–26.

Galaty, M. and W. Parkinson. 1999. "Putting Mycenaean Palaces in Their Place: An Introduction." In *Rethinking Mycenaean Palaces*, edited by M. Galaty and W. Parkinson, 1–8. Los Angeles: Cotsen Institute of Archaeology.

Galaty, M. et al., 2010. "Interaction amidst Diversity: An Introduction to the Eastern Mediterranean Bronze Age." In *Archaic State Interaction*, edited by W. Parkinson and M. Galaty, 29–52. Santa Fe, NM: School for Advanced Research Press.

Galaty, M., H. Thomas, and B. Parkinson. 2014. "Bronze Age European Elites: From the Aegean to the Adriatic and Back Again." In *The Cambridge Prehistory of the Bronze Age and Iron*

Age Mediterranean, edited by B. Knapp and P. van Dommelen, 157–177. Cambridge: Cambridge University Press.

Gale, N. 1991. "Copper Oxhide Ingots, Their Origin, and Their Place in the Bronze Age Metals Trade in the Mediterranean." In *Bronze Age Trade in the Mediterranean*, edited by N. Gale, 197–239. SIMA 90. Jonsered: P. Åströms Förlag.

Gale, N., M. Kayafa, and Z. Stos-Gale. 2008. "Early Helladic Metallurgy at Raphina, Attica, and the Role of Lavrion." In *Aegean Metallurgy in the Bronze Age*, edited by I. Tzachili, 87–104. Athens: Ta Pragmata.

Gale, N. and Z. Stos-Gale. 1982. "The Sources of Mycenaean Silver and Lead." *JFA* 9.4: 467–485.

——— 1986. "Oxhide Copper Ingots in Crete and Cyprus and the Bronze Age Metals Trade." *BSA* 81: 81–100.

——— 1995. "Comments on 'Oxhide Ingots, Recycling, and the Mediterranean Metals Trade'." *JMA* 8.1: 33–41.

——— 2012. "The Role of the Apliki Mine Region in the Post c. 1400 BC Copper Production and Trade Networks in Cyprus." In *Eastern Mediterranean Metallurgy and Metalworking in the Second Millennium BC*, edited by V. Kassianidou and G. Papasavvas, 70–82. Oxford: Oxbow.

Garfinkle, S. 2012. *Entrepreneurs and Enterprise in Early Mesopotamia: A Study of Three Archives from the Third Dynasty of Ur (2112–2004 BCE)*. Bethesda, MD: CDL Press.

Gates, M.-H. 2011. "Maritime Business in the Bronze Age Eastern Mediterranean: The View from Its Ports." In *Intercultural Contacts in the Ancient Mediterranean*, edited by K. Duistermaat and I. Regulski, 381–394. Leuven: Peeters.

Genz, H. 2011. "Foreign Contacts of the Hittites." In *Insights into Hittite History and Archaeology*, edited by H. Genz and P. Mielke, 301–331. Leuven: Peeters.

Georganas, I. 2000. "Early Iron Age Tholos Tombs in Thessaly (1100–700)." *MeditArch* 13: 47–54.

——— 2002. "Constructing Identities in Early Iron Age Thessaly: The Case of the Halos Tumuli." *OJA* 21.3: 289–298.

——— 2008. "Between Admetus and Jason: Pherai in the Early Iron Age." In *Dioskouroi*, edited by C. Gallou, M. Georgiadis, and G. Muskett, 274–280. BAR International Series 1889. Oxford: Archaeopress.

——— 2010. "Weapons and Warfare." In *The Oxford Handbook of the Aegean Bronze Age*, edited by E. Cline, 305–328. Oxford: Oxford University Press.

Giannopoulos, T. 2008. *Die Letzte Elite der mykenischen Welt: Achaia in mykenischen Welt: Achaia in mykenischer Zeit und das Phänomen der Kriegerbestattungen im 12.–11. Jahrhundert v. Chr.* Bonn: Habelt.

Giddens, A. 1984. *The Constitution of Society: Outline of the Theory of Structuration*. Berkeley: University of California Press.

Gillis, C. 1997. "The Smith in the Late Bronze Age: State Employee, Independent Artisan, or Both?" In *TEXNH. Craftsmen, Craftswomen, and Craftsmanship in the Aegean Bronze Age, Vol. II*, edited by R. Laffineur and P. Betancourt, 505–513. Aegaeum 16. Liège: Université de Liège.

Given, R. 2004. "Mapping and Manuring: Can We Compare Sherd Density Figures?" In *Side-by-Side Survey: Comparative Regional Studies in the Mediterranean World*, edited by S. Alcock and J. Cherry, 13–21. Oxford: Oxbow.

Gjerstad, E. 1977. "Pottery from Various Parts of Cyprus." In *Greek Geometric and Archaic Pottery Found in Cyprus*, edited by E. Gjerstad and Y. Calvet, 23–59. Stockholm: Swedish Institute at Athens.

Glowacki, K. and N. Klein. 2011. "The Analysis of 'Dark Age' Domestic Architecture: The LM IIIC Settlement at Kavousi Vronda." In *The "Dark Ages" Revisited*, edited by A. Mazarakis Ainian, 407–418. Volos: University of Thessaly.

Godart, L., A. Kanta, and A. Tzigounaki. 1996. "La bureaucratic palatiale: Naissance et évolution d'un système de pouvoir en Égée." In *Atti e memorie del secondo congress internazionale di micenologia*, edited by E. de Miro, L. Godart, and A. Sacconi, 581–598. Incunabula Graeca 98. Rome: Gruppo Editoriale Internazionale.

Goldstone, J. 1991. *Revolution and Rebellion in the Early Modern World*. Berkeley: University of California Press.

González de Canales, F., L. Serrano, and J. Llompart. "The Pre-Colonial Phoenician Emporium of Huelva ca. 900–770 BC." *BABesch* 81: 13–29.

Gorton, A. 1996. *Egyptian and Egyptianizing Scarabs: A Typology of Steatite, Faience, and Paste Scarabs from Punic and Other Mediterranean Sites*. Oxford: Oxford University Committee for Archaeology.

Gounaris, A. 2015. "Zagora: The 'Harvest'. The Contribution of Zagora to the Study of the Built Environment of the Geometric Period." In *Zagora in Context: Settlements and Intercommunal Links in the Geometric Period (900–700 BC)*, edited by J.-P. Descœudres and S. Paspalas, 1–28. *Mediterranean Archaeology* 25. Sydney: University of Sydney.

Grammenos, A. 1992. "The Ivories from Spata, Attica." In *Ivory in Greece and the Eastern Mediterranean from the Bronze Age to The Hellenistic Period*, edited by J. Fitton, 45–56. London: British Museum.

Gras, M. 1985. *Trafics Tyrrhéniens archaïques*. Rome: Ecole française de Rome.

Grote, G. 1846–1856. *A History of Greece*, 12 vols. New York: Harper.

Guglielmino, R., S. Levi, and R. Jones. 2010. "Relations between the Aegean and Apulia in the Late Bronze Age: The Evidence from an Archaeometric Study of the Pottery at Roca (Lecce)." *Rivista di Scienze Preistoriche* 60: 257–282.

Günel, S. 2008. "Çine-Tepecik Kazıları ve Bölge Arkeologisine Katkıları." In *Batı Anadolu ve Doğu Akdeniz Geç Tunç Çağı Kültürleri Üzerine Yeni Araştırmalar*, edited by H. Erkanal and S. Günel, 129–139. Ankara: Hacettepe Üniversitesi.

———. 2010. "Mycenaean Cultural Impact on the Çine (Marsyas) Plain, Southwest Anatolia Evidence from Çine-Tepecik." *AnatStud* 60: 25–39.

———. 2015. "Çine Tepecik: New Contributions on Late Bronze Age Cultures in Western Anatolia." In *NOSTOI: Indigenous Culture, Migration, + Integration in the Aegean Islands + Western Anatolia during the Late Bronze + Early Iron Ages*, edited by N. Stampolidis, Ç. Maner, and K. Kopanias, 627–646. Istanbul: Koç University Press.

Gunter, A. 2009. *Greek Art and the Orient*. Cambridge: Cambridge University Press.

Güterbock, H. 1983. "Hittites and the Aegean World: Part I. The Ahhiyawa Problem Reconsidered." *AJA* 87: 133–138.

Haarer, P. 2000. "Ὀβελοί and Iron in Archaic Greece." Ph.D. dissertation, Oxford University.

Haines, C. 1971. *Excavations in the Plain of Antioch II: The Structural Remains of the Later Phases, Chatal Hüyük, Tell Al-Judaidah and Tell Ta'yinat*. Chicago: The University of Chicago Press.

Hairfield, H. and E. Hairfield. 1990. "Identification of a Late Bronze Age Resin." *Analytical Chemistry* 62.1: 41–45.

Hakulin, L. 2004. *Bronzeworking on Late Minoan Crete: A Diachronic Study.* BAR International Series 1245. Oxford: Archaeopress.

——— 2013. "Metals in LBA Minoan and Mycenaean Societies on Crete: A Quantitative Approach." Ph.D. dissertation, University of Helsinki.

Halbherr, F. 1888. "Scavi e trovamento nell'Antro di Zeus sul Monte Ida in Creta." *Museo dell' Antichita Classico* 2: 689–766.

Halbherr, F. and P. Orsi. 1888. "Scoperte nell' Antro di Psychro." *Museo dell' Antichita Classico* 2: 905–910.

Haldane, C. 1993. "Direct Evidence for Organic Cargoes in the Late Bronze Age." *WorldArch* 24.3: 348–360.

Hall, E. 1914. *Excavations in Eastern Crete: Vrokastro.* Philadelphia: University of Pennsylvania Museum.

Hall, J. 2007. *A History of the Archaic Greek World.* Oxford: Wiley-Blackwell.

Hall, T., N. Kardulias, and C. Chase-Dunn. 2011. "World-Systems Analysis and Archaeology: Continuing the Dialogue." *JAR* 19.3: 233–279.

Hallager, B. 1985. "Crete and Italy in the Late Bronze Age III Period." *AJA* 89: 293–305.

——— 1988. "Mycenaean Pottery in LM IIIA1 Deposits at Khania, Western Crete." In *Problems in Greek Prehistory*, edited by E. French and K. Wardle, 173–181. Bristol: Bristol Classical Press.

——— 1993. "Mycenaean Pottery in Crete." In *Wace and Blegen: Pottery as Evidence for Trade in the Aegean Bronze Age, 1939–1989*, edited by C. Zerner, 263–269. Amsterdam: J.C. Gieben.

——— 2007. "Problems with LM/LH IIIB/C Synchronisms." In *LH IIIC Chronology and Synchronisms II: LHIIIC Middle*, edited by S. Deger-Jalkotzy and M. Zavadil, 189–202. Vienna: Verlag der Österreichischen Akademie der Wissenschaften.

——— 2010. "The Elusive Late IIIC and the Ill-named Subminoan." In *Cretan Offerings: Studies in Honour of Peter Warren*, edited by O. Krzsyzkowska, 141–156. BSA Studies 18. London: British School at Athens.

Hallager, E. 1988. "Khania and Crete ca. 1375–1200 BC." *Cretan Studies* 1: 115–124.

Hallager, E. and B. Hallager, eds. 2000. *The Greek-Swedish Excavations at the Agia Aikaterini Square, Kastelli, Khania, 1970–1987 II: The Late Minoan IIIC Settlement.* Jonsered: P. Åström Förlag.

———, eds. 2003. *The Greek-Swedish Excavations at Agia Aikaterini Square, Kastelli, Khania, 1970–1987 III: The Late Minoan IIIB:2 Settlement.* Jonsered: P. Åströms Förlag.

Halstead, P. 1988. "On Redistribution and the Origin of Minoan-Mycenaean Palatial Economies." In *Problems in Greek Prehistory*, edited by E. French and K. Wardle, 519–530. Bristol: Bristol Classical Press.

——— 1992. "The Mycenaean Palatial Economy: Making the Most of the Gaps in the Evidence." *PCPS* 38: 57–86.

Hankey, V. 1981. "The Aegean Interest in El Amarna." *Journal of Mediterranean Anthropology and Archaeology* 1: 38–49.

——— 1995. "Stirrup Jars at El-Amarna." In *Egypt, the Aegean and the Levant*, edited by L. Schofield and W. Davies, 116–124. London: British Museum.

Hansen, M.-H. 2006. *The Shotgun Method: The Demography of the Ancient Greek City-State Culture.* Columbia, MO: University of Missouri Press.

——— 2008. "An Update on the Shotgun Method." *GRBS* 48: 259–286.

Hasebroek, J. 1928. *Staat und Handel im alten Griechenland: Untersuchungen zur antike Wirtschaftsgeschichte*. Tübingen: J.C.B. Mohr.

Haskell, H. 1981. "Coarse-ware Stirrup-jars at Mycenae." *BSA* 76: 225–238.

———. 1997. "Mycenaeans at Knossos: Patterns in the Evidence." In *La Crète mycénienne*, 187–193. BCH Supplement 30. Paris: École française d'Athènes.

———. 1999. "Aspects of the Nature and Control of Mycenaean Foreign Trade." In *Meletemata*, edited by P. Betancourt et al., 339–342. Aegaeum 20. Liège: Université de Liège.

———. 2011a. "Chronology and Power." In *Transport Stirrup Jars of the Bronze Age Aegean and East Mediterranean*, edited by H. Haskell, R. Jones, P. Day, and J. Killen, 109–124. Prehistory Monographs 33. Philadelphia: INSTAP.

———. 2011b "Trade." In *Transport Stirrup Jars of the Bronze Age Aegean and East Mediterranean*, edited by H. Haskell, R. Jones, P. Day, and J. Killen, 125–132. Prehistory Monographs 33. Philadelphia: INSTAP.

Haskell, H., R. Jones, P. Day, and J. Killen, eds. 2011. *Transport Stirrup Jars of the Bronze Age Aegean and East Mediterranean*. Prehistory Monographs 33. Philadelphia: INSTAP.

Hasserodt, M. 2009. *Griechische und Orientalische Metallphialen des frühen ersten Jahrtausends v. Chr. in Griechenland*. Asia Minor Studien 62. Bonn: Habelt.

Hatzaki, E. 2004. "From Final Palatial to Postpalatial Knossos: A View from the Late Minoan II to Late Minoan IIIB Town." In *Knossos: Palace, City, State*, edited by G. Cadogan, E. Hatzaki, and A. Vasilakis, 121–126. BSA Studies 12. London: British School at Athens.

Hauptmann, A. 2009. "Lead Isotope Analysis and the Origin of Sardinian Metal Objects." In *Oxhide Ingots in the Central Mediterranean*, edited by F. Lo Schiavo, J. Muhly, R. Maddin, and A. Giumlia-Mair, 499–514. Rome: A.G. Leventis Foundation.

Hawkins, J. 1998. "Tarkasnawa King of Mira: 'Tarkondemos', Bogazköy Sealings, and Karabel." *AnatSt* 48: 1–31.

Hawkins, S. 2010. "Greek and the Languages of Asia Minor to the Classical Period." In *A Companion to the Ancient Greek Language*. Malden, MA: Wiley-Blackwell.

Hayden, B. 2003. *Reports on the Vrokastro Area*. Philadelphia: University of Pennsylania Museum.

Hegmon, M. 2003. "Setting Theoretical Egos Aside: Issues and Theory in North American Archaeology." *AmerAnt* 68: 213–243.

———. 2005. "No More Theory Wars: A Response to Moss." *AmerAnt* 70: 588–590.

Heizer, R. and S. Cook, eds. 1960. *The Application of Quantitative Methods in Archaeology*. New York: Quandrangle Books.

Helck, W. 1979. *Die Beziehungen Ägyptens und Vorderasiens zur Ägäis bis ins. 7. Jahrhundert v. Chr*. Darmstadt: Wissenschaftliche Buchgesellschaft.

Helms, M. 1979. *Ancient Panama: Chiefs in Search of Power*. Austin: University of Texas Press.

———. 1988. *Ulysses' Sail: An Ethnographic Odyssey of Power, Knowledge, and Geographical Distance*. Princeton, NJ: Princeton University Press.

———. 1993. *Craft and the Kingly Ideal*. Austin: University of Texas Press.

Heltzer, M. 1978. *Goods, Prices, and the Organization of Trade at Ugarit*. Wiesbaden: Reichert.

Hemingway, S. and P. Harrison. 1996. "Minoan Metalworking in the Postpalatial Period: A Deposit of Metallurgical Debris from Palaikastro." *BSA* 91: 213–252.

Henderson, J., J. Evans, and K. Nikita. 2010. "Isotopic Evidence for the Primary Production, Provenance, and Trade of Late Bronze Age Glass in the Mediterranean." *Mediterranean Archaeology and Archaeometry* 10.1: 1–24.

Herman, G. 1987. *Ritualized Friendship and the Greek City*. Cambridge: Cambridge University Press.

Herrmann, H.-V. 1966a. *Die Kessel der Orientalisierenden Zeit. Olympia VI*. Berlin: de Gruyter.

——— 1966b. "Urartu und Griechenland." *JdI* 81: 79–142.

Heurtley, W. and T. Skeat. 1930/1. "The Tholos Tombs of Marmariani." *BSA* 31: 1–55.

Heymans, E. and G. van Wijngaarden. 2009. "Low-Value Manufactured Exotics in the Eastern Mediterranean in the Late Bronze and Early Iron Ages." In *Exotica in the Prehistoric Mediterranean*, edited by A. Vianello, 124–136. Oxford: Oxbow.

Hiesel, G. 1990. *Späthelladische Hausarchitektur: Studien zur Architekturgeschichte des griechischen Festlandes in der späten Bronzezeit*. Mainz am Rhein: P. von Zabern.

Higgins, R. 1969. "Early Greek Jewellery." *BSA* 64: 143–153.

——— 1980. *Greek and Roman Jewellery*. London: Methuen.

Hiller, S. 1972. "Allgemeine Bemerkungen zur Jn-Serie." *SMEA* 15: 51–72.

——— 1988. "Dependent Personnel in Mycenaean Texts." *Orientalia Lovaniensia Analecta* 23: 53–68.

——— 1990. "The Miniature Frieze in the West House – Evidence for Minoan Poetry?" In *Thera and the Aegean World* III.1: *Archaeology*, edited by D. Hardy, 229–236. London: Thera Foundation.

Himmelhoch, L. 1990–1991. "The Use of the Ethnics *a-ra-si-jo* and *ku-pi-ri-jo* in Linear B Texts." *Minos* 25: 91–104.

Hirschfeld, N. 1992. "Cypriot Marks on Mycenaean Pottery." In *Mykenaïka: actes du IXe Colloque international sur les textes mycéniens et 'egéens*, edited by J.-P. Olivier, 315–319. *BCH* Supplément 25. Paris: L'École.

——— 1993. "Incised Marks (Post-Firing) on Aegean Wares." In *Wace and Blegen. Pottery as Evidence for Trade in the Aegean Bronze Age 1939–1989*, edited by C. Zerner, P. Zerner, and J. Winder, 311–318. Amsterdam: J. C. Gieben.

——— 1996. "Cypriots in the Mycenaean Aegean." In *Atti e Memorie del Secondo Congresso Internazionale di Micenologia, Roma-Napoli, 14–20 Ottobre 1991*. Vol. 1, edited by E. de Miro, L. Godart, and A. Sacconi, 289–297. Rome: Gruppo editoriale internazionale.

——— 1999. "Potmarks of the Late Bronze Age Eastern Mediterranean." Ph.D. dissertation, University of Texas at Austin.

——— 2000. "Marketing Late Bronze Age Pottery from the Kingdom of Ugarit." In *Céramiques mycéniennes*, edited by M. Yon, V. Karageorghis, and N. Hirschfeld, 163–210. *Ras Shamra-Ougarit* XIII. Paris: ERC-ADPF.

——— 2004. "Eastwards via Cyprus? The Marked Mycenaean Pottery of Enkomi, Ugarit, and Tell Abu Hawam." In *La Cerámique Mycénienne de l'Égée au Levant*, edited by J. Balensi, J.-Y. Monchambert, and S. Müller Celka, 97–104. Lyon: Maison de l'Orient et de la Méditerranée.

Hirth, K. 1978. "Interregional Trade and the Formation of Prehistoric Gateway Communities." *AmerAnt* 43.1: 35–45.

Hodder, I. 1982. "Theoretical Archaeology: A Reactionary View." In *Symbolic and Structural Archaeology*, edited by I. Hodder, 1–16. Cambridge: Cambridge University Press.

1984. "Archaeology in 1984." *Antiquity* 58: 25–32.

1985. "Post-Processual Archaeology." *Advances in Archaeological Method and Theory* 8: 1–25.

Hodder, I. and C. Orton. 1976. *Spatial Analysis in Archaeology*. Cambridge: Cambridge University Press.

Hodel-Hoenes, S. 2000. *Life and Death in Ancient Egypt*. Ithaca, NY: Cornell University Press.

Hodges, R. and D. Whitehouse. 1983 *Mohammed, Charlemagne and the Origins of Europe*. Ithaca, NY: Cambridge University Press.

Hodos, T. 2006. *Local Responses to Colonization in the Iron Age Mediterranean*. London and New York: Routledge.

Hodson, F., D. Kendall, and P. Tautu, eds. 1971. *Mathematics in the Archaeological and Historical Sciences*. Edinburgh: Edinburgh University Press.

Hoffman, G. 1997. *Imports and Immigrants: Near Eastern Contacts with Iron Age Crete*. Ann Arbor: University of Michigan Press.

Hofstra, S. 2000. "Small Things Considered: The Finds from LH IIIB Pylos in Context." Ph.D. dissertation, University of Texas at Austin.

Hogarth, D. 1899/1900. "The Dictaean Cave." *BSA* 6: 94–116.

1900. "The Cave of Psychro in Crete." *The Journal of the Anthropological Institute of Great Britain and Ireland* 30: 90–91.

Hölbl, G. 1979. *Beziehungen der ägyptischen Kultur zu Altitalien*. Leiden: Brill.

1987. "Zur kulturellen Stellung der Aegyptiaca in der mykenischen und frühgriechischen Welt." In *Forschungen xur Aegaeischen Vorgeschichte: Das Ende der mykenischen Welt*, edited by E. Thomas, 123–142. Koln: Habelt.

Hood, S., G. Huxley, and N. Sandars. 1958–1959. "A Minoan Cemetery on Upper Gypsadhes." *BSA* 53–54: 194–262.

Hooker, J. 1976. *The Coming of the Greeks*. Claremont, CA: Regina Books.

1982. "The End of Pylos and the Linear B Evidence." *Studi micenei ed egeo-anatolici* 23: 209–217.

Hope-Simpson, R. and O. Dickinson. 1979. *A Gazetteer of Aegean Civilization in the Bronze Age*. SIMA 52. Göteborg: Paul Åströms Förlag.

Hope Simpson, R. and J. Lazenby. 1970. *The Catalogue of Ships in Homer's Iliad*. Oxford: Clarendon.

Hopkins, T. and I. Wallerstein. 1982. *World Systems Analysis: Theory and Methodology*. Beverley Hills, CA: Sage Publications.

Hoppa, R. 2002. "Paleodemography: Looking Back and Thinking Ahead." In *Paleodemography: Age Distributions from Skeletal Samples*, edited by R. Hoppa and J. Vaupel, 9–28, Cambridge: Cambridge University Press.

Horden, P. and N. Purcell. 2000. *The Corrupting Sea: A Study of Mediterranean History*. Oxford: Wiley-Blackwell.

Horrocks, G. 1980. "The Antiquity of the Greek Epic Tradition: Some New Evidence." *Proceedings of the Cambridge Philological Society* 206 (NS 26): 1–11.

Hruby, J. 2013. "The Palace of Nestor, Craft Production, and Mechanisms for the Transfer of Goods." *AJA* 117: 423–427.

Huber, S. 2003. *L'Aire sacrificielle au nord du Sanctuaire d'Apollon Daphnéphoros. Eretria XIV*. Bern: Francke.

Hughes-Brock, H. 2011. "Exotic Materials Sent to – from? – The Bronze Age Aegean. Some Recent Work and Some Observations." In *Exotica in the Prehistoric Mediterranean*, edited by A. Vianello, 98–114. Oxford: Oxbow.

Hunt, P. 2007. Review of *The Shotgun Method: The Demography of the Ancient Greek City-State Culture*, by M.-H. Hansen. *BMCR* 2007.4.58.

Hurst, A. 1968. "A propos de forgerons de Pylos." *SMEA* 5: 92–96.

Huth, C. 2000. "Metal Circulation, Communication and Traditions of Craftsmanship in Late Bronze Age and Early Iron Age Europe." In *Metals Make the World Go Round: The Supply and Circulation of Metals in Bronze Age Europe*, edited by C. Pare, 176–193. Oxford: Oxbow.

Iakovidis, S. 1954. "Orientalisch Altertümer in einem mykenischen Grab bei Perati." *AfO* 17: 211–213.

———. 1966. "A Mycenaean Mourning Custom." *AJA* 70.1: 43–50.

———. 1967. "Ein Beschrifteter Siegelzylinder aus Cypern." In *Europa: Studien zur Geschichte und Epigraphik der Frühen Aegaeis*, edited by W. Brice, 143–151. Berlin: de Gruyter.

———. 1969. Περατή το νεκροταφείον Α. Athens: Library of the Archaeological Society.

———. 1970. Περατή το νεκροταφείον Β. Athens: Athens: Library of the Archaeological Society.

———. 1980. *Excavations on the Necropolis of Perati*. UCLA Institute of Archeology Occasional Paper 8. Los Angeles: Institute of Archaeology, UCLA.

———. 1982. "The Mycenaean Bronze Industry." In *Early Metallurgy in Cyprus, 4000–500 BC*, edited by J. Muhly, R. Maddin, and V. Karageorghis, 213–232. Nicosia: The Foundation.

———. 1983a. *Late Helladic Citadels on Mainland Greece*. Leiden: Brill.

———. 1983b. *Mycenae–Epidaurus*. Athens: Ekdotike Athenon.

———. 1987. "Perati, Eine Nekropole der Ausklingenden Bronzezeit in Attica." In *Ägäische Bronzezeit*, edited by H.-G. Buchholz, 437–477. Darmstadt: Wissenschaftliche Buchgesellschaft.

———. 2003. "Late Helladic IIIC in Perati." In *LH IIIC Chronology and Synchronisms I*, edited by S. Deger-Jalkotzy and M. Zavadil, 125–130. Vienna: Verlag der Österreichischen Akademie der Wissenschaften.

Ingram, R. 2005. "Faience and Glass Beads from the Late Bronze Age Shipwreck at Uluburun." M.A. thesis, Texas A&M University.

Jackson, C. and P. Nicholson. 2010. "The Provenance of Some Glass Ingots from the Uluburun Shipwreck." *JAS* 37.2: 295–301.

Jacobsson, I. 1994. *Aegyptiaca from Late Bronze Age Cyprus*. SIMA 112. Jonsered: P. Åströms Förlag.

Jacobsthal, P. 1956. *Greek Pins and Their Connexions with Europe and Asia*. Oxford: Clarendon.

James, P. et al., 1991. *Centuries of Darkness: A Challenge to the Conventional Chronology of Old World Archaeology*. London and New York: Jonathan Cape.

James, T. 1962. "The Egyptian-Type Objects." In *Perachora, the Sanctuaries of Hera Akraia and Limenia. II: Pottery, Ivories, Scarabs, and Other Objects*, edited by H. Payne, 461–516. Oxford: Clarendon.

Jameson, M., C. Runnels, and T. Van Andel. 1994. *A Greek Countryside. The Southern Argolid from Prehistory to the Present Day*. Stanford, CA: Stanford University Press.

Janeway, B. 2006–2007. "The Nature and Extent of Aegean Conact at Tell Ta'yinat and Vicinity in the Early Iron Age. Evidence of the Sea Peoples?" *Scripta Mediterranea* 27–28: 123–146.

Janko., R. 1982. *Homer, Hesiod and the Hymns*. Cambridge: Cambridge University Press.

Johnson, G. 1982. "Organizational Structure and Scalar Stress." In *Theory and Explanation in Archaeology*, edited by C. Renfrew, M. Rowlands, and B. Segraves-

Whallon, 389–421. New York: Academic Press.

Johnston, A. 2000. "The Iron Age Pottery from Kommos." *Hesperia* 69: 186–226.

——— 2005. "Kommos: Further Iron Age Pottery." *Hesperia* 74.3: 309–393.

Jones, D. 2000. *External Relations of Early Iron Age Crete, 1100–600 BC* Dubuque, IA: Kendall/Hunt Pub. Co.

——— 1993. "Phoenician Unguent Factories in Dark Age Greece: Social Approaches to Evaluating the Archaeological Evidence." *OJA* 12: 293–303.

Jones, M. 2007. "Oxhide Ingots, Copper Production, and the Trade in Copper and Other Metals in the Bronze Age." M.A. thesis, Texas A&M University.

Jones, R. 1980. "Analyses of Bronze and Other Base Metal Objects from the Cemeteries." In *Lefkandi I: The Iron Age*, edited by M. Popham, H. Sackett, and P. Themelis, 447–459. London: British School of Athens.

——— 1986. *Greek and Cypriot Pottery: A Review of Scientific Studies*. Athens: British School at Athens.

Jones, R., S. Levi, and M. Betelli. 2005. "Mycenaean Pottery in the Central Mediterranean: Imports, Imitations, and Derivatives." In *Emporia. Proceedings of the 10th International Aegean Conference*, edited by R. Laffineur and E. Greco, 473–484. *Aegaeum* 25. Liège: Université de Liège.

Jones, R. and L. Vagnetti. 1991. "Traders and Craftsmen in the Central Mediterranean: Archaeological Evidence and Archaeometric Research." In *Bronze Age Trade in the Mediterranean*, edited by N. Gale, 127–147. Stockholm: P. Åströms Förlag.

Jung, R. 2009. "Pirates of the Aegean: Italy – the East Aegean – Cyprus at the End of the Second Millennium." In *Cyprus and the East Aegean*, edited by V. Karageorghis and O. Kouka, 72–93. Nicosia: A.G. Leventis Foundation.

——— 2016. "Friede den Hütten, Krieg den Palästen!" – In the Bronze Age Aegean." In *Arm und Reich – Zur Ressourcenverteilung in prähistorischen Gesellschaften*, edited by H. Meller, H. Hahn, R. Jung, and R. Risch, 553–576. Halle: Landesmuseums für Vorgeschichte Halle.

Kanta, A. 1980. *The Late Minoan III Period in Crete: A Survey of Sites, Pottery, and Their Distribution*. Göteborg: P. Aströms Förlag.

——— 2003. "Aristocrats – Traders – Emigrants – Settlers: Crete in the Closing Phases of the Bronze Age." In *Ploes... Sea Routes...Interconnections in the Mediterranean 16th–6th c. BC*, edited by N. Stampolidis and V. Karageorghis, 173–184. Athens: University of Crete and the A.G. Leventis Foundation.

——— 2005. "The Gold Earring from the Cemetery of Krya." In *Emporia. Proceedings of the 10th International Aegean Conference*, edited by R. Laffineur and E. Greco, 701–706. *Aegaeum* 25. Liège: Université de Liège.

Karageorghis, V. 1963. "Une tombe de guerrier à Palaepaphos." *BCH* 91: 275–370.

——— 1972. "Two Built Tombs at Patriki, Cyprus." *RDAC* 1972: 161–180.

——— 1973. *Salamis Volume V: Excavations in the Necropolis of Salamis III*. Nicosia: Department of Antiquities Cyprus.

——— 1983. *Palaepaphos-Skales, an Iron Age Cemetery in Cyprus*. Konstanz: Universitätsverlag Konstanz.

Karageorghis, V. and M. Demas. 1988. *Excavations at Maa-Palaeokastro 1979–1986*. Nicosia: Cyprus Department of Antiquities.

Karageorghis, V. and V. Kassianidou. 1999. "Metalworking and Recycling in Late Bronze Age Cyprus – The

Evidence from Kition." *OJA* 18.2: 171–188.

Karageorghis, V. and E. Masson. 1975. "A propos de la découverte d'écuilles d'armure en bronze à Gostria-Alaas (Chypre)." *AA* 1975: 209–222.

Karantzli, E. 2009. "Local and Imported Late Bronze Age III Pottery from Ialysos, Rhodes: Tradition and Innovations." In *Δώρον: τιμητικός τόμος για τον Σπύρο Ιακωβίδη*, edited by D. Danielidou, 355–382. Athens: Akademia Athenon.

Kardulias, N. 2010. "World-Systems Applications for Understanding the Bronze Age in The Eastern Mediterranean." In *Archaic State Interaction*, edited by W. Parkinson and M. Galaty, 53–80. Santa Fe, NM: School for Advanced Research Press.

Karetsou, A., M. Andreadaki-Vlazaki, and N. Papadaki. 2000. *Κρήτη-Αίγυπτος: Πολιτισμικοί δεσμοί τριών χιλιετιών*. Heraklion: Υπουργείο Πολιτισμού.

Kassianidou, V. 2001. "Cypriot Copper in Sardinia. Yet Another Case of Bringing Coals to Newcastle?" In *Italy and Cyprus in Antiquity: 1500–400 BC*, edited by L. Bonfante and V. Karageorghis, 97–119. Nicosia: Costakis and Leto Severis Foundation.

——— 2006. "The Production, Use, and Trade of Metals in Cyprus and Sardinia: So Similar and Yet so Different." *Instrumentum* 23: 9–11.

Kayafa, M. 2000. "Bronze Age Metallurgy in the Peloponnese, Greece." Ph.D. dissertation, University of Birmingham.

——— 2008. "Copper-Based Artefacts in the Bronze Age Peloponnese: A Quantitative Approach to Metal Consumption." In *Aegean Metallurgy in the Bronze Age*, edited by I. Tzachili, 211–226. Athens: Ta Pragmata.

Kaza-Papageorgiou et al., 2011. "Κοντοπήγαδο Αλίμου Αττικής: Οικισμός της ΠΕ και ΥΕ χρόνων και ΥΕ εργασηριακή εγκατάσταση." *ArchEph* 150: 197–274.

Kelder, J. 2004–2005. "Mycenaeans in Western Anatolia." *Talanta* 36–37: 49–88.

——— 2009. "Royal Gift Exchange between Mycenae and Egypt: Olives as 'Greeting Gifts' in the Late Bronze Age Eastern Mediterranean." *AJA* 113.3: 339–352.

——— 2010. "The Kingdom of Mycenae: A Great Kingdom in the Late Bronze Age Aegean." Ph.D. dissertation, Vrije University.

Kenzelmann Pfyffer, A. 2005. "Graffiti d'époque géométrique provenant du Sanctuaire d'Apollon Daphnéphoros à Erétrie." *ZPE* 151: 76–77.

Kerschner, M. and I. Lemos, eds. 2014. *Archaeometric Analyses of Euboean and Euboean Related Pottery: New Results and Their Interpretations*. Vienna: Austrian Archaeological Institute.

Kiderlen, M., M. Bode, A. Hauptmann, and Y. Bassiakos. 2016. "Tripod Cauldrons Produced at Olympia Give Evidence for Trade with Copper from Faynan (Jordan) to South West Greece, c. 950–750 BCE." *JASR* 8: 303–313.

Kilian, K. 1978. "Ausgrabungen in Tiryns, 1976." *AA* 1978: 449–470.

——— 1979. "Ausgrabungen in Tiryns, 1977." *AA* 1979: 379–411.

——— 1981. "Ausgrabungen in Tiryns, 1978, 1979." *AA* 1981: 149–193.

——— 1982. "Zum Ende der mykenischen Epoche in der Argolis." *JRGZM* 27: 166–195.

——— 1983a. "Ausgrabungen in Tiryns, 1981." *AA* 1983: 276–328.

——— 1983b. "Weihungen aus Eisen und Eisenverarbeitung im Heiligtum zu Philia (Thessalien)." In *The Greek Renaissance of the Eighth Century BC. Tradition and Innovation*, edited

R. Hägg, 131–146. Stockholm: Swedish Institute at Athens.

1984. "Μυκηναϊκα εργαστήρια χαλκού στην Τίρυνθια." *Anthropologika* 6: 55–57.

1988a. "Ausgrabungen in Tiryns 1982/3. Bericht zu den Grabungen." *AA* 1988: 105–151.

1988b. "The Emergence of Wanax Ideology in the Mycenaean Palaces." *OJA* 7.3: 291–302.

Kilian-Dirlmeier, I. 1985. "Fremde Weihungen in griechischen Heiligtümern vom 8. Bis zum Beginn des 7. Jahrhunderts v. Chr." *JRGZM* 32: 215–254.

Killebrew, A. 2000. "Aegean-Style Early Philistine Pottery in Canaan during the Iron I Age: A Stylistic Analysis of Mycenaean IIIC:1b Pottery and Its Associated Wares." In *The Sea Peoples and Their World: A Reassessment*, edited by A. Oren, 236–253. Philadelphia: University of Pennsylvania Museum.

Killebrew, A. and G. Lehmann, eds. 2013. *The Philistines and Other "Sea Peoples" in Text and Archaeology*. Atlanta: Scholars Press.

Killen, J. 1983. "PY An 1." *Minos* 18: 71–79.

1984. "The Textile Industry at Pylos and Knossos." In *Pylos Comes Alive: Industry and Administration in a Mycenaean Palace*, edited by C. Shelmerdine and T. Palaima, 49–63. New York: Fordham University.

1985. "The Linear B Tablets and the Mycenaean Economy." In *Linear B: A 1984 Survey*, edited by A. Davies and Y. Duhoux, 241–305. Louvain-la-Neuve: Cabay.

1987. "Bronzeworking at Knossos and Pylos." *Hermathena* 1987: 61–72.

2008. "Mycenaean Economy." In *A Companion to Linear B: Mycenaean Greek Texts and Their World*, edited by Y. Duhoux and A. Morpurgo Davies, 159–200. Leuven: Peeters.

Kinet, D. 1981. *Ugarit-Geschichte und Kultur einer Stadt in der Umwelt des Alten Testamentes*. Stuttgart : Verlag Katholisches Bibelwerk.

King, C. 1970. "The Homeric Corslet." *AJA* 74.3: 294–296.

Kiriatzi, E. and C. Broodbank. n.d. Unpublished field report, British School at Athens. http://chronique.efa.gr/index.php/fiches/voir/1946/

Kitchen, K. 1998. "Amenhotep III and Mesopotamia." In *Amenhotep III: Perspectives on His Reign*, edited by D. O'Connor and E. Cline, 250–261. Ann Arbor: University of Michigan Press.

Knapp, A. 1986. *Copper Production and Divine Protection. Archaeology, Ideology, and Social Complexity on Bronze Age Cyprus*. Jonsered: P. Åströms Förlag.

1990. "Ethnicity, Entrepreneurship, and Exchange: Mediterranean Inter-Island Relations in the Late Bronze Age." *BSA* 85: 115–153.

1991. "Spice, Drugs, Grain, and Grog: Organic Goods in Bronze Age East Mediterranean Trade." In *Bronze Age Trade in the Mediterranean*, edited by N. Gale, 19–66. Göteborg: P. Åströms Förlag.

1993. "Thalassocracies in Bronze Age Eastern Mediterranean Trade: Making and Breaking a Myth." *WorldArch* 24: 332–347.

1998. "Mediterranean Bronze Age Trade: Distance, Power, and Place." In *The Aegean and the Orient in the Second Millennium*, edited by E. Cline and D. Harris-Cline, 193–207. Aegaeum 18. Liège: Université de Liège.

Knapp, A. and J. Cherry. 1994. *Provenance Studies and Bronze Age Cyprus: Production, Exchange, and*

Politico-Economic Change. Madison: University of Wisconsin Press.

Knapp, A. and S. Manning. 2016. "Crisis in Context: The End of the Late Bronze Age in the Eastern Mediterranean." *AJA* 120.1: 99–149.

Knapp, B. 1998. "Mediterranean Bronze Age Trade: Distance, Power, and Place." In *The Aegean and the Orient in the Second Millennium*, edited by E. Cline and D. Harris-Cline, 193–207. Aegaeum 18. Liège: Université de Liège.

——— 2008. *Prehistoric and Protohistoric Cyprus: Identity, Insularity, and Connectivity*. Oxford: Oxford University Press.

Knappett, C., T. Evans, and R. Rivers. 2008. "Modelling Maritime Interaction in the Aegean Bronze Age." *Antiquity* 82: 1009–1024.

Knappett, C. and I. Nikolakopoulou. 2008. "Colonialism without Colonies. A Bronze Age Case Study from Akrotiri, Thera." *Hesperia* 77:1–41.

Knappett, K. 1999. "Assessing a Polity in Protopalatial Crete: The Malia-Lasithi State." *AJA* 103: 615–639.

——— 2001. "Overseen or Overlooked? Ceramic Production in a Mycenaean Palatial System." In *Economy and Politics in the Mycenaean Palace States*, edited by S. Voutsaki and J. Killen, 80–95. Cambridge: Cambridge Philological Society.

——— 2011. *An Archaeology of Interaction: Network Perspectives on Material Culture and Society*. Oxford: Oxford University Press.

Knodell, A. 2013. "Small-World Networks and Mediterranean Dynamics in the Euboean Gulf: An Archaeology of Complexity in Late Bronze Age and Early Iron Age Greece." Ph.D. dissertation, Brown University.

Kohl, P. 1987. "The Ancient Economy, Transferable Technologies, and the Bronze Age World-System: A View from the Northeastern Frontier of the Ancient Near East." In *Centre and Periphery in the Ancient World*, edited by M. Rowlands, M. Larsen, and K. Kristiansen, 13–24. Cambridge: Cambridge University Press.

——— 2008. "Shared Social Fields: Evolutionary Convergence in Prehistory and Contemporary Practice." *American Anthropologist* 110: 495–506.

Kolia, E. 2011. "A Sanctuary of the Geometric Period in Ancient Helike, Achaea." *BSA* 106: 201–246.

Kolonas, L. 1998. "Νεώτερη μυκεναϊκή τοπογραφία της Αχαΐα." In *Acts of the Fifth International Congress of Peloponnesian Studies*, edited by T. Gritsopoulos and K. Kotsonas, 468–475. Athens: Society for Peloponnesian Studies.

Konsolaki-Giannopoulou, E. 2007. "Η Υστερομυκηναϊκή εγκατάσταση στην ερημονησίδα Μόδι του Σαρωνικού." *ΕΠΑΘΛΟΝ: Αρχαιολογικό Συνέδριο προς τιμήν του Αδώνιδος Κ. Κύρου*, edited by E. Konsolaki-Giannopoulou, 171–198. Athens: Demos Porou.

Kopanias, K. 2008. "The Late Bronze Age Near Eastern Cylinder Seals from Thebes (Greece) and Their Historical Implications." *AthMitt* 123: 39–96.

——— 2009. "Some Ivories from the Geometric Stratum at the Sanctuary of Artemis Orthia, Sparta: Interconnections between Sparta, Crete, and the Orient during the Late Eighth Century BC." In *Sparta and Laconia: from Prehistory to Premodern*, edited by B. Cavanagh, C. Gallou, and M. Georgiadis, 123–131. BSA Studies 16. London: British School at Athens.

Kopcke, G. 1990. *Handel*. Göttingen: Vandenhoeck & Ruprecht.

Korfmann, M. 1995. "Troia: A Residential and Trading City at the Dardanelles." In *Politeia. Society and State in the*

Aegean Bronze Age, edited by R. Laffineur and W.-D. Niemeier, 173–183. *Aegaeum* 12. Liège: Université de Liège.

Kotsonas, A. 2002. "The Rise of the Polis in Central Crete." *Eulimene* 3: 37–74.

———. 2006. "Wealth and Status in Early Iron Age Knossos." *OJA* 25.2: 149–172.

———. 2012. "'Creto-Cypriot' and 'Cypro-Phoenician' Complexities in the Archaeology of Interaction between Crete and Cyprus." In *Cyprus and the Aegean in the Early Iron Age: The Legacy of Nicolas Coldstream*, edited by M. Iacovou, 155–182. Nicosia: Bank of Cyprus Cultural Foundation.

———. 2015. "What Makes a Euboean Colony or Trading Station? Zagora in the Cyclades, Methone in the Thermaic Gulf and Aegean Networks in the 8th Century BC." *MeditArch* 25: 243–257.

———. 2016. "Politics of Periodization and the Archaeology of Early Greece." *AJA* 120.2: 239–270.

Kourou, N. 1990. "Εύβοια και Ανατολική Μεσόγειος στις αρχές της πρώτης χιλιετίας." *Archeion Euboikon Meleton* 29: 237–279.

———. 2000. "Phoenician Presence in Early Iron Age Crete Reconsidered." In *Actas del IV Congreso internacional de estudios fenicios y púnicos*, edited by E. Aubet and M. Barthélemy, 1067–1076. Cádiz: Universidad de Cádiz.

———. 2012. "Phoenicia, Cyprus, and the Aegean in the Early Iron Age: J.N. Coldstream's Contribution and the Current State of research." In *Cyprus and the Aegean in the Early Iron Age: The Legacy of Nicolas Coldstream*, edited by M. Iacovou, 33–50. Nicosia: Bank of Cyprus Cultural Foundation.

———. 2015. "Cypriots and Levantines in the Central Aegean during the Geometric Period: The Nature of Contacts." In *Zagora in Context: Settlements and Intercommunal Links in the Geometric Period (900–700 BC)*, edited by J.-P. Descœudres and S. Paspalas, 215–227. Sydney: University of Sydney.

Kowaleski, M. 1995. *Local Markets and Regional Trade in Medieval Exeter*. Cambridge: Cambridge University Press.

Kozal, E. 2003. "Analysis of the Distribution Patterns of Red Lustrous Wheel-Made Ware Mycenaean and Cypriote Pottery in Anatolia in the 15th-13th Centuries BC." In *Identifying Changes: The Transition from Bronze to Iron Ages in Anatolia and Its Neighboring Regions*, edited by B. Fischer, H. Genz, E. Jean, and K. Köroğlu, 65–77. Istanbul: Türk Eskiçağ Bilimleri Enstitüsü.

———. 2015. "Study of Imports in Late Bronze Age Anatolia: Identification, Definition, Chronological, and Spatial Analysis." In *NOSTOI: Indigenous Culture, Migration + Integration in the Aegean Islands + Western Anatolia during the Late Bronze + Early Iron Ages*, edited by N. Stampolidis, Ç. Maner, and K. Kopanias, 693–706. Istanbul: Koç University Press.

Kraiker, W. and K. Kübler. 1939. *Kerameikos I: Die Nekropolen des 12. bis 10. Jahrhunderts*. Berlin: de Gruyter.

Kramer-Hajos, M. 2008. *Beyond the Palace: Mycenaean East Lokris*. BAR International Series 1781. Oxford: Archaeopress.

———. 2016. *Mycenaean Greece and the Aegean World: Palace and Province in the Late Bronze Age*. Cambridge: Cambridge University Press.

Kristiansen, K. 1998. *Europe before History*. Cambridge: Cambridge University Press.

Kristiansen, K. and T. Larsson. 2007. "Contacts and Travels during the 2nd Millennium BC: Warriors on the Move." In *Between the Aegean and Baltic Seas: Prehistory across Borders*, edited by I. Galanaki, H. Tomas, Y. Galanakis, and

R. Laffineur, 25–34. *Aegaeum* 27. Liège: Université de Liège.

Krumme, M. 2015. "Geometric Miletus." In *NOSTOI: Indigenous Culture, Migration, + Integration in the Aegean Islands + Western Anatolia during the Late Bronze + Early Iron Ages*, edited by N. Stampolidis, Ç. Maner, and K. Kopanias, 581–591. Istanbul: Koç University Press.

Kryszkowska, O. 1992. "Aegean Ivory Carving: Towards an Evaluation of Late Bronze Age Workshop Material." In *Ivory in Greece and the Eastern Mediterranean from the Bronze Age to the Hellenistic Period*, edited by J. Fitton, 25–36. London: British Museum.

Ksifaras, N. 1998. *Η Κατάληψη του χώρου στην Πρωτογεωμετρική και Γεωμετρική Κρήτη*. Rethymno: University of Crete.

——— 2004. *Οικιστική της Πρωτογεωμετρικής και Γεωμετρικής Κρήτης, Η μετάβαση από την Μινωική στην Ελληνική κοινωνία*. Rethymno: University of Crete.

Kübler, K. 1943. *Kerameikos IV: Neufunde aus der Nekropole des 11. und 10. Jahrhunderts*. Berlin: de Gruyter.

——— 1954. *Kerameikos V: Die Nekropole des 10 bis 8 Jahrhundert*. Berlin: de Gruyter.

Kühne, C. 1973. *Die Chronologie der internationalen Korrespondenz von el-Amarna*. Kevelaer: Butzon & Bercker.

Kunze-Goette, E. 1933. Review of *The Sanctuary of Artemis Orthia at Sparta*, by R.M. Dawkins. *Gnomon* 9: 1–14.

Kurtz, D. and J. Boardman. 1971. *Greek Burial Customs*. Ithaca, NY: Cornell University Press.

Kyrieleis, H. 1977. "Stierprotomen: Orientalisch oder Griechisch." *AM* 92: 71–89.

——— 2002. "Zu den Anfängen des Heiligtums von Olympia." In *Olympia 1875–2000: 125 Jahre deutsche Ausgrabungen*, edited by H. Kyrieleis, 213–220. Mainz am Rhein: P. von Zabern.

Laffineur, R. 2005. "Imports/Exports in the Eastern Mediterranean: For a Specific Methodology." In *Emporia: Aegeans in the Central and Eastern Mediterranean*, 53–58. Liège: Université de Liège.

Laffineur, R. and E. Greco, eds. 2005. *Emporia: Aegeans in the Central and Eastern Mediterranean*. *Aegaeum* 25. Liège: Université de Liège.

Lamberg-Karlovsky, C. 1975. "Third Millennium Exchange and Production." In *Ancient Civilization and Trade*, edited by J. Sabloff and C. Lamberg-Karlovsky, 341–368. Albuquerque: University of New Mexico Press.

Lamberton, R. 1988. *Hesiod*. New Haven, CT: Yale University Press.

Lambrou-Phillipson, C. 1990. *Hellenorientalia: The Near Eastern Presence in the Bronze Age Aegean, ca. 3000–1100 BC: Interconnections Based on the Material Record and the Material Evidence*. Göteborg: P. Åströms Förlag.

Lang, M. 1996. *Archaische Siedlungen in Griechenland: Struktur und Entwicklung*. Berlin: Akademie Verlag.

Langdon, S., ed. 1997. *New Light on a Dark Age: Exploring the Culture of Geometric Greece*. Columbia: University of Missouri Press.

Lantzas, K. 2012. *Settlement and Social Trends in the Argolid and the Methana Peninsula, 1200–900 BC*. BAR International Series 2421. Oxford: Archaeopress.

Latacz, J. 2004. *Troy and Homer*. Translated by K. Windle and R. Ireland. Oxford: Oxford University Press.

Lavelle, B. 1997. "Epikouros and Epikouroi in Early Greek Literature and History." *GRBS* 38.3: 229–262.

Lazaridis, D. 1968. "Ἀνασκαφὴ Ἀναβύσσου." *ArchDelt* 21 Chr. B1: 97–100.

Lemos, I. 1998. "Lefkandi: What Is Not 'Dark' in the So Called 'Greek Dark Ages.'" In *Die Geschichte der hellenischen Sprache und Schrift vom 2. zum 1. Jahrtausend v.Chr.: Bruch oder Kontinuität?*, 279–300. Altenburg: Vereinigung zur Förderung der Aufarbeitung der hellenischen Geschichte.

— 2002. *The Protogeometric Aegean*. Oxford: Oxford University Press.

— 2003. "Craftsmen, Traders, and Some Wives in Early Iron Age Greece." In *PLOES: Sea Routes, Interconnections in the Mediterranean 16th–6th c. BC.*, edited by N. Stampolidis and V. Karageorghis, 187–195. Athens: University of Crete and the A.G. Leventis Foundation.

— 2007a. "Recent Archaeological Work on Xeropolis, Lefkandi: A Preliminary Report." in *Oropos and Euboia in the Early Iron Age: Acts of an International Round Table, University of Thessaly, June 18–20, 2004*, edited by A. Mazarakis Ainian, 123–134. Volos: University of Thessaly Press.

— 2007b. "Elite and Gender in Early Iron Age Greece." In *Keimelion: Elitenbildung und Elitarer Konsum von der Mykenischen Palastzeit bis zur Homerischen Epoche*, edited by E. Alram-Stern and G. Nightingale, 275–284. Wien: Verlag der Österreichischen Akademie der Wissenschaften.

— 2007c. "The Migrations to the West Coast of Asia Minor: Tradition and Archaeology." In *Frühes Ionien*, edited by J. Cobet et al., 713–727. Mainz am Rhein: P. von Zabern.

Lemos, I. and H. Hatcher. 1991. "Early Greek Pottery from Cyprus: Attic and Euboean." *OJA* 5: 323–337.

Leonard, A. 1981. "Considerations of Morphological Variation in the Mycenaean Pottery from the Southeastern Mediterranean." *BASOR* 241: 87–101.

— 1994. *An Index to the Late Bronze Age Aegean Pottery from Syria-Palestine*. SIMA 114. Jonsered: P. Åstroms Förlag.

— 1998. "Trade during the Late Helladic III Period." In *The Aegean and the Orient in the Second Millenium*, edited by E. Cline and D. Harris-Cline, 99–104. Aegaeum 18. Liège: Université de Liège.

Leonard, A., M. Hughes, A. Middleton, and L. Schofield. 1993. "The Making of Aegean Stirrup Jars: Technique, Tradition, and Trade." *BSA* 88: 105–123.

Leriou, N. 2002. "The Mycenaean Colonisation of Cyprus under the Magnifying Glass: Emblematic Indica versus Defining Criteria at Palaeopaphos." In *SOMA 2001: Symposium on Mediterranean Archaeology*, edited by G. Muskett, A. Koltsida, and M. Georgiadis, 169–177. BAR International Series 1040. Oxford: Archaeopress.

— 2007. "Locating Identities in the Eastern Mediterranean during the Late Bronze Age-Early Iron Age: The Case of Hellenised Cyprus." In *Mediterranean Crossroads*, edited by S. Antoniadou and A. Pace, 563–591. Athens: Pierides Foundation.

Liverani, M. 1972. "Elementi irrazionali nel commercio amarniano." *OA* 11: 297–317.

— 1987. "The Collapse of the Near Eastern Regional System at the End of the Bronze Age: The Case of Syria." In *Centre and Periphery in the Ancient World*, edited by M. Rowlands, M. Larsen, and K. Kristiansen, 66–73. Cambridge: Cambridge University Press.

— 1990. *Prestige and Interest. International Relations in the Near East ca. 1600–1100 B.C.* Padua: Sargon.

— 2001. *International Relations in the Ancient Near East, 1600–1100 BC*. Houndsmills and New York: Palgrave.

2003. "The Influence of Political Institutions on Trade in the Ancient Near East (Late Bronze to Early Iron Age)." In *Mercanti e politica nel mondo antico*, edited by C. Zaccagnini, 119–137. Rome: L'Erma di Bretschneider.

Lo Schiavo, F. 2003. "Sardinia between East and West: Interconnections in the Mediterranean." In *PLOES…Sea Routes…From Sidon to Huelva. Interconnections in the Mediterranean 16th–6th c. BC*, edited by N. Stampolidis, 152–161. Athens: Museum of Cycladic Art.

Lolos, Y. 2002. "Τάλαντα Χαλκού απο την Σαλαμίνα." *Enalia* 6: 73–79.

——— 2007. "Το Μυκηναϊκό άστυ της Σαλαμίνος." In *ΕΠΑΘΛΟΝ: Αρχαιολογικό Συνέδριο προς τιμήν του Αδώνιδος Κ. Κύρου*, edited by E. Konsolaki-Giannopoulou, 221–252. Athens: Demos Porou.

——— 2009a. "Salamis ca. 1200 BC: Connections with Cyprus and the Near East." In *From the Aegean to the Adriatic: Social Organizations, Modes of Exchange, and Interaction in postpalatial Times (12th–11th BC)*, edited by E. Borgna and P. Cassola Guida, 29–46. Rome: Quasar.

——— 2009b. "Kanakia." *Akamas* 3: 2–8.

——— 2011. *Land of Sikyon: Archaeology and History of a Greek City State*. Hesperia Supplement 39. Princeton, NJ: Princeton University Press.

Lolos, Y., Chr. Marabea, and V. Oikonomou. 2007. "Ajax's Capital. The Seat of the Maritime Kingdom of Salamis." In *Men, Lands and Seas, L' archeologia nel mare*, edited by C. Pepe, 114–127. Naples: Universita degli studi Suor Orsola Benincasa.

Lorimer, H. 1950. *Homer and the Monuments*. London: Macmillan.

Lucas, G. 2013. *Understanding the Archaeological Record*. Cambridge: Cambridge University Press.

Luce, J. 1975. *Homer and the Heroic Age*. London: Harper and Row.

Luce, J. and E. Blegen. 1939. "Archaeological News and Discussion." *AJA* 43.1: 107–132.

Luhán Martínez, R. and A. Bernabé. 2012. "Ivory and Horn Production in Mycenaean Texts." In *Kosmos: Jewellery, Adornment, and Textiles in the Aegean Bronze Age*, edited by M.-L. Nosch and R. Laffineur, 627–638. Aegaeum 33. Leuven: Peeters.

Luke, J. 2003. *Ports of Trade, Al Mina, and Greek Geometric Pottery in the Levant*. BAR International Series 1100. Oxford: Archaeopress.

Lynn, S. 1988. "The Ivory Trade in the Eastern Mediterranean Bronze Age: Background and Preliminary Investigation." Ph.D. dissertation, University of Minnesota.

Maftei, M. 1976. *Antike Diskussionen über die Episode von Glaukos und Diomedes im VI. Buch der Ilias*. Meisenheim am Glan: Hain.

Magiddis, C. 2007. "Mycenae Abroad: Mycenaean Foreign Policy, the Anatolian Frontier, and the Theory of Overextension – Reconstructing an Integrated Causal Nexus for the Decline and Fall of the Mycenaean World." In *Moving across Borders: Foreign Relations, Religion, and Cultural Interactions in the Ancient Mediterranean*, edited by P. Kousoulis and K. Magliveras, 71–98. Leuven: Peeters.

Maier, A., A. Fantalkin, and A. Zukerman. 2009. "The Earliest Greek Import in the Iron Age Levant: New Evidence from Tell Es-Safi/Gath, Israel." *Ancient West and East* 8: 57–80.

Malinowski, B. 1922. *Argonauts of the Western Pacific*. London: Routledge.

Malkin, I. 1987. Review of *La Naissance de la Cité grecque: Cultes, Espace, et Société*, by F. de Polignac. *JHS* 107: 227–228.

1998. *The Returns of Odysseus: Colonization and Ethnicity*. Berkeley and Los Angeles: University of California Press.

2002. "A Colonial Middle Ground: Greek, Etruscan, and Local Elites in the Bay of Naples." In *The Archaeology of Colonialism*, edited by C. Lyons and J. Papadopoulos, 151–181. Los Angeles: Getty Research Institute.

2011. *A Small Greek World: Networks in the Ancient Mediterranean*. Oxford: Oxford University Press.

Mangaloğlu-Votruba, S. 2015. "Liman Tepe during the Late Bronze Age," In *NOSTOI: Indigenous Culture, Migration, + Integration in the Aegean Islands + Western Anatolia during the Late Bronze + Early Iron Ages*, edited by N. Stampolidis, Ç. Maner, and K. Kopanias, 647–669. Istanbul: Koç University Press.

Mangou, H. and P. Ioannou. 2000. "Studies of the Bronze Age Copper-Based Ingots found in Greece." *BSA* 95: 207–217.

Manning, S. 2010. "Chronology and Terminology." In *The Oxford Handbook of the Bronze Age Aegean*, edited by E. Cline, 11–28. Oxford: Oxford University Press.

2014. *A Test of Time and a Test of Time Revisited: The Volcano of Thera and the Chronology and History of the Aegean and East Mediterranean in the Mid-Second Millennium BCE*. Oxford: Oxbow.

Manning, S. and L. Hulin. 2005. "Maritime Commerce and Geographies of Mobility in the Late Bronze Age of the Eastern Mediterranean: Problematizations." In *The Archaeology of Mediterranean Prehistory*, edited by E. Blake and B. Knapp, 270–302. Malden, MA: Wiley Blackwell.

Manning, S. et al., 2009. "Absolute Age of the Uluburun Shipwreck: A Key Late Bronze Age Time-Capsule for the East Mediterranean." In *Tree-Rings, Kings, and Old World Archaeology and Environment*, edited by S. Manning and M. Bruce, 163–188. Oxford: Oxbow.

Manning, S. and B. Weninger. 1992. "A Light in the Dark: Archaeological Wiggle Matching and the Absolute Chronology of the Close of the Aegean Late Bronze Age." *Antiquity* 66.252: 636 633.

Marakas, G. 2010. *Ritual Practice between the Late Bronze Age and Protogeometric Periods of Greece*. BAR International Series 2145. Oxford: Archaeopress.

Maran, J. 2004. "The Spreading of Objects and Ideas in the Late Bronze Age Eastern Mediterranean: Two Case Examples from the Argolid of the 13th and 12th Centuries BC." *BASOR* 336: 11–30.

2005. "Late Minoan Coarse Ware Stirrup Jars on the Greek Mainland. A Postpalatial Perspective from the 12th Century BC Argolid." In *Ariadne's Threads: Connections between Crete and the Greek Mainland in Late Minoan III (LM IIIA2 to LM IIIC)*, edited by A. D'Agata et al., 415–431. Athens: Italian School of Archaeology at Athens.

2006. "Coming to Terms with the Past: Ideology and Power in Late Helladic IIIC." In *Ancient Greece: From the Mycenaean Palaces to the Age of Homer*, edited by S. Deger-Jalkotzy and I. Lemos, 123–150. Edinburgh Leventis Studies 3. Edinburgh: Edinburgh University Press.

Marazzi, M. 1988. "La più antica marineria in occidente; dossier sulle rotte commerciali nel basso Tirreno fino al golfo di Napoli nei secoli XVI-XV a.C." *DialArch* n.s. 6: 5–22.

Marazzi, M. and S. Tusa. 2005. "Egei in Occidente. Le più antiche vie marittime alla luce dei nuovi scavi sull'isola di Pantelleria." In *Emporia. Aegeans in the Central and Eastern Mediterranean*, edited by R. Laffineur and E. Greco, 599–609. *Aegaeum 25*. Liège: Université de Liège.

Marketou, M. et al., 2006. "Pottery Wares from the Prehistoric Settlement at Ialysos (Trianda) in Rhodes." *BSA* 101:1–55.

Marketou, T. 2009. "Ialysos and Its Neighbouring Areas in the MBA and LB I Periods: A Chance for Peace." In *The Minoans in Central, Eastern, and Northern Aegean – New Evidence*, edited by C. Macdonald, E. Hallager, and W.-D. Niemeier, 73–96. Athens: Danish Institute at Athens.

Markoe, G. 1985. *Phoenician Bronze and Silver Bowls from Cyprus and the Mediterranean*. Berkeley: University of California Press.

1996. "The Emergence of Orientalizing in Greek Art: Some Observations on the Interchange between Greeks and Phoenicians in the Eighth and Seventh Centuries BCE." *BASOR* 1996: 47–67.

1998. "The Phoenicians on Crete: Transit Trade and the Search for Ores." In *Eastern Mediterranean: Cyprus-Dodecaness-Crete 16th–6th centuries BC*, edited by V. Karageorghis and N. Stampolidis, 233–240. Heraklion: University of Crete.

Martin, R. 1984. "Hesiod, Odysseus, and the Instruction of Princes." *TAPA* 114: 29–48.

1992. "Hesiod's Metanastic Poetics." *Ramus* 21.1: 11–33.

Martin Pruvot, C. et al., eds. 2010. *Cité sous terre: des archéologues suisses explorent la cité greque d'Eretrie*. Basel: Schwabe.

Mastrokosta, E. 1966. "Ἀνασκαφὴ Ἁγίου Ἠλία Μεσολογγίου-Ἰθωρίας." *Prakt* 1963: 203–217.

Matthäus, H. 1998. "Cyprus and Crete in the Early First Millennium BC" In *Eastern Mediterranean: Cyprus-Crete-Dodecanese, 16th–6th Centuries*, edited by V. Karageorghis and N. Stampolidis, 127–158. Athens: University of Crete and A.G. Leventis Foundation.

2001. "Studies on the Interrelations of Cyprus and Italy during the 11th to 9th centuries BC." In *Italy and Cyprus in antiquity, 1500–450 BC*, edited by L. Bonfante and V. Karageorghis, 153–214. Nicosia: Costakis and Leto Severis Foundation.

Matthäus, H. and G. Schumacher-Matthäus. 1986. "Zyprische Hortfunde. Kult und Metallhandwerk in der späten Bronzezeit." In *Gedenkschrift für Gero von Merhart zum 100. Geburtstag*, 129–191. Marburger Studien zur Vor- und Frühgeschichte 7. Marburg: Hitzeroth.

Matz, F. 1950. *Geschichte der griechischen Kunst. Die geometrische und die frühachaische Form*. Frankfurt am Main: Klostermann.

Mauss, M. 1923. "Essai sur le don. Forme et raison de l'échange dans les sociétés archaïques." *L'Année Sociologique* 1: 30–186.

Mazarakis Ainian, A. 1997. *From Rulers' Dwellings to Temples. Architecture, Religion and Society in Early Iron Age Greece*. Jonsered: P. Åströms Förlag.

1998. "Oropos in the Early Iron Age." in *Euboica: L'Eubea e la presenza euboica in Calcidica e in Occidente*, edited by M. Bats and B. d'Agostino, 173–209. Naples: Centre Jean Bérard.

2001. "Public and Private Space in Early Iron Age Greece." In *Building Communities: Settlement and Society in the Aegean and Beyond*, edited by R. Westgate, N. Fisher, and J. Whitley, 298–314. London: British School at Athens.

2002a. "Les fouilles d'Oropos et la fonction des péribles dans les agglomerations du début de l'Age du Fer." In *Habitat et urbanisme dans le* monde grec, de la fin des palais mycéniens a la prise de Milet (494 av. J.-C.), edited by J.-M. Luce, 183–227. *Pallas* 58. Toulouse: Presses universitaires du Mirail.

2002b. "Η συμβολή του Ωρωπού στη μελέτη των οικισμών του Αιγαίου της Πρώιμης Εποχής του Σιδήρου." In *Το Αιγαίο στην πρώιμη Εποχή του Σιδήρου*, edited by N. Stampolidis and A. Giannikouri, 369–387. Heraklion: University of Crete.

2006. "The Archaeology of *basileis*" In *From Mycenae to Homer*, edited by S. Deger-Jalkotzy and I. Lemos, 181–212. *Edinburgh Leventis Studies* 3. Edinburgh: University of Edinburgh Press.

ed. 2007. *Oropos and Euboia in the Early Iron Age*. Volos: University of Thessaly Press.

ed. 2011. *The Dark Ages Revisited*. 2 vols. Volos: University of Thessaly.

2012. "Euboean Mobility towards the North: New Evidence from the Sporades." In *Cyprus and the Aegean in the Early Iron Age*, edited by M. Iacovou, 53–75. Nicosia: Bank of Cyprus Cultural Foundation.

McDonald, W., D. Coulson, and J. Rosser, eds. 1983. *Excavations at Nichoria in Southwest Greece Volume III: Dark Age and Byzantine Occupation*. Minneapolis: University of Minnesota Press.

McKillop, I. 2005. *In Search of Maya Sea Traders*. College Station, TX: Texas A & M University Press.

Mee, C. 1978. "Aegean Trade and Settlement in Anatolia in the Second Millennium BC." *AnatSt* 28: 121–155.

1984. "The Mycenaeans at Troy." In *The Trojan War: Its Historicity and Context*, edited by L. Foxhall and J. Davis, 45–56. Bristol: Bristol Classical Press.

1998. "Anatolia and the Aegean in the Late Bronze Age." *The Aegean and the Orient in the Second Millennium*, edited by E. Cline and D. Harris-Cline, 137–146. *Aegaeum* 18. Liège: Université de Liège.

Mee, C. and B. Cavanagh. 2000. "The Hidden Landscape of Prehistoric Greece: A View from Laconia and Messenia." *JMA* 13: 102–107.

Melas, M. 2009. "The Afiartis Project: Excavations at the Minoan Settlement of Fournoi, Karpathos (2001–2004) – A Preliminary Report." In *The Minoans in the Central, Eastern, and Northern Aegean – New Evidence*, edited by C. MacDonald, E. Hallager, and W.-D. Niemeier, 59–72. Athens: Danish Institute at Athens.

Mele, A. 1979. *Il Commercio Greco Arcaico. Prexis ed Emporie*. Naples: Institut Français de Naples.

Melena, J. 1983. "Olive Oil and the Other Sorts of Oil in the Mycenaean Tablets." *Minos* 18: 89–123.

Melena, J. and J.-P. Olivier. 1991. *Tithemy: The Tablets and Nodules in Linear B from Tiryns, Thebes, and Mycenae: A Revised Transliteration*. Salamanca: Ediciones Universidad de Salamanca.

Menu, B. and A. Gasse. 2001. "Economy." In *The Oxford Encyclopedia of Ancient Egypt. Volume 1*, edited by D. Redford, 422–436. Oxford: Oxford University Press.

Meriç, R. and P. Mountjoy. 2002. "Mycenaean Pottery from Bademgediği Tepe (Puranda) in Ionia: A Preliminary Report." *IstMitt* 52: 79–98.

Meriç, R. and A. Öz, 2015. "Bademgediği Tepe (Puranda) Near Metropolis." In *NOSTOI: Indigenous Culture, Migration, + Integration in the Aegean Islands + Western Anatolia during the Late Bronze + Early Iron Ages*, edited by N. Stampolidis, Ç. Maner, and K. Kopanias, 609–626. Istanbul: Koç University Press.

Merkouri, C. 2005. "I contatti transmarini fra occidente e mondo miceneo sulla base del materiale ceramic d'importazione rinvenuto a Vivara (Napoli-Italia)." In *Emporia. Aegeans in the Central and Eastern Mediterranean*, edited by R. Laffineur and E. Greco, 611–621. Aegaeum 25. Liège: Université de Liège.

Middleton, G. 2015. "Telling Stories: The Mycenaean Origins of the Philistines." *OJA* 34.1: 45–65.

Milani, C. 1998. "Il bronzo per il tiempo. Note alla tavoletta micenea di Pilo Jn 829." *Aevum* 72: 29–35.

Miller, D. and C. Tilley. 1984. "Ideology, Power, and Prehistory: An Introduction." In *Ideology, Power, and Prehistory*, edited by D. Miller and C. Tilley, 1–15. Cambridge: Cambridge University Press.

Mills, J. and R. White. 1989. "The Identity of the Resins from the Late Bronze Age Shipwreck at Ulu Burun (Kaş)." *Archaeometry* 31.1: 37–44.

Mitchell, S. 1989/90. "Archaeology in Asia Minor 1985–1989." *AR* 36: 83–131.

Mommsen, H., T. Beier, and A. Hein. 2002. "A Complete Chemical Grouping of the Berkeley Neutron Activation Analysis Data on Mycenaean Pottery." *JAS* 29: 613–637.

Mommsen, H., P. Mountjoy, and A. Özyar. 2011. "Provenance Determination of Mycenaean IIIC Vessels from the 1934–1939 Excavations at Tarsus-Gözlükule by Neutron Activation Analysis." *Archaeometry* 53: 900–915.

Mommsen, H. and B. Sjöberg. 2007. "The Importance of the 'Best Relative Fit Factor' When Evaluating Elemental Concentration Data of Pottery Demonstrated with Mycenaean Sherds from Sinda, Cyprus." *Archaeometry* 49: 359–371.

Monroe, C. 2000. "Scales of Fate: Trade, Tradition, and Transformation in the Eastern Mediterranean, ca. 1350–1175 BCE." Ph.D. dissertation, University of Michigan.

——— 2009. *Scales of Fate, Trade, Tradition, and Transformation in the Eastern Mediterranean ca. 1350–1175 BCE*. Münster: Ugarit-Verlag.

——— 2011. "'From Luxuries to Anxieties': A Liminal View of the Late Bronze Age World-System." In *Interweaving Worlds: Systematic Interactions in Eurasia, 7th to 1st Millennia BC*, edited by C. Wilkinson, S. Sherratt, and J. Bennet, 87–99. Oxford: Oxbow.

——— 2015. "Tangled Up in Blue: Material and Other Relations of Exchange in the Late Bronze Age World." In *Traders in the Ancient Mediterranean*, edited by T. Howe, 7–46. Publications of the Association of Ancient Historians 11. Chicago: Ares.

Moran, W. 1992. *The Amarna Letters*. Baltimore: Johns Hopkins University Press.

Morgan, C. 1990. *Athletes and Oracles: The Transformation of Olympia and Delphi in the Eighth Century BC*. Cambridge: Cambridge University Press.

——— 1996. "From Palace to Polis? Religious Developments on the Greek Mainland during the Bronze/Iron Age Transition." In *Religion and Power in the Ancient Greek World*, edited by P. Hellström and B. Alroth, 41–57. Uppsala: Acta Universitatis Upsaliensis.

——— 1997. "The Archaeology of Sanctuaries in Early Iron Age and Archaic *Ethne*: A Preliminary View." In *The Development of the Polis in Archaic Greece*, edited by L. Mitchell and P. Rhodes, 168–198. London and New York: Routledge.

——— 2003. *Early Greek States beyond the Polis*. London and New York: Routledge.

——— 2006. "Ethne in the Peloponnese and Central Greece." In *From Mycenae to Homer*, edited by I. Lemos and S. Deger-Jalkotzy,

233–254. Edinburgh: Edinburgh University Press.

Morris, I. 1986. "The Use and Abuse of Homer." *ClAnt* 5: 81–138.

———. 1987. *Burial and Ancient Society*. Cambridge: Cambridge University Press.

———. 1989. "Circulation, Deposition, and the Formation of the Greek Iron Age." *Man* 23: 502–519.

———. 1991. "The Early Polis as City and State." In *City and Country in the Ancient World*, edited by J. Rich and A. Wallace-Hadrill, 25–58. London and New York: Routledge.

———. 1992. *Death Ritual and Social Structure in Classical Antiquity*. Cambridge: Cambridge University Press.

———. 1993. "Response to Papadopoulous: The Kerameikos Stratigraphy and the Character of the Greek Dark Age." *JMA* 6.2: 207–221.

———. 1997a. "Periodization and the Heroes: Inventing a Dark Age." In *Inventing an Ancient Culture: Historicism, Periodization, and the Ancient World*, edited by M. Golden and P. Toohey, 96–131. London and New York: Routledge.

———. 1997b. "Homer and the Iron Age." In *A New Companion to Homer*, edited by I. Morris and B. Powell, 535–549. Leiden: Brill.

———. 1998. "Archaeology and Archaic Greek History." In *Archaic Greece*, edited by N. Fisher and H. van Wees, 1–91. London: Duckworth.

———. 1999. "Iron Age Greece and the Meaning of 'Princely Tombs.'" In *Les princes de la protohistoire et l'émergence de l'état*, edited by P. Ruby, 57–80. Naples/Rome: Centre Jean Bérard and École française de Rome.

———. 2000. *Archaeology as Cultural History: Words and Things in Iron Age Greece*. Malden, MA: Wiley-Blackwell.

———. 2005. "Archaeology, Standards of Living, and Greek Economic History." In *The Ancient Economy: Evidence and Models*, edited by J. Manning and I. Morris, 91–126. Stanford, CA: Stanford University Press.

———. 2006. "The Growth of Greek Cities in the First Millennium BC." In *Urbanism in the Preindustrial World: Cross-Cultural Approaches*, edited by G. Storey, 27–51. Tuscaloosa: University of Alabama Press.

———. 2007. "Early Iron Age Greece." In *The Cambridge Economic History of the Greco-Roman World*, edited by W. Scheidel, I. Morris, and R. Saller, 211–241. Cambridge: Cambridge University Press.

———. 2013. *War: What Is It Good For?* Princeton, NJ: Princeton University Press.

Morris, S. 1989. "Daidalos and Kadmos: Classicism and Orientalism." *Arethusa* Supplement to vol. 22, Fall 1989: *The Challenge of Black Athena*: 39–54.

———. 1992. *Daidalos and the Origins of Greek Art*. Princeton: Princeton University Press.

———. 1995. "From Modernism to Manure." *Antiquity* 69: 182–185.

———. 1997. "Homer and the Near East." In *A New Companion to Homer*, edited by I. Morris and B. Powell, 599–623. Leiden: Brill.

Morris, S. and J. Papadopoulos. 1998. "Phoenicians and the Corinthian Pottery Industry." *Archäologische Studien in Kontaktzonen der antiken Welt*, edited by R. Rolle, K. Schmidt, R. Docter, 251–264. Göttingen: Vandenhoeck & Ruprecht.

Mountjoy, P. 1998. "The East Aegean-West Anatolian Interface in the Late Bronze Age: Mycenaeans and the Kingdom of Ahhiyawa." *AnatSt* 48: 33–67.

———. 1999. *Regional Mycenaean Decorated Pottery*. Rahden: M. Leidorf.

———. 2004. "Miletus: A Note." *BSA* 99: 190–200.

2011. "An Update on the Provenance by Neutron Activation Analysis of Near Eastern Mycenaean IIIC Pottery Groups with Particular Reference to Cyprus." In *Our Cups Are Full: Pottery and Society in the Aegean Bronze Age*, edited by W. Gauss, M. Lindblom, R. Smith, and J. Wright, 179–186. Oxford: Archaeopress.

2015. "The East Aegean-West Anatolian Interface in the 12th Century BC." In *NOSTOI: Indigenous Culture, Migration, + Integration in the Aegean Islands + Western Anatolia during the Late Bronze + Early Iron Ages*, edited by N. Stampolidis, Ç. Maner, and K. Kopanias, 37–80. Istanbul: Koç University Press.

Mountjoy, P. and H. Mommsen. 2001. "Mycenaean Pottery from Qantir-Piramesse, Egypt." *BSA* 96: 123–155.

Mühlenbruch, T. 2009. *Die Synchronisierung der nördlichen Levante und Kilikiens mit der ägäischen Spätbronzezeit*. Vienna: Verlag der Österreichischen Akademie der Wissenschaften.

2013. "Zum Phänomen der mykenischen Keramik und der Red Lustrous Wheelmade Ware im östlichen Mittelmeerraum des 2. Jahrtausends v. Chr." *Altorientalische Forschungen* 40: 282–294.

Mühlenbruch, T., J. Sterba, and D. Sürenhagen, 2009. "Neutronaktivierungsanalysen an Keramik aus Tell Djinderis/Gindaros." *Ägypten und Levante* 19: 219–227.

Muhly, J. 1973. *Copper and Tin: The Distribution of Mineral Resources and the Nature of the Metals Trade in the Bronze Age*. New Haven: The Connecticut Academy of Arts and Sciences.

1982. *The Nature of Trade in the LBA Eastern Mediterranean: The Organization of the Metals Trade and the Role of Cyprus*. Nicosia: Pierides Foundation.

1992. "The Crisis Years in the Mediterranean World: Transition or Cultural Disintegration." In *The Crisis Years*, edited by W. Ward and M. Sharp Joukowsky, 10–26. Dubuque, IA: Kendall/Hunt Publishing.

1998. "Copper, Tin, Silver, and Iron: The Search for Metallic Ores as an Incentive for Foreign Expansion." In *Mediterranean Peoples in Transition: Thirteenth to Early Tenth Centuries BCE*, edited by S. Gitin, A. Mazar, and E. Stern, 314–329. Jerusalem: Israel Exploration Society.

2003. "Trade in Metals in the Late Bronze Age and the Iron Age." In *ΠΛΟΕΣ...Sea Routes... Interconnections in the Mediterranean 16th–6th c. BC*, edited by N. Stampolidis and V. Karageorghis, 141–150. Athens: University of Crete and A. Leventis Foundation.

2005. "Kupfer und Bronze in der spätbronzezeitliche Ägäis." In *Das Schiff von Uluburun*, edited by Ü. Yalçin, C. Pulak, and R. Slotta, 503–515. Bochum: Deutsches Bergbau-Museum.

2008. "Metal Deposits in the Aegean Region." In *Anatolian metal IV*, edited by U. Yalçin, 67–75. Bochum: Deutches Bergbau-Museum Bochum.

2009. "Oxhide Ingots in the Aegean and in Egypt." In *Oxhide Ingots in the Central Mediterranean*, edited by F. Lo Schiavo et al., 17–39. Rome: A.G. Leventis Foundation.

Muhly, J., W. Stech, and R. Maddin. 1977. "The Cape Gelidonya Shipwreck and the Bronze Age Metals Trade in the Eastern Mediterranean." *JFA* 4: 352–362.

Muhly, J., T. Stech, and E. Özgen. 1985. "Iron in Anatolia and the Nature of the Hittite Iron Industry." *AnatSt* 35: 67–84.

Müller-Karpe, A. 1980. "Die Funde." AA 303–307.

——. 1994. "Anatolische Bronzeshwerter und Südosteuropa." In *Festschrift für Otto-Herman Frey zum 65. Geburtstag*, edited by C. Dobiat and O.-H. Frey, 431–444. Marburg: Hitzeroth.

Munn, M. and M. Munn. 1989. "Studies on the Attic-Boeotian Frontier: The Stanford Skourta Plain Project, 1985." In *Boeotia Antiqua I*, edited by J. Fossey, 73–127. Amsterdam: J.C. Gieber.

Murphy, J. 2014. "The Varying Place of the Dead in Pylos." In *KE-RA-ME-JA: Studies Presented to Cynthia W. Shelmerdine*, edited by D. Nakassis, J. Gulizio, and S. James, 209–221. Prehistory Monographs 46. Philadelphia: INSTAP.

Murray, A., A. Smith, and H. Walters. [1900] 1970. *Excavations in Cyprus*. London: British Museum.

Murray, G. 1907. *The Rise of Greek Epic*. Oxford: Oxford University Press.

Murray, O. 1993. *Early Greece*. 2nd ed. Cambridge, MA: Harvard University Press.

Murray, S. 2013. "Trade Imports and Society in Early Greece: 1300–900 BCE." Ph.D. dissertation, Stanford University.

——. 2015. "Quantitative Data, Hypothesis Testing, and the Construction of Archaeological Narratives: Was There Ever a Greek Dark Age?" In *Proceedings of the 1st Conference on Applications and Quantitative Methods in Archaeology. Greek Chapter (CAA-GR)*, edited by C. Papadopoulos et al., 46–49. Rethymno: IMS-FORTH.

——. forthcoming a. "Imported Exotica at the Cemetery of Perati in Late Helladic IIIC Attica: Elite Display or Evidence for Non-Local Mortuary Practice?" under revision for *AJA*.

——. forthcoming b. "Lights and Darks: Data, Language, Labels and the Progress of Scholarship on Early Greece." *Hesperia*.

——. forthcoming c. "Imports as Proxy Data for Change in Greek Trade after the Mycenaean Collapse: A Quantitative Analysis." In *EUDAIMON*, edited by P. Pavuk, V. Klonza, and A. Harding. Prague and Brno: Charles University and Masaryk University.

Muscarella, O. 1968. "Winged Bull Cauldron Attachments from Iran." *JNES* 26: 82–86.

——. 1992. "Greek and Oriental Cauldron Attachments: A Review." In *Greece between East and West*, edited by G. Kopcke and I. Tokumaru, 16–45. Mainz am Rhein: P. von Zabern.

Nakassis, D. 2007. "Reevaluating Staple and Wealth Finance at Mycenaean Pylos." In *Political Economies of the Aegean Bronze Age*, edited by D. Pullen, 127–148. Oxford: Oxbow.

——. 2013. *Individuals and Society in Mycenaean Pylos*. Leiden: Brill.

——. forthcoming. "The Economy of Land and Sea." In *The Blackwell Companion to Early Greece*, edited by A. Kotsonas and I. Lemos. London: Wiley-Blackwell.

Nakassis, D., M. Galaty, and B. Parkinson. 2011a. "State and Society." In *The Oxford Handbook of the Bronze Age Aegean*, edited by D. Pullen, 239–250. Oxford: Oxford University Press.

——. 2011b. "Redistributive Economies from a Theoretical and Cross-Cultural Perspective." *AJA* 115.2: 177–184.

Nam, R. 2012. *Gift Exchange in the Book of Kings*. Leiden: Brill.

Naroll, R. 1962. "Floor Area and Settlement Population." *AmerAnt* 27: 587–589.

Naumann, U. 1976. *Subminoische und protogeometrische Bronzeplastik auf Kreta*. Berlin: Mann.

Neeft, C. 1987. *Protocorinthian Subgeometric Aryballoi*. Amsterdam: Allard Pierson Museum.

Negbi, O. 1991. "Were There Sea Peoples in the Central Jordan Valley at the Transition from the Bronze Age to the Iron Age?" *TelAviv* 18: 205–243.

———. 2005. "Urbanism in Late Bronze Age Cyprus: LC II in Retrospect." *BASOR* 337: 1–45.

Netting, R. 1972. "Sacred Power and Centralization: Aspects of Political Adaptation in Africa." In *Population Growth: Anthropological Implications*, edited by B. Spooner, 219–244. Cambridge, MA: MIT Press.

Neve, P. 1993. *Hattuša. Stadt der Götter und Tempel*. Mainz am Rhein: P. von Zabern.

Niemeier, B. and W.-D. Niemeier. 1997. "Milet 1994–5: Projekt Minoisch-mykenisches bis protogeometrisches Milet: Zielsetzung und Grabungen auf dem Stadionhügel und am Athenatempel." *AA* 1997: 189–248.

Niemeier, W.-D. 2009. "LH IIIC Late: An East Mainland–Aegean Koine." In *LH IIIC Chronology and Synchronisms III. LHIIIC Late and the Transition to the Early Iron Age*, edited by S. Deger-Jalkotzy and A. Bächle, 289–312. Vienna: Verlag der Österreichischen Akademie der Wissenschaften.

Nightingale, G. 2000. "Die Kombination von Gold und Glas bei mykenischen Perlen." In *Österreichische Forschungen zur ägäischen Bronzezeit 1998*, edited by F. Blakolmer, 159–165. Vienna: Phoibos.

———. 2002. "Aegean Glass and Faience Beads: An Attempted Reconstruction of a Palatial Mycenaean High-Tech Industry." In *Hyalos-Vitrum-Glass. History, Technology and Conservation of Glass and Vitreous Materials in the Hellenic World*, edited by G. Kordas, 47–54. Athens: Glasnet Publications.

———. 2008. "Tiny, Fragile, Common, Precious: Mycenaean Glass and Faience Beads." In *Vitreous Materials in the Late Bronze Age Aegean*, edited by C. Jackson and E. Wager, 88–97. Oxford: Oxbow.

———. 2009. "Glass and Faience Beads from Perati: The End of the Mycenaean Tradition, the Beginning of the New Tradition of the Early Iron Age in Greece." In *Δώρον: Τιμητικός τόμος για τον Σπύρο Ιακωβίδη*, edited by D. Danielidou, 495–512. Athens: Academy of Athens.

Nikita, K., J. Henderson, and G. Nightingale. 2009. "Archaeological and Scientific Study of Mycenaean Glass from Elateia-Alonaki, Greece." In *Annales of the 17th Congress of the International Association for the History of Glass*, edited by K. Janssens et al., 39–46. Antwerp: University Press Antwerp.

Nikopoulou, Y. 1972. "Ἀβέρωφ καὶ 28ης Ὀκτωβρίου 101 (O.T. 104)." *ArchDelt* 25 B1 Chr: 101–102.

Nilsson, M. 1933. *Homer and Mycenae*. London: Methuen.

North, D. 1990. *Institutions, Institutional Change, and Economic Performance*. Cambridge: Cambridge University Press.

———. 1991. "Institutions." *Journal of Economic Perspectives* 5: 97–112.

———. 1996. "Epilogue: Economic Performance through Time." In *Empirical Studies in Institutional Change*, edited by L. Alston, T. Eggertsson, and D. North, 342–355. Cambridge: Cambridge University Press.

Nougayrol, J. 1955. *Le Palais royal d'Ugarit III*. Paris: Imprimerie Nationale.

———. 1956. *Le Palais Royal d'Ugarit IV*. Paris: Imprimerie Nationale.

———. 1970. *Le Palais Royal d'Ugarit VI*. Paris: Imprimerie Nationale.

Nougayrol, J. et al., 1968. *Ugaritica V: nouveaux textes accadiens, hourrites et ugaritiques des archives et bibliothèques privées d'Ugarit: commentaires des textes historiques, première partie*. Paris: Geuthner.

Nowicki, K. 2000. *Defensible Sites in Crete: c. 1200–800 BC. Aegaeum* 21. Liège: Université de Liège.

——— 2002. "From Late Minoan IIIC Refuge Settlements to Geometric Acropoleis: Architecture and Social Organization of Dark Age Villages and Towns in Crete." *PALLAS* 58: 149–174.

——— 2008. *Monastiraki Katalimata: Excavation of a Cretan Refuge Site, 1993–2000.* Prehistory Monographs 24. Philadelphia: INSTAP.

O'Connor, D. 2000. "The Sea Peoples and the Egyptian Sources." In *The Sea Peoples and Their World: A Reassessment*, edited by E. Oren, 85–102. Philadelphia: University of Pennsylvania Museum.

Ohly, D. 1953. *Griechische Goldbleche des 8 Jahrhunderts v Chr.* Berlin: Mann.

Oka, R. and C. Kusimba. 2008. "The Archaeology of Trading Systems, Part 1: Towards a New Trade Synthesis." *Journal of Archaeological Research* 16: 339–395.

Olivier, J.-P. 1990. "The Relationship between Inscriptions on Hieroglyphic Seals and Those Written on Archival Documents." In *Aegean Seals, Sealings, and Administration*, edited by T. Palaima, 11–19. *Aegaeum* 5. Liège: Université de Liège.

Olsen, B. 2014. *Women in Mycenaean Greece: The Linear B Tablets from Pylos and Knossos.* London: Routledge.

Osborne, R. 1996a. *Greece in the Making 1200–479 BC.* London and New York: Routledge.

——— 1996b. "Pots, Trade and the Archaic Greek Economy." *Antiquity* 70: 31–44.

——— 2006. "Demography and Survey." In *Side-by-Side Survey: Comparative Regional Studies in the Mediterranean World*, edited by S. Alcock and J. Cherry, 163–172. Oxford: Oxbow.

Otten, H. 1993. "Das Land Lukka in der Hethitischen Topographie." In *Akten des II. Internationalen Lykien-Symposiums*, edited by J. Borchhardt and G. Dobesch, 117–121. Vienna: Verlag der Österreichischen Akademie der Wissenschaften.

Owen, D. 1981. "An Akkadian Letter from Ugarit at Tel Aphek." *TelAviv* 8: 1–17.

Özgüç, T. 1978. *Maşat Höyük kazıları ve çevresindeki araştırmaları/Excavations at Maşat Höyük and Investigations in Its Vicinity.* Ankara: Türk Tarih Kurumu Basımevi.

——— 1982. *Maşat Höyük II. Boğazköy'ün kuzeydoğusunda bir Hitit merkezi/A Hittite Center Northeast of Boğazköy.* Ankara: Türk Tarih Kurumu Basımevi.

Özgünel, C. 1996. *Mykenische Keramik in Anatolien.* Asia Minor Studien 23. Bonn: Verlag Dr. Rudolf Habelt.

Özkan, T. and H. Erkaal. 1999. "Bakla Tepe Kazıları." In *Tahtalı Barajı Kurtama Kazısı Projesi*, edited by H. Erkanal, T. Özkan, 12–42. Izmir: T. C. Kültür Bakanlığı.

Paidoussis, M. and Ch. Sbarounis. 1975. "A Study of the Cremated Bones from the Cemetery of Perati (LH IIIC)." *OpAth* 11: 129–145.

Page, D. 1959. *History and the Homeric Iliad.* Berkeley: University of California Press.

Palaima, T. 1990. "Origin, Development, Transition, and Transformation: The Purposes and Techniques of Administration in Minoan and Mycenaean Society." In *Aegean Seals, Sealings, and Administration*, edited by T. Palaima, 83–112. *Aegaeum* 5. Liège: Université de Liège.

——— 1991. "Maritime Matters in the Linear B Tablets." In *Thalassa: L'Egée préhistorique et la mer*, edited by R. Laffineur and L. Basch, 273–310. *Aegaeum* 7. Liège: Université de Liège.

——— 1995. "The Last Days of the Pylos Polity." In *POLITEIA: Society and*

State in the Agean Bronze Age, edited by R. Laffineur and W.-D. Niemeier, 623–633. Aegaeum 12. Liège: Université de Liège.

Palaima, T. and J. Wright. 1985. "Ins and Outs of the Archives Rooms at Pylos: Form and Function in a Mycenaean Palace." *AJA* 89: 251–262.

Pamuk, S. 2007. "The Black Death and the Origins of the 'Great Divergence' across Europe, 1300–1600." *European Review of Economic History* 11: 298–317.

Panagiotaki, M. et al., 2005. "A Glass Workshop at the Mycenaean Citadel of Tiryns in Greece." In *Annales du 16ᵉ congres de l'Association internationale pour l'histoire du verre*, 14–18. Nottingham: L'Association.

Panvini, R. 1997. "Osservazioni sulle dinamiche socio-culturali a Dessueri." In *Prima Sicilia*, edited by M. Marazzi and S. Tusa, 492–501. Palermo: Assessorato al turismo.

——. 1997–1998. "Indagini e ricerche archaeologiche della Soprintendenza ai Beni culturali e ambientali di Caltanissetta." *Kokalos* 43/44: 17–40.

——, ed. 2003. *Butera: dalla preistoria all'età medievale*. Caltanissetta: Paruzzo.

Papadimitriou, A. 2003. "Οι Υπομυκηναϊκοί και Πρωτογεωμετρικοί τάφοι της Τίρυνθας. Ανάλυση και Ερμηνεία." In *ΑΡΓΟΝΑΥΤΗΣ: Τιμητικός Τόμος για τον καθηγητή Χρήστο Ντούμα*, edited by A. Vlachopoulos and K. Birtacha, 713–728. Athens: Academy of Athens.

——. 1963. "The Sanctuary of Artemis at Brauron." *Scientific American* 208: 111–122.

Papadimitriou, J. 1936. "Ausgrabungen auf Skyros." *AA* 51: 227–234.

Papadopoulos, J. 1993. "To Kill a Cemetery: The Athenian Kerameikos and the Early Iron Age in the Aegean." *JMA* 6.2: 175–206.

——. 1994. "Early Iron Age Potters' Marks in the Aegean." *Hesperia* 4: 437–507.

——. 1996. "Dark Age Greece." In *The Oxford Companion to Archaeology*, edited by B. Fagan, 253–255. Oxford: Oxford University Press.

——. 1997. "Phantom Euboeans." *JMA* 10: 191–219.

——. 2001. "Magna Achaea: Akhaian Late Geometric and Archaic Pottery in South Italy and Sicily." *Hesperia* 70.4: 373–460.

——. 2003. *Ceramicus Redivivus: The Early Iron Age Potters' Field in the Area of the Classical Athenian Agora*. Hesperia Supplements 31. Princeton, NJ: ASCSA.

——. 2011. "Phantom Euboeans – A Decade On." In *Euboea and Athens*, 113–133. Athens: Canadian Institute in Greece.

——. 2014. "Greece in the Early Iron Age: Mobility, Commodities, Polities, and Literacy." In *The Cambridge Prehistory of the Bronze and Iron Age Mediterranean*, edited by B. Knapp and P. van Dommelen, 178–195. Cambridge: Cambridge University Press.

Papadopoulos, J., B. Damaita, and J. Marston. 2011. "Once More with Feeling: Jeremy Rutter's Plea for the Abandonment of the Term Submycenaean Revisited." In *Our Cups Are Full: Pottery and Society in the Aegean Bronze Age*, edited by W. Gauß, M. Lindblom, R. Smith, and J. Wright, 187–202. Oxford: Archaeopress.

Papadopoulos, T. 1978–1979. *Mycenaean Achaea*. SIMA 55. Goteborg: P. Åstroms Förlag.

Papadopoulos, T. and L. Kontorli-Papadopoulou. 2000. "Four Late Bronze Age Italian Imports in Achaea." In *Periplus: Festschrift für Hans-Gunter Buchholz zu seinem achtzigsten Geburtstag*, edited P. Åstrom and D. Surenhagen, 143–146. Jonsered: P. Åstroms Förlag.

Papazoglou-Manioudaki, L. 1994. "A Mycenaean Warrior's Tomb at Krini Near Patras." *BSA* 89, 171–200.

Pappalardo, E. 2002. "Il *'Tripillar shrine'* di Kommos: alcune considerazioni." *CretAnt* 3: 263–274.

——— 2004. "Avori orientali da Creta. Il ruolo di Creta nella distribuzione degli avori nel Mediterraneo orientale." *CretAnt* 5, 207–47.

Pappi, E. 2012. "Οδός Ηρακλέους (οικόπεδο Α. Κουτρουμπή." *ArchDelt* 56–59 B4 Chr: 32–33.

Pare, C., ed. 2000. *Metals Make the World Go Round: The Supply and Circulation of Metals in Bronze Age Europe.* Oxford: Oxbow.

Parker, V. 1999. "Die Aktivitäten der Mykenäer in der Ost-Ägäis im Lichte der Linear B Tafeln." In *Floreant Studia Mycenaea*, edited by S. Deger-Jalkotzy, S. Hiller, and O. Panagl, 495–502. Vienna: Verlag der Österreichischen Akademie der Wissenschaften.

Parkinson, W. 2010. "Beyond the Peer: Social Interaction and Political Evolution in the Bronze Age Aegean." In *Political Economies of the Aegean Bronze Age*, edited by D. Pullen, 11–34. Oxford: Oxbow.

Parkinson, W. and M. Galaty. 2007. "Aegean States in Perspective: An Integrated Approach to State Formation in the Prehistoric Aegean." *American Anthropologist* 109.1: 113–129.

——— 2010. "Introduction: Interaction in Ancient Societies." In *Archaic State Interaction: The Eastern Mediterranean in the Bronze Age*, edited by W. Parkinson and M. Galaty, 3–28. Santa Fe, NM: School for Advanced Research Press.

Parkinson, W., D. Nakassis, and M. Galaty, eds. 2013. "Forum: Crafts, Specialists, and Markets in Mycenaean Greece." *AJA* 117: 413–459.

Payne, H. 1940. *Perachora I.* Oxford: Clarendon Press.

Peltenburg, E. 1986. "Ramesside Egypt and Cyprus." In *Acts of the International Archaeological Symposium "Cyprus between the Orient and the Occident,"* edited by V. Karageorghis, 147–79. Nicosia: Cyprus department of Antiquities.

——— 1991. "Greeting Gifts and Luxury Faience: A Context for Orientalizing Trends in Late Mycenaean Greece." In *Bronze Age Trade in the Mediterranean*, edited by N. Gale, 162–169. SIMA 90. Jonsered: P. Åstroms Förlag.

Pendlebury, J. 1930. *Aegyptiaca: A Catalogue of Egyptian Objects in the Aegean.* Cambridge: Cambridge University Press.

Perdrizet, P. 1908. *Fouilles de Delphes V.* Paris: A. Fontemoing.

Pernicka, E. 1995. "Crisis or Catharsis in Lead Isotope Analysis?" *JMA* 8: 59–64.

Persson, A. 1931. *The Royal Tombs at Dendra Near Midea.* Lund: C.W.K. Gleerup.

Petersen, W. 1975. "A Demographer's View of Prehistoric Demography." *CurrAnthr* 16: 227–245.

Petrie, F. 1886. *Naukratis. Part. I.* London: Trübner.

Petropoulos, M. 2002. "The Geometric Temple at Ano Mazaraki (Rakita) in Achaia." In *Gli Achei e l'Identita etnica degli Achei d'Occidente*, edited by E. Greco, 143–164. Paestum and Athens: Fondazione Paestum/Italian School at Athens.

Phappas, I. 2010. *Έλαιον ευώδες, τεθυωμένον: Τα αρωματικά έλαια και οι πρακτικές χρήσης τους στη μυκηναϊκή Ελλάδα και την αρχαία Εγγύς Ανατολή (14ος-13ος αι. π.Χ.).* Chania: Historical Folklore and Archaeological Society of Crete.

Phelps, W., Y. Lolos, and Y. Vlichos, eds. 1999. *The Point Iria Wreck: Interconnections in the Mediterranean ca. 1200 BC*. Athens: Hellenic Institute of Marine Archaeology.

Philadelpheus, A. 1923. "Ἀνασκαφή παρὰ τὸ χωρίον Σπάτα." *ArchDelt* 6: 131–138.

Philios, D. 1889. "Ἀρχαϊκαὶ κεφαλαὶ ἐξ Ἐλευσῖνος." *ArchEph* 1889: 171–194.

Philipp, H. 1981. *Bronzeschmuck aus Olympia. Olympia Forschungen 13*. Berlin: De Gruyter.

Phillips, J. 2008. *Aegyptiaca on the Island of Crete in Their Chronological Context: A Critical Review*. Vienna: Verlag der Österreichischen Akademie der Wissenschaften.

Pickles, S. and E. Peltenburg. 1998. "Metallurgy, Society, and the Bronze/Iron Transition in the East Mediterranean and the Near East." *RDAC* 1998: 67–100.

Piggott, S. 1965. *Ancient Europe, from the Beginning of Agriculture to Classic Antiquity*. Chicago: Aldine Publishing Company.

Pigott, V. 2012. "On Ancient Tin and Tin-Bronze in the Asian Old World: Further Comments." In *Eastern Mediterranean Metallurgy and Metalworking in the Second Millennium BC*, edited by V. Kassianidou and G. Papasavvas, 222–236. Oxford: Oxbow.

Pilali-Papasteriou, A. 1985. *Die bronzenen Tierfiguren aus Kreta*. Munich: Beck.

Platon, N. and E. Touloupa. 1964. "Oriental Seals from the Palace of Kadmus: Unique Discoveries in Boeotian Thebes." *Illustrated London News* Nov. 28, 1964: 859–861.

Pleiner, R. 1969. *Iron Working in Ancient Greece*. Prague: National Technical Museum.

Podzuweit, C. 1994. "Bemerkungen zur mykenischen Keramik von Tell el-Amarna." In *Festschrift für Otto-Herman Frey zum 65. Geburtstag*, edited by C. Dobiat, 457–474. Marburg: Hitzeroth.

Polanyi, K. 1957. "The Economy as Instituted Process." In *Trade and Market in the Early Empires*, edited K. Polanyi, C. Arensberg, and H. Pearson, 243–270. New York: The Free Press.

———. 1963. "Ports of Trade in Early Societies." *Journal of Economic History* 23.1: 30–45.

———. 1966. *Dahomey and the Slave Trade*. Seattle: University of Washington Press.

Polikreti, K. et al., 2011. "XRF Analysis of Glass Beads from the Mycenaean Palace of Nestor at Pylos, Peloponnesus, Greece: New Insight into the LBA Glass Trade." *JAS* 38.11: 2889–2896.

Popham, M. 1970. *The Destruction of the Palace at Knossos*. SIMA 12. Göteborg: P. Åström Förlag.

———. 1976. "Mycenaean-Minoan Relations between 1450 and 1400 BC" *BICS* 23: 119–121.

———. 1994. Precolonisation: Early Greek Contacts with the East." In *The Archaeology of Greek Colonization*, edited by G. Tzetkhadze and F. de Angelis, 11–34. Oxford: Oxford University Committee for Archaeology.

———. 1995. "An Engraved Near Eastern Bronze Bowl from Lefkandi." *OJA* 14.1: 103–107.

Popham, M. et al., 1984. *The Minoan Unexplored Mansion at Knossos*. Athens: British School at Athens.

Popham, M., P. Calligas, and H. Sackett. 1989. "Further Excavations of the Toumba Cemetery at Lefkandi, 1984 and 1986, a Preliminary Report." *AR* 35: 117–129.

———. eds. 1993. *Lefkandi II: The Protogeometric Building at Toumba. Part 2: The Excavation, Architecture, and Finds*. Athens: British School at Athens.

Popham, M. and I. Lemos. 1996. *Lefkandi II, Plates. The Early Iron Age Cemetery* at Toumba, the Excavations of 1981 to 1994. Athens: British School at Athens.

Popham, M. and E. Millburn. 1971. "The Late Helladic IIIC Pottery of Xeropolis: A Summary." *BSA* 66: 333–352.

Popham, M. and L. Sackett. 1968. *Excavations at Lefkandi, Euboea 1964–1966*. London: British School at Athens

Popham, M., H. Sackett, and P. Themelis, ed. 1979. *Lefkandi I. The Iron Age Settlement, the Cemeteries. Plates.* Athens: British School at Athens.

——— ed. 1980. *Lefkandi I. The Iron Age Settlement, the Cemeteries. Text.* Athens: British School at Athens.

——— eds. 1982. "Further Excavations of the Toumba Cemetery at Lefkandi, 1981." *BSA* 77: 213–248.

Popham, M., E. Touloupa and H. Sackett. 1982a. "The Hero of Lefkandi." *Antiquity* 56: 169–174.

——— 1982b. "Further Excavations of the Toumba Cemetery at Lefkandi, 1981." *BSA* 77: 213–248.

Porada, E. 1981. "The Cylinder Seals Found at Thebes in Boeotia." *Archiv fur Orientforschung* 28: 1–70.

Powell, B. 1991. *Homer and the Origin of the Greek Alphabet*. Cambridge: Cambridge University Press.

——— 2009. *Writing: Theory and History of the Technology of Civilization*. Malden, MA: Wiley-Blackwell.

Power, T. 2006. Review of *Le Prestige des Élites: Recherches sur les modes de reconnaissance sociale en Grèce entre les Xe et Ve siècles avant J.-C.* by A. Duplouy. *BMCR* 2006.08.22.

Pratt, C. 2016. "The Rise and Fall of the Transport Stirrup Jar in the Late Bronze Age Aegean." *AJA* 120.1, 27–66.

Prent, M. 2006. *Cretan Sanctuaries and Cults: Continuity and Change from Late Minoan IIIC to the Archaic Period*. Leiden: Brill.

Privitera-Bozza, S. 2013. *Principi, Pelasgi, e pescatori: L'Attica nella Tarda Età del Bronzo*. Paestum: Pandemos.

Pruss, A. 2002. "Ein Licht in der Nacht? Die Amuq-Ebene während der Dark Ages." In *Die nahöstlichen Kulturen und Griechenland an der Wende vom 2. Zum 1. Jahrtausend v. Chr.: Kontinuität und Wandel von Ktrukturen und Mechanismen kultureller Interaktion*, edited by W. Braun-Holzinger and H. Mattäus, 161–176. Möhnsee: Bibliopolis.

Pulak, C. 1998. "The Uluburun Ship: An Overview." *IJNA* 27, 188–224.

——— 2000. "The Copper and Tin Ingots from the Late Bronze Age Shipwreck at Uluburun." In *Anatolian Metal* I, edited by Ü. Yalçin, 137–157. Bochum: Dt. Bergbau-Museum.

——— 2008. "The Uluburun Shipwreck and Late Bronze Age Trade." In *Beyond Babylon: Art, Trade, and Diplomacy in the Second Millennium BC*, edited by J. Aruz, K. Benzel, and J. Evans, 289–310. New York: Metropolitan Museum of Art.

Pullen, D. 2013. "Exchanging the Mycenaean State." *AJA* 117.3: 437–445.

Qviller, B. 1981. "The Dynamics of Homeric Society." *SymbOslo* 56: 109–155.

Raaflaub, K. 1997. "Homeric Society." In *A New Companion to Homer*, edited by I. Morris and B. Powell, 624–648. Leiden: Brill.

Rahmstorf, L. 2003. "Kleinfunde aus Tiryns aus Terrakotta, Stein, Bein, und Glas/Fayence vornehmlich spätbronzezeitlicher Zeitstellung." *Archaeologisches Nachrichtenblatt* 8: 63–67.

——— 2005. "Clay Spools from Tiryns and Other Contemporary Sites. An Indication of Foreign Influence in LH IIIC?" In *Η Περιφέρεια του Μυκηναϊκού Κόσμου* 2, edited by

N. Kyparissi-Apostolika and M. Papakonstantinou, 397–416. Athens: Υπουργείο Πολιτισμού.

2008. "Tiryns XVI: Kleinfunde aus Tiryns. Terracotta, Stein, Bein, und Glas/Fayence, vornehmlich der späten Bronzezeit." Ph.D. dissertation, University of Heidelberg.

Rapp, G et al., 1978. "Analyses of the Metal Artifacts." In *Excavations at Nichoria in Southwest Greece: Volume I: Site, Environs, and Techniques*, edited by G. Rapp and S. Aschenbrenner, 166–181. Minneapolis: University of Minnesota.

Rathje, W. 1971. "The Origin and Development of Lowland Classic Maya Civilization." *AmerAnt* 36: 275–285.

Redfield, J. 1975. *Nature and Culture in the Iliad: The Tragedy of Hector*. Chicago: University of Chicago Press.

Redford, D. 1992. *Egypt Canaan, and Israel in Ancient Times*. Princeton, NJ: Princeton University Press.

2000. "Egypt and Western Asia in the Late New Kingdom: An Overview." In *The Sea Peoples and Their World: A Reassessment*, edited by E. Oren, 1–20. Philadelphia: University of Pennsylvania Museum.

Reed, C. 1984. "Maritime Traders in the Archaic Greek World." *AncW* 10: 31–44.

Rehak, P. 1999. "Aegean Natives in the Theban Tomb Paintings: The Keftiu Revisited." In *The Aegean and the Orient in the Second Millennium*, edited by E. Cline and D. Harris-Cline, 39–51. Aegaeum 18. Liège: Université de Liège.

Rehren, T. and E. Pusch. 2005. "Late Bronze Age Glass Production at Qantir-Piramesses, Egypt." *Science* 308 (5729): 1756–1758.

Renfrew, C. 1969. "Trade and Culture Process in European Prehistory." *CurrAnthr* 10: 151–169.

1972. *The Emergence of Civilization: The Cyclades and the Aegean in the Third Millennium BC*. London: Methuen.

1975. "Trade as Action at a Distance: Questions of Integration and Communication." In *Ancient Civilization and Trade*, edited by J. Sabloff and C. Lamberg-Karlovsky, 3–59. Albuquerque: University of New Mexico Press.

1977. "Alternative Models for Exchange and Spatial Distribution." In *Exchange Systems in Prehistory*, edited by T. Earle and J. Ericson, 71–90. New York: Academic Press.

Ridgway, D. 1992. *The First Western Greeks*. Cambridge: Cambridge University Press.

Risberg, C. 1995. "Production and Trade at Asine." In *Trade and Production in Premonetary Greece*, edited by C. Gillis, C. Risberg, and B. Sjöberg, 129–137. Jonsered: P. Åström Förlag.

Rizza G., ed. 2014. *Identità Culturale, Etnicità, Processi di Trasformazione a Creta fra Dark Age e Arcaismo*. Catania: Consiglio nazionale delle ricerche I.B.A.M.

Roebuck, C. 1972. "Some Aspects of Urbanization in Corinth." *Hesperia* 41: 96–127.

Rolley, C. 1977. *Fouilles de Delphes III. Les trépieds à Cuve Clouée*. Paris: Éditions de Boccard.

Romaiou, K. 1916. "Εκ τοῦ προϊστορικοῦ Θέρμου." *ArchDelt* 1: 225–279.

Rosen, R. 1990. "Poetry and Sailing in Hesiod's *Works and Days*." *ClAnt* 9: 99–113.

1997. "Homer and Hesiod." In *A New Companion to Homer*, edited by I. Morris and B. Powell, 463–488. Leiden: Brill.

Rössler, D. 1981. "Handwerker." In *Soziale Typenbegriffe III: Untersuchungen ausgewählter sozialer Typenbegriffe*, edited by E. Welkopf, 193–268. Berlin: Akademie-Verlag.

Roth, E. 1992. "Applications of Demographic Models to Palaeodemography." In *Skeletal Biology of Past Peoples: Research Methods*, edited by S. Saunders and M. Katzenberg, 175–188. New York: Wiley-Liss.

Rotstein, A. 1972. "Trade and Politics: An Institutional Approach." *West Canadian Journal of Anthropology* 3: 1–28.

Routledge, B. and K. McGeough. 2009. "Just What Collapsed? A Network Perspective on 'Palatial' and 'Private' Trade at Ugarit." In *Forces of Transformation: The End of the Bronze Age in the Mediterranean*, edited by C. Bachhuber and R. Roberts, 22–29. Oxford: Oxbow.

Rückl, S. 2008. "The Spatial Layout of the Protogeometric Settlement at Mitrou, East Lokris (Central Greece): Social Reality of a Greek Village in the 10th Century BC." M.A. thesis, University of Sheffield.

Rupp, D. 1988. "The Royal Tombs at Salamis (Cyprus): Ideological Messages of Power and Authority." *JMA* 1.1: 111–139.

Ruschenbusch, R. 1999. "Le Démographie d'Athènes au IVe siècle av. J.C." In *La Démographie historique antique*, edited by M. Bellancourt-Valdherand and J.-P. Corvisier, 91–95. Arras: Artois presses université.

Rutkowski, B. and K. Nowicki. 1996. *The Psychro Cave and Other Sacred Grottoes in Crete*. Warsaw: Art and Archaeology.

Rutter, J. 1983. "Some Thoughts on the Analysis of Ceramic Data Generated by Site 'Surveys.'" In *Archaeological Survey in the Mediterranean Area*, edited by D. Keller and D. Rupp, 137–142. BAR International Series 155. Oxford: B.A.R.

——. 1992. "Cultural Novelties in the Postpalatial Aegean World: Indices of Vitality or Decline?" In *The Crisis Years: The 12th Century BC from beyond the Danube to the Tigris*, edited by W. Ward and M. Joukowsky, 61–78. Dubuque, IA: Kendall/Hunt Publishers.

——. 2004. "Off-Island Imports to Kommos, Crete: New Discoveries and Identifications; Old Problems Unresolved." *BICS* 47: 189–190.

——. 2006. "Ceramic Imports of the Neopalatial and Later Bronze Age Eras." In *Kommos V: The Monumental Minoan Buildings*, edited by J. Shaw and M. Shaw, 646–688. Princeton, NJ: Princeton University Press.

——. 2014. "The Canaanite Transport Amphora within the Late Bronze Age Aegean: A 2013 Perspective on a Frequently Changing Picture." In *Ke-ra-me-ja: Studies Presented to Cynthia W. Shelmerdine*, edited by D. Nakassis, J. Gulizio and S. James, 53–69. Prehistory Monographs 46. Philadelphia: INSTAP.

Rystedt, E. 2006. "No Words, Only Pictures: Iconography in the Transition between the Bronze Age and the Early Iron Age in Greece." *OpAth* 24: 89–98.

Sackett, H. 1992. *Knossos from Greek City to Roman Colony*. BSA Supplementary Volume 21. Athens: British School at Athens.

Sakellarakis, G. 1992. "The Idaean Cave Ivories." In *Ivory in Greece and the Eastern Mediterranean from the Bronze Age to the Hellenistic Period*, edited by J. Fitton, 113–141. London: British Museum.

——. 1993. "Ivory Trade in the Aegean in the 8th Century BCE." In *Biblical Archaeology Today 1990*, edited by A. Biran, J Aviram, and A. Paris-Shadur, 345–366. Jerusalem: Israel Exploration Society.

——. 2006. "Με αφορμή κάποια λείψανα επίπλων στο Ιδαίο Άντρο." In *Ο Μυλοπόταμος από την αρχαιότητα ως σήμερα: περιβάλλον,* αρχαιολογία, ιστορία, λαογραφία, κοινωνολογία. III: Αρχαίοι Χρόνοι. Ιδαίο Άντρο, edited by E. Gavrilaki and G. Tzifopoulos, 137–181. Rethymno: Historical and Folklore Society of Rethymno.

———. 2013. Το Ιδαίο Άντρο: Ιερό και μαντείο. 3 vols. Athens: Athens Archaeological Society.

Sallares, R. 2007. "Ecology." In *The Cambridge Economic History of the Greco-Roman World*, edited by W. Scheidel, I. Morris, and R. Saller, 15–37. Cambridge: Cambridge University Press.

Salles, J.-F. 1995. *Rituel mortuaire et rituel social à Ras Shamra/Ougarit*. Oxford: Oxbow.

Salmon, J. 1984. *Wealthy Corinth: A History of the City to 338 BC*. Oxford: Oxford University Press.

Saltz, D. 1978. "Greek Geometric Pottery in the East." Ph.D. dissertation, Harvard University.

Sapouna-Sakellarakis, E. 1986. "Από την Εύβοια και τη Σκύρο." *AAA* 19: 27–44.

———. 2000. "Σκύρος." *ArchDelt* 50 B1 Chr: 316.

Sayre, E. et al., 2001. "Stable Lead Isotope Studies of Black Sea Anatolian Ore Sources and Related Bronze Age and Phrygian Artefacts from Nearby Archaeological Sites. Appendix: New Central Taurus Ore Data." *Archaeometry* 43.1: 77–115.

Sbonias, K. 2000a. "Introduction to Issues in Demography and Survey." In *Reconstructing Past Population Trends in Mediterranean Europe*, edited by J. Bintliff and K. Sbonias, 1–20. The Archaeology of Mediterranean Landscapes 1. Oxford: Oxbow.

———. 2000b. "Investigating the Interface between Regional Survey, Historical Demography, and Palaeodemography." In *Reconstructing Past Population Trends in Mediterranean Europe*, edited by J. Bintliff and K. Sbonias, 219–234. The Archaeology of Mediterranean Landscapes 1. Oxford: Oxbow.

Schachermeyr, F. 1979. *Kreta zur Zeit der Wanderungen: vom Ausgang der Minoïschen Ära bis zur Dorisierung der Insel*. Vienna: Verlag der Österreichischen Akademie der Wissenschaften.

———. 1980. *Griechenland im Zeitalter der Wanderungen: vom Ende der Mykenischen Ära bis auf die Dorier*. Vienna: Verlag der Österreichischen Akademie der Wissenschaften.

———. 1984. *Griechische Frühgeschichte: Ein Versuch frühe Geschichte wenigstens in Umrissen verständlich zu machen*. Vienna: Verlag der Österreichischen Akademie der Wissenschaften.

Schapp-Gourbellion, A. 2002. *Aux origines de la Grèce (XIIIe-VIIIe siècle avant notre ère). La genèse du politique*. Paris: Les Belles Lettres.

Scheibler, I. 1983. *Griechische Töpferkunst, Herstellung, Handel, und Gebrauch der antiken Tongefässe*. Munich: Beck.

Scheidel, W. 2003. "The Greek Demographic Expansion: Models and Comparisons." *JHS* 123: 120–140.

———. 2009. "Population and Demography." In *A Companion to Ancient History*, edited by A. Erskine, 134–146. Malden, MA: Wiley-Blackwell.

Schlörb-Vierneisel, B. 1966. "Eridanos–Nekropole." *AM* 81: 4–111.

Schneider, H. 1991. "Die Gaben des Prometheus. Technik im antiken Mittelmeerraum zwischen 750 v. Chr. und 500 n. Chr." In *Landbau und Handwerk 750 v. Chr bis 1000 n. Chr*, edited by H. Schneider and D. Hägermann, 17–313. Propyläen-Technikgeschichte 1. Berlin: Propyläen.

Schoep, I. 2006. "Looking beyond the First Palaces: Elites and the Agency of Power in EM III–MM II Crete." *AJA* 110: 37–64.

Schofield, A. 1991. *Interpreting Artefact Scatters. Contributions to Ploughzone Archaeology.* Oxford: Oxbow.

Schon, R. 2000. "On a Site and Out of Sight: Where Have Our Data Gone?" *JMA* 13: 107–111.

——— 2007. "Chariots, Industry, and Elite Power at Pylos." In *Rethinking Mycenaean Palaces II. Revised and Expanded Second Edition*, edited by M. Galaty and B. Parkinson, 133–145. Cotsen Institute of Archaeology at UCLA Monographs 60. Los Angeles: Cotsen Institute of Archaeology.

——— 2010. "Think Locally, Act Globally: Mycenaean Elites and the Late Bronze Age World-System." In *Archaic State Interaction*, edited by W. Parkinson and M. Galaty, 213–236. Santa Fe, NM: School for Advanced Research Press.

Schortman, E. and P. Urban. 1992. "The Place of Interaction Studies in Archaeological Thought." In *Resources, Power, and Interregional Interaction*, edited by E. Schortman and P. Urban, 3–25. New York: Plenum Press.

——— 2004. "Modeling the Roles of Craft Production in Ancient Political Economies." *JAR* 12: 185–226.

Schürmann, W. 1996. *Die Heiligtum des Hermes und der Aphrodite in Syme Viannou II: Die Tierstatuetten aus Metall.* Athens: Athens Archaeological Society.

Shaw, J. 1984. "Excavations at Kommos (Crete) during 1982–1983." *Hesperia* 53: 251–287.

——— 1989. "Phoenicians in Southern Crete." *AJA* 93: 165–183.

——— 1998. "Kommos in Southern Crete: An Aegean Barometer for East–West Interconnections." In *Eastern Mediterranean: Cyprus-Dodecanese-Crete, 16th–6th Century BC.*, edited by V. Karageorghis and N. Stampolidis, 13–27. Athens: University of Crete and A.G. Leventis Foundation.

——— 2000. "Ritual and Development in the Greek Sanctuary." In *Kommos IV: The Greek Sanctuary*, edited by J. Shaw and M. Shaw, 669–731. Princeton, NJ: Princeton University Press.

——— 2006. "Metals and Metalworking." In *Kommos V: The Monumental Minoan Buildings*, edited by J. Shaw and M. Shaw, 717–729. Princeton, NJ: Princeton University Press.

Shaw, J. and M. Shaw, eds. 1985. *A Great Minoan Triangle in Southcentral Crete: Kommos Haghia Triada, Phaistos.* Scripta Mediterranea 6. Toronto: Société d'études méditerranéennes.

——— eds. 1990. *Kommos I: The Kommos Region and Houses of the Minoan Town.* Princeton: Princeton University Press.

——— eds. 1995. *Kommos I: The Kommos Region and Houses of the Minoan Town, Part 1: The Kommos Region, Ecology, and the Minoan Industries.* Princeton, NJ: Princeton University Press.

——— eds. 2006. *Kommos V: The Monumental Minoan Buildings.* Princeton, NJ: Princeton University Press.

Shaw, M. 2000. "The Sculpture from the Sanctuary." In *Kommos IV: The Greek Sanctuary*, edited by J. Shaw and M. Shaw, 135–209. Princeton, NJ: Princeton University Press.

Shelmerdine, C. 1981. "Shining and Fragrant Cloth in Homeric Epic." In *The Ages of Homer: A Tribute to Emily Townsend Vermeule*, edited by J. Carter and S. Morris, 99–107. Austin: University of Texas Press.

——— 1985. *The Perfume Industry of Mycenaean Pylos.* Göteborg: P. Åströms Förlag.

——— 1997. "Workshops and Record Keeping in the Mycenaean World." In *TEXNH: Craftsmen, Craftswomen, and Craftmanship in the Aegean Bronze Age*, edited by R. Laffineur and P. Betancourt, 387–396. Aegaeum 16. Liege: Université de Liège.

1998. "Where Do We Go from Here? And How Can the Linear B Tablets Help Us Get There?" In *The Aegean and the Orient in the Second Millennium*, edited by E. Cline and D. Harris-Cline, 292–298. Aegaeum 18. Liège: Université de Liège.

2008. "Mycenaean Society." In *A Companion to Linear B: Mycenaean Greek Texts and Their World*, edited by Y. Duhoux and A. Morpurgo Davies, 115–158. Leuven: Peeters.

2011. "The Individual and the State in Mycenaean Greece." *BICS* 54: 19–28.

2013. "Economic Interplay among Households and States." *AJA* 117: 447–452.

Shelton, K. 2010. "Citadel and Settlement: A Developing Economy at Mycenae, the Case of Petsas House." In *Political Economies of the Aegean Bronze Age*, edited by D. Pullen, 184–204. Oxford: Oxbow.

Sherratt, A. and S. Sherratt. 1991. "From Luxuries to Commodities: The Nature of the Mediterranean Bronze Age." In *Bronze Age Trade in the Mediterranean*, edited by N. Gale, 351–386. SIMA 90. Jonsered: P. Åström Förlag.

2001. "Technological Change in the East Mediterranean Bronze Age: Capital, Resources, and Marketing." In *The Social Context of Technological Change: Egypt and the Near East, 1650–1550 BC*, edited by A. Shortland, 15–38. Oxford: Oxbow.

Sherratt, S. 1981. "The Pottery of LHIIIC and Its Significance." Ph.D. dissertation, University of Oxford.

1994. "Commerce, Iron, and Ideology: Metallurgical Innovation in 12th-11th Century Cyprus." In *Cyprus in the 11th Century BC*, edited by V. Karageorghis, 59–106. Nicosia: A.G. Leventis Foundation.

1998. "Sea Peoples and the Economic Structure of the Late Second Millennium in the Eastern Mediterranean." In *Mediterranean Peoples in Transition: Thirteenth to Early Tenth Centuries BCE*, edited by S. Gitin, A. Mazar, and E. Stern, 292–313. Jerusalem: Israel Exploration Society.

1999. "*E pur si muove*: Pots, Markets, and Values in the Second Millenium Mediterranean." In *The Complex Past of Pottery: Production, Circulation, and Consumption of Mycenaean and Greek Pottery (Sixteenth to Early Fifth Centuries BC)*, edited by J. Crielaard, V. Stissi, and G. van Wijngaarden, 163–211. Amsterdam: J.C. Gieben.

2000. "Circulation of Metals and the End of the Bronze Age in the Eastern Mediterranean." In *Metals Make the World Go Round: The Supply and Circulation of Metals in Bronze Age Europe*, edited by C. Pare, 82–98. Oxford: Oxbow.

2001. "Potemkin Palaces and Route-Based Economies." In *Economy and Politics in the Mycenaean Palace States*, edited by S. Voutsaki and J. Killen, 214–238. Cambridge: Cambridge Philological Society.

2003. "Visible Writing: Questions of Script and Identity in Early Iron Age Greece and Cyprus." *OJA* 22: 225–242.

2010. "The Aegean and the Wider World: Some Thoughts on a World-Systems Perspective." In *Archaic State Interaction*, edited by W. Parkinson and M. Galaty, 81–106. Santa Fe: School for Advanced Research Press.

2011. "Between Theory, Texts, and Archaeology: Working with the Shadows." In *Intercultural Contacts in the Ancient Mediterranean*, edited by K. Duistermaat and I. Regulski, 3–30. Leuven: Peeters.

Sherratt, S. and A. Sherratt. 1993. "The Growth of the Mediterranean Economy in the Early First Millenium BC." *WorldArch* 24.3: 361–378.

Shils, E. 1975. *Center and Periphery: Essays in Macrosociology*. Chicago: University of Chicago Press.

Simon, G. 1986. "The Archaic Votive Offerings and Cults of Ionia." Ph.D. dissertation, University of Michigan.

Singer, I. 1999. "A Political History of Ugarit." In *Handbook of Ugarit Studies*, edited by W. Watson and N. Wyatt, 603–733. Leiden: Brill.

——— 2000. "New Evidence on the End of the Hittite Empire." In *The Sea Peoples and Their World: A Reassessment*, edited by E. Oren, 21–34. Philadelphia: University of Pennsylvania Museum.

——— 2006. "Ships Bound for Lukka: A New Interpretation for the Companion Letters RS 94.2530 and RS 94.2523." *Altorientalische Forschungen* 33: 242–262.

——— 2011. "Schiffe nach Lukka: Eine Deutung des Briefpaares RS 94.2530 und RS 94.2523." In *Der Orient und die Anfänge Europas: Kulturelle Beziehungen von der Späten Bronzezeit bis zur Frühen Eisenzeit*, edited by H. Matthäus, N. Oettinger, and S. Schröder, 49–72. Wiesbaden: Harrassowitz Verlag.

Sjoberg, B. 2001. "Asine and the Argolid in the Late Helladic III Period: A Socio-Economic Study." Ph.D. dissertation, Uppsala University.

——— 2004. *Asine and the Argolid in the LHIII Period*. BAR International Series 1225. Oxford: Archaeopress.

Skias, A. 1898. "Παναρχαία ἐλευσινιακὴ νεκρόπολις." *ArchEph* 1898: 29–136.

Skon-Jedele, N. 1994. "Aigyptiaka: A Catalogue of Egyptian and Egyptianising Objects from Greek Archaeological Sites, ca. 1100–525 BC with Historical Commentary." Ph.D. dissertation, University of Pennsylvania.

Smith, A. 2010. *Mochlos IIB: Period IV, the Mycenaean Settlement and Cemetery: The Pottery*. Philadelphia: INSTAP.

Smith, J. 1992–1993. "The Pylos Jn Series." *Minos* 27/28: 167–259.

Smith, M. 2004. "The Archaeology of Ancient State Economies." *Annual Review of Anthropology* 33: 73–102.

Smith, T. 1987. *Mycenaean Trade and Interaction in the West Central Mediterranean, 1600–1000 BC*. BAR International Series 371. Oxford: B.A.R.

Smithson, E. 1968. "The Tomb of a Rich Athenian Lady, ca. 850 B.C." *Hesperia* 37.1: 77–116.

Snodgrass, A. 1971. *The Dark Age of Greece*. Edinburgh: Edinburgh University Press.

——— 1977. *Archaeology and the Rise of the Greek State*. Cambridge: Cambridge University Press.

——— 1980a. "Iron and Early Metallurgy in the Mediterranean." In *The Coming of the Age of Iron*, edited by T. Wertime and J. Muhly, 335–374. New Haven, CT: Yale University Press.

——— 1980b. *Archaic Greece: The Age of Experiment*. London: J.M. Dent.

——— 1983. "Heavy Freight in Archaic Greece." In *Trade in the Ancient Economy*, edited by P. Garnsey, K. Hopkins, and C. Whittaker, 16–26. London: Chatto and Windus.

——— 1985. "Greek Archaeology and Greek History." *ClAnt* 4.2: 193–207.

——— 1989. "The Coming of the Iron Age in Greece: Europe's Earliest Bronze/Iron Transition." In *The Bronze Age-Iron Age Transition in Europe: Aspects of Continuity and Change in European Societies c. 1200 to 500 BC*, edited by M. Stig Sørenson and R. Thomas, 22–35. BAR International Series 483. Oxford: Archaeopress.

1987. *An Archaeology of Greece.* Cambridge: Cambridge University Press.

1991. "Bronze Age Exchange: A Minimalist Position." In *Bronze Age Trade in the Mediterranean*, edited by N. Gale, 15–20. Göteborg: P. Åströms Förlag.

1993. "The Rise of the Polis." In *The Ancient Greek City-State*, edited by M.-H. Hansen, 30–40. Copenhagen: Royal Danish Academy of Sciences and Letters.

2000. *The Dark Age of Greece. An Archaeological Survey of the Eleventh to the Eighth Centuries BC.* 2nd ed. Edinburgh: Edinburgh University Press.

2006. *Archaeology and the Emergence of Greece.* Edinburgh: Edinburgh University Press.

Soles, J. 2008. "Metal Hoards from LMIB Mochlos, Crete." In *Aegean Metallurgy in the Bronze Age*, edited by I. Tzachili, 143–156. Athens: Ta Pragmata.

Sommer, F. 1937. "Ahhijawa und kein Ende?" *IGForsch* 55: 169–297.

Sommerfeld, W. 1995. "The Kassites of Ancient Mesopotamia: Origins, Politics, and Culture." In *Civilizations of the Ancient Near East*, edited by J. Sasson, 917–930. New York: Scribner.

Sotiriadis, G. 1900. "Ἀνασκαφαὶ ἐν Θέρμῳ." *ArchEph* 1900: 161–211.

Sourvinou-Inwood, C. 1993. "Early Sanctuaries, the Eighth Century and Ritual Space: Fragments of a Discourse." In *Greek Sanctuaries: New Approaches*, edited N. Marinatos and R. Hägg, 1–17. London and New York: Routledge.

Spartz, E. 1962. "Das Wappenschild des Herrin und der Herrin der Tiere in der minoisch-mykenischen und frühgriechischen Kunst." Ph.D. dissertation, Munich University.

Spaulding, A. 1953 "Statistical Techniques for the Discovery of Artifact Types." *AmerAnt* 18: 305–313.

Spriggs, M. 1984. "Another Way of Telling: Marxist Perspectives in Archaeology." In *Marxist Perspectives in Archaeology*, edited by M. Spriggs, 1–9. Cambridge: Cambridge University Press.

Spyropoulos, T. 1970. "Ἀγναντη." *ArchDelt* 25 B1 *Chr.* 235–237.

Stai, B. 1895. "Προϊστορικοὶ συνοικισκοὶ ἐν Ἀττικῇ καὶ Αἰγίνῃ." *ArchEph* 1895: 193–263.

Stamoudi, A. 1994. "Ταράτσα – Αγία Παρασκευή." *ArchDelt* 49 B1 *Chr.* 301–305.

Stampolidis, N. 1992. "Four Ivory Heads from the Geometric/Archaic Cemetery at Eleutherna." In *Ivory in Greece and the Eastern Mediterranean from the Bronze Age to the Hellenistic Period*, edited by J. Fitton, 141–162. London: British Museum.

1998. "Imports and Agalmata: The Eleuthernian Experience." In *Ανατολική Μεσόγειος. Κύπρος Δωδεκάνησα Κρήτη, 16ος-6ος αι. π. X.*, edited by N. Stampolidis and A. Karetsou, 175–185. Heraklion: University of Crete.

2003. "On the Phoenician Presence in the Aegean." In *Sea Routes...from Sidon to Huelva, Interconnections in the Mediterranean (16th–6th century BC)*, edited by N. Stampolidis, 217–232. Athens: Museum of Cycladic Art.

2004. *Eleutherna: Polis, Acropolis, Necropolis.* Athens: Ministry of Culture.

2008. *Ancient Eleutherna: West Sector*, T. Cullen and A. Oikonomou trans. Athens: Ministry of Culture.

2011. "Lux Cretensis: A Cretan Contribution to the Revision of the So-Called Dark Ages." In *The Dark Ages Revisited*, edited by A. Mazarakis Ainian, 760–768. Volos: University of Thessaly Press.

2014. "Eleutherna and the Idaean Cave: An Attempt to Reconstruct Interactions and Rituals." In *Identità Culturale, Etnicità, Processi di Trasformazione a Creta fra Dark Age e Arcaismo*, edited by G. Rizza, 395–420. Catania: Consiglio nazionale delle ricerche I.B.A.M.

Stampolidis, N. and A. Karetsou, eds. 1998. *Eastern Mediterranean: Cyprus-Dodecanese-Crete, 16th–6th cent. B.C.* Heraklion: University of Crete.

Stampolidis, N. and A. Kotsonas. 2006. "Phoenicians in Crete." In *Ancient Greece: From the Mycenaean Palaces to the Age of Homer*, edited by S. Deger-Jalkotzy and I. Lemos, 337–362. Edinburgh: Edinburgh University Press.

Starr, C. 1961. *The Origins of Greek Civilization*. New York: Knopf.

Stavropoulous, F. 1965. "Οδοῦ Καβαλόττι." *ArchDelt* 20 *Chr* 1: 75–85.

Steel, L. 1998. "The Social Impact of Mycenaean Imported Pottery on Cyprus." *BSA* 93: 285–296.

Stein, G. 1999a. *Rethinking World-Systems: Diasporas, Colonies, and Interaction in Uruk Mesopotamia*. Tucson: University of Arizona Press.

—— 1999b. "Rethinking World-Systems: Power, Distance, and Diasporas in the Dynamic of Interregional Interaction." In *World-Systems Theory in Practice: Leadership, Production, and Exchange*, edited by N. Kardulias, 153–177. Lanham, MD: Rowman & Littlefield Publishers.

—— 2002. "From Passive Periphery to Active Agents: Emerging Perspectives in the Archaeology of Interregional Interaction." *American Anthropologist* 104.3: 903–916.

Stern, B. et al., 2003. "Compositional Variations in Aged and Heated Pistacia Resin Found in Late Bronze Age Canaanite Amphorae and Bowls from Amarna, Egypt." *Archaeometry* 45.3: 457–469.

—— 2008. "New Investigations into the Uluburun Resin Cargo." *JAS* 35: 2188–2203.

Stockhammner, P. 2008. "Kontinuität und Wandel: Die Keramik der Nachpalastzeit aus der Unterstadt von Tiryns." Ph.D. dissertation, Ruprecht-Karls-Universität Heidelberg.

—— 2012. "Entangled Pottery: Phenomena of Appropriation in the Late Bronze Age Eastern Mediterranean." In *Materiality and Social Practice: Transformative Capacities of Intercultural Encounters*, edited by J. Maran and P. Stockhammer, 89–103. Oxford: Oxbow.

Stos-Gale, Z., M. Kayafa, and N. Gale. 1999. "The Origin of Metals from the Bronze Age Site of Nichoria." *OpAth* 24: 99–120.

Strøm, I. 1992. "Evidence from the Sanctuaries." In *Greece between East and West: 10th–8th Centuries BC*, edited by G. Kopcke and I. Tokumaru, 46–60. Mainz am Rhine: P. von Zabern.

Süel, A. 1998. "Ortaköy-Şapinuwa: Bir Hitit Merkezi." *Türkiye Bilimler Akademisi arkeoloji dergisi* 1: 73–80.

Süel, A. and M. Süel. 2000. "1998 yılı Ortaköy-Şapinuwa kazı çalişmaları." *Kazı Sonuçları Toplantısı* 21: 321–326.

Symeonoglou, S. 1973. *Kadmeia I: Mycenaean Finds from Thebes, Greece, Excavation at 14 Oedipus St*. Göteborg: P. Åströms Vörlag.

—— 1985. *The Topography of Thebes*. Princeton, NJ: Princeton University Press.

Syriopoulos, K. 1983–1984. *Ο Μεταβατικοί Χρόνοι από της μυκιναικής εις τήν αρχαικην περιoδον 1200 –700 π.Χ.* Athens: Archaeological Society of Athens.

—— 1995. *Η Προϊστορική Κατοίκησις της Ελλάδος και η Γένεσις του Ελληνικού*

Ἔθνους. Athens: Archaeological Society of Athens.

Tainter, J. 1988. *The Collapse of Complex Societies*. Cambridge: Cambridge University Press.

Tanasi, D. 2004a. "Per un Riesame degli Elementi di Tipo Miceneo nella cultura di Pantalica Nord." In *Le presenze micenee nel territorio siracusano*, edited by V. La Rosa, 337–381. Padua: Bottega D'Erasmo.

——— 2004b. "Per una Rilettura delle Necropoli sulla Montagna di Caltagirone." In *Le presenze micenee nel territorio siracusano*, edited by V. La Rosa, 399–445. Padua: Bottega D'Erasmo.

——— 2005. "Mycenaean Pottery Imports and Local Imitations: Sicily vs. Southern Italy." In *Emporia. Aegeans in the Central and Eastern Mediterranean*, edited by R. Laffineur and E. Greco, 561–569. Aegaeum 25. Liège: Université de Liège.

——— 2007. "A Late Bronze Age Upland Sanctuary in the Core of Sikania." In *Uplands of Ancient Sicily and Calabria*, edited by M. Fitzjohn, 157–170. London: Accordia Research Institute.

——— 2008. *La necropolis protostorica di Montagna di Caltagirone. Praehistorica Mediterranea* 1. Milan: Polimetrica.

——— 2010a. "A Mediterranean Connection: Nuovi dati sulle relazioni tra Malta e Creta agli Inizi dell'età del ferro." *CretAnt* 10.2: 519–538.

——— 2010b. "Vasellame metallico in Sicilia e nell'Arcipelago maltese nella seconda metà del II millennio a.C. Forme egee per pratiche religiose indigene." *Orizzonti: Rassegna di archeologia* 10: 11–28.

Tandy, D. 1997. *Warriors into Traders. The Power of the Market in Early Greece*. Berkeley: University of California Press.

Tandy, D. and W. Neale. 1996. *Hesiod, Works and Days: A Translation and Commentary for the Social Sciences*. Berkeley: University of California Press.

Taracha, P. 2003. "Is Tuthaliya's Sword Really Aegean?" In *Hittite Studies in Honor of Harry A. Hoffner Jr. on the Occasion of His 65th Birthday*, edited by G. Beckman, R. Beal, and G. McMahon, 367–376. Winona Lake, IN: Eisenbrauns.

Tartaron, T. 2004. *Bronze Age Landscape and Society in Southern Epirus, Greece*. BAR International Series 1290. Oxford: Archaeopress.

——— 2008. "Aegean Prehistory as World Archaeology: Recent Trends in the Archaeology of Bronze Age Greece." *Journal of Archaeological Research* 16: 83–161.

——— 2013. *Maritime Networks in the Mycenaean World*. Cambridge: Cambridge University Press.

Tartaron, T. et al., 2011. "The Saronic Harbors Archaeological Research Project (SHARP): Investigaions at Mycenaean Kalamianos, 2007–2009." *Hesperia* 80.4: 559–634.

Tartaron, T., D. Pullen, and J. Noller. 2006. "The Eastern Korinthia Archaeological Survey: Integrated Methods for a Dynamic Landscape." *Hesperia* 75: 453–523.

Taylour, W. 1958. *Mycenaean Pottery in Italy and Adjacent Areas*. Cambridge: Cambridge University Press.

——— 1970. "New Light on Mycenaean Religion." *Antiquity* 44: 270–280.

——— 1981. *Well Built Mycenae: The Helleno-British Excavations within the Citadel at Mycenae 1959–1969, fasc. 1: The Excavations*. Warminster: Aris & Phillips.

Terrenato, N. 2004. "Sample Size Matters! The Paradox of Global Trends and Local Surveys." In *Side-by-Side Survey: Comparative Regional Studies in the Mediterranean World*, edited by

S. Alcock and J. Cherry, 36–48. Oxford: Oxbow.

Themelis, P. 1979. "Γεωμετρικὸ νεκροταφεῖο." *ArchDelt* 26 Chr. B1: 108–110.

———. 1976. *Frühgriechische Grabbauten*. Mainz am Rhein: P. von Zabern.

———. 1983. "An 8th Century Goldsmith's Workshop at Eretria." In *The Greek Renaissance of the Eighth Century BC: Tradition and Innovation*, edited by R. Hägg, 157–165. Stockholm: Swedish Institute at Athens.

———. 2000. *Αρχαία Ελεύθερνα. Ανατολικός Τομέας*. Athens: ΤΑΠΑ.

Theocharis, D. 1961/2. "Ἀνασκαφαί εν Ιωλκό." *Prakt* 1961/2: 45–54.

———. 1963. "Νέα Ἀγχίαλος." *ArchDelt* 17 Chr: 179.

Theurillat, T. 2007. "Early Iron Age Graffiti from the Sanctuary of Apollo at Eretria." In *Oropos and Euboea in the Early Iron Age*, edited by A. Mazarakis Ainian, 332–335. Volos: University of Thessaly.

Thomatos, M. 2006. *The Final Revival of the Aegean Bronze Age: A Case Study of the Argolid, Corinthia, Attica, Euboea, the Cyclades, and the Dodecanese during LH IIIC Middle*. BAR International Series 1498. Oxford: Archaeopress.

Thompson, S. 2000. "The Still Hidden Landscape." *JMA* 13: 111–115.

Tite, M. et al., 2008. "The Scientific Examination of Aegean Vitreous Materials – Problems and Potential." In *Vitreous Materials in the Late Bronze Age Aegean*, edited by C. Jackson and E. Wager, 105–125. Oxford: Oxbow.

Todd, I. 2001. "Early Connections of Cyprus with Anatolia." In *The White Slip Ware of Late Bronze Age Cyprus*, edited by V. Karageorghis, 203–213. Vienna: Verlag der Österreichischen Akademie der Wissenschaften.

Toffolo, M. et al., 2013. "Towards an Absolute Chronology for the Aegean Iron Age: New Radiocarbon Dates from Lefkandi, Kalapodi, and Corinth." *PLoS ONE* 8(12): e83117. doi: 10.1371/journal.pone.0083117.

———. 2014. "Absolute Chronology of Megiddo, Israel, in the Late Bronze and Iron Ages: High-Resolution Radio-Carbon Dating." *Radiocarbon* 56.1: 221–244.

Tomlinson, J. 1995. "Chemical Analysis of Some Mycenaean Pottery from Perati, Attica." *ArchEph* 227–230.

Tomlinson, J., J. Rutter, and S. Hoffmann. 2010. "Mycenaean and Cypriot Late Bronze Age Ceramic Imports to Kommos: An Investigation by Neutron Activation Analysis." *Hesperia* 79.2: 191–231.

Touloupa, E. 1964a. "Bericht über die neuen Ausgrabungen in Theben." *Kadmos* 3/1: 25–27.

———. 1964b. "Ἀρχαιότητες καὶ μνημεία τῆς Βοιωτίας." *ArchDelt* 19 Chr. B2: 194–195.

———. 1965. "Ἀρχαιότητες καὶ μνημεία τῆς Βοιωτίας." *ArchDelt* 20 Chr. B2: 230–232.

———. 1966. "Ἀρχαιότητες καὶ μνημεία τῆς Βοιωτίας." *ArchDelt* 21 Chr. B2: 177–180.

Tournavitou, I. 1992. "The Ivories from the House of Sphinxes and the House of Shields: Techniques in a Palatial Workshop Context." In *Ivory in Greece and the Eastern Mediterranean from the Bronze Age to the Hellenistic Period*, edited by J. Fitton, 37–44. London: British Museum.

———. 1995. *The Ivory Houses at Mycenae*. Athens: British School at Athens.

Trundle, M. 2004. *Greek Mercenaries: From the Late Archaic Period to Alexander*. London and New York: Routledge.

Tsipopoulou, M. and K. Nowicki. 2003. "Μινωίτες και Μυκηναίοι στο τέλος του Χαλκού στην Ανατολική Κρητή." In *Η Περιφέρεια του Μυκηναϊκού Κόσμου 2*, edited by N. Kyparissi-Apostolika and

M. Papakonstantinou, 561–580. Athens: Υπουργείο Πολιτισμού.

Tsountas, C. 1891. "Ἐκ Μυκηνῶν." *ArchEph* 1–142.

Tylecote, R. 1987. *The Early History of Metallurgy in Europe*. London: Longman.

Uchitel, A. 1990. "Bronze-Smiths of Pylos and Silver Smiths of Ur." *Minos* 25: 195–202.

Vacek, A. 2014. "Euboean Imports at Al Mina in the Light of Recent Studies on the Pottery Finds from Woolley's Excavation." In *Archaeometric Analyses of Euboean and Euboean Related Pottery: New Results and Their Interpretations*, edited by M. Kerschner and I. Lemos, 141–156. Vienna: Austrian Archaeological Institute.

Vaessen, R. 2015. "The Ionian Migration and Ceramic Dynamics in Ionia at the End of the Second Millennium BC: Some Preliminary Thoughts." In *NOSTOI: Indigenous Culture, Migration, + Integration in the Aegean Islands + Western Anatolia during the Late Bronze + Early Iron Ages*, edited by N. Stampolidis, Ç. Maner, and K. Kopanias, 811–834. Koç University Press.

Vagnetti, L. 1993. "Mycenaean Pottery in Italy: Fifty Years of Study." In *Wace and Blegen: Pottery as Evidence for Trade in the Aegean Bronze Age 1939–1989*, edited by C. Zerner, 143–154. Amsterdam: J.C. Gieben.

——— 1998. "Variety and Function of the Aegean Derivative Pottery in the Central Mediterranean in the Late Bronze Age." In *Mediterranean Peoples in Transition. Thirteenth to Early Tenth Centuries BCE*, edited by S. Gitin, A. Mazar, and E. Stern, 66–77. Jerusalem: Israel Exploration Society.

——— 1999. "Mycenaean Pottery in the Central Mediterranean: Imports and Local Production in Their Context." In *The Complex Past of Pottery*, edited by J. Crielaard, V. Stissi, and G. van Wijngaarden, 137–161. Amsterdam: J.C. Gieben.

Vagnetti, L. and R. Jones. 1988. "Towards the Identification of Local Mycenaean Pottery in Italy." in *Problems in Greek Prehistory*, edited by E. French and K. Wardle, 335–348. Bristol: Bristol Classical Press.

——— 1991. "Traders and Craftsmen in the Central Mediterranean: Archaeological and Archaeometric Research." In *Bronze Age Trade in the Mediterranean*, edited by J. Cherry et al., 127–147. Jonsered: P. Åströms Förlag.

Vagnetti, L. et al., 2006. "Ceramiche egeomicenee dalle Marche: analisi archeometriche e inquadramento preliminare dei risultati." In *Atti della XXXIX Riunione Scientifica dell'Istituto Italiano di Preistoria e Protohistoria*, 1159–1172. Florence: Istituto italiano di preistoria e protostori.

——— 2009. "Ceramiche egee e di tipo egeo lungo i versanti adriatico e ionico della penisola italiana: situazioni a confront." In *From the Aegean to the Adriatic: Social Organizations, Modes of Exchange and Interaction in the Post-Palatial Times (12th–11th BC)*, edited E. Borgna and P. Cassola-Guida, 171–183. Rome: Quasar.

van de Mieroop, M. 2007. *The Eastern Mediterranean in the Age of Ramesses II*. Malden, MA: Wiley-Blackwell.

van den Hout, T. 2011. "The Written Legacy of the Hittites." In *Insights into Hittite History and Archaeology*, edited by H. Genz and D. Mielke, 47–84. Leuven: Peeters.

Van Effenterre, H. 1985. *Mycènes, vie et mort d'une civilization: la seconde fin du monde*. Paris.

van Soldt, W. 1995. "Ugarit: A Second Millennium Kingdom on the Mediterranean Coast." *CANE* 2: 1255–1266.

van Wijngaarden, G. 2002. *The Use and Appreciation of Mycenaean Pottery in the Levant, Cyprus, and Italy (ca. 1600–1200 BC)*. Amsterdam: Amsterdam University Press.

―― 2011. "Tokens of a Special Relationship? Mycenaeans and Egyptians." In *Intercultural Contacts in the Ancient Mediterranean*, edited by K. Duistermaat and I. Regulski, 225–252. Leuven: Peeters.

―― 2012. "Trade Goods Reproducing Merchants? The Materiality of Mediterranean Late Bronze Age Exchange." In *Materiality and Social Practice: Transformative Capacities of Intercultural Encounters*, edited by J. Maran and P. Stockhammer, 61–72. Oxford: Oxbow.

Varoufakis, G. 1982. "The Origin of Mycenaean and Geometric Iron." In *Early Metallurgy in Cyprus, 4000–500 BCE*, edited by J. Muhly, R. Maddin, and V. Karageorghis, 315–319, Nicosia: The Foundation.

Ventris, M. and J. Chadwick. 1956. *Documents in Mycenaean Greek*. Cambridge: Cambridge University Press.

―― 1973. *Documents in Mycenaean Greek*. 2nd ed. Cambridge: Cambridge University Press.

Verdan, S. 2013. *Le sanctuaire d'Apollon Daphnéphoros à l'époque géometrique. Eretria XXII*. Bern: Francke.

―― 2015. "Geometric Eretria: Some Thoughts on Old Data." In *Zagora in Context: Settlements and Intercommunal Links in the Geometric Period (900–700 BC)*, edited by J.-P. Descœudres and S. Paspalas, 181–190. *Mediterranean Archaeology 25*. Sydney: University of Sydney.

Verdelis, N. and K. Davaras. 1968. "Ἀνασκαφὴ Ἀναβύσσου." *ArchDelt* 21 B1 Chr: 97–98.

Verlinden, C. 1984. *Les Statuettes anthropomorphes crétoises en bronze et en plomb, du IIIe millénaire au VIIe siècle av. J.-C. Archaeologia transatlantica* 4. Providence: Brown University.

Vermeule, E. 1960. "The Mycenaeans in Achaia." *AJA* 64.1: 1–21.

Vetters, M. 2011. "A Clay Ball with a Cypro-Minoan Inscription from Tiryns." *AA* 2011/2: 1–49.

Vianello, A. 2005. *Late Bronze Age Mycenaean and Italic Products in the West Mediterranean. BAR International Series* 1439. Oxford: Archaeopress.

―― 2011. "One Sea for All: Intercultural, Social, and Economic Contacts in the Bronze Age Mediterranean." In *Intercultural Contacts in the Ancient Mediterranean*, edited by K. Duistermaat and I. Regulski, 411–426. Leuven: Peeters.

Virolleaud, C. 1957. *Le Palais Royale d'Ugarit II*. Paris: P. Geuthner.

―― 1965. *Le Palais Royale d'Ugarit V. Textes en cunéiformes alphabétiques des archives sud, sud-ouest et du petit palais*. Paris: P. Geuthner.

Voigtländer, W. 2004. *Teichiussa*. Rahden in Westfalen: VML, M. Leidorf.

Vonhoff, C. 2008. *Darstellungen von Kampf und Krieg in der minoischen und mykenischen Kultur*. Rahden: Verlag Marie Leidorf.

von Reden, S. 1995. *Exchange in Ancient Greece*. London: Duckworth.

Voskos, I. and B. Knapp. "Cyprus at the End of the Late Bronze Age: Crisis and Colonization or Continuity and Hybridization." *AJA* 112.4: 659–684.

Voutsaki, S. 1995. "Social and Political Processes in the Mycenaean Argolid: The Evidence from the Mortuary Practices." In *Politeia: Society and State in the Aegean Bronze Age*, edited by R. Laffineur and W.-D. Niemeier, 55–65. *Aegaeum* 12. Liège: Université de Liège.

―― 1997. "The Creation of Value and Prestige in the Aegean Late Bronze Age." *JEA* 5.2: 34–52.

1998. "Mortuary Evidence, Symbolic Meanings, and Social Change: A Comparison between Messenia and the Argolid in the Mycenaean Period." In *Cemetery and Society in the Aegean Bronze Age*, edited by in K. Branigan, 41–58. Sheffield: Sheffield Academic Press.

1999. "The Shaft Grave Offerings and Symbols of Power and Prestige." In *Bronze Age Elites: Symbols of Power and Prestige in the Bronze Age Aegean*, edited by I. Kilian, 103–117. Mainz: Römisch-Germanisches Zentralmuseums.

2001. "Economic Control, Power, and Prestige: The Archaeological Evidence." In *Economy and Politics in the Mycenaean Palace States*, edited by S. Voutsaki and J. Killen, 195–213. Cambridge: Cambridge Philological Society.

2010. "From the Kinship Economy to the Palatial Economy: The Argolid in the Second Millennium BC." In *Political Economies of the Aegean Bronze Age*, edited by D. Pullen, 86–111. Oxford: Oxbow.

Wace, A. 1956. "Mycenae, 1939–1955: Preliminary Report on the Excavations of 1955." *BSA* 51: 103–122.

1979. *Excavations at Mycenae, 1939–1955*. London: British School at Athens.

Wace, A. and F. Stubbings, eds. 1962. *A Companion to Homer*. London: Macmillan.

Wachsmann, S. 1987. *Aegeans in the Theban Tombs*. Leuven: Peeters.

Waldbaum, J. 1978. *From Bronze to Iron: The Transition from the Bronze Age to the Iron Age*. Göteborg: P. Åström.

1982. "Bimetallic Objects from the Eastern Mediterranean and the Question of the Dissemination of Iron." In *Early Metallurgy in Cyprus, 4000–500 BCE*, edited by J. Muhly, R. Maddin, and V. Karageorghis, 325–350. Nicosia: The Foundation.

1994. "Early Greek Contacts with the Southern Levant, ca. 1000–600 BC: the Eastern Perspective." *BASOR* 293: 53–66.

1999. "The Coming of Iron in the Eastern Mediterranean: Thirty Years of Archaeological and Technological Research." In *The Archaeometallurgy of the Asian Old World*, edited by V. Pigott, 27–57. Philadelphia: University of Pennsylvania.

Waldstein, C. 1902. *The Argive Heraeum I*. Boston, MA: Houghton Mifflin.

Wallace, S. 2000. "Case Studies of Settlement Change in Early Iron Age Crete." *AeA* 4: 61–99.

2003. "The Perpetuated Past: Re-Use or Continuity in Material Culture and the Structuring of Identity in Early Iron Age Crete." *BSA* 98: 251–277.

2005. "Last Chance to See? Karfi in the Twenty-First Century." *BSA* 100: 215–274.

2006. "The Gilded Cage? Settlement and Socioeconomic Change after 1200 B.C.: A Comparison of Crete and Other Aegean Regions." In *Ancient Greece: From the Mycenaean Palaces to the Age of Homer*, edited by S. Deger-Jalkotzy and I. Lemos, 619–664. Edinburgh Leventis Series 3. Edinburgh: Edinburgh University Press.

2010. *Ancient Crete: From Successful Collapse to Democracy's Alternatives, Twelfth to Fifth Centuries BC*. Cambridge: Cambridge University Press.

Wallerstein, I. 1974. *The Modern World System I: Capitalist Agriculture and the Origins of the European World-Economy in the Sixteenth Century*. New York: Academic Press.

Walløe, L. 1999. "Was the Disruption of the Mycenaean World Caused by Repeated Epidemics of Bubonic Plague?" *OpAth* 24: 121–126.

Walsh, V. and W. MacDonald. 1992. "House Construction and Town

Layout." In *Excavations at Nichoria in Southwest Greece: Volume II: The Bronze Age Occupation*, edited by W. MacDonald and N. Wilkie, 455–466. Minneapolis: University of Minnesota.

Wardle, K. 1973. "A Group of Late Helladic IIIB2 Pottery from within the Citadel at Mycenae." *BSA* 68: 297–348.

Wardle, K. and D. Wardle. 2003. "Prehistoric Thermon: Pottery of the Late Bronze Age and Early Iron Age." In *Η Περιφέρεια του Μυκηναϊκού Κόσμου 2*, edited by N. Kyparissi-Apostolika and M. Papakonstantinou, 147–156. Athens: Υπουργείο Πολιτισμού.

Warren, P. 1987. "Absolute Dating of the Aegean Late Bronze Age." *Archaeometry* 29: 205–221.

Warren, P. and V. Hankey. 1989. *Aegean Bronze Age Chronology*. Bristol: Bristol Classical Press.

Watkins, J. 2003. "Beyond the Margin: American Indians, First Nations, and Archaeology in North America." *AmerAnt* 68: 273–285.

Watrous, L. 1985. "Late Bronze Age Kommos: Imported Pottery as Evidence for Foreign Contact." In *A Great Minoan Triangle in South Central Crete: Kommos Haghia Triadha, Phaistos*, edited by J. Shaw and M. Shaw, 7–11. *Scripta Mediterranea* VI. Toronto: Society for Mediterranean Studies.

———. 1987. "The Role of the Near East in the Rise of the Cretan Palaces." In *The Function of Minoan Palaces*, edited by R. Hägg and N. Marinatos, 65–70. Stockholm.

———. 1989. "A Preliminary Report on Imported 'Italian' Wares from the Late Bronze Age Site of Kommos on Crete." *Studi micenei ed egeo-anatolici* 27: 69–79.

———. 1992. *Kommos III: The Late Bronze Age Pottery*. Princeton: Princeton University Press.

———. 1996. *The Cave Sanctuary of Zeus at Psychro: A Study of Extra-Urban Sanctuaries in Minoan and Early Iron Age Crete*. Aegaeum 15. Liège: Université de Liège.

———. 1998. "Egypt and Crete in the Early Middle Bronze Age: A Case of Trade and Cultural Diffusion." In *The Aegean and the Orient in the Second Millennium*, edited by E. Cline and D. Harris-Cline, 19–28. Aegaeum 18. Liège: Université de Liège.

Watrous, L., P. Day, and R. Jones. 1998. "The Sardinian Pottery from the Late Bronze Age Site of Kommos in Crete: Description, Chemical and Petrographic Analyses, and Historical Context." In *Sardinian and Aegean Chronology: Towards the Resolution of Relative and Absolute Dating in the Mediterranean*, edited by M. Balmuth and R. Tykot, 337–340. Oxford: Oxbow.

Webster, G. 1996. *A Prehistory of Sardinia, 2300–500 BC*. Sheffield: Sheffield Academic Press.

Wedde, M. 1998. "Across the Bronze/Iron Divide: Thoughts on Continuity and Discontinuity: Ship Building as a Case Study." Abstract of a lecture in *Trade and Production VIII: Crossing Borders*. Swedish Institute, Athens, December 12–13, 1998.

———. 2006. "Pictorial Evidence for Partial Survival in the Greek Bronze to Iron transition." In *Pictorial Pursuits. Figurative Painting on Mycenaean and Geometric Pottery*, edited by E. Rystedt and B. Wells, 255–269. Stockholm: Swedish Institute at Athens.

van Wees, H. 1992. *Status Warriors. War, Violence, and Society in Homer and History*. Amsterdam: J.C. Gieben.

———. 1999. "Introduction: Homer and Early Greece." In *Homer: Critical Assessments*, edited by I. de Jong, 1–32. London and New York: Routledge.

Weiler, G. 2001. *Domos Theiou Basileos: Herrschaftsformen und Herrschaftsarchitektur in den Siedlungen der Dark Ages*. Munich: Saur.

Wells, B., ed. 1983a. *Asine II, Fasc. 4. The Protogeometric Period, Part 2: The Analysis of the Settlement*. Stockholm: Swedish Institute at Athens.

———, ed. 1983b. *Asine II, Fasc. 4. The Protogeometric Period, Part 3: Catalogue of Pottery and Other Artefacts*. Stockholm: Swedish Institute at Athens.

———. 1996. *The Berbati-Limnes Archaeological Survey 1988–1990*. Jonsered: P. Åströms Förlag.

Weninger, B. and R. Jung. 2009. "Absolute Chronology and the End of the Aegean Bronze Age." In *LH IIIC Chronology and Synchronisms III*, edited by S. Deger-Jalkotzy and A. Bächle, 373–416. Vienna: Verlag der österreichischen Akademie der Wissenschaften.

Wertime, T. 1982. "Cypriot Metallurgy against the Backdrop of Mediterranean Pyrotechnology: Energy Reconsidered." In *Early Metallurgy in Cyprus 4000–500 BC*, edited by J. Muhly et al., 351–361. Larnaca: The Foundation.

———. 1983. "The Furnace versus the Goat: The Pyrotechnologic Industries and Mediterranean Deforestation in Antiquity." *JFA* 10: 445–452.

West, M. 1978. *Hesiod. Works and Days*. Oxford: Oxford University Press.

———. 1988. "The Rise of the Greek Epic." *JHS* 108: 151–172.

Whitelaw, T. 2001a. "From Sites to Communities: Defining the Human Dimensions of Minoan Urbanism." In *Urbanism in the Aegean Bronze Age*, edited by K. Branigan, 15–37. Sheffield Studies in Aegean Archaeology 4. Sheffield: Sheffield Academic Press.

———. 2001b. "Reading between the Tablets: Assessing Mycenaean Palatial Involvement in Ceramic Production and Consumption." In *Economy and Politics in the Mycenaean Palace States*, edited by S. Voutsaki and J. Killen, 51–79. Cambridge: Cambridge Philological Society.

———. 2004. "Estimating the Population of Neopalatial Knossos." In *Knossos: Palace, City, State*, edited by G. Cadogan, E. Hatzaki, and A. Vasilakis, 147–158. British School at Athens Studies 12. London: British School at Athens.

Whitley, J. 1986. "Style, Burial, and Society in Dark Age Greece: Social, Stylistic, and Mortuary Change in the Two Communities of Athens and Knossos between 1100 and 700 B.C." Ph.D. dissertation, Cambridge University.

———. 1988. "Early States and Hero Cults: A Re-appraisal." *JHS* 108: 173–182.

———. 1991a. *Style and Society in Dark Age Greece: The Changing Face of a Pre-Literate Society*. Cambridge: Cambridge University Press.

———. 1991b. "Social Diversity in Dark Age Greece." *BSA* 86: 341–365.

———. 1996. "Gender and Hierarchy in Early Athens: The Strange Case of the Disappearance of the Rich Female Grave." *Metis* 11: 209–231.

———. 2002. "Objects with Attitude: Biographical Facts and Fallacies in the Study of Late Bronze Age and Early Iron Age Warrior Graves." *CAJ* 12: 217–232.

Whitley, J. et al., 2005–2006. "Archaeology in Greece 2005–2006." *AR* 52: 1–112.

Williams, C. 1982. "The Early Urbanization of Corinth." *AsAtene* 60: 143–184.

Williamson, O. 1985. *The Economic Institutions of Capitalism: Firms, Markets, Relational Contracting*. New York: Free Press.

———. 1996. *The Mechanics of Governance*. New York: Oxford University Press.

Winter, I. 1976. "Phoenician and North Syrian Ivory Carving in Historical Context. Question of Style and Distribution." *Iraq* 38: 1–22.

1995. "Homer's Phoenicians: History, Ethnography, or Literary Trope? [A Perspective on Early Orientalism]." In *Ages of Homer*, edited by J. Carter and S. Morris, 247–271. Austin: University of Texas Press.

Wriedt Sørensen, K. 1988. "Greek Pottery Found in Cyprus." *Acta Hyperborea* 1: 12–32.

Wright, J. 2008. "Early Mycenaean Greece." In *The Cambridge Companion to the Aegean Bronze Age*, edited by C. Shelmerdine, 230–257. Cambridge: Cambridge University Press.

Xenaki-Sakellariou, A. 1985. *Ο θαλαμωτοί τάφοι τῶν Μυκηνῶν ἀνασκαφῆς Χρ. Τσούντα (1887–1898)*. Paris: de Boccard.

Yalouri, E. 1994. "Πήλινα σπαιρίδια." In *Eleutherna II.2*, edited by N. Stampolidis, 172–173. Rethymno: University of Crete.

Yasur-Landau, A. 2010. *The Philistines and Aegean Migration at the End of the Late Bronze Age*. Cambridge: Cambridge University Press.

Yasur-Landau, A. and Y. Goren. 2004. "A Cypro-Minoan Potmark from Aphek." *TelAviv* 31: 22–31.

Yener, K. 2000. *The Domestication of Metals: The Rise of Complex Metal Industries in Anatolia*. Leiden: Brill.

Yener, K. et al., 1989. "Kestel: An Early Bronze Age Source of Tin Ore in the Taurus Mountains, Turkey." *Science* 244.4901: 200–203.

1991. "Stable Lead Isotope Studies of Central Taurus Ore Sources and Related Artifacts from Eastern Mediterranean Chalcolithic and Bronze Age Sites." *JAS* 18.5: 541–577.

Yon, M. 1992a. "The End of the Kingdom of Ugarit." In *The Crisis Years: The 12th Century BC – From Beyond the Danube to the Tigris*, edited by W. Ward and M. Joukowsky, 111–122. Dubuque, IA: Kendall/Hunt Publishers.

1992b. "Ugarit: The Urban Habitat. The Present State of the Archaeological Picture." *BASOR* 286: 19–34.

Zaccagnini, C. 1973. *Lo scambio dei doni nel Vicino Oriente durante i secoli XV-XIII*. Rome: Centro per le antichità e la storia dell'arte del Vicino Oriente.

1983. "Patterns of Mobility among Ancient Near Eastern Craftsmen." *JNES* 42: 245–264.

2000. "The Interdependence of the Great Powers." In *Amarna Diplomacy: The Beginnings of International Relations*, edited by R. Cohen and R. Westbrook, 141–153. Baltimore: Johns Hopkins University Press.

Zimmermann, J.-L. 1989. *Les Chevaux de bronze dans l'art géométrique grec*. Geneva: P. von Zabern.

Zuckerman, S. D. Ben-Shlomo, P. Mountjoy, and H. Mommsen. 2009. "A Provenance Study of Mycenaean Pottery from Northern Israel." *JAS* 30: 1–8.

Zwicker, U. 1985. "Investigation of Samples from the Metallurgical Workshops at Kition." In *Excavations at Kition V. The Pre-Phoenician Levels*, edited by V. Karageorghis and M. Demas, 403–429. Nicosia: Department of Antiquities.

INDEX

Achaea, 7
  bronze rings in burials, 169
  bronze supply in IIIC, 173
  contacts with Italy during IIIC, 243
  flourishing in IIIC, 256
  IIIC imports in, 85, 91, 122, 174, 258, 259
  IIIC pottery in Italy, 200
  immigration in IIIC, 173
  possible Mycenaean state, 235
  warrior tombs in IIIC, 256
Achaea Klauss, 85
Aegina, 267
Aetolo-Akarnania
  IIIC imports in, 85
Agia Pelagia, 124
Agia Varvara, 85
Agios Elias, 185
Ahhiyawa, 43, 46, 252
  question, 36–38
Aigio, 85
Al Mina, 22, 203
Alaca Höyük, 252
Alašiya. See Cyprus
Amarna letters
  commercial exchange in, 44
  general background, 36
  gift-exchange in, 38–43
  interpretive problems with, 66
  objects exchanged in, 60–61
  relevance to Greek LBA, 36–38
Amathus, 201, 204
Ammurapi of Ugarit, 37, 46
Amnisos, 187, 267
Amuq plain, 200
Anatolia, 6, 9
  Cypriot finds from, 252
  Greek Geometric pottery in, 203, 204
  Greek PG pottery in, 201
  IIIC Mycenaean pottery in, 200
  pottery at Kommos, 82
Anavyssos, 188
  Geometric imports, 103, 105
andirons
  in Geometric graves, 268–270
Ano Mazaraki, 8
Anthedon, 85

Aphrati, 187, 267
Apulia, 198, 200, 202, 203, 205
Archaeological survey, 137–140, 250–251
Argive Heraion
  Geometric imports, 104
Argolid, 7
  concentration of IIIB imports in, 33, 76
  emigration in IIIC, 173
  hoarding, 172
  IIIB imports in, 259
  IIIC imports in, 85
  IIIC pottery in Italy, 200
  in the IIIC period, 256
  palaces in, 5
  PG gold, 185
  PG imports in, 100
  presence of Mycenaean state, 235
  source of ceramic exports in IIIB, 193, 197, 253
  Southern, PG sites from survey, 217
Argos, 5, 235
  andirons, 269
  gold in PG, 185, 188
  PG imports in, 100, 122
  spits, 269
Armenoi
  IIIB imports, 84
Artemis Orthia
  Geometric imports, 103, 104
  Geometric ivories, 186
Asarlik, 202
Ashdod, 193, 199, 257
Ashkelon, 189, 199, 257
Asine, 7
  bronzes, 175, 261
  ironworking, 242, 271
  PG imported objects in, 100, 122
Assyrians
  in Ugarit, 45
Atalanti, 185, 263
Athens, 8, 235, 236
  and Miletus in PG, 202
  EIA ceramic production, 243
  Geometric glass and faience, 187
  Geometric gold, 188
  Geometric imports, 103
  Geometric imports in tombs, 105

345

Geometric ivories, 186
hoarding, 172
PG bronzes, 181
PG gold, 185
population in EIA, 216, 237
Attic
  pottery abroad, 201, 203, 204
Attica
  IIIC imports in, 174

Bademgediği Tepe, 201
Bakla Tepe, 201
beads
  as trinkets, 145
  Geometric imports at Eretria, 105
  Geometric imports at Perachora, 104
  IIIC imports at Knossos, 91
  number known from IIIB period, 184
  on the Uluburun ship, 152, 183
  prominent among PG imports, 100
Boeotia, 197
  hoarding, 172
Boğazköy. See Hattuša
Broglio di Trebisacce, 193
bronze. See Metals
  Jn tablets, 173
bronze shortage. See Metals, bronze shortage
Bruttium, 269
Burnaburiash of Babylon, 38, 40, 41

Campania, 205
Canaanite jar
  at IIIA/B Mycenae, 79
  at IIIB Mochlos, 84
  at IIIB Tiryns, 79
  at IIIC Tiryns, 89
  at Mycenae, 77, 79
  Cypriot potmarks on, 193
  imports from IIIB mainland, 82, 124, 249, 263
  on the Uluburun ship, 152, 183
  sherds from IIIC deposits, 185
Canale, 205
Çatal Hüyük, 200, 201, 202
Chania, 7, 235, 236
  IIIB bronzes, 178
  IIIB imports, 84, 124
  IIIC bronzes, 179
  presence of Linear B tablets, 32
  production of TSJs, 197
Chios, 201
Chronology, 4
  and import counts, 113–116
  Protogeometric period, 115–116
Cilicia, 199
Çine Tepecik, 201
Collapse, 6, 46–47, 280
  and trade in IIIC Greece, 255–256

evidence for severance of trade routes during, 8, 9, 17, 260–262
commodities. See consumption of commodities
  exchange in LBA documents, 61
comparative history, 13–14
consumption
  and demography, 240–241
  as effective approach to import evidence, 24–25
  of bronzes
    significance of changes in, 165–172
  of commodities, 182–189
  of Greek pottery abroad
    Geometric, 201–208
    Mycenaean, 190–197
  of imports
    contextual change in, 120–124
    in PG Greece, 263
    significance of contextual change, 120–122
continuity, 16–18, 281
copper. See Metals
Corinth, 9, 110, 235
  Geometric fibulae, 169
  pottery abroad, 205
Corinthia
  Geometric imports, 105
Cumae, 204
cuneiform texts
  sites preserving, 35
Cyclades
  copper resources, 163
Cycladic
  pottery abroad, 27, 201, 202, 203, 204
Cypriot
  bronze amphora at Lefkandi, 95
  commodities in Linear B texts, 182
  craftsmen in Tiryns, 81, 90, 250, 258
  cylinder seals, 252
  imports
    at IIIB Chania, 124
    at IIIC Knossos, 91
    at IIIC Tiryns, 90
    at Perati, 86, 274
    from PG Knossos, 101
  in Anatolia, 252
  in IIIC Achaea, 91
  in IIIC Italy, 258
  in the PG period, 100
  individuals in Pylos, 65
  influence on Geometric goldwork, 188
  king Kinyras in Homer, 54
  merchants in PG, 202
  middlemen, 193, 253
  in Geometric Italy, 204
  pottery
    at Chania, 84
    at Geometric Knossos, 107
    at Huelva, 203
    at IIIB Tiryns, 79

at IIIC Tiryns, 90
at Kommos, 82
co-occurrence with Mycenaean pottery in the
    Near East, 193
co-occurrence with PG pottery in the
    Levant, 202
from Geometric Crete, 189
identification, 145
imports at Al Mina, 203
in Geometric Kommos, 107
on the Uluburun ship, 152
White Slip ware, 264
rings in Geometric Athens, 188
Cypro-Cretan pottery, 189
Cypro-Minoan, 36
clay ball at Tiryns, 90
inscriptions on seals from Thebes, 81
potmarks, 193
use through IIIC and PG periods, 46
Cyprus, 6, 8
as possible location of Homeric Temese, 269
bronze recycling, 173
contact with EIA Crete, 264
copper supply, 39, 163
Egyptianizing figurines, 126
Greek Geometric pottery in, 203
Greek PG pottery in, 201
IIIC Mycenaean pottery in, 199
in Homer, 53
local ceramics, 197
problems with interpreting artifact
    distributions, 190
source of ironworking knowledge, 175
spits, 269
tombs dominant in archaeological record, 203
trade with Yabninu, 257
TSJs on, 193
Ugaritian scribe in, 45

Danger at sea, 46–47, 256, 261
    pirates, 53
Dark Age
    as imaginative figment, 232
    continued support of, 18
    evidence for, 216
    in Messenia, 217
    traditional conception of, 9, 17, 75, 280
Deir el-Medina, 196
Delphi, 263
    Geometric imports, 105
    Geometric ivories, 186
Demography
    and burial evidence, 215
    and economic history, 211–214, 259–260, 263,
        268, 279–280
    and settlement size, 215–216
    and survey data, 250–251
    during the EIA, 241–245

estimates for early Greece, 238–246
Dendra
    bronze cuirass from, 170
depopulation, 7, 211–214, 241–245, 260, 279–280
Dikte, 8, 85, 187
    difficulty of dating bronzes from, 181
    Geometric imports, 106
    IIIC imports, 91
    PG imports, 101
Dimini, 235
Dipylon oinochoe, 264
Dirmil, 202
discontinuity, 16–18, 281
Dodecanese, 198, 201

Egypt, 6, 9
    absence of Mycenaean pottery in IIIC, 199
    fate of imports in Herodotus, 13
    Geometric scarabs, 104
    glass exports, 148
    glass ingots from, 147
    glass production, 184
    imported bead from Isopata, 148
    in Homer, 53, 55
    invasion by Sea Peoples, 47, 255
    Menelaos in, 52
    Mycenaean pottery in, 196
    pottery at Kommos, 82
    pottery on the Uluburun ship, 152
    relationship with Hatti, 251
Elateia, 7, 85, 169
Eleon, 7
Eleusis
    Geometric imports, 103
Eleutherna, 181, 187
    carved ivories, 187
    Geometric imports, 123
    imported objects in Geometric, 107
    Phoenicians buried at, 267
    spits, 269
élite contacts, 8, 58–59, 198, 204, 213, 251, 259,
    268–270
Ephesus, 199, 202
Eretria, 8, 9
    Geometric gold, 188
    Geometric imports in tombs, 105
    goldsmith's hoard, 270
    imported objects in sanctuary, 267
    inscribed skyphos, 264
    ironworking, 271
    population in EIA, 216
Etruria, 203, 204
    spits, 269
Euboea, 8, 33, 123
    concentration of PG imports on, 94
    early adopter of ironworking, 175, 271
    in Hesiod, 57
    iron sources, 263

pottery abroad, 190, 201, 203, 204
shipwreck off north coast, 183
Euphrates, 257
Excavation history of Greek sites, 137
exports, 190–208
   from Geometric Greece, 201–208
   from IIIB Greece, 190–197
   from IIIC Greece, 199–201
   from Protogeometric Greece, 201–202
   interpretive problems with, 190–192
   Mycenaean production of, 196–198

faience
   at Mycenae, 77, 79
   at Thebes, 81
   figurines from Geometric Kommos, 107
   figurines from Perati, 86
   Geometric imports, 104
   Geometric scarabs at Perachora, 104
   IIIC imports at Knossos, 91
   imports at Tiryns, 79
   plaque from Mycenae, 77
   production at Tiryns, 81
   production in IIIC Italy, 200
   prominent among PG imports, 100, 144
   rarity in PG, 186
firedogs. *See* andirons
Flimsy Settlements from the PG, 141–142
Francavilla Marittima, 205
Frattesina, 200
Function of imports, 124–126

Gelidonya, 152, 157, 162, 208
Geography
   LHIIIB imports, 77
   LHIIIC imports, 86
   limits of the study, 27
   LMIIIC imports, 84, 86
   of Geometric imports, 103–104
   of PG imports, 94–95
   origin of imported objects, 127–128
Gift exchange
   as public benefit, 43
   corruption of gifts within, 43
   Hittite, 251
   in Homer
      purpose, 63
   in the LBA, 38–43
      purpose, 63
   scale in Homer, 56
glass, 54, 241
   imports at Mycenae, 77
   in the Geometric period, 187
   ingots, 147, 148, 183, 184
   ingots on the Uluburun ship, 152
   manufacturing in the LBA, 148
   on the Uluburun ship, 183
   rarity in PG, 186

Gortyn, 7, 187
Gournia, 236
   tin ingot, 183

Hala Sultan Tekke, 90
Hattuša
   cuneiform documents from, 35
   imported objects in, 251–253
   letters from to Ugarit, 37
Hattusili III, 38, 40, 41, 251
hematite
   at Mycenae, 77
   weights at Perati, 86
Heraklion, 267
Herodotus, 272
   Greek mercenaries in Egypt, 272
   lavish dedications in sanctuaries, 267
   Phoenicians in, 264
   pottery imports in, 13
Hesiod, 156, 265
   historicity, 51
   risk mitigation in, 68
   trade in, 56–57
Hittites
   and Ugarit, 257
   archaeological evidence for long-distance exchange, 251–253
   documentary evidence, 35
   evidence for demise of, 47, 255
   inscriptions on seals from Thebes, 81
Homer
   commerce in, 52–54, 60, 61
   feasting in, 270
   funerals in, 264
   gift exchange, 54–56, 60, 61, 264
      purpose, 63
   historicity, 48–50
   interpretive problems with, 68–69
   movement of livestock in, 244
   objects exchanged in, 62, 154–156, 270
   Phoenicians in, 64, 267
   words for craftsmen in, 244
Homolion, 185
Huelva, 203

Iapygian wares, 202
Iasos, 198
Ida, 8
   difficulty of dating bronzes from, 181
   Geometric faience and glass, 187
   Geometric imports, 106
   Geometric ivories from, 187
   IIIC imports, 86
   ivory throne in, 270
   PG imports, 101
imported objects
   as an indirect observable, 151–158
   catalogues, 75–76, 143–144

definition, 26
excavation reports and, 150
identification of beads as, 146–150
identification of ceramics as, 145–146
in Greece
  at individual sites. *See* index entries for individual sites
  securely dated to the Geometric period, 103–112
  securely dated to the IIIB period, 76–85
  securely dated to the IIIC period, 85–94
  securely dated to the PG period, 94–103
in ritual contexts, 250, 258, 273, 274
quantitative analysis of, 18–21
Inatos, 123, 187
Ionian Migration, 204
Israel, 48
Italian
  IIIB imports
    at Chania, 84
    at Knossos, 84
    at Kommos, 82
  IIIC imports
    in Achaea, 91
    in Knossos, 91
  possibly unrecognized IIIC imports from, 75
  pottery at Huelva, 203
Italy, 6, 9
  contacts during IIIC, 7
  contacts with Achaea during IIIC, 243, 256
  copper supply, 163
  Geometric fibulae in Olympia, 105
  Greek Geometric pottery, 190, 203, 204–205
  Greek PG pottery in, 202
  IIIC Mycenaean imports, 200
  local ceramics, 197
  local imitations of Corinthian pottery, 205
  local imitations of Mycenaean pottery, 198, 243
  Mycenaean pursuit of commercial interest in, 254
  origins of Gray Ware carinated cup at Mochlos, 145
itinerant craftsmen
  and times of disruption, 259
  in Crete, 187, 267
  in Homer, 54
  in the Geometric period, 112
ivory
  and Levantine craftsmen in Crete, 267
  IIIC balance scale from Chania, 179
  imports
    at Geometric Artemis Orthia, 105
    at IIIB Mycenae, 77
    at IIIC Knossos, 91
    rod at IIIB Tiryns, 79
    scepter head at Thebes, 81
  in Geometric contexts, 186–187
  in Geometric Crete, 107
  in Geometric sanctuaries, 266

in IIIB contexts, 184
in IIIC contexts, 185
in LBA documents, 40, 61
in PG contexts, 185
in the Idaean cave, 270
lack of Greek sources, 161
on the Uluburun ship, 152, 183
production at Mycenae, 242
value as commodity in IIIB Greece, 249

Kadıkalesi, 201
Kalapodi Kokkalia, 185
Kanakia, 85, 235, 258
  hoarding, 172
  presence of ingots, 183
Karfi, 86, 180
Karkemish, 267
Kaş, 152
Kato Syme, 86, 179
Kavousi, 7, 123, 180, 187, 269
  industrial activity, 242
Kerameikos, 188
Kissamos, 123
Kition
  bronze recycling, 173
Klaros, 202
Klazomenai, 199
Klenia, 188
Knossos, 4, 8, 235, 236
  Agios Ioannis cemetery, 91
  élite tombs, 264
  evidence for imported commodities in Linear B texts, 182
  evidence for ivory production in Linear B texts, 184
  evidence for textile production in Linear B texts, 241
  evidence for treatment of oil in Linear B tablets, 196
  Fortetsa, 100
  funerary *cippi*, 267
  Geometric faience and glass, 187
  IIIB bronze consumption, 178
  IIIC bronze consumption, 179
  IIIC warrior burials, 258
  imports
    beads from the LBA, 148
    concentration of imports on PG Crete, 100
    Geometric, 107, 123
    IIIB period, 84
    IIIC period, 85, 91
    PG period, 94
    PG/G ceramic vessels as personal gifts, 263
  ironworking, 271
  Knossos North Cemetery, 91, 100
  PG bronze consumption, 170, 181
  PG faience bead consumption, 186
  PG faience vessels, 201

PG/Geometric bronze from cemeteries, 180
population in EIA, 237
population of Neopalatial, 216
presence of Linear B tablets, 32
production of Cypro-Phoenician pottery, 267
production of TSJs, 197
shipbuilding, 59
Syrian goldsmith, 188
Tekke tomb, 188
textile production, 241
Kolophon, 199
Kommos
  absence of material from IIIC, 86
  bronzes, 178
  concentration of ceramic imports, 253
  faience and glass in the Geometric period, 187
  glass production in, 148
  imports
    concentration of imports on PG Crete, 100
    Geometric, 107, 123
    IIIB period, 82, 124
    PG period, 94, 101, 186
    quantifying PG and Geometric, 94
    revisions of LBA ceramic imports by Rutter, 76, 144
  inscribed drinking cups, 264
  ironworking, 271
  production of TSJs, 197
Kontopigadi, 242
Korfos-Kalamianos, 59
Kourion, 204
Kouvaras Fyteion, 85
Krya, 86
Kuşaklı-Sarissa, 252

Lamia, 185
lapis lazuli
  absence from homer, 62
  at Thebes, 81
  in LBA documents, 39, 40, 61
  in the tomb of Rekhmire, 153
  of poor quality, 41
  value in the LBA, 82
Latium, 204
Lavrio
  copper ores, 172
  copper resources, 163
Lead Isotope Analysis, 163–165, 180
Lefkandi, 8, 215
  bronze
    composition and tin content in PG, 176, 177, 261
    quantity of bronze in PG tombs, 181
  distribution of wealth in burials, 99
  Geometric glass and faience, 187
  Geometric gold, 187
  Geometric ivories, 186
  importance of discoveries, 75, 137

imports
  Bes figurine, 104
  Geometric, 103, 106
  IIIC period, 85
  PG period, 95–100, 123
imports as trinkets, 144
metalworking, 242
PG faience vessels, 201
PG gold, 185
spits, 269
Lesbos, 202
Liman Tepe, 201
Linear A, 5
Linear B
  bronzeworkers in, 34, 274
  craftspeople in, 245
  evidence for foreign workers in, 34, 65
  evidence for trade, 32–34
  Levantine toponyms in, 193
  merchants in, 65
local imitations, 190
  in IIIC Anatolia, 201
  in IIIC Cyprus, 199
  in IIIC Italy, 200
  of Mycenaean pottery in the IIIC period, 209
Lokris, 7, 28, 123
  bronze supply in IIIC, 173
  IIIC warrior burials, 258
Lukka, 47, 257

Malia, 236
Malinowski, Bronisław, 12, 63
Malta, 202
Marmariani, 185
Maşat Höyük, 252
Mauss, Marcel, 12, 63
Megara, 188
Menidi, 185
mercenaries, 271
Messenia, 7, 85
metals
  bronze
    context of production in Geometric period, 246
    evidence for consumption on Crete, 177–181
    overall, 162–182
  Geometric imports, 104
  imports and orientalizing products on Geometric Crete, 107
  in exchange for humans, 244
  in Homer, 52, 55, 62
  in IIIC Achaea, 256
  in LBA documents, 40, 61
  in Linear B texts from Pylos, 47
  ingots, 249, 263
  Mycenaean acquisition of, 241
  production in IIIC, 242

quantitative change in deposition, 165–172
recycling, 172–174
relation of decline after IIIB to population, 238
shortage, 174–177, 261–263
spits, 269
value as commodity in IIIB Greece, 249
vessels among PG imports, 144
copper, 174–177
   acquisition, 163
   coals to Newcastle problem, 164
   Cypriot wealth in, 39
   in Homer, 52, 269
   in LBA documents, 42, 61, 68
   in the Satire on the Trades, 45
   in Ugarit, 44
   ingots, 173, 179
     at Ugarit, 45
     circulation in LBA Greece, 183
     in the tomb of Rekhmire, 153
     on the Uluburun ship, 143, 152
   ingots awaited in Lukka, 37
   on the Uluburun ship, 152
   shortage, 261–263
   Ugarit, 257
gold
   change in consumption patterns over time, 187–188
   in Geometric Knossos, 107
   in Homer, 52, 54, 55, 56, 61, 62
   in LBA documents, 39–44, 61, 68
   in Lefkandi *heroon* burial, 95
   in PG Greece, 185
   ingots, 188
     in Homer, 61
   lack of Greek sources, 161
   Mycenaean consumption of, 241
iron, 174–177
   adoption during the EIA, 8
   at Ugarit, 257
   early adopters, 244
   gift of blades from Hittites, 41
   Hittite possession of, 39
   in Geometric sanctuaries, 246
   in Homer, 52, 56, 62
   in LBA documents, 41
   ingots, 263, 269
   knife from Tiryns, 90
   production for export, 271
   replacement for bronze, 261–263
   spits, 269, 271
silver
   in Homer, 55
   in LBA documents, 40, 41, 42, 61
   in the Satire on the Trades, 45
   in Ugarit, 44
   Knossos Tekke tomb, 188
tin, 174–177
   acquisition, 163

   at Ugarit, 45, 257
   in Homer, 54
   in LBA documents, 61
   ingots, 173
     circulation in LBA Greece, 183
     in the tomb of Rekhmire, 153
     on the Uluburun ship, 143, 152
   lack of Greek sources, 161
   shortage, 261–263
middlemen, 43, 193, 204, 256–257, 258, 279
   absence in Homer, 70
   in LBA trade, 59, 69
migration
   IIIC Cyprus, 200
   to Italy in IIIC, 200
Miletus, 198, 199, 200, 201, 202, 203
Minet el-Beida, 192
Minimalist/Maximalist debate, 131, 211–214
Mitanni
   cylinder seals, 249
   cylinder seals imported to Greece in LBA, 82
   cylinder seals in Hattuša, 252
   in LBA documents, 39
   seal from IIIB Armenoi, 84
Mitrou, 7
   layout of settlement, 216
   PG imports, 123
   population in EIA, 237
Mochlos
   IIIB imports from, 84
   tin ingot, 183
Monastiraki Katalimata, 6
   access to bronze, 180
Mouliana, 180
Mycenae, 5, 6, 7, 235, 236, 248
   bronze recycling, 174
   bronze supply, 172
   cemeteries, 79, 121
   consumption of TSJs, 197
   glass from Egypt, 148
   glass production in, 148
   imports
     beads from the LBA, 148
     IIIB period, 77–79, 249–250
     IIIC period, 122
   industrial installations, 242
   ivory, 184
   ivory ingots, 184
   perfumed oil, 196
   population in the LBA, 216
   presence of Linear B tablets, 32
   presence of metal ingots, 183
   workshops, 184
Mycenaean state, 5, 248
   and Near Eastern states, 36–38
   control of long-distance trade, 253
   peer polities after 1300, 256

Nafplio, 188
Naukratis
  production of scarabs, 104
Neochorakion, 188
Nichoria, 7
  bronze recycling, 174
  bronzes, 175, 261
  composition of PG bronzes, 177

obeloi. *See* spits
octopus, 196, 200
olives, 183, 196
Olympia, 246
  Geometric imports, 103, 104
Orchomenos, 5, 235, 236
Oropos, 8
  ironworking, 271
Ortaköy-Şapinuwa, 252
Orthi Petra. *See* Eleutherna

Palaepaphos
  spits, 269
Palaikastro, 178, 180, 187, 236
Patso Cave, 86
Peloponnese
  bronzes in PG cemeteries, 177
Perachora
  Geometric imports, 103
  Geometric ivories, 186
  imported objects in, 104, 267
Perati, 7
  distribution of wealth in burials, 106
  imported objects in, 86–88, 122, 258, 273
  ivory, 185
  nature of imports from, 104
perfumed oil, 196, 241
  export from Argolid, 196
  export in IIIB and G periods, 205
  Geometric export from Corinth, 205
  in LBA documents, 61
  Linear B evidence, 196
  no evidence for export in PG Greece, 201
Phaistos, 86, 187, 236
Pherai, 185
Phoenician
  imports
    from PG Knossos, 101
    Geometric bowls, 104
    PG mainland, 100
  ivories in Geometric Crete, 186
  merchants, 202, 273
  pottery
    at Al Mina, 203
    at Geometric Knossos, 107
    at Geometric Kommos, 107, 189
    at Huelva, 203
    at PG Kommos, 186
  shrine at Geometric Kommos, 107

Phoenicians, 8
  in Homer, 53, 55, 58, 265
  on Geometric Crete, 107
  traders in Herodotus, 13
Phokis
  bronze supply in IIIC, 173
Pilavtepe, 201
Pithekoussai, 204, 205
  ironworking, 271
Pithekussai, 264
Point Iria, 157
Polanyi, Karl, 22, 23, 62
Politics
  and long-distance exchange, 93, 250, 274, 279
Poros-Katsambas, 59, 178
port of trade, 23
Portes, 85
Praisos, 123, 180, 187
primitivism/modernism, 12–13
Prinias, 187
production, 8
  and participation in exchange, 263
  archaeological evidence for, 211–214
Pylos, 5, 6, 7, 235, 236, 248
  bronze
    allotments to smiths, 173
    belonging to temple, 173
    evidence for smiths from Linear B texts, 34
    evidence for working, distribution,
      and taxation from Linear B texts, 162
    Jn tablets, 33, 34, 46, 162, 173, 182, 274
    recycling, 174
    workers belonging to temple, 274
  evidence for instability from, 46
  imports
    commodities, 182
    glass from Egypt and Mesopotamia, 148
    IIIC period, 85
    paucity in IIIB, 77
  ivory, 184
  population in the LBA, 216
  presence of Linear B tablets, 32
  shipbuilding, 59

Quantitative change
  in import numbers, 112–117, 277–279
  in scale of trade from textual evidence,
    69–71
  statistical significance of, 131–136

Ramesses III, 196
Rapanu, 257
Ras el-Bassit, 202
Rasap-abu, 257
Ras-Shamra, 36, 192
recycling. *See* metals, bronze recycling
Rekhmire
  tomb of, 153

Rhodes, 198, 200, 201
    production of scarabs, 104

Salamis (Cyprus), 204
    spits, 269
Salento, 205
Samos, 202, 267
sanctuaries
    and state formation, 265–267
    concentration of EIA imports in Cretan cave, 264
    concentration of Geometric imports in, 103–105
    Geometric emergence of, 8, 265–267
    imported objects in, 123
    metal production in the Geometric period, 246
Sardinia, 263
    copper resources, 163
    pottery at Huelva, 203
Sarepta, 193
Satire on the Trades, 45
Satyrion, 202
scarab
    at Geometric Aegina, 105
    at Geometric Eretria, 105
    at Geometric Perachora, 104
    at IIIB Chania, 84
    at IIIB Mycenae, 77
    identifiability of imports, 147
    imports in Geometric Greece, 111
    imports in Italy, 204
    in Geometric sanctuaries, 267
    on the Uluburun ship, 152
    possible Rhodian production, 105
    purpose of dedication, 273
Scoglio del Tonno, 193, 200, 254
Sicily, 200, 202, 203, 205
silver. See Metals
Skiathos, 271
Skourta plain survey, 140
Skyros, 188
slave trading, 43, 44, 244
    in Homer, 52
Smyrna, 202
Spata, 185, 188
spits
    and élite Geometric culture, 268–270
Submycenaean/Subminoan
    treatment of, 85
Sybaris, 205
Syria-Palestine, 6, 8, 9
    Geometric shipwreck from coast, 278
    Greek Geometric pottery in, 203
    IIIB Mycenaean imports in, 193
    IIIC Mycenaean imports in, 200
    production of scarabs, 104
Syro-Palestinian
    armor scale from Tiryns, 89
    craftspeople on Geometric Crete, 107
    imports at Perati, 274

    influence on fibulae in Geometric Italy, 263
    ivories in Geometric Crete, 186
    ivory scepter from IIIB Thebes, 81
    jars at Mochlos, 145
    pottery
        at IIIC Tiryns, 89
        at Kommos, 82
        on the Uluburun ship, 152

Tamassos, 269
taphonomy, 22, 25, 141, 154, 160, 161
Tarsus, 200
Taurus mountains, 163
Teichos Dymaion, 85
Tel Miqne, 199
Tel-Afis, 202
Tell Abu Hawam, 193
Tell el-Amarna, 196
Tell Es-Safi, 202
Tell Ta'yinat, 200
terebinth resin, 183, 249
textiles
    in Homer, 55
    in LBA documents, 40
Thebes, 5, 7
    consumption of TSJs, 197
    imports
        IIIB period, 81, 250
        ivory, 184, 185
        perfumed oil, 196
        presence of metal ingots, 183
theoretical approaches to exchange, 279–280
Theotokou, 185
Thessaly, 122
    bronzes in PG cemeteries, 177
    gold in PG, 185
    history of study, 138
    paucity of Geometric imports, 102
    PG imported objects in, 100
Thorikos, 185
Tiryns, 5, 6, 235, 236, 248
    bronze recycling, 174
    bronze supply, 172
    consumption of TSJs, 197
    glass production in, 148
    gold in PG, 185
    imports
        IIIB period, 79–81, 250
        IIIC period, 89–90, 122, 258
        PG period, 100
    in the IIIC period, 256
    industrial activity, 242
    metalworking and cult practice, 80
    presence of Linear B tablets, 32
    presence of metal ingots, 183
    wall brackets, 76, 79, 80, 144
Torre Galli, 204
transport stirrup jars, 196–198

INDEX

tripod cauldrons
  in Geometric Greece, 111
  in Geometric sanctuaries, 105, 266
  in Homer, 55, 62
Tudhaliya III, 255
Tychos Dymaion, 7
Tylissos, 86
  PG imports, 95
Tyre, 202

Ugarit, 192
  as commercial hub, 253
  destruction of, 46–47, 255
  documentary evidence from, 36, 256
  evidence for commercial exchange from, 44–45
  imported ceramics, 193
  merchants in, 65, 256
  relevance to Greek LBA, 36–38
Uluburun
  as confirmation of evidence from Amarna letters, 61
  cargo, 208
    commodities, 143, 157, 161, 182
    faience beads, 148
    glass ingots, 148
    metals, 162, 170, 181
    Mycenaean pottery, 198, 264
    summary, 152
  date of wreck, 114
  evidence for LBA long-distance exchange, 10
  independent of palatial exchange, 254
  unlikelihood of similarly laden vessels in PG, 182
Urtenu, 257

Veii, 204, 205
Vitsa, 205
Vrokastro, 86, 179, 187

warrior burials, 6, 91, 122, 258, 270
World Systems Theory, 23, 24

Yabninu, 257

Zagora, 8
Zagros mountains, 163
Zakros, 123, 236